Shaping language rights

**Commentary on the European Charter
for Regional or Minority Languages in light
of the Committee of Experts' evaluation**

Edited by

Alba Nogueira López
Eduardo J. Ruiz Vieytez
Iñigo Urrutia Libarona

Regional or Minority Languages, No. 9

Council of Europe Publishing

Cover design: Documents and Publications Production Department, Council of Europe
Layout: Jouve, Paris

Council of Europe Publishing
F-67075 Strasbourg Cedex
http://book.coe.int

ISBN 978-92-871-7216-7
© Council of Europe, February 2012
Printed at the Council of Europe

Contents

List of contributors

(in alphabetical order)

Dr György Andrássy
Professor and Head of the Department of Political Science and Social
Theory, Law Faculty, University of Pécs

Dr Santiago J. Castellà Surribas
Professor of Public International Law,
University Rovira i Virgili, Tarragona

Dr Elizabeth Craig
Lecturer in Law, University of Sussex

Dr Robert Dunbar
Senior Research Professor, University of the Highlands and Islands, Scotland

Dr Jutta Engbers
Lawyer, Friesoythe, Germany

Dr Iñaki Lasagabaster
Professor of Administrative Law, University of the Basque Country

Dr Tom Moring
Professor, Swedish School of Social Science, University of Helsinki

Dr Alba Nogueira López
Senior Lecturer in Administrative Law, Law Faculty, University of Santiago
de Compostela

Dr R. Gwynedd Parry
Senior Lecturer in Law, Swansea University

Dr José Manuel Pérez Fernández
Senior Lecturer in Administrative Law, University of Oviedo

Dr Anna M. Pla Boix
Lecturer in Constitutional Law, University of Girona

Dr Eva Pons Parera
Senior Lecturer in Constitutional Law, University of Barcelona

Dr Adriano Previtali
Professor of Law, University of Fribourg/Freiburg

Dr Eduardo J. Ruiz Vieytez
Senior Lecturer in Constitutional Law, Human Rights Institute,
University of Deusto, Bilbao

Dr Iñigo Urrutia Libarona
Senior Lecturer in Administrative Law, Law Faculty,
University of the Basque Country

Dr Márk Vogl
Assistant Lecturer, Department of Political Science and Social Theory,
Law Faculty, University of Pécs

Mr Jean-Marie Woehrling
Hon. President of the Administrative Tribunal and President of the Institute
for Local Legislation of Alsace-Moselle

Foreword

At the time of publication of this work, the European Charter for Regional or Minority Languages is in-between two anniversaries. Some 30 years ago, on 7 October 1981 to be exact, the Parliamentary Assembly adopted Recommendation 928 which initiated the Charter's drafting process. That process was completed 20 years ago, on 5 November 1992, when 11 member states of the Council of Europe signed the Charter as the first minority-related convention. The Framework Convention for the Protection of National Minorities, of which I am equally in charge, was subsequently drafted in the Council of Europe and entered into force in 1998. However, the Charter has remained the only convention dealing specifically with the languages used by traditional minorities or linguistic groups.

The Charter emerged at a time when the high hopes of some member states and many national minorities for the adoption of an additional protocol to the European Convention on Human Rights on minorities had just been deceived. While some observers praised the Charter's unprecedented thoroughness, sceptical remarks were voiced as well: How effective would a treaty be that allows the state to select the promotional measures at its own discretion? Could the state exclude languages from the Charter's scope of application?

Almost 14 years after the Charter's entry into force in 1998, we can conclude that these concerns have turned out to be mostly unfounded. This is the common achievement of the three stakeholders of the Charter process: the states parties, which in a number of cases have entered into quite ambitious undertakings, the linguistic groups as active participants during implementation and monitoring, and last, but not least, the Committee of Experts as the authoritative body in charge of interpreting the Charter and monitoring its application.

The present commentary is dedicated to the interpretation of the Charter by the Committee of Experts as a result of which many provisions have become clearer and taken shape. In its recommendations to the states parties, the Committee of Experts has spelled out in a concrete and practical manner what the Charter says, but also what it does not say explicitly. It is on the basis of that interpretative work that states are regularly urged not only to abstain from undermining regional or minority languages, but also to take active measures for their promotion.

Among the cases that have attracted Europe-wide attention is the Committee of Experts' view that high percentage thresholds established by national legislation, limiting the use of minority languages to certain parts of the language area, are incompatible with the Charter. Also, the Committee of Experts has included autochthonous languages within the Charter's scope of application even if they were still unrecognised in the respective states. When it felt that existing undertakings of a state were inadequate, the Committee of Experts has also recommended such parties to enter into higher obligations reflecting the real legal or sociolinguistic situation of the language.

These are but a few examples. It is the present publication's merit to present in detail how the Committee of Experts has shaped language rights by evaluating the Charter.

Ralf-René Weingärtner
Director of Human Rights and Anti-Discrimination

Preface

Enhancing regional and minority languages protection lays the foundations of a stronger Europe based on pluralist principles. This book shows the way that many regional or minority languages have striven to face the standardising risks of globalisation and have gained a presence in education, the media, administration, culture and every domain of public and private life.

The volume is based on the analysis of the provisions of the European Charter for Regional or Minority Languages and the implementation of the Charter within the states parties through the reports of the Committee of Experts and other available monitoring documentation. The study aims to describe and assess the content and potential of the provisions of the Charter in order to protect and promote regional or minority languages.

Through a collaborative pan-European project involving 18 researchers from 15 universities and research institutes, this volume proposes a scientific and independent assessment, compatible with a critical perspective about some issues. The main purpose of the study is to establish the current bases of interpretation of this instrument, to support the authority of the Committee of Experts in its responsible task of interpreting the Charter and to assess how states parties fulfil their undertakings under this instrument.

The book is addressed to the governments of the states (and the regions and other sub-national entities) that have signed or ratified the Charter, as well as to the states that are now preparing their signature or ratification. Such a work may also have interest for the Council of Europe's various bodies and be useful to civil servants and other public agents charged to apply the Charter in different sectors. NGOs that participate in the monitoring process of the Charter and foster its application in their states can also profit from the comparisons of experiences and interpretation of the provisions of the Charter. Scholars and citizens interested in linguistic matters at European level will find in this volume an in-depth study of the scope of language rights in the states that have ratified the Charter.

The methodology of the study is based on consideration of the Charter as a living instrument. On one side, the Charter is a useful instrument with a high degree of complexity subject to interpretation; on the other side, the interpretation of Charter, as a flexible instrument, is dependent on the different situations of the states and the languages to which it applies. The reports of the Committee of Experts are a major source of information for the study and interpretation and implementation of the Charter.[1]

We hope that this work will shed useful light on the scope of the European Charter for Regional or Minority Languages, a cornerstone for European language diversity with an outstanding role in the protection of linguistic rights.

Alba Nogueira López
Eduardo Ruiz Vieytez
Iñigo Urrutia Libarona

1. For the sake of clarity, the Committee of Experts' reports referred to in this work will be quoted as follows: for a given country and monitoring cycle, the first time they appear, they will be quoted in full, for example "Application of the Charter in Slovenia, 2nd monitoring cycle (2007), paragraph 11", and thereafter with just a reference to the country, year of the report and paragraph (in this case, "Slovenia 2007, 11"). All the Committee of Experts' reports may be consulted on the Charter's website: www.coe.int/minlang.

Introduction

Jean-Marie Woehrling

In 2011, the European Charter for Regional or Minority Languages has been in force for 13 years. This is quite a significant period of implementation, which involves today 25 states.[1]

The Charter is not a new document; it came into being long before it actually came into force. The draft version prepared by a working group was finalised and approved by the CLRAE in 1987.[2] While the text was considered at length by an ad hoc committee between 1988 and 1992, no further detailed amendments were made to it during this time, and so the Charter already possessed its main characteristics in 1987.

---

1. At 1 January 2011, 25 states had ratified the Charter, the last being Bosnia and Herzegovina in September 2010. Another eight states have signed but not ratified the Charter.
2. For the historical background, see J.-M. Woehrling (2005), *The European Charter for Regional or Minority Languages: a critical commentary*. Strasbourg: Council of Europe, pp. 11ff; M. Guskow (2009), *Entstehung und Geschichte der Europäischen Charta der Regional- oder Minderheitensprachen*, Frankfurt am Main: Peter Lang.

Thus the provisions of the Charter were formulated before both the fall of the Berlin Wall, which enabled the countries of central and eastern Europe to join the Council of Europe system, and the main onslaught of globalisation. Designed in the 1980s, the Charter has been applied to a Europe which is radically different from the Europe its authors knew. We should therefore ask ourselves whether the Charter is still suited to this new context.

The application of the Charter can be appraised in practical terms on the basis of the regular reports drawn up by the Committee of Experts. This is the main approach adopted in this publication. In the case of some countries, three or even four evaluation reports are already available, providing detailed outlines of the progress made and the difficulties encountered in implementing the Charter.

Other sources of information are the various studies of the situation of European regional and minority languages and the numerous projects conducted since 2000 relating to the status and protection of regional languages. Some of the most remarkable such studies were actually initiated and published by the Council of Europe.[3]

Despite these many sources of information, the kind of protection of regional or minority languages offered by the Charter is still not well known and often ill understood by large parts of the European population, including political leaders and legal experts. This is why it is so important to recall (in section 1 of this chapter) the originality of the Charter's approach. Then (in section 2 of this chapter) we look at the effects of contemporary developments on the Charter and its suitability to this new context and, generally its efficacy.

1. The originality of the Charter and its place in strategies to protect regional and/or minority languages

The working group responsible for developing the draft European Charter for Regional or Minority Languages based its discussions on the failure, which had been noted at the beginning of the 1980s, of all successive attempts since the end of the Second World War to integrate linguistic demands into conventional minority or human rights approaches. The Council of Europe had been presented with several proposals for conferring a European status on regional or cultural minorities, but all these proposals

---

3. Note especially the Council of Europe's Regional or Minority Languages series of publications on the Charter.

had come to nothing.[4] Nor has the idea been borne out in practice that entitling members of minority social groups to exercise their individual rights and freedoms as recognised by the European Convention on Human Rights would guarantee their capacity for proper development in a different culture. In the light of this admission of failure, the working group explored a third way, which consisted in designing a separate mode of protection for regional cultures and languages.

Following these observations, we can distinguish three different approaches to taking account of the situation of regional and/or minority cultures:

1.1. Recourse to the human rights technique to safeguard linguistic diversity

The human rights system is geared to protecting people in all their dimensions, so it must also cover the linguistic aspects of the human being. Human rights must therefore in principle enable individuals with linguistic specificities to fulfil their potential in their own language, under conditions equivalent to those enjoyed by speakers of the dominant languages, by exercising traditional individual rights: freedom of expression, freedom of education, respect for private life, equality and so on. All these aspects of human rights can be transposed to the linguistic dimension. This led to the idea that human rights could include language rights.[5]

Nevertheless, a passive concept of these freedoms is not very helpful in terms of the use of minority languages. It is often said that regional and minority languages are sufficiently guaranteed if there is no prohibition on speaking them. In France, for instance, we frequently hear the argument that regional languages are taken into account in a legally satisfactory manner because there is no prohibition on using them in the private sphere. Such an understanding of human rights clearly deprives minority languages of effective protection.

Some countries have interpreted the freedoms guaranteed by the human rights system more actively, as involving an effective right, a genuine,

---

4. On the Council of Europe's role in protecting minorities, see F. Ermacora (1972), "Der Minderheiten- und Volksgruppenschutz vor dem Europarat" in *System eines internationalen Völkergruppenrechts*. Vienna: Wilhelm-Braumüller-Universitäts-Verlagsbuchhandlung; H. Hartig (1994), "Les travaux du Conseil de l'Europe dans le domaine des minorités" in P. Grigourion (ed.), *Questions de minorités en Europe*, Collection l'Europe Plurielle No. 5. Brussels: Presses Interuniversitaires Européennes.
5. See F. de Varennes (2001), "Language rights as an integral part of human rights", *International Journal on Multicultural Societies*, Vol. 3, No. 1, p. 15, though the position taken by de Varennes does not reflect the state of positive law; see also X. Arzoz (2007), "The nature of language rights", *Journal on Ethnopolitics and Minority Issues in Europe*, No. 2, www.ecmi.de/jemie/download/2-2007-Arzoz.pdf.

non-discriminatory entitlement to speak a minority language. Where such a facility is jeopardised by facts on the ground, positive action is needed from the public authorities to give these rights real substance. It is a case of restoring effective equality in the use of languages by means of specific measures. This is what is sometimes called, somewhat infelicitously, "positive discrimination". This approach to minority languages is rare in European countries. Broadly speaking, when a state refrains from positive action to promote linguistic diversity, the courts do not consider such an omission as an infringement of human rights.

There is another restriction on using the human rights system to protect linguistic diversity. Such rights have limited application to public institutions in the field of regional or minority languages: the right to use a minority language in dealings with a public authority and the right to obtain teaching in such a language in state schools are not human rights as they are traditionally defined, which leaves it to individual states to establish the public status of the languages in question.

For all these reasons, the European Convention on Human Rights, which recognises individual rights, has not emerged as an appropriate basis for guarantees of respect for linguistic difference.[6] Despite a number of attempts to prepare the ground for protection in this area, the European Court of Human Rights has been unable to develop case law providing genuine protection for minority languages. The idea has sometimes been mentioned of an additional protocol to the Convention to incorporate protection for regional languages, but it has never had any real prospect of success. Despite some recent

---

6. The only provision of the European Convention on Human Rights which takes account of minority languages or linguistic minorities is Article 14, which mentions discrimination based on association with a minority or on grounds of language. However, this provision only concerns those rights whose enjoyment is recognised by the Convention, which has not been interpreted as including a right to one's language, e.g. in education. Article 14 only concerns types of discrimination which are deemed "unreasonable". The European Court of Human Rights has refrained from ruling that cultural standardisation policies in various states are unreasonable (cf. the language case in Belgium, judgment of 23 July 1968, Nos. 1474/62, 1677/62, 1691/62, 1769/63, 1994/63 and 2126/64: the Belgian State is not obliged to provide financial support for French-speaking schools in Flanders). As for the safeguard for a fair trial in criminal matters (Article 6.3 of the Convention), stipulating that everyone charged with a criminal offence is entitled to be informed of the nature of the accusation in a language which s/he understands, these provisions only cover individuals who do not understand the language used in proceedings, not individuals who feel more at ease with a different language. In connection with civil proceedings (Article 6.1), the Court has even held that an application could be legitimately rejected because it was not drafted in the official language of the judicial proceedings, if the applicant's lawyer was in a position to use the said language (ISOP case of 8 March 1962, No. 808/60). On these issues, see P. Leuprecht (1986), "Le Conseil de l'Europe et les droits des minorités", *Les Cahiers du Droit*, Vol. 27, No. 1.

favourable signs,[7] the human rights system has proved disappointing as a means of promoting linguistic diversity.

1.2. Minority rights as protection of linguistic minorities

Minority languages are the means of expression of minority groups. Specific legal protection can be organised for such linguistic groups, by entitling them to their own schools, their own media, and so on. They can also be granted a degree of autonomy in managing or organising public services so as to take account of their language or culture.

These specific rights as granted to minorities, particularly in the linguistic area, can take a number of forms:

• domestic law in a given state may have provisions legally protecting speci-fied linguistic groups: as, for instance, in Hungary, whose national legisla-tion includes laws on the country's linguistic minorities;

• bilateral international agreements can be concluded between two countries in order to protect minorities: this is the case, for example, of the Danish minority in Germany and the German minority in Denmark;

• multilateral conventions can protect the rights of minorities, as in the case of the Council of Europe's Framework Convention for the Protection of National Minorities, which provides for respecting the linguistic specificity of these minorities.

The traditional approach of drawing the requisite conclusions from the exist-ence of national, cultural or ethnic minorities and granting them a political status to provide them with a set of specific advantages that enable them to capitalise on their culture and their specific language, in the context of a state with a different culture and language, was in line with the development of an international status for minorities after the First World War,[8] and has recently

---

7. G. Gilbert (2002), "The burgeoning minority rights jurisprudence of the European Court of Human Rights", *Human Rights Quarterly*, Vol. 24, No. 2; P. Kovács (2009), "La protection des minorités dans la jurisprudence de la Cour européenne des Droits de l'Homme" in L. Trocsanyi and L. Congnard (eds), *Statuts et protection des minorités; exemples en Europe occidentale et centrale ainsi que dans les pays méditerranéens*. Brussels: Bruylant; K. Williams and B. Rainey (2002), "Language, education and the European Convention on Human Rights, in the twenty-first century", *Legal Studies: Journal of the Society of Legal Scholars*, Vol. 22, No. 4.

8. Re the historical background to measures to protect minorities in the wake of the First World War, under the League of Nations and then the UN, see I. O. Bokatola (1992), *L'organisation des Nations Unies et la protection des minorités*. Brussels: Bruylant, pp. 41ff; W. McKean (1983), *Equality and discrimination under international law*. Oxford: Clarendon Press; N. Lerner (1991), *Group rights and discrimination in international law*. Dordrecht, Boston, London: Martinus Nijhoff; E. Decaux (1991), "Le droit international et la protection des minorités" in *Minorités: quelles chances pour l'Europe, l'événement européen*. Paris: Seuil, No. 16, p. 1150.

been given concrete expression by the adoption of the aforementioned Council of Europe Framework Convention.[9] This type of procedure can also be used in order to recognise special local statuses.[10]

Adapting such statuses to linguistic groups, while striking a balance between national integration and regional specificity, can have very positive results because it combines linguistic, economic and political considerations. However, this type of instrument presupposes the adherence of the state in which it is to be implemented. But the fact is that the national legal traditions of some states are inimical to recognising minorities and granting them specific rights. For instance, the French Constitutional Council holds that such recognition would be incompatible with the principles of the equality of citizens and the oneness of the French nation. Beyond these objections of principle, the adaptation of particular statuses presupposes a situation of dispassionate and responsible protagonists. This restricts the possibility of recourse to such a minorities law instrument.

1.3. Direct protection of minority languages

In view of the relative ineffectiveness of using either human rights mechanisms or the instrument on minorities' rights, a third approach has gradually emerged, geared to providing legal protection not to individuals (via human rights) nor to groups (on the basis of minorities' rights), but to the languages themselves as collective cultural assets. This option, rather than creating rights for minorities or individuals, imposes obligations on states or public authorities, requiring them to actively promote minority languages.

This approach treats regional languages as a common asset shared by all citizens. It also facilitates protection of linguistic diversity, which is characterised by the fact that it avoids opposing the national language to the minority languages. It opts for a clear plurilingual approach, with an eye to cultural pluralism: the defence of regional or minority languages is not organised against the national language but rather aspires to the rational and positive cohabitation

---

9. The Framework Convention for the Protection of National Minorities was adopted on 10 November 1994 and came into force on 1 February 1998. It has been ratified by 39 states and signed by four others (only France, Turkey, Andorra and Monaco have neither signed nor ratified). The convention sets out principles for protecting individuals belonging to minorities in the fields of public life, including the language sector. Re this Framework Convention, see F. Benoît-Rohmer (1995), "La Convention-cadre du Conseil de l'Europe pour la protection des minorités nationales", *European Journal of International Law*, Vol. 6, No. 4, pp. 573ff.

10. This is the modern mode of protection of historical and cultural specificities of territorial national minorities, particularly in western Europe. See Institut du Droit Local Alsacien-Mosellan (1997), *Etat, régions et droits locaux: droits locaux et statuts particuliers en France et en Europe; actes du colloque des 6 et 7 juin 1996.* Strasbourg: IDL/Paris: Economica.

of all the languages involved. Languages are seen as mutually reinforcing rather than competing with each other. It is not enough for the states to refrain from linguistic repression in order to ensure the efficacy of such direct protection of languages. The public authorities must evince positive involvement and conduct an active policy of supporting and promoting these languages.

This is the approach adopted by the European Charter for Regional or Minority Languages, an instrument for the direct protection of languages and linguistic diversity as a cultural heritage.[11] Under this approach, protecting a minority language (e.g. Breton or Romansch) is a matter not just for the speakers of this language (Bretons or Romansch-speakers) but for all citizens, because this regional language is a common asset. Moreover, regional or minority languages are a vital component of European culture, that is to say its linguistic diversity, which justifies Council of Europe action to promote them.

However, the Charter also allows for differentiating among languages from the angle of their legal position and social function. While all languages are equal in dignity and value, they are not equal in terms of influence, demographic strength, their social and political role, or certain objective elements which must be taken into account in managing them. From the Charter's perspective, therefore, it is legitimate to organise policies and attribute statuses which differ according to the real-life situations of these languages, with a view to securing an appropriate legal framework for protecting each of them.

This third approach to languages protection, which might be called the "cultural approach", consists in promoting respect for cultural diversity and developing the concept of cultural rights.[12] It is a question not so much of protecting

---

11. P. Blair (2003), "La protection du patrimoine linguistique européen" in H. Giordan and T. Louarn (eds), *Les langues régionales ou minoritaires dans la république*. Toulouse: IEO Publications, p. 5.
12. The term "cultural rights" is clearly polysemous. It can be understood as defining, by their object, a category of rights which are traditional by nature: in this sense, the concept parallels that of social and economic rights, i.e. a set of programmatic principles which are not directly invocable, such as the right to one's own specific cultural life within the meaning of Article 27 of the UN Covenant on Civil and Political Rights. The original contribution of the term "cultural rights" is that it designates a variety of legal mechanisms directly protecting cultural assets. It is in this sense that we can speak of cultural rights in the context of the European Charter for Regional or Minority Languages: the text is intended to safeguard the use of languages considered as a cultural value in themselves, and develops legal rules accordingly. As with legal protection for natural assets (protected areas), architectural heritage (historic monuments) or threatened species (biodiversity), standards can be used to establish direct protection for cultural values. So it is not a case of rights to a cultural heritage but rather rights for a cultural heritage. The approach is the opposite of that adopted by instruments for protecting minorities: the Framework Convention for the Protection of National Minorities protects languages as attributes of minorities, whereas the Charter mentions speakers of minority languages as vehicles for a cultural asset that

minority groups or granting subjective rights to individuals as of ensuring that society respects certain cultural values. Among such values, language diversity is recognised as a cultural asset which must be preserved. This requirement is taken into account in the contemporary context of opening borders, population mobility, economic globalisation and cultural standardisation. Protecting regional or minority languages forms an integral part of this overall problem.

This original response to the phenomenon of linguistic pluralism inside states is not primarily political, in the sense of recognising national minorities or specific statuses; nor can it be fully covered by the safeguarding of individual liberties. It develops from a cultural fact.

From this angle, the European Charter for Regional or Minority Languages is designed to protect the European cultural heritage of regional and minority languages. Its context is not that of opposition between regional languages and the national language. It comes down clearly in favour of convivial, rational coexistence among the different languages in a context of plurilingualism and cultural pluralism. It does not devise specific rights for minority language speakers but rather imposes obligations on states to support regional languages via an active promotional policy.

2. Suitability of the Charter to the contemporary context

Drawing on 12 years of implementation, can we conclude that the philosophy of the Charter is still suited to the contemporary context in the second decade of the 21st century and that it has shown itself to be an efficacious instrument? To answer this question, we must first of all identify the major developments in the environment of the Charter since its initial drafting, and secondly attempt to appraise its impact in the states which have ratified it.

2.1. The context of implementation of the Charter

After the drafting of the Charter, radical changes occurred in Europe. Two developments in particular should be highlighted in broaching the question of the Charter's suitability to this new context. The first is European unification, and the second the triumph of globalisation.

---

must be preserved. These approaches are not contradictory. It might even seem artificial to differentiate them. But, in terms of protection technique, the difference is essential, because in one case the momentum starts from a social entity, viz the minority, while in the other, the impetus is conveyed by the overall legal and political system. See also P. Meyer-Bisch (ed.) (1991), *Les doits culturels: une catégorie sous-développée de droits de l'Homme*. Fribourg/Freiburg: Éditions Universitaires.

2.1.1. The accession of the countries of central and eastern Europe to the democratic system of the Council of Europe

The Charter had been designed for western Europe at a time when European unification looked like a far distant prospect. The experts who helped draft the Charter and the situations inspiring its authors were mostly to do with 1980s western Europe.

The instrument's extension to central and eastern Europe was facilitated by the fact that the applicant countries for Council of Europe membership had to undertake to accede to the *acquis* of the main Council conventions, including the Charter.[13] Accordingly, the central and east European states acceded to the Charter even more promptly than their western counterparts.[14] The national and ethnic tensions in former Yugoslavia and various other countries in central and eastern Europe also raised interest in the Charter to the extent that it could help reduce tensions between linguistic groups in conjunction with other Council of Europe principles (reinforcing human rights, developing local self-government and promoting respect for national minorities).

In addition, several central and east European countries already had a tradition of catering for linguistic minorities.[15] They quite naturally continued developing facilities for these minorities, considering that this was a means of honouring the commitments laid down in the Charter. However, they did not always sufficiently realise that the Charter protects languages, not linguistic minorities as such. This difference was reflected in the fact, which the Committee of Experts has frequently noted, that the percentages of speakers of a language required for validating the existence of a linguistic minority in a given area within the meaning of the Framework Convention do not correspond to the Charter's criteria for ascertaining whether a language is used in a specified area.

---

13. In the same spirit, in the 1993 Copenhagen Declaration, the European Union included respect for minorities, particularly linguistic ones, among the accession conditions for applicant countries in central and eastern Europe.

14. As has been rightly pointed out, dual standards were applied to countries which were already Council members and to the applicant countries: whereas countries such as France and Turkey, which were already members, could and can deny the existence of minorities and refuse to accede to the European Charter for Regional or Minority Languages, countries applying for membership have had to undertake to respect the Council of Europe's principles on the linguistic rights of minorities and the protection of regional or minority languages.

15. These include Hungary and Romania. In some respects, since many national minorities were recognised as such in various central and east European countries, action to promote minority languages and cultures was more easily accepted than in western Europe. In the 1990s such western countries as France rejected any obligation to linguistic minorities in their territory, but pressurised east European countries to develop a policy of recognising such minorities.

Moreover, in a number of cases the Charter was ratified more in order to fend off international criticism than out of any real conviction. Some new states have developed policies of promoting the national language which impede any open attitude towards regional or minority languages.[16]

Where it has been applied sincerely and effectively, the Charter has indeed helped to calm intercultural conflicts. However, it does not provide an absolute guarantee against the risks of linguistic plurality being hijacked to political ends. The instrument is based on sincere accession and application not only by the states but also by the population groups concerned, and is not backed up by any external coercion system. The Charter is based on mutual fair dealings on the part of the state vis-à-vis the regional or minority languages and of the speakers of these languages vis-à-vis the state.

When this basis is infringed and the Charter is accepted only on a formal and notional basis, it can be effective neither in preserving languages nor in calming intercultural relations. All in all, the eastward extension of the Council of Europe and accession to the Charter by most of the countries in central and eastern Europe has helped increase the Charter's influence and enrich the experience of implementing it.

2.1.2. Reinforced globalisation

The other major change in Europe since the 1980s, which has affected the west even more than the east of Europe, is globalisation. This process has considerably reduced states' cultural autonomy. The media system (television, the press, etc.) has been thrown wide open to international influences. The privatisation of the television and radio sector has helped this process along, and the Internet is international by definition.

Globalisation has been accompanied by privatisation of a number of public services to which the Charter ascribes a role in promoting regional or minority languages. This calls for a dynamic interpretation of the Charter. The Committee of Experts has accordingly had to reconsider its approach to implementing Article 11.1b and c of the Charter in the light of developments in the media sector, particularly broadcasting, since the adoption of the text. The traditional distinction between "public-service broadcasting" and "private broadcasting" has blurred somewhat. Several types of body might be deemed to be carrying out a "public-service mission" to varying degrees, without

---

16. In 1995 Slovakia adopted a law on the state language, amended several times since, most recently in 2009. The Committee of Experts of the Charter has considered that this law's restrictions and constraints on the use of regional and minority languages exceed what is required to ensure the position of Slovak as the national language.

having to belong to or be supervised by the public authorities. There is a broad associative sector operating along the boundaries of the public and private sectors. Broadcasting methods and platforms have evolved with the arrival of new technologies (Internet and digital TV). It is therefore necessary to re-interpret Article 11, preserving its effectiveness and facilitating attainment of the aims pursued by the Charter.

In addition to these technical aspects, new, extremely intense modes of migration have emerged. Whereas immigration used only to concern isolated workers, it now involves whole population groups; and while in the past these groups sought rapid integration, they now tend to retain their original cultural and linguistic features.

This development has transformed the whole issue of historic regional and minority languages. Owing to increased population mobility, especially recent immigration, many European regions now house new linguistic groups which are characterised by strong demographic expansion and efficiency in transmitting their language down the generations. The "strength" of these new linguistic communities contrasts with the frequent weakness of linguistic groups corresponding to traditional regional and minority languages.

The increasing presence of these new languages of migrant origin indirectly poses serious problems to traditional regional and minority languages. The public authorities often use this situation as a pretext for refusing to support historic regional or minority languages, arguing that for reasons of non-discrimination, such measures should also apply to immigrant languages, whereas they would in fact jeopardise the integration of the populations in question.

And yet, as the European Charter for Regional or Minority Languages has recognised, these two categories of languages cannot be placed on the same footing, firstly because they raise very different problems: speakers of historic regional or minority languages have no problems of integration. Secondly, the heritage and cultural issues are clearly separate. The Charter for Regional or Minority Languages is geared to preserving a regional heritage which is, so to speak, linked to a specific territory and history coming under the heritage of the state in question. All other things being equal, a regional language is naturally destined to enjoy a special status, on the same basis as the national language. Protecting this culture constitutes a political and moral imperative for the state structure which has historically superimposed on it. Like the native populations, therefore, regional language speakers can lay claim to anteriority. Conversely, migrants have chosen to settle in a new state where they are called upon to integrate. While it is legitimate, indeed desirable, that they continue to use their language of origin, provided they also know the language of their new state of residence, this language is not destined to enjoy the same public status.

21

Also in connection with support measures, languages of origin, historic languages and new languages in a given locality and languages of migrant populations all correspond to very different profiles. In one given area, the historic minority language has a legitimate claim on a specific public status. Although the languages of recently established migrant communities constitute an asset of interest to society in general, they are primarily a matter for the communities in question.

Nevertheless, the trend in public opinion and also among political leaders has been to lump these different problems together, subsuming them under the same highly theoretical eulogy of plurilingualism and the same pragmatic suspicion deriving from the financial and political difficulties of linguistic diversity. Generally, while globalisation has shown that monolingualism is not an over-riding necessity, it has nevertheless exacerbated the position of historic regional or minority languages by drowning the problem of their survival in an undif-ferentiated discussion of the attitude to be adopted to the multiplicity of languages used in a society open to mobility.[17]

2.2. Reflections on the efficacy of the Charter

Some observations on the mode of application of the Charter would suggest that it has not always been very convincing:

- a number of states which have ratified the Charter have basically continued their previous policy in the field of regional or minority languages, and their acceptance of the Charter has not really led to any in-depth reconsid-eration of this policy; in particular, some states which, before acceding to the Charter, had adopted measures aimed at cultural regionalisation or recognition of specific statuses in the language field, under a minimalist interpretation of the Charter, have deemed that their language promotion mechanisms already went beyond the requirements of the instrument;

- few states, when ratifying the Charter, revised their legislation and regula-tions on languages in substantive terms in order to guarantee genuinely dynamic implementation of the Charter;

- even those states which have devised active policies to promote regional or minority languages following ratification have often prioritised methods which are not those proposed by the Charter.

Discussion still continues whether it was appropriate for the Charter to opt for a flexible instrument enabling states to make undertakings to maintain and

---

17. For instance, the municipality of Strasbourg is discussing a plan to set up a *maison des langues et culture* covering Alsatian, Turkish, Arabic, Yiddish and sign language, all on an equal footing.

promote regional and minority languages as cultural assets. There are two specific categories of criticism of the efficacy of the Charter: the choice of protecting languages rather than their speakers; and the highly flexible wording of its provisions.

2.2.1. The "cultural" basis of the principle of protecting regional and minority languages

The "culturalist" approach of the Charter, the fact that it protects regional and minority languages as cultural assets rather than the linguistic minorities themselves, may be a weakness. While this approach is capable of defusing ethnic conflicts, it contains the risk of failing to recognise languages as a living social phenomenon and considering them as mere abstractions. This risk is reflected in the tendency to address regional or minority languages in a way that does not really ensure their protection as living, natural phenomena. A potential, even fairly common, deviation in the heritage treatment of regional and minority languages consists in taking a "museographical" view of them. Instead of restoring mechanisms for using, transmitting and learning regional languages, the authorities are sometimes tempted simply to implement such symbolic measures as organising "language festivals" or opening "regional or minority language centres". However congenial such measures might be, they cannot guarantee the use and survival of these languages. When natural transmission ceases to function for various sociological reasons, only intensive teaching in the regional or minority language can give it any serious chance of being learnt by upcoming generations.

There is also a danger of the question of regional languages being engulfed by the whole "linguistic diversity" issue. This kind of development is in evidence, for instance, in EU action regarding the qualified policy to promote plurilingualism. In the European Union, the regional language issue is merely one of many facets of linguistic diversity. Whereas in the past the European Commission initiated activities specifically geared to supporting "minoritised" European languages,[18] this concern has been subsumed under a very broad, vague theme

---

18. The item "promotion and protection of regional and minority languages" introduced into the Commission budget in 1983 was abolished in 2001, following a judgment by the Court of Justice in 1998. Since then, all efforts to secure an appropriate legal basis for this type of funding have failed; this is why EU strategy has been redirected towards a broader goal, regional and minority languages being now considered solely as vehicles for diversity. Funding for such languages has therefore become indirect, channelled through Interreg, Leader and programmes promoting multilingualism, etc. On the Commission's activity in the field of regional or minority languages, see its presentation at http://ec.europa.eu/education/languages/languages-of-europe/doc139_en.htm.

relating to cultural and linguistic diversity.[19] Under the terms of the new Article 3 of the Treaty on the European Union, the Union "respects the wealth of its cultural and linguistic diversity". Article 165 of the Treaty on the Functioning of the European Union comprises a similar reference with regard to education. Article 22 of the European Charter of Fundamental Rights also affirms that the "Union shall respect cultural, religious and linguistic diversity". These formulations are of no use to regional and minority languages, and can even have a negative effect on them by obscuring the lack of effective consideration of these languages. For instance, French policy in this area adopts the same approach of making a very broad reference to linguistic diversity and plurilingualism, serving as an alibi for the absence of any substantial policy of supporting regional or minority languages. The authorities claim to wish to promote plurilingualism, a theme under which French historical linguistic plurality is engulfed, or indeed smothered.

The mechanism of granting specific rights to a linguistic group may, as mentioned above, seem more effective. However, its implementation is subject to a political context which only exists in very few cases. Moreover, it is tailored to situations of "national minorities", which are socially separate groups, aware of their specificity and wishing to retain it, whereby the linguistic difference combines with such other elements as specific cultural and educational institutions, or sometimes even a specific administrative and political administration. Such situations only account for a few of the regional or minority languages spoken in Europe. In many cases, the language is no longer an identifying factor for specific linguistic groups.

The Charter mechanism is better suited to such more and more frequent situations, where the existence of a regional or minority language no longer corresponds to a population group which is clearly split off from the rest of the population and to which specific rights can be granted because they use a regional or minority language.

The use of the regional or minority languages often needs to be restored rather than protected, because natural transmission is no longer functioning. So it is a case not so much of protecting existing speakers as of building up a stock of future speakers. Owing to population mobility and acculturation, moreover, it has often become difficult to pinpoint a language-specific population group in order to apply a special legal regime to it. Furthermore, in contemporary European societies, applying such a regime is seen as tendentious in terms of

---

19. Cf. O. Amiel (2008), "Diversité culturelle et droit communautaire", *Revue du droit public et de la science politique en France et à l'étranger*, No. 1; B. Nabli (2005), "Le principe de la diversité culturelle et linguistique au sein d'une Union élargie", *Revue française de droit administratif*, No. 1.

anti-discrimination regulations.[20] Even if we can get round this difficulty, application of such a specific regime cannot be imposed but must be based on the convictions and choices of those concerned. Yet many of the latter also wish to retain their affiliation with the larger group. Furthermore, the aim is not to replace one language by another but to add an extra linguistic dimension.

In such cases, regional language policy must strive not only to defend but also to rehabilitate these languages. Granting rights to their speakers is not enough. Effective incentives are needed to recruit new speakers for these languages. For instance, what would increase the use of the languages is the presence of regional or minority languages in the media and public institutions, more than the right to use them in dealings with the administration or justice.

2.2.2. The highly flexible wording of the Charter's provisions

Another possible cause of ineffective application of the Charter is its deliberately flexible wording. Part II of the Charter sets the objectives, but leaves the state to choose the means of attaining these objectives. Part III leaves it to the states to choose which undertakings they wish to accept. They can also stipulate the languages to which Part III is to apply. All these elements may suggest that the Charter's undertakings are too vague to be effective.

However, the flexibility of the Charter does not mean that the states can interpret and apply it as they see fit; it merely leaves them room for adaptation for which they remain accountable. As in the case of other non-specific rules, such as the equality and proportionality principles, practice, doctrine and case law must gradually provide increasingly specific criteria for interpretation. The Committee of Experts has a major central role to play here. Of course the committee is not a judicial body empowered to impose its interpretation of the Charter in specific cases. The criteria for the committee's action and the force of its reports prevent its appraisals from being legally binding. Nevertheless, the committee issues more or less official interpretations of the Charter. Such a body is necessary, and is the only possible response to this need. It must do its utmost to fulfil this function of providing authoritative interpretations of the Charter. To that end, it must adopt clear options of interpretations of the Charter provisions and apply them consistently, so that states that have ratified the Charter can refer to them and find increasingly precise rules on implementing the Charter.

---

20. In Alsace, for example, employment agencies reject job offers requiring knowledge of the Alsatian dialect on the ground that such a requirement discriminates unduly against persons who do not speak this language. Though such an argument is clearly spurious, it is approved by the Haute Autorité de Lutte contre les Discriminations.

In this respect some of the Committee of Experts' reports arouse some feeling of dissatisfaction. The committee has not devoted as much attention as it might to its role as official interpreter of the Charter, with a view to gradually fleshing out its scope in its successive reports. It has apparently preferred to concentrate on analysing the admittedly widely varying national situations which it is called upon to appraise, rather than using the reports to develop an increasingly precise interpretation of the requirements of the Charter.

Of course, the Charter does not provide for a system of judicial supervision of the way states implement it. The idea underlying supervision of its application as provided for by the Charter corresponds primarily to a combination of synergy and emulation which is supposed to grow up among states implementing the principles of the Charter. Supervision of application of the Charter should therefore involve exchanges of experience and mutual encouragement in devising actions to promote the less widespread languages. However, the aim is also to make states face up to their responsibilities and commitments to the international community. To that end, the committee's reports must clarify these undertakings by taking account of the situations on the ground, but also by gradually building up the relevant doctrine. The interpretation formulated by the Committee of Experts is made public and is indirectly approved by the Committee of Ministers of the Council of Europe. This interpretation should be made more systematic in order to enhance the effectiveness of the Charter.

In its supervision of the application of the Charter, the Committee of Experts has consistently stressed the importance of Part II. Despite some superficial or erroneous interpretations of the Charter, this part is not a mere catalogue of guidelines with only a moral or political scope rather than legal force. Part II sets out actual legal undertakings on the part of the states, even though the said undertakings are couched in fairly general terms. The scope and consequences of these undertakings are relatively precise, when one considers on the one side the clear objectives of the Charter and on the other the actual situation of each state and each language. The Committee of Experts is therefore wholly justified in systematically verifying compliance with Part II in its periodical reports.

Where Part III is concerned, the committee has frequently recalled that it is not the Charter's intention to leave states an arbitrary choice of undertakings to adopt under this section. The idea is to acknowledge the wide diversity of the situations in which regional and minority languages find themselves and the need to treat them differently. The same measures cannot be applied to all languages in all European states. It is therefore left to the states concerned to select the measures. However, this choice must not be arbitrary: it must take account of the specific situation of each language from the angle of its institutional situation and its potential area of influence.

In the case of the more influential regional languages, for example, it is quite feasible to devote a television channel to them, broadcasting primarily or exclusively in this language. In the case of less widespread languages, such a measure would be impossible, and a local radio station would be better. Part III of the Charter is intended to show states the full range of possible measures to support regional and minority languages, inviting them to choose effective and efficacious undertakings but leaving it to them to decide what is possible in their individual case.

The Charter does not demand excessive or disproportionate undertakings in this section. Even for the undertakings which have been accepted, it specifies that they must be understood as having to be implemented "as far as this is reasonably possible", "according to the situation of each of these languages" or provided that the use of the facilities afforded is not considered to hamper the proper administration of justice or the efficacy of teaching of the national language. Moreover, most of the articles in Part III must be implemented only in the territory in which each language is sufficiently intensively used.

It is noticeable that this part of the Charter endeavours to ascribe a high level of importance to fields which are often neglected by international texts on the protection of minority situations. For instance, in addition to traditional issues relating to schools, justice and administration, the Charter deals with the place of regional or minority languages in the media, in cultural activities and amenities, and in economic and social life. In the latter field, the Charter conceives of positive promotional measures to restore the presence of regional or minority languages in everyday life. There is no doubt that the place of regional languages in cultural, economic and social life is decisive in terms of their future. This is particularly true in the case of the media. In these fields, however, it is not enough to remove prohibitions restricting the use of these languages; given the weakness of their position, they must be granted positive support and special attention.

Nevertheless, many commentaries have concentrated on the provisions on administration and justice. The goal of the Charter in these sectors is not to prompt intensive use of the regional or minority languages, since the national language is prioritised in these fields. The Charter only asks that regional and minority languages be given an effective public life, so that they can secure scope for expression in the activities of the public and judicial authorities. It suggests "reasonable accommodations" under which regional and minority languages can be granted a relative position in the functioning of the public institutions, without disrupting these institutions or challenging the status of the national language.[21] In this field, as elsewhere, the Charter aspires to convivial, positive coexistence rather than sectarian or intransigent confrontation.

Nor can the efficacy of the Charter's system for promoting regional and minority languages be appraised in isolation. The Charter is part of an overall strategy linked up to other international instruments such as the Framework Convention for the Protection of National Minorities, the Reference Framework for Regional Democracy and the language learning policies promoted by the Council of Europe. The Charter sets out a philosophy of cultural rights, regional identity promotion and linguistic diversity, which form a whole.

Each state can develop this philosophy on the basis of its domestic legislation, without needing first to ratify European conventions like the European Charter for Regional or Minority Languages: this international instrument does not give states any new powers which they would not be in a position to implement directly. However, experience shows that collective action packs more punch than isolated action at the national level. Like the environment, preserving traditional linguistic diversity is a value which does not stop at national boundaries. The feeling of responsibility for this value and the desire to defend it is easier to guarantee within the framework of international action as defined in the Charter.

3. Final consideration

For all its weaknesses and ambiguities, the Charter clearly sets out all the necessary ingredients for an effective policy of promoting a regional or minority language:

- a legal framework guaranteeing a status protecting this language;
- availability of bodies representing this language capable of objectively analysing the situation of this language and defining the criteria for a support policy;
- appropriate financial support;

---

21. See J.-M. Woehrling (1998), "Problems raised by the use of regional or minority languages before public and judicial authorities" in *International Conference on the European Charter for Regional or Minority Languages*, Regional or Minority Languages No. 1. Strasbourg: Council of Europe Publishing. Consideration of the first ratifications shows that most states agreed to allow speakers of regional languages to submit written or oral requests in the regional language or to use it in deliberative assemblies. However, the authorities are less often required to use the regional or minority languages themselves, except in signposting or place names, translating specified texts into the regional language and, in some cases, in replying to requests submitted by citizens.

- a school system guaranteeing the acquisition or reappropriation of the language;

- media facilities capable of giving the language a cultural and social reality.[22]

There is a further element which is less clearly asserted by the Charter but which is implicit in it, namely the provision of mechanisms to guarantee some degree of independent management for the population corresponding to the language in question.

Where these facilities are properly implemented, the Charter is properly complied with and the language in question has optimum chances of preservation. Although the Charter does not contain any means of coercion to impose implementation of these facilities, at least it provides a mechanism for finding against states which have failed to honour their commitments.

In conclusion, it should be stressed that the Charter's many ratifications, and the fact that it is very widely recognised in doctrine and public debate, mean that the instrument is now the main European reference in terms of good practice for public policies on regional languages. Even Part III of the Charter, which consists solely of options, serves as a criterion for assessing national action in the field of regional and minority languages. The Charter acts as a catalyst for demands relating to regional and minority languages, as we can clearly see from the ongoing debate in France: the demand for a status for regional languages has taken the form of a demand for French ratification of the Charter; conversely, hostility to regional languages has crystallised into opposition to the Charter. This effectively ensures its function of legitimising demands for protection of regional and minority languages, and constitutes a strong legal argument for granting legal statuses at national level to protect such languages.

---

22. The Committee of Experts has on several occasions stressed that "resolute action to promote regional or minority languages in order to safeguard them covers, among other things, the following aspects: the creation of a legal framework for the promotion of regional or minority languages, the establishment of bodies which are responsible for the promotion of these languages, and the provision of adequate financial resources; Application of the Charter in Germany, 2nd monitoring cycle (2006), paragraph 24; Application of the Charter in Sweden, 2nd monitoring cycle (2006), paragraph 28; Application of the Charter in Norway, 3rd monitoring cycle (2007), paragraph 34; Application of the Charter in Spain, second monitoring cycle (2008), 103.

References

Amiel, Olivier (2008), "Diversité culturelle et droit communautaire", *Revue du droit public et de la science politique en France et à l'étranger,* No. 1, p. 247.

Arzoz, Xabier (2007), "The nature of language rights", *Journal on Ethnopolitics and Minority Issues in Europe*, No. 2.

Benoît-Rohmer, Florence (1995), "La Convention-cadre du Conseil de l'Europe pour la protection des minorités nationales", *European Journal of International Law*, Vol. 6, No. 4.

Blair, Philip (2003), "La protection du patrimoine linguistique européen" in Henri Giordan and Tangi Louarn (eds), *Les langues régionales ou minoritaires dans la république*. Toulouse: IEO Publications.

Bokatola, Isse Omanga (1992), *L'Organisation des Nations Unies et la protection des minorités*. Brussels: Bruylant.

Decaux, Emmanuel (1991), "Le droit international et la protection des minorités" in *Minorités – Quelles chances pour l'Europe, l'événement européen*, No. 16. Seuil: Paris.

Ermacora, Felix (1972), "Der Minderheiten- und Volksgruppenschutz vor dem Europarat" in *System eines internationalen Völkergruppenrechts*. Vienna, Wilhelm-Braumüller- Universitäts-Verlagsbuchhandlung, pp. 73-89.

Gilbert, Geoff (2002), "The burgeoning minority rights jurisprudence of the European Court of Human Rights", *Human Rights Quarterly*, Vol. 24, No. 2, p. 736.

Guskow, Meike (2009), *Entstehung und Geschichte der Europäischen Charta der Regional- oder Minderheitensprachen*. Frankfurt am Main: Peter Lang.

Hartig, Hanno (1994), "Les travaux du Conseil de l'Europe dans le domaine des minorités" in Panazyatis Grigourion (ed.), *Questions de minorités en Europe*, Centre hellénique d'études européennes, Collection l'Europe Plurielle No. 5. Brussels: Presses Interuniversitaires Européennes, pp. 281ff.

Institut du Droit Local Alsacien-Mosellan (1997), *Etat, régions et droits locaux: droits locaux et statuts particuliers en France et en Europe; actes du colloque des 6 et 7 juin 1996*. Strasbourg: IDL/Paris: Economica.

Kovács, Péter (2009), "La protection des minorités dans la jurisprudence de la Cour européenne des Droits de l'Homme", in Laszlo Trocsanyi and Laureline Congnard (eds), *Statuts et protection des minorités; exemples en Europe occidentale et centrale ainsi que dans les pays méditerranéens*. Brussels: Bruylant, p. 49.

Lerner, Natan (1991), *Group rights and discrimination in international law.* Dordrecht. Boston, London: Martinus Nijhoff.

Leuprecht, Peter (1986), "Le Conseil de l'Europe et les droits des minorités", *Les Cahiers du Droit*, Vol. 27, No. 1, pp. 203-13.

McKean, Warwick (1983), *Equality and discrimination under international law.* Oxford: Clarendon Press.

Meyer-Bisch, Pierre (ed.) (1991), *Les doits culturels: une catégorie sous-développée de droits de l'Homme; actes du VIIIe colloque interdisciplinaire sur les droits de L'Homme de l'université de Fribourg/Suisse.* Fribourg/Freiburg: Éditions Universitaires.

Nabli, Beligh (2005), "Le principe de la diversité culturelle et linguistique au sein d'une Union élargie", *Revue française de droit administratif*, No. 1, p. 177.

Varennes, Fernand de (2001), "Language rights as an integral part of human rights", *International Journal on Multicultural Societies*, Vol. 3, No. 1.

Williams, Katherine and Rainey, Bernadette (2002), "Language, education and the European Convention on Human Rights, in the twenty-first century", *Legal Studies: Journal of the Society of Legal Scholars* (Butterworth), Vol. 22, No. 4, p. 625.

Woehrling, Jean-Marie (1998), "Problems raised by the use of regional or minority languages before public and judicial authorities" in *International Conference on the European Charter for Regional or Minority Languages*, Regional or Minority Languages No. 1. Strasbourg: Council of Europe Publishing.

Woehrling, Jean-Marie (2005), *The European Charter for Regional or Minority Languages: a critical commentary.* Strasbourg: Council of Europe Publishing.

Part I
General provisions

Article 1. Definitions

Eduardo J. Ruiz Vieytez
University of Deusto, Bilbao

1. Introduction

2. General scope
   2.1. Language as the subject matter of the Charter
   2.2. The Charter definitions

3. Comments on the relevant provisions: analysis of the Committee of Experts' position
   3.1. Regional or minority languages
   3.2. Territory and non-territorial languages
   3.3. Less widely used official languages

4. Recommendations and good practices

References

Article 1 – Definitions

For the purposes of this Charter:

a. "regional or minority languages" means languages that are:

   i. traditionally used within a given territory of a State by nationals of that State who form a group numerically smaller than the rest of the State's population; and

   ii. different from the official language(s) of that State;

   it does not include either dialects of the official language(s) of the State or the languages of migrants;

b. "territory in which the regional or minority language is used" means the geographical area in which the said language is the mode of expression of a number of people justifying the adoption of the various protective and promotional measures provided for in this Charter;

c. "non-territorial languages" means languages used by nationals of the State which differ from the language or languages used by the rest of the State's population but which, although traditionally used within the territory of the State, cannot be identified with a particular area thereof.

1. Introduction

As a general rule the purpose of legal definitions is to delimit the subject matter or scope of a given legal instrument. In the case of standards concerning cultural objects, the introduction of a number of defining parameters is virtually inevitable in view of the difficulties inherent in determining cultural categories. At the same time, where international legal instruments are concerned, the diversity of national criteria and the plurality of interpretations of some key synonyms frequently plead for the inclusion in treaties of defining parameters that are formulated as clearly as possible. The European Charter for Regional or Minority Languages contains a series of initial definitions intended to delimit its scope with the greatest possible accuracy. Nonetheless this does not prevent many questions arising with regard to both application of the instrument itself and its exegesis.

In Europe we are confronted with a complex variety of linguistic situations, in the sociolinguistic characteristics particular to each language and its legal recognition under each national system of law. For these reasons it was advisable that the Charter begin with a conceptual definition of the categories of languages it is intended to protect. Although the Charter contains few definitions, they are of manifest importance since they determine the treaty's subject matter. Indeed its underlying philosophy clearly shows a desire to protect the European cultural heritage, which therefore has to be defined as far as possible within the treaty itself. It can be – and this applies to the Charter – that, along with the explicit definitions set out in an instrument, other indirect or implicit definitions may be inferred from its wording. This section analyses the Charter's main operational definitions, contained in Article 1, in the light of subsequent interpretations placed on them by the Committee of Experts responsible for monitoring its application.

2. General scope

2.1. Language as the subject matter of the Charter

Language constitutes one of the most remarkable elements of collective identity in present-day Europe. At the same time, virtually all the countries of Europe have to contend with some form of linguistic diversity within their population, given the many linguistic minorities to be found throughout the continent and the number of communities that speak languages different from the official or majority languages of the states in which they live. The fundamental purpose of the Charter, as set out in the Explanatory Report, is to protect as far as possible the use of the regional or minority languages of Council of Europe member states, thereby guaranteeing the preservation of the cultural wealth inherent in our continent's linguistic diversity. It is accordingly a legal instrument with a clear cultural protection role that deals with the regional or minority languages of Europe as a cultural heritage. From this standpoint, regional or minority languages are regarded as an endangered component of the cultural heritage that needs to be protected via an international legal instrument, which one way or another requires the adoption of a definition – whether or not explicit – of that category of languages.

Nowadays, language is essential to the performance of many of the functions incumbent on any state. However, there is a great disparity worldwide between the number of living languages and the number of sovereign states, and this mismatch is mirrored at European level. The sharp distinction between official state languages and other languages would therefore leave largely devoid of protection a rich cultural and social heritage which still exists in variable forms and to different degrees. Indeed, the importance of regulating language use lies not only in the symbolic and instrumental role played by languages in the organisation of political communities but also in their close link with identity and with their speakers' individual and collective development.[1]

It should nonetheless be pointed out that the law's capacity to influence linguistic processes is limited. Those processes usually have social and economic causes that are very often hard to counter via legislation.[2] While language law is the set of legal standards that govern the use of languages in a given political community,[3] its consistency and systematic nature are not always guaranteed,[4] no doubt partly on account of the difficulties of regulating such a particularly complex matter. Nevertheless, there can be no question that language laws are tending to increase both in number and in rank. In recent decades, language-related rules have been adopted, including at the highest constitutional level, by many countries that previously had no explicit law in such matters,[5] to which the international standards, of which the Charter is the most perfect example, must be added.

Regulating linguistic situations via legal standards poses many methodological and operational problems. The complexity of language issues, which normally

---

1. C. O'Reilly (2003), "When a language is just symbolic: reconsidering the significance of language to the politics of identity" in G. Hogan-Brun and S. Wolff (eds), *Minority languages in Europe: frameworks, status, prospects.* New York: Palgrave Macmillan, p. 20; A. Patten (2003), "What kind of bilingualism?" in W. Kymlicka and A. Patten (eds), *Language rights and political theory.* Oxford: Oxford University Press, p. 313.
2. G. Hogan-Brun and S. Wolff (2003), *Minority languages in Europe: frameworks, status, prospects*, p. 5.
3. J. Vernet (ed.) (2003), *Dret lingüístic.* Valls: Cossetània, p. 22.
4. C. Fernández Liesa (1999), *Derechos lingüísticos y Derecho internacional.* Madrid: Dykinson, p. 14.
5. E. Ruiz Vieytez (2005), "Lenguas y constitución: una visión del derecho lingüístico comparado en Europa", *Revista Vasca de Administración Pública*, No. 72, p. 234.

involve hard-to-objectify parameters, makes them difficult to reduce to legal categories. It is hard to determine valid categories, including for a single legal standard. For example, one need but bear in mind the difficulties encountered in defining each individual's own language in view of the combination of personal, social and psychological factors that come into play. It might be considered that a person's own language is the language of his or her parents (together or separately), the language spoken within his or her family, the language he or she knows best, the language he or she uses most in his or her daily life, the language with which he or she identifies most or with which most people identify him or her. Any of these parameters could be adopted to determine the concept of an individual's own language, or various parameters could be applied simultaneously, which would require that they be assigned an appropriate weighting.

In the same way, many difficulties can arise when it comes to determining the legal definition of a language in contradistinction to other forms of expression such as dialects, local variants and jargons. Such a definition would doubtless take account of scientific factors, as well as political or symbolic ones. Similar problems can occur with glottonyms, spellings, alphabets or other elements linked to public usage of languages. Whatever definition is being aimed for in a legal instrument, serious difficulties will be encountered on account of the social, psychosocial, political and cultural complexities inherent in linguistic situations. The problems will be all the greater if it is an international legal instrument that has to be implemented against different social and legal backgrounds, a factor which simultaneously makes it all the more necessary to have operational definitions in place.

At all events, since the Charter's declared objective is to protect the European linguistic heritage, a definition of this concept is needed, or at least of the Charter's subject matter. It can be said that virtually all the fundamental defining questions posed by the Charter have their origin in this principle and are linked to the definitions contained in Article 1 thereof. Four fundamental questions have to be raised on the basis of those definitions. Firstly, it has to be asked whether the Charter determines a single category of languages deserving of protection or whether it establishes different groups of languages to be safeguarded. Secondly, determining what is to be protected brings one directly to the issue of the difference between languages and dialects, since some dialects are not part of the linguistic heritage the Charter sets out to protect. Thirdly, when it comes to defining this European linguistic heritage, a dilemma arises with regard to the so-called immigrant languages, which need to be expressly defined to exclude them from the protection afforded by the Charter. Lastly, it is necessary to clarify the relationship that exists under the Charter between the category of official languages and that of regional or minority languages.

All these questions of definition ensue from the very purpose of the Charter and are reflected only to a partial extent in the document itself, which makes the task of interpreting its first article all the more necessary.

2.2. The Charter definitions

Article 1 of the Charter contains express definitions and at the same time mentions a series of concepts and language-related terms that are linked to those definitions without being expressly defined themselves. The concepts for which Article 1 gives proper, express definitions are as follows:

- regional or minority language;
- territory (in which the regional or minority language is used);
- non-territorial languages.

The language-related concepts with no express definition that are mentioned in the text of the Charter, whether in the above explicit definitions or in Article 3, are these:

- official language;
- languages of migrants;
- dialects (of official languages);
- official language which is less widely used (Article 3).

One of the consequences of the international nature of this instrument is that, although the Charter includes terms such as "regional or minority languages", "non-territorial languages" or "official languages", these concepts do not necessarily have the same meanings when they are utilised in the domestic law of the countries of Europe. This makes it necessary to adapt the categories found in the Charter to those that may be used in domestic law and to again proceed with the necessary interpretations. The fact that the Charter is intended to cover the entire European continent, with its huge diversity of linguistic and social situations, makes this interpretation exercise particularly complex. In view of all these difficulties the chief task of the Committee of Experts is the gradual adoption of criteria that can constitute points of reference in this matter, which makes the analysis of the reports and opinions issued to date in this field particularly relevant.

Consequently, when interpreting the definition of regional or minority languages or completing the Charter's definition of official languages, it is necessary to lay down criteria that go beyond the categories utilised in the various European language laws. The categories mentioned in those laws coincide to some extent with those utilised in the Charter (above all as regards the concepts official language, regional languages and minority languages), but that does not mean that the content must necessarily be the same in every case. On the other hand, in comparative European language law other concepts corresponding to language objects can be found, such as "state language",[6] "national language",[7] "language of the republic",[8] "linguistic regions",[9] "language in parity,"[10] "language of equal status",[11] "own language",[12] "language of the indigenous population",[13] "principal language",[14] "language of interethnic communication",[15] "linguistic minorities"[16] or "own languages of the national minorities".[17]

The states' instruments of ratification of the Charter offer some indication of matches between the categories provided for in the Charter and those in force in the different constitutional systems. However, the adoption of common criteria for interpreting the Charter is principally the work of the Committee of Experts, as the key source of guidance regarding the Charter. The various categories used in the Charter are in fact linked to the definition of regional or minority languages given in Article 1. Therefore an appropriate analysis is required of this definition and its component elements. Such an analysis, linked to implementation of the Charter to date, will supplement the interpretation given to the other two definitions found in the same article.[18]

3. Comments on the relevant provisions: analysis of the Committee of Experts' position

3.1. Regional or minority languages

The key definition of the entire Charter is unquestionably that which appears first in the text and which defines nothing less than the subject matter protected by the treaty. Three of the linguistic concepts that are not expressly defined (official language, languages of migrants and dialects of official languages) are

---

6. Constitutions of Armenia (Article 12), Azerbaijan (Article 21), Georgia (Article 8), Lithuania (Article 14), Russian Federation (Article 68), Ukraine (Article 10) and Slovakia (Article 6).
7. Constitutions of Finland (Article 17), Moldova (Article 13), Ireland (Article 8), Liechtenstein (Article 6), Malta (Article 5) and Switzerland (Article 4).
8. Constitution of France (Article 2).
9. Constitution of Belgium (Article 4).
10. Statutes of Autonomy of Valle d'Aosta/Vallée d'Aoste and the region of Trentino-Alto Adige/Südtirol, Italy.
11. Government of Wales Act (Article 47).
12. Statutes of autonomy of Galicia, Catalonia, the Basque Country, Navarra, Valencia and the Balearic Islands, Spain.
13. Official Language Law of Latvia (Article 4).
14. Self-Government Acts of the Faroe Islands and Greenland (Denmark).
15. Law on the Languages of the Republic of Moldova (Article 3).
16. Constitutions of Italy (Article 6), Sweden (Chapter 1, Article 2.4) and Austria (Article 8).
17. Constitutions of Hungary (Article 68), Ukraine (Article 53) and Poland (Article 35).
18. See E. Ruiz Vieytez (2009), "Constitutions, languages, definitions and the European Charter for Regional or Minority Languages", *Llengua i Dret*, No. 51, pp. 227-53.

present in the very definition of regional or minority languages, and the fourth (less widely used official language) can be seen to be indirectly linked to this definition. At the same time, of the two other express definitions contained in Article 1 (territory and non-territorial languages) the first also refers to an element of the principal definition, whereas the second follows from the exclusion of this same element.

First of all, it should be clear that the Charter's definition of regional or minority languages is functional, not substantive, in nature. In other words, the purpose of this definition is not so much to delimit the concept of a given type of language as to clarify the Charter's scope and which languages can be placed under the protection of Part III, as provided for in Article 3.[19] The Charter does not include a list of regional or minority languages, which could have obviated the need for a definition.[20] An analysis of the instruments of ratification of the states parties and of the reports issued to date by the Committee of Experts leads to the conclusion that the Charter presently[21] covers 84 languages which are used by 206 minorities/linguistic groups[22] in 23 of the 25[23] states parties. Of these 206 groups, 76 are covered by Part II of the Charter only (i.e. the language concerned is a "Part II language") and 122 groups are covered by parts II and III ("Part III languages"). The languages of eight linguistic groups are both Part II and Part III languages in the same country, depending on the region.[24]

This figure can be arrived at only thanks to the Committee of Experts' interpretation of the elements composing the definition given in Article 1, though this interpretation is not entirely clear or consistent, as I shall attempt to show by analysing in detail the separate elements of the definition of regional or minority languages as used when implementing the Charter.

So as to analyse the interpretation that has been given so far to the principal definition of the Charter, I shall adopt as systematic an approach as possible. Firstly, since this is a concept or category that is not unambiguous in its formulation (regional or minority languages), it is necessary to examine whether the definition proposed corresponds to a single conceptual category with two indistinct names or whether the Charter draws a significant distinction between

---

19. Woehrling (2005), *The European Charter for Regional or Minority Languages: a critical commentary*. Strasbourg: Council of Europe Publishing, p. 53.
20. Ibid., p. 56.
21. August 2011.
22. One language may be used by several minorities (for example, Hungarian in eight states).
23. Without Liechtenstein and Luxembourg, where no regional or minority languages are used.
24. Low German in Germany, for example, is a Part III language in the *Land* of Schleswig-Holstein, *inter alia*, but only a Part II language in the *Land* of Brandenburg.

regional and minority languages. Secondly, I shall break down the definition into its component elements and analyse them individually.

3.1.1. Regional languages and minority languages

The Charter protects regional or minority languages, and Article 1 thereof contains a single definition for both categories.[25] It can therefore be asked whether there is something in the definition itself that helps to separate regional languages from minority languages or whether we are really in the presence of a single legal concept which takes on two meanings. Given the diversity of categories that can, and indeed do, exist in the European countries' legal systems, the duality may simply be intended as a means of more fully clarifying the subject matter of the Charter.

In principle, from a literary analysis standpoint, the definition is unambiguous and the joint reference to both categories of languages constitutes an invitation to consider that they actually are interchangeable for the purposes of the Charter, without it being possible for the use of one or the other, or both together, to have different implications. However, on referring to the Explanatory Report, one finds a difference in meaning for each of the categories. According to the Explanatory Report, the adjective "regional" denotes languages spoken in a limited part of the territory of a state, within which, moreover, they may be spoken by the majority of the citizens,[26] whereas minority languages are non-territorial languages or those spoken in a given territory by a minority of those living there. Nonetheless no clear legal or sociolinguistic basis for this distinction can be found in any internationally recognised document and it does pose certain problems of implementation. It will not always be easy to determine the territory within which we have to analyse whether the language in question is a majority one or not. Applying a strict definition of the territory, it may be the case that a language is spoken by the majority of those living there; if we take a more flexible view of its traditional territory, it may be spoken by a minority. Also, it is a known fact that determining the number of people who speak a given language poses problems, especially when it is a question of languages that are not official state languages. In a not insignificant number of cases there may be a huge gap between the number of people who understand a language and those who can read, speak and write it. Nor is it clear whether the term "majority" means that the language must be that used to the greatest extent in social exchanges within the area or whether merely some knowledge of it among the majority of the population is enough.

---

25. "Minority language" is an ancient concept, whereas that of regional languages appeared in the second half of the 20th century. Woehrling (2005), op. cit., p. 54.
26. Explanatory Report, paragraph 18.

In any case, the distinction drawn in the Explanatory Report has not been incorporated in the Charter, nor have other sub-categories been created within those noted above. The terms "regional languages" and "minority languages" are used to refer to distinct factual situations, not to legally differentiated categories.[27] According to the wording of the Charter, in reality each state is free to consider its languages as regional languages or minority languages provided it complies with its obligations under the Charter and thereby sets out to protect, at least through the provisions of Part II, all languages traditionally spoken in its territory which are not the official state language. All these languages should fit into the generic category of "regional or minority languages", and all the states are free to utilise this expression in full or in part. This is reflected, to some extent, in an analysis of the instruments of ratification deposited by the different states.

It is true that, most of the states party to the Charter draw no distinction between the language categories – regional or minority – in their declarations of ratification. Of the 25 countries that have ratified the Charter, eight use the two categories interchangeably in their instruments of ratification.[28] Four countries refer solely to their minority languages[29] and one uses only the expression "regional languages" (Ukraine). Another eight confine themselves to referring to "languages" to be protected, without specifying whether they are regional or minority languages.[30] In the final analysis, only two countries draw any express distinction between the two categories.[31] However, even in the case of Poland it can be objected that the declaration made at the time of ratification is confusing in this regard since, though it declares Kashub as a minority language along with others, in a subsequent paragraph it identifies it as a regional language, a situation which has more to do with the domestic legislation governing the country's minorities than with the spirit and sense of the Charter itself. Similarly, in the case of Germany the distinction does not give rise to any further specifications or consequences.

In the end, despite what is said in the Explanatory Report, for the purposes of the Charter it must be understood that regional or minority languages form a single category that can best be characterised by the languages' traditional features and their exclusion from the official languages of the state. A vast majority of countries have used both categories interchangeably or else just one of them without attaching different meanings to them. The Committee of

---

27. Woehrling (2005), op. cit., p. 54.
28. Finland, Romania, Liechtenstein, Slovakia, the United Kingdom, Sweden, Spain and Slovenia.
29. Denmark, the Czech Republic, Armenia and Austria.
30. Bosnia and Herzegovina, Serbia, the Netherlands, Norway, Croatia, Montenegro, Switzerland, Hungary and Cyprus.
31. The 25th state party, Luxembourg, has no declaration on protected languages in its instrument of ratification.

Experts has also refrained from raising a controversial issue that the states themselves have not brought up and has evaded the question, confining itself to interpreting which languages correspond to the definition in Article 1. The committee has not analysed any alleged difference among the languages concerned, which would anyway have been of little practical significance given the way the Charter is structured.

3.1.2. Classification and analysis of the defining elements

The definition of regional or minority languages proposed in Article 1 is admittedly complex, but it can be analysed in terms of a number of substantive elements, which can in turn be broken down into five main categories. These elements, in order of appearance, are:

- languages;
- used;
- traditionally;
- within a given territory of a state;
- by nationals of that state;
- who form a group numerically smaller than the rest of the state's population;
- different from the official language(s) of that state;
- not including dialects of the official language(s) of the state;
- (or) the languages of migrants.

On the basis of their subject matter these nine elements can be assigned to five categories:

a) Language-related elements: the concepts of language and dialect of an official language (elements 1 and 8).

b) Numerical or demographic elements: minimum or maximum number of speakers (elements 2 and 6).

c) Elements of traditionalism or elements linking the language and the European cultural heritage: traditional nature and nationality of speakers (elements 3, 5 and 9).

d) Territorial elements: the concept of a given state territory (element 4); this links up with the subsequent definitions laid down in Article 1 (territory and non-territorial languages).

e) Elements concerning legal status: the concept of official language of the state (element 7); this links up with the category of less widely used official languages, to be found in Article 3.

In this way, a relation is established between all the language-related categories utilised in the initial articles of the Charter and the definition of regional or minority languages. Some of the elements are merely defining in nature; others serve to exclude. As a result of the diversity of sociolinguistic situations of European minority languages, when implementing the Charter doubts and questions can arise concerning any of the foregoing elements. The work of the Committee of Experts helps us to identify tangible guidelines for their interpretation.

a) Language-related elements

This first group of elements concerns those that are specifically language-related. This is unquestionably the most substantive part of the definition and the one that has the greatest practical implications for the work of the Committee of Experts. It follows from the operative definition of Article 1 that there are two linguistic contents to be clarified, one inclusive and the other exclusive. The first is the very fact of being a language, necessary to qualify for the Charter's protection. This brings us to the need to associate the concept of language as used in the Charter with other neighbouring concepts and with distinct European linguistic situations. Secondly, there is an excluding element of the definition that is closely linked to the former, since the Charter denies protection to dialects of official languages, which leads to the question of the relationship between language and dialect for this purpose.

Languages and dialects in the context of the Charter

The Charter does not propose any definition of language. This is partly due to the fact that the instrument's underlying philosophy is protection of languages with regard to their cultural role[32] rather than recognition of individual or collective rights in connection with given languages. However, while the spirit of the Charter is that of a treaty whose subject matter is cultural rather than human-rights-related, an attempt could have been made to define the linguistic phenomenon it sets out to safeguard. To that end it would have been necessary to distinguish between the categories of language and dialect, which would have been particularly complicated. The Charter in fact uses both concepts in the definition contained in Article 1, but without giving any objective clues to the content of either of them.[33]

---

32. Explanatory Report, paragraph 17.
33. R. Dunbar (2008), "Definitively interpreting the European Charter for Regional or Minority Languages: the legal challenges" in *The European Charter for Regional or Minority Languages: legal challenges and opportunities*. Strasbourg: Council of Europe Publishing, p. 43.

As stated in the Explanatory Report, the Charter also does not attempt a definition of dialect and says nothing about the difference between the two. However, the Explanatory Report, in recognising that this difference is not just influenced by factors of a linguistic nature but also depends on psycho-sociological and political factors, grants the authorities of each state a key role in deciding what forms of expression constitute languages at any given time.[34] The report also states that although the national authorities are not free to deny the existence of regional or minority languages with a view to their minimum protection under Part II, it will be left to the authorities concerned within each state to determine whether a particular form of expression constitutes a regional or minority language within the meaning of the Charter,[35] which seems to allow the authorities a broad margin of discretion. The states cannot deny the existence of languages in their territory, but they can question their individuality by regarding them as dialects. This would seem to indicate that there is some objective leeway as regards linguistic realities and a degree of subjective leeway in their definition, effectively corresponding to the distinction between classification as a language for the purposes of the Charter or consideration as a dialect.

This viewpoint must, however, be fleshed out in the light of the work done by the Committee of Experts. In general, the committee, adopting a more pragmatic approach, has opted to steer clear of complicated discussions on the concepts of language and dialect. So as to recognise the existence of different languages for the purposes of the Charter, it decided to focus on both the consistency of subjective feelings of speakers of a given language and on the seriousness of the issue of the linguistic difference.[36]

This is because discussions as to whether given language variants are different in nature raise real identity-related conflicts that are usually bound up with debates that transcend the linguistic or cultural area. As mentioned above, linguistic realities are difficult to objectify. Linguistics and philology do not offer unequivocal answers that are accurate in all cases, and the symbolic or identity-related functions of language variants are also of political relevance. In reality, the difference between language and dialect is more a political issue than a genuinely linguistic question.[37] Not surprisingly, many of the languages identified in Europe today are but a standardised form of the most widely spoken variants, which have benefited from the official status conferred by state policy,

---

34. Explanatory Report, paragraph 32.
35. Explanatory Report, paragraph 40.
36. Woehrling (2005), op. cit., p. 63.
37. S. May (2003), "Misconceiving minority language rights: implications for liberal political theory" in W. Kymlicka and A. Patten (eds), *Language rights and political theory*. Oxford: Oxford University Press, p. 128.

a situation reflected in the aphorism "a language is a dialect that has its own army and navy." Beyond its artful formulation, what this expression means is that, linguistic conditions being equal, the smaller the political power of a group using a variant, the greater proof is required of the latter's specificity. Or, seen from another angle, that the political sphere plays a part in determining whether language variants are commonly accepted or rejected as established languages, depending on the circumstances.

For instance, when drawing up a list of the languages of modern-day Europe we would not include Luxembourgish if Luxembourg had not emerged as an independent entity. This language would very possibly be regarded in the same way as other variants of the common core German spoken in the southern half of Germany, in Austria, in Switzerland and in South Tyrol. The same could possibly be said of other "state" languages such as Norwegian, Macedonian, Bosnian or Maltese, which could have been regarded as dialects of other languages if their territory had belonged to Sweden, Bulgaria, Serbia and Tunisia respectively. It is in any case clear that the drawing of national borders influenced the identification of a number of variants as languages in their own right or, conversely, the relegation of other variants to the category of dialects of the national language.

Nonetheless, the stated aim of the Charter – protecting Europe's linguistic heritage – has helped to ensure that many variants are considered as separate languages in the light of this treaty. While the interpretative work of the Committee of Experts offers examples of all kinds, it reveals a prevailing tendency to recognise the specificity of regional or minority languages first and foremost when their speakers offer evidence of that specificity. In this sense, through its interpretation of the objective leeway for identifying the traditional languages of a given country, the committee has to a large extent deprived states of the capacity to decide whether given variants should be considered as dialects for the purposes of the Charter. This does not preclude the existence of many complex and uncertain situations that the committee tends to deal with in the most prudent way possible and always based on the assumption that the aim of the Charter is the protection of a linguistic heritage, not its classification.

Separation of languages and use of glottonyms

In the light of the instrument's application to date, the problem of the identity of the languages protected by the Charter can be seen to take various forms. There are a number of cases which raise the question of the existence of one or more separate languages because of the way they are named. These are cases where, in principle, most linguists seem to consider that there is a single language, but as a result of the use of different glottonyms this unity is called into question, at least by some groups of speakers or institutions. The

47

difficulties deriving from languages' identity accordingly also extend to the glottonyms or the names by which they are designated. In fact, the controversy surrounding glottonyms is similar to that already referred to above concerning the difference between languages and dialects.

There are a number of linguistic situations in Europe that are relevant to this issue. In some cases, Romanian and Moldovan for instance, the Committee of Experts has not yet addressed the problem – in this case quite simply because Moldova has not yet ratified the Charter.[38] Other cases have already been addressed in whole or in part. According to the declarations made by Croatia and Serbia on ratifying the Charter and in the light of the Committee of Experts' reports, it can be concluded that the committee has acknowledged the difference between Serbian, Croatian and Bosnian for the purposes of the Charter. It is also true that the mutual resemblance of these languages has been recognised by the committee itself, which acknowledges that they are regarded as separate languages due to the political changes that took place in the region.[39] In regarding Serbian, Croatian and Bosnian as separate languages the committee attaches importance to the linguistic self-identification of each ethnic group with its respective language.[40]

In this connection, the key obstacle to the Charter's application in Spain is the use in the Statute of Autonomy of the Valencian Community (and indirectly in the declaration made by Spain at the time of ratification) of the glottonym "Valencian" to refer to the form of Catalan spoken in that region. In the case of Catalan and Valencian, the Valencian Academy of Language has recognised the language's unity, a fact to which the committee attaches relevance.[41] Nonetheless, the debate continues within society, and the committee is seeking to downplay it while achieving appropriate levels of protection.[42] It has not definitively settled the question, especially since it has decided to treat Catalan and Valencian separately in its reports, despite having noted the unity of the Catalan language. As a result of the committee's position, the variant of Catalan spoken in certain municipalities of the region of Murcia is also referred to in the second report on Spain as the "Valencian language in Murcia".[43]

---

38. On the ratification of Moldova, see Centrul pentru Problemele Minorităţilor (ed.) (2008), *Carta Europeană a Limbilor, Comrat-Taraclia-Briceni-Chişinău – Materialele seminarelor.* Chişinău: Vector.
39. Application of the Charter in Slovenia, 2nd monitoring cycle (2007), paragraph 11.
40. Application of the Charter in Slovenia, 1st monitoring cycle (2004), paragraphs 28-31.
41. Application of the Charter in Spain, 1st monitoring cycle (2005), paragraph 36.
42. Application of the Charter in Spain, 2nd monitoring cycle (2008), paragraphs 82-84.
43. Ibid., paragraph 47.

Another similar outstanding issue concerns the name of the language spoken by the Yezidi group in Armenia. Kurds claim they speak the same language as them, and the Committee of Experts has noted that Yezidi and Kurd were included in the same group until Armenia's independence and that both communities speak the same variant of Kurmanji.[44] The problem, therefore, again concerns the use of a different glottonym by the Yezidi group, as well as the use of different alphabets, though it is stressed that they speak the same language.[45] The debate is ongoing, and in this case the committee has based its approach on the fact that the state decided to treat them differently in its instrument of ratification; it thus considers them as separate languages for the purpose of evaluating application of the Charter.[46]

Unity or diversity of given language families

Another form taken by the debate on identity and languages concerns their possible grouping, for reasons of linguistic similarity, in larger dialectological units. The committee sometimes confines itself to recognising a degree of linguistic similarity between two languages, without this preventing their separate consideration for the purposes of the Charter. This applies, for example, to the cases of Galician and Portuguese,[47] and Czech and Slovakian,[48] whose similarity, according to the committee, is a factor that explains their "special status".[49]

However, in other cases the committee can be seen to regard the grouping of languages or language variants as more self-evident. This concerns situations where political borders have not resulted in distinct standards, but a group of interrelated variants tends to display a degree of cross-border linguistic unity, which is sometimes more symbolical than real. This of course concerns linguistic systems without official state backing which have developed through variants that are not always interrelated but are usually referred to as a whole.

The most complex set of European languages or language variants is those spoken by the Roma. In principle, Romani refers to a language of the Indo-Iranian family, but the geographical dispersion of these communities has had a significant impact on the identification of their language as an unambiguous whole or as diverse variants that can be regarded as separate languages for the purpose of the Charter. In addition, there are the different designations used by

44. Application of the Charter in Armenia, 1st monitoring cycle (2006), paragraphs 1-7.
45. Ibid., paragraph 14.
46. Application of the Charter in Armenia, 2nd monitoring cycle (2009), paragraph 25.
47. Spain 2005, 41.
48. Application of the Charter in the Czech Republic, 1st monitoring cycle (2009), paragraph 21.
49. Application of the Charter in Slovakia, 1st monitoring cycle (2007), Finding O.

the states for the Romani language in their declarations and reports, which are generally respected and simply reused by the Committee of Experts. For instance, in the English versions the following designations can be found: Roma (Slovakia), Romanes (Finland, Norway and the Netherlands), Romaní (Norway and Romania), Romany (Austria, Germany, Hungary, Montenegro, Serbia and Slovenia) and Romani Chib (Sweden). In the case of the Netherlands, the government reports talk of the Roma and Sinti languages,[50] but the instrument of ratification solely uses the term Romanes, which was adopted by the Committee of Experts from its second evaluation report concerning this country.[51] Norway draws a distinction between Romanes, the language of the Roma, and Romani, the language of the Travellers.[52] On other occasions, as for instance in the first evaluation report concerning the United Kingdom, reference is made to the Romani languages in the plural,[53] which leads to the conclusion that their position under the Charter is not clear, and as things stand today the UK does not consider them to enjoy the Charter's protection. The plurality of Roma languages or variants can again be observed in the case of Sweden.[54]

This tends to confirm the opinion that all the designations utilised so far in fact refer to the same language or a group of closely related languages, and there is a strong tendency to consider the Romani language, in its separate forms, as a single language for the purpose of its inclusion in the European linguistic heritage. That being the case, the Committee of Experts usually abides by the designation that each state gives to these languages. Conversely, other languages spoken by Roma communities, such as Beás in Hungary or Caló in Spain, can be more clearly distinguished from this common core.[55] It is clear that the unfavourable living conditions of the Roma communities throughout the length and breadth of the continent have made it difficult for a standardised form of their languages to emerge and have fostered the diversity of these languages not only in their use but also in their names. This explains why only six states (Bosnia and Herzegovina, Poland, Slovakia, Montenegro, Germany and Serbia) protect the Romani language by measures referred to in Part III of the Charter and a larger number of countries protect this language group solely via the provisions of Part II.

A more or less similar situation, but not so complex from a geographical or linguistic standpoint, is that of the Sami languages in the north of Europe. These

---

50. Application of the Charter in the Netherlands, 1st monitoring cycle (2001), paragraph 10.
51. Application of the Charter in the Netherlands, 2nd monitoring cycle (2004), paragraph 22.
52. Application of the Charter in Norway, 1st monitoring cycle (2001), paragraphs 12-13.
53. Application of the Charter in the United Kingdom, 1st monitoring cycle (2004), paragraph 12.
54. Application of the Charter in Sweden, 1st monitoring cycle (2003), paragraph 15.
55. Spain 2008, 60-61.

languages are spoken in territories of the Russian Federation, Finland, Sweden and Norway, and the latter three countries have ratified the Charter. Unlike Romani, it is easier to accept that there is a common thread to the Sami languages, which justifies making general reference to the Sami language and considering the different variants as branches of the same language tree. In English the term "Sami" is used by Norway and Sweden, whereas Finland uses the designation "Saami". For Norway, the Committee of Experts' first report recognises the presence of three variants of the Sami language: North Sami, Lule Sami and South Sami, which in the declaration appended to Norway's instrument of ratification are cited as a single language.[56] However, the Committee of Experts' second evaluation report on Norway mentions a fourth variant, Eastern Sami,[57] referred to in the third evaluation report as Skolt Sami.[58] In Sweden's case too, the Sami languages are referred to in the plural.[59] In Finland, Sami is divided into three variants: North, Skolt and Inari Sami.[60] Another variant comes to the fore in the third evaluation report on Sweden, which refers to a movement for the revival of Ume Sami, on which the committee requests more information from the Swedish authorities.[61] In any case, it can be seen that for the purposes of the Charter the decision has been taken to consider Sami or Saami as a single minority language, without prejudice to the protection enjoyed by its separate variants.

Inclusion of dialects of minority languages

The issue of the distinction between a language and a dialect for the purposes of the Charter has been raised with greater or lesser insistence on numerous occasions. Beyond the controversies surrounding the use of glottonyms or a group of variants' membership of a common linguistic reference framework, in the presence of a given linguistic form the question that usually arises is whether it can be considered a regional or minority language within the meaning of the Charter or whether it is a dialect of another language that is already protected or recognised as an official language. There are indeed a good number of languages that may display a low level of linguistic standardisation or whose independent existence is questioned in some quarters. The question to be asked in such cases is whether these variants can be regarded as languages within the meaning of the Charter.

As we have seen, the definition set out in Article 1 of the Charter excludes dialects of official languages, which suggests that the Charter may cover dialects

---

56. Norway 2001, 9.
57. Application of the Charter in Norway, 2nd monitoring cycle (2003), paragraph 11.
58. Application of the Charter in Norway, 3rd monitoring cycle (2007), paragraph 10.
59. Sweden 2002, 12.
60. Application of the Charter in Finland, 1st monitoring cycle (2001), paragraph 11.
61. Application of the Charter in Sweden, 3rd monitoring cycle (2009), paragraph 21.

of non-official languages.[62] In a way this is what happens with languages such as Sami, although in many other cases whether a form of expression qualifies as a mere dialect or an authentic language is not so clear. Taking into account the Charter's structure in this regard, I set out below a number of cases in which the distinction between a language and a dialect has been addressed, in the light of the status of the language of reference in each individual case. This makes it possible to identify the situations in which a given language variant has been considered a dialect of an official language, distinguishing them from those situations where the language of reference of the presumed dialect is itself another minority language. In accordance with this criterion, four different types of situation can be noted: languages or dialects of the official language of the state itself; languages or dialects of an official language of another state; languages or dialects of a minority language of the state itself; languages or dialects of a minority language of another state or of several states.

Languages or dialects of the official language of the state itself

According to Article 1, dialects of this kind are excluded from the Charter's protection. This means that, if they are to be protected, we must necessarily consider them as distinct languages. Woehrling nonetheless asserts that dialects of an official state language can enjoy protection via the category of less widely used official languages referred to in Article 3.[63] In view of the Charter's wording this theory is debatable, nor does the Explanatory Report appear to endorse it.[64] However, with regard to the Charter's practical application, Norway has qualified Nynorsk as a dialectal variant of the official language and decided to accord it protection under the Charter in the category of less widely used official languages,[65] a state of affairs which the Committee of Experts accepted without raising further questions.

Other cases that raised (with greater or lesser justification) the question whether a given language or linguistic variant might be a dialect of an official language were resolved in the affirmative or the negative, as the case may be, without having recourse to the protection afforded by Article 3. In fact, the negative responses were confined to only two cases, both in Sweden. Scanian was identified by the Swedish authorities as a dialect of the Swedish language, and the committee did not appear to challenge this decision.[66] A somewhat different case is that of Elfdalian, whose speakers requested that it be recognised as a language separate from Swedish. The committee took no decision on this matter,

---

62. Woehrling (2005), op. cit., p. 64.
63. Ibid., p. 65.
64. Explanatory Report, paragraph 51.
65. Norway 2001, 14.
66. Sweden 2003, 17.

but requested more information from the Swedish authorities, asking them to look further into the possibility.[67]

In other cases, a number of languages that, in some people's opinion, are dialects or mere variants of official languages have been granted express recognition under the Charter. These are usually not exactly less widely used languages, but those whose similarity to an official language has all too often led them to be considered in a derogatory way as a kind of patois. The Charter is accordingly the instrument that enables them to flourish and to secure some legal recognition, which would otherwise be very limited. We can include in this group languages like Asturian or Aragonese,[68] which for years were neglected by Spanish textbooks. A similar situation is that of Scots and Ulster Scots, recognised as languages under the Charter although their similarity to English had for many years prevented any form of official recognition within the United Kingdom.[69] Low Saxon has also been recognised as a minority language for the purposes of the Charter,[70] despite the reluctance of certain authorities in the Netherlands to accord it a higher level of protection.[71] A similar case is that of Low German, recognised as the ancestral language of northern Germany.[72] The Committee of Experts denounced the fact that Low German was regarded as a mere variant of German, not as a distinct language,[73] despite the fact that it was described as a regional language in Germany's instrument of ratification. In the same family of Germanic languages, the Limburger language is recognised as a separate language by the Netherlands authorities but not by the Dutch Language Union, causing some uncertainty about its status,[74] though its consideration as a separate minority language for the purposes of the Charter is undeniable. Similarly in Finland, Karelian, a language historically close to Finnish, has been recognised by the Finnish authorities as a separate language for the purposes of the Charter.[75] Lastly, in the case of Switzerland, in agreement with the Committee of Experts, the authorities have recognised that the Yenish speak a non-codified language that belongs to the Germanic family, a hybrid language resulting from a combination of Romani, Yiddish and German.[76] Nonetheless, the Committee

---

67. Sweden 2009, 19-20.
68. Spain 2005, 46-9.
69. United Kingdom 2004, 26-7.
70. The Netherlands 2001, 10, Finding D; the Netherlands 2004, 16.
71. Application of the Charter in the Netherlands, 3rd monitoring cycle (2008), paragraph 11.
72. Application of the Charter in Germany, 1st monitoring cycle (2002), paragraph 31.
73. Ibid., Finding G.
74. The Netherlands 2001, Finding E.
75. Application of the Charter in Finland, 3rd monitoring cycle (2007), paragraph 17, Finding M.
76. Application of the Charter in Switzerland, 1st monitoring cycle (2001), paragraph 19.

of Experts is in favour of considering Yenish to be a specific minority language traditionally spoken in Switzerland.[77]

Languages or dialects of an official language of another state

In other cases the question that arises is whether a given language variant must be considered a separate language or a dialect of the official language of a foreign state. In principle, the definition contained in Article 1 of the Charter does not rule out the granting of minority language status to dialects of official languages of other states. However, it must be clear that, where a mere dialect is considered in this way, the name of the protected minority language must match that of the official language of the other state, whereas if it is designated by a different name for the purpose of implementing the Charter this is because it is understood that it in itself constitutes a distinct language.

There are a good number of languages in this situation. One of the most wide-ranging cases is that of the Ruthenian language, which was long considered in conjunction with the Ukrainian-speaking community,[78] with religion as the true distinguishing factor. This is the approach applied in Ukraine, whose authorities deny the existence of a separate Ruthenian language. However, other countries have included Ruthenian among the languages to be protected (this is the case in Slovakia, Serbia, Romania, Croatia and Hungary). The Committee of Experts has recognised that the Ruthenian language does not always command sufficient recognition as a language separate from Ukrainian.[79] Ruthenian was nonetheless standardised in 1995,[80] and today there can be no doubt about its specificity as compared with Ukrainian, especially since the five above-mentioned states simultaneously protect Ukrainian as a distinct language.

In the far north of Europe, a fairly similar situation occurs with the Meänkieli language (also known as Tornedal Finnish) and the Kven language (also known as Kven Finnish). Both languages are considered in some quarters as mere dialectal variants of the Finnish language. However, Meänkieli is protected as a minority language in Sweden (which also regards Finnish as a separate language) and Kven in Norway. Kven is recognised as an ancient variant of the Finnish language,[81] and discussions on its specificity continued throughout the first two monitoring cycles.[82] However, through the third evaluation report on Norway, Kven was recognised as a separate language.[83] Meänkieli, which is

---

77. Application of the Charter in Switzerland, 2nd monitoring cycle (2004), paragraphs 45-50.
78. Slovakia 2007, 20.
79. Ibid., Finding M.
80. Ibid., 22.
81. Norway 2001, 11.
82. Norway 2001, 19-20; Norway 2003, 23.
83. Norway 2007, 13.

also acknowledged to have the same roots as Finnish, was recognised as a separate language in Sweden only very recently.[84]

Another similar case concerns the Beás language, spoken by a Roma minority in Hungary, which is considered as an archaic version of Romanian but is specifically protected under the Charter.[85] A comparable situation is that of the Arabic language spoken by the Maronite community in Cyprus. The country's government maintains that Maronite Arabic is usually regarded as a dialect, is not codified and has few speakers.[86] The Committee of Experts, however, considers that the Maronite language may be a dialect of Arabic, but not of the official languages of Cyprus, and that it is one of the country's traditional languages, which means that it must be considered as a regional or minority language for the purposes of the Charter.[87]

Lastly, three more borderline cases can be found in Austria and Serbia. The difference between the Croatian language of Burgenland and Croatian itself is questionable at the very least. As the committee itself stated, the distinction between Croatian and Burgenland-Croatian is a very recent one, and the instrument of ratification is the first official reference thereto.[88] In fact, the committee tends to use both terms as alternatives, though it generally adheres to the expression "Croatian of Burgenland" as established in the instrument of ratification. Another confused situation regarding the Croatian language is that of the Bunjevac language, spoken in Serbia, which some people consider as a separate language while others regard it as a mere variant of Croatian. As a consequence, the status of Bunjevac remains undetermined,[89] and in this case the committee has confined itself to requesting more information from the Serb authorities.[90] The committee has also requested more information on the situation of Vlach in Serbia, which does not, however, preclude its protection under Part II of the Charter.[91] The committee points out that speakers of Vlach are divided over its status and that the National Council of the Vlach Minority supported the view that Vlach is a variant of Romanian and need not be standardised, which led the committee to request a clarification of the situation by the authorities in co-operation with the speakers of this language form.[92]

---

84. Sweden 2003, 14.
85. Application of the Charter in Hungary, 1st monitoring cycle (2001), paragraph 13.
86. Application of the Charter in Cyprus, 1st monitoring cycle (2006), paragraph 46.
87. Ibid., 30 and 47.
88. Application of the Charter in Austria, 1st monitoring cycle (2005), paragraph 15.
89. Application of the Charter in Serbia, 1st monitoring cycle (2009), paragraph 12.
90. Ibid., 35-6.
91. Ibid., 23.
92. Ibid., 34.

Languages or dialects of a minority language of the state itself

The third group of cases concerns the possibility that a given language form may be considered as a separate language or as a dialect of another minority language existing within the state itself. As already mentioned, the existence of dialects within the same minority language does not prevent their protection under the same head (as is the case with Sami), though the protection is more straightforward when they are considered as separate languages. Some cases that could be included in this category have been referred to above in connection with disputes over the use of separate glottonyms, which actually conceal differences over the independent or non-independent status of a given language variant. Reference can be made here to cases like that of Catalan in relation to Valencian and the Kurd language in relation to Yezidi. As we have seen, the committee in both cases opted for separate treatment of the two languages, which means they are seen as different languages for the purposes of the Charter.[93]

With regard to the Sorbian language spoken in the easternmost parts of Germany, the internal dialectal difference is clearly reflected in the fact that, under the Charter, two different minority languages are taken into consideration, Upper Sorbian and Lower Sorbian. In this case the geographical separation of the two variants helped to permit this clear distinction, since, despite their obvious linguistic similarity, they have evolved independently.[94] Conversely, the Limburger language, while it is acknowledged to have six different variants,[95] is regarded as a single minority language for the purposes of the Charter. Other related cases that may cause some controversy are those surrounding the Galician language in Spain. In the case of so-called Asturian-Galician, the committee stated in its first evaluation report that this form is not clearly recognised as a variant of Galician, as it should be.[96] However, in the second evaluation report on Spain, the committee seemed to nuance its position. Galician-Asturian continues to be dealt with in separate paragraphs, and the committee states that there is a lack of recognition of its specific identity, but without making express mention of Galician.[97] Lastly, the same evaluation report addresses the existence of the language known as Fala, which it designates "Galician in Extremadura",[98] which could open up the debate on the linguistic or dialectal specificity of Fala in relation to Galician, but would in any case not detract from its protection under Part II of the Charter.

---

93. Spain 2008, 28.
94. Germany 2002, 16.
95. The Netherlands 2008, 16.
96. Spain 2005, Finding Q.
97. Spain 2008, 36-7.
98. Ibid., 45-6.

Languages or dialects of a minority language of another state or of several states

In yet other cases the debate over the category – language or dialect – of a given language form can occur with regard to a minority language present in another state or in several states at the same time. In these cases the practical consequences of the classification exercise are certainly not so important, but if we are effectively talking about traditional languages they should be protected as independent minority languages, regardless of whether their linguistic unity with, or difference from, variants found in other countries can be debated. One example is the Frisian languages, which encompass the variants North Frisian (Germany), Sater Frisian (Germany) and Frisian proper (Netherlands).[99] Their geographical separation over the centuries has led them to develop in different ways and today they must be considered as different languages. More or less the same can be said of Crimean Tatar (Ukraine) and the Tatar languages protected in Finland or Romania. The committee recognises that Tatar is a language of the Turkish family,[100] as is Crimean Tatar, and the existing relations with the Autonomous Republic of Tatarstan,[101] but has made no finding that the two language forms can be considered to constitute a single language. On the other hand, we still do not have the committee's views regarding Romania, which could affect the relationship between the Tatar spoken in that country and the Tatar of Finland or Ukraine.

The minority languages spoken in Spain are a different matter. On one hand, Aranese, which is fully recognised in Spanish law through the Statute of Autonomy of Catalonia, is clearly acknowledged to be a variant of Occitane,[102] a minority language in France currently not protected by the Charter, except as regards its Aranese dialect. Similarly, the committee mentions Tamazight as a traditional language of Spain to be protected under the Charter, but Tamazight could be regarded as a local variant of the Berber language, and the committee in fact uses the term "Berber" on more than one occasion when referring to Tamazight.[103]

b) Numerical elements

The definition of regional or minority languages also encompasses numerical elements which refer to the number of speakers. While with regard to the classification of languages and dialects the key disciplines are philology and

---

99. Germany 2002, 23.
100. Finland 2001, 13.
101. Finland 2007, 56.
102. Spain 2005, 53.
103. Spain 2008, 12 and 51.

psycho-sociology, here reference can primarily be made to sociolinguistic data. In tangible terms, the definition stipulates two requirements: that the language should be "spoken", that is to say that there should be a minimally significant number of speakers, and that the speakers should constitute a minority within the state where they live.

Minimum number of speakers

For a regional or minority language to exist there must be a sufficient number of speakers for us to be able to consider that it is effectively a living language. From the standpoint of the Charter this can be expressed as the minimum number of speakers justifying the adoption of the various protective and promotional measures.[104] This minimum number or percentage is not laid down in the Charter, which leaves the states to determine, in the light of the nature of the measures they intend to implement, the minimum number of speakers required for the adoption of those measures.[105] This means that these numerical minima must be established case by case; alongside the state concerned, the Committee of Experts will have a say in the matter in the context of its monitoring of the Charter's application.

There have indeed been cases where the possible existence of a regional or minority language was raised, but the language was ruled out for the purposes of the Charter as it did not have a sufficient number of speakers or had virtually died out. This applies to Prussian, historically spoken in areas of Germany or Poland.[106] Similarly, in Norway Yiddish is not regarded as a language within the meaning of the Charter for lack of a sufficient number of speakers,[107] though it qualifies as a language protected by the Charter in Sweden, Romania and Switzerland; the situation in Finland is ambiguous since the committee noted a low number of speakers (the figure of 200 is cited), which is tending to decrease.[108] Yiddish is also protected in the Netherlands, though the committee notes that it has only a few hundred speakers.[109]

In other cases, a small number of speakers or even a language's earlier disappearance does not preclude taking it into consideration if its speakers show enthusiasm for its conservation or revival. It seems, therefore, that the attitude shown by groups of speakers is critical for the committee, which also appears to be guided by the criterion of the dominant trend in a language's recent

---

104. To use the terms employed in subparagraph b of Article 1.
105. Explanatory Report, paragraph 35.
106. Application of the Charter in Germany, 2nd monitoring cycle (2006), paragraph 11.
107. Norway 2003, 17.
108. Finland 2007, 15.
109. The Netherlands 2008, 30.

development. If that trend is towards its increased use, the committee tends to take a positive view of an application for protection as a minority language. This is the case, for example, with Cornish, which died out in the 17th century but is today protected under the Charter on the basis of a revival in recent decades, with the result that there may now be about 100 speakers of this language.[110] A similar case is that of Manx: its last native speaker died in 1974, but by 2001 there were 1 689 people who again had some knowledge of the language.[111] Another instance of a language's revival, in this instance not of a language that had died out but that was in a very critical situation, is that of Aragonese in Spain.[112] In Austria, the committee considers that, with over 4 000 speakers of Romani according to the 2001 census,[113] there is justification in according this language the Charter's protection in that country as a non-territorial minority language.[114] In Armenia's case the committee has called on the government to make an effort since the Greek community, though small, is very dynamic.[115] Lastly, according to the third evaluation report on Finland, Tatar is spoken by a community of 800-900 people, a small number that nevertheless does not prevent recognition of Tatar as a minority language in Finland according to the Charter definition.[116]

There are also circumstances in which the committee does not adopt a definitive position and attempts to obtain more information before deciding whether a minority language is really "spoken" in a given country. For example, the Cypriot Government asserted that the Roma population there speaks Turkish with a few words of Kurbetcha, but does not make much use of the latter language. In this case the committee requested more information and refrained from adopting a position on the question.[117] In the case of Finland, the same situation arose with the Roma community's language, known as Caló.[118] Apart from a shortage of reliable data on the number of speakers, a further difficulty is the poverty and advanced age of the population potentially concerned.[119] In

---

110. United Kingdom 2004, 31.
111. Application of the Charter in United Kingdom, 2nd monitoring cycle (2007), paragraph 14.
112. Spain 2005, 52.
113. Austria 2005, 109.
114. Ibid., 110.
115. Armenia 2009, 24 and 15. The same report states that the committee noted an interest in the Charter among a number of groups of speakers of Georgian, German, Polish, Ukrainian and Belarusian, and, due to the lack of data on the number of speakers and their traditional presence, requested more information from the government. The committee nonetheless included these languages in the analysis of Part II. Armenia 2009, 22-3.
116. Finland 2007, 13.
117. Application of the Charter in Cyprus, 2nd monitoring cycle (2009), paragraph 1.
118. Finland 2007, 12.
119. Ibid., 13.

Spain's case, Caló is mentioned as a language spoken by some 4 000 persons and as a specific language when compared with Romani.[120] However, during the second monitoring cycle no new information was obtained. The committee nonetheless seems to consider that Caló should be considered a minority language in Spain,[121] unlike Romani itself of which there seem to be fewer than 100 speakers. In any case, the debate is now open. Similarly, in Armenia the Assyrian, Kurd and Greek languages are spoken by few people and there is a lack of reliable data on the number of native speakers.[122] Lastly, in Croatia the committee found evidence of the traditional presence of a small community of Istrian-Romanian speakers,[123] concerning which it requested more concrete data from the authorities.

In general, the committee regrets the scarcity of data concerning the speakers or native speakers of a good number of languages that could be afforded protection under the Charter, of which the authorities either have, or claim to have, no knowledge owing to the small number of speakers concerned. One of the recommendations most frequently issued by the committee is the reliable, ongoing collection of sociolinguistic data, since that may determine whether a language does or does not come within the definition of Article 1 of the Charter.[124]

Minority status

The other element required under the definition set out in Article 1 is that the language in question should be spoken by nationals of the state concerned who form a group numerically smaller than the rest of the state's population. This therefore rules out the possible protection under the Charter of non-official languages that are nonetheless spoken by a majority of the population of the state party.[125] In fact, in the current linguistic situation of the states that have ratified the Charter, this situation does not arise. No language spoken by the majority of the population has ceased to be an official language (whether or not expressly declared as such) of the state concerned, so the hypothesis envisaged here is currently not borne out. This means that all state non-official languages come under the definition of the Charter if they also meet the other requirements.

However, the possibility that the majority language of a country may have no official status is not entirely hypothetical, but in fact corresponds to the

---

120. Spain 2005, 58.
121. Spain 2008, 59-61.
122. Armenia 2006, 8-9.
123. Application of the Charter in Croatia, 3rd monitoring cycle (2008), paragraph 48.
124. Spain 2008, 32-3; Sweden 2009, 9-10; Armenia 2009, 16-17 and 22-3.
125. Woehrling (2005), op. cit., p. 60.

situation in certain European countries that could potentially ratify the Charter. This principally concerns certain former republics of the Soviet Union, which found themselves caught up in a process of expansion of the Russian language before they gained their political independence. Russian is the official language only in the Russian Federation, Belarus and the autonomous regions of the Crimea (Ukraine), Transnistria and Gagauzia (Moldova). In a number of communities that formerly belonged to the Soviet Union, Russian functions as a language of intercultural or interethnic communication.[126] To date, two ex-Soviet states have ratified the Charter, Ukraine and Armenia, and both have included Russian as one of their minority languages in accordance with the Charter definition. In other cases, however, this question may pose greater difficulties. One of the obstacles to the Charter's ratification by Moldova is in point of fact the place to be occupied by Russian. In this country, Russian is really the majority language and the lingua franca between ethnic groups, whereas Moldovan (Romanian) is the official state language. Lacking official status, Russian could not satisfy the definition of Article 1 of the Charter, since it is not a minority language. On the other hand, it cannot be protected in the category of less widely used official languages, although that category could be applied to Moldovan, at least in some regions. At the same time, it seems shocking that the other languages of Moldova should be granted some level of protection which is denied to Russian. It is clear that the authors of the Charter could not have imagined a situation of this kind, but as things stand at present the Russian language in Moldova could only enjoy the Charter's protection as part of the European linguistic heritage if it were granted official language status, which will depend on the political will existing within the country. Not surprisingly, the language issue is a recurring theme in Moldovan politics and the country's particular linguistic situation constitutes an obstacle to its ratification of the Charter.

c) Elements of traditionalism or linking elements

As already mentioned, the Charter sets out to protect and promote the traditional linguistic heritage of Europe, excluding from its scope linguistic situations that do not correspond to this concept. This is reflected in three defining elements forming part of the definition of Article 1. One of these elements is the exclusion of migrants' languages. The other two are inclusive elements: the notion of traditionalism and the nationality of the speakers of languages. The three elements are related to a large extent and the issues they raise are frequently interconnected.

---

126. Armenia 2006, 13. Article 3 of the Law of the Parliament of the Republic of Moldova of 1 September 1989 on use of the languages spoken in the Moldavian SSR.

Traditionalism

Protection under the Charter only concerns historical languages: those that have been spoken for a long time in the country in question.[127] However, just as for the numerical elements, neither the Charter nor its Explanatory Report provides objective insights into the traditionalism requirement. Traditionalism seems to refer to a given lapse of time, and yet it is related to the speakers' nationality or non-immigrant status. Determining the lapse of time for recognition of the traditional nature of a language is extremely complex, especially when one is confronted with languages brought into a country by immigrants many years ago. An additional question is whether the time span should be measured by the same parameter for all languages or whether other factors influence it, such as the number of speakers or the linguistic similarity of the language in question and the state's official language.

Woehrling asserts that the required period for recognising a language as traditional also depends on the closeness or distance of the language or culture of those who immigrated long ago to the majority language or culture.[128] However, this standpoint, which is not endorsed by the Committee of Experts, can be deemed rather unfortunate since it seems merely to reflect an assimilationist attitude, laying emphasis not on the time that has elapsed but on absorption of the majority culture by the minority group. Traditionalism, like the minimum number of speakers, can be determined case by case according to the tangible circumstances, but it would be difficult to justify differential treatment of two languages that arrived in a country at about the same time simply because they belong to two separate language families. From the point of view of the Charter the question is not whether the speakers of these languages find it easier or harder to acquire the majority language (which can also have to do with other social, educational or demographic factors), but whether the language in question is part of the European linguistic heritage.

The Committee of Experts is very prudent on this matter and does not propose clear criteria that could serve as a general guideline. Nonetheless, reference can be made to a number of cases to determine the committee's position. For example, with regard to the Slovenian language in Croatia, the committee states that, on account of its traditional presence, this language deserves protection under the Charter, regardless of its legal status under Croatian domestic law.[129] Similarly, the committee has stated that Part II of the Charter applies to Croatian, German and Serbian due to fact that they are autochthonous languages used on

---

127. Explanatory Report, paragraph 31.
128. Woehrling (2005), op. cit., p. 59.
129. Croatia 2008, 43-7.

the present territory of Slovenia since the 14th (German) and 16th centuries (Croatian, Serbian) respectively. Furthermore, the Committee of Experts urged Slovenia to clarify whether Bosnian has a traditional presence or not.[130] With regard to the Romani language in Denmark, the Committee of Experts has concluded that this language has no traditional presence in this country as its speakers arrived only from the end of the 1960s.[131] These examples confirm that the Committee of Experts is guided by the theory of a minimum period of 100 years to be found in certain laws concerning European minorities.[132] The Committee of Experts has also recognised that Part II of the Charter applies to Portuguese, Berber and Arabic, not mentioned in Spain's declaration of ratification.[133] However, in the second evaluation report, the committee asks the government to clarify whether the presence of Tamazight (Berber) in Melilla is traditional "and continuous",[134] without it being clear whether this last expression refers to a new requirement or can be considered to be implicitly included in the adjective "traditional".

Another doubt that subsists concerns languages that may have been spoken in the past within a country, which then subsequently died out and are now re-emerging as a consequence of recent migratory movements. For instance, it could be possible to consider Arabic as traditional not only in Ceuta but in other parts of Spain, although it seems that the way the Charter is predominantly interpreted tends to rule out its traditional nature in mainland Spain. A similar question could arise should there be a renewed presence in Spain of speakers of Ladino, or Judeo-Spanish, which has been absent for centuries but has a clear historical link with the country. Conversely, the situation of Yiddish in Spain could raise many doubts as regards a traditional presence, although the committee has cautiously confined itself to requesting more information in this respect.[135]

Nationality of the speakers

The condition that speakers must be nationals, stipulated in Article 1 of the Charter, must be understood to refer to legal nationality or citizenship, as the legal relationship between individuals and the state, not to other non-legal concepts of nationality or the nation. What is required by the Charter is therefore that the language in question should be spoken by nationals of the state, that is

---

130. Slovenia 2004, 35-40; Slovenia 2007, 24-25.
131. Application of the Charter in Denmark, 2nd monitoring cycle (2007), paragraph 29.
132. Article 1.2 of Hungary's Law No. LXXVII of 1993 relating to the rights of ethnic and national minorities.
133. Spain 2005, 54-6; Spain 2008, 48-50 and 56.
134. Spain 2008, 53.
135. Ibid., 16.

to say not by foreigners resident there. The Charter does not set out to protect languages spoken by foreign nationals or foreign languages.[136]

However, this apparently very clear requirement also does not fail to raise serious problems of interpretation. On one hand, there is the need to determine the relationship between the concepts of "national" and "migrant". Since the Charter definition excludes the languages of migrants, it would seem that the latter must be understood as synonymous with foreigners or non-nationals. Although "migrant" is a concept that is more sociological than legal in nature, in this context it is clear that the status of migrant is equated with nationality. Even so, serious classification difficulties arise when certain sectors of the immigrant communities have with the passage of time acquired the nationality of the host state, because there will then be a good number of languages that are spoken in part by nationals and in part by foreigners, and the category "foreign languages" will be more difficult to define.

In any case, it should be made clear that the requirements of traditionalism and nationality of the speakers are cumulative not separate. A fairly hypothetical case would be that of a language traditionally spoken in a country, but always by persons who are not its nationals. Given the functioning of nationality law in the majority of European countries, this occurs relatively infrequently. Conversely, it is common for there to be communities of speakers who already have the nationality of the host country, but whose language does not satisfy the traditionalism requirement already discussed above. This obviously excludes that language from the scope of the Charter, but, in view of the parameters the committee appears to apply to the traditionalism requirement, it is very possible that in a few years' time a good number of non-European languages in the historical sense may qualify to be considered as regional or minority languages spoken by European nationals with a sufficient traditional presence (a number of decades or more than one generation, for example). This issue, which has not been broached to date, undoubtedly portends a subsequent stage in the Charter's development, although the instrument's authors wished to avoid it, since the social changes taking place on the international scene seem to indicate that it will be necessary to reconsider these concepts within a reasonable period of time. The committee has, however, not got to grips with this thorny question so far.

Exclusion of the languages of migrants

In a similar vein, the exclusion of the languages of migrants involves the same kind of problem as the requirement concerning the speakers' nationality. The Explanatory Report to the Charter states that it does not protect "new, often

---

136. Woehrling (2005), op. cit., p. 57.

non-European languages which may have appeared in the signatory states as a result of recent migration flows".[137] An obvious issue of interpretation concerns the meaning of the term "recent", a question that can be linked to the interpretation we have given of the term "traditional". In any case, one of the problems with the Charter is that it may suggest that it protects a European linguistic heritage that primarily corresponds to a snapshot of the situation at a given moment in time, with scarce flexibility or capacity to evolve, which would imply that the instrument could eventually lose some of its legitimacy. On account of its cultural philosophy the Charter cannot become a mere instrument for the conservation of the European "linguistic ecosystem" of the late 20th century; the very concept of the European linguistic heritage must in fact be open to a certain capacity to evolve.[138]

One obvious aspect of this need is the interaction that is already taking place between given migratory processes and the historical presence of certain traditional minority languages. For instance, the traditional presence of Russian in Finland justifies its protection under the Charter, but at the same time its social position has been significantly reinforced by recent immigration from neighbouring Russia. The committee decided to protect this language as such on the basis of its traditional character, but without drawing any distinction between its old and its new speakers.[139] In the same way, in Austria, and particularly in Vienna, the distinction between traditional languages and their variants as languages of immigrants is becoming increasingly blurred. This means that migratory movements from Slovenia, Croatia and other neighbouring countries can reinforce the position of these languages, and, according to the committee, the protection of their languages can help promote immigrants' integration.[140]

This means that where immigrants add new speakers to traditional languages, they can benefit from the provisions of the Charter in respect of their language. What is more, their mere presence will help reinforce the position of that language with regard to the adoption of some of the measures figuring on the full menu of the Charter. In addition to the above-mentioned cases of Russian immigrants to Finland and Slovenia, or Croat immigrants to Austria, a similar dynamic process is also tending to occur with the migration of Italians to Switzerland, Russians to Armenia or Ukraine, Serbs to Slovenia and Arabs and Berbers to Spain. From this standpoint, a question likely to arise is whether it is legitimate to exclude entirely from the Charter's protection other languages of former immigrants, whose presence in Europe is already fairly long-standing.

---

137. Explanatory Report, paragraph 15.
138. R. Dunbar, "Definitively interpreting the European Charter", pp. 44-6.
139. Finland 2001, 14.
140. Application of the Charter in Austria, 2nd monitoring cycle (2009), paragraph 16.

For the time being, some languages of immigrants (those that coincide with traditionally spoken languages) benefit from the Charter's protection, sometimes including cases where the immigrant community has far more members than the community that gives the language the element of traditionalism required under Article 1 of the Charter.

d) Territorial elements

Article 1 requires that regional or minority languages should be spoken "within a territory of the state". In turn, the sense to be conferred on "territory" is determined by the following subparagraph of the same article. Therefore, here it is a matter of determining whether the language in question has a reference territory within the state, in the sense of the definition of territory of Article 1b. This means that the definition of regional or minority languages excludes those languages which, while fulfilling the other requirements, do not have a tangible reference territory, even if they are spoken within the territory of the state. These languages which are excluded from the definition will be those that come under the head of "non-territorial languages".[141]

This requires us to refer at this juncture to the definition of territory given in subparagraph b of the same article. In accordance with that definition, it is the geographical area in which the language under consideration is the mode of expression of a number of people that justifies the adoption of the various protective and promotional measures provided for in the Charter. According to the Explanatory Report, it is the area in which the language is spoken to the largest extent, even if only by a minority, and which corresponds to its historical base.[142] For example, the Committee of Experts has considered Polish in Hungary a territorial language because most persons belonging to the small Polish minority are concentrated in a few places.[143] Although Polish is used by a tiny proportion of the population of these places, that presence was seen as sufficient to apply Part II of the Charter. With regard to Croatia, the Committee of Experts noted that the Roma are a recognised national minority and live in definable areas where their languages have a traditional presence and are afforded a certain degree of protection. On the basis of these four criteria, the Committee of Experts considered the Roma languages as territorial.[144] The concept accordingly does not entail that the language in question should be the language most used in that territory, but that the latter should constitute the geographical area with which it can traditionally be linked. According to the report, more precisely determining this territory for each language is a matter

---

141. Explanatory Report, paragraph 36.
142. Ibid., paragraph 34.
143. Hungary 2001, 19, 24 and 26.
144. Croatia 2010, 85-6.

for the states. However, this is not a discretionary power, nor does it evade control, since respect for the geographical area defined is one of the obligations stipulated in the Charter itself, to be precise in Article 7.1b thereof, and the Committee of Experts will accordingly be competent to monitor appropriate compliance with this obligation. Accordingly, for the analysis of the concept and its application, reference can in fact be made to the comments on the relevant principle of the Charter.

Nonetheless, at this stage in the analysis it must be noted that five states have made declarations on the concept of "territory" referred to in subparagraph b of Article 1. Slovakia and Romania have set a minimum percentage of 20% of the inhabitants of a territory for it to be considered a territory of the language in question under the Charter. Croatia refers to its proposed domestic legislation, which is in fact less strict than the former rules. Serbia and Montenegro refer to those areas in which the minority language is in official use in accordance with domestic law, which in practice entails new minimum thresholds of speakers of between 1% and 25% of the inhabitants of each municipality.

The Committee of Experts' position concerning these minimum thresholds is clearly negative. The committee considers that setting minimum thresholds of speakers as a screening measure for recognition of a minority language is incompatible with the Charter, and that the declarations made by these countries, if interpreted literally, would constitute a reservation not permitted by the Charter itself.[145] The committee makes it clear that it evaluates the Charter's application in the territories of the different languages according to realities on the ground and without regard to the constraints of domestic legislation, and this approach is valid for all the countries that have chosen this solution.[146] The committee accordingly tends to interpret the territory of each language with the same flexibility it requires of the governments[147] and is particularly concerned when it finds that a traditional territory of a language has been excluded from the Charter's application.[148]

Another type of question linked to territory brings us to the need to clarify the Charter's geographical scope. The initial question was whether the territory of the states parties was confined to their territories located in Europe or whether it included all the territories under their jurisdiction. The first option would be more geographical and the second more legal or official in nature. The Preamble

---

145. Slovakia 2007, 42-7.
146. Serbia 2009, 29; Application of the Charter in Slovakia, 2nd monitoring cycle (2009), paragraphs 12-13; Application of the Charter in Hungary, 3rd monitoring cycle (2007), paragraph 12. We do not yet have an opinion on Romania.
147. Austria 2009, 15.
148. Sweden 2009, 11-14.

to the Charter talks of the historical languages of Europe, a concept which can be interpreted in the geographical sense or as the sum of all the countries of Europe. For Woehrling, languages that are not strictly European which are spoken in a European sovereign territory can be covered by the Charter.[149] In fact the committee accepts this possibility in so far as it applies to the Arabic spoken in Ceuta and the Berber spoken in Melilla, Spanish sovereign territories that are clearly part of the African continent. Since geographical distance would seem to be a less consistent criterion, it is not very clear why some non-European languages could be protected by the Charter but not others. At all events, what some countries term their overseas territories or dependencies could lead to some doubts. In fact the states parties that might have raised this question – the United Kingdom and the Netherlands – have both issued statements restricting the application of the Charter to their European territories.[150] Although the Charter does not permit reservations to be entered in this matter, the Committee of Experts has not addressed the issue of a possible extension of its territorial scope. In the case of Denmark, the exclusion of the languages of the Faroe Islands and Greenland is due to other criteria which will be analysed below.

e) Elements relating to legal status

Under the Charter a regional or minority language cannot be the official state language. This makes it necessary to define this last legal concept in a manner that can encompass the diverse situations of the countries of Europe. Fundamentally, two questions can be raised when determining the meaning of official language of the state, as utilised in Article 1 of the Charter, one relating to its application in national legal systems that do not utilise this concept and the other concerning those legal systems that use the concept of official language for more than one language. It is ultimately a matter of bringing the terms used in the Charter into harmony with the diversity of legal concepts applied by the countries likely to accede to it.

Official language in fact and in law

It is possible to say that for 36 of the current 47 Council of Europe member states an express definition of the official language or languages can be found in their constitutional law. The translations of the various constitutional or legal texts concerned utilise the following equivalent expressions: "state language", "official language" and "language of the republic". However, the expression "national language", utilised by six states, is more debatable. In

---

149. Woehrling (2005), op. cit., p. 59.
150. In the case of the United Kingdom this includes the Isle of Man, but not the Channel Islands (which are not part of the UK, having the status of Crown dependencies) or Gibraltar.

four of the countries concerned (Liechtenstein, Ireland, Malta and Switzerland), this term is used alongside that of official language, which means that there are no doubts concerning the languages that enjoy this or that status. However, in both Finland and Moldova, the expression "national language" is used alone, making it the equivalent of what is termed the "official language" in other legal systems. Similarly, in the case of Belgium the term "linguistic regions" used in the constitution denotes the official territory of each of the corresponding languages. Other language-related legal concepts to be found elsewhere in Europe, such as "language in parity", "language of equal status", "own language", "language of the indigenous population", "principal language", "language of interethnic communication" or "own languages of the national minorities", in principle cannot be equated with the official language of the state within the meaning of the Charter.

In all of these countries there is therefore no reasonable doubt as to their official languages which are accordingly excluded in principle from the definition of regional or minority language under the Charter. The problem could arise with the remaining 11 Council of Europe member states which have not expressly defined their official language in any legal category (this concerns the Netherlands, the Czech Republic, Norway, San Marino, Iceland, Sweden, Hungary, the United Kingdom, Denmark, Greece and Germany). The Explanatory Report to the Charter recognises the need for each state to determine its official language,[151] but this does not necessarily have to be done expressly. In fact, all of the states have one or more official languages in the substantive sense, even if they have not formally declared them as such in a written text. The states referred to above all have an official language within the meaning of Article 1 of the Charter, which accordingly cannot enjoy protection as a regional or minority language. This is confirmed by the Committee of Experts' interpretation of the situation in the Czech Republic, since it states that, as a result of the dominance of Czech in that country and the privileges accorded to it under its legislation, this language is considered official for the purposes of the Charter,[152] an approach that can quite easily be extended to the other countries on the list.

Conversely, the fact that a non-official language is sociologically recognised as a language of interethnic communication or lingua franca does not make it an official language for the purposes of the Charter where there is already an official language in the same country and it could therefore be protected as a minority language if appropriate.[153]

---

151. Explanatory Report, paragraph 29.
152. Czech Republic 2009, 11.
153. Armenia 2009, 27-8.

Official status for the entire territory

In Europe there are a number of languages falling within one of the aforementioned categories that are official languages of distinct territories, from municipalities to entire states, via autonomous territorial entities. However, from the standpoint of the Charter a language is not official merely because it is expressly recognised as such.[154] The territorial scope of this official status will play an important role here, since what is excluded under the Charter is not all official languages, but official languages of the state, that is to say solely those whose official status extends to the entire state territory.

By converse implication, non-state official languages, enjoying this status only in certain more or less extensive areas of the state concerned, can for the purposes of the Charter fall within the category of regional or minority languages, rather than official languages.[155] Hence, languages like Galician, Welsh or Gagauz can be placed under the Charter's protection despite their official status in certain self-governing territories.

To date, the application of the Charter has encountered no major obstacles in this respect, apart from the situation of Denmark. The Committee of Experts has urged the Danish authorities to include the languages of the Faroe Islands and Greenland under the Charter's protection, since neither of them is covered in the state reports.[156] The committee finds it surprising that these languages are not included, since they perfectly correspond to the type of language for which the Charter was drawn up.[157] According to the Danish authorities, the Faroe Islands' institutional bodies have shown absolutely no interest in extending the Charter's application to their language, while the Greenland authorities have expressed some interest, as indicated in the second state report.[158] In any case, the fact that the autonomous authorities of these territories have expressed little or no interest in the Charter should not be a relevant factor for precluding its application, since Denmark as a whole is a state party to this treaty. It should also not be forgotten that this is an instrument designed for the protection not of speakers' rights, but of a cultural heritage belonging to all Europeans.

Official status in form or in substance

In relation to the exclusion of official state languages, a specific case has arisen with regard to the Charter's application in Cyprus that raises new questions. The country's constitution recognises the existence of two official languages

---

154. Woehrling (2005), op. cit., p. 61.
155. Explanatory Report, paragraph 14.
156. Application of the Charter in Denmark, 1st monitoring cycle (2004), paragraph 26.
157. Ibid., Finding C.
158. Denmark 2007, 24.

for the entire country, Greek and Turkish. This would tend to exclude Turkish from the Charter's protection, at least as a regional or minority language, but leaves the door open to its protection as a less widely used official language. The problem is posed by the specific conflict situation prevailing in Cyprus, in that the country is in fact divided into two zones which in practice act is if they each had only one official language, Greek in the south and Turkish in the north.

With a view to implementing the Charter, the Cypriot Government is responsible for the part of the country under its effective control, which in practice means that, although Turkish is formally an official language nationwide, in the current situation (which has now endured for more than three decades), the sole active official language is Greek, leaving Turkish in a very weak position within the territory controlled by the Cypriot authorities. The Committee of Experts has arrived at the conclusion that Turkish has in fact ceased to be an official language,[159] which could pave the way for a new interpretation of this require-ment. If, in the positive sense, a possible and indeed accepted interpretation is that some countries have official languages that are not expressly declared, it would also be possible to assert that in a given country a language does not exist as an official language, despite its express declaration as such. However, the committee has for the time being not dared to go so far in its findings.

In this connection the committee has stated that Turkish must be guaranteed no less favourable treatment than the regional or minority languages of Cyprus.[160] This could be achieved by considering it a less widely used official language, but this is a decision for the state concerned, since this category is not based on objective criteria or on a definition, unlike the situation of regional or minority languages. So far, the committee has continued to request information on this matter,[161] while observing that Turkish is indeed in a situation equivalent to the minority languages.[162] How this situation will develop remains to be seen, since it could indeed give rise to a less formal, more substantive interpretation of the concept of official state language, as is the case with countries where no express declaration has been made.

3.2. Non-territorial languages

As pointed out above, the languages which fulfil the remaining requirements of the definition set out in Article 1 subparagraph a, but which do not have a territorial basis, are considered for the purposes of the Charter to be non-territorial languages, in keeping with the definition set out in subparagraph c

---

159. Cyprus 2006, 40.
160. Ibid., 41.
161. Cyprus 2009, 25.
162. Ibid., 19.

of the same article. These languages are therefore protected under Part II of the Charter and form part of the European linguistic heritage, but they are not strictly speaking either regional or minority languages within the meaning of the Charter. This is corroborated by the Explanatory Report[163] and the logic of the treaty.[164] Nevertheless, another interpretation is also possible in keeping with the philosophy of the Charter and that is that non-territorial languages should be considered as a sub-category of regional or minority languages. Whatever the case, neither interpretation has any practical consequences.

Only three countries expressly mention non-territorial languages in their instrument of ratification, namely Sweden, Poland and Cyprus, but this does not mean that the national authorities of other countries have not subsequently recognised non-territorial languages or that the Committee of Experts has not detected the presence of such languages. The only country which, in accordance with Article 21.1 of the Charter, has made a reservation to Article 7.5 in its instrument of ratification and therefore to the application of the Charter to its non-territorial languages is Croatia. Therefore, although Croatia has recognised the traditional presence of the German, Hebrew and Romani languages on its territory, the condition of non-territorial languages within the meaning of the Charter excludes them from its scope as a result of the aforementioned reservation.[165]

Under Article 7.5, non-territorial languages are only protected by the provisions of Article 7, not by Part III. Accordingly, once the application of Part III to a specific language has been accepted, it is not possible subsequently to reconsider it as a non-territorial language, as the Armenian authorities claimed when they wished to consider Russian as a non-territorial language.[166] However, in the specific case of the division of Cyprus into two zones, the Committee of Experts recognised that Maronite Arabic, which could be considered a minority language within the meaning of the Charter, had in fact become a non-territorial language.[167] In another case, the question arose of whether a language which was considered to be a minority language in one area of the country could be considered a non-territorial language in other parts of the same country, although no decision has yet been taken in this matter.[168]

There are currently 13 European languages, spoken in 12 different countries, which are protected as non-territorial languages: Armenian (Cyprus and Hungary), Maronite Arabic (Cyprus), Beás (Hungary), Bulgarian (Hungary),

---

163. Explanatory Report, paragraph 36.
164. Woehrling (2005), op. cit., p. 69.
165. Application of the Charter in Croatia, 1st monitoring cycle (2001), paragraphs 27-8.
166. Armenia 2009, 75.
167. Cyprus 2006, 58.
168. Austria 2009, 92-4.

Caló – a Gypsy dialect (Spain), Greek (Hungary), Karaim (Poland), Romanes or Romani (the Netherlands, Norway, Austria, Finland, Hungary, Poland, Spain and Slovenia), Russian (Armenia, Finland), Tatar (Finland), Ukrainian (Hungary), Yenish (Switzerland) and Yiddish (Finland, the Netherlands, Norway, Poland, Sweden and Switzerland).[169]

With regard to the future, the "non-territorial languages" category may raise problems in changing social circumstances. For example, although the family of Romani languages can today clearly be considered non-territorial, the sedentarisation of a growing percentage of the Roma population in many parts of Europe, in the same way as happens with some traditionally itinerant communities, may in the long run mean that these languages can no longer be placed in the "non-territorial languages" category, unless the concept of reference territory is confined in all cases to historical periods predating the Charter.

3.3. Less widely used official languages

The final linguistic category mentioned in the Charter is found in the reference in Article 3 to an "official language which is less widely used", which is, however, not clearly defined. When drafting the Charter, it was decided to include this reference to cover the situation of some official national languages which might, nevertheless, require some protection given their sociolinguistic vulnerability. According to the Explanatory Report, there are national languages which have the status of an official language of the state but may in other respects be in a comparable situation to regional or minority languages.[170] Irish Gaelic was paradigmatic of this category and the first language that fell therein. Ironically, Ireland's failure to ratify the Charter has prevented the application of this provision as the authors of the Charter may have intended.

Given the wording of this provision, this category can be applied not only in states which proclaim more than one official language for the whole country,[171] but also in the other states when it is considered that, in some part of the country, the official national language is in a situation comparable to regional or minority languages. Indeed, Woehrling cited, as possible candidates for using this article, countries with different legal-linguistic situations such as Finland, Switzerland, Croatia or Spain.[172] One of the problems that the article raises is that its wording

---

169. In the case of Romani and Gypsy dialects in Spain, the Committee of Experts pointed out that it was possible to consider them as non-territorial languages, but it also asked for more information on this subject: Spain 2008, 14-15.
170. Explanatory Report, paragraph 51.
171. Ireland, Malta, Luxembourg, Finland, Switzerland and Cyprus. Also in Europe, but not included among the Council of Europe member states, there are Belarus and Kosovo.
172. Woehrling (2005), op. cit., p. 79.

is sufficiently vague for very different situations to fit into this category without any objective criteria being identified. Although the term must be used in accordance with the underlying philosophy of the Charter, this category should always be applied while taking account of the national legal framework and the overall sociolinguistic situation so that it cannot be used to protect sufficiently consolidated official languages to the detriment of the development of regional or minority languages.

Only two countries make any reference to this category in their instrument of ratification. Switzerland states that it will apply this provision to the Italian and Romansh languages, and Finland places Swedish in this category. Nevertheless, in practice, the application of this category has also been extended to Norway where, despite the fact that no explicit reference is made in the instrument of ratification, this category applies to the Nynorsk variant of Norwegian.[173] In the case of Switzerland, the term "less widely used official language" does not apply to German or French given that Switzerland decided when ratifying the Charter not to apply the provisions of Part III of the Charter. However, Part II applies to French in the Canton of Bern/Berne and to German in the cantons of Fribourg/Freiburg, Valais/Wallis, Ticino (municipality of Bosco-Gurin) and Jura (municipality of Ederswiler).[174]

The Norwegian example is not lacking in interest as it illustrates two important consequences. The first is that, contrary to what is provided in Article 3, it has been accepted that a country may make undertakings under Part III in respect of any linguistic variant without stipulating this either in the instrument of ratification or in a subsequent acceptance. On the other hand, it can be concluded from such a case that the "less widely used official language" category can be applied to dialects of the official language which cannot be considered to be regional or minority languages.[175] Indeed, Nynorsk has always been regarded as one of the two variants of the Norwegian language and not as a separate language,[176] but this has not prevented the committee from accepting it as a less widely used official language.

---

173. Norway 2001, 14 and 21; Norway 2003, 9.

174. 1st Periodical Report of Switzerland, pp. 9-10; Application of the Charter in Switzerland, 3rd monitoring cycle (2008), paragraph 15; Application of the Charter in Switzerland, 4th monitoring cycle (2010), paragraph 11.

175. Woehrling (2005), op. cit., p. 65.

176. The Norwegian law of 11 April 1980 on the use of languages in public services establishes the official bilingualism of Norwegian institutions (Article 1): "The Bokmål and Nynorsk languages are linguistic variants of equal value and have equal status in the written communications of all national bodies and municipal and regional councils" (my translation of the French version taken from the website of *L'aménagement linguistique dans le monde*).

4. Recommendations and good practices

From the analysis of the Committee of Experts' work to date, we can conclude that, with regard to the majority of the questions raised, the committee has avoided determining objective rigid parameters and has sought in all cases to establish flexible criteria that can easily be adapted to the actual situation in each country and, where appropriate, of each language protected under the Charter. The committee has therefore neither fixed nor established strict numerical criteria for determining the minimum number of speakers of a regional or minority language, or a specific period of time for which a language must have been spoken in order to be considered traditional, or a general criterion for distinguishing between separate languages or dialects of the same language.

On the contrary, the stance taken by the speakers appears to be very important for the Committee of Experts. Although it is not clear how this stance can be interpreted in groups which may prove to be heterogeneous, what is certain is that on numerous occasions the committee has based its decision on the wishes expressed by speakers or groups of speakers with which it has had contact during study visits or on an informal basis. The wishes of the speakers of the languages concerned are therefore, in the eyes of the committee, not so much decisive information as an element to be taken into account and on which it either bases its own position or which leads it to request more explanations from the relevant authorities. The committee's subjectivity is, however, not always "neutral" since one of the consequences is an increase in the number of languages protected by the Charter given that there is a tendency to consider as separate languages linguistic variants which are defended as such by the speakers of those variants. The fact that other speakers of the same language or of a similar language have a different opinion does not seem to be as important to the committee when it comes to allowing each variant its own space, which also extends to the issue of glottonyms.

Lastly, it is important to point out that the committee seeks to foster a concrete and not merely formal concept of an official language, which is undoubtedly an appropriate position from the point of view of the underlying philosophy of the Charter.

As regards recommendations, there is still a need to clarify the exact identity of certain languages, particularly when there is a linguistic relationship between them. The clearest example in this connection is that of Romani languages. The overall situation regarding these languages should be clarified so that they can be given more effective protection under the Charter. Similarly, it would be better if the committee avoided sterile discussions on the number of languages or their identity and if it also established a clear position when available linguistic evidence allows it to do so.

The concept "official language" should in future be clarified once and for all; such a definition should be extended to include the use that may be made of the concept "less widely used official language" found in Article 3. The aim should be to ensure that its use does not undermine the philosophy of the Charter and to clarify the possibility that less widely used official languages should include dialects of such languages.

Finally, the most complex problem that should be addressed in the course of time is that of the inevitable adjustment of the concept of the European linguistic heritage, which will at some point require a reinterpretation of what access to the protection offered by the Charter should be accorded to those numerous languages currently excluded because they are spoken by migrants or non-nationals. The distinction between territorial and non-territorial languages in the Charter offers possibilities of reinterpretation. Whatever the case, given the rapidly changing social situation in Europe, it will be necessary to devise an approach which ensures the continuity of the Charter as an instrument, without the rigidity that would condemn it in the medium or long term. Above all, the demands which may gradually emerge in this connection should be addressed in the same way the committee currently handles such problems, that is, through dialogue with the authorities and the speakers of the new language communities demanding the same protection as their fellow European citizens. Not only must the Committee of Experts and the Council of Europe play a long-term role in this work but there will also be a major responsibility for academics, who must continue to ensure the effectiveness of the Charter through their reflection and in particular by protecting the most vulnerable aspects of the European linguistic heritage.

References

Centrul pentru Problemele Minorităților (2008), *Carta Europeană a Limbilor, Comrat-Taraclia-Briceni-Chişinău – Materialele seminarelor*. Chişinău: Vector.

Dunbar, Robert (2008), "Definitively interpreting the European Charter for Regional or Minority Languages: the legal challenges" in *The European Charter for Regional or Minority Languages: legal challenges and opportunities*, Regional or Minority Languages No. 5. Strasbourg: Council of Europe Publishing, pp. 37-61.

Fernández Liesa, Carlos (1999), *Derechos lingüísticos y derecho internacional*. Madrid: Dykinson.

Hogan-Brun, Gabrielle and Wolff, Stefan (2003), "Minority languages in Europe: an introduction to the current debate" in Gabrielle Hogan-Brun and Stefan Wolff (eds), *Minority languages in Europe: frameworks, status, prospects*. New York: Palgrave Macmillan.

Kymlicka, Will and Patten, Alan (2003), "Language rights and political theory: context, issues, and approaches" in Will Kymlicka and Alan Patten (eds), *Language rights and political theory*. Oxford: Oxford University Press.

May, Stephen (2003), "Misconceiving minority language rights: implications for liberal political theory" in Will Kymlicka and Alan Patten (eds), *Language rights and political theory*. Oxford: Oxford University Press.

O'Reilly, Camille (2003), "When a language is just symbolic: reconsidering the significance of language to the politics of identity" in Gabrielle Hogan-Brun and Stefan Wolff (eds), *Minority languages in Europe: frameworks, status, prospects*. New York: Palgrave Macmillan.

Patten, Alan (2003), "What kind of bilingualism?" in Will Kymlicka and Alan Patten (eds), *Language rights and political theory*. Oxford: Oxford University Press.

Ruiz Vieytez, Eduardo (2005), "Lenguas y constitución: una visión del derecho lingüístico comparado en Europa", *Revista Vasca de Administración Pública*, No. 72, pp. 231-75.

Ruiz Vieytez, Eduardo (2009), "Constitutions, languages, definitions and the European Charter for Regional or Minority Languages", *Llengua i Dret*, No. 51, pp. 227-53.

Vernet, Jaume (ed.) (2003), *Dret lingüístic*. Valls: Cossetània.

Woehrling, Jean-Marie (2005), *The European Charter for Regional or Minority Languages: a critical commentary*. Strasbourg: Council of Europe.

Article 1c. Non-territorial languages

György Andrássy
Márk Vogl
University of Pécs

1. Introduction

2. Analysis: protection and promotion of non-territorial languages

3. Commentary

4. Recommendations

References

Appendix: Number of speakers of non-territorial languages

> ### *Article 1*
>
> **c.** *"non-territorial languages" means languages used by nationals of the State which differ from the language or languages used by the rest of the State's population but which, although traditionally used within the territory of the State, cannot be identified with a particular area thereof.*

1. Introduction

The Charter is designed to protect and promote threatened historical languages of Europe as parts of Europe's cultural heritage, underlining that the protection and promotion of these languages are in accordance with – and a supplement of – the existing human rights principles of the United Nations and the Council of Europe. The Charter protects and promotes most of these languages as territorial languages, but there are also some languages which so far have always counted, and several other languages which count in some instances, as non-territorial languages within the meaning of the Charter.

This chapter does not analyse the concept of non-territorial languages; such an analysis and a discussion of the related issues is provided in another chapter. Instead, this chapter focuses on how the languages identified as non-territorial have actually been protected and promoted in the states parties so far.

In the process of implementation of the Charter relating to non-territorial languages, the states parties and the committee have faced several difficulties; this chapter analyses and comments on two such difficulties from a theoretical and a practical point of view. These comments are then supplemented by putting some issues in a broader context, with two recommendations that concern non-territorial and territorial languages alike.

2. Analysis: protection and promotion of non-territorial languages

2.1. Protected and promoted non-territorial languages under the Charter

Article 21 of the Charter allows states parties to make one or more reservations to paragraphs 2 to 5 of Article 7. The fact that only one state party has made such a reservation and, in particular, excluded the application of Article 7 paragraph 5, means that all other states parties undertook "to apply, *mutatis mutandis,* the principles listed … in paragraphs 1-4 of Article 7 to non-territorial languages".[1]

Although there has been some uncertainty and dispute about both the presence and the territorial or non-territorial status of some languages in the overall process of implementing the Charter, it seems that the most important non-territorial languages identified in one way or another are the Romani varieties[2]

---

1. Croatia 2001, 35.
2. "Romani varieties" is probably the most appropriate term to use in this context and, for the sake of simplicity, we use it here. We must note, however, that there is at least one language, the Boyash, whose situation is unique: this language is defined by its speakers as a Gypsy language but it cannot be considered as a variety of the Romani language: "Most Boyash people define their own ethnicity and language as 'Boyash' in their mother tongue in intra-group communication. This endo-definition is used when they talk both about Romani-speaking groups, whom they

and the Yiddish language: the Romani varieties (or one of them at least) are present traditionally in most states parties,[3] and the Yiddish language is present at least in five of them.[4]

Those languages of which the non-territorial status was identified either by the states parties or the Committee of Experts are as follows: Armenian (Cyprus, Hungary, Poland), Beás (Hungary), Bulgarian (Hungary), Caló (Spain), Cypriot Maronite Arabic (Cyprus), German (Croatia), Greek (Hungary), Hebrew (Croatia, Poland), Karaim (Poland), Karelian (Finland), Romanes (Netherlands (as Romanes languages), Norway), Romani (Austria, Finland, Germany, Hungary, Norway, Poland, Serbia, Slovenia, Spain, Sweden (as Romani Chib)), Russian (Armenia, Finland), Tatar (Finland), Ukrainian (Hungary), Yenish (Switzerland) and Yiddish (Finland, Netherlands, Poland, Slovakia, Sweden, Switzerland).

The situation of these languages differs substantially throughout Europe, which is reflected, *inter alia*, in the number of their users. However, there is a high degree of obscurity about the number of speakers of non-territorial languages.[5] Therefore it seems expedient to refer only to a few categories relating to the number of speakers. The first group may be the languages which count roughly 100-1 000 speakers; these are Romani in Spain, Yiddish in the Netherlands and Finland, Armenian in Hungary, Romanes and Romani in Norway and Tatar in Finland. The second group is languages with 1 001-10 000 speakers; they are Bulgarian, Greek and Ukrainian in Hungary, Armenian and Cypriot Maronite Arabic in Cyprus, Yiddish in Sweden, Caló in Spain, Karelian in Finland, Romani in Slovenia and Austria,[6] and the Romanes varieties in the Netherlands.

---

unanimously call 'lakatar', and about non-Gypsies. In intergroup communication, and when using the majority language, they refer to themselves and their own language as 'Gypsi', in opposition to Romani-speaking groups and in opposition to non-Gypsies as well" (A. Szalai (1999), "Linguistic human rights problems among Romani and Boyash-speakers in Hungary with special attention to education" in M. Kontra, R. Phillipson, T. Skutnabb-Kangas and T. Várady, *Language: a right and a resource*. Budapest: Central University Press, p. 308). So while "their ethnic and linguistic internal identification is 'Boyash', and their external (self-) definition is 'Gypsi'" (ibid.), the language of these Boyash people is actually "an archaic version of the Romanian language" (Hungary 2001, 19), which is not a variety of Romani.

3. The status of the Romani language in Denmark is still pending, since the committee received contradictory information about the traditional and continuous presence of this language in the country. Cf. Denmark 2007, 26-9.

4. The presence of Yiddish is somewhat uncertain in some states party to the Charter, notably Slovakia, Norway, Armenia and Spain; it is present in Germany but the committee concluded that this language in Germany is not "covered by the Charter". Germany 2002, 8-9.

5. This follows from the fact that the figures originate from various sources and they are not comparable in many cases; also, in some cases the committee does not refer to the number of speakers at all. For more details see the Appendix to this chapter.

6. According to official data, Austria has 4 348 Romani-speakers; but Romani-speakers estimate their numbers at 20 000 to 25 000. Cf. Austria 2004, 36.

Languages in the third group count 10 001-150 000 speakers; these are Russian in Armenia and Finland, Beás in Hungary and Romani in Sweden, Hungary, Germany and Serbia. The number of speakers of the Roma community in Finland is not known.[7]

This picture must be supplemented with the fact that the official and the estimated numbers of speakers differ significantly in certain countries.[8] In addition, there is a remarkable difference between the number of speakers of some languages and the number of persons belonging to their respective minority groups.[9]

2.2. Non-territorial languages under Article 7 paragraph 1a

The Parties shall base their policies, legislation and practice on the recognition of the regional or minority languages as an expression of cultural wealth.

According to the committee the term "recognition", in terms of the subparagraph, covers two meanings: it can either mean "formal" or "practical" recognition. The committee's practice shows that it insists on the fulfilment of formal recognition in every instance; this may follow from the fact that it is this subparagraph which gives expression to the underlying philosophy of the Charter in a very clear and simple form.

When the committee evaluates "formal recognition" in the states parties, it mostly examines whether there are such provisions in their legal systems which designate each regional or minority language, one by one,[10] through declaration of their value and the corresponding level of protection.[11] It also occurs sometimes that the committee considers it satisfactory if the state party explicitly undertakes to apply the Charter to the respective languages in its instrument of

---

7. There are about 10 000 Kaale Roma in Finland. Cf. Finland 2007, 13.

8. Besides the Austrian case (see note 6), we may mention that some estimates put the number of Beás and Romani-speakers together as possibly 200 000 in Hungary, while official data from the 2001 census refer to only 48 689 speakers. Cf. Application of the Charter in Hungary, 2nd monitoring cycle (2004), paragraphs 15 and 41. It is worth noting that most of the evaluation reports lack either official data or estimated numbers of speakers of certain languages. For the lack of official data, see for example: Germany 2002, 29 (lacks official data for Romani); Sweden 2003, 15 (lacks official data for Romani languages); the Netherlands 2008, 19 (lacks official data for Romanes languages); Finland 2007, 17 (lacks official data for Karelian). For the lack of estimated data, see for example: Serbia 2009, 18 (lacks estimated numbers for Romani); Finland 2007, 14 (lacks estimated numbers for Russian); Armenia 2006, 7 (lacks estimated numbers for Russian).

9. For the sake of simplicity this note contains only examples based on official data (giving first the number of speakers and then the number of persons belonging to the given minority): Romani in Serbia: 78 980/108 193; Russian in Armenia: 29 563/14 660. Cf. Serbia 2009, 18; Armenia 2006, 7 and 9.

10. Armenia 2006, 21.

11. Switzerland 2004, 45.

ratification.[12] Nevertheless, the practice of the committee varies and this may, to a certain extent, be attributable to the differing state practices.[13]

In most cases the committee regards Article 7 paragraph 1a fulfilled if all regional or minority languages are formally recognised as part of cultural wealth.[14] However, if a language suffers from prejudice and has a very low prestige, and this appears to be typical in the case of some non-territorial languages, in particular the Romani varieties, the committee stresses the need to supplement "formal recognition" with certain forms of "practical recognition".[15] Practical recognition may consist in funding of cultural activities and organisations, enhancing the presence of the language in the media,[16] teaching the language and teaching the culture of which it is an element and a main carrier.[17] Last but not least, these measures must be taken within the framework of a structured policy.[18]

In connection with "formal recognition", the committee does not consider it satisfactory if a state party, instead of recognising the cultural wealth of minority languages, prefers to protect its national minorities[19] or religious groups[20] without an explicit mention of their languages as representing cultural wealth which deserves special protection. Nor does the committee deem it sufficient if a state recognises cultural diversity or multilingualism in general only;[21] in this respect the committee also stresses and urges that each regional or minority language be appraised as an expression of cultural wealth. The committee is of the view, on the other hand, that "practical recognition" requires a structured language policy and not merely measures with an ad hoc character.

2.3. Non-territorial languages under Article 7 paragraph 1b

The Parties shall base their policies, legislation and practice on the respect of the geographical area of each regional or minority language in order to ensure that existing or new administrative divisions do not constitute an obstacle to the promotion of the regional or minority languages in question.

---

12. The Netherlands 2001, 15; Cf. Application of the Charter in Cyprus 1st monitoring cycle (2006), 52.
13. Norway 2001, 29; Cyprus 2009, 34.
14. Spain 2005, 78; Armenia 2009, 31.
15. Hungary 2001, 21.
16. Hungary 2007, 10.
17. Serbia 2009, 38.
18. National minorities and minority language policy can also "recognise" non-territorial languages as being integral elements of cultural wealth. Cf. Sweden 2003, 33.
19. Switzerland 2008, 20-1.
20. Cyprus 2006, 51.
21. Ibid.

Evaluating the application of Article 7 paragraph 1b, the committee does not deal with non-territorial languages, most probably because these languages are dispersed and this excludes the possibility that their protection might be hindered by administrative divisions of the states. In other words, the committee may be of the view that, if the administrative division of a state party could hinder the protection of a language, this language would probably count as territorial instead of non-territorial in the given territorial unit.

In any case, it seems that the committee does not consider Article 7 paragraph 1b relevant in the implementation of the Charter in relation to non-territorial languages.

2.4. Non-territorial languages under Article 7 paragraph 1c

The Parties shall base their policies, legislation and practice on the need for resolute action to promote regional or minority languages in order to safeguard them.

The committee made it clear in several evaluation reports how the term "resolute action" shall be interpreted. Accordingly, resolute action covers, among other things, the following aspects: the creation of a legal framework for the promotion of regional or minority languages, the establishment of bodies which are responsible for the promotion of these languages, and the provision of adequate financial resources.[22] A recognised commentator holds that these are the three main kinds of measure from which it can be apparent that actions taken in the interest of regional or minority languages have overall coherence (which is needed for an action to be resolute).[23] Therefore, the lack or insufficiency of these measures can entail the need of further implementation of Article 7 paragraph 1c.

The committee's practice shows that all the measures mentioned above, and insufficiencies regarding them, apply both to territorial and non-territorial languages. Insufficiencies may be: there is not an overall legal instrument which provides a general framework for any particular language;[24] there are not proper institutions or organisations which are responsible for the promotion of these languages;[25] or the organisations of the respective linguistic minorities or the activities of these minorities are not financed appropriately.[26]

---

22. Spain 2008, 103; Germany 2006, 24; Sweden 2006, 28; Norway 2007, 34.
23. J.M. Woehrling (2005), *The European Charter for Regional or Minority Languages: a critical commentary*. Strasbourg: Council of Europe Publishing, p. 112.
24. Finland 2007, 40; Slovenia 2004, 87.
25. Sweden 2009, 15-6.
26. See previous notes.

In regard to non-territorial languages, while the first two kinds of measure raise problems less often, the third, funding, seems to be quite problematic: states do not have funds earmarked for this purpose,[27] the allocation of funds lacks transparency,[28] or it is provided after considerable delay,[29] the amount of resources is not sufficient,[30] or it is not adapted to the different situation[31] or to the changing needs of these languages.

Finally, there are special difficulties which arise mainly in relation to non-territorial languages. The most complex among them is when the speakers do not accept, in one way or another, the protection and promotion provided by the Charter.[32] It can also happen that the committee has insufficient information[33] about the situation of a language and therefore it cannot evaluate whether actions taken for the protection and promotion of that language can be considered appropriate or not. Non-territorial languages are in most cases dispersed and this also hinders states parties from taking adequate resolute action in those states where the promotion of languages is tied to concentrations of speakers in territorial units.

2.5. Non-territorial languages under Article 7 paragraph 1d

The Parties shall base their policies, legislation and practice on the facilitation and/or encouragement of the use of regional or minority languages, in speech and writing, in public and private life.

In connection with this subparagraph, the committee focuses primarily on public use of non-territorial languages. This probably follows from the fact that the Charter understands and specifies the term "public life" in quite a wide sense; as Woehrling puts it, public life includes "whatever is not part of private life".[34] Therefore, the undertaking of the states parties under Article 7 paragraph 1d can be considered fulfilled if the use of a protected language is "generally encouraged in the various aspects of public life and if restrictions are acceptable and do not undermine the promotion of regional or minority languages"[35] and if the use of the language is, in principle, encouraged in the field of private life as well.

---

27. Cyprus 2009, 36; Sweden 2009, 25.
28. Cyprus 2009, 36.
29. Austria 2009, 35.
30. Austria 2009, 34; Serbia 2009, 45.
31. Austria 2009, 35.
32. There is discussion and comment on this issue under subheading 3.1. of this chapter, so it seems sufficient here to provide only some references: Germany 2002, 58; Switzerland 2008, 30; the Netherlands 2008, 32.
33. Sweden 2003, 39.
34. Woehrling (2005), op. cit., pp. 113-14.
35. Ibid., p. 114.

A characteristic feature of the practice of the committee is that within the fields of public life enumerated in Part III of the Charter[36] it gives priority to mass media. This means that the committee makes just a few references to other issues and then only if there is a clear need for the presence of the language[37] or this presence is expressly required by the speakers,[38] or the legal system of a state party ensures this kind of presence of the language (i.e. the committee assesses how domestic law is implemented in this respect),[39] or the committee intends to point out certain positive examples.[40] This practice of the committee is understandable at least to the degree that the rest of the provisions of Article 7 cover the remaining fields specified in Part III of the Charter, as, for example, Article 7 paragraph 1f does education.

Although in principle Article 7 paragraph 1d covers all forms of mass media, the committee puts the emphasis on radio: it is more inclined to decide on whether certain non-territorial languages are present in radio broadcasting in an appropriate way and to a satisfactory degree than to consider these issues, for example, in the field of television broadcasting or in the written press. The committee insists that radio broadcasting come to fruition in the case of all non-territorial languages, and it does not consider it sufficient if the programmes are only about the language[41] or the linguistic community[42] but not in the language concerned. Besides, when the broadcasting is hindered, for example because it is difficult to gain access to the radio frequency[43] or the frequency cannot be received,[44] the committee expects that the situation be resolved. Nonetheless, this undertaking is usually considered at least partly fulfilled,[45] even if programmes are only partly in the given languages.[46]

The committee usually ascertains whether there is a lack of television broadcasting in the non-territorial languages concerned,[47] but it encourages the authorities to ensure broadcasting in the given languages only in a few cases.[48]

---

36. Cf. Hungary 2001, 24.
37. Sweden 2003, 42 (in the fields of justice and health care).
38. Cyprus 2009, 55 (in the field of culture).
39. Hungary 2004, 19-20 (the use of non-territorial languages in justice and administration).
40. In the field of culture, see for example Sweden 2006, 43; Sweden 2009, 35; in the field of care and health care, see Sweden 2009, 35; Cyprus 2009, 50.
41. Sweden 2009, 37 (as regards Yiddish).
42. Cyprus 2006, 76 (Cypriot Maronite Arabic community).
43. Austria 2005, 70-1.
44. Hungary 2004, 25.
45. See for example: Sweden 2009, 35 (in Romani); Finland 2004, 45 (in Russian); Cyprus 2006, 74 (in Armenian); Hungary 2007, 21 (in Armenian, Beás, Bulgarian, Greek, Romani and Ukrainian).
46. Slovenia 2007, 66 (partly in Romani); Cyprus 2009, 59 (partly in Cypriot Maronite Arabic).
47. Sweden 2009, 35 (in Romani); Sweden 2009, 37 (in Yiddish).
48. Cyprus 2009, 61 (in Cypriot Maronite Arabic and Armenian).

Actually, the presence of non-territorial languages as the medium of television programmes is very thin.[49]

It can be established in general that magazines and periodicals are published in most non-territorial languages,[50] even if in several cases only some of the articles published[51] are in the given language. It seems that the committee settles for this, since it often states only that there is a lack of state funding[52] or that state funding seems insufficient,[53] and encourages the authorities only exceptionally to consider the need for structured financial support.[54]

Within the meaning of the Charter, private media count – to some degree at least – as a field of public life. Therefore, it is not surprising that the committee examines the presence of non-territorial languages in private media, too. In doing so, the committee considers it unacceptable if the authorities claim they are not allowed to "interfere" in the operation of private media.[55] In addition, the committee considers that regional or minority languages must be present both in traditional and new media.[56]

As already mentioned, the committee does not pay much attention to the implementation of Article 7 paragraph 1d in the field of private life. An exception is that, when observing a need to increase the awareness of Roma parents of the importance of using their language at home and to support the language clubs in Finland, the committee encouraged the authorities to develop strategies to facilitate the use of Romani both in public and private life.[57]

While examining fulfilment of Article 7 paragraph 1d, the committee has faced certain difficulties on the part of the speakers. For example, speakers are opposed to the opportunity that the use of their languages be promoted

---

49. Finland 2004, 46 (programmes in Russian are received from Russia); Slovenia 2007, 66 (in Romani language in certain territories); Hungary 2007, 21 (in Armenian, Beás, Bulgarian, Greek, Romani and Ukrainian).

50. Sweden 2009, 35 (in Romani); Sweden 2009, 37 (in Yiddish); Armenia 2006, 27 (Polish magazine published also in Russian); Finland 2007, 57 (in Russian); Finland 2007, 60 (in Yiddish); the Netherlands 2008, 49 (in Yiddish); Cyprus 2009, 47 (in Armenian).

51. Finland 2004, 42 (articles in Romani); Slovenia 2004, 85 (partly in Romani); Cyprus 2009, 54 (articles in Cypriot Maronite Arabic).

52. Finland 2001, 39; Cyprus 2006, 78.

53. Finland 2007, 58; Cyprus 2009, 47.

54. The Netherlands 2008, 49.

55. Cf. for example, Germany 2002, 59 and 118; Germany 2006, 30-1 and 129; Application of the Charter in Germany, 3rd monitoring cycle (2008), paragraph 437.

56. Germany 2002, 59.

57. Finland 2007, 52 and 54 (Romani).

in some fields[58] or in all of the fields[59] of public life; sometimes they simply do not wish state support for their languages.[60]

It can also happen that speakers would like the use of their language to be facilitated and/or encouraged by the state, but the broadcaster requires the status of that language to be cleared for ensuring programmes in the given language.[61]

2.6. Non-territorial languages under Article 7 paragraph 1e

The Parties shall base their policies, legislation and practice on the maintenance and development of links, in the fields covered by this Charter, between groups using a regional or minority language and other groups in the State employing a language used in identical or similar form, as well as the establishment of cultural relations with other groups in the State using different languages.

The Charter requires in general that states participate actively in the protection and promotion of regional or minority languages spoken on their territories.[62] However, it is also common in relation to non-territorial languages that the organisational and institutional guarantees which make possible the continuous fulfilment of the two obligations in Article 7 paragraph 1e have already been established in the given states. In such cases the committee simply acknowledges these forms and may note in the following evaluation report that, in the absence of any new information requiring reassessment of the application of this provision, it just reserves the right to evaluate the situation again at a later stage.[63]

The links in question can be maintained and developed in several ways. Linguistic groups develop these links through their cultural associations;[64] the organisation of administration is structured in a way which supports the development of these connections – for example by a multilevel minority self-government system,[65] by a government council for national minorities or by the system of national minority councils;[66] besides, in fostering these connections the national committees of the European Bureau for Lesser Used Languages (EBLUL) can also play a very important role.[67]

---

58. Switzerland 2008, 33-4 (Yenish); Finland 2001, 37 (Romani).
59. Germany 2002, 60 (Romani); Norway 2007, 68-9 (Romani and Romanes).
60. Finland 2001, 38 (Tatar and Yiddish).
61. Finland 2007, 50 (the Finnish broadcasting company in the case of the Karelian language).
62. Cf. ECRML, Article 7 paragraph 1c.
63. Hungary 2004, 22. Incidentally, there have been cases where the committee has re-evaluated the situation at a later stage. Cf. the Netherlands, 1st, 2nd and 3rd monitoring cycles (2001, 2004, 2008).
64. Finland 2001, 41 (Russian, Tatar, Romani).
65. Hungary 2001, 25.
66. Serbia 2009, 55.
67. Finland 2001, 42.

The authorities contribute to the inculcation of Article 7.1e in several ways, for instance via organising consultations[68] and conferences[69] with organisations representing groups speaking non-territorial languages, on which occasions these organisations can exchange experiences. The committee encourages the authorities to continue such initiatives with particular emphasis on the protection and promotion of the relevant languages, which can become necessary because these events concern primarily national minorities instead of linguistic groups.[70] Nonetheless, the committee monitors the implementation of both obligations, so it examines not only the development of links between groups employing a language used in identical or similar form, whether or not these are all non-territorial languages, but it also encourages the establishment of cultural relations with other groups using different non-territorial languages when it is necessary.[71]

Application of Article 7.1e can be prevented if co-operation with the speakers is insufficient[72] or the authorities are not active enough in this field.[73]

2.7. Non-territorial languages under Article 7 paragraph 1f

The Parties shall base their policies, legislation and practice on the provision of appropriate forms and means for the teaching and study of regional or minority languages at all appropriate stages.

Education plays an extremely important role in transmission of languages to new generations. However, this line of language transmission is quite problematic and confusing in the case of non-territorial languages. In many cases there is no teaching and study, either in or of the language,[74] not even when there is an expressed wish for it.[75] However, there are also examples which show that, even when education in or of a particular non-territorial language is made available, only a few speakers avail themselves of these opportunities; the reason can be that parents are not sufficiently informed[76] or that providing mother-tongue education is tied to certain conditions, for instance to a certain

---

68. The Netherlands 2008, 52 (Romanes).
69. Germany 2002, 61 (Romani).
70. The Netherlands 2008, 52 (Romanes); Norway 2003, 67 (Romani and Romanes).
71. Cyprus 2006, 82 (Armenian and Cypriot Maronite Arabic).
72. Switzerland 2001, 41 (Yenish and Yiddish).
73. Slovenia 2007, 42.
74. Switzerland 2001, 43 (Yiddish); Sweden 2002), 50 (Yiddish); Germany 2005, 38 (where Romani language is covered only by Part II of the Charter – with the exception of Hamburg).
75. Spain 2008, 173 (Romani); Netherlands 2008, 65 (Romanes); Slovenia 2007, 62 (Romani); Switzerland 2001, 42 (Yenish); Austria 2009, 66 (Romani language outside Burgenland); There is no general teaching support scheme: Norway 2007, 91 (Romani and Romanes) and 94 (Romani is not offered as a subject in schools anywhere in Norway).
76. Sweden 2006, 52; Finland 2007, 68; Serbia 2009, 58.

concentration, minimum number of pupils[77] or minimal language skills.[78] It also occurs, however, that speakers of some languages do not demand state support for the education of their languages at all or they expressly oppose the teaching of the language through state support or outside their group[79]. Finally, it also happens sometimes that the information at the disposal of the committee proves not to be unequivocal.[80]

When the committee examines whether education of non-territorial languages is carried out in the appropriate stages, it emphasises especially the importance of pre-schools and primary schools in language acquaintance and maintenance, and deals with higher stages of education mainly if there exists teaching in or of the language at these stages in the state party.[81]

Teaching of non-territorial languages is usually organised outside the regular state school-system. In such cases the committee urges states to include instruction of or in the relevant languages in the normal curriculum.[82] This indicates that the committee does not consider this state practice appropriate, as it causes for example additional strain on pupils.

The structure of Article 8 of the Charter suggests, in accordance with common sense, that studying in a language is more favourable than study of a language, from the viewpoint of language transmission. Despite this fact the committee deals with this issue not so often,[83] most likely because the main obstacles preventing the implementation of Article 7 paragraph 1f arise not as much from the forms as the means: in many cases there is a lack of teachers and teaching materials, let alone qualified teachers[84] and appropriate teaching materials.[85]

---

77. Sweden 2006, 50 (Yiddish); Austria 2009, 64 (Romani in Burgenland).
78. Sweden 2006, 52.
79. Switzerland 2004, 48 (Yenish); Germany 2002, 65 (Romani); Norway 2001, 43 (Romanes).
80. Hungary 2007, 30 (Romani and Beás).
81. Hungary 2007, 30 (Romani and Beás), 32 (Bulgarian); Cyprus 2009, 70-4 (Armenian); Finland 2001, 44 and 49 (Romani and Russian). For an exception, see the Greek language in Hungary: Hungary 2007, 36.
82. Hungary 2004, 52; Hungary 2007, 26 (Armenian); Hungary 2007, 45 (Ukrainian); Cyprus 2006, 102 (Cypriot Maronite Arabic); the Netherlands 2004, 62 (Yiddish); Sweden 2009, 41; Austria 2009, 64 (Romani in Burgenland); Finland 2004, 53 (Romani).
83. Hungary 2001, 26 (Beás and Romani).
84. Spain 2008, 174 (Romani); Slovenia 2004, 87 (Romani); Sweden 2006, 55 (Romani); Cyprus 2009, 76 (Armenian); Cyprus 2009, 82 (Cypriot Maronite Arabic); Hungary 2001, 26 (Romani and Beás); Sweden 2009, 47 (Romani); Slovenia 2007, 64 (Romani); Austria 2009, 64 (Romani in Burgenland), Finland 2007, 69 (Romani); Norway 2007, 94 (Romani and Romanes).
85. Hungary 2001, 26 (Romani and Beás); Cyprus 2006, 103 (Cypriot Maronite Arabic); Switzerland 2004, 49 (Yenish); Sweden 2006, 55 (Romani); Austria 2005, 89 (Romani in Burgenland); Finland 2007, 69 (Romani); Slovenia 2004, 87 (Romani).

2.8. Non-territorial languages under Article 7 paragraph 1g

The Parties shall base their policies, legislation and practice on the provision of facilities enabling non-speakers of a regional or minority language living in the area where it is used to learn it if they so desire.

The Preamble of the Charter declares that "the protection and encouragement of regional or minority languages should not be to the detriment of the official languages and the need to learn them"; Article 8 of the Charter reinforces this by setting out that "with regard to education, the Parties undertake, … without prejudice to the teaching of the official language(s) of the state, to" promote the teaching in or of the regional or minority languages. These expressions of respect for teaching in and of the official languages refer to two facts: one is that most speakers of the regional or minority languages in most states parties have to learn the official language(s) under the relevant legal provisions; the other is that the overwhelming majority of the speakers of regional or minority languages also "know that, for their own personal fulfilment, they need to know the official language".[86] However, the "spirit of receptiveness to several languages should not be confined to the speakers of regional or minority languages",[87] but should be extended to speakers of the official languages as well. Accordingly, the idea of desirable mutual receptiveness implies that the states parties should also provide facilities enabling the speakers of official languages to learn regional or minority languages if they so desire. Nevertheless, the idea of desirable mutual receptiveness implies that the states parties should provide these facilities not only to the speakers of the official language(s) but to any other non-speakers of a particular regional or minority language, too. And this is exactly what Article 7 paragraph 1g requires from the states parties.

In accordance with this requirement the scheme of education in some states parties allows non-speakers to learn certain regional or minority languages. For example, the Slovene or (Burgenland) Croatian languages can be and are in fact studied by non-speakers, *inter alia* by native German-speakers in Austria, and the German language can be and is in fact studied by a significant number of native Hungarian-speaking children in Hungary.[88]

However, the implementation of Article 7 paragraph 1g appears to be much more difficult in the case of non-territorial languages, especially the Romani varieties. One of the obstacles the authorities face is the opposition of the speakers or some speakers of certain Romani varieties to the teaching of their languages: these speakers usually tolerate, for example, research being carried

---

86. ECRML, Explanatory Report, paragraph 65.
87. Ibid.
88. Austria 2005, 93-4; Hungary 2001, 27. For a further example, see Serbia 2009, 64.

out on their language or that their own language learning be supported by the state,[89] but they often insist that their language remain unknown outside their community.[90]

Another important obstacle is the lack of codification. This prevents not only education of the language within but outside the groups as well.[91]

A third obstacle is that the prestige of Romani varieties is very low in most states parties; this low prestige is likely to be closely related to the marginal and disadvantageous social status of the Roma/Gipsy themselves in most states parties.[92] In any case, it seems certain that this low prestige of these languages does not enhance the demand for learning these languages on the part of non-speakers.

On the other hand, the committee found that in almost all cases there is a remarkable difference between the number of speakers of Romani varieties and the number of persons belonging to the Roma/Gipsy population.[93] Therefore, the committee pointed out that within the wide group of non-speakers of the Romani varieties those individuals who belong to the Roma/Gipsy population but have lost their Romani varieties comprise a distinct group and stated that the states parties must ensure that these persons also have the possibility to learn the relevant Romani variety, to recover their language if they so wish.[94]

In some cases there is no specific provision of facilities enabling non-speakers to learn the given non-territorial languages, but the scheme of minority language education at public schools is in principle open for pupils from other linguistic groups.[95] This can also cause problems, for example if the teaching level is not suitable or appropriate for non-speakers,[96] or if financial difficulties of a minority language school hinder the satisfaction of demand from non-speakers.[97] It has also happened that the committee could not evaluate implementation of the undertaking at all due to the lack of information.[98]

---

89. Ibid; Finland 2004, 63 (teaching materials have been distributed to the Roma).
90. Germany 2002, 68 (Romani); Norway 2003, 72 and 75 (Romani and Romanes); the Netherlands 2004, 69 (Romanes). Switzerland 2004, 33 (Yenish); Switzerland 2008, 38 ("due to the widespread opposition among the Yenish-speakers concerning state action to promote Yenish outside their group, the project of standardising and including Yenish in the ordinary teaching framework could not be pursued further").
91. Slovenia 2004, 91; Hungary 2004, 42; Switzerland 2004, 49.
92. See for example, Hungary 2001; Hungary 2004; Slovenia 2004; Slovenia 2007.
93. Serbia 2009, 18; Hungary 2001, 11; the Netherlands 2008, 19; Spain 2005, 58; Switzerland 2004, 14; Cf. Switzerland 2008, 30.
94. Hungary 2007, 46.
95. Hungary 2004, 27; Cyprus 2006, 108.
96. Cyprus 2006, 108.
97. Hungary 2007, 47; Cf. Hungary 2007, 48 (no capacity problems seem to exist).
98. Serbia 2009, 64 (Romani).

2.9. Non-territorial languages under Article 7 paragraph 1h

The Parties shall base their policies, legislation and practice on the promotion of study and research on regional or minority languages at universities or equivalent institutions.

Implementation of Article 7 paragraph 1h is essential to the development of all regional or minority languages in terms of vocabulary, grammar and syntax. The promotion of study of and research into these languages is part of the general effort to promote regional or minority languages in order to encourage their intrinsic progress.[99]

As regards non-territorial languages, there is a particularly important aspect of the undertaking laid down in Article 7 paragraph 1h, namely that inclusion of these languages in the ordinary teaching framework presupposes a minimum degree of codification of the given language, allowing the preparation of teaching materials. Therefore the committee is of the view that research efforts should be aimed more clearly at achieving such a minimum degree of codification of non-territorial languages.[100] Codification also affects study of the language at universities,[101] which in turn is a strategic priority in view of the lack of teachers.[102]

Nevertheless, codification should be pursued in close co-operation with the speakers themselves and, as it is often the case that non-territorial languages are present in more than one European state, with the other states where the given language is also spoken. The committee is of the opinion that the latter requirement is vital also because a purely "national" codification could risk cutting ties between the respective communities.[103]

Article 7 paragraph 1h is applied to various extents in different states. It can happen that neither the study of nor research into the language is ensured.[104] In some cases the given language is not studied at universities (or is not known),[105] but research is carried out on it,[106] although permanent support to the relevant institutions may not be guaranteed.[107] There are also examples which show that certain states meet both undertakings.[108]

---

99. Cf. ECRML, Explanatory Report, paragraph 64.
100. Switzerland 2004, 49 (Yenish).
101. Slovenia 2004, 91.
102. Sweden 2009, 57.
103. Slovenia 2004, 91.
104. Cyprus 2009, 88 (Cypriot Maronite Arabic); the Netherlands 2004, 69 (Romanes); Switzerland 2001, 47 (Yiddish); Finland 2007, 77 (Karelian); Norway 2003, 78 (Romanes).
105. Hungary 2007, 49 (Armenian, Bulgarian, Greek and Ukrainian).
106. Finland 2007, 79 (Romani); Switzerland 2004, 33 (Yenish), Cf. Switzerland 2008, 38.
107. Sweden 2009, 54 (Romani and Yiddish).
108. The Netherlands 2001, 39 (Yiddish); Sweden 2009, 54 and 59 (Yiddish).

2.10. Non-territorial languages under Article 7 paragraph 1i

The Parties shall base their policies, legislation and practice on the promotion of appropriate types of transnational exchanges, in the fields covered by this Charter, for regional or minority languages used in identical or similar form in two or more States.

According to Woehrling, the Charter leaves states free to define the "appropriate types" in the light of the particular situation.[109] In accordance with this statement, transnational exchanges can take several forms. Participation in international cultural events[110] or international conferences[111] and exchanges between schools, via teacher training exchange programmes or via twinning programmes between towns in different countries can also be regarded as transnational exchanges. In several cases transnational exchanges are carried out in institutionalised forms, for example through the co-operation of organisations representing groups using the same non-territorial languages,[112] within the framework of international organisations,[113] through EU regional co-operation programmes or in a form which is defined in a bilateral agreement.[114]

Transnational exchanges are mostly supported by the states parties;[115] however, unlike the obligation laid down in Article 7 paragraph 1i, the committee does not always explore whether they happen or not. It reflects only on the existence of these exchanges,[116] encourages states to promote appropriate types of transnational exchanges in the fields covered by this Charter when these sorts of connections have not yet been developed,[117] or it asks for further information if the fulfilment of Article 7 paragraph 1i cannot otherwise be evaluated.[118]

---

109. Woehrling (2005), op. cit., p. 120.
110. Finland 2007, 86 (Russian); Norway 2007, 107 (Romanes).
111. Norway 2007, 107 (Romani).
112. Germany 2002, 74 (Romani).
113. Finland 2007, 85 (Romani); Germany 2002, 75.
114. Cyprus 2006, 111 (Armenian); Cyprus 2009, 95 (Cypriot Maronite Arabic).
115. Sweden 2003, 56 (Romani languages); Finland 2001, 54, Finland 2007, 85 (Romani); Finland 2001, 55, Finland 2007, 86 (Russian); Norway 2001, 50, Norway 2003, 80, Norway 2007, 107 (Romani); Norway 2001, 50, Norway 2003, 80, Norway 2007, 107 (Romanes); Cyprus 2006, 112 (Armenian).
116. Sweden 2003, 57 (Yiddish); Germany 2002, 74 (Romani); Finland 2001, 56 (Yiddish and Tatar); Cyprus 2006, 114 (Cypriot Maronite Arabic).
117. Switzerland 2001, 48, Switzerland 2004, 50 (Yenish); Finland 2007, 84 (Karelian); the Netherlands 2008, 72-3 (Romanes).
118. Hungary 2004, 30; Hungary 2007, 53.

2.11. Non-territorial languages under Article 7 paragraph 2

The Parties undertake to eliminate, if they have not yet done so, any unjustified distinction, exclusion, restriction or preference relating to the use of a regional or minority language and intended to discourage or endanger the maintenance or development of a regional or minority language. The adoption of special measures in favour of regional or minority languages aimed at promoting equality between the users of these languages and the rest of the population or which take due account of their specific conditions is not considered to be an act of discrimination against the users of more widely-used languages.

The principle of non-discrimination is a fundamental element in contemporary international law and plays a fundamental role in the philosophy of the Charter too.[119] By comparison, it may seem that the committee discusses this issue quite briefly in most cases.

The committee focuses primarily on those provisions of the legal systems of the states parties which prohibit discrimination: that is, it first takes into account the relevant constitutional provisions[120] and then the more specific regulations of the issue in various laws[121] and other legal instruments.[122] In doing so the committee also refers to international obligations of the states parties. For example, in its first report on Austria the committee notes that "Article 66 of the State Treaty of St. Germain expressly prohibits discrimination on the ground of language and guarantees the free use of any language in private and public life for Austrian nationals. Article 67 of the same treaty provides for equal treatment of linguistic minorities and allows them to establish their own organisations within which a regional or minority language can be spoken freely."[123]

Moreover, the committee notices whether some international instruments, such as the Convention for the Protection of Human Rights and Fundamental Freedoms, the UN Covenant on Civil and Political Rights and the UN Covenant on Economic, Social and Cultural Rights, constitute an integral part of the legal systems of the states parties[124] and whether the EU directives on

---

119. Explanatory Report, paragraph 71; Woehrling (2005), op. cit., pp. 120-6.
120. See for example: Switzerland 2001, 50; Austria 2005, 99; Norway 2001, 51; Cyprus 2006, 115 .
121. See for example: Finland 2007, 87 (Non-Discrimination Act); Hungary 2001, 30 (Criminal Code), Hungary 2007, 55 (Act on Equal Treatment and Promotion of Equal Opportunities); Armenia 2009, 64 (Criminal Code).
122. Slovakia 2009, 44 (Action Plan for the Prevention of All Forms of Discrimination, Racism, Xenophobia, Anti-Semitism and Other Expressions of Intolerance, for the period 2006-08).
123. Austria 2005, 99.
124. Norway 2001, 51.

anti-discrimination and equal treatment are transposed into their internal law.[125] Last but not least, the committee also mentions the organisations which can participate in the struggle against discriminatory practices,[126] for example the Minorities Ombudsman.[127]

The committee deals with the "phenomena of social and economic discrimination"[128] as well. In connection with this the committee points out that integration of Roma into the wider society may lead to "a loss of language and cultural identity" and it underlines that "integration in line with the principles set out in the Charter is one which allows for a full participation in economic, social and political life, combined with the preservation of one's linguistic and cultural identity".[129]

Most likely because the committee observes in several cases that continuous efforts are being made to combat discrimination,[130] it rarely emphasises that the undertaking under Article 7 paragraph 2 requires not only a legislative framework which prohibits discrimination on the grounds of language, but also practical steps to eradicate it.

2.12. Non-territorial languages under Article 7 paragraph 3

The Parties undertake to promote, by appropriate measures, mutual understanding between all the linguistic groups of the country and in particular the inclusion of respect, understanding and tolerance in relation to regional or minority languages among the objectives of education and training provided within their countries and encouragement of the mass media to pursue the same objective.

According to the committee, experience shows that the motivation of speakers plays a crucial role in the protection and promotion of a language, and that this motivation is closely linked to the social prestige which a language enjoys. Fostering the social prestige of the given language in turn raises other linguistic communities' awareness of that language, and this has overall significance.[131] As indicated by Article 7 paragraph 3 of the Charter, two fields are especially relevant in this respect: education and the media.[132]

In the first place, states must include respect, understanding and tolerance in relation to regional or minority languages among the objectives of education

---

125. Austria 2009, 79.
126. Finland 2007, 87 (Discrimination Board); Hungary 2007, 55 (Agency of Equal Opportunities).
127. Finland 2007, 87; Hungary 2001, 30.
128. Cf. for example, Hungary 2001, 30; Serbia 2009, 70.
129. Hungary 2004, 43.
130. See for example Hungary 2001, 30.
131. Switzerland 2004, 50 (Yenish).
132. See also: Sweden 2006, 63; Germany 2008, 64; Finland 2007, 88; Cyprus 2009, 98.

and training, while encouraging the mass media to pursue the same objective. In this respect the committee examines not only the existence of internal regulations requiring education and the media to comply with the above-mentioned principles, but it also explores the extent of the actual presence of these principles in teaching materials, in teacher training and in the programmes offered by the media. In other words, if there is relevant information at its disposal, the committee follows with attention both legislation and practice. Hence, the implementation of Article 7 paragraph 3 has certain stages in the states parties.

In connection with education it may happen that the committee has not been informed of any inclusion of respect, understanding and tolerance in relation to regional or minority languages among the objectives of education and training.[133] It can also happen that the teaching materials are not sufficient, because they do not deal with the long tradition of the given languages; these languages receive only marginal attention or are stereotypically described;[134] another weakness may be that the value of multilingualism is emphasised only in general, without specification and sufficient reference to the respective languages;[135] in some cases the choice of teaching materials depends on the individual teacher who in turn may not be bound in this choice at all[136] and this may also cause problems, especially if teaching about regional or minority languages and the corresponding history and culture is absent from teacher training.[137]

Although the committee often lacks sufficient information about whether the media adopt the principles laid down in Article 7 paragraph 3,[138] the media are likely to be a more sensitive area than education. What this suggests is that the committee has received information that the media portrayal of certain non-territorial languages is in many cases expressly negative[139] and therefore the committee holds that there is a need for an awareness campaign to improve the image of these languages.[140]

The fact that the committee has made several recommendations – even in boxes between the paragraphs[141] in the body of its evaluation reports – indicates that it deems the protection and promotion of regional and minority languages in this respect really important. On the other hand, however, the committee has also

---

133. Finland 2007, 90; the Netherlands 2008, 74-6.
134. Sweden 2006, 66.
135. Cyprus 2006, 117 and 119 (Armenian and Cypriot Maronite Arabic).
136. Sweden 2006, 66.
137. Ibid.; Sweden 2009, 61; Finland 2004, 68.
138. Austria 2005, 101; the Netherlands 2008, 74-6; Armenia 2006, 40.
139. Slovenia 2007, 67 (Romani).
140. Slovenia 2004, 90 (Romani).
141. Switzerland 2004; Sweden 2006; Sweden 2009; Finland 2007; Serbia 2009; Slovenia 2007; Cyprus 2006; the Netherlands 2004.

found satisfactory arrangements in relation to both the legal framework or regulation[142] and practice in the education[143] and the media.[144] In addition, the committee has come to the conclusion that positive changes are under way in a number of cases.[145] Nevertheless, the committee holds that awareness by the linguistic majority of non-territorial languages is still very low in several states.[146]

2.13. Non-territorial languages under Article 7 paragraph 4

In determining their policy with regard to regional or minority languages, the Parties shall take into consideration the needs and wishes expressed by the groups which use such languages. They are encouraged to establish bodies, if necessary, for the purpose of advising the authorities on all matters pertaining to regional or minority languages.

As already mentioned, most states parties have already established the organisational and institutional guarantees which make possible the continuous fulfilment of some obligations included in the Charter. As Woehrling put it, "in some countries, institutions have been formed to take responsibility at the national level for the interest of all regional or minority languages.[147] Some of these institutions are federations of bodies set up for each language.[148] They are sometimes created by the public authorities themselves,[149] in which case they tend to represent linguistic minorities rather than regional or minority languages."[150]

According to Woehrling, it is recommended that for each regional or minority language there should be a body to represent its interests, suggest practical measures for promoting it and monitor charter observance.[151] It can be added

---

142. Hungary 2001, 31; Finland 2001, 58.
143. Germany 2002, 77 (Romani); Norway 2003, 82 (Romani and Romanes); Norway 2007, 111 (further efforts are needed in relation to Romani and Romanes).
144. Serbia 2009, 75 (Romani).
145. Serbia 2009, 74 (in education); Cyprus 2006, 121 (Armenian and Cypriot Maronite Arabic languages in the media); Cyprus 2009, 99 (Armenian and Cypriot Maronite Arabic languages in education); Finland 2007, 90 (in education); Finland 2007, 93 (in the media); Austria 2009, 82 (in education); Slovenia 2007, 63 (Romani language in education); Sweden 2006, 64 (in the media).
146. For example: Sweden 2006, 65 (Romani); Finland 2007, 94 (Romani and Russian); Cyprus 2009, 100 (according to the speakers: Cypriot Maronite Arabic).
147. See for example: Finland 2001, 59 (Finnish Bureau of Lesser-Used Languages: FiBLUL).
148. Austria 2005, 80 (Austrian Centre for Ethnic Groups).
149. For example: Sweden 2006, 69 (Interministerial Working Group on issues relating to national minorities); Austria 2005, 106 (advisory councils); Slovenia 2004, 81 (Government Office for Nationalities); Serbia 2009, 77 (Republic of Serbia Council for National Minorities); Hungary 2001, 32 (Government Office for National and Ethnic Minorities).
150. Woehrling (2005), op. cit., p. 129.
151. Ibid.

that it is helpful if these bodies are present at all levels of administration. The committee is also of the opinion that a system of bodies connected to the regular body of administration – for example the minority self-government system,[152] the committees for national minorities or the national minority councils[153] – represents a particularly appropriate way of taking into consideration the needs and wishes expressed by groups which use regional or minority languages, even if this system is still to be improved.[154]

As regards non-territorial languages, one shortcoming of the aforementioned solutions can be that the speakers of these languages do not reach certain thresholds which are required for the setting-up of these bodies. In addition, these are mainly languages which tend to suffer from prejudice and have very low prestige. Therefore it seems that groups which use non-territorial languages have particular need of separate advisory bodies at central level with which the authorities consult on a regular basis on the issues concerning these languages.

Naturally, in many cases speakers of non-territorial languages do have their separate advisory bodies which deal also with linguistic issues,[155] although the consultations with these bodies are not frequent enough in every instance.[156]

2.14. Non-territorial languages under Article 7 paragraph 5

The Parties undertake to apply, mutatis mutandis, *the principles listed in paragraphs 1 to 4 above to non-territorial languages. However, as far as these languages are concerned, the nature and scope of the measures to be taken to give effect to this Charter shall be determined in a flexible manner, bearing in mind the needs and wishes, and respecting the traditions and characteristics, of the groups which use the languages concerned.*

The general logic of the committee position on the implementation of Article 7 of the Charter, including some typical differences between territorial and non-territorial languages, can be reconstructed as follows.

The first step for the protection and promotion of a given non-territorial language is the recognition of its existence, which should include certain forms of "practical recognition" in addition to "formal recognition" (application of Article 7 paragraph 1a).

---

152. Hungary 2001, 32.
153. Serbia 2009, 76.
154. To function, the national minority councils need a stable legal basis in Serbia.
155. See for example: Finland 2001, 59 (Finnish Islamic Congregation/as regards the Tatar language); Finland 2001, 59 (Advisory Board on Romani Affairs/as regards also the Romani language); Hungary 2007, 61 (a council to advise the prime minister on affairs pertaining to the Roma/as regards also the Romani and Beás languages).
156. Sweden 2009, 62; Serbia 2009, 77.

If a certain regional or minority language has already been recognised as part of the cultural wealth of the state where it is spoken, the Charter determines in more detail what the state should and should not do in order to sufficiently protect and promote the given language.

Taking the negative aspects first, states should not hinder the protection and promotion of a language by administrative divisions (application of Article 7 paragraph 1b); this naturally does not apply to non-territorial languages.[157]

Then, in accordance with a coherent and structured language policy, states should create the legal, organisational and financial frameworks for the language's protection and promotion (application of Article 7 paragraph 1c).

Within these frameworks, states must ensure the possibility of language acquaintance and maintenance by ensuring the possibility of language transmission in education (application of Article 7 paragraph 1f). With regard to non-territorial languages, this means that teaching in or of these languages should be included in the regular curriculum, at least in pre-school and primary school education.

The inclusion of these languages in the ordinary teaching framework presupposes a minimum degree of codification of the given language, allowing the preparation of teaching materials. Therefore, research efforts should be aimed more clearly at achieving such a minimum degree of codification of non-territorial languages. Codification also affects study of the language at universities (application of Article 7 paragraph 1h), which in turn is a strategic priority in view of the lack of teachers.

If the possibility of language transmission is guaranteed, states should aspire to realise this possibility: they should foster the motivation of speakers for language learning, which in turn can be achieved by enhancing of the prestige of the given non-territorial language.

Since the prestige of non-territorial languages, and the awareness of the majority about them, is extremely low in many cases, it is necessary to improve and consolidate the presence of these languages, and also the presence of the history and culture which they reflect, in education (application of Article 7 paragraph 3) and in the media (application of Article 7 paragraph 3 and 1d). In the latter case, radio broadcasting has overriding importance, which means that the authorities must encourage broadcasters to offer programmes both about and in the language, in conformity with the principles laid down in Article 7 paragraph 3.

---

157. However, it may apply to a language which generally counts as non-territorial, but in that particular state it shows territorial characteristics, for example the Romani language in Slovakia.

Promoting, maintaining and developing links between groups speaking a language in identical or similar form, be these groups in the same state (application of Article 7 paragraph 1e) or in different states (application of Article 7 paragraph 1i), can also contribute to fostering the prestige of that language through the establishment of a common identity of the respective linguistic groups, since these groups can recognise the importance of their language in building such identity. In this way, the application of the above-mentioned subparagraphs can raise linguistic groups' awareness of the value of their language.

This identity can be consolidated by developing cultural relations with other linguistic groups (application of Article 7 paragraph 1e) in which relations these groups are present as equal partners, capable of co-operating in reaching common aims. In addition, if these groups live in the same territory, the state must ensure greater mutual permeability between them by facilitating communication and understanding in an institutionalised form, also enabling non-speakers of a non-territorial language to learn this language if they so desire (application of Article 7 paragraph 1g).

Article 7 paragraph 1g also applies to persons who have lost their language, that is, they too must have the opportunity to learn their lost language if they so desire. If such persons lost their language partly because of social discrimination from which the group they belong to traditionally suffers, the authorities should take measures which allow their full participation in economic, social and political life (application of Article 7 paragraph 2) to allow Article 7 paragraph 1g to be applicable.

Because of the traditionally low prestige of non-territorial languages and the fact that the interests of linguistic groups may remain invisible at local and regional levels because they are dispersed, it is of overriding importance that these languages have their separate bodies at the central level of the given state, which bodies are capable of sufficiently articulating the needs and wishes of the respective linguistic groups (application of Article 7 paragraph 4).

In addition to this more or less general framework of the application of Article 7 to non-territorial languages, it is also important to explore the more specific content of the *mutatis mutandis* application of Article 7 paragraph 5. For such an investigation, two ways are possible. One is to analyse how the states parties, the Committee of Experts and the Committee of Ministers interpret and conceive the meaning of this *mutatis mutandis* application in particular issues; however, it is not easy to find such direct or explicit interpretations.[158] The other approach would be to provide a detailed comparative analysis of the application of the provisions of Part II of the Charter to territorial languages and non-territorial languages in the states parties. This chapter does not undertake this task; it confines itself to commenting on a single aspect of the history of the protection of territorial and non-territorial languages and especially the Romani varieties in the states party to the Charter.

As already mentioned in various contexts, the states parties and the Committee of Experts have faced several obstacles in the implementation of the Charter provisions in relation to non-territorial languages, especially the Romani

---

158. A relevant example is the Yenish language in Switzerland. In its first report, the Committee of Experts found that "Swiss Gypsies" or Yenish are "regarded by the authorities as a cultural minority and not as a linguistic minority". While acknowledging that financial support for this minority group "may be used by the organizations concerned to develop projects concerning the Yenish language", it considered that "an official recognition of the value of this language and the interest of protecting it is still necessary" (Switzerland 2001, 34-5). Commenting on the committee's report, the Swiss authorities pointed out that "the existence of these two minorities [the Yiddish and the Yenish] is recognised in Switzerland but the travelling people are supported by the Federal Council as a cultural minority and not as part of the country's language policy, within the meaning of Article 7 of the Charter" (ibid., p. 70). In its second report, the committee insisted that the Yenish language "has not yet been recognised as a regional or minority language in Switzerland within the meaning of the Charter" and "the Committee of Ministers also recommended this kind of recognition" (Switzerland 2004, 33 and 40). Commenting on this recommendation, the Swiss authorities stated that "the issue of recognition for Yenish beyond the current level first needs to be discussed with reference to the practical needs of the individuals actually concerned" (ibid., p. 38), but in their third report they reiterated their former view; the Committee of Experts then observed that "the recognition of the Yenish as a national minority does not necessarily imply a recognition of the Yenish language" and so it encouraged the competent Swiss authorities "to consult with the representatives of the users of Yenish on measures to protect and promote the language" (Switzerland 2008, 20-1); the Committee of Ministers also recommended that the Swiss authorities "pursue the dialogue with the representatives of the Yenish-speakers with a view to identifying the field of Article 7 that could be applied to Yenish with the greatest possible support by the speakers" (ibid., paragraph 32). Commenting on the Committee of Experts' report, the Swiss authorities confined themselves to the issue of formal recognition of the Yenish language, but changed their reasoning when stating that "in ratifying the Framework Convention for the Protection of National Minorities, Switzerland recognised Travellers as a national minority. With the ratification of the Charter, Switzerland grants Yenish the status of a non-territorial language of Switzerland" (ibid., paragraph 31). This dispute shows that neither the Committee of Experts nor the Committee of Ministers has been willing to accept that recognition of the speakers' group as a national minority amounted to adequate recognition of the value of their language itself, though the Committee of Experts has in some cases accepted that the instrument of ratification of the Charter may serve as an acceptable form of recognition of the wealth of the language (cf. the Netherlands 2001, 15; Cyprus 2006, 52). Therefore, it seems probable that the Committee of Experts will accept such a form of recognition of the Yenish language in the case of Switzerland, too.

varieties. But we have not yet highlighted the fact that active protection of the Romani varieties is a relatively new phenomenon, even in those states parties where other historical languages have been protected for some 160 years[159] or those where certain language rights of minority language speakers have been recognised for 160 or 140 years,[160] or 90 years.[161]

In particular, Switzerland, which has developed its multilingual national and official language system since 1848, has granted, within this system, national language status to four of its historical languages, giving official language status to three of them and a semi-official status to the fourth; but Switzerland has not extended this very strong protection of historical languages to its non-territorial languages, such as the Yenish language. Instead, by ratifying a number of international conventions in the 1990s,[162] it undertook to prohibit discrimination on the ground of language, to recognise certain minority language rights, to provide some protection for persons belonging to national minorities and to provide some direct protection for historical minority languages, including the Yenish language.

In those states where certain language rights of minority language speakers have been recognised for almost a century, or even longer, the situation has become even more complex. This follows from the fact that, while the

159. It was Switzerland which first started to protect its historical minority languages by declaring them national (and official) languages in 1848. Cf. U. Altermatt (1998), "A többnyelvű Svájc – minta Európának?" in A. Oplatka and S. Szalayné, *A többnyelvűség scájci modellje*. Budapest: Osiris Kiadó, p. 33.

160. Austria has protected linguistic minorities since 1867 (H. Baltl and G. Kocher (1995), *Österreichische Rechtsgeschichte*, Graz: Leykam, p. 228). Hungary adopted an act protecting its national minorities in 1849 and it has protected them in practice since the adoption of Act XLIV of 1868 on the subject of Equality in National (Ethnic) Rights (*Magyar Törvénytár*, Vol. I, 1000-1873, Franklin Társulat, Budapest, 1912, pp. 422-7).

161. Such countries are Czechoslovakia (now the Czech Republic and Slovakia) and Yugoslavia (at present Serbia, Croatia and Slovenia as states party to the Charter). In the interwar period these countries were obliged, along with Austria, Hungary and several other states in central and eastern Europe, to protect their minorities under the international minority protection system of the League of Nations; cf. P. Thornberry (1991), *International law and the rights of minorities*. Oxford: Clarendon Press, pp. 41-2. After the Second World War it was uncertain whether these countries were still obliged by these undertakings; but, even after the Secretary General of the UN stated in his report that these undertakings were not considered valid in relation to most countries and "generally speaking, the system should be considered as having ceased to exist", several countries maintained this kind of minority protection, to some extent, for decades (cf. "Study on the Legal Validity of the Undertakings Concerning Minorities": UN-Doc. E/CN. 4/367, p. 71). For further international obligations in relation to Austria, see Austria 2005, 11 and 22.

162. Switzerland became a state party to the International Covenant on Civil and Political Rights in 1992, the European Charter for Regional or Minority Languages in 1997 and the Framework Convention for the Protection of National Minorities in 1998.

recognition of these language rights provided strong indirect protection for the historical minority languages – including, in principle, Romani – from the very beginning, it seems that this kind of indirect protection had little practical relevance in the case of the Romani varieties until the 1990s. This weakness of practice may have arisen from various causes, for instance, from that unwillingness of Roma to avail themselves of language protection, which they show sometimes even today, or from their traditional travelling way of life,[163] or the lack of the codification of their languages; it cannot be excluded either that they were denied the possibility of practising their language rights.

In the light of what has been said, the main elements of the overall picture appear to be these: first, direct protection for historical minority languages has been provided in one state party,[164] but this direct protection did not extend, in any form, to non-historical languages, including the Romani varieties, until the 1990s; second, indirect protection of historical minority languages, including the Romani varieties, has been provided in a number of states parties in the form of recognition of certain minority language rights, but these long-established language rights seem to have been hardly operative in relation to the Romani varieties until the late 20th century; third, a number of states parties had not provided either direct or indirect protection for historical minority languages, including the Romani varieties, until the late 20th century. This overall picture suggests that the Romani varieties were, for one reason or another, not protected either in law or in practice as much as the historical minority languages or the languages of migrants.[165]

---

163. To get an impression of what kind of obstacles may have arisen, let us take the example of the educational provisions of the minority protection system of the League of Nations. Article 8 of the Polish Minority Treaty – which, as Thornberry says, "served as a model for others" – said: "Poland will provide in the public educational system in towns and districts in which a considerable proportion of Polish nationals of other than Polish speech are residents adequate facilities for ensuring that in the primary schools the instruction shall be given to the children of such Polish nationals through the medium of their own language. This provision shall not prevent the Polish Government from making the teaching of the Polish language obligatory in the said schools" (P. Thornberry (1991), *International law and the rights of minorities.* Oxford: Clarendon Press, p. 42; for the text of the Polish Minority Treaty, see ibid., pp. 399-403). It is interesting that the Committee refers to the travelling way of life of the Roma and to the expression of "special treatment" as a characteristic feature of minority protection in the interwar period in connection with Switzerland, which was not a state party to this system: Amid the tide of nationalism that swept through Europe after the First World War, people with a lifestyle centred on travelling were singled out for "special treatment". See Switzerland 2001, 18.
164. Since the adoption of its new constitution in 1978, Spain also has provided strong direct protection for historical minority languages, but this kind of direct protection does not extend to the Roma languages.
165. Sometimes the situation was much worse. The committee refers to an example in Switzerland 2001, 18.

In any case, it seems that there has been in recent years a real shift concerning the protection of the Romani varieties in almost all the states parties where at least one Roma variety has been traditionally spoken. In Switzerland, where there has been a strong tradition of direct protection of historical minority languages, this shift is seen in the fact that the Yenish language, being a historical minority language, has now been granted certain direct and indirect protection. In those states in which there has been a tradition of indirect protection of historical minority languages, this shift is shown by the fact that the Romani varieties as historical minority languages have gained, in addition to their indirect protection, some direct protection, and that both forms of protection have become noticeably operative. Finally, in those states in which there has not been a tradition of protecting historical minority languages in any form, the shift is in the fact that the historical languages, including the Romani varieties, have gained certain protection simultaneously.

It seems that these historical circumstances deserve some attention in relation to Romani and other non-territorial languages as well as in relation to territorial languages. At any rate, these circumstances certainly underline how, in the process of implementing the Charter in accordance with Article 7 paragraphs 4 and 5, "the needs and wishes" of Roma-speakers must really be taken into consideration.[166]

3. Commentary[167]

3.1. Reluctance of speakers to accept Charter protection

Certain speakers and/or representatives of some non-territorial languages have shown reluctance to accept protection and promotion of their languages under the Charter in their respective states parties. This kind of aversion has taken various forms, from refusal of all possible means of Charter protection and

---

166. Re implementing the Charter for non-territorial languages, Kovács noted the Roma's special needs and wishes in 1996: P. Kovács (1996), *Nemzetközi jog és kisebbségvédelem*. Budapest: Osiris Könyvkiadó, p. 71, n.80.

167. As noted in the introduction to this chapter, the states party to the Charter and the Committee of Experts have faced several difficulties relating to non-territorial languages. We comment on only two difficulties here, though this section could be an opportunity to comment on other issues, e.g. the consistency between approaches applied by the Committee of Experts in its reports on particular states. We considered discussing that here but we abandoned the idea in the end. Nevertheless, we agree with those commentators who think there are some inconsistencies in this respect and that the issue deserves attention. For more details, see F. de Varennes (2008), "Language protection and the European Charter for Regional and Minority Languages: *quo vadis?*" in R. Dunbar and G. Parry, *The European Charter ... legal challenges and opportunities*. Strasbourg: Council of Europe Publishing, pp. 30-1; R. Dunbar, "Definitively interpreting the European Charter: the legal challenges" in ibid., pp. 59-60.

promotion to refusal of some possible measures, especially those protecting or promoting the language outside the group concerned.[168]

The problem is that these phenomena of reluctance seem to contradict some provisions of the Charter. For illustration let us take Article 7.1g, which states that the states parties must provide "facilities enabling non-speakers of a regional or minority language living in the area where it is used to learn it if they so desire". However, given the objection made by the speakers to the teaching of their language outside their group, how is it possible to implement this provision or principle of the Charter? In other words, how to evaluate such expressions of the wishes of the speakers and to what extent should these wishes be taken into consideration?

It would hardly be justifiable not to respect, at least to some degree, the will or choice of the speakers in relation to their own languages. Article 7 paragraph 4, which applies to non-territorial languages *mutatis mutandis*, also supports this view by stating that "in determining their policy with regard to regional or minority languages, the parties shall take into consideration the needs and wishes expressed by the groups which use such languages". In addition, Article 7 paragraph 5 (which concerns only non-territorial languages) stresses that "as far as these languages are concerned, the nature and scope of the measures to be taken to give effect to this Charter shall be determined in a flexible manner, bearing in mind the need and wishes, and respecting the traditions and charac-teristics, of the groups which use the languages concerned". As a result, two kinds of contradiction occur: one between Article 7 paragraphs 4-5 and certain other provisions of the Charter, and one between some expressions of wishes or choices of the speakers of a few non-territorial languages and certain Charter provisions.[169] In the former case the contradiction itself, in the latter the potential for contradiction, is inherent in the Charter. Consequently, the phenomena of reluctance on the part of the speakers just make the contradiction or the potential for contradiction explicit, or put it into practice.

It is probable that both kinds of contradiction originated from an unconscious presupposition, by those who drafted the Charter, that the speakers and repre-sentatives of territorial and non-territorial languages traditionally spoken in Europe would agree with the idea of protecting and promoting their languages

---

168. In this case the speakers/representatives consider their language a secret asset of their group or its members.

169. Re implementation of Charter provisions on the Romani language in Hesse, the committee pointed out the existence of this latter kind of contradiction: "The Committee of Experts is … aware that part of the speakers do not wish the Romani language to have a presence in public life outside the Sinti and Roma community, which is in contradiction with the aims of a number of provisions of the Charter" (Germany 2006, 745).

under the Charter. At any rate, it is this assumption which is, according to all indications, reflected in several provisions and the logic of the Charter.[170]

The underlying presupposition or assumption has not so far caused serious problems in implementing the Charter. On the contrary, it might seem as if the process of implementation has justified this idea or means of standard-setting of the drafters. The verifying fact has been, first and foremost, that reluctance to see protection and promotion of languages under the Charter has been very exceptional in the overall process of implementation: such reluctance has been in sharp contrast with the prevailing attitude of speakers and representatives of territorial languages and has not been general among the speakers and representatives of non-territorial languages either. There are only three non-territorial languages whose speakers have shown such reluctance: Romani, Yiddish and the Tatar languages. Undoubtedly, Romani and Yiddish are the two most important non-territorial languages, but their speakers have not shown reluctance in all the states parties where these languages are present; as for Tatar, it is spoken traditionally only in three states parties: Finland, Poland and Romania.

It may not be redundant to add a note here about official languages in this respect, even though official languages (or at least the widely used ones among them) are outside the scope of the Charter. What is remarkable about official languages and the issue of unwillingness is that all the states party to the Charter designated their official language(s) – or language(s) for official use – exclusively from historical languages of Europe and that all the signs are that the speakers of these languages are not dissatisfied with the official status of their languages, that is, with this kind of protection and promotion of them. In other words, official language status as a kind of protection and promotion of historical European languages seems also to be in accordance with the will or choice of the speakers of the respective languages.

To sum up, in the light of all the ways that the will or choice of the speakers of historical European languages concurs with the idea of protection and promotion of these languages, the cases of reluctance to accept the protection and promotion provided by the Charter appear to be extraordinarily exceptional indeed. Therefore, the main lesson to draw from what has been said may be that the Charter rests much more on the respect of the will or choice of the speakers of traditionally spoken languages of Europe than may appear at first glance.[171]

---

170. In this context, Article 7 paragraph 4 would respect not so much those wishes of the speakers or their groups that contradicted the Charter provisions as those wishes of the speakers or their groups that concerned various issues of implementation of several provisions of the Charter.
171. This does not mean, of course, that the speakers are always satisfied with the forms and level of protection and promotion that their own languages enjoy under the Charter in a particular place at a given time.

Naturally, however exceptional the cases of reluctance have been in the implementation of the Charter so far, the states parties and the committee had to face them and handle them somehow. Under the circumstances described above it is not surprising that the practice of the states parties and the committee is still somewhat precarious, but it seems that the committee has already managed to develop some elements of a proper and consistent practice. A basic element of this practice is likely to be that the committee does not consider the expressions of the wishes of the speakers showing reluctance in relation to the protection of their languages under the Charter a fact that would preclude such a protection on the part of the states parties. The only exception so far has been the case of the Yiddish language in Switzerland. In its second report the committee concluded that "as long as there is no indication that a need for protecting the Yiddish language is expressed inside the Jewish community, the Committee of Experts considers that there is no scope for the protection of Yiddish in Switzerland under the Charter".[172] Interestingly, the committee settled its usual practice as a principled view also in relation to the Yiddish language. In its first report on Finland the committee stated that "the absence of a request for support from the users of a language does not, in principle, release the state from the obligation to fulfil the undertakings of the Charter".[173]

An argument for this principled view of the committee can be derived from the reasoning for the main aim of the Charter. If the threatened historical languages of Europe belong to the cultural heritage of Europe, they comprise part of Europe's wealth and for this reason they must be protected and promoted, which is the main aim of the Charter. Consequently, if a state becomes a party to the Charter, its obligations in the protection and promotion of a particular language depend on objective rather than subjective criteria; in particular, they depend on, first and foremost, whether or not the language is a non-territorial language under the provisions of the Charter. If it is, the state party must in principle fulfil the undertakings concerned. In so doing, however, the state party must take into consideration, in accordance with Article 7 paragraphs 4 and 5, "the needs and wishes" expressed by the group which uses the language. As a result, if the speakers show reluctance to accept protection and promotion, the scope for state action becomes limited but supposedly not impossible. For example, the speakers have not objected to the recognition of the cultural wealth of their languages, viz. Romani, Yiddish or the Tatar languages (Article 7 paragraph 1a) or to research into these languages at universities (Article 7 paragraph 1h), so

---

172. Switzerland 2004, 53.
173. Finland 2001, 46.

this kind of protection can be provided without any difficulty.[174] But even if speakers in the future object to recognition of the cultural wealth of their languages or research into these languages at universities, these forms of protection of these languages may nevertheless prove to be justifiable.

Naturally, such a justification must include an analysis of claims of the individual speakers of the languages concerned and possible claims of the groups which use these languages; further, the analysis must extend to the relationship between these claims and the relationship of these claims to the obligations of the state, representing the wider society under the Charter. In this chapter it is not possible to provide such an analysis, but it is possible to raise one of the key issues: the claims of the individual versus the wider society. The question is likely to be whether individual speakers who own their own language own this language as their exclusive property or not? This question is exactly the same as the one that John Stuart Mill put in general terms as follows: "What then, is the rightful limit to the sovereignty of the individual over himself? Where does the authority of society begin?" The answer, according to Mill, is that "Each will receive its proper share, if each has that which more particularly concerns it. To individuality should belong the part of life in which it is chiefly the individual that is interested; to society, the part which chiefly interests society."[175]

From this perspective the task is to define these proper shares and to draw the demarcation line between them or between their underlying interests, not only in general, but also in the language question within and outside the context of the Charter. As regards implementation of the Charter, it seems that the committee is more or less on the right track.

3.2. Local and migrant speakers and protection of languages under the Charter

It sometimes happens that certain speakers of a language protected under the Charter belong to the group that uses the language traditionally in a state party and that the other speakers of the same language are immigrants in that state. Among such languages are Italian in Switzerland, Russian in Finland and Hungarian, Slovene, Croat, Czech and Slovak in Austria. Let us take the issue of Italian in Switzerland: "The results of the federal census of 1990 indicate that there were, at that time, 524 116 persons who considered Italian to be their main language. This figure includes the 279 273 persons living outside of the

---

174. The case of the Yenish language is confusing in this respect. Cf. Switzerland 2004, 33; Switzerland 2008, 30 and 43.
175. J. S. Mill (1991), "On liberty" in J. S. Mill, *On liberty and other essays*. Oxford: Oxford University Press, p. 83.

traditional Italian language area, of whom 85.6% are migrants."[176] In connection with Russian in Finland the committee stated: "Russian is a traditional language in Finland. The Russian-speakers form a rather heterogeneous group of about 5 000 so-called Old Russians, of whom only a part has maintained the Russian language, and 15 000 to 25 000 New Russians, depending on the time of their arrival in Finland."[177]

These examples illustrate that, in the case of certain languages protected under the Charter, these two kinds of group of speakers really exist. Here, for the sake of simplicity, those speakers who belong to the group that uses the language traditionally in the state party are called "local speakers" in contrast with migrant speakers of the same language in that state. The term "local" – which refers primarily to the speakers' link with an area – is obviously qualified in this case by the term "traditional" within the meaning of Article 1a.i.[178] Naturally, "local" conceived in this sense also covers, in most cases, speakers of the official language(s); however, the discussion here is limited to the local and migrant speakers of those languages that enjoy protection under the Charter.

The main problem of interpretation, concerning languages that enjoy protection under the Charter and have not only local but migrant speakers, derives from the fact that Article 1a.ii excludes "the languages of migrants" from the Charter protection provided for regional or minority languages. Therefore the question is whether these languages count, within the meaning of Article 1a.ii of the Charter, as "the languages of migrants" when spoken by migrants or not? To put it another way, the question is: if the language of a number of migrants is identical with a language protected under the Charter in a state party, should this Charter protection extend to the use of this language by these migrants or not? After all, is it possible within the meaning of the Charter that one and the same language can be both protected and non-protected, depending on who the users of it are? The answer, it seems, depends on whether the protected language when used by migrants counts as "the language of migrants" within the meaning of Article 1a.ii of the Charter or not. If it does, the protection provided by the Charter may not extend to its use by these migrants; otherwise it does, at least to those among these migrants who are citizens of the state.

Whichever interpretation is proper, further difficulties arise. If the Charter protection did not cover the use of a protected language by migrants in the

---

176. Switzerland 2001, 16.
177. Finland 2001, 14.
178. Nationality is also a qualifying term within the meaning of Article 1a.i, but migrants (and, in exceptional cases, local speakers) may be nationals or non-nationals; therefore it seems to be proper to take nationality into account, together with other qualifications included in Article 1a.i separately.

states parties, it would often be difficult to differentiate between protected and non-protected uses of the language in practice, let alone the fact that such a differentiation sometimes would not appear reasonable at all.[179] On the other hand, if the Charter protection did cover the use of protected languages by migrant citizens in the states parties, it might happen that the Charter protection of a protected language with only a small number of local speakers could suddenly extend to a large number of migrants, causing practical problems and calling into question whether this remarkably increased use of the language could still be considered a legitimate object of the protection of the linguistic heritage of the state party.

The issue appears to be even more complex in the case of non-territorial languages. This follows from the fact that, while Article 1a.ii excludes "the languages of migrants" from the protection the Charter provides to regional or minority languages, Article 1c does not contain this exclusion in relation to non-territorial languages. Therefore, if a non-territorial language that enjoys Charter protection has both local and migrant speakers, the protection of the Charter is likely to automatically extend to the use of the language by these migrants, or at least to those among them who are citizens of the state party. Nevertheless, this could be true only on condition that non-territorial languages are conceived as being not regional or minority languages. However, it seems that the provisions of the Charter allow another interpretation of the concept of non-territorial languages, and according to this interpretation non-territorial languages are nonetheless regional or minority languages.[180] In this case the answer to the question – whether the Charter protection of languages that have both local and migrant speakers extends to the use of this language by migrant speakers, or not – would probably be the same as in the case of regional or minority languages.[181]

The committee has not yet stated its position on these issues in its reports. Nevertheless, it has developed certain practice and, in so doing, has tended to

---

179. For example, where a migrant speaker of a language protected under the Charter is a party before a court, it is questionable whether the court should allow the migrant to produce documents and evidence in the protected language if it is different from the language of the proceedings; however, if the other party is a local speaker of the same protected language, and therefore the local speaker is entitled to produce documents and evidence in the protected language, it would probably be unreasonable as well as contradictory to procedural justice to deny the same opportunity to the migrant speaker of the same language.
180. For more detail on these interpretations, see Woehrling (2005), op. cit., pp. 68-71.
181. For a more detailed interpretation of the lack of the condition "the languages of migrants" in Article 1c, see ibid., p. 70.

adopt the position, for one reason or another, that non-territorial languages must be considered regional or minority languages.[182]

In the case of Russian in Finland, the committee pointed out that the Russian-speakers included so-called Old Russians (local speakers) and New Russians (migrant speakers) and that their estimated numbers were about 5 000 for the first group and 15 000 to 25 000 in the second group. Further, the committee took the view that Russian must be considered a non-territorial language in Finland, concluding: "The Committee has however decided to consider this language without the distinction of whether its users are 'new' or 'old'."[183]

This decision means that, according to the committee, the Charter protection in Finland is not limited to the use of the Russian language by old or local Russians but extends to the use of this language by new or migrant Russians as well. This decision of the committee resembles some judgments of the European Court of Justice in which the Court found that the right to use a minority language in criminal proceedings granted by the law of a member state of the European Community or European Union only for certain individuals might extend to a migrant national of another member state or even to non-migrant nationals of other member states in virtue of Community law.[184] It is remarkable, however, that unlike the Court the committee refrained from providing the reasons on which its decision was based; instead, the drafting of the decision suggests that the committee maintained the right to change its view on the issue.

In its second report on Austria the committee stated that:

> in the case of Austria and most notably Vienna the distinction between traditional regional or minority languages and varieties of the same languages as migrant languages is becoming increasingly blurred. The committee is of the view that advantages can be drawn from this development for the benefit of the traditionally spoken regional or minority languages. The migratory flow of speakers from Croatia, Slovenia and other neighbouring countries can lead to a reinforcement of regional or minority languages, which is especially important considering the ongoing trend towards assimilation in Austria … At the same time, strengthening regional or minority languages can also lead to a better integration of migrants.[185]

Obviously, the committee put the emphasis in this analysis on possible and mainly desirable consequences rather than interpretation of the relevant provisions of the Charter; this is understandable given the specific context. However, it cannot

---

182. Cf. ibid., p. 69.
183. Finland 2001, 14.
184. Cf. *Ministere Public v. Mutsch*, Case 137/84 [1985] ECR 2681 and *Criminal Proceedings against Bickel and Franz* [1998] ECR I-7637.
185. Austria 2009, 16.

be excluded that the consequences might differ from the scenario described by the committee, either in Austria or elsewhere, in the future and that the issue of Charter protection of languages spoken both by local and migrant speakers could lead to fears and tensions and inhibit some states parties from protecting historical languages under the Charter.[186] Therefore, beyond the theoretical need for a more detailed and consistent interpretation of Charter provisions on these issues, practical considerations also point to the need to address and answer them in the foreseeable future. This seems urgent because the underlying philosophy of the Charter is increasingly challenged both in theory and practice.[187]

4. Recommendations

4.1. The principle of non-discrimination

Non-discrimination is a fundamental principle which, however, seems to be complex and somewhat confusing both within and outside the context of the Charter.[188] The Explanatory Report interprets non-discrimination outside the

---

186. It is worth noting here that in *Mutsch* the Public Prosecutor's office appealed, "maintaining that since the accused was a Luxembourg national, he did not have the right to be tried through German" in virtue of the relevant Belgian statute which granted this right only to Belgian nationals residing in a German-speaking municipality. Remarkably, the Italian Government made a submission arguing that "national legislation for the benefit of language minorities applies only to members of the minority in question and to the area where the language is spoken"; N. Nic Shuibhne (2004), *EC law and minority language policy*. The Hague: Kluwer Law International, pp. 72-3. In *Bickel and Franz*, the Italian Government argued in a similar way. For a detailed analysis of these cases see Nic Shuibhne, op. cit., pp. 72-80 and 278-84.

187. For example, Tom Cheesman heavily criticises the philosophy of the Charter, raising various arguments and stating, *inter alia*, that Europe protects marginalised indigenous, autochthonous languages while it has marginalised new, immigrant, allochthonous languages; T. Cheesman (2001), "'Old' and 'new' lesser-used languages of Europe: common cause?" in C. C. O'Reilly, *Language, ethnicity and the state*, Vol. 1. Houndmills: Palgrave, pp. 147-68. This shift, however, may result in a shift in understanding of some basic principles, which may also be a warning for the philosophy of the Charter, but from the opposite direction. For illustration, let us note a remark by the Finnish authorities, commenting on the report of the committee: "The Non-Discrimination Act is intended to foster and safeguard equality and enhance the protection provided by law to those who have been discriminated against in cases of discrimination that fall under the scope of the Act. The commentary to the bill for this Act states, *inter alia*, that authorities drafting anti-discrimination plans must not only take into account immigrants but also the traditional national minorities in Finland." Finland 2004, 37.

188. For a comprehensive and detailed analysis of non-discrimination as a principle of international law, see F. de Varennes (1996), *Language, minorities and human rights*. The Hague: Martinus Nijhoff, pp. 54-128; for a comprehensive and detailed analysis of non-discrimination in the context of the Charter, see Woehrling (2005), op. cit., pp. 120-6, and J.M. Woehrling (2008), "The European Charter for Regional or Minority Languages and the principle of non-discrimination" in R. Dunbar and G. Parry, *The European Charter ... legal challenges and opportunities*, pp. 63-81.

context of the Charter as a minimum standard, which is mainly negative in nature. Accordingly, non-discrimination "creates only a right for individuals not to be subjected to discrimination, but not a system of positive protection for minority languages and the communities using them".[189] Within the context of the Charter the report repeats, on the one hand, that "the prohibition of discrimination in respect of the use of regional or minority languages constitutes a minimum guarantee for the speakers of such languages. For this reason, the parties undertake to eliminate measures discouraging the use or jeopardising the maintenance or development of a regional or minority language."[190] However, the report adds that the purpose of Article 7 paragraph 2 of the Charter "is not to establish complete equality of rights between languages".[191] This statement suggests that the principle of non-discrimination must in this respect be seen not as a minimum guarantee with only negative, eliminative implications; on the contrary, in this respect it must be considered nearly a maximum standard which implies positive protection and action.

So far the committee has discussed the issue of non-discrimination in most cases very briefly and has considered the principle almost always a minimum standard. Accordingly, there seems to be still a great potential inherent in the principle of non-discrimination that could and ought to be, step by step, capitalised on in the process of implementing the Charter. It is the committee which could and ought to give stimulus to this higher-level interpretation and application of the principle.

A relatively simple way to develop this kind of interpretation and application could be as follows: if there are, under the protection of the Charter, languages whose situations are very similar while their legal statuses are very different, the committee can and ought to remind the state party that similar situations need similar regulations; otherwise, at least one of the regulations must be considered discriminatory.[192] Then the question would often be merely whether higher or lower status is justifiable; presumably the principle of non-discrimination and the underlying philosophy of the Charter would imply[193] the higher legal status as appropriate in most cases at present.

---

189. *European Charter for Regional or Minority Languages and Explanatory Report* (Strasbourg, Council of Europe Publishing, 1993), Explanatory Report, paragraph 3. For similar statements, see paragraphs 10, 27 and 61.
190. Ibid., paragraphs 71 and 61.
191. Ibid., paragraph 72.
192. For such an interpretation of the principle of non-discrimination, and for such a comparative analysis, see G. Andrássy (2010), "A hivatalos nyelvek száma és az emberi jogok: amiről még nem esett szó a szlovák államnyelv törvényről folyó vitában", *Jogtudományi Közlöny*, Vol. LXV, No. 9, pp. 403-14.
193. That is to say, it seems that the highest reasonably possible protection for the threatened historical languages as an ultimate purpose derives from the Charter or its underlying philosophy.

Naturally, this approach would require a focus on the similarities of actual language situations rather than their differences. Therefore, this approach would involve a certain shift from the usual attitude of always emphasising the differences between actual situations of languages spoken in different countries.[194] Nevertheless, this approach does not of course question that there exist differences and that these differences are very often significant.

In any case, the principle of non-discrimination implies or offers this kind of approach which appears to be promising for the establishment of more precise standards for protecting threatened historical languages.

4.2. Freedom of language

The Charter, without calling a spade a spade, respects freedom of language in various ways. The most obvious way is found in Article 11 paragraph 2, where the states parties undertake "to guarantee freedom of direct reception of radio and television broadcast from neighbouring countries in a language used in identical or similar form to a regional or minority language" and "to ensure that no restrictions will be placed on the freedom of expression and free circulation of information in the written press in a language used in identical or similar form to a regional or minority language", though "the exercise of the above-mentioned freedoms" may be subject to "some formalities, conditions, restrictions or penalties". In other cases the Charter allows the states parties to undertake to apply some provisions only if speakers of the protected languages express some demand, for example "if they so request"[195] or "if they so wish"[196] or "at the request of" them.[197] However, it is evident that when the states parties undertake to make possible, for example, education in or of a minority language without such a condition, they also respect the will or the choice of the eligible persons insofar as in these cases it is also these persons who are entitled to decide whether to avail or not to avail themselves of these opportunities. Hence, as already pointed out in section 3.1 above, respect of the will or choice of the speakers, that is respect of freedom of language, really permeates the Charter.

---

194. Originally, this attitude emerged not in relation to the protection of languages but the protection of minorities. For example, the General Assembly of the United Nations, immediately after the adoption of the Universal Declaration of Human Rights, adopted another resolution on the fate of minorities, and this specified why it did not include an article on the rights of minorities. One of the reasons was: "it is difficult to adopt a uniform solution of this complex and delicate question, which has special aspects in each state in which it arises" (United Nations A/RES/3/217 C, General Assembly, "Fate of minorities", 10 December 1948). Almost 50 years later, in *Language, minorities and human rights* (1996), p. 90, de Varennes wrote: "What is reasonable in the particular context of one state may be completely unacceptable in another".
195. Article 8 paragraphs 1a.iii and 1b.iv.
196. Article 8 paragraphs 1c.iv and 1d.iv.
197. Articles 9b.i and 9c.i, Article 10 paragraph 5, and Article 11 paragraph 2.

It is even possible that freedom of language is a universal human right, as the author of this section of this chapter holds,[198] although this freedom, unlike other freedoms, is not recognised as such in either the Charter or other international instruments at present.

Whatever the case, it is a fact that there is a state party to the Charter, Switzerland, whose constitution recognises freedom of language among the enumerated fundamental rights in its Article 18: "Freedom of language is guaranteed".

In its first report on Switzerland the committee stated that "the new Constitution has introduced both the principle of linguistic freedom (Article 18) and the principle of territoriality (Article 70.2). The principle of territoriality, as applied in Switzerland, means that each canton or municipality has the right to preserve its traditional distinctive character and to determine its official language(s). This implies that the linguistic boundaries, once established, must not be deliberately shifted, and that cantons must endeavour to safeguard the homogeneity of the language areas. The Federal Tribunal has recognised the right of the cantons to limit the linguistic freedom of those who move into a particular linguistic area. In practice, it means that such citizens are expected to adapt to the linguistic environment of the canton (or municipality), by acquiring sufficient knowledge of the local language and sending their children to the local schools teaching in that language. Linguistic rights can therefore be exercised only on those territories where the language concerned has been declared official."[199] It may not be redundant to add that the limitations apply naturally to official and educational language rights only. In its first report the committee held that:

---

198. For more details, see G. Andrássy (2009), "Nyelvszabadság: egy elismerésre váró emberi jog", *Jogtudományi Közlöny*, Vol. LXIV, No. 11, pp. 445-56. (A longer version of this paper entitled "Freedom of language: a universal human right to be recognised" is forthcoming in the *International Journal on Minority and Group Rights* in 2011/12.) It must be added that freedom of language is a universal human right with certain non-universal implications: the right derives from international human rights law and moral/political philosophy; the implications of the right derive both from the right itself and, again, from international human rights law and political/moral philosophy. Thus, freedom of language conceived in this way differs both from various theories of linguistic human rights developed by de Varennes and some sociolinguists, and from Kymlicka's theory of minority rights. For an overview of linguistic human rights, see R. Phillipson, M. Rannut and T. Skunabb-Kangas (1995), "Introduction" in T. Skutnabb-Kangas and R. Phillipson, *Linguistic human rights: overcoming linguistic discrimination*. Berlin/New York: Mouton de Gruyter, pp. 1-22, and T. Skutnabb-Kangas (2000), *Linguistic genocide in education – Or worldwide diversity and human rights?* Mahwah NJ/London: Lawrence Erlbaum. For a philosophical criticism of the theory of de Varennes and of other linguistic human rights theories, see A. Patten and W. Kymlicka (2004), "Language rights and political theory: context, issues and approaches" in A. Patten and W. Kymlicka (eds), *Language rights and political theory*. Oxford: Oxford University Press, pp. 32-7.

199. Switzerland 2001, 26.

the measures undertaken by Switzerland in accordance with the Charter reflect the very high standard of protection and promotion of the four national languages in this country. The deeply rooted respect for the inherited linguistic and cultural diversity of the country, together with the strong federalist tradition, have created an institutional environment that has effectively preserved the linguistic and cultural richness of Switzerland.[200]

Therefore, if one of the aims of the Charter is, as Woehrling holds, "to bring about change in national law in order to improve the legal status of regional languages",[201] Switzerland is likely to be close to the point where, according to Woehrling, "no new legal provision is needed to implement the charter".[202] However, the aims of the Charter seem also to include the aim that its overall implementation must contribute to the development of more precise or more specified international standards for protecting threatened historical languages. And from this perspective, the implementation of the Charter in Switzerland offers an extremely important opportunity to study how freedom of language and the regulation of official languages play their role and interact with each other, and how this process contributes to the protection and promotion of threatened historical languages.

References

Altermatt, Urs (1998), "A többnyelvű Svájc – minta Európának?" in András Oplatka and Erzsébet Szalayné Sándor (eds), *A többnyelvűség scájci modellje* [The Swiss model of multilingualism]. Budapest: Osiris Kiadó.

Andrássy, György (2009), "Nyelvszabadság: egy elismerésre váró emberi jog" [Freedom of language: a human right to be recognised], *Jogtudományi Közlöny*, Vol. LXIV, No. 11.

Andrássy, György (2010), "A hivatalos nyelvek száma és az emberi jogok: amiről még nem esett szó a szlovák államnyelv törvényről folyó vitában" [The number of official languages and human rights: what has not yet been discussed in the debate on the State Language Act of Slovakia], *Jogtudományi Közlöny*, Vol. LXV, No. 9.

Baltl, Hermann and Kocher, Gernot (1995), *Österreichische Rechtsgeschichte*. Graz: Leykam.

Cheesman, Tom (2001), "'Old' and 'new' lesser-used languages of Europe: common cause?" in Camille C. O'Reilly (ed.), *Language, ethnicity and the state*, Vol. 1. Houndmills: Palgrave.

---

200. Ibid., paragraph 62.
201. Woehrling (2005), op. cit., p. 99.
202. Ibid., p. 101.

Dunbar, Robert (2008), "Definitively interpreting the European Charter for Regional or Minority Languages: the legal challenges" in Robert Dunbar and Gwynedd Parry (eds), *The European Charter for Regional or Minority Languages: legal challenges and opportunities.* Strasbourg: Council of Europe Publishing.

Kovács, Péter (1996), *Nemzetközi jog és kisebbségvédelem* [International law and protection of minorities]. Budapest: Osiris Könyvkiadó.

Mill, John Stuart (1991), "On liberty" in John Stuart Mill, *On liberty and other essays.* Oxford: Oxford University Press.

Nic Shuibhne, Niamh (2004), *EC law and minority language policy.* The Hague: Kluwer Law International.

Patten, Alan and Kymlicka, Will (2004), "Language rights and political theory: context, issues and approaches" in Alan Patten and Will Kymlicka (eds), *Language rights and political theory.* Oxford: Oxford University Press.

Phillipson, Robert, Rannut, Mart and Skunabb-Kangas, Tove (1995), "Introduction" in Tove Skutnabb-Kangas and Robert Phillipson (eds), *Linguistic human rights: overcoming linguistic discrimination.* Berlin/New York: Mouton de Gruyter.

Skutnabb-Kangas, Tove (2000), *Linguistic genocide in education – Or world-wide diversity and human rights?* Mahwah NJ/London: Lawrence Erlbaum Associates.

Szalai, Andrea (1999), "Linguistic human rights problems among Romani and Boyash speakers in Hungary with special attention to education" in Miklós Kontra, Robert Phillipson, Tove Skutnabb-Kangas and Tibor Várady (eds), *Language: a right and a resource.* Budapest: Central University Press.

Thornberry, Patrick (1991), *International law and the rights of minorities.* Oxford: Clarendon Press.

Varennes, Fernand (de) (1996), *Language, minorities and human rights.* The Hague: Martinus Nijhoff.

Varennes, Fernand (de) (2008), "Language protection and the European Charter for Regional or Minority Languages: *quo vadis?*" in Robert Dunbar and Gwynedd Parry (eds), *The European Charter for Regional or Minority Languages: legal challenges and opportunities*, Regional and Minority Languages No. 5. Strasbourg: Council of Europe Publishing.

Woehrling, Jean-Marie (2005), *The European Charter for Regional or Minority Languages: a critical commentary.* Strasbourg: Council of Europe Publishing.

Woehrling, Jean-Marie (2008), "The European Charter for Regional or Minority Languages and the principle of non-discrimination" in Robert Dunbar and Gwynedd Parry (eds), *The European Charter for Regional or Minority Languages: legal challenges and opportunities*, Strasbourg: Council of Europe Publishing.

Appendix: Number of speakers of non-territorial languages

Non-territorial language	State party	Official numbers	Numbers estimated by the authorities	Numbers estimated by the speakers	Estimates from other sources	Official numbers of the respective minority	Estimated numbers of the respective minority
1. Romani	Serbia	78 980				108 193	
2. Romani	Germany				70 000		500 000–800 000
3. Romani	Hungary	Romany + Beás→ 48 438			Romany→ 100 000–150 000		500 000–800 000
4. Beás	Hungary	Romani + Beás→ 48 438			Beás→ 50 000		500 000–800 000
5. Russian	Finland	37 253*					
6. Russian	Armenia	29 563				14 660	
7. Romani languages	Sweden		20 000				
8. Romanes languages	Netherlands		7 000				16 000–20 000**
9. Karelian	Finland		5 000				
10. Ukrainian	Hungary	4 885				5 070	2 000–5 000
11. Romani	Austria	4 348		20 000–25 000			
12. Caló	Spain		4 000				450 000
13. Romani	Slovenia	3 834					
14. Yiddish	Sweden		3 000				20 000–30 000
15. Armenian	Cyprus		3 000§				
16. Yenish	Switzerland				2 000–3 000		30 000–35 000
17. Greek	Hungary	1 921				2 509	4 000–4 500

119

Non-territorial language	State party	Official numbers	Numbers estimated by the authorities	Numbers estimated by the speakers	Estimates from other sources	Official numbers of the respective minority	Estimated numbers of the respective minority
18. Cypriot Maronite Arabic	Cyprus		1 300	2 000–2 500			4 650/150§§
19. Bulgarian	Hungary	1 299				1 358	3 000–3 500
20. Tatar	Finland				800–900		800–900
21. Romani	Norway		100–a few thousand	700			
22. Romanes	Norway		400				
23. Armenian	Hungary	294				620	3 500–10 000
24. Yiddish	Netherlands		a few hundred				
25. Yiddish	Finland				50–200		1 500
26. Romani	Spain				≤100		450 000
27. Romani	Finland						10 000
28. Romani	Poland	15 657					
29. Yiddish	Poland	243†					
30. Karaim	Poland	43‡					
31. Armenian	Poland	321					

* No differentiation by the Committee of Experts between Old Russians, New Russians and Ingrian returnees.
** Including the Roma who have migrated to the Netherlands since the 1990s.
§ Including about 400 recent immigrants.
§§ In the government controlled/non-government-controlled area.
† Speakers of Hebrew and Yiddish are counted together in the 1st report on Poland.
‡ People belonging to minority.

Article 2. Undertakings
and Article 3. Practical arrangements

José Manuel Pérez Fernández
University of Oviedo

1. Flexibility as a guideline for undertakings from the ECRML
2. Minimum state undertakings and obligations: the objectives and principles of Part II
   2.1. Defining the regional or minority language as a restrictive criterion for discretionary state recognition
   2.2. General scope of Part II and its variations
3. Optional undertakings and obligations: various and graduated acceptance of the provisions of Part III
   3.1. The factors affecting states' choice of specific undertakings: the minimum and how it is calculated
   3.2. Examining the case literature deriving from undertakings accepted by states in connection with Part III
4. Conclusions
References

Article 2 – Undertakings

1. *Each Party undertakes to apply the provisions of Part II to all the regional or minority languages spoken within its territory and which comply with the definition in Article 1.*

2. *In respect of each language specified at the time of ratification, acceptance or approval, in accordance with Article 3, each Party undertakes to apply a minimum of thirty-five paragraphs or sub-paragraphs chosen from among the provisions of Part III of the Charter, including at least three chosen from each of the Articles 8 and 12 and one from each of the Articles 9, 10, 11 and 13.*

Article 3 – Practical arrangements

1. *Each Contracting State shall specify in its instrument of ratification, acceptance or approval, each regional or minority language, or official language which is less widely used on the whole or part of its territory, to which the paragraphs chosen in accordance with Article 2, paragraph 2, shall apply.*

2. *Any Party may, at any subsequent time, notify the Secretary General that it accepts the obligations arising out of the provisions of any other paragraph*

of the Charter not already specified in its instrument of ratification, acceptance or approval, or that it will apply paragraph 1 of the present article to other regional or minority languages, or to other official languages which are less widely used on the whole or part of its territory.

3. *The undertakings referred to in the foregoing paragraph shall be deemed to form an integral part of the ratification, acceptance or approval and will have the same effect as from their date of notification.*

1. Flexibility as a guideline for undertakings from the ECRML

The European Charter for Regional or Minority Languages (ECRML) is a multilateral international convention which requires the signatory states to enter into a number of undertakings and legal obligations (principles, objectives and rules) in a graduated manner taking account of their national situation, with the ultimate aim of protecting the historical regional and minority languages of Europe insofar as they contribute to "the maintenance and development of Europe's cultural wealth and traditions" (the cultural dimension of linguistic diversity), and "considering that the right to use a regional or minority language in private and public life is an inalienable right" (Preamble to the Charter);[1] in other words, though flexibility and the principle

---

1. In connection with the choice of the international convention format for the ECRML, M.-À. Clotet I Miró (1994), "La Carta Europea de las lenguas regionales o minoritarias", *Revista de Instituciones Europeas*, Vol. 21. No. 2, p. 535, points out that the precedents of the European Social Charter and the European Charter of Local Self-Government provided "a notable example both for their binding nature in international law and for the flexible aspect which they incorporate, enabling the states to adopt measures in a graduated manner", noting also that, of the three possibilities considered by the group of experts set up by the Standing Committee of the Congress of Local and Regional Authorities (resolution, recommendation or convention) for the legal nature of the document, the experts opted for a convention "for three reasons: because it is the kind of text which has the greatest legal force, because the convention formula most resembles that of a law, and because conventions provide for supervisory mechanisms for their implementation". The group of experts comprised Herbert Kohn, Lluís Maria de Puig (rapporteurs), Pietro Ardizzone, Félix Ermacora, Ivo Peeters, Mervyn Phillips, Modest Prats and Jean-Marie Woehrling. Of interest in this context are J.-M. Woehrling (1989) "La promotion des langues régionales et minoritaires dans le Projet de Charte du Conseil de l'Europe" in P. Pupier and J. Woehrling (eds), *Langue et droit: actes du Premier Congrès de l'Institut International de Droit Linguistique Comparé*. Montreal: Wilson & Lafleur, pp. 133-81; and L. M. de Puig (1986), "Informe provisional sobre la preparació d'un projecte de Carta Europea de les llengües regionals e minoritàries", *Revista de Llengua i Dret*, No. 8, pp. 79-92, and (1991), "Debat i elaboració de la Carta Europea de les Llengües", *Revista de Llengua i Dret*, No. 16, pp. 153-77. See also J. Triadú i Vila-Abadal (2002) "Perspectiva constitucional i Carta Europea de les llengües Regionals o Minoritàries", *Revista de Llengua i Dret*, No. 37, pp. 136-7. On the question whether the Charter has an exclusively cultural purpose rather than protecting language rights, we may consider arguments advanced by S. Petschen Verdaguer (1989), "Entre la politica y el Derecho: la Carta de las lenguas regionales o minoritarias", *Revista de Estudios Politicos*, No. 66,

of free disposal are certainly the criteria governing the acceptance of undertakings by states – the à la carte system – this does not mean that the Charter sets out mere moral recommendations or political goals devoid of any legal force.[2]

The Charter contains genuine legal rules requiring the signatory states to adopt legal and administrative measures to facilitate its effective and actual implementation, and all such measures must be adopted with respect for the principles set forth in the Charter. Moreover, some of the undertakings set out in the ECRML place obligations on the states to create particular rights for their citizens.[3]

---

pp. 127-35, and H. Kohn and L. Maria de Puig, quoted by X. Deop Madinabeitia (2000), *La protección de las minorias nacionales en el Consejo de Europa*. Oñati: Basque Institute of Public Administration, pp. 234-5.

2. The flexibility of the ECRML's structure has induced some writers to speak of an "à la carte system" or "à la carte Charter"; for instance, D. Christopoulos (1992), *La question de la protection des minorités dans un ordre public européen: analyse critique des travaux élaborés au sein du Conseil de l'Europe, de la CSCE, et de la CEE*. Strasbourg: Université R. Schuman, p. 101, quoted by S. Castellà Surribas (2002), "La ratificació de l'Estat espanyol a la Carta europea de llengües regionals o minoritàries", *Mercator-Documents de Treball*, No. 8, www.ciemen.org/mercator/pdf/wp8-cat-def.pdf, p. 4; A. Viaut (2004), "The European Charter for Regional or Minority Languages: sociolinguistic particularities and the French configuration", *Mercator-Documents de Treball*, No. 15, www.ciemen.org/mercator, p. 19; F. Palermo and J. Woelk (2008), *Diritto costituzionale comparato dei gruppi e delle minoranze*. Padova: CEDAM, p. 87; F. de Varennes (2008), "Language protection and the European Charter for Regional or Minority Languages: *quo vadis?*" in R. Dunbar and G. Parry, *The European Charter for Regional or Minority Languages: legal challenges and opportunities*. Regional or Minority Languages No. 5. Strasbourg: Council of Europe Publishing, pp. 27-8, and J. M. Pérez Fernández (2009), "La protection des langues régionales ou minoritaires en Espagne: Le statut juridique de la langue asturienne", *Opinio Iuris*, Vol. 2, Paper No. 2, http://lider-lab.sssup.it/opinio, online publication, October, p. 11, note 23. In any case, flexibility enables member states that wish to accede to the instrument to accept undertakings in accordance with their specific domestic situation and later on to extend the scope of their obligations. This is because, as Peter Kovács (1993) points out in "La protection des langues minoritaires ou la nouvelle approche de la protection des minorités?", *RGDIP*, Vol. 97, No. 2, p. 411, on the one hand, the Charter protects languages rather than the actual rights of minorities, and, on the other, since it is not an additional protocol to the European Convention on Human Rights but a straightforward semi-open multilateral convention, it escapes the system of judicial supervision provided for in the aforementioned Convention.

3. As pointed out in Jean-Marie Woehrling (2005), *The European Charter for Regional or Minority Languages: a critical commentary*. Strasbourg: Council of Europe Publishing, p. 18, "The question arises whether the charter has a direct effect on the law of states parties, and whether it directly creates rights for citizens of those states. This question is usually – and rightly – answered in the negative. However, in some cases the charter makes it obligatory for states to confer such rights. It may therefore be said that in certain cases applying the charter will involve states in creating new rights."

The reason invariably given for the flexibility of the ECRML is the enormous variety of sociolinguistic situations in Europe;[4] the instrument must cater for all the contexts in which regional and minority languages may be used, and also facilitate the accession of states to the Charter.

In connection with the undertakings to be accepted by signatory states, according to Articles 2 and 3 of the ECRML, which are the subject of this analysis, the Charter breaks down into two main sections:

- First of all, there is the common core or basic legal statute of minimum obligations to be accepted by all states parties in relation to all the regional or minority languages spoken in their territories, whether nationwide or in specific linguistic areas. In any case, the minimum obligations are fleshed out in the objectives and principles of Part II, which are detailed in Article 7 of the Charter. Implementation of the minimum obligations and their real effectiveness in protecting and promoting the relevant languages raise an interesting problem which, as we shall see, involves such issues as the state's capacity to recognise whether the form of expression used in its territory is a regional or minority language within the meaning of the Charter,[5] the overly general definition of the obligations and the resultant broad interpretative margin left to the states, or the reduction of its binding character to cater for the specific situation of each language and the possibility of entering reservations to paragraphs 2 to 5 of Article 7.

- Secondly, there is a series of optional undertakings and obligations involving differential treatment for each regional or minority language, linking up with the idea of European social-linguistic diversity. This involves seeking the most suitable formula for protecting each language and limiting the state's freedom to choose which languages to protect, in order to prevent arbitrariness. The optional obligations are specified in Part III (Article 8 to 13), referring to the public and private spheres of daily life which are of most importance for language use.

The important thing here, as we shall see, is the state's choice of regional or minority languages to be covered by Part III. This decision will be subject to

---

4. Lluís Maria de Puig ("Informe provisional...", p. 88) highlights the need for flexibility to adapt the ECRML to the wide variety of situations of minority languages in Europe: "it would be absurd, and certainly pointless, to apply to a language without any real potential the same promotional standards as for languages which can be used for mass communication and cultural activity in the short to medium term". See also R. Dunbar (2008), "Definitively interpreting the European Charter for Regional or Minority Languages: the legal challenges" in R. Dunbar and G. Parry, *The European Charter ... legal challenges and opportunities*, pp. 37-61, at p. 41.
5. Regarding the concept of official language which is less widely used on the whole or part of the territory of the state (Article 3 paragraph 1), see *supra* the commentary on Article 1 of the Charter by Eduardo Ruiz Vieytez.

a number of "minimum" undertakings vis-à-vis the languages, in terms of numbers and areas of use, a further requirement being that no reservations may be entered for Part III.

In the analysis of the questions put and any other matters which may arise during the exercise, we devote particular attention to the case law developed by the Committee of Experts and endorsed by the Committee of Ministers of the Council of Europe. This case law corresponds to a number of simple criteria which are anchored in the provisions of the ECRML and other international texts such as the Framework Convention for the Protection of National Minorities and the OSCE treaties on national minorities.

2. Minimum state undertakings and obligations: the objectives and principles of Part II

2.1. Defining the regional or minority language as a restrictive criterion for discretionary state recognition

Article 2.1 of the Charter establishes the scope and degree of applicability of the objectives and principles of Part II, stipulating that the provisions of the said part apply to "all the regional or minority languages spoken within its territory and which comply with the definition in Article 1".[6]

The first question is the power of states ratifying the Charter in their (discretionary or regulated) recognition of the regional or minority languages existing in their territory. In this context, the states parties to the Charter do not enjoy freedom to grant or refuse for a given language which is spoken in their territory and which complies with the criteria set out in Article 1 the status of regional or minority language.[7] Paragraph 40 of the Explanatory Report appears, albeit in a rather confused and confusing manner, to limit the power of the states parties to decide whether the form of expression used in a part of

---

6. With the exception, as pointed out at the end of Article 1a.ii of the Charter, of dialects of the official languages of the state and the languages of immigrants, which can under no circumstances be granted the status of regional or minority languages.

7. As Maria-Àngels Clotet I Miró points out on p. 539 of "La Carta Europea…", "the terminology used, viz 'regional or minority languages', refers to *de facto* situations within a specific State, not to any legal concepts. This means that the adjective 'regional' applies to the languages spoken in a specific part of the territory of a State, where these languages may possibly be spoken by the majority of the citizens. The epithet 'minority' refers either to situations where a language is spoken by individuals who are not concentrated in a specified part of the State or else who are so concentrated but are numerically inferior to the population of the region speaking the majority State language". With regard to the concepts used in the Charter, in addition to the analysis presented here, see also P. Thornberry and M. A. Martin Estébanez (2004), *The Council of Europe and minorities*. Strasbourg: Council of Europe Publishing, pp. 32, 33.

its territory or by a specific group is a "regional" or "minority" language within the meaning of the Charter.[8]

The Committee of Experts' case law clarifies the states' role in recognising the regional or minority languages spoken in their territory. According to the committee, any language which complies with the basic criterion set out in Article 1a of the Charter (to the effect that for the purposes of the Charter a regional or minority language is one that is "traditionally used within a given territory of a State") must be protected, as a minimum, by the principles and objectives set out in Part II of the Charter (Article 7). Recognition and minimum application of Part II are therefore not an objective consequence of the implementation of the Charter, which means that the fact that a language which meets the criteria of the Charter is not mentioned by a state in its instrument of ratification or in the first periodical report in no way deprives it of the protection afforded by Part II of the Charter.[9]

---

8. Explanatory Report, paragraph 40: "Although the States Parties are not free to grant or to refuse a regional or minority language the status which it is guaranteed under Part II of the charter, they are responsible, as authorities for the application of the charter, for deciding whether the form of expression used in a particular area of their territory or by a particular group of their nationals constitutes a regional or minority language within the meaning of the charter". Germany, for example, in its instrument of ratification deposited on 16 September 1998, drew a distinction, for the purposes of the Charter, between minority languages and regional languages: "Minority languages within the meaning of the European Charter for Regional or Minority Languages in the Federal Republic of Germany shall be the Danish, Upper Sorbian, Lower Sorbian, North Frisian and Sater Frisian languages and the Romany language of the German Sinti and Roma; a regional language within the meaning of the Charter in the Federal Republic shall be the Low German language". Other states, such as Austria, Denmark and the Czech Republic, only use the expression "minority language". Alongside the term "regional or minority language", taken collectively or individually, other terms have come in: "national minority language", "ethnic minority language", "less widespread official language", "stateless language", "primary language" and "less frequently used official language"; see A. Viaut, "The European Charter", pp. 25-8.
9. See Slovenia 2007, 15: "It follows from these two provisions that, while states can restrict the application of Part III undertakings to the languages specified in their instruments of ratification, the application of Part II to all regional or minority languages may not be restricted and is automatic. Accordingly, the fact that a regional or minority language corresponding to the Charter's definition is not explicitly mentioned in the declaration(s) of a state party does not preclude the application of Part II of the Charter to that language"; and "the Committee of Experts is competent, *inter alia*, to assess the application of Article 2, paragraph 1 of the Charter. It therefore has the task of monitoring the application of Part II of the Charter to all regional or minority languages which correspond to the definition contained in Article 1.a of the Charter". See also Denmark 2007, 20: "The Danish authorities maintain the position that the Charter applies only to the German language in South Jutland. In its first evaluation report, the Committee of Experts raised the question as to whether the definition regional or minority languages under Article 1.a of the Charter applies to the Greenlandic, Faeroese and Romani languages, which would entail the obligation for Denmark to apply the provisions of Part II of the Charter to these languages in accordance with Article 2, paragraph 1 of the Charter". See, *inter alia*, Spain 2005, 77; Spain 2008, 13.

We can therefore conclude that if a language which is spoken in part or all of the territory of a state which has ratified the Charter complies with the criteria of Article 1, that state must recognise the language for the purposes of applying the principles and objectives of Part II, confining itself, if it so wishes, to specifying its status as a regional or minority language or, if appropriate, a non-territorial language (formal and non-substantive delimitation). For the purposes of applying the provisions of Part III, as we shall see below, the state's capacity is also confined to specifying its area of application, which regional or minority languages existing in its territory should be covered by the provisions of Part III and which actual paragraphs or subparagraphs the state accepts as undertakings in relation to these languages.[10]

The second question, which is closely linked to the first, is whether the states must effect their recognition in an explicit nominal manner, that is, whether they must fulfil the obligation of recognising its linguistic realities by expressly mentioning the regional or minority languages spoken in their territory in their instruments of ratification, acceptance or approval. Obviously, Article 3.2 of the Charter requires explicit specification for the purposes of applying the provisions of Part III. However, the question remains concerning regional or minority languages which are protected solely by Part II. Some consider that in such cases, given that the Charter applies automatically to all regional or minority languages, it is unnecessary to name or expressly identify any individual languages,[11] an argument endorsed by the clear position maintained in this regard by the Committee of Experts. Nevertheless, we feel that in order to improve the legal security of the users of the languages in question in terms of the scope of the Charter, and also to guarantee more effective supervision of the signatory states' compliance with the latter, it would be better for the states to explicitly indicate which regional or minority languages the Charter is to cover – whether in parts II and III or only in Part II[12] – and also in which areas they are spoken.[13]

---

10. See Slovakia 2007, 42: "In ratifying, the matters of real choice for the authorities are (1) the languages to be covered under Part III (see Article 2 paragraph 2 of the Charter) and (2) undertakings to be entered into under Part III (the choice of which should of course take account of the situation of the language in the territories concerned; see paragraph 79 of the Explanatory Report)."
11. See A. Viaut, "The European Charter", pp. 24 and 28.
12. As Germany, Austria, Holland and other states did in their instruments of ratification, acceptance or approval. On the matter of whether the regional or minority languages to be covered by Part II have to be specified or not, Jean-Marie Woehrling points out on p. 66 of *The European Charter for Regional or Minority Languages: a critical commentary* that the "Charter does not oblige states to declare a list of these languages". But it follows indirectly from Article 15 that states must draw one up: this article requires them to submit a periodical report "on their policy pursued in accordance with Part II of this Charter", and such a report must necessarily mention the languages covered by the policy.
13. See I. Agirreazkuenaga (2006), "La Carta Europea de Lenguas Regionales o Minoritarias del Consejo de Europa como Derecho interno" in J. M. Pérez Fernández (ed.), *Estudios sobre el estatuto jurídico de las lenguas en España*. Barcelona: Atelier, p. 110.

At all events, as already mentioned, the absence or omission of any of the regional or minority languages from the instruments of ratification, acceptance or approval does not prevent these languages from being protected by the principles and objectives set out in Part II of the Charter (Article 7). The Committee of Experts, endorsed by the recommendations of the Committee of Ministers of the Council of Europe, has done excellent work on this matter. The languages protected under Part II of the Charter were established *ex officio* by the Committee of Experts, which has used its reports to advise the states parties to extend their official recognition to regional or minority languages which were not covered in their instruments of ratification either by deliberate or accidental omission or because they use indirect or open expressions (e.g. the Spanish instrument of ratification states "For the same purposes, Spain also declares that the languages protected by the Statutes of Autonomy in the territories where they are traditionally spoken are also considered as regional or minority languages").[14]

The work of the Committee of Experts in this field has not been confined to promoting the incorporation into the Charter's field of protection of languages with a low level of legal and/or sociolinguistic protection, but has also embraced situations in which the regional or minority languages in question enjoy a high level of protection under domestic law. This means that the protection provided by the Charter under Part II is unaffected by the legal status of the language under domestic law. For instance, the Committee of Experts asked the Danish authorities to incorporate the languages of Greenland and the Faroe Islands into the ambit of the Charter[15] because it considered that the system of protection provided for in Danish domestic law (expressed in the laws on self-governing powers in Greenland and the Faroes) and the special protection provided by the Charter were not incompatible, also in view of the overriding principle of applying those provisions which are more favourable or which provide higher levels of protection, in accordance with Article 4.2 of the Charter.

---

14. See, re Slovene, Application of the Charter in Croatia, 4th monitoring cycle (2010), paragraph 8; re German in the municipalities of Bosco-Gurin (Canton of Ticino) and Ederswiler (Canton of Jura), Switzerland 2001, 15, and Switzerland 2008, 13, 15, and, with the Yenish language, in Recommendation of the Committee of Ministers: Switzerland (2004), 5; re Croat and German, Slovenia (2004), 35-7, and recommendations of the Committee of Ministers: Slovenia (2004), 1, and Slovenia (2007), 1-2; re Serbian in Slovenia, Slovenia 2010, 19; re Galician in Castilla y León, Portuguese in the city of Olivenza, Tamazight (Berber) in the Autonomous City of Melilla, and Arabic in the Autonomous City of Ceuta, see Spain 2005, 75-7; and, re Galician in Extremadura and Valencian (Catalan) in Murcia, see Spain 2008, 12; re Maronite Arabic, Cyprus 2006, 45-9, and Recommendation of the Committee of Ministers: Cyprus (2006), 1.
15. See Denmark 2004, 22-7, and Recommendation of the Committee of Ministers: Denmark (2004), 2.

Lastly, the Committee of Experts assert that increasing the number of regional or minority languages recognised by the states parties fits in perfectly with the flexible, dynamic and graduated character of the Charter.[16]

2.2. General scope of Part II and its variations

The objectives and principles set out in Part II are general in scope, as can be clearly inferred from Article 2.1 of the Charter, which requires this part to be applied in its entirety to all the regional or minority languages spoken in the territory of all states parties. The latter therefore cannot waive the objectives and principles of Part II, nor can they choose among the languages or prioritise some of them over others.[17] Nevertheless, the effectiveness of the general applicability clause governing the minimum obligations set out in Part II is conditioned or tempered, at least, by three closely linked factors:

- Firstly, there is the differing legal/political and sociolinguistic situation of each of the regional or minority languages, which is recognised in Article 7.1 ("and according to the situation of each language").[18] The need to cater for the practical situation of each language enables the states parties to design a policy tailored to the actual needs of each language community, adapting the principles and objectives of Part II of the Charter to them. Conversely, designing a homogeneous policy for all regional languages

---

16. For instance, re Romani and Frisian, see Germany 2006, 13, which mentions a "dynamic approach to the instrument of ratification". In the case of the historical regional or minority languages of Austria, the numbers of users of which are increasing (especially in Vienna) because of the influx of immigrants speaking them (Croats, Slovenes, etc.), the Committee of Experts urged the Austrian authorities "to consider applying as far as possible a more flexible approach to the Charter", in Austria 2009, 15-6. See also Application of the Charter in the UK, 1st monitoring cycle (2004), paragraphs 36-7.

17. Explanatory Report, paragraph 39: "Part II is general in scope and applies in its entirety to all regional or minority languages spoken on the territory of a State Party". Case law is virtually unanimous on this point; see e.g. J. M. Castells (2004), "Efectos jurídicos de la ratificación por España de la Carta Europea de Lenguas regionales o minoritarias", *Revista Vasca de Administración Pública*, No. 69 (II), p. 228; S. Castellà Surribas, "La ratificació de l'Estat espanyol", p. 4.

18. Explanatory Report, paragraph 39: "It will be noted, however, that the use of the expression 'according to the situation of each language' shows that this part is drafted so as to cater for the very great variety of language situations that may be encountered in the various European countries and within each country". As regards "according to the situation of each language", according to F. de Varennes (2008), "Language protection and the European Charter for Regional or Minority Languages: *quo vadis*", p. 28: "This has been described as 'a crucial phrase in the ECRML', since the measures adopted must be those best adapted to the objective needs and possibilities of each language situation, meaning that: ... in the absence of other relevant factors, the larger the number of users of a regional or minority language and the more homogeneous the regional population, the stronger the option which should be adopted. A weaker alternative should be adopted only when the stronger option cannot reasonably be applied owing to the situation of the language in question."

could lead to a practice incompatible with the spirit of the Charter, particularly where such homogeneity obstructs or hinders the real effectiveness of the ECRML's provisions.[19]

• Secondly, states parties can enter reservations to modify or exclude the application of these provisions; this possibility, by virtue of Article 21 of the Charter, is confined exclusively to Article 7 paragraphs 2 to 5.[20] This enables a state to enter reservations to the whole of Article 7 apart from paragraph 1, which lays down the objectives and principles which must guide legislative and administrative activity, as well as state practice in the territories where regional or minority languages are spoken. At all events, the possibility of entering reservations does not include the capacity of states to make interpretative declarations modifying the legal effects of the Charter, because the Committee of Experts is the only body competent to interpret and apply the ECRML.[21]

---

19. Even though it refers to the application of Part III, the approach which follows from the Committee of Experts' report is, in our opinion, perfectly applicable to the languages protected under Part II of the Charter. See Croatia 2001, 17: "The instrument of ratification has been drawn up in such a manner as to provide exactly the same level of protection for all the seven languages under Part III: Italian, Hungarian, Slovak, Czech, Serbian, Ruthenian and Ukrainian. The Charter, however, is constructed in such a way that the state can adapt the protection of the various languages to the real situation of each language. That is indeed the principal justification for the possibility offered to each state in Article 2.2 to choose among the provisions of Part III. This is clearly stated in paragraph 43 of the Explanatory Report of the Charter, which specifies that the state in question has to determine which paragraphs of Part III are to be applied to each particular language. The instrument of ratification indicates on the other hand that all the languages chosen should receive equal protection. This is, however, contrary to the actual situation of the languages because they in fact do have a different legal status in Croatia". In keeping with this approach, the Committee of Experts, in Slovakia 2009, 13, stressed the need to adopt flexible and specific measures in line with the situation of each language to achieve coherent application of the Charter, in this case, of Article 10 paragraph 15; and Recommendation of the Committee of Ministers: Slovakia (2009), 1. See also Armenia 2006, 17.

20. Article 21 paragraph 1 of the Charter: "Any State may, at the time of signature or when depositing its instrument of ratification, acceptance, approval or accession, make one or more reservations to paragraphs 2 to 5 of Article 7 of this Charter. No other reservation may be made". Explanatory Report, paragraph 135: "The CAHLR considered that contracting states should not have the possibility to make reservations with regard to Article 7, paragraph 1, since this paragraph contains objectives and principles. As far as Part III is concerned, it took the view that, in a text which already allowed the parties so much choice as to the undertakings they entered into, reservations would be inappropriate". CAHLR (Comité ad hoc langues régionales) is the ad hoc committee.

21. Slovakia 2007, 37: "However, given that pursuant to its Article 21 paragraph 1 the Charter only admits reservations to paragraphs 2 to 5 of Article 7, the above declarations constitute simple interpretative declarations. As such, they cannot modify the legal effects of the Charter provisions to which they refer, as interpreted by the Committee of Experts, which is the authoritative body in charge of interpreting the Charter and monitoring its implementation."

- Thirdly, while, by their very nature, the objectives and principles set out in Article 7.1 of Part II cannot be the subject of any waiver or reservation by states ratifying the Charter, they do confer on states parties a wide margin of discretion in their application and interpretation, which makes it difficult to supervise their implementation and blurs their binding force.[22] We might consider these as "behavioural obligations" to be understood as "standards" or "guidelines" requiring states to engage in specific behaviour aimed at a given result, under the motto of "the duty of care".[23]

This being the case, the objectives and principles of Part II, as a whole, undeniably fulfil a "guiding" or "informative" function for state public action in pursuing the ultimate aim of the ECRML, the protection of languages.[24] Consequently, in our view, interpretations that were so lax as to empty the Charter of its substance would not be admissible: there would be no point in restricting the freedom of states parties vis-à-vis recognition of a language spoken in part or the whole of its territory as a regional or minority language, in the aforementioned terms,[25] only to allow states not to take practical action to ensure the effective protection of this language, on the pretext of its "specific" situation (low number of speakers), excessive spread or fragmentation of speakers, extremely low or non-existent social demand, excessive economic cost of the requisite measures, etc. Ratifying the Charter obliges the states to tailor their domestic law to its provisions, including obviously those of Part II; this means that in the absence of a reservation in the instrument of ratification, acceptance or approval, the states' domestic legislation and regulations must be adapted to the provisions of the Charter. We need only think here of the boost in the effectiveness of protecting regional or minority languages provided

---

22. Explanatory Report, paragraph 39: "These [principles and objectives] are fairly generally defined and allow the states concerned a broad measure of discretion as regards interpretation and application". Nonetheless, as Iñaki Agirreazkuenaga points out in "La Carta Europea de Lenguas...", p. 114, "Article 7 of the Charter is a key provision because it singles out the objectives and principles, so that it might be considered as the hard core of the European Charter", which explains its compulsory nature.

23. The Part II obligations and the measures in Part III laid on administrative authorities, public services, media, cultural activities/facilities, economic/social life and cross-border relations are called "behavioural obligations" whereas educational and judicial measures are "obligations to achieve a specific result". See M.-À. Clotet I Miró, "La Carta Europea...", pp. 550, 555; P. Reuter (1961), "Principes de Droit International Public", *RCADI*, No. 103, pp. 472-5, 598-9, quoted by Clotet. See also S. Castellà Surribas, "La ratificació de l'Estat espanyol...", p. 5.

24. Explanatory Report, paragraph 57: "These provisions [Article 7, paragraph 1] concern essentially objectives and principles and not precise implementing rules. These objectives and principles are considered to constitute the necessary framework for the preservation of regional or minority languages. They fall under six main headings".

25. Explanatory Report, paragraph 58: "Admitting the existence of a language is a pre-condition for taking its specific features and needs into consideration and for action on its behalf."

by the principle of prohibiting discrimination on the grounds of language, as enshrined in Article 7.2, which is one of the major achievements of the Charter and an example of explicit stipulation of the need to change domestic law.[26]

The Committee of Experts was keenly aware of the serious problems which would sometimes arise from the fact of protecting regional or minority languages exclusively under Part II, which is why it repeatedly affirmed that the states parties had to adopt a coherent, structured policy for the protection and promotion of these languages, so as to create the requisite conditions for using them in public life.[27] The work of the Committee of Experts did not, however, stop at this general imperative: it has produced a series of criteria establishing the framework for state action in applying the principles and objectives of Part II. These criteria are obviously transposable to the application of Part III, but it is preferable to deal with them here because of the general applicability of Part II.

The Committee of Experts has made very clear that it is not enough for a state to ratify the ECRML, even with constitutional provisions at national level guaranteeing the use of regional or minority languages, unless the state adopts legislative measures effectively guaranteeing the use of the languages in question and establishes mechanisms to supervise implementation of these measures.[28] The measures proposed include drawing up language policy plans (see Application of the Charter in the Netherlands, 1st monitoring cycle (2001), paragraph 4, and Recommendation of the Committee of Ministers: Netherlands (2008), 3), and the adoption of a common language strategy, with reference to financial bodies and resources (cf. the case of regional or minority languages covered by Part II of the Charter in Application of the Charter in Spain, 2nd monitoring cycle (2008), paragraphs 64 and 66).

---

26. Article 7 paragraph 2 of the Charter: "The Parties undertake to eliminate, if they have not yet done so, any unjustified distinction, exclusion, restriction or preference relating to the use of a regional or minority language and intended to discourage or endanger the maintenance or development of it". Explanatory Report, paragraph 71: "The prohibition of discrimination in respect of the use of regional or minority languages constitutes a minimum guarantee for the users of such languages. For this reason, the parties undertake to eliminate measures discouraging the use or jeopardising the maintenance or development of a regional or minority language". We would refer to the analysis of this undertaking in the present text.
27. See Austria 2005, 43, and Recommendation of the Committee of Ministers: Austria (2005), 1. Similarly, though with particular reference to the situation in Vienna, see Recommendation of the Committee of Ministers: Austria (2009), 1.
28. See Recommendation of the Committee of Ministers: Croatia (2001), 1: "Adopt and effectively apply the legal acts and regulations necessary to implement the existing constitutional provisions and basic statutory acts aimed at protecting and ensuring the use of regional or minority languages". See too Croatia 2001, 18; recommendations of the Committee of Ministers: Switzerland (2001), 1, and (2004), 1; Recommendation of the Committee of Ministers: Norway (2001), 2; Recommendation of the Committee of Ministers: United Kingdom (2004), 2; and Recommendation of the Committee of Ministers: Slovakia (2007), 1.

Furthermore, the Committee of Experts, with the endorsement of the Committee of Ministers of the Council of Europe, has listed a series of arguments which the states parties may not use to justify non-adoption of measures to protect and promote regional or minority languages. First of all, the "weak status" of the regional or minority language is considered as a factor requiring states parties to adopt positive and effective measures. Where the regional or minority language is in a particularly weak situation, owing to the small number, dispersal or fragmentation of users of the language, the low or non-existent social demand for its use, or any other circumstance, the Committee of Experts, far from excusing inertia on the part of the state authorities, considers that the latter must adopt measures conducive to promoting the use of the languages in question, knowledge of their historical and cultural importance and the values of tolerance and respect.[29]

Secondly, the fact that a state party has a federal or decentralised structure does not exempt it from guaranteeing compliance with the obligations and undertakings accepted under the ECRML, although responsibility here goes mainly to the local and/or regional authorities. While in principle the Committee of Experts approves, in pursuing the objectives of the Charter, the fact of assigning responsibility for its application to the local and/or regional authorities in the name of the principle of proximity to the communities using these languages and to their problems, it is also true that this sometimes leads to serious problems or tensions, such as: differing levels of protection for the same language community distributed across different regions or municipalities, or protection levels which vary between different language communities; obstacles created by the local and/or regional authorities to compliance with the Charter; or lack of effective protective or promotional measures by the local and/or regional authorities. Committee of Experts case law has consistently recalled that, from the angle of international law, the state which ratified the Charter is the authority responsible for ensuring its implementation; this obliges it, with respect for domestic apportionment of responsibilities, to take the requisite steps to guarantee observance of the obligations set out in the Charter and accepted by the state in question. For instance, in connection with the German minority, in Application of the Charter in Denmark, 1st monitoring cycle (2004), paragraph 20 reads:

> The responsibility for the implementation of the Charter rests with the central authorities, despite the fact that German is spoken mainly at the regional and local levels. In many policy areas, local and regional authorities merely receive

---

29. See, in connection with the Sami language, recommendations of the Committee of Ministers: Finland (2001), 1, and (2004), 1; Recommendation of the Committee of Ministers: Germany (2001), 6; in connection with the Lule language and southern Sami, Recommendation of the Committee of Ministers: Norway (2003), 4; Recommendation of the Committee of Ministers: the Netherlands (2004), 3; recommendations of the Committee of Ministers: Croatia (2005), 2, and (2008), 2; Recommendation of the Committee of Ministers: Serbia (2009), 1.

recommendations from the central state and are otherwise free to take their own decisions. Bearing in mind that Denmark has a "dualist" system under which international agreements to which Denmark becomes a party are not automatically incorporated into domestic law, the Committee of Experts considers that a more proactive stance from the central authorities is necessary to ensure Denmark's compliance with its undertaking ensuing from the Charter.

The case of the Netherlands is enlightening too. The central authorities do not feel responsible for the disparities in protection of regional or minorities languages because this is basically a provincial responsibility. Nevertheless, the Committee of Experts once again stresses the state's responsibility for honouring the undertakings entered into (see Application of the Charter in the Netherlands, 2nd monitoring cycle (2004), paragraph 12, and Recommendation of the Committee of Ministers: Netherlands (2004), 3). This is made even clearer in Application of the Charter in Netherlands, 3rd monitoring cycle (2008), paragraph 10:

> the Committee of Experts considers that division of labour between the national authorities and the provincial authorities regarding the promotion of regional or minority languages, in particular the competence for education, should be reconsidered with a view to making it more effective ... The Committee of Experts underlines, however, that the national authorities have to ensure the application of the Charter in practice even if responsibilities are delegated to local and regional authorities. Under international law, the state is responsible for the fulfilment of its obligations under international treaties. In the absence of a national language policy, the provincial authorities, however, lack any overall guidance with regard to the application of the Charter.[30]

Thirdly, the precedence of the ECRML in domestic law (having the "force of a Federal Law", according to the German Government) does not detract from the need to adopt effective (legal) measures (in the administrative and judicial fields) to realise the application of the Charter, rather than transferring to the users of the languages protected the "burden" of lodging a complaint under the Charter about possible "unfavourable practices". This is why, according to the Committee of Experts, when a regional government (*Land*) fails to adopt the relevant measure, from the international law angle it is the state that must guarantee the honouring of the obligations set out in the Charter.[31]

---

30. Among others, see United Kingdom 2004, 34, and United Kingdom 2007, 31; Austria 2005, 41; Sweden 2006, 20-22; and Spain 2008, 62 and 65.

31. See recommendations of the Committee of Ministers: Germany (2002), 1; (2006), 15-16, (2006), 1; (2008), 19, and (2008), 1.

Fourthly and lastly, since the basic aim of the ECRML is to stimulate public and private use of regional or minority languages, the lack of a specific policy to promote these languages cannot be justified on the pretext that users of the minority language can speak the majority official language (the argument advanced by Denmark in relation to the German minority).[32]

3. Optional undertakings and obligations: various and graduated acceptance of the provisions of Part III

The clearest expression of the principle of free disposal of the Charter is to be found in the acceptance of the undertakings set out in Part III. This is, firstly, because the states are entitled to specify in the instrument of ratification, acceptance or approval the regional or minority languages to which the provisions of Part III (Article 3.1) are to apply. It should be noted, however, that any decision to exclude specific regional or minority languages from Part III must not be arbitrary, but must be based on objective reasons compatible with the spirit, objectives and principles of the Charter.[33]

Secondly, the signatory states must specify which actual obligations they are accepting in connection with each of the languages they recognise (Article 2.2). In other words, where the undertakings of Part II are concerned, the states' action follows from various graduated criteria facilitating, in principle, the introduction of a specific system of protection for each of the regional or minority languages which have been recognised in the instrument of ratification, acceptance or approval. This system can subsequently be enlarged in terms of numbers of languages and of undertakings accepted (Article 3.2).[34] Nevertheless, as we shall see below, the signatory states' freedom of choice is limited in terms of the number and scope of the undertakings which they have to accept vis-à-vis regional or minority languages.

---

32. See Denmark 2004, 21, and Recommendation of the Committee of Ministers: Denmark (2004), 1. Finland constitutes a diametrically opposed example here: the Finnish Government has decided to apply some of the protective and promotional measures set out in Article 2.2 of the Charter to Swedish, which is a second official language alongside Finnish (governed by a combination of the territoriality and personality principles in public relations); see Finland 2001, 19.

33. See Explanatory Report, paragraph 42: "Clearly, however, the reasons which prompt a state to exclude a recognised regional or minority language completely from the benefit of Part III must be reasons compatible with the spirit, objectives and principles of the charter". See also X. Deop Madinabeitia, *La protección de las minorías...*, p. 231.

34. According to Woehrling (2005), op. cit., p. 71, "It should be borne in mind that a State may make an additional declaration accepting fresh undertakings, but cannot revoke those it has already accepted".

3.1. The factors affecting states' choice of specific undertakings: the minimum and how it is calculated

Once the signatory state has specified the regional or minority languages to be covered by Part III of the Charter in its instrument of ratification, acceptance or approval, the system for choosing undertakings describe in Article 2.2 operates as follows:

- The "minimum" is defined as the 35 paragraphs or subparagraphs to be applied to each regional or minority language, chosen from the provisions of Part III. In principle, the choice of the 35 (sub-)paragraphs may lead to a uniform system for all the languages recognised or to different systems for each.[35] The provisions are highly graduated, ranging from minimum undertakings to obligations of a considerable magnitude.

- The 35 (sub-)paragraphs must include a minimum number for each area of use covered by the Charter: three each from articles 8 (education) and 12 (cultural activities and facilities), one each from articles 9 (judicial authorities), 10 (administrative authorities and public services), 11 (media) and 13 (economic and social life).[36] As paragraph 46 of the Explanatory Report says, "The role of the states will be, not to choose arbitrarily between these alternatives, but to seek for each regional or minority language the wording which best fits the characteristics and state of development of that language". It adds that "in the absence of other relevant factors, this would imply, for instance, that the larger the number of users of a regional or minority language and the more homogeneous the regional population, the 'stronger' the option which should be adopted; a weaker alternative should be adopted only when the stronger option cannot be applied owing to the situation of the language in question".

As highlighted in both the Explanatory Report (paragraph 45) and the relevant case law,[37] the calculation of the 35 paragraphs or subparagraphs may give rise to doubts and questions, beginning with the definition of a paragraph and subparagraph.

---

35. See M. A. Clotet i Miró, "La Carta Europea…", p. 547. Cf. also the Explanatory Report, paragraph 43: "The role of the state in the choice between these different paragraphs will consist in matching the charter as closely as possible to the particular context of each regional or minority language".

36. See Explanatory Report, paragraph 42: "For this purpose the conditions stipulated by Article 2, paragraph 2 are kept to a minimum designed to provide for a reasonable distribution of the parties' undertakings among the different articles of the charter and thus ensure that they do not ignore any of the major fields of protection of regional or minority languages (education, judicial authorities, administrative authorities and public services, media, cultural activities and facilities, economic and social life)."

37. See for all references, Woehrling (2005), op. cit., pp. 67-70.

A paragraph is a numbered sub-division of an Article (1, 2, 3, etc.), and a subparagraph is a sub-division of a paragraph, characterised by the fact that it starts on a new line. In the Charter not all paragraphs have sub-divisions, but where they do, the latter are assigned letters (a, b, c, etc.). In principle, for the purposes of Article 2.2, these are the sub-divisions which must be taken into account in calculating the 35 paragraphs or subparagraphs which are to apply to each regional or minority language, chosen from the provisions of Part III. The fact is that most subparagraphs of the Charter are themselves sub-divided, and these sub-divisions are numbered i, ii, iii, etc. In the light of this, the 35 (sub-)paragraphs required as a minimum number of undertakings for signatory states under Article 2.2 are calculated by these rules:

- If the sub-divisions comprise undertakings which, though not separate, are alternative in nature – expressed by the conjunction "or" – only one of them counts for the purposes of Article 2.2. These sub-divisions express a varying degree of undertaking on the state's part to protect and promote the language in question, with the most extensive degree encompassing the narrowest or lowest level of undertaking. For instance, Article 8.1a on pre-school education in the regional or minority language has alternative sub-divisions i, ii, iii and iv; and Article 9.2 on the validity of legal documents drawn up in regional or minority languages has alternative sub-divisions a, b and c.

- If the sub-divisions comprise undertakings which are cumulative in nature – expressed by the conjunction "and/or" – for the purposes of Article 2.2 the calculation may be more complicated, considering that in such cases the criterion to be taken into account must be the autonomy of the undertaking entered into:

  - In the case of separate undertakings which may be accepted concurrently, each of them will be counted separately. This applies, for instance, to Article 9.1a on the use of regional or minority languages in criminal proceedings, which covers three different types of undertakings in sub-divisions ii, iii and iv. However, in the same provision, the undertaking set out in sub-division i encompasses the other three (to provide that the courts, at the request of one of the parties, shall conduct the proceedings in the regional or minority languages; and/or), which means that its acceptance by a state must exclude, for the purposes of calculation, the other three and therefore only count as one subparagraph within the meaning of Article 2.2 of the Charter.

  - If the alternative is set out within the same sub-division, in our view, it should not be counted separately. For instance, Article 8.1e.iii, "if, by reason of the role of the State in relation to higher education

137

institutions, subparagraphs i and ii cannot be applied, to encourage and/or allow the provision of university or other forms of higher education in regional or minority languages or of facilities for the study of these languages as university or higher education subjects". The same applies to articles 8.1f.iii, 11.1a.ii and 11.1b.i.

• Lastly, if the sub-divisions include separate undertakings, each of them counts separately for the purposes of Article 2.2. This applies to the measures laid down in Article 10 on the use of regional or minority languages in the public services.

Apart from the possible problems win counting paragraphs and/or subparagraphs, which the Committee of Experts must help solve, it is certain that Article 2.2 of the Charter limits the margin of discretion available to signatory states in choosing which obligations to accept in relation to the regional or minority languages which they recognise. This provision is geared to tailoring states' obligations to the particular situation of each language and prevent states from evading international obligations in relation to regional or minority languages. What we need, therefore, is a definition of a European minimum standard of linguistic rights.[38]

3.2. Examining the case literature deriving from undertakings accepted by states in connection with Part III

As we have seen above, Article 2.2 requires states to accept a minimum of 35 paragraphs or subparagraphs from among the provisions of Part III. Nevertheless, a number of questions might arise in the application of this provision: what happens if a state falls short of the minimum number of undertakings required for some or all of the regional or minority languages recognised in its instrument of ratification, acceptance or approval? And what if the terms in which the undertaking is expressed are so ambitious or ambiguous as to hamper the application of Part III? In the light of the rules adopted by the Committee of Experts in its reports on the application of the Charter, we shall now analyse these and other questions relating to the undertakings accepted by the states parties.

First of all, we might address the situation where a signatory state has failed to accept the minimum undertaking of 35 (sub-)paragraphs required under Article 2.2 of the Charter, which means that the instrument of ratification, acceptance or approval is invalid. If such non-compliance is noted at the time of deposit of the instrument of ratification, acceptance or approval, in accordance with articles 76 and 77 of the Vienna Convention on the Law of Treaties of 1969, the Secretariat of the Council of Europe, as depositary body, must

---

38. See S. Castellà Surribas, "La ratificació de l'Estat espanyol...", p. 6.

request the state in question to honour its undertakings. If the disagreement between the state and the Council Secretariat persists, the latter may refer the matter to the Committee of Ministers.

If, however, non-compliance is noted at a later stage, it is for the Committee of Ministers to inform the state in question that it has fallen short of the minimum 35 (sub-)paragraphs, on the occasion of its examination and supervision of the application of the ECRML. In practice, the Committee of Experts has adopted special approaches to cases where, in connection with specific regional or minority languages, the state has fallen short of the minimum required under Article 2.2, by means of a compromise solution not provided for in the Charter.

For instance, in Application of the Charter in Austria, 1st monitoring cycle (2005), paragraphs 51-2, the Committee of Experts noted that in the case of the Czech, Hungarian and Slovak languages in the *Land* of Vienna, the Slovene language in the *Land* of Styria and the Romani language in the *Land* of Burgenland, the Austrian Government's undertaking falls short of the minimum 35 paragraphs/subparagraphs, and therefore opted, to avoid any confusion between the languages protected under Part II and Part III, to consider the languages in question as being protected exclusively by the objectives and principles of Part II. In order to draw up the report, therefore, it took account of all the additional data and information at its disposal.

The Committee of Experts adopted the same solution to the problem arising from the Spanish instrument of ratification vis-à-vis regional or minority languages which are protected by law but do not have "co-official" status.[39] In

---

39. The Spanish instrument of ratification reads: "All the provisions of Part III of the Charter which can reasonably apply according to the objectives and principles set out in Article 7 shall apply to the languages mentioned in the second paragraph." In this connection, paragraphs 60 and 61 of the 2005 report on Spain state: "60. As to the question of identifying the languages covered by Part III of the Charter, the Committee of Experts notes that the first paragraph of the declaration appended to the instrument of ratification states that 'for the purposes of the mentioned articles', i.e. presumably the articles of Part III of the Charter explicitly listed in the third paragraph of the declaration, the following are considered as regional or minority languages: the languages recognised as official languages in the statutes of autonomy of the Basque Country, Catalonia, the Balearic Islands, Galicia, Valencia and Navarra. The second paragraph of the declaration then states that '(f)or the same purposes, Spain also declares that the languages protected by the Statutes of Autonomy in the territories where they are traditionally spoken are also considered as regional or minority languages'. These languages are Bable/Asturian, Asturian Galician, Aragonese ('Fabla'), Catalan in Aragon and Aranese. The phrase 'for the same purposes' seems at first sight to suggest that the purposes in question are the same as those mentioned in the first paragraph, i.e. with regard to the articles of Part III which are explicitly mentioned in the declaration. This would seem to imply that these languages too are protected by Part III provisions. However, the third paragraph of the declaration corrects this apparent reading by stating that the provisions of Part III listed therein will apply to the languages mentioned in the

our view, the solution adopted by the Committee of Experts, especially in the case of Spain, confining its analysis to the undertakings accepted under Part II for regional or minority languages which fall short of the minimum number of undertakings required by Article 2.2, is not really consonant with the spirit of the Charter. We feel that the Committee of Experts should have explored other possibilities, ranging from conducting an *ex officio* examination of the application of the minimum standard of protection, through requesting/requiring the state to amend its instrument of ratification, especially as it does not comply with the terms specified in the Charter because it creates an unnecessary "third type" of protection. Ultimately, this interpretative approach does not provide regional or minority languages which have a lower level of legal protection at the national level with the necessary international safeguards.

On other occasions where the state authorities have chosen a subparagraph which contains alternative undertakings without specifying which of them they are accepting, the Committee of Experts has acted *ex officio* to apply one of the possible options, which, as a general rule, has to be the most extensive or the most favourable for the protection of the language. This is what happened when Slovenia fell short of the undertakings in connection with Article 8.1a, b, c and d of the Charter (see Application of the Charter in Slovenia, 1st monitoring cycle (2004), paragraph 33). Obviously, where such non-compliance is noted at the time of deposit of the instrument of ratification, acceptance or approval, as we have seen above, it is for the Secretariat of the Council of Europe to invite the state to complete its choice.

Secondly, there are cases were the ambiguity of the wording of the instrument of ratification or the over-ambitiousness of the targeted protection produces a

---

first paragraph, i.e. those recognised as official languages by the statutes of autonomy of the mentioned autonomous communities. According to the combined reading of the first three paragraphs of the declaration, the languages mentioned in the second paragraph appear to be protected only under Part II of the Charter.

61. The declaration appended to the instrument of ratification contains nevertheless an additional and final clause, stating that all the provisions of Part III of the Charter which can reasonably apply according to the objectives and principles laid down in Article 7 will apply to the languages mentioned in the second paragraph, i.e. those covered only by Part II of the Charter. However, since the Spanish authorities have not indicated a minimum of 35 paragraphs or sub-paragraphs of Part III, as required by Article 2 paragraph 2 of the Charter, which should apply to these languages in order for them to be covered by Part III of the Charter, these languages remain only covered by Part II. When evaluating compliance with Article 7 (Part II) in respect of these languages the Committee of Experts will therefore confine itself to taking into consideration, where relevant, the information provided by the Spanish authorities with regard to certain Part III provisions, but will not actually evaluate compliance with the latter." See also X. Arzoz (2008), "The implementation of the European Charter for Regional or Minority Languages in Spain" in R. Dunbar and G. Parry, *The European Charter … legal challenges and opportunities*, pp. 89-98.

similar problem, i.e. in effectively applying Part III of the Charter. In the event of ambiguity, the case law established by the Committee of Ministers in its reports on Croatia is most enlightening. In *Application of the Charter in Croatia*, 2nd monitoring cycle (2005), paragraph 13, the Committee of Experts highlights the fact that the ambiguity of the Croatian instrument of ratification in terms of geographical scope has had serious consequences:[40] on the one hand, the inability to delimit the areas covered by the obligations of Part III, and on the other, the inability to implement Part III in many of the areas, despite the strong traditional presence of the regional or minority languages there. Far from nearing a solution, the problem is worsening, as illustrated by *Application of the Charter in Croatia*, 3rd monitoring cycle (2008), paragraphs 11-14. According to the Committee of Experts, Croatia's instrument of ratification is liable to have effects or consequences contrary to the spirit of the Charter and the honouring of its fundamental obligations (paragraph 11). The fact that, in pursuance of domestic law, it is for the local authorities to decide on the territorial application of the Charter does not lead to a valid limitation of Croatia's obligations under parts II and III of the Charter. Accordingly, the Committee of Experts also evaluates the situation in areas where there is a traditional presence and a sufficient number of users of regional or minority languages covered by Part III (paragraph 12). The committee concludes by once again asking Croatia to revise its instrument of ratification (paragraph 14).

Over-ambitiousness in efforts to protect regional or minority languages can also cause problems. Ambitious instruments of ratification attempting to protect a large number of languages may clash with the fragmented, scattered situation of the users of the languages nationwide, which raises enormous difficulties in applying Part III. In the case of Slovakia, for instance, the Committee of Experts urged the authorities to specify or determine the areas in which users of the protected regional or minority languages actually exist in sufficient numbers for the purposes of the undertakings accepted in Part III in relation to such languages (see *Application of the Charter in Slovakia*, 1st monitoring cycle (2007), paragraph 34).[41]

---

40. The Croatian instrument of ratification reads as follows: "The Republic of Croatia declares that, in accordance with Article 2, paragraph 2, and Article 3, paragraph 1, of the European Charter for Regional or Minority Languages, it shall apply to Italian, Serbian, Hungarian, Czech, Slovak, Ruthenian and Ukrainian languages ... The Republic of Croatia declares, with regard to Article 1, paragraph b., of the Charter, that pursuant to Croatian legislature, the term 'territory in which the regional or minority languages is used' shall refer to those areas in which the official use of minority language is introduced by the by-laws passed by the local self-government units, pursuant to Article 12 of the Constitution of the Republic of Croatia and Articles 7 and 8 of the Constitutional Law on Human Rights and Freedoms and the Rights of National and Ethnic Communities or Minorities on the Republic of Croatia."
41. See also Hungary 2001, 16.

Thirdly, the Committee of Experts is critical of cases where the state's undertaking to apply the protection provided for in Part III is apparently subject to restrictions: sometimes a minimum percentage of speakers is required in a given municipality;[42] sometimes there are territorial limits which can lead to different levels of protection for the same language in the same state.[43] In such cases, what the Committee of Experts demands is that the thresholds in question be implemented in a manner compatible with the spirit, objectives and general principles of the Charter.

Lastly, we should consider the hypothesis of a state agreeing, in its instrument of ratification, acceptance or approval, to apply all the undertakings provided for in Part III. Although this is theoretically possible, it seems obvious that such a choice would be incompatible with the spirit of the Charter, given that Part III contains alternative undertakings with differing degrees of intensity.[44]

4. Conclusions

The ECRML requires signatory states to accept a series of legal undertakings and obligations (some minimum and others optional); these undertakings are accepted in a graduated manner, taking account of the domestic situation, but they have (or should have) the ultimate aim of protecting the historical regional or minority languages spoken in their territories. To this end they must adopt genuine and effective legal and administrative measures applicable to these territories, as the Committee of Experts has repeatedly stressed.

The Committee of Experts' reports have enshrined the principle of the general applicability of Part II of the ECRML to all regional or minority languages which fulfil the requirements of Article 1a and are spoken in the territory of a signatory state, whether or not they are explicitly mentioned in the instrument of ratification. Being aware of the possible variations on this general principle, the Committee of Experts has concentrated firstly on expanding the list of languages eligible for protection under Part II of the Charter, and secondly on establishing

---

42. The Committee of Experts considers the limit provided for in Slovak legislation, viz that users of the regional or minority language must constitute at least 20% of the municipal population to benefit from the measures laid down in Article 10 of the Charter, an excessively high threshold: see Slovakia 2009, 13. Application of the Charter in Montenegro, 1st monitoring cycle (2010), paragraph 28, reads as follows: "In general, the Committee of Experts considers that percentage thresholds may prevent the Charter from being applied to those regional or minority languages which may be present in sufficient numbers in municipalities or localities for the application of provisions of the Charter." See also Czech Republic 2009, 46; Serbia 2009, 29.
43. In connection with Sami and Finnish, see Sweden 2006, 16, and Recommendation of the Committee of Ministers: Sweden (2006), 1, repeated in Sweden 2009, 12. In this context, the problem of the "territorial co-official status of Basque in Navarra is enlightening: see Spain 2005, 64-74.
44. See Woehrling (2005), op. cit., p. 67.

a series of criteria for the efforts of states to implement the principles and objectives of Part II (the need to adopt a language policy or strategy, the "weakness of the language" as a decisive factor for active policies, and so on).

In connection with the undertakings accepted under Part III of the Charter, the Committee of Experts has managed, not without committing a number of contradictions (e.g. broadening its scope to include regional or minority languages with a weaker domestic legal status), to establish criteria which flesh out or clarify the scope and real efficacy of the undertakings accepted by the signatory states: rejecting ambiguities, interpreting or questioning the setting of thresholds for numbers of speakers or territorial limits. The aim of the commendable work of the Committee of Experts is, by accepting the principle of free disposal governing relations between the states and Part III of the Charter, to prevent arbitrary decisions and exclusions from protection incompatible with the spirit, objectives and principles of the ECRML.

References

Agirreazkuenaga, Iñaki (2006), "La Carta Europea de Lenguas Regionales o Minoritarias del Consejo de Europa como Derecho interno" in José Manuel Pérez Fernández (ed.), *Estudios sobre el estatuto jurídico de las lenguas en España.* Barcelona: Atelier.

Arzoz, Xabier (2008), "The implementation of the European Charter for Regional or Minority Languages in Spain" in Dunbar, Robert, and Parry, Gwynedd (eds), *The European Charter for Regional or Minority Languages: legal challenges and opportunities*. Strasbourg: Council of Europe Publishing.

Castellà Surribas, Santiago (2002), "La ratificació de l'Estat espanyol a la Carta europea de llengües regionals o minoritàries", *Mercator-Documents de Treball*, No. 8, www.ciemen.org/mercator/pdf/wp8-cat-def.pdf.

Castells, José Manuel (2004), "Efectos jurídicos de la ratificación por España de la Carta Europea de Lenguas regionales o minoritarias", *Revista Vasca de Administración Pública*, No. 69 (II).

Christopoulos, Dimitris (1992), "La question de la protection des minorités dans un ordre public européen: analyse critique des travaux élaborés au sein du Conseil de l'Europe, de la CSCE, et de la CEE". Strasbourg: Université R. Schuman (thesis).

Clotet I Miró, Maria-Àngels (1994), "La Carta Europea de las lenguas regionales o minoritarias", *Revista de Instituciones Europeas,* Vol. 21, No. 2.

Deop Madinabeitia, Xabier (2000), *La protección de las minorias nacionales en el Consejo de Europa*. Oñati: Basque Institute of Public Administration.

Dunbar, Robert (2008), "Definitively interpreting the European Charter for Regional or Minority Languages: the legal challenges" in Robert Dunbar and Gwynedd Parry (eds), *The European Charter for Regional or Minority Languages: legal challenges and opportunities*. Strasbourg: Council of Europe Publishing.

Kovács, Péter (1993), "La protection des langues minoritaires ou la nouvelle approche de la protection des minorités?", *Revue Générale de Droit International Public*, Vol. 97, No. 2.

Palermo, Francesco and Woelk, Jens (2008), *Diritto costituzionale comparato dei gruppi e delle minoranze*. Padua: CEDAM.

Pérez Fernández, José Manuel (2009), "La protection des langues régionales ou minoritaires en Espagne: Le statut juridique de la langue asturienne", *Opinio Iuris,* Vol. 2, No. 2, http://lider-lab.sssup.it/opinio.

Petschen Verdaguer, Santiago (1989), "Entre la politica y el derecho: la Carta de las Lenguas Regionales o Minoritarias", *Revista de Estudios Politicos*, No. 66.

Puig, Lluís Maria (de) (1986), "Informe provisional sobre la preparació d'un projecte de Carta Europea de les llengües regionals e minoritàries", *Revista de Llengua i Dret*, No. 8.

Puig, Lluís Maria (de) (1991), "Debat i elaboració de la Carta Europea de les Llengües", *Revista de Llengua i Dret*, No. 16.

Reuter, Paul (1961), "Principes de droit international public", *Recueil des Cours de l'Académie de Droit International*, No. 103.

Triadú i Vila-Abadal, Joaquim (2002), "Perspectiva constitucional i Carta Europea de les llengües Regionals o Minoritàries", *Revista de Llengua i Dret*, No. 37.

Varennes, Fernand (de) (2008), "Language protection and the European Charter for Regional or Minority Languages: *quo vadis?*" in *The European Charter for Regional or Minority Languages: legal challenges and opportunities*, Regional or Minority Languages No. 5. Strasbourg: Council of Europe.

Viaut, Alain (2004), "The European Charter for Regional or Minority Languages: sociolinguistic particularities and the French configuration", *Mercator-Documents de Treball*, No. 15, www.ciemen.org/mercator.

Woehrling, Jean-Marie (1989), "La promotion des langues régionales et minoritaires dans le Projet de Charte du Conseil de l'Europe" in Paul Pupier and José Woehrling (eds), *Langue et droit: actes du Premier Congrès de l'Institut International de Droit Linguistique Comparé*. Montréal: Wilson & Lafleur.

Woehrling, Jean-Marie (2005), *The European Charter for Regional or Minority Languages: a critical commentary*. Strasbourg: Council of Europe Publishing.

Article 4. Existing regimes of protection

R. Gwynedd Parry
Swansea University/Prifysgol Abertawe

1. Introduction

2. Interpretation
   2.1. Article 4 and the European Convention on Human Rights
   2.2. Article 4 and the rule of interpretation

3. Commentary

4. Conclusion

References

Article 4 – Existing regimes of protection

1. Nothing in this Charter shall be construed as limiting or derogating from any of the rights guaranteed by the European Convention on Human Rights.

2. The provisions of this Charter shall not affect any more favourable provisions concerning the status of regional or minority languages, or the legal regime of persons belonging to minorities which may exist in a Party or are provided for by relevant bilateral or multilateral international agreements.

1. Introduction

The European Charter for Regional or Minority Languages (ECRML) operates within the context of an expanding body of international jurisprudence with an interest in minority language protection. It also functions in the context of considerable diversity at the domestic level, with the legal relationship between the minority or regional language and the state differing quite considerably from state to state. Because there are now a number of international and domestic instruments which offer protection to speakers of minority languages in various ways, the chief objective of Article 4 is establishing the ECRML's place and role within the jurisprudential firmament.

Article 4 sets out certain principles governing the ECRML's relationship with other legal instruments and international agreements. In doing so, it establishes certain ground rules of interpretation. The main purpose of Article 4 is to affirm the principle of compatibility. It provides reassurance, if reassurance is needed, that the ECRML is a benign instrument which is not in conflict with either international or domestic law, and that it is one which promotes rather than imposes standards. This chapter examines the content of Article 4 and determines to what extent its inclusion was necessary for the ECRML to gain the support of ratifying states.

2. Interpretation

2.1. Article 4 and the European Convention on Human Rights

Article 4 paragraph 1 contains an explicit declaration of non-derogation from the European Convention on Human Rights (ECHR). According to the Explanatory Report, this paragraph "seeks to exclude the possibility that any of the provisions of the charter might be so interpreted as to detract from the protection accorded thereby to the human rights of individuals".[1]

This declaration of compatibility is echoed elsewhere in the treaty. The Charter also declares itself and its mission to be in communion with international human rights jurisprudence in its Preamble: "The right to use a regional or minority language in private and public life is an inalienable right conforming to the principles embodied in the United Nations International Covenant on Civil and Political Rights, and according to the spirit of the Council of Europe's Convention for the Protection of Human Rights and Fundamental Freedoms".[2] Why is there a need to declare this principle of compatibility, and is there a genuine potential for the ECRML to be interpreted in a way that contravenes the provisions of the ECHR?

The ECHR governs the relationship between the individual and the state. It is a product of its period in history, a necessary innovation from a time when Europe and the world were recovering from the destruction and human suffering caused by those fascist regimes which had subsumed individual freedom and dignity in the name of extreme collectivist ideologies. The ECHR was thus conceived as part of the international community's rejection of state totalitarianism and was created in order to lay down a series of minimum, fundamental and individual human rights intended to protect all human beings from future oppression. The history of its genesis is the key to understanding why the ECHR has an individualistic emphasis and why it is concerned with fundamental, individual human rights.

It is sometimes assumed that the ECHR has little or no impact on minority language rights. Although the ECHR does not support linguistic freedom in the sense of facilitating language choice, it counters and prevents discrimination

---

1. See *European Charter for Regional or Minority Languages and Explanatory Report* (1993). Strasbourg: Council of Europe Publishing, and Explanatory Report, paragraph 54.
2. ECRML, Preamble.

or degrading treatment towards individuals who belong to particular linguistic groups.[3] It is thus an important contributor to the maintenance of the rights of linguistic minorities, even if those rights are mostly confined to the private sphere and are essentially a prohibition on discrimination. As one commentator observes, "state measures which have the effect of preventing the use of a minority language in private activities can be in breach of a number of well-established rights in international law", because, "in the private sphere what are involved are in fact the application of basic individual human rights which impact in the arena of language".[4] Accordingly, "Government attempts to regulate the language used in the private sphere ... may run foul of the right to private and family life, freedom of expression, non-discrimination or the rights of persons belonging to a linguistic minority to use their language with other members of their group".[5]

Of course, the ECHR is mainly a preventative instrument concerned with the maintenance of fundamental freedoms and rights, laying down a bottom line below which states must not fall. The ECRML is a totally different sort of instrument. It encourages and promotes positive initiatives and measures for the benefit of minority languages.[6] Its promotion of minority languages is also couched in collective rather than individualistic terms. Whereas the ECHR protects individual speakers of minority languages from human rights infringements, it does not provide active promotion of multilingualism as a social objective. To this extent, the ECHR is a limited instrument. As Kymlicka puts it, "The right to free speech does not tell us what an appropriate language policy is".[7]

The ECRML is more directly focused on the appropriate language policy for European states, albeit in a very particular way. It promotes not merely minority languages, but the indigenous or historical languages of European people, which it seeks to protect in the name of European heritage. The languages of new, migrant peoples do not come under its remit.[8] As is clearly stated in Article 1, the languages that are protected are those which are not "official languages", which are spoken by a minority, are traditionally used by part of the population of a state and which are not languages of migrants, dialects or artificially created

---

3. See S. M. Poulter (1997), "The rights of ethnic, religious and linguistic minorities", *EHRLR*, Vol. 3, p. 254.
4. See F. de Varennes (2001), "The linguistic rights of minorities in Europe" in S. Trifunovska (ed.), *Minority rights in Europe: European minorities and languages*. The Hague: T.M.C. Asser Press, p. 9.
5. Ibid.
6. W. Kymlicka (1995), *Multicultural citizenship: a liberal theory of minority rights*. Oxford: Clarendon Press, p. 6.
7. Ibid., pp. 2-5.
8. ECRML, Explanatory Report, paragraphs 10 and 15.

languages.[9] The ECRML is concerned with "the historical regional or minority languages of Europe", because, it maintains, they contribute "to the maintenance and development of Europe's cultural wealth and traditions".[10] Therefore, its interest in multilingualism does not include new linguistic minorities, such as those minorities of Asian or African origin which are now well established in most European states. Repeatedly, the emphasis is on the "common heritage" and on the "traditional regional and minority languages".[11]

This distinction between "old minorities" and "new minorities" is replicated in the domestic legislation of many of the ratifying states, which have granted civic rights to certain indigenous minority linguistic groups but not to the more recently formed minority linguistic groups. Some observers have questioned whether this differentiation between linguistic groups is undermining the integrity and validity of claims for recognising language rights as fundamental rights, and see it as being contrary to liberal, rights-based principles.[12] More specifically, this selective approach to minority language protection might give the ECRML the appearance of being at odds with the universal emphasis in the ECHR. But it is doubtful whether this focus on the historical languages runs counter to ECHR principles. Justifying discrimination or preferential treatment always appears counter-intuitive to notions of universal equality. However, affirmative action or positive discrimination for minority or neglected groups has also been recognised as being justified and necessary in given situations.

Where the minority culture is unfairly disadvantaged when compared with the dominant culture, the way of rectifying that disadvantage is by the creation of a "group differentiated right".[13] In other words, bringing about social equality requires special measures/positive discrimination/affirmative action in favour of the minority group. It has also been said that, provided that the group-

---

9. ECRML, Article 1: "For the purposes of this Charter: a 'regional or minority languages' means languages that are: i. traditionally used within a given territory of a State by nationals of that State who form a group numerically smaller than rest of the State's population, and ii. different from the official language(s) of that State; it does not include either dialects of the official language(s) of the State or the languages of migrants".
10. ECRML, Preamble.
11. ECRML, Explanatory Report, paragraph 26.
12. See R. Dunbar (2000), "Implications of the European Charter for Regional or Minority Languages for British linguistic minorities", *European Law Review*, No. 25, Human Rights Survey, p. 50; T. Cheesman (2001), "Old and new lesser-used languages of Europe: common cause?" in C. C. O'Reilly (ed.), *Language, ethnicity and the state*, Vol. 1. Basingstoke: Palgrave, pp. 147-66; P. Keller (1998), "Re-thinking ethnic and cultural rights in Europe", *Oxford Journal of Legal Studies*, Vol. 18, No. 1, pp. 29-59; R. Baubock (1996), "Cultural minority rights for immigrants", *International Migration Review*, Vol. 30, No. 1, pp. 203-50.
13. W. Kymlicka (1995), *Multicultural citizenship...*, pp. 108-16.

differentiated right does not infringe other basic, individual, human rights and that it is proportional to meet the deficit, then such affirmative action in favour of the minority language group can be justified.[14] Indeed, such affirmative action has been argued to be consistent with basic liberal and more universal principles of individual freedom, namely the freedom to belong to a cultural group, and the right to cultural (and linguistic) self-expression. Group-differentiated rights are therefore argued to be necessary in order to provide a climate whereby the minority culture can function in the way the dominant culture takes for granted.[15]

The ECRML does not offend or contravene the ECHR because it does not restrict or invade the rights of individuals who speak dominant or official languages. Neither does it undermine the rights of those who speak other minority languages which are not protected by it. Fears that it might somehow be in conflict with individual human rights are therefore unfounded.[16] Its particular emphasis on the promotion of indigenous minority languages does not infringe the universal principles of the ECHR, but builds on those principles so that minority language speakers enjoy a greater equality with speakers of official languages. Instead of representing a divergence from the values of the ECHR, the ECRML is a logical development of the ECHR and enhances its core principles. The difference is that the ECRML marks a shift from an anti-discriminatory, minimalist emphasis to an affirmative and proactive approach towards linguistic minorities. Indeed, it is arguably a part of a well-established political tradition which has sought to bring about the emancipation of minorities and those marginal groups who were historically excluded from mainstream society.

Therefore, to claim a tension between universal human rights and more partic-ular linguistic rights is arguably a conceptual fallacy. To quote one observer, "the 'linguistic rights' of minorities actually refer to the application of universal human rights and freedoms in specific situations … as part of an evolving, comprehensive framework based on respect for human worth and dignity."[17] Indeed, such a view sees the relatively recent acknowledgement of the case for linguistic rights as being an inevitable consequence of the maturing of human rights jurisprudence. To quote:

> It is therefore an often repeated error to assume that the protection of the rights of minorities is somehow inconsistent with or different from "individual" human rights. On the contrary, by being founded on the recognition of the intrinsic value of the

---

14. J. Castellino (2003), "Affirmative action for the protection of linguistic rights: an analysis of international human rights; legal standards in the context of the protection of the Irish language", *Dublin University Law Journal*, Vol. 25, No. 1, pp. 1-43.

15. W. Kymlicka (1995), *Multicultural citizenship*, p. 126.

16. J.-M. Woehrling (2005) *The European Charter for Regional or Minority Languages: a critical commentary*. Strasbourg: Council of Europe Publishing, pp. 83-4.

17. See F. de Varennes (2001), "The linguistic rights of minorities in Europe", p. 4.

human person's dignity and worth, human rights have gone beyond mere tolerance of human differences: respect of the individual includes valuing human diversity.[18]

There is a body of scholarship which is sceptical of the very idea of "human rights" with its universalist perspective and its claim to express self-evident, objective and metaphysical truths about human values.[19] The rights sceptics see it as a creation of a Western, neo-liberal, individualist mindset. Others are sceptical of how ethereal human rights can permeate to the ground level and influence policy in real situations. For some, the maintenance of language rights is more a bottom-up rather than a top-down process, one which depends more on the socio-political situation of the particular linguistic community than on general, universal and international policy initiatives.[20] This chapter cannot enter into a philosophical assessment of the validity of the notion of "human rights" or its practical impact. It must proceed on the basis that there is an international consensus in support of human rights instruments as being one of the means of protecting individuals against state oppression. What is important for present purposes is to recognise that there is neither a conceptual nor a practical conflict between the ECHR and the ECRML.

Setting aside these conceptual issues and turning to some hard law, the most significant factor dictating the legal relationship between the two instruments is the fact that the ECHR has legal force whereas the ECRML does not. Although the ECHR creates individual legal rights, which can be enforced through legal processes in the European Court of Human Rights, the ECRML does not grant such legal rights and does not provide a means of judicial adjudication or remedy. Therefore, the legal reality does not enable any direct legal conflict between the ECHR and the ECRML to arise. On the other hand, it is also possible that, by signing up to the Charter's obligations, states will consequently create laws which then create legal rights for speakers of those languages.[21] This is because states that adopt the Charter's measures may need to legislate at a domestic level for that adoption to be effective. But it is not the Charter that is the sovereign or authority for the laws created internally by states parties, even if those laws were inspired by the Charter's provisions. Therefore, even if some claim of incompatibility with the ECHR were to arise, any legal challenge or remedy would have to be sought through domestic court processes and/or the European Court of Human Rights.

---

18. Ibid., p. 29.
19. For a critique of the idea of human rights, see M.-B. Dembour (2006), *Who believes in human rights? Reflections on the European Convention*. Cambridge: Cambridge University Press, *in toto*.
20. See X. Arzoz (2009), "Language rights as legal norms", *European Public Law*, Vol. 15, No. 4, pp. 541-74.
21. Woehrling (2005), op. cit., p. 31.

2.2. Article 4 and the rule of interpretation

Article 4 paragraph 2 provides a rule of interpretation that governs the relationship between the ECRML and existing guarantees or measures in both the international and the domestic context. The Explanatory Report states:

> Where certain languages or the minorities who practise them already enjoy a status defined in domestic law or under international agreements, the purpose of the charter is clearly not to reduce the rights and guarantees recognised by those provisions. However, the protection afforded by the charter is additional to the rights and guarantees already granted by other instruments.[22]

Woehrling explains that this is a rule for interpreting the ECRML which is in accordance with the provisions of Article 30.2 of the Treaty of Vienna of 1969.[23] Article 30 of the Treaty of Vienna deals with the difficulties of interpretation and implementation that can arise where there are successive treaties on the same subject or the same subject matter.[24] Article 30.2 provides that, when a treaty is drafted so that it contains a provision which makes it "subject to, or that it is not to be considered incompatible with, an earlier or later treaty, the provisions of that other treaty will prevail".[25]

The exact wording in Article 4 is "shall not effect", which in Woehrling's opinion must be taken to put into effect the principle in Article 30.2 of the Treaty of Vienna and which effectively means that the ECRML must be interpreted in such a way that it is either compatible with other applicable treaties or else the other treaties take precedence. Therefore, this is a rule of compatibility to prevent conflict with other international treaties. Another effect of Article 4.2 is that it makes it clear that the Charter does not interfere with or undermine provisions in either domestic law or international law, nor in other international agreements which affect regional or minority languages. If, for example, a regional or minority language enjoys greater protection than that provided by the ECRML, the ECRML does not seek to interfere with that or undermine it in any way.

The Explanatory Report goes further, and states:

> For the application of all these undertakings, where competing provisions exist on the same subject the most favourable provisions should be applied to the minorities or languages concerned. Thus the existence of more restrictive provisions in domestic law or under other international undertakings must not be an obstacle to the application of the charter.[26]

---

22. See ECRML, Explanatory Report at paragraph 53.
23. The Vienna Convention on the Law of Treaties (1969).
24. For analysis of the 1986 Vienna Convention on the Law of Treaties between states and international bodies, see C. Brolmann (2007), *The institutional veil in public international law.* Oxford: Hart, pp. 197-247.
25. Woehrling (2005), op. cit., p. 82.
26. See ECRML, Explanatory Report, paragraph 53.

A literal interpretation of this latter part of paragraph 53 of the Explanatory Report might support the view that there may be situations where the ECRML's provisions take precedence if they are more favourable than other provisions. However, this would contradict the principle in Article 30.2 of the Treaty of Vienna. The more viable interpretation of this paragraph is that it encourages the most favourable approach towards the relevant languages, and that it is aspirational rather than prescriptive. This is the interpretation which is compatible with the ECRML's legal status in international law.

In the context of the first evaluation report on Ukraine, the Committee of Experts and the Committee of Ministers interpreted Article 4.2 in such a way that every regional or minority language must at least get the level of protection under the Charter that it already enjoys in accordance with national legislation, policies and practice at the time of ratification. Provisions of national legislation must therefore be mirrored in related Charter provisions. Obviously, the Charter menu may also go beyond a mere reflection of the level of national protection.

3. Commentary

Since 1945, there has been a proliferation of international treaties and legal instruments concerned to varying degrees and in different ways with the rights and interests of regional and minority languages and of the individuals who speak those languages. On the global stage, the United Nations has played a leading role in setting standards. The International Covenant on Civil and Political Rights, Article 27, provides that linguistic minorities should not be denied their culture and the right to use their own language.[27] The United Nations Declaration on the Rights of Persons belonging to National or Ethnic, Religious and Linguistic Minorities also supports the rights of minority cultures, although it does not amount to a binding instrument.[28] If we add the draft United Nations Declaration on the Rights of Indigenous Peoples to the mix, we can fairly conclude that the United Nations has had a sustained interest in the rights of minorities, including minority languages.[29]

This chapter does not provide a guided tour of the international jurisprudence in this field. However, looking at the situation in the round, the common thread

---

27. See ICCPR, Article 27. The actual scope of this right is, however, somewhat uncertain.

28. Even so, the United Nations' contribution to international human rights law is often regarded as one of its "great accomplishments": see H. Herman (1998), "Human rights" in C. C. Joyner (ed.), *The United Nations and international law*. Cambridge: Cambridge University Press, pp. 130-54, at p. 153.

29. For a more detailed guide to the range of applicable international instruments, see F. de Varennes (2007), "Linguistic identity and language rights" in M. Weller, *Universal minority rights: a commentary on the jurisprudence of international courts and treaty bodies*. Oxford: Oxford University Press, at pp. 255-8.

and the general emphasis within many of these instruments and their provisions is to declare and uphold the principle of non-interference. They maintain the principle that linguistic minorities should not be prevented from, say, setting up societies, engaging in cultural festivals or publishing literature in their languages.[30] In essence, speakers of minority languages are protected to the extent that they are entitled to enjoy freedom to use their language in the private sphere. Non-interference is, of course, not the same as active promotion of linguistic minorities on the part of the state.

In the context of European Union law, a degree of support for minority language interests can also be discerned.[31] A multicultural entity composed of other multi-cultural entities, the EU has an important role in providing a vision for a multicul-tural and multilingual society. As a logical extension of the principle of subsidiarity, the rationale of the EU's policy can be summed up in the words of one particular commentator: "minorities cannot be considered to exist merely on the sufferance of the majority; the ethos of multiculturalism is that of unbiased coexistence".[32] It is the case that European law has for some time, albeit perhaps tentatively, supported the principle of cultural diversity, particularly Article 151 EC, although there was no specific mention of linguistic diversity in this provision. However, European law has provided limited support for linguistic rights within the notion of European citizenship, particularly following the case of *Re Criminal Proceedings against Horst Otto Bickel and Ulrich Franz.*[33] That case upheld the principle that Article 6 EC precludes national rules which confer on its own citizens the right to require that criminal proceedings be conducted in a particular language, without conferring the same right on nationals of other member states who may be subject to criminal proceedings in the relevant region.

More recent developments may herald greater support for linguistic diversity in EU law. The European Charter of Fundamental Rights enshrines the core values of the European Union in a consolidating instrument.[34] The EU's Reform Treaty (the Lisbon Treaty)[35] provides a legal base for the Charter of Fundamental Rights (provided that member states ratify both).[36]

---

30. For an interpretation of the scope of the ICCPR, Article 27, see *Ominayak v. Canada*, UN 167/1984, Doc. A/42/40.
31. For commentary on the position of linguistic rights in European Law, see I. Urrutia and I. Lasagabaster (2008), "Language rights and Community law", *European Integration Online Papers*, Vol. 12, No. 4 – http://eiop.or.at/eiop/texte/2008-004a.htm.
32. N. Nic Shuibhne (2002), *EC law and minority language policy: culture, citizenship and fundamental rights*. London: Kluwer Law International, p. 55.
33. Case C-274/96) ECJ [1999] 1 C.M.L.R. 348.
34. See http://europa.eu.int/comm/justice_home/unit/charte/en/charter-equality.html.
35. http://europa.eu/lisbon_treaty/index_en.htm.
36. The United Kingdom and Poland have opted out of the Charter of Fundamental Rights.

Article 21 of the Charter of Fundamental Rights advances the principle of linguistic rights within the European Union and creates means of redress and appeal in cases of discrimination on the grounds of language or where an individual is a "member of a national minority". Such appeals will go to the European Court of Justice in Luxembourg. Article 21.1 states:

> Any discrimination based on any ground such as sex, race, colour, ethnic or social origin, genetic features, language, religion or belief, political or any other opinion, membership of a national minority, property, birth, disability, age or sexual orientation shall be prohibited.

Article 22 states that "The Union shall respect cultural, religious and linguistic diversity." In addition, Article 3.3 of the Lisbon Treaty itself states that the European Union "shall respect its rich cultural and linguistic diversity, and shall ensure that Europe's cultural heritage is safeguarded and enhanced." Linguistic groups are thus provided with some grounds for redress if they are discriminated against in any European Union legislation. The Charter of Fundamental Rights is intended to complement other international instruments such as the European Convention on Human Rights. A Fundamental Rights Agency (FRA) will be able to monitor and make reports on discrimination, as well as promoting general awareness of minority language issues. The Lisbon Treaty, by giving a binding effect to the Charter of Fundamental Rights, broadens the influence of the EU in the field of individual rights. It also unequivocally engages the jurisdiction of the European Court of Justice in cases of discrimination.

Of course, it remains to be seen to what extent these recent developments will advance the cause of linguistic rights in a positive and practical way in the medium to long term. The emphasis is largely on preventing discrimination rather than on conferring any rights to speakers of minority languages, and in that sense replicates UN activity in this field. The Council of Europe, however, has been the source of more proactive standards on minority language promotion.

The Council of Europe's Framework Convention for the Protection of National Minorities addresses language rights within the broader context of minority rights.[37] For example, Article 10.1 of the Framework Convention recognises the right to use a minority language in public and private life. Article 14.1 of the Framework Convention appears to deal with education, but it is couched in very conservative terms. Article 14.1 requires "the parties undertake to recognise that every person belonging to a national minority has the right to learn his or her

---

37. For an overview of the Framework Convention, see M. Weller (ed.) (2005), *The rights of minorities: a commentary on the European Framework Convention for the Protection of National Minorities*. Oxford: Oxford University Press; see also S. Wheatley (1996), "The Council of Europe's Framework Convention on National Minorities", *Web JCLI*, No. 5.

minority language", and Article 14.2 requires parties, as far as possible, in areas where the minority language is spoken, if there is sufficient demand, and within the existing framework of their education systems, to endeavour to provide adequate opportunities for being taught in the minority language.

The difficulty with many of these instruments is that, though they promote worthy sentiments towards minority languages and cultures, they are weak on detail and fail to set out specific measures that need to be undertaken by states in the interests of linguistic minorities.[38] The ECRML is far more detailed and specific than any of these other instruments. It is also flexible in its capacity to take into account the diversity that exists between minority languages within European states.[39] The often repeated criticism of the Charter, that it gives states too much discretion to apply it according to their own political interests, can also be a virtue in the context of the complex and diverse linguistic landscape in Europe as a whole.[40] The monitoring process, despite its limitations,[41] provides a mechanism for ensuring a level of public accountability for the implementation of the Charter by party states.[42]

The ECRML's detail and proactive emphasis marks it out from the other international instruments. Take, for example, the use of a minority language in a court trial. Article 6 of the ECHR simply guarantees basic comprehension on the basis of a principle of linguistic necessity. It guarantees the right to use a minority language as part of the basic tenets of a fair trial.[43] Article 6 ECHR provides that a person on trial must be understood and has a right to understand the proceedings. But the right under Article 6 to an interpreter where the defendant does not understand the language of the court is not the same as a right to use the language of choice, or the right to a tribunal that speaks the defendant's language.[44] This principle of necessity has been maintained in other

---

38. For a study of the mechanisms to implement and monitor minority rights, see R. M. Letschert (2005), *The impact of minority rights mechanisms*. The Hague: T.M.C. Asser Press.

39. See R. Dunbar (2008), "Definitely interpreting the European Charter for Regional or Minority Languages: the legal challenges" in R. Dunbar and G. Parry, *The European Charter for Regional or Minority Languages: legal challenges and opportunities*. Strasbourg: Council of Europe Publishing, pp. 37-61, at p. 40.

40. See R. Dunbar (2000), "Implications… for British linguistic minorities", p. 69.

41. See T. Skutnabb-Kangas (1999), "Linguistic diversity, human rights and the 'free' market" in M. Kontra, R. Phillipson, T. Skutnabb-Kangas and T. Varady, *Language: a right and a resource*. Budapest: CEU Press, pp. 204-6.

42. ECRML, Article 15.

43. See ECHR, Article 6.

44. This has been made clear in a number of judgments; see, for example *A v. France* (1984) 6 EHRR CD 371. In this case, the applicant was a French citizen who appeared before a military tribunal in Rennes charged with military insubordination. He insisted on answering all charges put to him in the Breton language and requested an interpreter. The request was refused

situations where individuals have unsuccessfully sought the support of the ECHR when seeking to use the language of their choice.[45]

Article 10.3 of the Framework Convention for the Protection of National Minorities requires party states to guarantee the right of an individual to be informed, in a language that he or she understands, of the reasons for his or her arrest and the nature of the accusation, and to be able to defend himself or herself in that language (if necessary, with the assistance of an interpreter). The wording of Article 10.3 is so similar to that of Article 6 of the ECHR, that it is doubtful that it creates any further right at all, as it appears to promote linguistic comprehension rather than linguistic choice, which is no more than the basic human right protected by Article 6 of the ECHR. Again, as with the ECHR, it is the principle of linguistic necessity which the Framework Convention upholds.

The ECRML, however, goes much further. Article 9 ECRML takes the position from one of linguistic necessity to one of linguistic equality. It requires that subscribing states undertake in respect of those judicial districts where the numbers who use the minority language justify it, and according to the situation of the language concerned, to allow speakers of the minority language to use it in court and tribunal hearings (provided that it does not hamper the proper administration of justice).[46] The right to use the minority language in court proceedings applies to defendants, witnesses and all parties. Furthermore, it contains provisions stipulating that states provide that the criminal courts, at the request of one of the parties, shall conduct the proceedings in the minority or regional language[47] and guarantee the accused the right to use his or her minority language.[48] There are similar provisions in the context of civil proceedings[49] and in administrative courts.[50] The Charter provides that the use of the

---

because, *inter alia*, he was a fluent French speaker. He was eventually convicted and sentenced to two years' imprisonment. When the matter came before the European Commission of Human Rights, one issue was whether the refusal to allow the applicant to present his case in Breton was a breach of Articles 6.3e and 14 (that is, the right not to be discriminated against on the basis of language) of the Convention. The Commission held the complaint to be inadmissible as the relevant articles of the Convention only apply where the individual concerned cannot understand or speak the language used in court.

45. In *Fryske Nasjonale Partij and Others v. Netherlands* (1987) 9 EHRR CD 261, speakers of Frisian complained about the refusal of authorities in the Netherlands to allow them to use the Frisian language when submitting relevant parliamentary election registration documents. The Commission again held that there had been no breach of Convention rights, and there was no right to use the language of one's choice within the articles of the Convention.

46. ECRML, Part III, Article 9.

47. Ibid., Article 9, paragraph 1a.i.

48. Ibid., paragraph 1a.ii.

49. Ibid., paragraph 1b.

50. Ibid., paragraph 1c.

minority language be facilitated, if necessary, by the use of interpreters and translation.[51] The key difference is that the provisions of Article 9 do not depend on the individual not being able to understand the dominant language, but introduce the principle of choice on the basis of equality.

The ECRML, in light of its emphasis and detail, is unlike other international instruments, and this means that there is little likelihood of incompatibility. Of course, as has been already stated, it is not part of European law, and does not grant individual legal rights nor does it create legal obligations. It has no judicial enforcement mechanism in the event of non-compliance. Its important role is in setting out agreed standards which can provide a reference point or bench-mark for promoting multilingualism and cultural diversity as a social value.[52] Its effect is that it requires party states to undertake measures in the interests of the minority or regional languages within their frontiers, rather than create rights for speakers of those languages. While recognising that minority languages may not enjoy the same status as the official language(s), its objec-tive is to promote the concept of a multilingual society based on principles of respect and harmonious coexistence.[53]

The ECRML is therefore more in the nature of a policy document which provides a set of values, international norms, to guide European states in their policies towards the indigenous minority languages within their boundaries. It provides a shopping list in the form of practical measures that can facilitate minority language protection and promotion. The challenge posed by the Charter's concept of multilingual citizenship is citizenship which promotes political unity without promoting cultural assimilation, one which recognises the value of linguistic diversity as a common value shared by the political community as a whole.

4. Conclusion

The inclusion and wording of Article 4 are indicative of the fact that the authors of the ECRML were anxious to reassure those who were hostile or sceptical towards its creation that it is an essentially benign instrument which respects human rights principles and which observes established principles of inter-national law.

Despite its collective and particular emphasis, which might seem counter to the more individualist emphasis found in most other instruments, it is not intended to undermine or be in conflict with the universal and individual

---

51. ECRML, Article 1, paragraph b.
52. Woehrling (2005), op. cit., pp. 19-23.
53. Ibid., pp. 33, 36-7.

objectives of the ECHR. Neither is it intended to be in conflict with other instruments or legal provisions in either international law or domestic law which apply to minority or regional languages. It explicitly defers authority to these other instruments, by providing this rule of interpretation in Article 4.

References

Arzoz, Xabier (2009), "Language rights as legal norms", *European Public Law*, Vol. 15, No. 4.

Bauböck, Rainer (1996), "Cultural minority rights for immigrants", *International Migration Review*, Vol. 30, No. 1.

Brolmann, Catherine (2007), *The institutional veil in public international law*. Oxford: Hart.

Castellino, Joshua (2003), "Affirmative action for the protection of linguistic rights: an analysis of international human rights; legal standards in the context of the protection of the Irish language", *Dublin University Law Journal*, Vol. 25, No. 1.

Cheesman, Tom (2001), "Old and new lesser-used languages of Europe: common cause?" in Camille C. O'Reilly (ed.), *Language, ethnicity and the state*, Vol. 1. Basingstoke: Palgrave.

Dembour, Marie-Benedicte (2006), *Who believes in human rights? Reflections on the European Convention*. Cambridge: Cambridge University Press.

Dunbar, Robert (2000), "Implications of the European Charter for Regional or Minority Languages for British linguistic minorities", *European Law Review*, Vol. 25, Human Rights Survey, pp. 46-69.

Dunbar, Robert (2008), "Definitely interpreting the European Charter for Regional or Minority Languages: the legal challenges" in Robert Dunbar and Gwynedd Parry (eds), *The European Charter for Regional or Minority Languages: legal challenges and opportunities*. Strasbourg: Council of Europe Publishing.

European Charter for Regional or Minority Languages and Explanatory Report (1993), Strasbourg: Council of Europe Publishing.

Herman, Hurst (1998), "Human rights" in Christopher C. Joyner (ed.), *The United Nations and international law*. Cambridge: Cambridge University Press.

Keller, Perry (1998), "Re-thinking ethnic and cultural rights in Europe", *Oxford Journal of Legal Studies*, Vol. 18, No. 1.

Kymlicka, Will (1995), *Multicultural citizenship: a liberal theory of minority rights*. Oxford: Clarendon Press.

Rianne M. Letschert (2005), *The impact of minority rights mechanisms*. The Hague: T.M.C. Asser Press.

Nic Shuibhne, Niamh (2002), *EC law and minority language policy: culture, citizenship and fundamental rights*. London: Kluwer Law International.

Poulter, Sebastian M. (1997), "The rights of ethnic, religious and linguistic minorities", *European Human Rights Law Review*, Vol. 3, p. 254.

Skutnabb-Kangas, Tove (1999), "Linguistic diversity, human rights and the 'free' market" in Miklós Kontra, Robert Phillipson, Tore Skutnabb-Kangas and Tibor Várady (eds), *Language: a right and a resource*. Budapest: CEU Press, pp. 187-222.

Urrutia, Iñigo and Lasagabaster, Iñaki (2008), "Language rights and community law", *European Integration Online Papers*, Vol. 12, No. 4, http://eiop.or.at/eiop/texte/2008-004a.htm.

Varennes, Fernand (de) (2001), "The linguistic rights of minorities in Europe" in Snežana Trifunovska (ed.), *Minority rights in Europe: European minorities and languages*. The Hague: T.M.C. Asser Press, pp. 3-30.

Varennes, Fernand (de) (2007), "Linguistic identity and language rights" in Marc Weller (ed.), *Universal minority rights: a commentary on the jurisprudence of international courts and treaty bodies*. Oxford: Oxford University Press, pp. 253-323.

Weller, Marc (ed.) (2005), *The rights of minorities: a commentary on the European Framework Convention for the Protection of National Minorities*. Oxford: Oxford University Press.

Wheatley, Steven (1996), "The Council of Europe's Framework Convention on National Minorities", *Web Journal of Current Legal Issues*, No. 5.

Woehrling, Jean-Marie (2005), *The European Charter for Regional or Minority Languages: a critical commentary*. Strasbourg: Council of Europe Publishing.

Article 5. Existing obligations

R. Gwynedd Parry
Swansea University/Prifysgol Abertawe

1. Introduction

2. Interpretation

3. Commentary

4. Conclusion

References

> **Article 5 – Existing obligations**
>
> *Nothing in this Charter may be interpreted as implying any right to engage in any activity or perform any action in contravention of the purposes of the Charter of the United Nations or other obligations under international law, including the principle of the sovereignty and territorial integrity of States.*

1. Introduction

Article 5 provides a further rule for interpreting the European Charter for Regional or Minority Languages (ECRML), which is closely related to and complements Article 4. In summary, it prevents any interpretation of the Charter that conflicts with the Charter of the United Nations. In particular, it prevents the ECRML being used to undermine principles of international law governing national sovereignty or territorial integrity. In this regard, Article 5 makes it clear that the Charter is not an instrument to undermine the authority of European states by promoting political autonomy for national/linguistic groups or justifying intervention on behalf of those groups by other states or the international community.

2. Interpretation

The Explanatory Report enlarges on the provisions of Article 5 by stating that "the protection and promotion of regional or minority languages which is the objective of the charter must take place within the framework of national sovereignty and territorial integrity".[1] The Preamble outlines the overriding

---

1. See *European Charter for Regional or Minority Languages and Explanatory Report* (1993). Strasbourg: Council of Europe Publishing. Explanatory Report at paragraph 55.

purpose and rationale of the Charter in upholding the values of "inter-cultur-alism and multilingualism" and proclaims that "the protection and promotion of regional or minority languages in the different countries and regions of Europe represent an important contribution to the building of a Europe based on the principles of democracy and cultural diversity within the framework of national sovereignty and territorial integrity."[2]

Woehrling comments that Article 5 affirms the Charter's commitment to a principle of international law as it applies to international treaties, in that "commitments entered into under international agreements can only be changed by a new international agreement between the same parties".[3] He adds that "the charter cannot legally have the effect of calling into question the aims of the Charter of the United Nations (or other agreements concluded with states which are not parties.)".[4]

It is a well-established principle of international law that states should enjoy respect for their sovereignty and territorial integrity. This was the foundation for world peace as declared in the Charter of the United Nations. After all, the overriding objective in setting up the United Nations was:

> To maintain international peace and security, and to that end: to take effective collective measures for the prevention and removal of threats to the peace, and for the suppression of acts of aggression or other breaches of the peace, and to bring about by peaceful means, and in conformity with the principles of justice and international law, adjustment or settlement of international disputes or situations which might lead to a breach of the peace.[5]

The creation of the United Nations was a key component of the post-1945 reconstruction agenda and at the very heart of the new world order. Its cardinal purpose was to prevent war and aggression, and to guarantee the security of all state members. As has been said,

> Most of the fundamental norms, rules and practices of international relations rest on the premise of state sovereignty ... non-intervention is the duty correlative to the right of sovereignty. Other states are obliged not to interfere with the internal actions of a sovereign state.[6]

2. ECRML, Preamble.
3. J.-M. Woehrling (2005), *The European Charter for Regional or Minority Languages: a critical commentary*. Strasbourg: Council of Europe Publishing, pp. 85-6.
4. Ibid.
5. UN Charter, Article 1.1.
6. See J. Donnelly (1995), "State sovereignty and international intervention: the case of human rights" in G. M. Lyons and M. Mastanduno (eds), *Beyond Westphalia? State sovereignty and international intervention*. Baltimore: Johns Hopkins University Press, p. 118.

Interference with the domestic jurisdiction of states could thus amount to a breach of Article 2.7 of the Charter of the United Nations, and the threat or use of force against the territorial integrity of states could likewise contravene Article 2.4 of the Charter of the United Nations. Article 2.4 states that:

> All Members shall refrain in their international relations from the threat or use of force against the territorial integrity or political independence of any state, or in any other manner inconsistent with the Purposes of the United Nations.[7]

These are the provisions of the United Nations Charter which Article 5 ECRML refers to and upholds. The Explanatory Report gives further guidance on what exactly Article 5 is seeking to achieve:

> the fact that, by ratifying the charter, a state has entered into undertakings with respect to a regional or minority language may not be used by another state having a special interest in that language or by the users of the language as a pretext for taking any action prejudicial to the sovereignty and territorial integrity of that state.[8]

Perhaps it is this particular passage in the Explanatory Report which is most instructive in explaining the inclusion and content of Article 5 in the Charter. It ensures that the ECRML cannot be interpreted in such a way that it gives the authority to a state to interfere in the interests of a linguistic group in another state.

The need to declare this injunction, and thus compatibility with the United Nations Charter, may have historical resonances, and may be a response to the inter-war experience of minority protection in international affairs. In the inter-war period (1918-39), the purported claims of linguistic and national minorities had been manipulated to justify military intervention in neighbouring states.[9] The ECRML rejects this form of political manipulation of its objectives and declares its compatibility with the principle of national sovereignty and state integrity. As Woehrling explains, "There is no provision in the charter allowing challenges to territorial boundaries in the states parties or which seeks to identify distinctive territorial entities which would present a challenge to state integrity".[10]

3. Commentary

The ECRML came into existence when the fragmentation of established political order in the Balkans was reaching its climax with the disintegration of

---

7. UN Charter, Article 2.4.
8. See ECRML, Explanatory Report at paragraph 55.
9. F. de Varennes (2007), "Linguistic identity and language rights" in M. Weller (ed.), *Universal minority rights: a commentary on the jurisprudence of international courts and treaty bodies.* Oxford: Oxford University Press, pp. 254-5.
10. Woehrling (2005), op. cit., p. 86.

Yugoslavia.[11] This may have created wariness in some quarters of a treaty which promoted the rights of linguistic minorities and which might, indirectly and by extension, also promote the cause of national minorities seeking self-determination. The provisions of Article 5 were thus necessary as part of the diplomatic trade-off to provide reassurance that those who drafted the ECRML had no such agenda. Consequently, as Woehrling states, "The purpose of Article 5 is primarily to forestall misinterpretation of the charter as a means of creating a right for linguistic groups to satisfaction of separatist claims".[12]

Of course the position of international law on state sovereignty and territorial integrity is complex and not always easy to determine. The concept of sovereignty is controversial and has been the subject of much debate as to its meaning. It is acknowledged that sovereignty is relative and malleable, and can mean different things in different contexts.[13] The principle of non-intervention is not absolutely sacrosanct and can be overridden in certain circumstances. After all, another important principle in international law is that which recognises the right of peoples to self-determination.[14] Indeed, the United Nations Charter provides that one of the primary purposes of the United Nations is "to develop friendly relations among nations based on respect for the principle of equal rights and self-determination of peoples".[15] It is conceded that the right of nations within established states to unilateral secession has been held to be justified only in extreme cases.[16] However, although commentators claim that "self determination cannot be used to further larger territorial claims in defiance of internationally accepted boundaries of sovereign states", it is also acknow-ledged that "it may be of some use in resolving cases of disputed frontier lines on the basis of the wishes of the inhabitants".[17]

The position is further complicated by the fact that, in recent times, there has been steady erosion of the sovereignty and territorial integrity principle due to an escalation in situations where the use of force against sovereign states has

---

11. Much has been written on this subject. See, for example, B. Magas (1993), *The destruction of Yugoslavia: tracking the break-up 1980-1992*. London: Verso; M. Glenny (1992), *The fall of Yugoslavia: the Third Balkan War*. London: Penguin.
12. Woehrling (2005), op. cit., p. 86.
13. For a detailed consideration of the concept of sovereignty in international law, see D. Sarooshi (2005), *International organisations and their exercise of sovereign powers*. Oxford: Oxford University Press.
14. For further discussion, see K. Knop (2005), *Diversity and self-determinations in international law*. Cambridge: Cambridge University Press.
15. UN Charter, Article 1.2.
16. *Reference Re Secession of Quebec* (1998) 161 DLR (4th) 385, 438.
17. M. Shaw (2003), *International law*, 5th edn. Cambridge: Cambridge University Press, p. 445.

either been justified or has not been condemned by the UN.[18] The use of force against terrorism in the name of collective security and international stability has provided disputed legitimacy for military interventions in Iraq and Afghanistan. The emergence of the humanitarian intervention justification for the use of force, particularly following NATO action in Kosovo in 1999, has made the advancement of human rights a potential basis for breaching the state sovereignty principle. This has set a precedent which potentially justifies intervention for the protection of minorities within states, particularly where such interference is necessary to preserve wider stability and where there is some risk of escalation in international conflict in the event of non-action.[19]

These recent conflicts have thus added to the wariness among states that well-established international law principles have been undermined and that the territorial integrity principle may be less robust than in the past.[20] A lack of clarity and certainty in international law on the right to secession[21] might have also fuelled anxiety that minority language campaigners could use linguistic claims as a pretext for the claims of national self-determination. If language rights are presented as an extension of human rights principles, then the unease and concern that either internal instability or external interference might be consequences of the recognition of such rights at some future point is understandable.

Yet, it is easy to exaggerate these concerns and anxieties. As one commentator has remarked, "sovereignty remains the central norm in the politics of international human rights. The international community, except in rare circumstances, does not have the right to exercise the power to intervene on behalf of human rights, nor has it been willing to do so."[22]

But the need for Article 5 betrays the political sensitivity surrounding the advent of the ECRML. Of course, there is no provision in the Charter which undermines states or promotes political campaigns for separation. Its authors clearly wished to respect states' authority and to reassure them that the ECRML has not in any way taken over states' powers to legislate for languages within their territories.

---

18. For reflections on the United Nations' position on the use of force, see J. F. Murphy (1998), "Force and arms" in C. C. Joyner (ed.), *The United Nations and international law*. Cambridge: Cambridge University Press.
19. See S. D. Krasner (1995), "Sovereignty and intervention" in G. M. Lyons and M. Mastanduno (eds), *Beyond Westphalia? State sovereignty and international intervention*. Baltimore: Johns Hopkins University Press.
20. See, generally, C. Gray (2004), *International law and the use of force*. Oxford: Oxford University Press, and Y. Dinstein (2005), *War, aggression and self-defence*. Cambridge: Cambridge University Press.
21. See A. Buchanan (2006), "The morality of secession" in W. Kymlicka (ed.), *The rights of minority cultures*. Oxford: Oxford University Press.
22. See J. Donnelly (1995), "State sovereignty and ... human rights", p. 115.

It does not in any way derogate or diminish the right of states to legislate for languages within their territories. Indeed, for its provisions to be implemented and for them to acquire legal force, states must create domestic legislation for that purpose. We are thus reassured that ratification of the ECRML does not raise difficult constitutional questions about transfer of powers.

Another way of making the point is to say that Article 5 depoliticises the instrument so that it cannot be interpreted in such a way that it is deemed to grant political power to any group. To quote Woehrling, "none of the charter provisions gives linguistic minorities the right to powers of political decision-making that might challenge public authority in the states parties".[23] Yet, somewhat paradoxically, the need to respect and observe the rights of minority language speakers arguably has an inherent political quality. Indeed, as was pointed out by one commentator, the European Union has "gone as far as to make respect for minority rights one of the 'political criteria' for admissions of new States to the Union".[24] In many states, the political and the linguistic are inextricably linked.[25]

At the root of the matter is a fundamental, self-evident truth, which is that many of the languages protected by the charter are, put simply, the languages of nations which were at a point in history incorporated into larger states. The linguistic agenda at a local level can therefore be an aspect of a broader nationalist movement rather than a product of some non-political cultural diversity agenda.[26] In Wales, for example, the language issue has traditionally been driven by groups or individuals who have also promoted a nationalist, political drive for political self-determination.[27] This close nexus between the language revitalisation and political autonomy agendas has, potentially, been detrimental to both the linguistic and political causes, *mutatis mutandis*. The political argument for greater self-determination has sometimes been treated with suspicion by the non-Welsh speaking majority due to fears of hidden linguistic agendas that

---

23. Woehrling (2005), op. cit., p. 86.
24. See F. de Varennes (2001), "The linguistic rights of minorities in Europe" in S. Trifunovska (ed.) *Minority rights in Europe: European minorities and languages.* The Hague: T.M.C. Asser Press, p. 3.
25. See J. Muller (2008), "The European Charter for Regional or Minority Languages and the current legislative and policy contexts in the north of Ireland" in R. Dunbar and G. Parry, *The European Charter for Regional or Minority Languages: legal challenges and opportunities*, pp. 219-37.
26. W. Kymlicka (2007), "Language policies, national identities, and liberal-democratic norms" in C. Williams (ed.), *Language and governance.* Cardiff: University of Wales Press, pp. 509-15.
27. The cultural dimension in the story of national reawakening has been the subject of several major historical studies: e.g. K. O. Morgan (1981), *Rebirth of a nation: a history of modern Wales.* Oxford: Oxford University Press; or D. G. Evans (2000), *A history of Wales 1906-2000.* Cardiff: University of Wales Press.

might eventually lead to their marginalisation as a monoglot linguistic group. Conversely, the language revitalisation agenda has sometimes encountered opposition based on a fear that it might lead to claims for political separation.

Of course, the link between language and nationhood is not always clear or straightforward. Not every linguistic community is harbouring serious ambition for self-governance as a linguistic group. In Scotland, for example, there is no political drive for independence on the part of either Gaelic-speakers or Scots-speakers in an effort to somehow undo the unity of Scotland brought about in the 11th century. Gaelic-speakers and Scots-speakers do not regard themselves as nations by virtue of language. The claim of these linguistic communities is for recognition and protection within a larger, multilingual political entity, be that Scotland or the United Kingdom.[28] But there can be no doubt that by looking at Europe as a whole we see that there is a tangible political nexus between language, culture and national identity.[29]

Kymlicka argues that the demands of "small nations" for greater national and political autonomy, of which cultural and linguistic autonomy is an important aspect, has become acceptable in western Europe, and seen as being compatible with liberal-democratic values and notions of justice. Conversely, however, such nationalist claims are not as sympathetically considered by central and eastern European states, which see secessionist movements as being a threat to state security and a menace to international stability.[30] The Charter's position is that it distances itself from this political hot potato and promotes multilingualism, but within the unitary state.

The ECRML's agenda is the recognition and promotion of linguistic diversity within European states as being an important and normalised component of European society and of membership of the European political community.[31]

---

28. For some legal-historical perspectives, see H. MacQueen (2002), "Laws and languages: some historical notes from Scotland", Vol. 6.2, *Electronic Journal of Comparative Law* (http://law.kub.nl/ejcl/62/art62-2.html).
29. For further reflections, see K. Henrard (2001), "The interrelationship between individual human rights, minority rights and the right to self- determination and its importance for the adequate protection of linguistic minorities", *Global Review of Ethnopolitics*, Vol. 1, No. 1, pp. 41-8.
30. See W. Kymlicka (2004), "Justice and security in the accommodation of minority nationalism" in S. May, T. Modood and J. Squires (eds), *Ethnicity, nationalism and minority rights*. Cambridge: Cambridge University Press, pp. 144-75.
31. W. Kymlicka (1995), *Multicultural citizenship: a liberal theory of minority rights*. Oxford: Clarendon Press, pp. 174-6.

The underlying rationale is to promote recognition of equality in diversity.[32] Linguistic minorities are afforded the status, obligations and privileges of full citizenship without sacrificing their linguistic identity. Of course, this vision of "multicultural citizenship" has benefits for the linguistic minority. However, it may also benefit the dominant group and, in particular, may serve the interests of preserving political hegemony and unity. As Kymlicka puts it, having recognised language as one of the key components of national identity,

> if there is a viable way to promote a sense of solidarity and common purpose in a multinational state, it will involve accommodating, rather than subordinating national identities. People from different national groups will only share an allegiance to the larger polity if they see it as the context within which their national identity is nurtured, rather than subordinated.[33]

This argument maintains that, instead of promoting political fragmentation along linguistic/national lines, an agenda for linguistic equality supports the concept of multilingual and multinational political entities. Accordingly, the grievance felt by the minority linguistic group, which might develop into an ambition for political autonomy and, possibly, secession, is defused if the state concept of citizenship recognises and protects the linguistic identity of that group.

The linguistic plurality which this concept of citizenship promotes challenges the traditional, one-dimensional and homogeneous understanding of state citizenship. It also encourages an approach whereby it is appreciated "that citizenship is not just a legal status, defined by a set of rights and responsibilities, but also an identity, an expression of one's membership in a political community".[34] This is arguably a form of self-determination which is compatible with the maintenance of state sovereignty and territorial integrity. This, as is made clear in Article 5, is the agenda which the ECRML promotes and supports.

Has Article 5's commitment to honouring state sovereignty and national integrity been a source of actual controversy for the Charter in practice? There have been few cases where territorial disputes have resulted in states finding themselves at odds with the provisions of Article 5, and, therefore, unable to fully ratify or implement the ECRML. Azerbaijan's long-running dispute with Armenia resulted in it refusing to ratify, declaring that it is "unable to guarantee

---

32. One commentator summed up the approach thus: "With the politics of equal dignity, what is established is meant to be universally the same, an identical basket of rights and immunities; with the politics of difference, what we are asked to recognize is the unique identity of this individual or group, their distinctiveness from everyone else"; C. Taylor (1994), "The politics of recognition" in C. Taylor et al. (eds), *Multiculturalism: examining the politics of recognition*. Princeton NJ: Princeton University Press, pp. 25-73, at p. 38.
33. W. Kymlicka (1995), *Multicultural citizenship*, p. 189.
34. Ibid., pp. 191-2.

the application of Article 5 of the Charter in the territories occupied by the Republic of Armenia until these territories are liberated from that occupation".[35]

Cyprus recognises the Cypriot Maronite Arabic language as a language which it protects in accordance with Part II and Article 2 paragraph 1 of the ECRML. However, because the language is also used in the village of Kormakitis which is situated in that part of Cyprus under Turkish military occupation, and therefore an area over which it does not exercise effective political control, it excludes any interpretation of the ECRML that would be contrary to Article 5's provisions on respecting territorial integrity and sovereignty.[36] In other words, it declares that it has no control over the fate of the Cypriot Maronite Arabic language in the area under Turkish control.

As for Turkey, neither its government nor Greece's has ratified either the Framework Convention or the ECRML, failures which reflect both states' problematic attitude towards their respective Turkish and Greek minorities.[37] But these rare instances where there have been failures, to varying degrees, to ratify the ECRML are a symptom rather than the cause of conflict.

4. Conclusion

The ECRML is an instrument which respects the cardinal tenets of international law on sovereignty and territorial integrity. In its task of setting standards and promulgating international norms for the protection of regional or minority languages, it facilitates good practice through constructive dialogue and diplomacy. It advances the notion that promoting linguistic diversity is not incompatible with respecting sovereignty and territorial integrity. Indeed, it is the only international instrument which provides a comprehensive road map of the way to the idea of the multinational and multilingual unitary state.

Article 5 is therefore necessary to immunise the Charter from the charge of harbouring a political pretext. It might therefore be regarded as a pre-emptive, anticipatory provision to reassure the sceptics more than a genuine, practical provision that is likely to be the source of dispute or discordance. On the whole, the immunisation strategy has been successful because the ECRML has not been the source of inter-state dispute or internal political controversy, even if some states have used such political conflicts as a basis for not ratifying it.

---

35. List of declarations made with respect to Treaty No. 148: see http://conventions.coe.int/ Treaty/Commun/ListeDeclarations.asp?NT=148&CM=1&DF=&CL=ENG&VL=1.
36. Ibid.
37. Their failure to honour the rights of minorities has been the subject of repeated criticism by the Council of Europe. See http://assembly.coe.int/ASP/NewsManager/EMB_ NewsManagerView.asp?ID=4493; also www.aina.org/news/20100127195356.htm.

References

Buchanan, Allen (2006), "The morality of secession" in Will Kymlicka (ed.), *The rights of minority cultures*. Oxford: Oxford University Press, pp. 350-74.

Dinstein, Yoram (2005), *War, aggression and self-defence*. Cambridge: Cambridge University Press.

Donnelly, Jack (1995), "State sovereignty and international intervention: the case of human rights" in Gene M. Lyons and Michael Mastanduno (eds), *Beyond Westphalia? State sovereignty and international intervention*. Baltimore: Johns Hopkins University Press, pp. 115-46.

European Charter for Regional or Minority Languages and Explanatory Report (1993), Strasbourg: Council of Europe Publishing.

Evans, D. Gareth (2000), *A history of Wales, 1906-2000*. Cardiff: University of Wales Press.

Glenny, Misha (1992), *The fall of Yugoslavia: the Third Balkan War*. London: Penguin.

Gray, Christine (2004), *International law and the use of force*. Oxford: Oxford University Press.

Henrard, Kristin (2001), "The interrelationship between individual human rights, minority rights and the right to self-determination and its importance for the adequate protection of linguistic minorities", *Global Review of Ethnopolitics*, Vol. 1, No. 1.

Knop, Karen (2005), *Diversity and self-determination in international law*. Cambridge: Cambridge University Press.

Krasner, Stephen D. (1995), "Sovereignty and intervention" in Gene M. Lyons and Michael Mastanduno (eds), *Beyond Westphalia? State sovereignty and international intervention*. Baltimore: Johns Hopkins University Press, pp. 228-49.

Kymlicka, Will (1995), *Multicultural citizenship: a liberal theory of minority rights*. Oxford: Clarendon Press, pp. 174-6.

Kymlicka, Will (2004), "Justice and security in the accommodation of minority nationalism" in Stephen May, Tariq Modood and Judith Squires (eds), *Ethnicity, nationalism and minority rights*. Cambridge: Cambridge University Press, pp. 144-75.

Kymlicka, Will (2007), "Language policies, national identities, and liberal-democratic norms" in Colin Williams (ed.), *Language and governance*. Cardiff: University of Wales Press, pp. 505-15.

MacQueen, Hector (2002), "Laws and languages: some historical notes from Scotland", *Electronic Journal of Comparative Law*, Vol. 6, No. 2, http://law.kub.nl/ejcl/62/art62-2.html.

Magas, Branka (1993), *The destruction of Yugoslavia: tracking the break-up, 1980-1992.* London: Verso.

Morgan, Kenneth O. (1981), *Rebirth of a nation: a history of modern Wales.* Oxford: Oxford University Press.

Muller, Janet (2008), "The European Charter for Regional or Minority Languages and the current legislative and policy contexts in the north of Ireland" in Robert Dunbar and Gwynedd Parry (eds), *The European Charter for Regional or Minority Languages: legal challenges and opportunities.* Strasbourg: Council of Europe Publishing, pp. 219-37.

Murphy, John F. (1998), "Force and arms" in Christopher C. Joyner (ed.), *The United Nations and international law.* Cambridge: Cambridge University Press, pp. 97-130.

Sarooshi, Dan (2005), *International organisations and their exercise of sovereign powers.* Oxford: Oxford University Press.

Shaw, Malcolm (2003), *International law*, 5th edn. Cambridge: Cambridge University Press.

Taylor, Charles (1994), "The politics of recognition" in C. Taylor et al. (eds), *Multiculturalism: examining the politics of recognition.* Princeton: Princeton University Press.

Varennes, Fernand de (2001), "The linguistic rights of minorities in Europe" in S. Trifunovska (ed.), *Minority rights in Europe: European minorities and languages.* The Hague: T.M.C. Asser Press, pp. 3-30.

Varennes, Fernand de (2007), "Linguistic identity and language rights" in Marc Weller (ed.), *Universal minority rights: a commentary on the jurisprudence of international courts and treaty bodies.* Oxford: Oxford University Press, pp. 253-323.

Woehrling, Jean-Marie (2005), *The European Charter for Regional or Minority Languages: a critical commentary.* Strasbourg: Council of Europe Publishing.

Article 6. Information

José Manuel Pérez Fernández
University of Oviedo

1. Introduction

2. Scope of the obligation to provide information
   2.1. The intended recipients of the information
   2.2. Purpose of the information and how it is provided

3. Monitoring fulfilment of the commitment to provide information

4. Conclusion

References

Article 6 – Information

The Parties undertake to see to it that the authorities, organisations and persons concerned are informed of the rights and duties established by this Charter.

1. Introduction

Parts I and IV of the European Charter for Regional or Minority Languages (ECRML) set out a number of commitments to be entered into by the states parties in addition to those laid down in parts II and III. There is an overall consistency in the scope and effectiveness of these commitments, and states have to honour them without the possibility of making any reservations or making any distinction between any of the regional and minority languages spoken in their country and protected by the Charter.

Article 6, which is contained within Part I – General provisions, stipulates that states must provide information on the rights and duties established by the Charter and, at the same time, verify that the said information is effectively transmitted to those affected.[1] The obligation to provide information is closely linked to ensuring that the Charter is fully operational and is therefore justified by the need to guarantee the full effectiveness of the rights and duties established therein, as stated in the Explanatory Report (paragraph 56):

---

1. Other than the obligation to provide information, set out in Article 6, and those in parts II and III, the other obligations are those in Article 3 (Part I), obliging states to specify the languages concerned and the paragraphs they have accepted for the purposes of applying Part III; and those in articles 15 to 17 (Part IV), obliging states to draw up regular reports on the application of the Charter and to co-operate with the Committee of Experts.

The motive for the undertaking to provide information which is established by this Article lies in the fact that the charter can never become fully effective if the competent authorities and interested organisations and individuals are not aware of the obligations which derive from it.

2. Scope of the obligation to provide information

The scope of states' obligation to provide information, established in Article 6, must be considered from two points of view:[2]

- a subjective point of view, in other words by determining who the intended recipients of the information are;

- an objective point of view, by specifying what the exact content of the information should be and, what in my opinion is more relevant, how such information should be provided, given that it is the means which determines the real effectiveness of the information.

2.1. The intended recipients of the information

According to the terms used in Article 6, the intended recipients of the information are a combination of public and private entities, in three groups: the public authorities responsible for applying the Charter, the organisations involved in safeguarding the languages in question, and the persons affected by the provisions of this international convention, in other words, the speakers of traditionally recognised regional or minority languages.

The term "authorities" obviously comprises public authorities as a whole, that is, both their political and administrative bodies, and also all the public law bodies and entities subordinate to the public authorities. In practice, the information must be provided to those public authorities which, in accordance with the internal attribution of responsibilities, are tasked with applying the provisions of the Charter (in other words, the regional or local authorities, in the case of states with devolved government). At all events, it is up to the signatory state to provide precise and detailed information to all tiers of administration on the general measures recommended in the Charter and the specific undertakings it has entered into in respect of all or each of the regional or minority languages spoken in the country, and the consequences deriving from those undertakings.[3]

---

2. With regard to Article 6, see J.-M. Woehrling (2005), *The European Charter for Regional or Minority Languages: a critical commentary*. Strasbourg: Council of Europe Publishing, pp. 87-8.
3. See Woehrling (2005), op. cit., pp. 83-4: "This information requirement means that states cannot merely go through the motions of committing themselves without taking any steps to ensure that the resultant opportunities are known to the authorities translating them into action."

The term "organisations" refers to all non-governmental organisations which protect and promote regional or minority languages and, in a relevant and significant manner, safeguard the interests of the speakers of those languages. These organisations are the public authorities' key partners in fulfilling the undertakings entered into under the Charter. The ECRML itself makes several references to the role of these partners: for example, in Article 7.4, to help in determining policy with regard to regional or minority languages;[4] in Article 11.3, to ensure that account is taken of the interests of the speakers of regional or minority languages in the media;[5] and in Article 16.2, to ensure that they have the opportunity to submit their opinions on the application of the Charter to the Committee of Experts.[6]

Finally, the persons affected by the provisions of the Charter are the community at large and, more specifically, the speakers of regional or minority languages protected by the Charter. To ensure that the undertakings entered into by each state in the instrument of ratification, acceptance or approval are effectively met, it is essential that the linguistic community protected by the Charter be aware of its content and the undertakings entered into by its government, for it is difficult to expect anyone to fulfil an obligation of which they are unaware.

2.2. Purpose of the information and how it is provided

Having looked at the subjective aspect of the obligation to provide information, I now look at the objective aspect: exactly what information states have to provide and how they should do so.

With regard to the first question – "the type of information" – Article 6 contains something obvious and something surprising. The obvious thing is that the state party must first of all provide information on the duties, in other words, the undertakings it has entered into in the instrument of ratification,

---

4. Article 7.4: "In determining their policy with regard to regional or minority languages, the Parties shall take into consideration the needs and wishes expressed by the groups which use such languages. They are encouraged to establish bodies, if necessary, for the purpose of advising the authorities on all matters pertaining to regional or minority languages."

5. Article 11.3: "The Parties undertake to ensure that the interests of the users of regional or minority languages are represented or taken into account within such bodies as may be established in accordance with the law with responsibility for guaranteeing the freedom and pluralism of the media."

6. Article 16.2: "Bodies or associations legally established in a Party may draw the attention of the committee of experts to matters relating to the undertakings entered into by that Party under Part III of this Charter. After consulting the Party concerned, the committee of experts may take account of this information in the preparation of the report specified in paragraph 3 below. These bodies or associations can furthermore submit statements concerning the policy pursued by a Party in accordance with Part II."

adoption or approval in respect of each of the regional or minority languages spoken on its territory. The surprise lies in the fact that the state must not only provide information on the duties but also the rights involved. The term "rights" is used only in this provision of the Charter and raises the question of how it should be understood, given that the Charter gives precedence to the cultural dimension of the use of regional or minority languages, which is why it does not establish any individual or collective rights for the speakers of such languages.[7]

From the standpoint of this analysis, it is more important to specify how states should fulfil the obligation to provide information given that the Charter does not further explain this. Accordingly, the states parties have a free hand because it is they who decide on the measures to be taken, which leads us to ask whether any criteria might be established to determine the state's choice of measures.

In my opinion, the state's choice of means for meeting its undertaking to provide information on the content of the ECRML is governed by the need to achieve results: in other words appropriate means must be used to ensure that there is sufficient awareness of the Charter in the signatory states. Therefore, as is the case with some of the obligations set out in Part III (articles 8 and 9), the nature of the obligation to provide information means that it could be considered one of the so-called obligations of result.[8]

An examination of the states parties' periodical reports on the application of the Charter shows that there is a huge variety of measures taken to ensure fulfilment of the obligation established in Article 6 and significant differences in the number of measures taken by each state. Taking as a minimum step publication in all states parties of the text of the ECRML, as an international

---

7. "The charter sets out to protect and promote regional or minority languages, not linguistic minorities. For this reason emphasis is placed on the cultural dimension and the use of a regional or minority language in all the aspects of the life of its speakers. The charter does not establish any individual or collective rights for the speakers of regional or minority languages. Nevertheless, the obligations of the parties with regard to the status of these languages and the domestic legislation which will have to be introduced in compliance with the charter will have an obvious effect on the situation of the communities concerned and their individual members"; Explanatory Report, paragraph 11. See too F. de Varennes (2008), "Language protection and the European Charter for Regional or Minority Languages: *quo vadis*?", pp. 27-8; Woehrling (2005), op. cit., pp. 18-21.

8. See M.-À. Clotet I Miró (1994), "La Carta Europea de las lenguas regionales o minoritarias", *Revista de Instituciones Europeas*, Vol. 21, No. 2, pp. 550, 555; P. Reuter (1961), "Principes de droit international public", *RCADI*, No. 103, pp. 472-5, 598-9, quoted by Clotet; S. Castellà Surribas (2002), "La ratificació de l'Estat espanyol a la Carta europea de llengües regionals o minoritàries", *Mercator-Documents de Treball*, No. 8, www.ciemen.org/mercator/pdf/wp8-cat-def.pdf, p. 5.

treaty, in their Official Gazette, the other methods used to provide information on the content of the Charter include:[9]

- Dissemination of the text and its practical consequences among the various government authorities at national, regional and local level, and in the linguistic communities themselves (national and/or regional bodies representing linguistic minorities and NGOs) by holding conferences and seminars of different territorial scope and content, organising meetings between public officials responsible for the protection of the languages and the representatives of the linguistic minorities in question, etc.

- Publication – also in digital form on the Internet – of not only the text of the Charter (in different languages, including obviously the regional or minority languages concerned), but also information on numerous aspects of its content, the problems inherent in its application or the situation of the intended recipients. These include scientific or academic case studies, press releases, reports on linguistic minorities, information brochures, etc.

- Conferences, programmes, interviews and other specific information activities in the mass media (written and digital press, radio and television).

3. Monitoring fulfilment of the commitment to provide information

Monitoring fulfilment of the commitment to provide information under Article 6 of the Charter is carried out by the Committee of Experts, which examines the reports submitted by the national authorities. As stipulated in Article 15.2, these reports must be made public.

The Committee of Experts has sometimes limited its monitoring activity to a simple verification of the basic means used to provide information about the rights and duties established by the Charter, in other words, its official publication.[10] In some cases, it has gone a step further by assessing the real effectiveness of the measures taken by the states parties: even if the means used – official and digital publication of the text, information brochures, etc. – merit a positive appraisal, in practice they have often proved to be insufficient, both in quality (publication of the text in only one language) and quantity (limited number of

---

9. Among others, see Initial State Periodical Report of Armenia (03/09/2003), Austria (14/02/2003), Czech Republic (30/04/2008), Denmark (03/12/2002), Finland (10/03/1999), Germany (20/11/2000), Serbia (11/11/2007), Slovakia (05/12/2003) and Sweden (18/06/2001); Second Periodical Report of Austria (12/12/2007) or Finland (31/12/2002), and Third Periodical Report of Finland (13/03/2006).
10. See Hungary 2001, 1: "The Charter entered into force for Hungary on 1 March 1998. The Hungarian authorities published the text of the Charter in the Official Gazette in Volume 1999, No. 34". See too, The Netherlands 2001, 1; Norway 2001, 1.

publications distributed or limited number of activities undertaken at local level),[11] or because the scope is much more limited than indicated by states in their periodic reports.[12]

In a large number of cases, the shortcomings in fulfilling the obligation established in Article 6 is linked to states' total or partial failure to honour their commitment to make their periodical reports public (Article 15.2) because, in the eyes of the Committee of Experts, such shortcomings in the preparation of the periodical reports and the limited awareness of its contents are a clear indication of the difficulties encountered by communities of linguistic minorities in gaining knowledge of the substance of the Charter and the undertakings entered into by their national authorities.[13]

---

11. See Finland 2001, 2: "In accordance with Article 15.1, the Finnish authorities presented their Initial Periodical Report to the Secretary General of the Council of Europe in April 1999. They published the text of the Charter in the official publication Treaty Series 23/1998. The Initial Periodical Report was made available on the official website of the Finnish government but only in English. Given the economic situation and the language skills of most of the speakers of Sami or Romany, the Committee considers that the Report has not been made public in accordance with the requirement in Article 15.2. A limited distribution of printed copies of the draft report in Finnish was made among the experts, authorities and associations involved in the consultation process leading to the acceptance." See too Czech Republic 2009, 4: "The text of the Charter was published in the official Collection of International Treaties and on the website of the Government Council for National Minorities, as was the initial periodical report. The Secretariat of the Government Council distributed an information brochure on the Charter (*Charta – co bychom měli vědět?* [*The Charter – what should we know?*]) to the regions and municipalities. However, during the on-the-spot visit, several representatives of the regional or minority language-speakers as well as the authorities expressed the view that the Charter may not have been distributed widely enough and that many municipalities were not sufficiently aware of the Charter."

12. See Initial Periodical Report of Austria (14/02/2003): "Moreover, in the ratification procedure the Charter was presented to the Advisory Councils of all ethnic groups. The Charter was also subject to a consultation procedure. For this purpose, the bodies and persons concerned were informed of this Charter"; however, in Austria 2005, Finding A, the Committee of Experts say: "However, contrary to the common practice in Austria, the participation of the Advisory Councils for the ethnic groups and the regional or minority language speakers in the ratification process and in the preparation of Austria's initial periodical report appears to have been very limited." See too Croatia 2001, 2 and Finding A: "Moreover, the Croatian authorities did not publish the initial periodical report and therefore the speakers of the regional or minority languages were not in a position to react to its contents as the Charter provides in its Article 16.2. As a result, the monitoring procedure in Croatia has not been fully operational."

13. See Application of the Charter in Montenegro, 1st monitoring cycle (2010), paragraph 5: "The Committee of Experts was not informed whether the Montenegrin authorities made their initial periodical report public. According to representatives of the regional or minority language-speakers, the local authorities and the speakers had not been fully informed of their rights and duties deriving from the Charter."

Although there are admittedly not many examples, there are a number of cases in which the Committee of Experts makes an extremely positive assessment of the action taken by states. For example, the Committee of Experts makes very favourable observations in the report on the Application of the Charter in Serbia, 1st monitoring cycle (2008), paragraph 6:

> The Committee of Experts wishes to express its gratitude to the Serbian authorities for the active and fruitful co-operation it has enjoyed. Immediately after ratifying the Charter, and in co-operation with the Council of Europe and the Organization for Security and Co-operation in Europe (OSCE), Serbia organised several seminars in different parts of Serbia with a view to actively informing the authorities, organisations and speakers of the regional or minority languages of the rights and duties established by the Charter. Serbia also submitted its very comprehensive initial report on time. The co-operation with the authorities and with the bodies and associations representing the speakers of the regional or minority languages during the on-the-spot visit was exemplary.[14]

Finally, it should be pointed out that there are cases in which the monitoring does not appear to be particularly effective. Spain, for example, should be mentioned in this connection. Part One, paragraph II.6, of the Spanish authorities' *Report on the application in Spain of the European Charter for Regional or Minority Languages* states:

> The wide dissemination of the Statutes of Autonomy, most of which have been in force for more than twenty years, the public's detailed knowledge of them and the consolidation of autonomous organisation itself all mean that there is no need to take special measures to make the European Charter for Regional [or] Minority Languages more widely known.[15]

And later on in the report, subparagraph 7 also underlines the same idea:

> As we have seen, the level of legal protection already existing was considered sufficient. It was therefore not considered necessary to conduct a specific policy of informing the authorities that have to apply the Charter, in view of the fact that its application coincides with the application of laws already in force in Spain.

---

14. See too Germany 2002, 2: "The German version was published in October 2000 by the Federal Ministry of the Interior, which is the department responsible for the drafting of the State Report. The Report was printed and also included in the Ministry's Internet site. Anybody interested in the document can order it – and extensive use is being made of this offer. At the annual Implementation Conference on the Charter, the *Länder* and the umbrella organizations of the linguistic groups were provided detailed information on the Report and were – and still are – offered the opportunity to order as many copies of the Report as they like for their staff, members and affiliates."

15. Initial periodical report on the application of the European Charter for Regional or Minority Languages, Spain, 2002, Part One, paragraph II subparagraph 6.

No observation was made by the Committee of Experts in response to the Spanish Government's claims concerning fulfilment of the obligation imposed under Article 6. At most, some conclusions could be drawn from the general criticism of the government's report in the committee's evaluation report on the Application of the Charter in Spain, 1st monitoring cycle (2005), paragraph 63, and more indirectly, in Finding T, in which it suggests a number of lines of action to the government:

> 63. An additional difficulty derives from the basic approach taken by the Spanish Government in providing information to the Committee of Experts. Most of the information provided especially in the initial periodical report is in fact of a formal nature, in that it refers essentially to the formal regulatory framework, but very little is said concerning the practice. An additional difficulty comes from the fact that in several cases the Spanish Government submitted overall comments referring to various undertakings at the same time instead of specifically commenting on the fulfilment of each individual undertaking. In a number of cases the mentioned difficulties have prevented the Committee of Experts from reaching a conclusion. The Spanish authorities are encouraged to take account of these remarks in the preparation of their next periodical report and in their further contribution to the next monitoring round.

> T. Finally, the Committee of Experts considers that there is still a need for awareness-raising in Spain about regional or minority languages. In particular, very little attention is devoted to linguistic diversity by the national Spanish media and there still seems to be a lack of awareness among the Castilian-speaking majority population and especially in the autonomous communities other than those directly concerned, that Spain is a plurilingual country. More efforts therefore seem to be needed in education for the majority Castilian-speaking population and in the national media with a view to fostering a greater acceptance and respect by the majority vis-à-vis the specificities of regional identities as an integral part of the Spanish heritage. There is also a need to improve mutual understanding, with a view to promoting the virtues of plurilingualism and linguistic diversity and, in both majority and minority language groups, the fundamental idea of peaceful and harmonious co-existence.[16]

Finally, in fairness to the Spanish Government, the 2nd Periodical Report (30 April 2007) takes account of these criticisms by providing a whole list of measures that have been taken both by central government and by the governments of the autonomous communities to ensure compliance with Article 6.

---

16. See also Spain 2008, Finding T.

4. Conclusion

The simplicity of the wording used in Article 6, to express the obligation for signatory states to provide information on the rights and duties established by the Charter, should not obscure the importance of this obligation. One of the main ways of ensuring that the aims of the Charter are fully achieved is to ensure the widest possible dissemination of its content and of the commitments entered into by each of the states parties and the steps taken to ensure their fulfilment. Linguistic communities will only be able to ensure that the Charter is fully effective if they have exhaustive information about its content. That is why the Committee of Experts should increase its monitoring of the measures taken by states and the concrete results achieved through these measures.

References

Castellà Surribas, Santiago (2002), "La ratificació de l'Estat espanyol a la Carta europea de llengües regionals o minoritàries", *Mercator-Documents de Treball*, No. 8. www.ciemen.org/mercator/pdf/wp8-cat-def.pdf.

Clotet I Miró, Maria-Àngels (1994), "La Carta Europea de las lenguas regionales o minoritarias", *Revista de Instituciones Europeas,* Vol. 21, No. 2.

Reuter, Paul (1961), "Principes de droit international public", *Recueil des Cours de l'Académie de Droit International*, No. 103.

Varennes, Fernand (de) (2008), "Language protection and the European Charter for Regional or Minority Languages: *quo vadis?*" in *The European Charter for Regional or Minority Languages: legal challenges and opportunities*, Regional or Minority Languages No. 5. Strasbourg: Council of Europe Publishing.

Woehrling, Jean-Marie (2005), *The European Charter for Regional or Minority Languages: a critical commentary.* Strasbourg: Council of Europe Publishing.

Part II
Objectives and principles

Article 7. Objectives and principles

Robert Dunbar
University of the Highlands and Islands

1. Introduction

2. Contextual analysis

3. The scope of the provisions: analysis of the position taken by the Committee
   of Experts
   3.1. Subparagraph 1a
   3.2. Subparagraph 1b
   3.3. Subparagraph 1c
   3.4. Subparagraph 1d
   3.5. Subparagraph 1e
   3.6. Subparagraph 1f
   3.7. Subparagraph 1g
   3.8. Subparagraph 1h
   3.9. Subparagraph 1i
   3.10. Paragraph 2
   3.11. Paragraph 3
   3.12. Paragraph 4
   3.13. Paragraph 5

4. Good practice

5. Conclusions

References

Article 7 – Objectives and principles

1. *In respect of regional or minority languages, within the territories in which such
   languages are used and according to the situation of each language, the Parties
   shall base their policies, legislation and practice on the following objectives and
   principles:*

   a. *the recognition of the regional or minority languages as an expression of
      cultural wealth;*

   b. *the respect of the geographical area of each regional or minority language in
      order to ensure that existing or new administrative divisions do not constitute
      an obstacle to the promotion of the regional or minority language in question;*

    c. *the need for resolute action to promote regional or minority languages in order to safeguard them;*

    d. *the facilitation and/or encouragement of the use of regional or minority languages, in speech and writing, in public and private life;*

    e. *the maintenance and development of links, in the fields covered by this Charter, between groups using a regional or minority language and other groups in the State employing a language used in identical or similar form, as well as the establishment of cultural relations with other groups in the State using different languages;*

    f. *the provision of appropriate forms and means for the teaching and study of regional or minority languages at all appropriate stages;*

    g. *the provision of facilities enabling non-speakers of a regional or minority language living in the area where it is used to learn it if they so desire;*

    h. *the promotion of study and research on regional or minority languages at universities or equivalent institutions;*

    i. *the promotion of appropriate types of transnational exchanges, in the fields covered by this Charter, for regional or minority languages used in identical or similar form in two or more States.*

2. *The Parties undertake to eliminate, if they have not yet done so, any unjustified distinction, exclusion, restriction or preference relating to the use of a regional or minority language and intended to discourage or endanger the maintenance or development of it. The adoption of special measures in favour of regional or minority languages aimed at promoting equality between the users of these languages and the rest of the population or which take due account of their specific conditions is not considered to be an act of discrimination against the users of more widely-used languages.*

3. *The Parties undertake to promote, by appropriate measures, mutual understanding between all the linguistic groups of the country and in particular the inclusion of respect, understanding and tolerance in relation to regional or minority languages among the objectives of education and training provided within their countries and encouragement of the mass media to pursue the same objective.*

4. *In determining their policy with regard to regional or minority languages, the Parties shall take into consideration the needs and wishes expressed by the groups which use such languages. They are encouraged to establish bodies, if necessary, for the purpose of advising the authorities on all matters pertaining to regional or minority languages.*

5. *The Parties undertake to apply,* mutatis mutandis, *the principles listed in paragraphs 1 to 4 above to non-territorial languages. However, as far as these languages are concerned, the nature and scope of the measures to be taken to give effect to this Charter shall be determined in a flexible manner, bearing in mind the needs and wishes, and respecting the traditions and characteristics, of the groups which use the languages concerned.*

186

1. Introduction

In many respects, Article 7 is the single most important provision in the European Charter for Regional or Minority Languages ("the Charter"). First, it applies to all of the state's regional or minority languages (RMLs), a point which, as we shall see, the Committee of Experts has confirmed. This is in contrast to the various Part III commitments, which only apply in respect of those RMLs specifically designated by the state. Second, all of the provisions of Article 7 apply to all of the state's RMLs. This is again in contrast to the 68 options contained in the paragraphs and subparagraphs in Part III of the Charter, which will only apply to any particular RML to the extent that the state has chosen the particular commitment. Third, Article 7 sets out broad objectives and principles on which the state's "policies, legislation and practices" must be based. As the Explanatory Report to the Charter makes clear, Article 7 does not contain precise implementing rules – these can be found in Part III – but it does set out "the necessary framework for the preservation of regional or minority languages".[1]

Sometimes it is thought that because the obligations of Article 7 are less detailed and precise than those in Part III, they are somehow less important. This is an incorrect view. For those RMLs which are not designated for the protection of Part III, as well as the state's "non-territorial languages", which cannot benefit from the protection of Part III, Article 7 constitutes "front-line protection". Also, there are some provisions in Article 7 which have no equivalent in Part III – for example, Article 7, subparagraphs 1b, 1e, 1g, arguably 1h (which, in referring to "study and research on" RMLs goes beyond Article 8 paragraph e, which focuses mainly on teaching though the medium of RMLs, or the study of RMLs as a subject, at universities and other higher education facilities), as well as paragraphs 2 to 5 – and therefore these also represent "front-line protection" for all RMLs, even those designated for Part III protection. In any case, even in respect of those RMLs which are designated for Part III, as Jean-Marie Woehrling has noted, on more detailed examination of Article 7 it becomes clear that "the principles are precise and place considerable demands on states which are serious about putting them into practice".[2]

To this I would add some other considerations, on which I shall expand in my concluding remarks. The first is that the very precision of the Part III obligations may in some cases be a limiting factor, and the very breadth of the Article 7 commitments may be a strength. There is both a technical and a broader policy-based aspect to this point. The Charter was drafted at a particular point in time,

---

1. Paragraph 57.
2. Woehrling (2005), op. cit.

but the world that it describes is constantly changing, and the very precise commitments of Part III often make it difficult to respond to this changing environment.[3] This is particularly clear with respect to the media, where, since the time the Charter was first being drafted in the 1980s, there has been an explosion of new developments.[4] The media world which Article 11 describes – television channels and radio stations and newspapers – is almost quaint. What do we do with new media and communications technologies, on which Article 11 is almost silent? The very breadth of Article 7 gives us the tools to get to grips with such change: the requirement in Article 7 paragraph 1d that the state facilitate and/or encourage the use of RMLs, in speech and writing, in public and private life provides us with all we need, I suggest, to allow for a consideration of the issues raised by such new technologies, and the changing environment in which RMLs will have to exist.

With regard to policy, we must be aware of the limits, and even the pitfalls of Part III. My starting point here is the purpose of the Charter itself. The Explanatory Report claims that, as is made clear in the Charter's preamble, its overriding purpose is "cultural".[5] This, in my view, gives only a partial description of the Charter's overriding, albeit somewhat more specific, purpose. The Explanatory Report makes clear that the Charter is "designed to protect and promote regional or minority languages as a threatened aspect of Europe's cultural heritage". Thus, the ultimate concern may be cultural – the protection of Europe's cultural heritage – but the immediate concern is sociolinguistic – the protection and promotion of RMLs. This aspect of Europe's cultural heritage will be protected only to the extent that the Charter (as one of many possible instruments) is successful in furthering the maintenance of RMLs. In this sense, as I have argued elsewhere,[6] the Charter must be interpreted and applied in a sociolinguistically sensitive manner. In this context, Article 7 takes on added importance, because only it, among all of the Charter's provisions, allows us to address the "big picture" and measure state performance based on what is actually happening to the RMLs and on what measures need to be taken, based on an understanding of sociolinguistics and, in particular, policy and planning for minority languages.

There are several considerations here. First, while the Explanatory Report provides that the role of states in making their choices of Part III obligations will not be to choose arbitrarily between alternatives but to seek for each RML

---

3. See, generally, R. Dunbar (2008), "Definitively interpreting the Charter: the legal challenges".
4. T. Moring and R. Dunbar (2008), *The European Charter for Regional or Minority Languages and the media.*
5. Paragraph 10.
6. R. Dunbar (2008), "Definitively interpreting the Charter…".

the wording which best fits the characteristics and the state of development of that language,[7] it is, in my view, patently the case that states do not always make these choices on this basis. They are not always, and perhaps not mainly, guided by what combination of measures in Part III will be ideally suited to having maximum impact on the health of the RMLs. More frequently, it appears that choices are made on an ad hoc basis, based not on an assessment of what is necessary for the language from a sociolinguistic perspective but on an assessment of what the state is already doing in respect of its RMLs, or on what it could do to satisfy the requirements of the Charter most conveniently in present circumstances. Part II takes on a much greater importance in these circumstances, as its breadth permits an holistic assessment to be made of policy, legislation and practice.

A second consideration is that the Part III obligations force the Committee of Experts, of necessity, to focus on the details of the extent to which the commitments are being implemented. They do not invite a consideration of what effect the measures, both in isolation and together, are having on the vitality of the relevant language. They focus attention on details, rather than the big picture, and the linkages between policy areas that are essential in any effort to maintain minoritised languages. It may be that all commitments are being fully implemented, and yet the RML continues to lose numbers of speakers or valuable domains. What then? Again, Part II, through its very breadth, allows attention to be focused on the "big picture".

Third, as detailed as Part III is, it still contains some significant gaps, aside from the gaps, referred to above, opened up by the changing nature of the world which the Charter is meant to regulate. There are relatively few provisions which deal explicitly with use of language in certain domains which are of absolutely crucial importance to the maintenance and revitalisation of minority languages, such as the home, the local community, the private and voluntary sectors and so forth. There are few provisions which allow us to step back and think about the indirect impact on the vitality of RMLs of state policies which are apparently unrelated to RMLs, such as economic and social development policies – policies which can nonetheless have a significant impact on a language community by affecting the social and economic environment in which it must survive.[8] Article 7, by contrast, allows us to consider all these matters. Its

---

7. Paragraph 46.
8. Article 13 subparagraph 2b does provide, for example, that states (that accept this provision) undertake, with regard to economic and social activities, to organise activities to promote the use of RMLs, but only "in the economic and social sectors directly under their control (public sector)"; there is no similar undertaking in respect of the non-state sector, although this provision is probably sufficiently wide to allow states to require, for example, economic and social development agencies, regional economic development bodies and similar public institutions to

breadth allows us to take a holistic look at the entire scope of policy that impinges on RMLs and their speakers. In this sense, Article 7 is, in my view, the real powerhouse of the Charter. The question is, to what extent is its potential in this regard being exploited?

2. Contextual analysis

With regard to the languages to which Article 7 applies, the treaty itself seems reasonably clear: all the languages which satisfy the definition of "regional or minority language" set out in Article 1a, or for the purposes of Article 7 paragraph 5, all the languages which satisfy the definition of "non-territorial languages". Unlike Part III, where the state designates the languages to which that part applies, no designation is required for a language to benefit from the protection of Article 7.

The obligations imposed by the undertakings in paragraph 1 of Article 7 only apply, however, "within the territories in which such languages [RMLs] are used", and not throughout the territory of the state; thus, as with many other provisions of the Charter, the delineation of the territory or territories of the RMLs is important. The obligations are also interpreted and applied "according to the situation of each language". What is meant by the "situation of each language" is not entirely clear, but it would seem likely, given the purposes of the Charter, that the phrase refers to the social and demographic situation of the language. Thus, considerations such as the numbers of speakers, their age profile, their distribution in the population – and particularly whether the speakers are concentrated in certain areas or are scattered – the extent to which the languages are used in different domains,[9] and the vitality, the extent to which the languages are passed on to the next generation in the home and community, and attitudes to the language among speakers and non-speakers would be relevant considerations here. Article 7 paragraph 1 refers to a number of general objectives and principles on which states must base their "policies", "legislation" and "practice"; as the Explanatory Report makes clear, these are not "precise implementing rules" but rather "the necessary framework

---

take into account linguistic issues in their activities and in exercising any grant-making or other similar powers.

9. The concept of "domains" was originally developed by Joshua Fishman. They are the sociolinguistic contexts in which language is used, and they are defined by three dimensions: the location in which discourse is taking place, the participants in the discourse and the topic of the discourse. He identified the home, the church, the local neighbourhood, the school and the workplace as important domains, and he showed how language use can change in any domain – where, for example, the participants change (e.g. entry into the home of a non-speaker of the language of the home): see J. A. Fishman, R. L. Cooper and R. Ma (1971), *Bilingualism in the barrio*, or for a useful discussion of Fishman's ideas, B. Spolsky (2004), *Language policy*, Ch. 4, pp. 39-56.

for the preservation of regional or minority languages".[10] The use of the word "framework" brings to mind the Council of Europe's Framework Convention for the Protection of National Minorities, which itself contains a range of rather broad principles which require more precise formulation by states in practice.

Some of the objectives and principles set out in Article 7 paragraph 1 are very broad, and relate to the general policy orientation of the state: subparagraph 1a requires "recognition" of RMLs as an expression of "cultural wealth" and subparagraph 1c requires an acceptance of the need for "resolute action" to promote and safeguard them. Another, subparagraph 1b, is rather specific and, in a sense, practical, as it requires states to respect the geographical area of RMLs in order to ensure that administrative divisions do not constitute an obstacle to their promotion. Other objectives and principles set out in paragraph 1, while broad, are also somewhat more specific than those set out in subparagraphs 1a and c as they refer to the sorts of action which are required of states, and clearly relate to the main sorts of language planning activity that are recognised in the language planning literature: acquisition planning, status planning and corpus planning.[11]

With regard to acquisition planning, both subparagraph 1f, which refers to the provision of appropriate forms and means for the teaching and study of RMLs at all appropriate stages, and subparagraph 1g, which refers to the provision of facilities enabling non-speakers of an RML living in the area in which it is used to learn the language, are of obvious relevance because both aim to expand the number of people who are able to communicate in RMLs.

With regard to status planning (or the closely related concept of "use" or "usage planning"), subparagraph 1d, for example, is of obvious relevance because it

---

10. Paragraph 57.
11. See, for example, R. Cooper (1989), *Language planning and social change*. Acquisition planning concerns planning for the increase in the number of users – speakers, writers, listeners, or readers – of the language (ibid., pp. 33-4). Status planning has to do with modifying the functions which a particular language is meant to serve (or, to put it another way, modifying the domains in which a language is used), and therefore relates to the social (and political) position of the language (ibid., pp. 32-3). More recently, the concept of "use" or "usage" planning has appeared alongside "status planning", with use planning subsuming those aspects of status planning relating to the encouragement of the practical use of the language in a greater number of domains, and "status planning" restricted to planning to enhance the prestige (through visibility and audibility, for example) of the language (what could perhaps be described as "prestige planning"): see, for example, Welsh Language Board (2000), *The Welsh language: a vision and a mission for 2000-2005*. Corpus planning refers to activities such as coining new terms, reforming spelling and adopting a new script. It refers, in short, to the creation of new forms, the modification of old ones or the selection from alternative forms in spoken or written code (Cooper, op. cit., p. 31).

requires "facilitation" and/or "encouragement" of the "use" of RMLs in speech and writing, in public and private life. As we shall see below, "public and private life" is a very broad term, and encompasses most of the domains in which a language can be used. The reference to "use" is significant, as it illustrates that the Charter is not merely concerned with whether people can use an RML for a variety of reasons because they are able to speak, understand, read or write it, but whether they do in fact put it to use, a clear recognition that the lack of opportunities and contexts in which an RML can be put to use is one of the main reasons why such languages are vulnerable. In some ways, subparagraph 1e, which refers to the maintenance and development of links, in fields covered by the Charter, between groups using an RML and other groups in the state using essentially the same RML, as well as the establishment of cultural relations with other groups in the state using different languages, embodies elements of use planning as well as status planning (and as we shall see, the Committee of Experts has interpreted this provision, and subparagraph 1i, which is similar to subparagraph 1e in that it involves the promotion of contacts between users of an RML in fields covered by the Charter, albeit those who are located in different states, in ways that are relevant for corpus planning and even acquisition planning).

Subparagraph 1h, which obliges states to promote the study of and research into RMLs at universities and equivalent institutions has, as we shall see, been interpreted in a way that is highly relevant to corpus planning, as the sorts of initiatives which the Committee of Experts has considered in the context of this subparagraph relate to things like standardisation of the language, the development of grammars, dictionaries and so forth. As already noted, and as will be seen below, the committee has also commented on cross-border initiatives to standardise RMLs which are found in several states, or to jointly develop teaching materials, in the context of subparagraph 1i, illustrating how that provision is also relevant to corpus planning.

Paragraphs 2, 3 and 4 of Article 7 could all be understood to further in various ways status planning goals for RMLs. Paragraph 2 requires states to eliminate any unjustified distinction, exclusion, restriction or privilege relating to the use of an RML and intended to discourage or endanger its maintenance and development, and it makes clear that the adoption of special measures in favour of an RML aimed at promoting equality between its users and the rest of the population is not considered to be discrimination. By aiming to ensure equal treatment of languages which have often been marginalised, this paragraph is clearly directed at increasing the status, the prestige, of RMLs. Paragraph 3 requires states to promote mutual understanding between linguistic groups and the inclusion of respect, understanding and tolerance in relation to RMLs in the education system and the mass media. Often RMLs and their speakers are stigmatised, and their low social status engenders a sense of inferiority and lack of self-confidence which works against their maintenance. Thus, this provision also clearly aims at increasing the status of RMLs and could therefore be seen as a mechanism of status planning. Paragraph 4 requires states to consider the needs and wishes of users of RMLs in determining their policies with respect to such languages. Often, speakers of RMLs are themselves marginalised and excluded from processes that affect them, and this provision, by attempting to redress to some extent power differentials, could also be viewed as a status planning mechanism. Finally, paragraph 5 of Article 7 is a *sui generis* provision which applies only in respect of "non-territorial languages", a special category defined in Article 1 of the Charter, and simply confirms that the rest of Article 7 applies to such languages as well as to RMLs.

3. The scope of the provisions: analysis of the position taken by the Committee of Experts

As already noted, Article 7 of the Charter applies to all of a state's RMLs, and a preliminary matter which the Committee of Experts has sometimes had to consider is the identity of a state's RMLs. The Committee of Experts has made clear that the determination of a state's RMLs be made objectively, and based on the definition of an RML laid down in Article 1a of the Charter.[12] As this is a matter for consideration under Article 1, this issue is dealt with more comprehensively in that chapter. However, it is worthwhile recalling certain basic principles here. First, where a state has not provided any information in its periodical reports about the existence of any regional or minority languages other than those it has designated for the purposes of Part III, the Committee of Experts will ask for additional information in subsequent periodical reports on any languages which could be covered by Article 7.[13]

Second, in some cases, there has been a question as to whether Article 7 applies to a language because of uncertainty as to whether the language has had a traditional presence. In the case of Denmark, for example, this uncertainty applied in respect of Greenlandic, Faroese and Romani; the Committee of Experts noted a lack of statistical information, making the factual basis of the assessment unclear, and asked for additional information from the state.[14] In its first report on Slovenia, however, the Committee of Experts rejected the position advanced by the Slovenian authorities, that Croatian, Serbian and Bosnian were not RMLs because these linguistic communities only settled on

---

12. Cyprus 2006, 45.
13. Armenia 2006, 19.
14. Denmark 2007, 25-9.

Slovenian territory from the mid-1960s. In respect of Croatian language and culture, the Committee of Experts noted that the information at their disposal (whose source and nature they did not specify) pointed to "an ancient and continuous presence" in Slovenia to the present, referring to the particular territories in question; based on their conclusion that Croatian qualified as an RML, they encouraged the authorities to identify the territories in which Croatian is covered by the Charter and comment on the implementation of Article 7 in these territories in its next state report.[15] In regard to Serbian and Bosnian, the Committee of Experts found "indications of a traditional presence" in Slovenia, and they encouraged the authorities "to clarify these elements in co-operation with the speakers and to comment on the results of this process in the next periodical report".[16]

Third, the Committee of Experts has also considered the question of whether, in accordance with the definition of regional or minority languages in Article 1a of the Charter, a language should be denied the status of an RML because it is a "dialect". Cyprus, for example, had sought to exclude Cypriot Maronite Arabic from the protection of the Charter on the basis that it was a dialect of Arabic. In addition to its very long presence in Cyprus, the Committee of Experts noted that Cypriot Maronite Arabic differs from the official languages of Cyprus, Greek and Turkish, and as a result, it must be considered an RML.[17]

Fourth, where no specification has been made by a state, in its instrument of ratification or in its initial periodical report, of the state's RMLs, the Committee of Experts will look at other sources to determine the identity of these languages, such as relevant domestic legislation.[18]

A very important preliminary issue with which the Committee of Experts has had to deal concerns the relationship between parts II and III of the Charter. As has already been noted and as will be discussed further below, particularly in the context of Article 7 subparagraph 1d, Article 7 provisions often cover subject matter which is also dealt with in more detailed and specific provisions in Part III. Generally, the Committee of Experts has taken the view that where an RML is also covered by obligations under Part III, it will generally leave a discussion of those aspects which are subject to Part III obligations to the

---

15. Slovenia 2004, 38.
16. Slovenia 2004, 39-40. The Committee of Experts has meanwhile recognised the Croatian and Serbian languages as regional or minority languages covered by Part II; clarification of the status of Bosnian is still pending.
17. Cyprus 2006, 47.
18. In its first report on Hungary, for example, the Committee of Experts looked to Act LXXVII of 1993 on the Rights of National and Ethnic Minorities to identify Hungary's RMLs: Hungary 2001, 19.

section of their reports which deal with those Part III obligations.[19] On occasion, however, the Committee of Experts notes that they reserve the right to carry out a comprehensive evaluation of the implementation of Part II in respect of languages also subject to Part III obligations.[20]

When a language is designated for the protection of Part III, this generally is done only in respect of certain regions or territories within the state. In some cases, such designation can leave some speakers outside the protection of Part III, and the Committee of Experts has made clear that it may treat the language as being subject to Part II in areas in which there are some concentrations of speakers. In some cases, this can extend to a language which is an official language of the state (and therefore generally not entitled to protection of the Charter), if, due to the federal structure of the state, the language is not an official language in certain sub-state administrative or political units and is in a vulnerable position.[21]

A final preliminary matter relates to the need for reliable data on RMLs for the purposes of assessing compliance with Part II (and other) Charter obligations. In its second report on Slovakia, for example, the Committee of Experts noted that the lack of reliable data was problematical. They noted that census data often serve as the basis for allocation of funding, broadcasting time and the use of RMLs in relations with the administrative authorities, and they said that the inaccuracy of the available data and the volatility inherent in 10-yearly censuses limited the capacity of the Slovak authorities to plan and take consistent and constant action. Their comments on 10-yearly censuses are particularly interesting, as many states (including, for example, the UK) take a census of the population only every 10 years. The Committee of Experts encouraged the Slovak authorities to take steps to collect reliable data concerning the number of users of RMLs and their geographic distribution.[22] The committee did not specify what form such data would take, but their reference to numbers of users and geographic distribution give fairly clear guidance on the nature of the data required.

---

19. See, e.g., Hungary 2001, 26; Germany 2002, 50; Slovenia 2004, 42; Finland 2007, 30.
20. For example, Hungary 2004, 24.
21. See, e.g., Switzerland 2004, 41-3; and Switzerland 2008, 13, 15, respectively, where the committee treated German in two cantons (Ticino, Jura) in which German was not an official language as a Part II language for these units. In the case of Ticino, as they had noted a sharp decline in the numbers of speakers of the Walser German dialect, it would appear that the vulnerable social situation of the language was a relevant consideration here.
22. Slovakia 2009, 9; see, also, Sweden 2009, 10.

3.1. Subparagraph 1a

Subparagraph 1a of Article 7 requires states to base their policies, legislation and practices on the recognition of RMLs as an expression of cultural wealth. Most of the comments of the Committee of Experts have been directed at what constitutes sufficient "recognition" for the purposes of this provision. What appears to be the present approach of the Committee of Experts has been expressed in the following terms:

> This provision requires States Parties to recognise in their domestic legal order, a regional or minority language as an expression of cultural wealth, without specifying what specific legal form this recognition should take. This does not necessarily require a constitutional provision. Ordinary legal acts or political measures, in combination with existing bilateral treaties may also suffice in this regard.[23]

In the same report, the Committee of Experts also noted that the Charter does not require the official recognition of minority groups, but of RMLs, and therefore a recognition of minorities in the domestic legal order in a fashion which does not make reference to the languages of such groups may not be sufficient. In practice, generally, the Committee of Experts will consider whether the RML benefits from any constitutional or legislative protection (such as a language act) or any general policy document in order to determine whether this paragraph has been fulfilled.[24]

In some of its earlier reports, the Committee of Experts was willing to accept that the identification by the state of some of its languages under Part III of the Charter itself constitutes sufficient recognition of the value of such languages.[25] More controversially, the Committee of Experts had interpreted the mere ratification of the Charter, with explicit reference to a language as a Part II (but not a Part III) language, as constituting specific recognition of that language as an expression of wealth.[26] In some ways, this is understandable. In many cases, mere recognition by a state of the existence of such languages represented a step forward. As noted in the Explanatory Report to the Charter, admitting the existence of a language is a precondition for taking its specific features and needs into consideration and for action on its behalf.[27] However, acceptance of mere ratification of the Charter as constituting recognition of an RML is problematic: if mere ratification of the Charter constituted sufficient recognition for

---

23. Slovenia 2007, 31.
24. Armenia 2006, 20-22; Austria 2005, 53; Finland 2001, 27.
25. See, for example, Croatia 2001, 30.
26. For example, Cyprus 2006, 52, in respect of Armenian, and the Netherlands 2001, 15, in respect of Frisian, Lower Saxon, Limburger, Yiddish, Romani and Sinti.
27. Paragraph 58.

the purposes of subparagraph 1a, it would effectively deprive the subparagraph of all meaning, because it would never be possible to find that a state has not satisfied its obligations. Surely, subparagraph 1a requires more, and this seems to be recognised in the more recent approach, quoted above. Thus, while the Committee of Experts noted in its initial report on Norway that the recognition of Romanes and Romani was "in itself a certain recognition of these languages by the authorities",[28] in its third report, the committee noted that no specific legislative measures had been adopted to ensure the promotion and protection of those two languages; they felt there was "room for improvement" and looked forward to seeing more information in the next state report.[29]

The insufficiency of an international treaty, by itself, was highlighted in the Committee of Experts' second report on Slovenia, from which the above quotation was taken. In that report, the Committee of Experts noted that the only legal text which made reference to the protection of German in Slovenia was a treaty between Slovenia and Austria. The Committee of Experts found that such a treaty, on its own, cannot be a sufficient basis for implementing the undertaking, noting that something must also exist within the domestic legal order.[30] By the same token, promotion of RMLs in international organisations (against the backdrop of significant domestic legal measures) has been referred to by the Committee of Experts; in its third report on the UK, for example, the committee noted that the Welsh and Scottish Gaelic languages had gained status within the European Union bodies as they could now be used in meetings of the Council of the European Union, and Welsh-speakers and Scottish Gaelic-speakers could now write and receive a response to EU bodies in their mother tongue.[31]

As is indicated in the earlier quote, recognition in the domestic legal order does not necessarily require recognition of an RML in the constitution of the state. However, the Committee of Experts has also repeatedly cited such provisions as being the highest form of recognition which could be given.[32] For example, in their initial report on Spain, the Committee of Experts concluded that Article 3 paragraph 3 of the Spanish Constitution, which makes reference to the richness of the linguistic varieties of Spain as a cultural patrimony that will be the object of special respect and protection, "represents one of the most exemplary formal recognitions of regional or minority languages as an expression of cultural

---

28. Norway 2001, 29.
29. Norway 2007, 28.
30. Slovenia 2007, 29-30.
31. Application of the Charter in the United Kingdom, 3rd monitoring cycle (2010), paragraph 35.
32. The Explanatory Report to the Charter makes clear, however, that "recognition" within the meaning of subparagraph 1a "must not be confused with recognition of a language as an official language": paragraph 58.

wealth that can be found in Europe".[33] The committee also noted in the context of Spain, in reference to recognition in the statutes of autonomy of several autonomous communities of the official status of the historic languages of those communities, that "the granting of co-officiality to a regional or minority language constitutes the strongest way of officially recognising its value".[34]

The Committee of Experts has also placed considerable importance on the creation of legislation, in particular language legislation, in assessing state compliance with subparagraph 1a. Thus, in its third report on Finland, for example, the Committee of Experts noted that despite the official recognition of Karelian as an RML, the authorities had not yet granted any "specific status" to the language, and encouraged them "to adopt legal measures in order to create a basis for the protection of the language concerned".[35] The notion of legislation as creating a "basis" or a "platform" for protection of an RML has been a recurrent theme. In its initial report on Sweden, for example, the Committee of Experts noted that the ratification "and especially the adoption of the legal acts on the use of Sami, Finnish and Meänkieli in administrative authorities and courts of law ... have created a platform where it is clear that the Swedish authorities recognise these three languages as an expression of cultural wealth".[36] By contrast, in its initial report on the Ukraine, the Committee of Experts noted that the constitution and even a number of laws recognise "the cultural wealth of minority languages"; however, it noted, particularly in the context of the restoration of Ukrainian as the official language and the promotion of its use in different fields, that "the lack of an operational language law is not satisfactory" and invited the authorities, in consultation with the speakers, "to draft a law that fits with today's reality in Ukraine and that gives clear legal guidelines to authorities and citizens".[37]

---

33. Spain 2005, 78-9. In its initial report on Serbia, the committee noted that according to the Statute of the Autonomous Province of Vojvodina, several languages are official languages of that province, and that this was "a high level of recognition" for those RMLs: Serbia 2009, 38. In its second report on Switzerland, the committee stated that the recognition of Italian and Romansch as official languages in the new constitution of the Canton of Graubünden represented "a very strong recognition of the value of these two languages": Switzerland 2004, 25. In its first report on Slovenia, the committee noted that the constitution of the state provides specific rights for members of the Hungarian and Italian-speaking minorities, "including a significant number of linguistic rights", and that in municipalities where communities of those speakers reside, the languages are official, and commented that "the granting of co-official status to these two minority languages, at the local level, is a very strong recognition of their value": Slovenia 2004, 45. There are other similar examples.

34. Spain 2005, 84, 86, 88 and 90.

35. Finland 2007, 32.

36. Sweden 2003, 33.

37. Ukraine 2010, 90, 92 and 93.

It is notable that, in some cases, even where there is some constitutional recognition of an RML, the Committee of Experts has noted the importance of further legislation; this is especially the case where the committee is of the view that the constitutional protection is rather vague. In its second report on Switzerland, the committee noted that Article 70 of the constitution provides that German, French and Italian are the official languages of the state and that Romansch is to be officially used to communicate with persons speaking that language,[38] but in its third report, the committee, in a box recommendation,[39] urged the federal authorities "to adopt legislation which would ensure the practical implementation of Article 70 of the Federal Constitution",[40] and in its fourth report, it welcomed the adoption by the Swiss Parliament of a Federal Law on the National Languages and Understanding between the Language Communities.[41] Even where there is constitutional protection which the Committee of Experts considered to be "a very strong recognition" of the value of RMLs, it has welcomed further legislation. Thus, in its third report on Switzerland, noting that the Canton of Graubünden had adopted a language law which aimed to strengthen the canton's trilingualism, increase individual, public and institutional awareness of multilingualism, improve mutual understanding between linguistic groups, preserve and promote Romansch and Italian, and apply particular promotional measures to Romansch, the committee described this law as "a remarkable step forward", clearly implying their view that such legislation represented an optimal and, indeed, exemplary approach under subparagraph 1a.[42] In its initial report on Slovakia, the Committee of Experts noted a range of important protections under the state's constitution, including language rights, but also mentioned legislation on the Use of Languages of National Minorities, and stated that, taken as a whole, "these provisions represent an optimal compliance with the present obligation from a formal perspective".[43] The reference to a "formal perspective" is important, because the Committee of Experts has on occasion noted the importance of not just the legal framework but its actual implementation.

---

38. Switzerland 2004, 25.
39. Recommendations of the Committee of Experts are all requests contained in the evaluation report which "encourage" (also invite, etc.) the state to take concrete action in support of a regional or minority language. The Committee of Experts weights the recommendations with a view to indicating priorities to the authorities: While "simple" recommendations are in the text, particularly important or urgent recommendations appear in a box at the end of a paragraph. If the state does not implement a recommendation, the Committee of Experts usually repeats it in the following evaluation report(s). However, it then formulates the recommendation more firmly: The first repetition "urges" the authorities to take the respective measure, and the second repetition "strongly urges" the authorities to do that.
40. Switzerland 2008, after 16.
41. Switzerland 2010, 14.
42. Switzerland 2008, 17.
43. Slovakia 2007, 48.

For weaker languages, the Committee of Experts will still place emphasis on the creation of a legal framework,[44] At very least, the committee seems to place emphasis on the formulation of a coherent policy for the language.[45] The committee has, however, commented on the importance of significant measures in support of such languages:

> Because the traditional prestige of these two Roma/Gypsy languages had been extremely low, much more effort is needed to raise their reputation as a means of communication. Without an energetic effort and constant symbolic gestures, it will be difficult to overcome deeply rooted historical prejudice against the two Roma/Gypsy languages. The practical recognition of these two languages as an expression of cultural wealth of Hungary and as part of the European cultural heritage needs a high political profile in order to have positive consequences in the public consciousness.[46]

This is a good illustration – and one of many evident in its work in respect of Article 7 – of the awareness of sociolinguistics and of principles of language planning which the Committee of Experts brings to its work; though it does not make specific reference to status planning, the need for such planning is clearly implicit in this passage. In this regard, reference should be made to the Committee of Experts' comments on the treatment of Aranese in Catalonia. The committee noted that the Statute of Autonomy of Catalonia recognises the language and states that it shall be the subject of special teaching, respect and protection, and in particular that the Autonomous Community of Catalonia has developed "a special legal and administrative system for the Aran valley, which has led in practice to Aranese being co-official in the area concerned", and observed that "this is a particularly strong recognition for a language spoken on a limited portion of the territory of the autonomous community concerned".[47]

Another example of the understanding of sociolinguistic realities which informs the work of the Committee of Experts was evident in its initial report on Hungary. In explanation of the lack of recognition of certain of its RMLs, the Hungarian authorities had noted that there was virtually no demand for the use of such RMLs; the Committee of Experts commented:

---

44. See, for example, Finland 2004, 29, where the committee encouraged a "legal framework" for Romani.
45. See for example the first report on Sweden, in which the Committee of Experts noted a new national minorities and minority language policy which, in their view, recognised the Yiddish and Romani languages "as being integral elements of Swedish cultural wealth": Sweden 2003, 33.
46. Hungary 2001, 21.
47. Spain 2005, 97.

Given the practical impossibility to use these languages in education and before public authorities, such reluctance by the speakers of these languages to insist on language rights is understandable. But one should not deduce from such reluctance a lack of will on their part to preserve their cultural and linguistic identity.[48]

In order to determine real levels of demand, and in particular whether users of RMLs want special protection and/or promotion, the Committee of Experts has stressed the importance of consultation with representatives of the users of RMLs.[49]

3.2. Subparagraph 1b

The Committee of Experts has consistently expressed concern where changes in the borders of administrative areas can have a negative impact on the delivery of minority language services. In this, they are reinforced by the Explanatory Report to the Charter, which explains that this subparagraph condemns practices which devise territorial divisions so as to render the use or survival of a language more difficult, or to fragment a language community among a number of administrative or territorial units.[50] In their initial report on Denmark, for example, the Committee of Experts mentioned the concerns of the German minority about the severe repercussions that would result from a possible consolidation of the county in which they resided into a much larger administrative unit, and the committee urged the Danish authorities to give full consideration to their undertakings under the Charter before implementing any changes.[51] In their initial report on Austria, the Committee of Experts heard evidence that changes in the boundaries of school districts were threatening the viability of Slovene schools, and the committee encouraged the Austrian authorities to ensure that such changes did not have a negative impact on the protection and promotion of Slovene in public life.[52] In its second report on Croatia, the Committee of Experts reported complaints that the way in which administrative divisions were made in 1993 resulted in Croatian speakers mostly being in the majority even in those areas in which Hungarian is spoken, a situation which the Committee of Experts described as "unsatisfactory".[53]

The Committee of Experts has also consistently emphasised the importance of consultation with users of RMLs whenever a merger of administrative areas could

---

48. Hungary 2001, 20. See also Norway 2001, 29.
49. Norway 2001, box recommendation after 29.
50. Paragraph 60.
51. Denmark 2004, 34-5. See also Finland 2007, 35.
52. Austria 2005, 60. See also Switzerland 2008, 22-25, Switzerland 2010, 16 and in a box recommendation immediately thereafter.
53. Application of the Charter in Croatia, 2nd monitoring cycle (2005), paragraphs 18-19.

have a negative impact on RMLs. In their second report on Denmark, for example, following up on concerns raised in their initial report about the potential negative consequences for the German minority of a merger of administrative areas, the committee noted that the German minority had been consulted throughout the process and their needs and wishes had been carefully considered by the authorities, leading to unspecified "special solutions" in order to safeguard their interests.[54] In its second report on Slovenia, the Committee of Experts noted concerns about an attempt to split a municipality into two entities against the wishes of the Italian minority, and while the proposal had been rejected, there were similar proposals in other municipalities. The committee made the following comment:

> The Committee of Experts trusts that the authorities will take full account of the views and concerns of the Italian-speakers and refrain from taking measures relating to administrative divisions which would constitute an obstacle to the promotion of the Italian language.[55]

With regard to pre-existing administrative or territorial boundaries, the Explanatory Report to the Charter, while noting the desirability of ensuring a consistency between the territory of an RML and an appropriate territorial administrative entity, recognised that this could not be achieved in all cases, as settlement patterns may be too complex and the determination of territorial administrative entities may legitimately depend on other considerations than linguistic ones.[56] Where, however, administrative boundaries were established long ago based on patterns of settlement of linguistic minorities at the time, the committee has noted the need to update such boundaries to reflect changing patterns of settlement. In its initial report on Slovenia, for example, Hungarian and Italian had co-official status in "ethnically mixed areas", in the territories of the historical settlement of these minorities as defined by the statutes of the municipalities in question. However, these had been established in 1954 and populations had shifted since then, so these areas now corresponded only in part to the current distribution of speakers. As a result, no protection was granted to the languages outside the 1954 settlements. The Committee of Experts noted that an RML "is a living reality and that its framework of protection and promotion should always be seen in the socio-economic context in which it lives and be adapted/developed accordingly".[57] It concluded that an effective policy of language maintenance would therefore require "the progressive extension of the framework for protecting the Italian

---

54. Denmark 2007, 32. See also Finland 2007, 37, where the committee invited the authorities "to take all appropriate measures in consultation with the speakers", and made particular reference to the Swedish Assembly and the Sami Parliament. See also Norway 2001, 30.
55. Slovenia 2007, 35.
56. Paragraph 59.
57. Slovenia 2004, 52.

language ... to other areas in the territories of the municipalities [in question] where there is a stable presence of Italian speakers".[58]

More generally, the Committee of Experts has been concerned where significant numbers of speakers are left outside the protection of the Charter because of the definition of the territory of an RML. In its second report on Norway, for example, the Committee of Experts observed that the existing definition of the Sami administrative district excluded the application of relevant legislation in support of Sami from being applied to South, Lule and possibly Eastern Sami, all of which were in a precarious situation and in need of special protection. The committee noted that it was "especially concerned" about these three languages and expressed the hope that the Norwegian authorities would "look carefully into their situation with a view to securing their protection and promotion".[59]

In a similar vein, the Committee of Experts has expressed concern where, as in Slovakia, the application of measures of support and the creation of measures to allow for use of RMLs is defined by reference to the speakers of an RML exceeding a certain percentage – in the case of Slovakia, 20% – of the local population. The committee made the following comment:

> The Committee of Experts has already observed that the 20% rule cannot be invoked to prevent the relevant obligations under the Charter from being operational where the speakers are traditionally present in sufficient numbers, irrespective of the said threshold and therefore even below 20% .... In other words, an administrative division which has the effect of bringing the percentage of regional or minority language speakers below the 20% threshold does not affect the operation of the relevant obligations under the Charter if in the territory concerned the speakers are present in sufficient numbers for the purposes of those undertakings.[60]

While this is clearly a principle of importance, the Committee of Experts refrained from defining what would be "sufficient numbers"; this is sensible, as what would be sufficient would depend on circumstances, and any more precision would run the same sort of risk as specifying a percentage. The committee has raised the question of the use of percentages, and has taken a similar approach, under other subparagraphs of Article 7 paragraph 1.[61]

---

58. Ibid., 54, followed by a box recommendation to similar effect.
59. Norway 2003, 46. In its third report on Norway, the committee was pleased to note that amendment of the relevant legislation, the Sami Act, simplified the procedures for extending the Sami administrative district, and that at least one municipality which had a large concentration of Lule Sami speakers had been included: Norway 2007, 30.
60. Slovakia 2007, 50.
61. See, for example, Switzerland 2008, 27, the Committee of Experts thought that a threshold of 20% of the population of a municipality was required in order to impose an obligation on the municipality to use Romansch might be "problematical from the point of view of the Charter".

The Committee of Experts has noted that where an RML is split between two different administrative entities within the same state – Basque, which is present in both the Basque Autonomous Community and Navarra, and Catalan, split into different autonomous communities, are examples – there is a need for close co-ordination between the administrative entities, and that such co-ordination can, in fact, be essential to the fulfilment of commitments under the Charter.[62] In the context of Spain, the committee also noted that the creation of separate linguistic zones in Navarra for the Basque language meant that the "mixed zone" there had to be excluded from Part III protection.[63] In this regard, the Committee of Experts noted that, in principle, it is possible for a state not to extend the provisions of Part III to a given language, or to a given territory, as long as such a decision is compatible with the spirit, objectives and general principles of the Charter. Consequently, the committee therefore encouraged the Spanish authorities to provide more detailed information on the characteristics of the presence of Basque in the "mixed zone", making specific reference to places concerned, degree of concentration of speakers and the proportion of such speakers compared to the population of such places as a whole, and to reflect on "whether there may be a need for an appropriate level of Part III protection within the mixed zone".[64]

Finally, the Committee of Experts has, in the context of subparagraph 1b, noted the need for broader economic development (and other public policy) decisions to include consideration of the effects of such decisions. In its initial report on Germany, the Committee of Experts noted that the dissolution of an administrative division of a municipality in which the Sorbian language had a strong presence, to allow lignite mining to occur, suggested that respect for the geographical area of minority languages might take a secondary place to other interests, and it took the view that "appropriate and strong measures" should be taken to compensate for the adverse impact on the Lower Sorbian language. It emphasised the importance, in planning decisions of this kind, of ensuring that adequate provision is made for weighing the interests of RMLs against economic considerations.[65] As will be discussed at the end in the concluding

---

62. Spain 2005, 100-1. This issue has also arisen in Germany. In its initial report, the Committee of Experts noted that the speech area of Low German comprised eight German *Länder*; noting that there was a "danger" of them acting in isolation, the committee suggested that measures should be taken to ensure co-operation between the *Länder*; with the aim of strengthening the impact of the measures taken to promote the language: Germany 2002, 52. In its second report, the committee noted that the *Länder* had taken up this suggestion and that officials now met for consultation: Germany 2006, 21.
63. Spain 2005, 99.
64. Ibid., 71-2.
65. Germany 2002, 54; in the following box recommendation, the committee strongly encouraged the authorities "to take all appropriate measures aimed at remedying the adverse effects on the Lower Sorbian language". Similar statements followed in the second report: Germany 2006, 23, and the box recommendation following.

section of this chapter (and as mentioned in the introductory section), the integration of language planning considerations in broader public policy, and in particular economic and regional development policy decisions is crucial in any attempt to maintain an RML, and the Committee of Experts' reflections here illustrate the potential, only partly realised here, for Article 7 to be applied to effect this integration.

3.3. Subparagraph 1c

The Explanatory Report offers relatively little additional guidance on the substantive content of subparagraph 1c. It merely indicates that, owing to the weakness of many RMLs, the "mere prohibition of discrimination is not sufficient to ensure their survival" and they "need positive support". The report states only that it is left up to the states to determine the manner in which they intend acting to promote RMLs, noting only that such action must be "resolute".[66] In an early report, the Committee of Experts noted that "[i]n light of the variety of language situations that may be encountered in the various European countries, the authors of the Charter did not regard it as feasible to provide a list of the actions which might be considered to be 'resolute'".[67] Generally, though, the Committee of Experts seems to be looking for evidence of a "structured approach" to the protection of RMLs, rather than simply measures indicative of goodwill and a positive dialogue with users of the RMLs.[68]

In its second report on the Netherlands, for example, the Committee of Experts noted the recommendation in its first report that the Dutch authorities should develop a general national policy for the languages covered by Part II, and commented that the province of Limburg had adopted a plan drawn up by the Regional Language Officer and the province's advisory body on the Limburger language.[69] They also noted, however, that their attention had been drawn to "the absence of a clear national language policy" and consequently to the lack of financial support from the central authorities.[70] In its third report on Finland, in relation to the Karelian language, the Committee of Experts encouraged the authorities "to look into" the recommendations of a report by the University of Joensuu on strengthening the status of Karelian "and develop a strategy and

---

66. Paragraph 61.
67. Croatia 2001, 32.
68. Austria 2005, 65-6.
69. The Netherlands 2004, 38.
70. The Netherlands 2004, 40. In a similar vein, in its second report on Norway, the committee expressed concern for the South Sami and Lule Sami languages; and, in observing that the Sami Parliament had drafted an action plan for South Sami, they noted that some suggestions for action had been implemented, but many had not: Norway 2003, 51.

measures to promote the language".[71] In the same report, in relation to Romani, the committee urged the authorities, in a box recommendation, to strengthen the promotion of Romani "by developing a language planning programme, in co-operation with the speakers";[72] here, again, we see the principle of consultation with the speakers of RMLs emerging in the work of the committee. In some cases, however, the committee has set a markedly lower standard, and has therefore arguably weakened the requirements of the paragraph. For example, in its first report on Cyprus, the committee noted that, though there was no overall language plan or any national strategy aiming at the promotion of RMLs in Cyprus, "the government has shown resolute action to promote Armenian".[73] The action referred to in subsequent paragraphs primarily involved Armenian primary schools which were being funded by the government.

It is extremely important that the Committee of Experts have emphasised the need for a strategy and a structured approach to the maintenance and promotion of RMLs, as expressed in a formal language policy of some sort. Even if there is not necessarily full agreement on what form any such strategy should take, there is a consensus (in the literature on language policy and planning for minoritised languages) on the need for a structured and coherent approach.[74] However, the Committee of Experts has generally refrained from considering whether the strategies or policies which it observes are sensible or appropriate. As discussed further in the concluding section of this chapter, it may now be time for the Committee of Experts to reflect more critically on the precise content of any strategy or policy embodying a structured approach and to explore whether the strategy or policy is in fact suitable in the circumstances of the language in question. As noted elsewhere in this chapter and discussed in the conclusions, the purpose of the Charter is to ensure that RMLs are maintained and promoted. If a strategy or policy in respect of an RML is not succeeding in maintaining the language in question,

---

71. Finland 2007, 39.
72. Finland 2007, 42.
73. Cyprus 2006, 61.
74. See, for example, Joshua Fishman, *Reversing language shift* (Clevedon: Multilingual Matters, 1991), which is still the most influential model in this area. In its third report on the UK, the Committee of Experts noted, for example, the publication by the Welsh Language Board in 2005 of its 10-year Strategic Plan, making reference to priorities like extending the influence of Welsh-language schemes and strengthening the use of Welsh in business and education, and among young people, and also the development by Bòrd na Gàidhlig in 2007 of a National Plan for Gaelic, approved by the Scottish Government, which "delivers a basic strategy for the development of the language and identifies four key target areas to strengthen the language: language acquisition, usage, status and corpus planning": United Kingdom 2010, 48 and 50 respectively.

or if, based on current understanding of the principles of language policy relevant to such languages, the strategy or policy has no reasonable prospect of achieving the goals sought by the Charter, the Committee of Experts should be willing to point this out. Indeed, it is difficult to conclude that a strategy or policy constitutes "resolute" action if it is not, in fact, actually succeeding in promoting the maintenance and revitalisation of the language or has little prospect of doing so. Of course, to engage in such an assessment requires a much more sophisticated knowledge of the actual position of the language, and this would require far more data than the Committee of Experts has at its disposal. This is another issue to which I shall return.

Since its second report on Germany in 2005, it has become standard for the Committee of Experts to note in its reports that, in addition to a structured approach, "resolute action" to promote and safeguard RMLs covers several aspects, three in particular: the creation of a "legal framework" for the promotion of the languages; the "establishment of bodies" which have responsibility in this field; and the provision of "adequate financial resources".[75]

With regard to the first requirement, creation of a "legal framework", there is obvious overlap with subparagraph 1a of Article 7, and considerable repetition or cross-referencing emerges here. Constitutional recognition of an RML as an official language of the state, as in the case of Swedish in Finland, has been interpreted by the Committee of Experts as clearly amounting to "resolute action".[76] Legislation in support of RMLs has generally been interpreted by the Committee of Experts as evidence of resolute action, though they have expressed concerns where they have found that significant groups of speakers of RMLs are partly left out of the legislative framework.[77] Indeed, the committee has encouraged the adoption of "a specific legal framework" for the protection and promotion of some RMLs, such as Aragonese and Catalan in Aragon.[78] The committee has also noted that the lack of constitutional and legislative provisions indicates a lower level of commitment to action in favour of RMLs.[79]

With regard to the second requirement, the "establishment of bodies" with responsibility for promoting RMLs, various bodies have been deemed

---

75. Germany 2006, 24; see also, for example, Sweden 2006, 28; Norway 2006, 34; Denmark 2007, 33; Spain 2008, 103; Serbia 2009, 43; Ukraine 2010, 100, and others.
76. Finland 2001, 31.
77. Croatia 2005, 20. See also, for example, the second report on Sweden, where, in a box recommendation, the committee encouraged Sweden to take measures to secure implementation of the Charter throughout Sweden, "including where necessary the adoption of specific legislation" on RMLs: Sweden 2006, 31.
78. Spain 2005, 113-15 and box recommendation thereafter.
79. See, for example, Germany 2006, 26.

satisfactory. The establishment of language planning bodies, with formal powers grounded in legislation, has been welcomed by the Committee of Experts.[80] Establishment of a language planning body with the aim of "studying and developing" the language has also been considered by the Committee of Experts to be evidence of "resolute action".[81] In some cases, the appointment of a regional language officer has been considered by the committee as a "major step".[82] In its first report on Hungary, the committee stated that Hungary had taken "important initiatives that raise the awareness of the need to protect and promote" RMLs, citing the establishment of the Government Office for National and Ethnic Minorities and the work of the Parliamentary Committee for Human Rights, Minorities and Religions, and talked of "particular significance" in the establishment of a Minorities Ombudsman and the development of the scheme of minority self-governments.[83]

The Committee of Experts has described the third requirement, the provision of adequate financial resources, as "a crucial aspect of safeguarding regional or minority languages".[84] While they have recognised that economic difficulties can have an impact, the Committee of Experts has nonetheless emphasised the importance of financing, in the case of Croatia noting in particular the sociolinguistic realities, namely "the dramatic decline in the number of speakers that the most recent statistics have shown".[85] This implies that the degree to which action could be said to be "resolute" may be affected by the degree to which a particular RML is particularly vulnerable. In its second report on Sweden, in a box recommendation the committee simply encouraged the authorities to reverse the trend of diminishing support for the associations of Finnish-speakers.[86]

The Committee of Experts has frequently considered states where authority for matters relating to RMLs is split between two levels of government, as a result either of a federal constitutional structure or of devolved decision making. In such cases, the committee has noted cases where one level is satisfying the requirements of paragraph 1c and another is not.[87] The committee has noted

---

80. See, for example, United Kingdom 2007, 48, where the committee was "pleased to note" the passage of a Gaelic Language Bill which, *inter alia*, gave a statutory role to the Gaelic Language Board charged with a variety of tasks, including the development of a national language plan and, with local authorities, local language plans to promote the use of Gaelic.
81. Finland 2001, 33: the Roma Language Board, established under the auspices of the Research Centre for the Languages of Finland.
82. Appointed by the Province of Limburg in respect of the Limburger language: the Netherlands 2004, 38.
83. Hungary 2001, 23.
84. Croatia 2005, 22.
85. Ibid.
86. Sweden 2006, after 37.
87. Austria 2005, 62.

that, in these circumstances, the need for resolute action involves participation of various levels of government, including the central authorities and municipalities, and has been critical when, for example, many of the former do not implement policies adopted at the level of the autonomous community.[88] The committee has noted that there can often be considerable confusion among speakers of RMLs as to which authorities are responsible for protection and promotion of their languages and for implementation of the Charter, which causes problems, particularly with regard to financing.[89]

Indeed, the implementation of commendable legislation and policy is an issue on which the Committee of Experts has commented under subparagraph 1c. For example, in its comments on the Basque language in the Basque Country, the Committee of Experts noted that the substantial number of legislative and practical measures resulting from the granting of co-official status to Basque is undoubtedly a "significant response" to the need for resolute action to promote Basque, but they also noted that actual implementation of the legislative measures "may still be unsatisfactory in specific areas".[90]

The Committee of Experts has noted that one of the reasons why implementation is often poor is that the likely users of services provided in the RML lack information about the availability of such services.[91] In its third report on Finland, the committee noted that few Roma children were yet receiving the teaching of Roma, and stated that "more visible measures are needed to improve the status of this language". In particular, they noted that "Roma people must be informed more effectively of their linguistic rights and the importance for the children to learn Romani".[92] Here, the committee is referring to the very important language planning principle of "active offer": it is not sufficient simply to provide a service if the potential users are not informed of the existence of the minority language service and actively encouraged to take advantage of that service. Here again we see a keen understanding developing in the work of the committee of sociolinguistic realities and appropriate responses from a language planning perspective, which is salutary.

Three final aspects of the Committee of Experts' work in respect of subparagraph 1c should be mentioned. The first is that where a language that has only received Part II protection has enjoyed relatively little support in terms of

---

88. Spain 2005, 105-6.
89. See Germany 2006, 25; the committee also welcomed, however, the federal government's provision of funds to assist the *Länder*, which had primary responsibility for action under the Charter, in promoting RMLs.
90. Spain 2005, 105-6.
91. See, for example, Sweden 2003, 35.
92. Finland 2007, 41.

legislation or even policy, the taking of steps to lay the necessary groundwork for the development of policy has been commended. In the case of Scots, for example, the committee noted that there had been no overarching language policy for the language. It noted that, with the change of government in Scotland in 2007, the new government undertook an audit "(or rather a survey)", of the current provision of the Scots language in public life, based on the seven articles of Part III of the Charter. The committee also noted that as a result of the audit, the Scottish Government had put together "a strategic task force, with the aim to promote Scots, raise public awareness of Scots, and support it in the fields of education, culture and media". The committee commended "the resolute action taken by the Scottish authorities" and looked forward to receiving more information about the activities of the task force in the next UK periodical report.[93] Similarly, the committee noted in that same report that the Cornish Language Partnership was set up in 2005 to promote and support the Cornish language and to oversee the development of the Cornish Language Strategy. It noted that the partnership was led by Cornwall Council and included Cornish-language NGOs and other representatives. The committee observed that "this model of collaboration between representatives of the speakers and the authorities has worked well for the Cornish language, and could be considered as a model for other languages in similar situations" (the Cornish language being a highly threatened language which is, in fact, being revived). The committee noted that one of the main achievements of the partnership had been the agreement on a Standard Written Form of Cornish, which it welcomed and commended as an example of "concerted and resolute action".[94]

Second, the Committee of Experts has commented on the importance of corpus planning initiatives in the context of this paragraph, in recognition of the fact that the linguistic development of the language, and particularly standardisation and lexical expansion, are preconditions for greater use in a wider range of domains, including in formal ones such as education, public services and so forth. Thus the committee noted with satisfaction the recognition by the Norwegian Government of the need to set up a linguistic infrastructure for the Kven language, including its standardisation, the development of a grammar, dictionaries, textbooks and teaching materials.[95]

---

93. United Kingdom 2010, 53.
94. Ibid., 62.
95. Norway 2007, 36. Highlighting again the importance of adequate funding, though, the committee noted the shortages of funds for research on Kven, and encouraged the authorities to provide adequate funding to support the development of the language, including funds for research: paragraph 38. In it second report on Slovakia, the committee noted that the standardisation of Romani by the state clearly represented "resolute action" to promote Romani, and commended the authorities on this achievement: Slovakia 2009, 32.

Finally, the Committee of Experts has again shown its willingness to consider the impact of broader policy areas on language maintenance, which is a very significant development, given the ways in which diverse policy areas can affect language use.[96] In its fourth report on Switzerland, the committee considered the Yenish language, spoken by travelling people. They heard that Yenish use was linked to the traditional nomadic way of life, which requires the possibility to assemble groups at stopover facilities. The committee noted that such facilities were not provided in some cantons, though they "represented the most important precondition for the maintenance and transmission of Yenish", and encouraged the authorities to consider the provision of such facilities "and to come to flexible solutions".[97]

3.4. Subparagraph 1d

This subparagraph requires the facilitation and/or encouragement of the use of RMLs, in speech and writing, in public and private life. As Jean-Marie Woehrling has pointed out, there is rarely any formal challenge or obstacle to the use of RMLs in the private sphere.[98] Indeed, it is likely that core civil and political rights, such as the right to freedom of expression and the right to freedom of association provide sufficient protection against any attempt by the state to limit the use of any particular language in "private" contexts.[99] In this context, then, the reference to "public life" takes on particular importance. However, it is not immediately clear to what the term "public life" actually refers.

From its earliest reports, the Committee of Experts has made it clear that it will interpret "public life" in an expansive way, one which in effect overlaps with the Charter's Part III commitments. For example, in its initial report on Croatia, the Committee of Experts noted that the term "public life" "is fairly wide and can include the use of the language in education, justice, administration, economic and social life, cultural life, the media and in transfrontier exchanges".[100] This formulation has been followed in many other reports.[101] The list of domains reproduces, of course, the subject matter covered by Part III of the Charter, but the term can certainly go beyond those domains, as is implied

---

96. For an excellent discussion of these complexities from a sociolinguistic perspective, see B. Spolsky (2004), *Language management*.
97. Switzerland 2010, 19-20.
98. Woehrling (2005), op. cit., p. 113.
99. See, for example, R. Dunbar (2007), "European traditional linguistic diversity and human rights: a critical assessment of international instruments" in E. J. Ruiz Vieytez and R. Dunbar (eds), *Human rights and diversity: new challenges for plural societies*. Bilbao: Humanitarian Net, University of Deusto, pp. 85-110.
100. Croatia 2001, 34.
101. See, for example, Hungary 2001, 24, and Denmark 2004, 36.

in the formulation itself – "can include" – and it has been suggested that it covers whatever is not part of private life, so that communal activities, the activities of associations, cultural and social organisations and so forth would also be covered.[102] The Committee of Experts has sometimes followed this formulation by emphasising that the obligation under subparagraph 1d does not only imply "passive permission to use regional or minority languages in public and private life, but requires the State Party to facilitate and/or encourage the use of the languages" in the specific public spheres referred to, such as education, the courts, administration, and so on,[103] and has pointed out that "facilitation and/or encouragement" goes beyond mere tolerance, but calls for positive action to give RMLs a place in public life.[104]

Among the domains referred to, the Committee of Experts makes most frequent reference to use of RMLs in the context of administrative or judicial authorities and the media, probably because other subparagraphs in paragraph 1 of Article 7 deal with education and transfrontier exchanges. The committee has noted that the failure to specify measures which allow the use of RMLs with the administrative and judicial authorities can lead to problems, and that the need to be able to serve users of RMLs in these settings has implications for the language competence of civil servants.[105] The Committee of Experts has often referred particularly to the use of RMLs in the health care system. In its first report on Sweden, for example, the committee noted that there was a clear need for interpreters in the Romani varieties, which was often "a real social need for elderly people especially in health care", while also noting the need for interpreters and translators in the courts.[106]

We have seen in the context of other subparagraphs in paragraph 1 that the Committee of Experts has been critical of the use of thresholds defined in percentage terms for the purpose of determining whether provision of services through the medium of RMLs should be made available, and it has commented on this issue in the context of subparagraph 1d as well. In its second report on Croatia, the committee noted that Croatia required that speakers of an RML must constitute at least one third of the population of a municipality in order

---

102. Woehrling (2005), op. cit., pp. 113-14.
103. Denmark 2004, 36.
104. United Kingdom 2003, 57.
105. Germany 2006, 29-30.
106. Sweden 2003, 42. The need for minority-language services in the health care sector was highlighted in Sweden 2006, 40, and Sweden 2009, as well, with the committee asking the authorities in the third report to investigate whether undertakings concerning health care and the care of the elderly "could be part of an extended ratification instrument", because both the authorities and the representatives of the speakers of RMLs see the use of RMLs in this area "as an acutely growing need": Sweden 2009, 34.

to be entitled to use their language in official contexts. Noting that this excluded a number of communities where the population of speakers of an RML is sizeable and significantly concentrated, but does not meet the threshold, the committee considered this an unacceptable outcome.[107]

The Committee of Experts has frequently taken a very close look at the use of RMLs in the media, particularly in broadcasting, under this subparagraph. The committee has been clear about the importance of media, and particularly of television. In its second report on Sweden, it emphasised "the importance of varied and extensive television broadcasting for the maintenance and promotion" of RMLs, and in this context was concerned about the negative impact of reducing the amount of time devoted to them.[108] In its initial report on Austria, the committee welcomed an amendment to broadcasting legislation to include the provision of RML programmes in the public service mandate of the state broadcaster, again noting "the importance of the media for regional or minority languages".[109]

The Committee of Experts has generally shown concern where the amount of broadcast time devoted to an RML is very limited: for example, six minutes of television time every month, plus 25 minutes once a year, based on an "obsolete" programme structure was considered "particularly limited",[110] while 12 minutes per week of regional radio broadcasts for the Kven minority in Norway in standard Finnish rather than Kven was considered "quite limited".[111] Where an RML – even a small one – has been completely excluded from the media, the Committee of Experts has expressed concern. In its third report on Sweden, for example, it considered that the relatively low number of Yiddish-speakers should not lead to the complete exclusion of this RML from public broadcasting, and it encouraged the authorities to investigate the possibilities of providing at least radio broadcasts in Yiddish.[112] It has also been critical where provision is made for an RML in the media, but in a format that is not accessible to the audience: provision must be effective. Thus, where an increase in radio programming in an RML took place on medium wave, which was not accessibly to very

---

107. Croatia 2005, 23-4, 26.
108. Sweden 2006, 39.
109. Austria 2005, 69.
110. Ruthenian, as noted in Hungary 2004, 25. By contrast, in its initial report on Serbia, after noting that Serbian authorities provided assistance to one hour per month of television programmes on one regional station and one hour per week on another one, as well as 30 minutes per week of radio programming on one regional station, acknowledged the "good situation" of Macedonian in the media of the relevant province, Vojvodina: Serbia 2009, 52.
111. Norway 2007, 55. The committee added that there was an urgent need for radio programmes in Kven, particularly for children and young people who are learning the language, and in a box recommendation the committee urged the authorities to take appropriate measures to facilitate and encourage radio broadcasting in Kven: Norway 2007, 57 and subsequent box recommendation.
112. Sweden 2009, 38.

many people, the Committee of Experts made reference to the "importance of a widely accessible media provision on the visibility" of RMLs.[113] It has also noted that the "broadcasting media" are an "important area" of public life, and has commented where the presence of a language in these media is limited.[114]

Some states – Germany in particular – have argued that they are not allowed to "interfere" with private media outlets and therefore cannot take any action to improve the presence of RMLs in this field. The Committee of Experts has been critical of such arguments:

> Freedom of expression in the media is not compromised by facilitating or promoting use of regional or minority languages in the media. By reason of their relative economic and political weakness, minority languages are at an inherent disadvantage when it comes to opportunities to be seen and heard in the media. It is necessary and appropriate for this imbalance to be redressed by positive measures.[115]

Thus, the committee has been critical of a lack of positive measures being taken by states to promote the visibility of RMLs in the media, and has made reference to mechanisms such as the provision of financial assistance.[116]

As noted at the start of this chapter, one advantage which Article 7 may have over the more detailed and specific provisions of Part III is flexibility: the relatively broad formulation of the Article 7 commitments allows for scrutiny of matters which are relevant to the maintenance and promotion of RMLs but do not fit easily within a Part III obligation. A good example is new media. When the Charter was drafted, many new media had not yet been developed. Article 11 contains rather detailed provisions on older media such as television, radio and newspapers, but it does not easily accommodate new media. Subparagraph 1d does, and the Committee of Experts has taken advantage of this to comment on new media issues in the context of that provision, noting in the context of subparagraph 1d:

> The new information technology has opened possibilities for new flexible and cheap ways of communicating compared to traditional media. Chat rooms and electronic newspapers on the internet and texting on mobile phones are examples of this. These new communication channels are in particular used by young people. They are also much used by young speakers of regional or minority languages

---

113. Austria 2005, 74; also Hungary 2004, 25, where the committee noted that minority language programmes are still broadcast on the very low east Europe FM frequency, "which modern radio sets cannot even receive".
114. Denmark 2007, 40.
115. Germany 2002, 59.
116. Germany 2006, 31.

because of their flexibility, informality and economical use, but also because it is in many cases difficult to use regional or minority languages in the traditional media for a number of reasons.[117]

The committee has also stated that the active use of RMLs "in the new media environment is important for sustaining these languages and it may contribute positively to the use of regional or minority languages in private and public life",[118] and has therefore encouraged the authorities, in co-operation with the speakers, to explore ways and means to stimulate the use of RMLs in the new media.[119]

Where a language (for example, Cypriot Maronite Arabic) has not been codified or standardised, the Committee of Experts has noted that corpus planning initiatives for the language, such as codification and standardisation, are "crucial for its maintenance since [this] facilitates its teaching at school, enhances its visibility in public life, for example in the press, and raises its cultural status", and therefore the committee has encouraged the authorities to find means, in co-operation with the speakers, to engage in such corpus planning.[120] Where the linguistic minority is dispersed, the Committee of Experts have noted the special importance of establishing institutions which will facilitate opportunities to meet to use the language, such as cultural and youth centres.[121] In all these cases, the Committee of Experts has shown a real sensitivity to sociolinguistic realities and an application of sound principles of language planning for minoritised languages.

3.5. Subparagraph 1e

Subparagraph 1e has two aspects. The first is the maintenance and development of links between groups in different parts of the state which use the same or a similar RML; this recognises that users of RMLs are sometimes found in quite different parts of the country, and might have tenuous links. Maintaining and developing relations between them allows them to pool resources more effectively and learn from each others' experiences.[122] The second is the establishment of cultural relations between groups in the state which use different languages.

On the first aspect of this subparagraph, the Committee of Experts has regularly pointed out the importance of the existence of umbrella organisations, grouping together speakers of RMLs, and the role that they can play in facilitating links

---

117. Norway 2007, 60.
118. Ibid., 61; see also Finland 2007, 49, where the very same formulation was used.
119. Norway 2007, 61.
120. Cyprus 2006, 71.
121. Ibid., 72.
122. See Woehrling (2005), op. cit., pp. 115-6.

between such groups.[123] Among the sorts of initiative upon which the committee has commented favourably are the multilevel system of minority self-govern-ments in Hungary, which "ensures that users of the same minority language inside Hungary have close links with each other",[124] and the Sami Parliament.[125] Where no organisations exist, the committee has encouraged the authorities to support the establishment of a cultural organisation of speakers of the RML.[126]

With regard to the second aspect, the Committee of Experts has regularly stressed the benefits for speakers of different RMLs of having a forum in which they can maintain a dialogue and create constructive links.[127] The committee has welcomed efforts by the authorities to provide such a forum where repre-sentatives of RMLs can co-operate, and institutions which foster such links, such as a Commissioner for Minorities and a Commissioner for Matters relating to Repatriates and National Minorities.[128]

The Committee of Experts has noted that this provision is particularly relevant where, as with the Basque language, its speakers are split between two regional entities, the Basque Autonomous Community and Navarra. In this context, they noted that links between speakers in the two communities exist, but that "there seems to be room for improving co-operation between the two communities concerned". They also noted, in this context, that retransmission in Navarra of programming of the Basque-language television channel in the Basque Autonomous Community "appears to be problematical". They also noted as a problem the lack of a common framework for sharing teaching materials in Basque in the educational systems of the two communities, and they generally encouraged the authorities to seek ways to foster closer co-operation.[129] In a similar vein, the committee observed in its first report on the Netherlands that, as concerns Lower Saxon, "the administrative divi-sion of the provinces where these languages are spoken results in an obstacle to the links between communities, especially as regards cable television".[130] With regard to precise modalities for satisfying this obligation, the Committee of Experts has looked, for example, at umbrella bodies which represent all the national minorities or other relevant groups and which play an advisory function for the authorities.[131]

---

123. See, for example, the second report on Germany, 2006, paragraph 34.
124. Hungary 2001, 25.
125. Norway 2001, 37.
126. Slovakia 2007, 55 and box recommendation thereafter, in respect of Ruthenian.
127. See, for example, Norway 2007, 70.
128. See, for example, Germany 2006, 32-3.
129. Spain 2005, 133-4 and the box recommendation thereafter.
130. The Netherlands 2001, 25.
131. Armenia 2006, 28.

3.6. Subparagraph 1f

The Committee of Experts has made clear its view that education is one of the most crucial factors in promoting an RML, especially at the pre-school, primary and secondary levels,[132] and has made reference to the particular importance of primary school in the protection and development of an RML.[133] The Explanatory Report to the Charter indicates that the arrangements for the teaching of RMLs "will obviously vary according to the level of education concerned" and that in some cases provision will need to be made for teaching "in" the RML – the reference appears to be to the use of the RML as the medium of instruction – and in others only for the teaching "of" the language – the reference appears to be to the teaching of the RML as a subject.[134] The Committee of Experts has, however, commented positively on the provision of bilingual or mother-tongue education in separate schools such as the Armenian Nareg primary schools in Cyprus.[135] The committee has been critical of attempts by a state to limit access to education through the medium of the RML to children who already have a basic knowledge of the language, on the basis that this "appears to be in contradiction with the aims of the Charter, which seeks to promote the teaching of these threatened languages".[136] Typically, numbers of speakers of RMLs have declined over a period of time and, in order for them to survive, new speakers, including those produced through the education system, are essential.

Although the committee has generally not been prescriptive with regard to the form which teaching in or of the RML should take, it has indicated on occasion where provision is inadequate. In its second report on Hungary, for example, the committee noted that the system for teaching Ruthenian was still based on only four Sunday schools and some very short summer language camps, and stated that it considered this system "to be unsatisfactory, as it requires a considerable effort on the part of the pupils and offers very limited possibilities for language development".[137] In its third report on Slovenia, the committee considered that the amount of time devoted to the existing Croatian classes – two hours per week – was "too limited to ensure the transmission of Croatian as a living language" and that teaching of Croatian was made available too late – it started in the seventh grade, "which excludes pre-school and most parts of primary education".[138] As elsewhere in its work, the committee shows here a sophisticated understanding of broader linguistic issues, in this case the

---

132. Croatia 2001, 37.
133. Germany 2002, 66.
134. Paragraph 63.
135. Cyprus 2006, 84-7.
136. Sweden 2006, 52.
137. Hungary 2004, 27.
138. Slovenia 2010, 61.

217

mechanics of language acquisition in schools, and this also illustrates the committee's concern with actual effectiveness, the real linguistic impact, of measures taken under the Charter; provision will not be satisfactory if it is not effective. As Woehrling has noted, given the goal of the Charter to increase numbers of users of an RML, teaching of an RML must be designed to permit effective and full command of the language, and a superficial introduction would not meet the requirements of this subparagraph.[139] Another point the Committee of Experts has made is the importance of continuity of provision, particularly from primary to secondary, with the result that when provision at secondary level has been abolished, the committee has been critical.[140] And on occasion, the Committee of Experts has, in the context of strongly encouraging a state to take necessary measures to develop the teaching of an RML at primary and secondary level, asked the state to consider the possibility of extending the scope of Part III protection for the language under the state's instrument of ratification to Article 8.[141]

The Committee of Experts has noted on several occasions the importance of a structured education policy, and with it the collection of relevant education data, in satisfying the obligations imposed under subparagraph 1f. In its second report on Germany, for example, the committee made the following comment: "The lack of a systematic approach to Low German teaching, as well as the lack of statistical data and adequate supervision, hampers the development of a structured education policy for Low German".[142] Where an RML is, like Low German in the Netherlands, spoken in different provinces, regions and munici-palities, the Committee of Experts has noted a lack of co-ordination between such units and the need for co-ordination.[143]

Perhaps the most recurring theme in the reports of the Committee of Experts is the shortage of qualified teachers of, and suitable teaching materials in, RMLs.[144] The importance of qualified teachers is obvious, and the committee has indicated that this must be dealt with in the teacher training system itself.[145] With regard to

---

139. Woehrling (2005), op. cit., p. 117.
140. See, for example, Germany 2006, 37, in respect of Sater Frisian.
141. See Germany 2006, box recommendation after 37.
142. Germany 2006, 36. See also the Netherlands 2001, box recommendation after 30, where reference was made to the need to adopt a "coherent strategy" for the teaching and study of a variety of RMLs.
143. The Netherlands 2004, 52.
144. See, for example, Hungary 2001, 26; Sweden 2003, 47 and 48 and the box recommendation thereafter; Norway 2003, 70; Austria 2005, 89 and box recommendation thereafter; Cyprus 2006, 98 and box recommendation thereafter; Finland 2007, 64; Norway 2007, 78, 90.
145. In Germany 2006, 36, for example, the committee noted in respect of the teaching of Low German that "the fact that Low German is not systematically included in basic and further teacher training has an adverse effect on the quality and quantity of Low German teaching".

teaching materials, this comment of the Committee of Experts is typical: "the importance of the availability of appropriate teaching materials, as a foundation of good teaching in and of the languages, has to be stressed".[146] In keeping with the theme of the importance of consultation with speakers of RMLs which is recurrent in its work, the Committee of Experts has urged the authorities to develop solutions in co-operation with the speakers of RMLs.[147] Of course, both teacher training and production of teaching materials depend on sufficient funding and technical support from both local and national governments, a point which the committee has reinforced on a number of occasions.[148]

A further barrier to the teaching of RMLs is that in many cases, the language in question has not been standardised, and is often in need of corpus planning initiatives of various sorts – corpus planning is, as we have seen, an issue which emerges under other subparagraphs of Article 7 paragraph 1 in respect of languages such as Ruthenian and, particularly, forms of Romani. The Committee of Experts has noted that standardisation of an RML is often a precondition to its inclusion in the education system, and has recognised cataloguing of varieties, standardising and codifying the language, development of grammars and so forth as important measures.[149] The committee has also mentioned the promotion of research into RMLs, for example suggesting the creation of a language board with the aim of developing and researching a language, though in this case they also encouraged the relevant government to further develop its support for education in the language, and especially to explore the possibilities of promoting the teaching of the language and relevant teacher training.[150] By the same token, the Committee of Experts has noted that a regional or minority language may have a particular character in a particular place, and it is important that this be reflected; thus, it has noted that the reference in paragraph f to providing "appropriate forms" and means for the teaching and study of regional or minority languages implies the development of an educational model "which takes the traditional character of the given language into account, for example by covering the local culture which is reflected by the language".[151]

The concept of "active offer" – a very important concept in planning for minoritised languages – has been referred to in discussion of other subparagraphs in Article 7 paragraph 1, and the need for it has been raised by the Committee of Experts in the context of this subparagraph as well. In its third report on Finland,

---

146. Hungary 2001, 26.
147. Finland 2007, 70 and box recommendation thereafter.
148. See, for example, Sweden 2003, 48, and Norway 2007, 78.
149. See, for example, Sweden 2008, 49, and Norway 2003, 72.
150. Finland 2001, 44-5 and box recommendation thereafter.
151. Slovenia 2010, 55.

for example, the committee noted that a major obstacle to teaching in or of Romani was that parents were not informed of the right for their children to be taught in it; as a result there was a lack of demand for such education.[152] As we shall see below, the Committee of Experts found commendable the Serbian practice of allowing RML classes to be set up even where there was less than the requisite level of demand, as required by relevant legislation; however, they noted that they had been informed that the authorities did not sufficiently inform pupils of this possibility, commenting: "The Committee of Experts encourages the Serbian authorities to inform pupils and parents more actively of the right to education in regional or minority languages and to encourage them to make use of it".[153] This summarises well the concept of "active offer": not only must speakers be notified of services available through RMLs but, to overcome an understandable reluctance that often exists to take advantage of such services, speakers need to be encouraged to take advantage of such services. In the education sphere, such reluctance is sometimes based on old-fashioned ideas – now thoroughly discredited by research on the cognitive and other benefits of bilingualism flowing from bilingual education – about how RML education may inhibit children's development; the Committee of Experts has noted, for example, the "urgent need" for information on bilingualism and bilingual language development among parents and educational staff at all levels of the education system.[154]

Unsurprisingly, given the comments it has made on the importance of active offer, the Committee of Experts has noted that simply because users of an RML have not asked the authorities for teaching and study of their language does not release the state from the obligation to fulfil the undertakings of the Charter.[155] This recognises the sociolinguistic reality that people generally do not request provision which they do not know exists or do not expect to be provided. However, if speakers have been given access to information on support measures available and even legislation they may rely upon, and they have informed the authorities that they need not take action, the commitment is considered to have been fulfilled.[156]

The Committee of Experts has consistently expressed concerns where instruction in the RML is not offered on the same terms as similar forms of education. In its second report on Croatia, the committee was critical of a teaching programme which took place on Saturdays, on the basis that it required extra effort from the pupils and that the schools did not offer the same buildings on

---

152. Finland 2007, 68.
153. Serbia 2009, 58; see, also, the similar formulation in Slovenia 2010, 55.
154. The Netherlands 2004, 52.
155. Finland 2001, 46, in respect of Yiddish.
156. Ibid., 46, 48.

Saturdays that were used during the week.[157] In its initial report on Spain, the committee noted that, even if teaching in schools of an RML is optional, this is not in itself contrary to the provision, on condition that the teaching is not provided in such a way that the RML is at a clear disadvantage, which is the case when, as with Aragonese and Catalan in Aragon, pupils are required to follow the class in the RML outside regular school hours, or when the teaching has no recognition in the normal curriculum[158] or, as with Asturian, when the course in the RML has to compete for students with other subjects.[159]

The Committee of Experts has taken the view that states should relax rules of general application where these would impact negatively on the provision of education in RMLs. In its initial report on Austria, for example, it encouraged the Austrian authorities to allow more flexibility regarding the regulations applying to all private schools on the minimum number of pupils required for the establishment of a class.[160] In its first report on Serbia, the committee noted that, at the beginning of each school year, a survey is carried out among pupils and parents to ascertain the demand for RML classes. Relevant education legislation requires that at least 15 pupils or parents request the establishment of such classes, though classes can be set up even where such levels of demand are not met if the minister for education approves them; the committee noted that the minister had never refused such a request and commended the authorities on what it described as an "exemplary practice".[161]

Finally, the Committee of Experts has commented at length under this subparagraph on practices, particularly in certain central and eastern European states, in the education of Roma children. In its first report on Slovakia, for example, the Committee of Experts noted that the educational authorities for the most part still pursued a "fundamentally assimilatory approach with regard to education for Roma". The authorities' main argument for doing so was that Romani-speakers themselves give priority to their children having full command of the Slovak language to have better chances at full integration. In response to this, the committee made an important statement of policy. It recalled that the Charter does not question the need to acquire command of the official language, and recognises that parents want their children to successfully integrate. They also noted, however: "integration should not be confused with assimilation and all the information at the Committee of Experts' disposal indicates that full recognition of the linguistic and cultural specificities of Roma is conducive to their

---

157. Croatia 2005, 30 and box recommendation thereafter.
158. Spain 2005, 155; see also Hungary 2004, 27, 34.
159. Spain 2005, 149.
160. Austria 2005, 85 and box recommendation thereafter.
161. Serbia 2009, 58.

successful integration in society".[162] They followed this up with some observations on the benefits of first-language teaching in school, which reveal once again that the committee has a fairly sophisticated understanding of sociolinguistics and related research:

> Furthermore, language policy experts confirm that acquiring multiple linguistic skills from a very early age, or even better as a mother-tongue bilingual speaker, enhances the child's intellectual and linguistic ability. This, however, presupposes the recognition in particular by the school authorities of such added value, which is not yet the case in Slovakia, especially as far as the Romani language is concerned. In fact, many school authorities in Slovakia tend to perceive the Romani language as an obstacle rather than an asset of linguistic and cultural richness for those who speak it.[163]

The committee concluded that the development of a curriculum for the Romani language is an essential step in ensuring that Roma children receive the sort of education that the Charter requires.[164]

The Committee of Experts also commented on the practice of effectively segregating Roma children in schools for children with educational "special needs". That practice has now been found by the European Court of Human Rights to be in violation of the European Convention on Human Rights.[165] In their first report on Slovakia, the committee found that Roma children were disproportionately placed in special needs schools solely because of their insufficient knowledge of Slovak. Once again, the committee made an important statement of policy:

> This practice infringes basic human rights, has disastrous effects on the development of the children concerned and their future integration into the society, is totally contrary to the principle of the Charter that regional and minority languages should be treated with dignity and respect, and must be stopped without delay.[166]

The committee concluded, from the information that it had at its disposal and the views that it has gathered "from language policy and Roma experts", that it was convinced "that integration of the Romany-speaking people into the Slovak society implies inclusion of teaching of and in Romany in the Slovak school system".[167]

---

162. Slovakia 2007, 57-8.
163. Ibid., 59.
164. Ibid., 60.
165. See, for example, *D.H. and Others v. the Czech Republic*, Application No. 57325/00, 13 November, 2007, the so-called "Ostrava" case, which is the leading case on these practices.
166. Slovakia 2007, 61; see, also, Hungary 2004, 49.
167. Slovakia 2007, 62; a significant box recommendation, reinforcing the foregoing points, appeared after 63.

3.7. Subparagraph 1g

The Committee of Experts has clarified that this provision applies to two different kinds of non-speakers: those who define themselves as part of the language community and those who are not part of it.[168] The first category would appear to include people who have a cultural link to the language and the language community, and may consider themselves to be members of the ethnic group with which the language is associated, but who do not speak it, because of the breakdown in "intergenerational transmission", the passing of the language by parents to the next generation in the home, which is a common feature of many RMLs.[169] The second category would probably include people living in an area where an RML is used but who do not know the language, including migrants to such areas from other parts the state or from abroad.[170] As Woehrling has pointed out, the acquisition of an RML by both categories of non-speakers is very important, as every policy to promote RMLs seeks to increase the numbers speaking them.[171] In the Explanatory Report to the Charter, it is noted that in some states the objective of the authorities is that the RML should be the language normally and generally spoken in the region, and that measures are taken to ensure that the language is known by those for whom it is not a native language. The report notes that this sort of policy is not contrary to the Charter, but that this is not the purpose of subparagraph 1g, which "seeks only to ensure greater mutual permeability between language groups".[172]

The Committee of Experts has made clear that subparagraph 1g envisages both instruction in the RML for scholars enrolled in the school system and various forms of language instruction for adults. In its first report on Slovenia, for example, the committee noted that the system of Hungarian bilingual education was offered not only to ethnic Hungarians but also to ethnic Slovenes living in the area, and this was an "excellent" way of fulfilling the obligation under this subparagraph. They also noted that students who did not belong to the Italian-speaking community were allowed to attend Italian-speaking schools, and that the curriculum for ethnic Slovenes residing in "ethnically-mixed areas" included two hours of instruction in Italian per week: "these are excellent ways for fulfilling this obligation and Slovenia must be congratulated".[173] With regard to adult learners, sometimes the committee has referred to the teaching of RMLs

---

168. Cyprus 2006, 107.
169. See Woehrling (2005), op. cit., p. 118.
170. Ibid.
171. Ibid.
172. Paragraph 66.
173. Slovenia 2004, 64-5.

in adult education or in universities,[174] signalling that these forms of education are also considered to be means of satisfying the obligation set out in this subparagraph.

3.8. Subparagraph 1h

The Committee of Experts has made the following comment about the general importance of the commitment set out in this subparagraph:

> The Committee considers the promotion of study and research to be central in the context of promoting regional or minority languages. Study and research enable proper assessment to be made of the needs of minority language speakers in order to develop the language and to plan for the provision of education and other services. The Committee notes with concern the apparent decline in study and research at a time when there is resurgence in linguistic consciousness.[175]

The teaching of RMLs at university is certainly a central aspect of the commitment set out in subparagraph 1h, and there is frequent mention by the Committee of Experts of things like the establishment of university chairs in RMLs, as well as courses in the languages, and lectures and seminars on RMLs and their related cultures.[176] Unsurprisingly, then, the committee has been critical of the failure of states to support the study of RMLs at university level and has noted some systemic problems for RMLs at university level. For example, in its third report on Sweden, the committee stated that "[t]he basic problem for all regional or minority languages in higher education is the lack of a structured policy and long-term planning", referring to the failure to fill two chairs relating to Sami and the cancellation of the teaching of Finnish at two universities.[177] They have noted that often a problem is a shortage of trained personnel capable of carrying out the relevant activities, particularly research.[178] Funding is also critical, and the Committee of Experts has commented positively where, as in Sweden, money was provided to two universities specifically to fund the introduction of courses.[179]

Research into RMLs is also crucial, and the Committee of Experts has on occasion noted the linkages between study and research at universities and other aspects of RML education policy. In this context, corpus planning is particularly

---

174. Sweden 2003, 52.

175. Germany 2002, 72, reiterated in Germany 2006, 41.

176. See, for example, Sweden 2003, 53-4; Switzerland 2004, 33; and Serbia 2009, 66.

177. Sweden 2009, 53. The problem with the courses that had been cancelled was the break-even number of students required (30-5) if the university was to offer a course; the number was considered to be too high.

178. See, for example, Norway 2007, 97.

179. Sweden 2009, 57, 59; the government provided €150 000 for courses in Romani and in Yiddish.

important, a point which is recognised in the Explanatory Report to the Charter, which stipulates that such work "is essential to the development of [RMLs] in terms of vocabulary, grammar and syntax".[180] Corpus planning has often been referred to by the committee, and the Committee of Experts has praised various types of corpus projects. One example is as an Austrian project on the codification and standardisation of the language of the Burgenland Roma, to promote the use of Romani as a written medium.[181] In its first report on Slovakia, it noted that there is considerable linguistic pluralism in Roma society, and the committee praised the Slovakian authorities for achieving the codification of a written form, which other countries had not yet achieved. The committee also noted, though, that codification efforts would be "greatly facilitated if they were supported at a European level, by co-ordinating in a European context the action that individual countries are taking".[182] In its reports on Hungary and Croatia, the Committee of Experts has noted that the Ruthenian language is confronted by some fundamental problems, like a lack of proper standardisation in the national context of both states, and that promotion of the study of and research into Ruthenian in higher education is therefore very relevant to improving the teaching of the language.[183] Establishment of a research institute to examine the languages of a state, including its RMLs, will be considered as contributing to the fulfilment of this obligation.[184] As with instruction in the language, funding for research is important; where this has been forthcoming, the committee has responded encouragingly.[185]

3.9. Subparagraph 1i

There is considerable overlap between this subparagraph and Article 14; for languages which have been designated for Part III protection, the Committee of Experts will usually deal with issues relating to transnational exchanges under the latter provision. As is often the case under paragraph 1 obligations, the Committee of Experts looks for a "structured policy" for the promotion of appropriate types of transnational exchanges,[186] although the committee has not been prescriptive as to the form which such a policy should take.

When a Part II language is spoken in different states and is in need of corpus planning initiatives, the Committee of Experts has pointed to transnational co-operation as a means of accomplishing this. The case of Ruthenian provides

---

180. Paragraph 64.
181. Austria 2005, 97.
182. Slovakia 2007, 69, with a box recommendation immediately thereafter in support.
183. See, for example, Hungary 2004, 29, and Croatia 2005, 33.
184. Finland 2001, 52, in respect of the Research Institute for the Languages of Finland.
185. Hungary 2001, 28.
186. See, for example, Serbia 2009, 69.

a good example. As noted in the context of paragraph 1g, the situation of Ruthenian, and in particular the need for corpus planning for the language, has been a feature of Committee of Experts' reports on Croatia and Hungary. In its second report on Croatia, the committee noted that there was no state in which Ruthenian was an official language, but that it was spoken in several countries of central and eastern Europe, and that in this context, co-operation between these countries could be useful in the process of fostering standardisation of the language.[187]

The Committee of Experts has also been concerned where television and radio broadcasts in a minority language are hindered by borders. In particular, it has noted in reports on Slovenia and Croatia that Italian-language radio and television broadcasting from Koper/Capodistria in Slovenia had, in the days of the former Yugoslavia, received wide coverage and reached the Italian audience in Italy (allowing it to generate advertising revenue to support the service) and Croatia but since the dissolution of Yugoslavia the channels have been deprived of relays, meaning that coverage has effectively been lost in both Italy and Croatia, with particularly serious consequences for Italian-speakers in Croatia.[188] The committee encouraged the Slovenian authorities to adopt a policy in co-operation with Italy and Croatia, aimed at promoting the broadcasting of Italian-language television in both countries,[189] and the Croatian authorities to investigate the possibilities for co-operation with Slovenia to address this issue.[190]

3.10. Paragraph 2

There are two parts to this provision: the first is a non-discrimination provision, and the second provides that special measures adopted in favour of RMLs to promote equality between their users and the rest of the population are not considered an act of discrimination. The first part of the provision overlaps considerably with non-discrimination provisions in international human rights instruments.[191] To determine whether a state has satisfied this provision, the Committee of Experts will generally look to non-discrimination and/or equality

---

187. Croatia 2005, 37. The committee had made a similar comment in its second report on Hungary, noting that co-operation between the countries of central and eastern Europe where Ruthenian is spoken "could be useful in particular with a view to fostering the process of standardisation of the language": Hungary 2004, 30.
188. See Slovenia 2004, 71-2.
189. Slovenia 2004, box recommendation after 73.
190. Croatia 2005, 34-6, and the box recommendation thereafter.
191. See Woehrling (2005), op. cit., pp. 121-2, for a summary of these provisions.

clauses in constitutional texts and human rights legislation;[192] the committee has even welcomed the adoption of government action plans for the prevention of all forms of discrimination, racism and other forms of intolerance as contributing to the achievement of this provision.[193] In some cases, such as Denmark, the Committee of Experts has noted that the domestic legal framework does not have a provision prohibiting discrimination on the specific grounds of language, but has noted the views of the domestic authorities that prohibition of discrimination on other grounds, such as a person's descent, provides adequate protection to linguistic minorities.[194]

An interesting issue has arisen under paragraph 2 in relation to the Irish language in Northern Ireland. The Administration of Justice (Language) Act 1737 regulates the use of languages in court in Northern Ireland and states that the administration of justice "shall be in the English tongue and language, and not in Latin or French or any other tongue or language whatsoever". The Committee of Experts noted that the effect of this act is a prohibition on the use of Irish in court, "and this is how it has been interpreted and implemented".[195] The Committee of Experts noted that, while the UK had made no commitment under Article 9, Judicial authorities, with respect to the use of Irish in the courts, nonetheless "ratifying Part III undertakings in relation to a regional or minority language implies a will on the part of the state to place on itself obligations to protect and promote this language, in addition to the general protection and promotion delivering from Part II of the Charter".[196] The Committee of Experts noted that, in this light, legislation which actively prohibited the use of Irish "from an important field of one of the Articles under Part II is, in the view of the Committee of Experts, contrary to the spirit and objectives of the Charter and the general commitment of the UK authorities to protect and promote Irish", and as a result the committee decided to deal with the issue under Article 7 paragraph 2. It noted in its second report that it had encouraged the UK authorities to remove this obstacle to the use of Irish, a position which it reinforced in its third report.[197]

The Committee of Experts also uses this provision to examine possible inequities in the treatment of different regional or minority languages. In its third report on the UK, the committee noted that, since 2004, applicants for citizenship in the UK could take their citizenship test in English, Welsh or Scottish

---

192. See, for example: Hungary 2001, 30; Croatia 2001, 41; Finland 2001, 57; Switzerland 2001, 50; Norway 2001, 51; Germany 2002, 76; Austria 2005, 99; Armenia 2006, 38; Cyprus 2006, 115; Serbia 2009, 70.
193. See Slovakia 2009, 45.
194. Denmark 2004, 43.
195. United Kingdom 2010, 117.
196. Ibid., 119.
197. Ibid., 120-1.

Gaelic, but not in Irish. It noted that, since 2007, this had been extended to applications for residence. The committee noted that the UK authorities were unable to explain "why this distinction between Part III languages exists" – implying, perhaps, that such a distinction between Part III and Part II languages might be justifiable – concluding that the committee could not "see how this restriction is justified".[198]

With regard to the second part of this paragraph, in its third report on the UK, the Committee of Experts noted that it had been informed about several instances, "especially within local councils where it was decided not to promote or use the Irish language within their services", on the grounds that it would contravene a provision of the Northern Ireland Act, the legislation which created the devolved institutions in Northern Ireland, which states that public authorities "should take due regard of the need to promote equality of opportunity, among others between persons of different religious belief or political opinion". The committee emphasised that paragraph 2 states that the adoption of special measures in favour of RMLs aimed at promoting equality between the users of such languages and the rest of the population or which take due account of their specific conditions is not considered to be an act of discrimination against the users of more widely-used languages.[199]

Finally, as is noted in the Explanatory Report to the Charter, measures laid down in a state in favour of the use of national or official languages do not constitute discrimination against RMLs solely because these same measures are not taken for the benefit of RMLs; however, the report also notes that such measures in support of national or official languages "must not constitute an obstacle to the maintenance or development of the regional or minority languages".[200] In its first report on Slovakia, for example, the Committee of Experts found a number of instances in which the State Language Act expressly imposed the use of Slovak, and therefore had the effect of discouraging the use of RMLs in the relevant areas, and stated that a modification of the language law was necessary to bring it into conformity with the obligations under the Charter.[201]

3.11. Paragraph 3

It has now become commonplace for the Committee of Experts to preface its comments with respect to Article 7 paragraph 3 with the following comment, or a comment having very similar content to this:

---

198. Ibid., 122.
199. Ibid., 123.
200. Paragraph 72.
201. Slovakia 2007, 76, and the box recommendation immediately thereafter.

The Committee of Experts recalls that the extent to which a minority language is protected or promoted is, in many respects, a reflection of the majority language speakers' approach and perception and that awareness-raising within the majority is therefore of the utmost importance. As this provision indicates, education and the media are especially relevant in this respect.[202]

In some recent reports, the Committee of Experts has gone on to emphasise that the purpose of the obligation is not just knowledge of the existence of the regional or minority languages in one's country, but also "understanding and tolerance in relation to these languages and their speakers".[203] In some cases, the committee has stressed that such awareness-raising "requires constant efforts in both the educational and the media field".[204] The committee has emphasised that such promotion must be directed at the general public, and not simply the wider public living in the regions associated with users of RMLs.[205] In its second report on Spain, for example, the Committee of Experts noted that they had received evidence that the general state administration had become "more positive as regards the plurilingual nature of the country" since its first report, and in this regard they noted "several important steps forward", such as the conclusion of bilateral agreements with the European institutions (i.e. EU institutions) to ensure the right to use the various co-official languages in Spain before European bodies, and the amendment of the Spanish Senate's Rules of Procedure in 2005 to allow the gradual introduction of co-official languages in parliamentary debates.[206] The committee noted, however, that it was

> still necessary to convey to the general population the cultural value of this pluri-lingualism as the exclusively Castilian-speaking population living in autonomous regions with no co-official language tend to see it more as a problem to be over-come than as an indication of cultural wealth to be fostered.[207]

Illustrating again its sound understanding of sociolinguistic realities, the committee has noted, in the context of a consideration of Roma, for example, that there is a link between how an RML and its community of speakers are viewed and the self-esteem of its speakers, and that low self-esteem may itself be a barrier to full integration.[208] The committee has noted that two sets of measures are generally envisaged here:

---

202. Spain 2005, 182; see also, for example, Switzerland 2004, 38; Slovenia 2004, 76; Croatia 2005, 39; Sweden 2006, 63; Slovakia 2007, 77; and Serbia 2009, 74.
203. Slovenia 2010, 70; Ukraine 2010, 131.
204. Slovakia 2007, 81.
205. Cyprus 2006, 119 and the box recommendation at end of the section.
206. Spain 2008, 194.
207. Ibid., 195.
208. Slovakia 2007, 83.

(a) the inclusion of elements of the culture expressed by the regional or minority languages spoken in [the State] in the general curriculum for ... pupils [of that State], as an integral part of [the State's] cultural heritage;

(b) measures aimed at encouraging the media to eliminate stigmatising approaches toward the members of the [linguistic minority] community.[209]

With regard to education, from its earliest reports the Committee of Experts has provided examples of the sorts of positive measure which could be taken under this paragraph, such as "informing the whole population of the existence and value of the regional or minority languages and the inclusion in the national curricula of the culture and history of the users of these languages".[210] In some reports, the Committee of Experts has referred to the extent to which the presence of RMLs in the state, in its history and its traditional (or autochthonous) character are explained in the curriculum for children speaking the majority language living in other parts of the country.[211] Where the curriculum does not contain explanations for the majority language community as to why RMLs are traditionally present in the state and are therefore just as "at home" as the majority, the committee has been critical.[212]

The Committee of Experts has therefore commented favourably where legislation and government policy requires that scholars learn the history of a country's national minorities, their culture, language and religion, and where the curriculum and the school syllabi have been revised accordingly.[213] It has welcomed the intention to introduce a multi-ethnic manual for primary and secondary schools which would include elements from the history, geography, tradition, folklore and culture of different national minorities living in the state.[214] In its initial report on Slovenia, the committee noted that pupils from the Slovenian-speaking majority population were able to demonstrate a good awareness of most of the RMLs spoken in Slovenia, and that teaching tools such as the use of bilingual place names on maps of Slovenia used in classes could be considered to be model practice.[215] They also noted, however, that it was unclear if and how the autochthonous character of RMLs spoken in Slovenia is explained to Slovenian-speaking pupils across the country – thereby emphasising the importance of such material in the national curriculum and not simply in the

---

209. Croatia 2005, 45.
210. Croatia 2001, 42; for a recent report which uses precisely this formulation, Ukraine 2010, 130.
211. Spain 2005, 186.
212. See, for example, Slovakia 2007, 81.
213. See, for example, Sweden 2003, 59.
214. See, for example, Serbia 2009, 74.
215. Slovenia 2004, 78.

regions in which RMLs may be found – and encouraged the authorities to address this issue.[216] The committee also commended a pilot project in Norway in which young Sami visit secondary schools throughout the country to raise awareness of Sami culture and identity among other pupils, noting that the project was "successful and has had a positive impact", and they encouraged the authorities to pursue the project over a longer term, and to consider extending it to other RMLs.[217]

The Committee of Experts has, however, been critical in cases where legislation and policies which aim at inclusion of reference to RMLs in the curriculum were not being implemented, and in one case pointed to a range of factors which were responsible for poor implementation:

> There is a lack of adequate teaching materials, which is a view shared by the authorities: regional or minority languages receive only marginal attention or are stereotypically described in mainstream teaching materials at primary and secondary school level. The history and culture reflected by regional or minority languages is also absent from teacher training.[218]

These point to structural weaknesses underlying positive curriculum developments, and although the committee did not make reference to the need for a strategic approach – a common theme in its approach to many of the Article 7 commitments – such an approach is clearly implied by these comments.

The media clearly also have a role to play, though it has been noted that states generally do not have the same direct control over the media, particularly print media, as they have over the curriculum, and therefore can often only encourage.[219] However, as the Explanatory Report to the Charter notes, encouragement of the mass media to pursue aims such as the development of a spirit of tolerance towards RMLs and their users is not considered to constitute illegitimate state influence, and concepts such as respect for human rights, tolerance of minorities and avoidance of incitement to hatred "are the kinds of objective which most European states do not hesitate to impose as obligations upon the media".[220] Thus, the Committee of Experts has commended Sweden on the fact that the licences of its public sector broadcasters prescribe that they must take into account the needs of minority languages and ethnic minorities, and that there were programmes about minority language groups.[221] Similarly, it has noted with apparent approval that the broadcasting programming principles

---

216. Ibid., 79.
217. Norway 2007, 110.
218. Sweden 2006, 66.
219. See Woehrling (2005), op. cit., p. 127.
220. Paragraph 74.
221. Sweden 2003, 60.

embodied in various broadcasting acts and state treaties explicitly lay down that programmes should help to reduce xenophobia and to achieve protection and promotion of minorities. The Committee of Experts has also noted that awareness of regional or minority languages should be raised as a component "and as an expected result" of mainstream journalist training.[222]

The Committee of Experts has expressed concern on occasion about the potential negative impact on mutual understanding between linguistic groups of stereotyping in ways that perpetuate the image among the majority that speakers of RMLs are "backward",[223] and also about negative statements by politicians.[224] In its initial report on Spain, for example, the committee expressed concern about complaints that it had heard that promoters of the Basque language can suffer from stigmatisation, and of being accused of supporting terrorism because of their commitment to the Basque language and culture. The committee concluded that efforts are needed "with a view to giving full legitimacy, both in the Spanish society and within the two autonomous communities concerned, to the protection and promotion of the Basque language when this is clearly independent from any form of political violence or terrorism".[225] In its third report on the UK, the Committee of Experts noted that it had gained the impression that, in Northern Ireland, the climate had worsened since the previous monitoring round and that, according to representatives of Irish-speakers, debates in the Northern Ireland Assembly and public statements of some ministers had been "polemic, negative, if not hostile towards the Irish language", mentioning that a member of the assembly had put forward a motion in 2007 to prohibit the use of the language in Assembly debates. The committee concluded that such actions and statements were, in its view, "adverse to the aim of creating mutual understanding, respect and tolerance towards the speakers of regional or minority languages in Northern Ireland", and emphasised "that it is important to refrain from making any of the languages a playing field for party politics".[226]

3.12. Paragraph 4

The Committee of Experts has on occasion discussed the nature of this paragraph and has noted that its general purpose is to "develop an understanding for language plurality within the State", and that development of this spirit of tolerance and receptiveness through the education system and the media "would

---

222. Slovenia 2010, 76.
223. See, for example, Switzerland 2008, 49.
224. Austria 2005, 102, in reference to statements made by the Minister-President of Carinthia about a constitutional court ruling on minority language signage.
225. Spain 2005, 188.
226. United Kingdom 2010, 127.

be an important factor in the preservation of regional or minority languages".[227] Since the Charter came into force, both the Committee of Experts and members of the Charter's Secretariat have frequently noted that the Charter's monitoring process is meant to establish a three-way dialogue, involving the state, the users of RMLs and the Council of Europe, and as we have seen, the need for states to consult users of RMLs has become an important theme in the implementation of many provisions in Article 7, and as other chapters in this book will demonstrate, in implementation of the Charter as a whole.

Thus, unsurprisingly, the Committee of Experts has noted that Article 7 paragraph 4 is "of great importance in creating, maintaining and enhancing a constructive dialogue between the authorities ... and the speakers" of RMLs. The Committee of Experts has implied the desirability of such consultations taking place at the time of the ratification of the Charter itself, as well as when legislation on the use of RMLs is being adopted[228] and when periodical reports are being prepared.[229] They have also noted that it requires the authorities to consult representatives of RMLs when minority language policy is being determined.[230] While this latter position is certainly an understandable and wholly appropriate one, it could be argued that it is also an excessively narrow one which fails to capture the paragraph's full potential. In particular, paragraph 4 refers to the establishment of bodies for the purpose of advising the authorities "on all matters pertaining to" RMLs whereas the Committee of Experts referred only to "minority language policy". While minority language policy clearly impacts on RMLs, as is discussed elsewhere in this chapter, including in its concluding section, there are a great many other policy areas, such as economic and social development policy, regional development policy and so forth, which can also have an impact on communities in which users of RMLs live, and on the use and vitality of RMLs in such communities. Certainly, the indirect impact of such policy development on RMLs should be considered and where possible anticipated, and bodies which satisfy the requirements of paragraph 4 should certainly advise on such matters as well.

There are essentially two aspects to paragraph 4. The first is the requirement that the authorities take into consideration the needs and wishes expressed by users of RMLs when the authorities determine policies with regard to RMLs. The second relates to one way in which the authorities can do so, through the establishment of bodies to advise the authorities on all matters relating to RMLs. With regard to consultation, the Committee of Experts has noted its satisfaction

---

227. Denmark 2004, 44.
228. Croatia 2001, 43.
229. Finland 2001, 60.
230. Austria 2005, 103.

when it has found that non-governmental organisations (NGOs) representing language groups are consulted.[231] In its first report on Sweden, the committee noted that, before ratification, Sweden had established a special Minority Language Committee to look at the situation of languages in Sweden and to evaluate how the Charter could be ratified, and, after it had presented its conclusions, special conferences were organised with participation of representatives of regional or minority languages, which "have been occasions for them to express their needs and wishes". The committee concluded that it "considers this way of finding out the real needs of the minority language speakers to be a good practice, provided such contacts are regular and rigorous",[232] thereby giving a good idea of what the committee has in mind. In its first report on Norway, the Committee of Experts noted the following:

> Associations and bodies to further the Sami language and culture have been consulted in the policy making of the Norwegian authorities. They were made aware of the ratification of the Charter and were also consulted when the authorities drafted the initial periodical report.[233]

In its second report, the committee noted that

> [a]ssociations and bodies to further the Sami language and culture have been consulted during the policy-making process of the Norwegian authorities. They were made aware of the ratification of the Charter and were also consulted when the authorities drafted the initial periodical report.[234]

With regard to the second aspect of paragraph 4, the Committee of Experts has indicated that the lack of an umbrella organisation for users of an RML makes it difficult for the authorities to maintain dialogue with users of an RML.[235] Where no such organisation exists, the committee has not always been too prescriptive about the precise nature of the organisation which is anticipated: in its second report on Switzerland, it referred simply to "a permanent framework, actively involving speakers themselves".[236] It has, however, discussed such bodies, for example the Council of the Government of the Slovak Republic for National Minorities and Ethnic Groups, which is a self-governing authority of the national minorities,[237] in relation to which the committee made this statement of general principle:

---

231. See, for example, the Netherlands 2001, 48.
232. Sweden 2003, 61.
233. Norway 2001, 53.
234. Norway 2003, 83.
235. Germany 2002, 80.
236. Switzerland 2004, 49.
237. Slovakia 2007, 85.

The Committee of Experts considers that the role of the said Council and the method of appointment of its members, who are nominated by the regional or minority language groups themselves, fulfils in principle the requirements of the present obligation.[238]

The Committee of Experts has also referred to provisions in the constitution of the state which give members of certain minorities the right to elect a representative to the national legislature, suggesting that this may be an acceptable modality for satisfying the requirements of the paragraph.[239] Thus, the committee has noted that it is impressed by the Hungarian system of minority self-government:

> The whole system of minority self-governments created by Hungarian legislation during the last decade secures participation of the minorities in the formulation of minority-related policies. These self-governments have the possibility to take over responsibilities in education and culture from the local and central governments, and could thus decide on their own administrative policies. Moreover, also in the other fields that remain in the competence of municipalities or the State, the legal framework guarantees a far-reaching participation of the representatives of the minorities in determining the policies with regard to the minorities.[240]

Similarly, in its first report on Serbia, the committee was of the view that the national minority councils created pursuant to the constitution and elected by persons belonging to national minorities to exercise self-governance in culture, education, information and official use of the language and script "represent a particularly appropriate way of taking into consideration the needs and wishes expressed by the groups which use regional or minority languages", and they encouraged Serbia to establish a stable legal basis for their functioning. From these comments, a number of features emerge, including the fact that the bodies are representative in some sort – usually, elected by members of a national minority – that they have some formal basis in law – usually in legislation, sometimes even in a constitution – and that they can have some formal decision-making power. Significantly, perhaps, they are not necessarily bodies representing users of RMLs, but minorities or national minorities. However, in some reports, notably on the United Kingdom, the Committee of Experts has discussed rather different sorts of bodies, such as government-appointed language boards: in addition to being more closely focused on the relevant RMLs, they are also technical language planning bodies; but, as they are appointed by the authorities, they could not necessarily be said to be representative of users of RMLs in the same way that, say, the Hungarian minority self-governments are. There

---

238. Ibid., 87.
239. Cyprus 2006, 123.
240. Hungary 2001, 32.

is, in fact, an important distinction between these two types of groups, and the extent to which one or the other sort is necessary for the satisfaction of paragraph 4 – and, given the content of the paragraph, it may be that both types of bodies are needed – needs further clarification.

3.13. Paragraph 5

In the Explanatory Report to the Charter, the languages of the Roma and also Yiddish are given as examples of "non-territorial languages" and any comments which have been made by the Committee of Experts on paragraph 5 – and in very many reports, few if any comments are made, presumably because no "non-territorial languages" have been found to be present in the state – have overwhelmingly been in respect of Roma languages. In several reports, the Committee of Experts has commented at considerable length about the general situation of the Roma population of the state, and how both this and present state policies towards the Roma, both in respect of language and more generally, have affected the language. Thus, in its first report on Hungary, the committee discussed the general demographic position of the Roma in Hungary and considered the state of the Romani language, noting an estimate that only about 30% of Roma spoke it. They then commented that there had been "practically no efforts to upgrade the standing of the two Roma/Gypsy languages in public life", and that there were few educational programmes fostering the linguistic capabilities of Roma children in the language of their families. They noted that this was "undoubtedly due to traditional conceptions of anti-discrimination policy as entailing assimilation and past efforts to free the Roma population from its marginal status". Thus, for a long time, integration was actually aimed at assimilation of Roma into the wider population. The committee noted that such an approach had been "only partly successful", because much discrimination and social exclusion still existed, but it had also deprived the majority of Roma of their traditional culture and language "without becoming really integrated". They therefore concluded:

> Under Article 7.5 of the Charter, the Republic of Hungary should pay primary attention to the problem and should take measures to preserve the languages of the Roma/Gypsy population, without endangering the important goal of putting an end to the marginalisation and social discrimination that have traditionally plagued members of this community. The measures to be developed could include intensified efforts in Romani and Beás language planning and an attempt to draw up a viable model of bilingual education for children of Roma/Gypsy background. The aim should be at the same time to preserve the language and cultural identity of the community and to enhance the social integration of its members into Hungarian society.[241]

---

241. Ibid., 34. These comments were repeated in a box recommendation that followed this paragraph.

236

The committee followed up on these themes in its second report on Hungary, and emphasised many of the points of principle it had made in its first report, particularly the notion that full integration involves full participation in the economic, social and political life of the state, as well as the preservation of one's linguistic and cultural identity. In its reports on other states with significant Roma populations, similarly detailed and wide-ranging discussion of the Roma situation, linguistic and more generally, has taken place, and similar themes and policy positions with regard to the nature of integration required under the Charter, and the nature of particular programmes, such as greater use of mother-tongue education, have emerged.[242]

Finally, but significantly, Croatia made a reservation to this paragraph when ratifying the Charter, which raises the issue of the legality and propriety of such a reservation. The Charter seems clearly to contemplate the possibility of such a reservation, because Article 21 paragraph 1 permits a state to "make one or more reservations to paragraphs 2 to 5 of this Charter".[243] Woehrling argues that the possibility of formulating a reservation to paragraph 5 "is justified by the very delicate situation which may exist in some states where many languages are used that have no specific territorial link".[244] However, he notes that allowing reservations to the other paragraphs seems "surprising", noting that, given the fundamental importance of these provisions – he views them as "forming part of the basic undertakings of any state which seeks to develop an effective policy of protecting regional or minority languages in the spirit of the charter" – any reservation in respect of them would seem inconsistent with accomplishing the fundamental aims of the Charter itself. Thus he suggests that, in spite of the formal provisions of Article 21, "reservations which exclude these paragraphs entirely from the undertakings of an acceding state will therefore be incompatible with genuine acceptance of the charter", and Article 21 "should be regarded as envisaging only partial reservations affecting some of the provisions of paragraphs 2 to 5 of Article 7".[245]

I agree with this analysis, but would argue that a blanket reservation in respect of paragraph 5 would be equally "surprising". I would consequently suggest that the possibility of formulating a complete reservation in respect of paragraph 5 is not justified. At paragraph 135 of the Explanatory Report to the Charter, the ad hoc committee (CAHLR: Comité ad hoc langues régionales) considered that contracting states should not be able to make reservations with regard to Article 7 paragraph 1, since this paragraph contains objectives and

---

242. See, for example, Slovenia 2004, 83-91.
243. Article 21 paragraph 1 permits no other reservations in respect of Charter obligations.
244. Woehrling (2005), op. cit., p. 266.
245. Ibid., and note 471, p. 271.

principles. However, a blanket reservation in respect of Article 7 paragraph 5 would have precisely that effect for non-territorial languages. This would mean that there is a category of languages, "non-territorial languages", which are specifically recognised under the Charter and whose only means of protection is under Article 7 paragraph 5, but whose protection could, by virtue of a blanket reservation, be completely eviscerated. Given that these are among the most vulnerable of all the languages protected by the treaty, an interpretation that would permit their complete exclusion from the Charter's protection seems absurd. Upon closer inspection, one could argue that Article 21 paragraph 1 is somewhat ambiguous. It provides, as noted, that a state may make "one or more reservations to paragraphs 2 to 5" and a reservation "to" a paragraph could be understood to permit a blanket reservation in respect of that paragraph, but it could also be understood to permit a partial reservation in respect of a paragraph. Given that Article 31 paragraph 1 of the 1969 Vienna Convention on the Law of Treaties requires that treaties be interpreted in good faith, in the light of their object and purpose, and given the object and purpose of the Charter, it is suggested that Article 21 paragraph 1 of the Charter be interpreted, as Woehrling suggests, in a manner which does not permit a blanket reservation; such a reading would also be consistent with the fundamental legal principle that a provision should not be interpreted in a manner which allows an absurd result if another interpretation which avoids such a result is possible.

It should be noted that Croatia's reservation may be challenged on the basis that some of the languages to which the reservation would apply are not in fact "non-territorial" languages but are rather regional or minority languages.[246] In their first state report, the Croatian authorities considered Romani, Hebrew and German to be non-territorial languages. Representatives of the speakers of Romani and German have argued that they are not non-territorial languages because these languages have a traditional territorial base in Croatia. With regard to Romani, the Committee of Experts has encouraged Croatia to withdraw its reservation.[247] In the absence of a response from the Croatian authorities, the Committee of Experts subsequently concluded that the reservation does not apply to languages which, like Romani in Croatia, have a traditional presence in definable areas, and in light of the fact that Roma are a recognised national minority in Croatia and are therefore afforded a certain degree of protection, including in respect of their language, the committee invited the Croatian authorities to consider applying Part II of the Charter to the Roma languages.[248]

---

246. See a similar conclusion in D. Rein (2011), "Artikel 21" in *Handkommentar zur Europäischen Charta der Regional- oder Minderheitensprachen*, Zurich.
247. Croatia 2005, 14.
248. Croatia 2010, 85-6.

Although the Committee of Experts has not yet addressed the issue of whether the Croatian reservation wrongly excludes German from the scope of application of the Charter, it has encouraged the Croatian authorities to "strengthen efforts to promote" it and the other non-territorial languages.[249] While it is most welcome that the Committee of Experts is willing to consider whether a language is a non-territorial language and effectively to reclassify it as a regional or minority language where it finds objective evidence of a traditional presence in definable areas, it is to be hoped that they will clarify that Article 21 paragraph 1 only permits partial reservations to any of paragraphs 2 to 5 of Article 7, and will not permit a reservation that would frustrate in a fundamental way the object and purpose of the Charter.

4. Good practice

From the foregoing, it is clear that a number of good practices are emerging from the scrutiny that has been conducted by the Committee of Experts. Consultation with speakers of RMLs is specifically provided for in Article 7 paragraph 4; however, the importance of consultation has been highlighted by the Committee of Experts in relation to several other Article 7 provisions, such as in the determination of administrative divisions, and even in threshold issues such as the determination of whether an RML exists. Consultation on all aspects of policy, legislation and practice seems to be assuming almost the status of an unwritten quasi-constitutional principle or convention under the Charter.

Another principle which is almost assuming the status of an unwritten convention is the Committee of Experts' reluctance to use fixed percentages as thresholds for determining levels of provision of services through an RML. Any rule which may arbitrarily exclude a significant number and/or concentration of users of an RML from benefiting from services in that RML will be viewed with suspicion.

The Committee of Experts has also made reference to the need for reliable data, and in particular information about numbers of users and their geographic concentrations. This is an important development, and a crucial consideration in the development and assessment of policy with regard to RMLs. Article 7 paragraph 1 requires states to base their policies, legislation and practice on a variety of objectives and principles, but according to the "situation" of each language. As noted earlier in this chapter, it is likely that the "situation" of an RML concerns its sociolinguistic and in particular its demographic situation, and an understanding of that situation requires reliable data.

---

249. Croatia 2001, 46.

While not requiring the enactment of legislation, the Committee of Experts has also made clear, in the context of several subparagraphs of Article 7 paragraph 1, that a "legal framework" of some kind is highly desirable, and although that phrase does not necessarily mean legislation, in the form of a language act or other relevant legislation, such legislation could clearly constitute a "legal framework". And while the conferral of official status in relevant regional political institutions is not necessary in order to achieve recognition under subparagraph 1a of RMLs as an expression of cultural wealth, the Committee of Experts has made clear that such recognition represents the highest form of recognition possible.

In a number of provisions, most notably subparagraphs 1c and 1d, the Committee of Experts are often looking for evidence of a "structured approach", which will typically involve a strategy of some sort. And, in determining whether action is "resolute" within the meaning of subparagraph 1c, the Committee of Experts now generally considers three factors: whether a "legal framework" for the promotion of the languages has been created, whether bodies have been established which have responsibility in this field and whether "adequate financial resources" have been provided for the task. In respect of subparagraph 1c and several other subparagraphs, including those which deal with the teaching of RMLs, the committee will now generally consider not only whether states are fulfilling their undertakings, but whether they are creating the conditions necessary to fulfil undertakings. In the educational sphere, for example, the committee is increasingly considering whether sufficient resources are being directed to the task, whether sufficient numbers of teachers are being trained, whether other support materials are being created and whether necessary corpus planning steps like linguistic standardisation, terminological development and so forth are taking place. Generally, the Committee of Expertise is scrutinising not only legislation and policy, but also implementation; its overarching concern is with actual effectiveness of delivery.

Effectiveness of delivery of services via the medium of an RML also depends on the degree to which users know that the possibility of receiving such services exists, and are confident that by opting for such services, they will not be in any way disadvantaged. Ensuring that users of RMLs know what is available to them and are encouraged to use such services is known as "active offer", and this concept too appears to be taking on for the Committee of Experts the status of an unwritten but profoundly important convention.

Another important development is that the Committee of Experts is beginning to take advantage of the breadth of the provisions of paragraph 1, particularly provisions such as subparagraphs 1c and 1d, to consider wider policy areas, where such policy areas can have a profound, albeit indirect, impact on the state of an RML.

In relation to subparagraph 1d, which is particularly important, the Committee of Experts has made clear that "public life" is a very broad term but one that certainly includes all areas dealt with in Part III of the Charter. They have given particular attention to the use of RMLs in health care, particularly with older patients, for whom the ability to receive service in their RML is particularly important. They have also used this provision to scrutinise broadcasting; although they have referred to the importance of "varied and extensive television broadcasting for the maintenance and promotion" of RMLs and have been critical of very minimal amounts of broadcast time, it is unclear how far standards have been applied consistently to different languages and their treatment by different states. One positive development is that the committee has used the inherent flexibility created by the rather general nature of paragraph 1 provisions to address issues relating to new media forms, something less easily scrutinised in the context of the more precise and arguably somewhat static commitments of Part III.

5. Conclusions

The Charter is still a relatively young instrument, and the Committee of Experts is only at an early stage in its work. The committee has already done a significant amount of good work in enriching our understanding of the scope and meaning of the Charter's provisions, and this is certainly true in respect of Article 7. However, their work is difficult, for a variety of reasons. First, it is by its very nature reactive: the Committee of Experts is responding to information which is put before it. They have to react to particular issues in the context of particular states and particular languages, and this does not lend itself easily to broad comparative analyses of trends across a variety of states and languages. Second, the work of the Committee of Experts is not that of either a court of law or an academic think-tank. They are required to interact with states and representatives of language communities and enter into an ongoing tripartite dialogue. Their findings must, of necessity, be tempered by what is possible, rather than what is ideal. Both these considerations work against a slavish consistency.

By the same token, considerations of effectiveness argue for some coherence and those of fairness argue for some degree, at least, of consistency. Furthermore, the Committee of Experts has, as we have seen, sought to create some general principles to guide the application of various provisions in Article 7; where they have done so, there is, one would think, a good argument for such principles to be followed.

So, for example, in our consideration of Article 7 paragraph 1a we have seen that the Committee of Experts has accepted a wide range of acts as constituting "recognition" of RMLs as an expression of cultural wealth, ranging from constitutional guarantees and legislation to policy pronouncements and ratification of the Charter itself. However, it is not so clear why one such act constitutes an acceptable form of recognition in one context and another type of act constitutes an acceptable form of recognition in another. The same comment could be made in respect of what constitutes "resolute" action to promote RMLs under Article 7 paragraph 1c. As we have seen, the types of activity which have been found to be "resolute" action are diverse, and once again it is not clear why one sort of activity constitutes "resolute" action in one set of circumstances and another quite different, and arguably more limited sort of activity represents "resolute" action in another. With respect to Article 7 paragraph 1d, we have seen that the Committee of Experts has taken a broad and expansive interpretation of what constitutes "public life", and that there is considerable overlap with Part III obligations. As with those Part III obligations, though, the question arises whether standards are being applied consistently between different languages and across different states. Again, slavish consistency is neither possible nor desirable. However, I suggest that some broad consistency of approach here is desirable.

And what of the potential of Article 7, which was discussed at the beginning of this chapter? First, I believe that Article 7 has the scope to allow for an assessment by the Committee of Experts of the overall impact of state policy, legislation and practice on RMLs. I believe that subparagraph 1c, which requires states to base their policies, legislation and practice on the need for "resolute" action, is particularly relevant. The question which could be asked is this: to what extent are the policies, legislation and practices being employed by the state in respect of an RML actually safeguarding them? Even where Article 7 and Part III commitments are being implemented, are the policies, legislation and practices being put in place actually having an effect?

Second, against such an assessment of actual effectiveness, there is a question whether the overall strategy of a state with regard to its RMLs – as indicated by the mix of policies, legislation and practices that it has put in place – can be considered. Once again, provisions like Article 7 subparagraphs 1c and 1d can easily provide a platform for this sort of holistic analysis of the overall policy mix. As noted, the Committee of Experts is now looking, in respect of these and other Article 7 provisions, for evidence of a "structured approach" and a strategy; however, once such an approach or strategy has been identified, there has tended not to be serious consideration whether such an approach or strategy is adequate to the task of minority language maintenance at hand. In this context, the Committee of Experts could make reference to other considerations, such as the insights provided by a growing literature on minority language maintenance, reversing language shift and so forth. While a proper theory of reversing language shift has not yet emerged, there is now a range of hypotheses and considerable experience of what works – and, as importantly, what is not likely to work. As has been noted in this chapter, the Committee of Experts has shown in a variety of areas a quite sophisticated understanding of sociolinguistics, and it therefore should be able to engage in a much more intensive scrutiny of the actual quality of any strategy that is in place for an RML. In order to do so, however, the committee will generally need much more information than it currently has at its disposal. While it has, as noted, highlighted the need for good data, it is not clear that even the data which the committee has sought are sufficiently detailed to support the sort of close analysis of the coherence of policy that is being suggested here.

Third, as noted, there are many policy areas not directly concerned with minority language policy, which may appear to be quite irrelevant to minority language maintenance but which can have a profound impact. Clear examples are economic development policy, regional development policy, rural development policy, transport policy, social policy, health policy and so forth. The discipline of language planning has shown us that economic development policy can have a profound effect on the health of an RML. One of the ironies of government policy for the Irish Gaeltacht, for example – these are the fragile rural enclaves, primarily on Ireland's west coast, in which Irish is still widely spoken – was that the effort to preserve those communities by creating employment in some cases actually did considerable damage to the language because, where it succeeded, it tended to bring a non-Irish-speaking managerial class, non-Irish-speaking job seekers and Irish-speaking returnees accompanied by non-Irish-speaking families to the Gaeltacht. When it comes to RMLs, all policy areas which impinge on users of the language must be sensitive to linguistic issues and the linguistic implications of policy development, and only Article 7 has the breadth to allow this much more wide-ranging assessment to take place. Once again, the Committee of Experts has demonstrated that it has the sort of sophisticated understanding of sociolinguistics that is necessary for this sort of analysis, and as we have seen, has already begun considering impacts of wider policy on language policy. It is now, perhaps, time for the Committee of Experts to be somewhat more robust and energetic in exploring these issues.

References

Cooper, Robert (1989), *Language planning and social change*. Cambridge: Cambridge University Press.

Dunbar, Robert (2008), "Definitively interpreting the Charter: the legal challenges" in Robert Dunbar, Gwynedd Parry and Simone Klinge (eds), *The European Charter for Regional or Minority Languages: legal challenges and opportunities*. Strasbourg: Council of Europe Publishing.

Dunbar, Robert, Parry, Gwynedd and Klinge, Simone (eds) (2008), *The European Charter for Regional or Minority Languages: legal challenges and opportunities*. Strasbourg: Council of Europe Publishing.

Fishman, Joshua A. (1991), *Reversing language shift: theoretical and empirical foundations of assistance to threatened languages*. Clevedon: Multilingual Matters.

Fishman, Joshua A., Cooper, Robert L. and Ma, Roxana (1971), *Bilingualism in the barrio*. Bloomington, IN: Research Center for the Language Sciences, Indiana University.

Grin, François (2003), *Language policy evaluation and the European Charter for Regional or Minority Languages*. Basingstoke: Palgrave Macmillan.

Moring, Tom and Dunbar, Robert (2008), *The European Charter for Regional or Minority Languages and the Media*, Regional or Minority Languages No. 6. Strasbourg: Council of Europe.

Rein, Detlev (2011), "Artikel 21" in *Handkommentar zur Europäischen Charta der Regional- oder Minderheitensprachen*. Zürich: Dike.

Spolsky, Bernard (2004), *Language policy*. Cambridge: Cambridge University Press.

Welsh Language Board (2000), *The Welsh language: a vision and a mission for 2000-2005*. Cardiff: Welsh Language Board.

Woehrling, Jean-Marie (2005), *The European Charter for Regional or Minority Languages: a critical commentary*. Strasbourg: Council of Europe Publishing.

**Part III
Measures to promote the use of regional
or minority languages in public life**

Article 8.1. Education (I)

Alba Nogueira López
University of Santiago de Compostela

1. Education as a crucial factor in the protection and promotion of regional or minority languages (RMLs)

2. General considerations on the implementation of Article 8.1

3. Scope and assumptions regarding the protection of languages in the education field in the territories in which they are traditionally spoken

4. Undertakings under Article 8.1
   4.1. Education in regional or minority languages (8.1a.i, b.i, c.i, d.i, e.i, f.i)
   4.2. Offer of a substantial part of education in regional or minority languages (8.1a.ii, b.ii, c.ii, d.ii)
   4.3. The teaching of regional or minority languages as an integral part of the curriculum (b.iii, c.iii, d.iii, f.ii)
   4.4. Language teaching if there is sufficient demand (8.1a.iii, b.iv, c.iv, d.iv)
   4.5. Protection of languages when the state has no direct competence in organising the educational stage in question (8.1a.iv, e.ii, f.iii)
   4.6. Teaching of history and culture (8.1g)
   4.7. Teacher training (8.1h)
   4.8. Supervision and evaluation bodies

5. Problems of consistency regarding the undertakings entered into
   5.1. Lack of continuity in undertakings for different educational levels
   5.2. Lack of precision and consistency in the undertakings entered into

6. Prejudices and other organisational matters that hinder the fulfilment of undertakings
   6.1. Prejudice
   6.2. Demographic problems and remoteness of schools
   6.3. Costs of education provision in regional or minority languages
   6.4. Other organisational measures with disincentive effects

7. Best practice in implementation of the ECRML in education

8. Conclusions

References

Appendix: Ratifications

Article 8 – Education

1. *With regard to education, the Parties undertake, within the territory in which such languages are used, according to the situation of each of these languages, and without prejudice to the teaching of the official language(s) of the State:*

   a. *i.* *to make available pre-school education in the relevant regional or minority languages; or*

       ii. *to make available a substantial part of pre-school education in the relevant regional or minority languages; or*

       iii. *to apply one of the measures provided for under i and ii above at least to those pupils whose families so request and whose number is considered sufficient; or*

       iv. *if the public authorities have no direct competence in the field of pre-school education, to favour and/or encourage the application of the measures referred to under i to iii above;*

   b. *i.* *to make available primary education in the relevant regional or minority languages; or*

       ii. *to make available a substantial part of primary education in the relevant regional or minority languages; or*

       iii. *to provide, within primary education, for the teaching of the relevant regional or minority languages as an integral part of the curriculum; or*

       iv. *to apply one of the measures provided for under i to iii above at least to those pupils whose families so request and whose number is considered sufficient;*

   c. *i.* *to make available secondary education in the relevant regional or minority languages; or*

       ii. *to make available a substantial part of secondary education in the relevant regional or minority languages; or*

       iii. *to provide, within secondary education, for the teaching of the relevant regional or minority languages as an integral part of the curriculum; or*

       iv. *to apply one of the measures provided for under i to iii above at least to those pupils who, or where appropriate whose families, so wish in a number considered sufficient;*

   d. *i.* *to make available technical and vocational education in the relevant regional or minority languages; or*

       ii. *to make available a substantial part of technical and vocational education in the relevant regional or minority languages; or*

       iii. *to provide, within technical and vocational education, for the teaching of the relevant regional or minority languages as an integral part of the curriculum; or*

       iv. *to apply one of the measures provided for under i to iii above at least to those pupils who, or where appropriate whose families, so wish in a number considered sufficient;*

e. i. to make available university and other higher education in regional or
minority languages; or

    ii. to provide facilities for the study of these languages as university and
higher education subjects; or

    iii. if, by reason of the role of the State in relation to higher education institu-
tions, sub-paragraphs i and ii cannot be applied, to encourage and/or
allow the provision of university or other forms of higher education in
regional or minority languages or of facilities for the study of these
languages as university or higher education subjects;

f. i. to arrange for the provision of adult and continuing education courses
which are taught mainly or wholly in the regional or minority languages;
or

    ii. to offer such languages as subjects of adult and continuing education; or

    iii. if the public authorities have no direct competence in the field of adult
education, to favour and/or encourage the offering of such languages as
subjects of adult and continuing education;

g. to make arrangements to ensure the teaching of the history and the culture
which is reflected by the regional or minority language;

h. to provide the basic and further training of the teachers required to implement those of paragraphs a to g accepted by the Party;

i. to set up a supervisory body or bodies responsible for monitoring the measures taken and progress achieved in establishing or developing the teaching
of regional or minority languages and for drawing up periodic reports of
their findings, which will be made public.

1. Education as a crucial factor in the protection and promotion of regional or minority languages (RMLs)

The European Charter for Regional or Minority Languages (ECRML) is a major
step in the development of an international framework for the protection of
languages, which hitherto had been limited to the linguistic content of certain
human rights, minority rights or the protection of cultural and linguistic diversity.[1] The difficulties in inferring language rights from human rights as protected

---

1. On the creation of a framework for the protection of linguistic rights in international and Community
law, see E. Pons Parera (2006), "Los derechos lingüísticos en el marco internacional y comunitario
europeo" in J. M. Pérez Fernández (ed.), *Estudios jurídicos sobre el estatuto jurídico de las lenguas
en España*. Barcelona: Atelier; F. de Varennes (2001), "Language rights as an integral part of human
rights", *International Journal on Multicultural Societies*, Vol. 3, No. 1; R. Dunbar (2001), "Minority
language rights in international law", *International and Comparative Law Quarterly*, No. 50;
P. Thornberry (1991), *International law and the rights of minorities*. Oxford: Clarendon Press;
I. Urrutia and I. Lasagabaster (2008), "Language rights and community law", *European Integration
Online Papers*, Vol. 12 (http://eiop.or.at/eiop/index.php/eiop/article/view/2008_004a); X. Arzoz
(2009), "Language rights as legal norms", *European Public Law*, Vol. 15, No. 4.

by international treaties and the scant references to language rights in international law confer significant added value to the ECRML. Although the Charter was not intended to grant rights to speakers but to protect linguistic diversity, it is clear that the provisions relating to education set out a number of unconditional undertakings (resulting from demand by speakers, the presence of a sufficient number of speakers, etc.) which, insofar as the Charter has been ratified by states, make it possible to speak of a genuine right to teaching in and of regional or minority languages (RMLs).

It could be argued that under the Charter the preferred route for the protection of linguistic diversity is education. A clear indication of the importance attached to education can be seen in the placing of the article in the structure of the Charter – the first article in Part III – and the linkage between Article 8 and most of the paragraphs of Article 7, and the scope and detail of the undertakings set out in Article 8, which show the central role it plays in the Charter.

Education is the cornerstone for the protection and promotion of regional and minority languages. Numerous Charter monitoring reports make statements along the following lines: "Education is the fundamental basis of the protection and promotion of RMLs. In general terms, more precise planning seems to be needed in this area";[2] "Considering education to be one of the most crucial factors in promoting a language, and especially in pre-school, primary or secondary education".[3]

Although all sectors are relevant to the preservation of minority languages, it is clear that a key aim is to ensure transmission from generation to generation and that education plays a central role to this end. This is a general conclusion drawn by the Council of Europe in assessing the practical implementation of undertakings relating to education, and one that is frequently repeated in Charter evaluation reports. The statement that "education is a key factor in the promotion and protection of RMLs" illustrates the fact that this article probably constitutes the core of the Charter.[4] In societies such as those in Europe where compulsory education is widespread, reaching almost the whole population, the socialising dimension is one shared between families and schools. Any breakdown in the intergenerational transmission of languages which are in a vulnerable state reinforces the importance of education for the protection of minority languages.

---

2. Germany 2002, Findings; also Slovenia 2004, 96.
3. Croatia 2001, 38.
4. ECRML, Committee of Experts (2006), *The Committee of Experts' interpretation and evaluation practice concerning the implementation of articles on education of the European Charter for Regional or Minority Languages*. Strasbourg: Council of Europe Publishing, 3 June 2006 (MIN-LANG (2006) 3), p. 2.

The Council of Europe has, through various bodies and statements, emphasised the importance of education for the preservation of minority languages as a European value. It asserts that "regional and minority languages are not luxuries: as well as being an integral part of Europe's rich cultural heritage, they have a vital role to play in increasing the integration and economic prosperity of the greater European area".[5] Education is a priority action area in the process of European integration through its linguistic diversity, which is the driving force behind the Charter.

2. General considerations on the implementation of Article 8.1

The ECRML is an international text which applies automatically to those states having ratified it, although many of the undertakings require regulatory action at domestic level. It is not enough to have a non-discrimination policy; there has to be a proactive improvement-oriented approach. De Varennes states that "promotion means more than being satisfied with the status quo".[6]

In the field of education, the Committee of Experts has specified the need to adopt such an active position by means of positive measures to ensure compliance with the Charter: "The German authorities work on the assumption that the Charter, as an international treaty, contains provisions of a self-executing nature. But even if the national law provisions of the Charter are self-executing, many of the undertakings accepted under the Charter need specific implementing legal provisions in order to become operational in practice".[7] The Committee of Experts noted, even though the education authorities had claimed in the second Charter monitoring cycle that there was no necessity to adopt

---

5. Minority languages: an asset for regional development, Rec. 286 (2010), 18th Session, Congress of Local and Regional Authorities of the Council of Europe. The importance of education is seen in the many references to it in recommendations in Rec. 286: "The Congress invites the Committee of Ministers to ask member states to:

a. take action to prevent the decline of regional and minority languages by ensuring shared responsibility between central government and relevant regional and local authorities;

b. ensure that all children have the opportunity to learn these languages from a very early age (pre-school) and to continue learning them up to higher education and vocational training;

c. encourage and support the provision of regional and minority language courses in adult, continuing education and vocational training;

d. encourage and promote the use of regional and minority languages in the media, cultural industries and cultural tourism;

e. promote education in the mother tongue for all minority groups;

f. set up language promotion councils to encourage language diversification and the development of regional and minority language use in regions;

g. sign and ratify the Framework Convention for the Protection of National Minorities and the European Charter of Regional or Minority Languages if they have not yet done so".

6. F. de Varennes, (2008), "Language protection and the European Charter ... *quo vadis?*" in R. Dunbar and G. Parry (eds), *The European Charter ... legal challenges and opportunities*, p. 33.

7. Germany 2002, Findings D.

further measures, that the absence of implementing measures entailed repercussions for public employees and citizens. It stated that "it is unrealistic to expect civil servants dealing with regional or minority language speakers on a daily basis to apply the provisions of the Charter directly." It added that such measures were "necessary to avoid legal uncertainties and to fill legislative gaps". Finally, it made a particularly interesting reference to the position of the speakers themselves, as they "are not likely to challenge possible unfavourable practices by invoking the Charter, in order not to be seen as 'troublemakers' and on account of the legal costs they would incur".[8] The education-related undertakings must be implemented by the educational authorities in a sufficiently clear way, without imposing burdens on the speakers by obliging them to demand compliance with the obligations deriving from the Charter.

States which ratify the Charter must carry out the required legal and organisational changes to ensure that their education system is in line with the commitments entered into. The changes in question will prevent the sort of problems which have been identified: the existence of loopholes that may cause implementation problems for civil servants and, especially, the fact that these loopholes become a burden on citizens requiring them to demand compliance with the Charter. Insofar as the Charter does not create individual rights but obligations to protect languages, it is logical that ordinary citizens should not have to adopt an active position to demand compliance with its provisions (which is usually costly in money and time).[9] The internal political and institutional organisation is used by member states to justify the failure to honour the commitments of the Charter, arguing that it is not the responsibility of the central government authorities to guarantee implementation of undertakings in the field of education. The ECRML monitoring reports show that the division of responsibilities and internal organisational reform have a clear influence on the degree of compliance with the Charter.[10] Nonetheless, the Committee of Experts has emphasised the requirement to comply with the undertakings entered into by the state, holding that, for this purpose, the authority which has responsibility for application in practice is irrelevant.[11] Accordingly, the prin-

---

8. Germany 2006, 16.
9. F. de Varennes (2008), "Language protection and the European Charter ... *quo vadis?*", p. 27: "It is based on state obligations rather than individual or collective rights."
10. In Finland there was concern about the impact of municipal reform on the teaching of Swedish: Finland 2007, 102.
11. "In Spain, the responsibility for the practical application of the Charter rests largely in the Administration of the Autonomous Communities. However, the Committee of Experts recalled that the Spanish State has overall and final responsibility for ensuring the implementation of the Charter (in this point, see the Second Assessment Report of the Committee of Experts on the UK-ECRML (2007) 2 paragraph 31 and the second evaluation report on the Netherlands-ECRML (2004) 8, paragraph 12)": Spain 2008, 62.

ciple of a state's institutional autonomy should not be used as justification for failure to honour the undertakings entered into.

The greatest problems, in view of the wide variety of solutions involved, are in states where responsibility for education lies with the municipalities. In such cases, it is difficult to adopt measures of a global scope and the protection afforded to languages is excessively fragmented.[12] This lack of territorial continuity in the organisation of the education system for teaching of or in minority languages affects the very survival of languages since protection policies require temporal stability and sufficient territorial scope. The high degree of municipal discretion in organising the teaching of minority languages can lead to situations where there is a failure to ensure that "this as a right in the relevant territories".[13] Further, additional persuasion effort is being undertaken in respect of states where responsibility for education lies with the regional authorities.[14]

The education undertakings contained in Part III of the Charter are an extension and practical expression of some of the undertakings set out in Article 7, an important article in Part II, which apply to all RMLs found in the ratifying states.

3. Scope and assumptions regarding the protection of languages in the education field in the territories in which they are traditionally spoken

Article 8.1 sets out the undertakings that states can enter into with regard to education in the territories where the languages in question are traditionally spoken, in contrast to the provisions of Article 8.2 which extend the possibility of protection for those languages outside the territory in which they are traditionally used. The fact that there are education-related undertakings which can go beyond the general framework of protection restricted to the "traditional homeland", provided for in the Charter, gives an idea of the importance attached to education for the preservation of languages.

There are two factors which affect the undertakings which states can enter into in relation to the teaching of languages in the territory in which they are traditionally spoken. These are the situation of the language in question and the statutory guarantee of the teaching of the official language of the state. Accordingly, the first paragraph of Article 8.1 specifies these two conditions which will have an impact on the protection of the RMLs in the state concerned.

---

12. Sweden 2003, 24; United Kingdom 2004, 207, with respect to Gaelic.
13. Croatia 2001, Finding F.
14. For Russian as a non-territorial language: "the authorities confirm that there is a need to convince the municipalities of the importance of providing education in Russian": Finland 2004, 60.

The first, the situation of the language, concerns sociolinguistic considerations like the number of speakers, geographical distribution, the age of speakers and the value they attach to their language (presence or absence of prejudice). The choice of undertakings is also influenced by matters relating to legislation and the way education is organised (i.e. public or private education) insofar as the term "situation" of the languages would also appear to refer to both their vitality and any legal constraints which may affect the protection afforded. The situation of the languages becomes the parameter of many of the undertakings of the Charter, making it possible to adjust the level of commitment entered into, which should prevent lower protection than is appropriate to the actual situation of the language. This principle of differentiation between language protection systems, according to the actual situation of the languages concerned, is aimed, as Woehrling puts it, at "something more than a strict, standardised form of equality".[15]

The diversity of actual situations, and the very concept of the Charter as a flexible instrument is reflected in the wording of each of the undertakings in relation to the different stages of education. It is the "situation of each of these languages" which must be assessed in choosing between a widespread offer of teaching of/in the minority language, the provision of instruction if there is "sufficient demand" from speakers or, finally, merely a policy of support where the requisite skills are not available because of the way the education system is organised. Even subjective considerations such as the wishes of the speakers are taken into consideration to decide the level of undertaking entered into.

Some of the undertakings in Article 8.1 are in practice conditional on there being a sufficient number of speakers to warrant provision of education in that language.[16] In an attempt to avoid the application of excessively strict numerical criteria, the Committee of Experts notes that "although the numer-

---

15. J.-M. Woehrling (2008), "The European Charter for Regional or Minority Languages and the principle of non-discrimination", in *The European Charter ... legal challenges and opportunities*, p. 65.

16. Xabier Arzoz classifies models of language rights by distinguishing between models for the protection of minorities, and human rights and official-language protection models, pointing out that under the former rights protection is dependent upon certain qualifiers. See "Accommodating linguistic difference: five normative models of language rights", *European Constitutional Law Review*, Vol. 6 (2010), pp. 102-22, at p. 121: "In the three cases, legal norms (both international and domestic) and administrative practices make language rights or accommodations dependent on certain qualifiers: the size of the group, a significant demand, proportionality and reasonableness in the circumstances. In addition, belonging to a minority needs to be defined as to legal effects. By contrast, human rights and official-language rights are not subject to any qualifiers: human rights are accorded to any person anywhere; after their proclamation, official-language rights are to the benefit (or the constraint) of anyone subject to the relevant jurisdiction."

ical criteria are useful for the application of Part III provisions, languages spoken by a low number of speakers are also protected by the Charter".[17] Ultimately, the Charter protects linguistic diversity regardless of the number of speakers of languages, although certain undertakings may be modulated according to numerical criteria.

The situation of the languages in question should therefore serve as a guide for states in the ECRML ratification process. As the Explanatory Report states: "this stipulation is especially relevant to the choice of which option to accept for which language in sub-paragraphs *a* to *f*".[18] As discussed below, a comprehensive assessment of the actual situation of languages prior to ratification would make it possible for states to select the most appropriate undertakings from among those set down in the Charter, thereby avoiding any shortcomings in the instruments of ratification which might hinder the ECRML monitoring process.

Secondly, the opening paragraph of Article 8.1 provides a guarantee of the teaching of the official language(s) of the state, in an apparent attempt to overcome any reservations in states with RMLs in connection with the acceptance of undertakings in the education sector. As a number of languages classified as RMLs within the meaning of the Charter are backed by feelings of national identity and nationalist movements, this article (with others, especially Article 5) seeks to provide states with a guarantee that they are fully able to decide on the level of protection they wish to give to each of the languages concerned and that their political sovereignty and the official language will not be affected by the ECRML.[19]

The terms of the Explanatory Report are straightforward and clear about the purpose of this guarantee: it "is intended to avert any possibility of interpreting the provisions of Article 8, paragraph 1 – and in particular the first option in each of sub-paragraphs *a* to *f* – as excluding the teaching of the language(s) spoken by the majority". Furthermore, it considers that the learning of the official language(s) avoids the creation of ghettos and is in the interests of the minority language speakers, and that failing to act in this way would be contrary to the principles of interculturalism and multilingualism underlined in the preamble.[20]

---

17. Application of the Charter in Ukraine, 1st monitoring cycle (2010), paragraph 62.
18. Council of Europe, *European Charter for Regional or Minority Languages and Explanatory Report*, Council of Europe, 2000, p. 24.
19. As Gwynedd Parry argues above (p. 128) in discussing Article 5, the Charter tries to depoliticise the links between language protection and nationalist disputes.
20. Council of Europe, *European Charter for Regional or Minority Languages and Explanatory Report*, p. 24.

Guaranteeing the teaching of the official language, which, as stated in the Explanatory Report should contribute to the integration of speakers of RMLs, must not be confused with assimilation.[21] The integration of linguistic minorities in states with another official language to be learned cannot justify policies aimed at eliminating the outward signs of the identity of such minorities.

In the light of the above, Article 8.1 seeks primarily to regulate the undertakings relating to the teaching in and of RMLs at all educational levels (pre-school, primary and secondary education, technical education and vocational, university and adult education). It also includes three undertakings, which do not specify various levels of protection, concerning the teaching of history and culture, teacher training and the setting up of supervisory bodies.

In view of its relatively homogeneous structure, Article 8.1 makes it possible to offer education in RMLs for all or a substantial part of education, and to make this offer conditional on the existence of sufficient demand in terms of numbers. It also encourages measures to promote some of these arrangements where the public authorities have no competence to organise the education system (in those levels of education which might not be part of compulsory education).

4. The undertakings in Article 8.1

4.1. Education in regional or minority languages (8.1a.i, b.i, c.i, d.i, e.i, f.i)

The highest level of undertaking that states can subscribe to in relation to the languages to which Part III of the Charter applies is that of teaching in RMLs. The ECRML reflects this undertaking for all levels of education and includes an immersion-teaching model – along with a guarantee of teaching the official majority language.

The significance of this undertaking is that the different stages of education should be taught primarily in RMLs; thus, "balanced" bilingual educational models (i.e. 50%) would not be regarded as sufficient to comply with this undertaking.

The case of Spain is a telling example of what this undertaking means, as the uniformity of the instrument ratifying this undertaking in respect of all the languages to which Part III applies conflicts with the diverse situation of those languages, both from the sociolinguistic point of view and with regard to the way the education system is organised. The Committee of

---

21. Slovakia 2007, 59.

Experts has been unequivocal in stating that those autonomous communities with education systems in which only 50% of teaching, or of certain subjects, is taught in the regional language do not meet the required level of the undertaking given.[22]

In contrast, it notes that systems entirely in the regional or minority language do comply with the undertakings given and also have a clear effect in reversing the decline of these languages. "The Committee of Experts observes that this system points to an impressive reversal of the trend: a regional/minority language that was still oppressed just 30 years ago has become the default language in the education system in its traditional territory and the first language of instruction for the larger part of the last generation of young people who have been educated in Catalonia. Such a development is extremely rare in Europe's history and confirms the special interest of Spain in this domain."[23] In tune with the statements about the importance of education for the protection of RMLs, education systems entirely in these languages seem to have a clear effect on the recovery of languages and also on the recovery of social prestige.

This higher level of undertaking to education primarily in the RMLs need not be mandatory for all students in the territory where the language is traditionally spoken. The competent authorities may offer various educational models in the

---

22. "The Committee of Experts considers that the current educational model does not attain the level required by the specific undertakings entered into by Spain, which imply the offer of an instruction essentially in Catalan in the Balearic Islands and not limited to half of the curriculum. The form of education currently available in the Balearic Islands actually corresponds to the lower level of obligation laid down in Article 8 paragraph 1.a/b/c (therefore, to the obligations contained in Article 8 paragraph 1.a.ii, 1.b.ii and 1.c.ii), implying that a substantial part of the education is made available in the language and representing in practice a bilingual model", Spain 2005, 624.
"Irrespective of the uncertainty as to the practice followed in pre-school and early primary school, consisting of using the language which predominates among the pupils, the Committee of Experts considers that the information at its disposal indicates that the current educational model does not attain the level required by the specific undertakings entered into by Spain, which imply the provision of an instruction essentially in Galician and not just a number of subjects, or a substantial part of the curriculum, being taught in Galician. The form of education currently available in Galicia actually corresponds to the lower level of obligation laid down in Article 8 paragraph 1.a/b/c (therefore, to the obligations contained in Article 8 paragraph 1.a.ii, 1.b.ii and 1.c.ii). In addition, the Committee of Experts received complaints, during the 'on-the-spot' visit, according to which in reality Galician is rarely a language of instruction, many primary and secondary schools do not teach all the subjects that should normally be taught in Galician and in many educational centres textbooks in Galician are not available. Finally, Galician does not seem to be present outside classes. 875. In the light of the specific undertakings entered into by Spain, i.e. the highest under Article 8 of the Charter, the Committee of Experts considers that these are not fulfilled." Spain 2005, 874-5.
23. Spain 2005, 208.

territories in which these languages are traditionally spoken, at least one of which must include teaching in the RMLs.[24]

However, the provision of teaching in the RMLs as part of this undertaking cannot be conditional on sufficient demand from the speakers because this would be a different undertaking available in the Charter (8.1a.iii; and option iv in paragraphs b,c,d). There has to be provision by the public authorities covering all speakers who wish to study primarily in the minority languages without the need for prior demand or a specified number of interested speakers.[25] This level of undertaking, entailing an obligation on the part of the education authorities to provide education in the RMLs, produces an unconditional right to receive education in these languages. In contrast to the undertakings in Article 8.1a.iii and option iv in paragraphs b, c, d, e, under which the authorities may limit access to education in the RMLs depending on whether or not there is sufficient demand, it is clear that this cannot be a condition for fulfilling option i in subparagraphs a to e.

The lack of continuity or the absence of sufficient provision for speakers who want an education primarily in the regional or minority language is one of the problems with this undertaking.[26] It can also be difficult to assess the compliance with this undertaking of educational models in which the choice of

---

24. "The basic structure of the educational framework is in principle an impressive one and the competent authorities must be praised in this regard .... Whether any other models also pursue the objective of achieving bilingualism in general in the territory concerned goes beyond the concrete undertaking entered into" (Spain 2005, 484), on the Euskera teaching model, which has one immersion model in Euskera, another bilingual model and a third primarily in Spanish.
25. "In most of the Autonomous Communities, education in the co-official languages is based on a structured model of bilingualism. However, this does not correspond to the undertakings chosen by Spain, which implies an offer also of the models of education given essentially in the regional or minority languages. The development of a 'full immersion' model on top of the bilingual model is the objective towards which all the autonomous communities concerned should aim, with a view to gradually fulfilling the undertakings entered into" (Spain 2008, Finding H).
26. "According to the information received by the Committee of Experts, this decreasing curve is due to a decreasing availability of model D as the curriculum progresses. The problem is particularly serious at secondary school level. In any event, it was stressed to the Committee of Experts that in some places not all demands are catered for owing to a problem of space. However, the efforts clearly being made to make education in Basque available both in principle and in practice result in the fact that 40% of the pupils speak Basque" (Spain 2005, 486). Also, "not being able to pursue their technical or vocational studies in Basque represents a serious linguistic setback for those pupils who have had their education in Basque until that stage. As a result, according to the figures made available to the Committee of Experts, 81.6% of the pupils who have received education in Basque cannot pursue their education in this language because there is no offer in the field of technical and vocational training (Spain 2005, 489). In Wales, almost half of the parents who would choose Welsh-medium education do not have schools to do so (United Kingdom 2004, 105).

language may vary, because it depends on the wishes of families, but where there is only one model (education through the medium of the official language or through the medium of the regional or minority language) that the speakers wishing to be schooled in the RMLs may opt for.[27]

4.2. Offer of a substantial part of education in regional or minority languages (8.1a.ii, b.ii, c.ii, d.ii)

The second level of intensity in the education-related undertakings is the offer of a substantial part of education in the relevant RMLs. This undertaking is available for all pre-university educational levels (pre-school, primary and secondary) and technical or vocational education. However, it does not appear as an undertaking for university or for adult education. In these two areas, the undertakings go from full education in the RMLs to provision of the study of these languages as a subject. This jump in the level of protection in university and adult education between the education systems in the regional or minority language and the mere existence of some form of teaching of the language at these educational levels seems too large. Encouragement should be given to include "a substantial part of education in regional or minority languages" in higher and adult education.

Determining what constitutes a substantial part of education in RMLs is relatively open and the Committee of Experts has accepted different solutions regarding the degree of the undertaking. It is clear that a residual presence of RMLs in education cannot be considered a substantial part of education. Nor too, can the simple teaching of these languages as a subject, as this would be another ECRML undertaking.

This has been the line taken by the Committee of Experts with regard to various languages, stating, for example, that "one lesson per week, which cannot be interpreted as a 'substantial part of primary education'".[28] It accepts, however, that bilingual education in Hungarian and German in Austria constitutes satisfactory compliance with this undertaking, in that Hungarian must be used no less than six hours a week in pre-school education.[29] Given the importance of language in pre-school education in that the development of oral skills, essential

---

27. "It is not clear what using the language that predominates among pupils in pre-school and early primary education actually means in practice" (Spain 2005, 871).
28. The Netherlands 2001, 61. The second compliance report reiterated that "the average time dedicated to the teaching of the Frisian language in primary schools is 25 minutes per week, which is insufficient for achieving the attainment targets"; the Netherlands 2004, 86. Cf. "meaning that in addition to teaching of the language [Ruthenian], other subjects must be taught in the language" (Slovakia 2007, 382).
29. Austria 2005, 283.

for reading and writing, lies at the heart of education, six hours a week does not seem sufficient to qualify as a "substantial" part of education.

Bilingual systems providing 50% of education in the relevant RMLs and the other 50% in the official majority language of the state may fulfil this level of undertaking. In fact, the Committee of Experts points out that Spain has failed to fulfil the undertaking entered into (intended to fulfil option i: education in an RML) in the case of several regional languages in 50% bilingual education systems since the models offered equate rather to an education substantially in the regional or minority language.

The internal logic of grading in the undertakings of the Charter means that the interpretation of the concept "substantial part" requires a qualitative leap in relation to the undertaking to provide education in the language as an integral part of the school curriculum (option iii for 8.1b,c,d). Additionally, the adjective "substantial" clearly implies that a large proportion of education will be in the regional or minority language.

It would be helpful if, with regard to the situation of languages, the Committee of Experts applied parameters setting out the percentages it considers acceptable to fulfil these undertakings. There should also be a qualitative examination of the presence of languages at each educational level. Limiting the use of RMLs to matters deemed to be of lesser importance for the education system or linked exclusively to historical and cultural aspects can reinforce prejudices about these languages. The RMLs should be seen as appropriate for all types of uses and contexts relating to modern life and economically competitive sectors (maths, science, technical subjects, etc.).

4.3. The teaching of regional or minority languages as an integral part of the curriculum (b.iii, c.iii, d.iii, f.ii)

The teaching of RMLs as an integral part of the curriculum is the lowest-level undertaking of those referred to in the Charter, and is not subject to any specific conditions, whether quantitative or in the way the teaching is organised. Where it has been entered into, this undertaking guarantees that RMLs will be included as subjects in the education system, without any requirement for a demand to this effect from speakers of those languages. The wording of this undertaking ("as an integral part of the curriculum") indicates that the teaching of such languages should be part of the mainstream education curriculum, regardless of other forms of non-formalised education, such as Sunday schools, classes taught by cultural associations, etc.

It is also an undertaking that applies only to primary, secondary, vocational and adult education. One might wonder why pre-school education is not included under this level of undertaking, since it prevents continuity in the undertakings entered into for states unable or unwilling to commit to a regional or minority language forming a substantial part of education or being the normal medium of instruction.

Nor, in this case, does the Charter lay down indicators as to how much teaching of RMLs should be included in the school curriculum. Woehrling states that "if the measure is not to be merely a formal one of little real use to the language taught, there must be at least a minimum level of intensiveness. Experience shows that below three hours a week, such teaching has little impact".[30]

The monitoring reports also show that, over and above the reduced nature of the undertaking, there are cases where implementation is unsatisfactory. One example referred to is Germany's justification for Low German, where the undertaking in practice equates simply to the teaching of a song, poem and short story. The Committee of Experts comments that this remains below the level required by the undertaking but nevertheless constitutes a step forward.[31]

A problem that emerges in respect of this and other undertakings is the possibility that the teacher will decide unilaterally whether to conduct classes in the regional or minority language. The Committee of Experts recommends that measures be taken "to ensure that Low German forms a part of the curriculum in its own right".[32] Allowing teachers to decide whether to teach in the minority languages is an obstacle to compliance with the undertakings entered into and is at odds with the unconditional nature of this undertaking, which – once ratified – parties should fulfil by adopting all necessary organisational measures.[33]

The similarity between the official majority language and the minority language in some cases has led the Committee of Experts not to conclude a failure to fulfil the undertaking, accepting the argument that there was insufficient demand.[34] This statement appears somewhat inconsistent with the role of the

---

30. J.-M. Woehrling (2008), "The European Charter … and the principle of non-discrimination", p. 150. The author notes that even three hours a week is not effective if there is no family or external reinforcement.

31. Germany 2006, 471-2.

32. Germany 2002, 255.

33. "The German Government has informed the Committee that the Framework Curriculum recommends the use of Low German in literature and texts, but teachers have no legal obligation to follow these instructions" (Germany 2002, 103). Also, "most of the Frisian school initiatives still depend on the good will and interest on the part of the teachers and school leaders and the motivation of the parents" (Germany 2002, 174).

34. "According to the information received by the Committee of Experts, no teaching of Czech or in Czech is available at any level of education …. During the 'on-the-spot' visit the Committee of Experts was informed that there is at present no demand on the part of the speakers in respect of the relevant provisions under this article" (Slovakia 2007, 544).

Committee of Experts, which is to assess whether the undertakings entered into have been fulfilled. In this case, it is clear that the argument used by the state not to comply refers to an undertaking which was not entered into, and consequently the committee should indicate this discrepancy.

4.4. Language teaching if there is sufficient demand (8.1a.iii, b.iv, c.iv, d.iv)

Undertakings to provide teaching of and in RMLs if there is sufficient demand can be entered into for pre-school, primary, secondary and technical/vocational training in the territories in which they are traditionally spoken.[35] Making the protection of language in education conditional on the existence of sufficient demand is also contained in the Framework Convention for the Protection of National Minorities (Article 14).[36]

This undertaking, conditional on the existence of demand from speakers and the educational authorities' stipulating a number deemed sufficient for them to be bound by it, provides for the possibility of education systems partly or wholly in RMLs or the teaching of RMLs. Education authorities may choose the degree of presence of these languages in the education system (wholly, substantially or as an integral part of education) and determine whether there is sufficient demand to perform this service.[37]

It requires therefore an active demand from the speakers, or their families in the case of children, for education in their languages. There is a problem with the requirement for speakers to express their demand, which is those speakers' unawareness of the Charter and the rights they could claim for education to be provided in their languages if there were sufficient demand. The Committee of Experts would need to verify, as a subsidiary measure to this undertaking, whether speakers have this information. In some reports,

---

35. In relation to education outside the territory in which they are traditionally spoken (Article 8.2), several states make this also conditional on there being sufficient demand by setting a minimum number of students. Norway sets a minimum number of three students to be taught Sami and 10 for classes in Sami (Norway 2001, 67). Slovenia sets a number between five and seven students for education outside the traditional territory (Slovenia 2004, 114).

36. I. Urrutia Libarona (2005), *Derechos lingüísticos y euskera en el sistema educativo*. Iruña: Lete, p. 258, notes the wide margin of appreciation granted by the convention to the parties in its delivery component, on account of both the undertaking's lack of precision and the introduction of assessment criteria – sufficient demand, as far as possible – allowing different possibilities for action.

37. "Depending on the socio-linguistic situation and the resulting needs and wishes of parents, three different models are used that correspond to the three variants listed in Article 8 paragraph 1b of the Charter. Primary education is either provided purely in the minority language, or it is organised bilingually, with a substantial part taught in the minority language but another part in Hungarian, or Hungarian is used as the medium of instruction, with supplementary teaching of the minority language as an integral part of the curriculum"; Hungary 2001, 36.

it is indeed noted that authorities "should raise awareness of the right to mother tongue instruction".[38]

In the ECRML monitoring process, it is clear that probably the most problematic issue is precisely the setting of the minimum number of students to ascertain whether there is sufficient demand. Here, too, the Charter allows flexibility and does not lay down any standards regarding this minimum number. Woehrling considers this ability to be flexible about the number of students needed to maintain classes in the regional language as belonging to positive action measures "which go beyond the principle of equality" and among the cases in which it is permissible to make exceptions to the principle of non-discrimination.[39]

Most of the monitoring reports indicate that the authorities adopt relatively low numbers that are applied flexibly (about seven students in several countries).[40] Although the Charter adopts a flexible rather than prescriptive approach in terms of setting a numerical standard common to all languages, which would be at odds with the principle of adaptation to the situation of the language, the Committee of Experts takes the view that excessively high numbers are contrary to the spirit of the ECRML.[41]

A common problem in respect of this undertaking that affects various linguistic minorities is that in many cases they live in impoverished areas from which large-scale emigration has taken place. This brings with it depopulation and closures of schools due to insufficient demand, with the result that in the new areas they move to, there may not be any offer of teaching in RMLs.[42]

The Committee of Experts raised the question of whether this is "a right which families can invoke, should they request pre-school education in a certain language in sufficient numbers".[43] It would appear from the text of the Charter that education authorities have an obligation to provide teaching of and in RMLs and that the only margin for appreciation available to them concerns specifying the number of students required to constitute "sufficient demand". In more recent reports this appears to be the interpretation of the Committee of Experts which seeks to clearly

---

38. Sweden 2006, 84.
39. J.-M. Woehrling (2008) "The European Charter … and the principle of non-discrimination", p. 80.
40. In Armenia, the requirement is for seven students, although this is flexible and can be fewer (Armenia 2006, 52). Although Croatian law does not indicate the required number, the authorities speak of seven families in order to provide education in the minority languages (Croatia 2001, 50). In Hungary, requests from eight families are required (Hungary 2001, 36).
41. "Having regard to the Charter and its Explanatory Report, the Committee of Experts reiterates its view that the required number of 20 pupils is excessively high for the purposes of the present undertaking" (Germany 2006, 98).
42. Hungary 2004, 56; Slovakia 2007, 186.
43. Croatia 2001, 51.

identify the objective conditions that oblige education authorities to create classes or schools in the RMLs. Reference is also made to the need for authorities to establish an "effective legal remedy", which would indicate quite clearly that this undertaking gives rise to an obligation for the education authorities, the corollary of which is the families' right, which can be relied upon and defended, to an effective appeal system in the event of non-fulfilment.[44]

4.5. Protection of languages when the state has no direct competence in organising the educational stage in question (8.1a.iv, e.ii, f.iii)

The Charter includes an undertaking for the protection of languages at educational stages in which many states have forms of provision which do not directly fall within the competence of the education authorities. They are stages that, generally speaking, are not part of compulsory education, in which there is a private offer organised in a way that limits the authorities' influence (e.g. university autonomy). For this reason the measures provided for may be any of those specified in the other undertakings, of varying intensity, in relation to the teaching of/in the languages in question. It would appear that the education authorities' role in such cases is more one of funding or promotion than of laying down mandatory measures for educational institutions.

For example, Denmark took steps to ensure that changes in financing pre-school education would not affect the German language minority regardless of whether such education was privately run. The rules adopted guaranteed the continuation of funding at previous levels provided that quality requirements were fulfilled.[45]

One factor that needs to be verified in this connection is whether indeed the education authorities have no direct competence over the teaching institutions. In some states, such as Spain, this undertaking has been entered into in respect of universities; it appears that the autonomy which universities enjoy in certain spheres does not preclude powers at state and autonomous community level to regulate other aspects of university organisation, such as the language of instruction.

4.6. Teaching of history and culture (8.1g)

The stated aim of the ECRML is to protect regional or minority languages as part of the European cultural heritage. In addition to teaching the language, the Charter also contains a commitment to teaching the history and culture of which that language is a part. Languages are the form of expression of a unique culture

---

44. "The Committee of Experts notes that the obligation for the authorities to provide for the creation of a class or a school with education in a minority language if certain objective conditions are met is currently not provided for in clear terms and no effective legal remedy seems to be available in the regional or minority languages" (Ukraine 2010, 152).
45. Denmark 2007, 57-60.

and history. It is extremely important to teach the cultural and historical roots of these languages in order to fight prejudice that often contributes to the loss of speakers. From the point of view of ecolinguistics, the preservation of linguistic diversity requires there to be positive functions and positive space for the language, an environment in which to develop, and this means that the necessary favourable social and political conditions must be in place.[46] The awareness of being part of a historical and cultural tradition itself is essential if people are to take an active stance to protect regional and minority languages. In many monitoring reports, the Committee of Experts refers to intense prejudice, on the part of both speakers and non-speakers, which creates the risk of assimilation for linguistic minorities. This process has accelerated since the 1980s, spurred on by the information society and use of new communication technologies.

The problems in implementing this undertaking have in common the absence of a systematic and comprehensive approach to the teaching of culture and history. The undertaking in the Charter requires the education authorities to ensure the teaching of culture and history for all students systematically within the school curriculum.[47] This means there must be appropriate teaching material and teachers who have received suitable training. In connection with this undertaking, it has been noted in some cases that compliance is complicated by the fact that some systems allow teachers to choose whether or not to teach the language and culture.[48]

This undertaking is not limited solely to speakers of RMLs but must also be aimed at students who may be in an education system which does not provide teaching of the RMLs but who live in the territory in which these languages are traditionally spoken.[49] It is also important for the history and culture

---

46. "In all probability, the secret of preservation must be the provision for the group code of certain important functions for the community and in which the self-perceptions of these groups can be invariably positive and not negative, as happens in human groups with a tendency to abandon their historical codes. Obviously, such groups are not subjected to demeaning and stigmatising discourse on their forms of communication, with the result that, despite having had to acquire wholesale other languages, the latter are seen as appropriate for other uses – usually external or for clearly defined specific purposes", A. Bastardas Boadas (2003), "Ecodinámica sociolingüística: comparaciones y analogías entre la diversidad lingüística y la diversidad biológica", *Llengua i Dret*, No. 39, p. 129.
47. "Notably through measures such as clearer guidelines for the implementation of the relevant sections of school curricula, the inclusion of this aspect in the monitoring of the Folkeskole, as well as an increased attention to this issue in the context of teaching materials and mainstream teacher training" (Denmark 2007, 65).
48. Sweden 2003, 90.
49. "The Committee of Experts recalls that the present undertaking concerns not only education for pupils using regional or minority languages but also education for non-speakers about the specific history and traditions of the regional or minority languages spoken in the relevant territory" (Spain 2005, 492).

accompanying the RMLs to be more visible in the school curriculum and not limited to optional subjects, and to ensure continuity of the teaching in the whole education system for all students.[50]

4.7. Teacher training (8.1h)

The training of teachers is essential to ensure compliance with the undertakings of Article 8 of the Charter and some of the undertakings in Article 7. This undertaking is so central that shortcomings in this respect are frequently highlighted in the compliance reports, for example: "The most pressing problem seems to be teacher training, since the further development of minority language education depends on the availability of sufficient numbers of teachers trained in the minority languages".[51]

It is clear that there is an urgent need for structured, long-term training of teachers given the crucial importance of education for the future of RMLs.[52] This undertaking should be mandatory for all states ratifying the Charter since without trained teachers it would be extremely difficult to fulfil any of the education-related undertakings with any degree of success.

In countries where the minority language is present in another neighbouring state, usually as a majority language, sometimes teachers are trained there.[53] This is the case in Denmark, where training takes place in Germany. The Committee of Experts believes this to be a valid approach, presupposing that Denmark covers the cost of that training in another state.[54] In contrast, Italy even covers the cost of the salary difference for Italian teachers teaching in Slovenia.[55]

The lack of universities in the territory where minority languages are spoken has implications for the professional training of speakers of those languages and for research into those languages.[56]

Some states attempt to find other ways of ensuring that there are trained teachers, such as recognition of foreign degrees obtained in countries with the same

---

50. Finland 2007, 113-4.
51. Hungary 2001, Finding E.
52. Croatia 2005, 107, Recommendations.
53. Sweden 2003, 202.
54. Denmark 2004, 67.
55. Slovenia 2004, 181. The difficulty in the recognition of diplomas obtained in other countries with the same language is one of the problems identified at university level (Finland 2007, 111; Slovenia 2004, 177). The situation regarding fulfilment of undertakings on university education tends to improve where such recognition is straightforward (Hungary 2007, 88; Slovenia 2004, 105). It should also be mentioned that some states receive financial help from others to fund university education in the minority language where that language is the state language (Slovakia 2007, 193).
56. Switzerland 2001, 71.

language. The fact that many states ratifying the Charter now belong to the European Union has in recent years facilitated the recognition of degrees from other countries.[57] Even so, making teacher training dependent on other countries creates its own problems, as the teaching of/in the languages in question is closely linked to the organisation and content of the education system.

A greater problem is created where there are differences in the recognition of training qualifications in the same country between speakers of the same language who come under two different administrative authorities.[58] Such is contrary to the provisions of Article 7.1b of the Charter, which sets forth the principle of respect for the geographic area of languages in order to ensure that existing administrative divisions do not constitute an obstacle to their promotion.

One factor which has a significant effect on teacher training is the way the education system was organised in the past. If only limited scope is given for RMLs in education systems, this means that there are fewer linguistically qualified people who may subsequently wish to become teachers.

A further relevant factor will be teachers' working conditions when it comes to encouraging people to retrain as teachers of minority languages. The fact of belonging to communities which are small in number can mean that teachers have complex timetables or have to cover several schools, involving a great deal of travel. This makes teaching a considerably less attractive option.[59] The Committee of Experts encourages states to introduce appropriate incentives to obviate such situations.

Clearly linked to this issue is the lack of any prospects or incentives to increase the level of training required for access to public employment if knowledge of RMLs is not compulsory.[60]

Another problem common to various languages is the fact that teachers may not be obliged to follow the curriculum as laid down.[61] In such cases, this can lead not only to situations where because of decisions taken at an individual level the international commitments entered into by the state may not be complied with but also to serious implications for the consolidation of RMLs because it makes it impossible to plan objectives.

---

57. Slovenia 2007, 76. Prior to this, the Committee of Experts had observed that there should be no bureaucratic hindrances to the recognition of qualifications (Slovenia 2004, 105).
58. "Reference was also made, by another source, to the lack of qualified teachers and to problems in having a diploma obtained in Catalonia recognised in Valencia" (Spain 2005, 757).
59. Sweden 2006, 97.
60. For university teachers: "It is also unclear how the teachers are selected for this level of education. In this regard, it was reported to the Committee of Experts that knowledge of Valencian counts as a simple advantage" (Spain 2005, 748).
61. United Kingdom 2004, 69.

4.8. Supervision and evaluation bodies

One way of helping the monitoring of compliance with the Charter would be ratification and implementation of the undertaking to set up bodies overseeing the honouring of commitments entered into in the education field. This undertaking includes, among the roles of such bodies, assessment of the progress made and the drafting and publication of regular reports. Clearly, having bodies evaluating the honouring of commitments in the education field and producing public reports regularly is extremely useful for speakers, NGOs involved in monitoring the Charter and the Committee of Experts itself.

However, most of the reports of the Committee of Experts repeatedly point to a failure to comply with this undertaking. In some cases the educational authorities indicate that these functions are carried out by existing bodies.[62] In general, however, no regular reports are drafted, and consequently it would appear that this type of body tends rather to ensure partial fulfilment of the undertaking, in form only, without really implementing its objectives.[63]

On occasion, some education authorities acknowledge failure to comply with this undertaking, stating that the absence of such bodies makes it impossible to assess the effectiveness of their language policies in the education field.[64]

5. Problems of consistency regarding the undertakings entered into

The large number of reports by the Committee of Experts and as many as three monitoring cycles for some member states highlight certain problems or imbalances in the undertakings entered into. Inconsistencies between the level of undertaking and the actual situation of the languages or organisational models of the education system, a lack of continuity in the level of protection provided in the different education stages and doubts about the undertakings made are some of the issues raised in the reports of the Committee of Experts.

---

62. "The Swedish Department of the National Board of Education has certain supervisory functions with regard to the teaching of Swedish. In addition, the Swedish Assembly is the national body with the competence to look after the interests of the Swedish speaking population"; Finland 2001, 72.

63. For example, there are references to the fact that it is not clear whether periodic reports are produced (Austria 2005, 308; Germany 2002, 181).

64. "The Hungarian authorities admitted to the Committee of Experts during the on-the-spot visit that the absence of a supervisory body as required by the Charter made it difficult to assess the quality of education and to control how the funding devoted to teaching (in) minority languages is actually spent" (Hungary 2007, 104).

5.1. Lack of continuity in undertakings for different educational levels

One issue seen in many of the Charter monitoring reports is a lack of continuity – visible in various forms – in the undertakings entered into, which poses problems for the preservation of languages. The perception that education is a key sector for the vitality of languages should lead to a certain level of uniformity in the undertakings entered into, both in the level chosen and the absence of undertakings for one or more stages of education, especially in compulsory education. The Council of Europe itself is aware of "the need for continuity in the provision of education from pre-school to higher education".[65]

In general, most member states have entered into more stringent undertakings for the early stages of the education system (pre-school and primary education) and there is a subsequent decrease in the degree of protection of languages in the higher levels of education. There are also cases of states where, despite clear consistency in the undertakings entered into, in practice that continuity is non-existent in what is actually available in higher education levels,[66] often related to material problems, space or the need for students to travel long distances to attend establishments where the language in question is on offer. There are also statutory limits on the percentage of teaching of RMLs, imposing fewer hours as students progress to higher-level education. The Committee of Experts has expressed its concern "as to the possible negative effects this might have on the protection and promotion of regional or minority languages".[67] This lack of continuity in the teaching of RMLs in secondary education and/ or university may have an impact on the survival of languages in other environments, like work, since it limits the acquisition and consolidation of advanced and technical linguistic concepts.

Although this lack of continuity has obvious problems for the maintenance of languages as students approach adulthood, ratifications which comprise no undertakings in the first levels of education make it even harder to achieve the Charter's aim of the preservation of languages. On occasion, the Committee of Experts has called for a reconsideration of the undertakings entered into in

---

65. ECRML, Committee of Experts, *The Committee of Experts' interpretation and evaluation practice concerning the implementation of articles on education of the European Charter for Regional or Minority Languages*, Council of Europe, Strasbourg, 3 June 2006 (MIN-LANG (2006) 3), p. 2.
66. See United Kingdom 2004, 110: "Both the Welsh Language Board and RhAG point to an alarming pattern of lack of continuity between primary and secondary education in largely Welsh-speaking areas, where, of those pupils who have studied Welsh as a first language in primary school, a large percentage (40 or 50%) do so only as a second language in secondary schools". See also Spain 2005, 485-6; Norway 2003, 94; and United Kingdom 2007, 192.
67. Sweden 2003, 66. The School Ordinance sets a maximum of 50% in the regional or minority language, and this percentage decreases as students progress to higher grades.

order to also cover primary education, pointing out that "primary school is of course a very important domain if a language is to be protected and developed".[68] The absence of minority languages in the early stages of education has a decisive impact on later stages. This is borne out by the fact that in most European states "in primary education, the language of instruction is clearly the most important subject in terms of taught time".[69]

Such situations, which would appear to leave responsibility for transmitting the language to the family, result in a lack of language skills in later educational levels and therefore can dissuade students from opting for education in the minority language where such instruction is offered later on in secondary education. It should also be borne in mind that many of these RMLs have already experienced generational transmission problems; thus the family environment alone may not be sufficient for maintaining the language.[70]

Furthermore, this lack of prior language training has an influence on educational results and the general tests which all students sit, usually in secondary education. Established evaluation procedures may dissuade students from opting for being taught in the language or studying the language, fearing lower results in those general assessments.[71] This is sometimes clearly the case since there are no other factors, such as the non-availability of trained teachers, which could explain the decision not to pursue the study of minority languages. This has led the Committee of Experts to suggest changes to the instrument of ratification to include higher-level undertakings.[72]

5.2. Lack of precision and consistency in the undertakings entered into

The Committee of Experts has also noted inconsistencies in the instruments of ratification either as a result of a lack of precision about the level of undertaking entered into or the fact that the undertakings are inappropriate to the actual situation of the language concerned.

With regard to cases where there is a lack of precision in the level of specific undertakings entered into for some languages,[73] the committee's practice is to automatically apply the highest option "unless specific circumstances make the highest option appear as manifestly incompatible with the needs of the regional

---

68. Germany 2002, 66.
69. Eurydice, "Key data on education in Europe 2009", 16 July 2009, http://eacea.ec.europa.eu/education/eurydice/documents/key_data_series/105EN.pdf, p. 15.
70. Germany 2002, 391.
71. See the Netherlands 2001, 64.
72. See Germany 2006, 37.
73. In the case of Slovenia in Article 8.1, paragraphs a and c do not specify the level of protection chosen.

or minority language concerned and/or with the expressed wishes of the speakers".[74] For Hungarian in Slovenia, the second level of protection has been opted for precisely because of apparent incompatibility with the language situation and the wishes of the speakers (in accordance with Article 7.4 of the Charter). A similar situation occurs where an instrument of ratification specifies two options which should be alternatives (8.1c.iii/iv); in such cases, the Committee of Experts points out that only one of the two options should have been ratified.[75] This applies to Germany in connection with Frisian in Schleswig-Holstein, although the Committee of Experts indicates that the requirement for state funding where there is no private provision could justify the ratification of two alternative undertakings.[76] The option of the highest level of protection coupled with flexibility in the application of this criterion when not warranted by the situation of the language or the organisation of the education system is therefore one way of solving the problems of the lack of precision of undertakings.

On the other hand, there are inconsistencies between the instruments of ratification and the organisation of the education system. The Charter contains several protection options (for pre-school and university) for education systems in which the provision of education services may not be in the hands of the public authorities. This incongruity between the undertaking and the organisation of the education system is evident in some states where such education is indeed the responsibility of public authorities, although the experts do not appear to attach great significance to this issue.[77]

Both the lack of correlation between the instrument of ratification and the organisational form of the education system and the failure to choose between the different levels of protection, or the ratification of options which should be alternatives, point to the need at the time of ratification for verification by the Council of Europe of the undertakings entered into. Woehrling referred to a satisfactory procedure to ensure that the undertakings entered into were appropriate to the actual situation of the languages concerned, which was that a committee or expert should be tasked with drafting a preliminary report analysing the situation of the language and the expectations of the speakers, evaluating the actions already taken or being adopted and the measures that seem advisable.[78]

This is not a question of interfering with the sovereign will of states, but rather of seeking to ensure that ratification does not present any problems which would

---

74. Slovenia 2004, 94.
75. Denmark 2004, 59.
76. Germany 2002, 173.
77. Hungary 2001, 41; Spain 2005, 342.
78. J.-M. Woehrling (2008), "The European Charter ... and the principle of non-discrimination", p. 77.

hamper the subsequent monitoring work. Paradoxically, if this formal control of the instrument of ratification is not carried out, then subsequently the Committee of Experts decides the level of undertaking assumed to have been chosen, in accordance with the practice referred to above, or is obliged to observe that the undertaking is incompatible with the organisational aspects of the education system or the actual situation of the languages in question.

In some cases, concern is expressed that the adoption of unambitious undertakings can be exploited to reduce the level of protection afforded to minority languages, which would be contrary to Article 4.2 of the Charter.[79] The maintenance of the most favourable provisions existing in the ratifying states is one of the principles of the Charter that cannot be undermined through the adoption of reduced undertakings. The opposite case is also seen, in which the undertakings entered into are too ambitious for the actual situation of the language.[80]

There are also cases of incompatibilities between the highest level of undertakings accepted and the actual situation of the teaching of the languages in question (non-existent) where the Committee of Experts chooses not to issue conclusions, accepting the argument that there is no demand by the speakers.[81] In such cases, it is more appropriate to recommend an amendment to the instrument of ratification by choosing the option available under the Charter whereby the provision of education in/of RMLs is subject to the existence of specific demand by the speakers.

A further problem noted is that the ratification by some states contains identical undertakings for all languages regardless of their actual situation; as a result the undertakings are less ambitious than they should be for the stronger minority languages.[82]

6. Prejudices and other organisational matters that hinder the fulfilment of undertakings

The reports of the Committee of Experts highlight a number of problems that manifest themselves across the board in all stages of education and for various regional and minority languages. These concern issues relating to the organisation and costs of access to education in regional and minority languages, and also deeper problems which are more difficult to solve, such as the way the education system may reinforce prejudices towards these languages rather than promoting their social prestige.

---

79. Ukraine 2010, 154.
80. Slovakia 2007, 593.
81. Ibid., 544.
82. Ukraine 2010, 155.

It should be noted that the first Charter monitoring cycles for all member states tend to make an initial assessment in relation to overall compliance with the undertakings entered into – essentially, the provision of teaching in/of the minority language. A positive step would be for subsequent evaluation cycles to consider more indirect factors (teaching material covering the whole curriculum, design of assessment tests, exemption mechanisms, activities) which, even where they comply with the undertakings entered into, may have an impact on or pose obstacles to the learning of the minority languages.

6.1. Prejudice

The existence of prejudice towards the minority language can result in this being considered "unnecessary and bad" for the children, consequently requiring positive teaching action that also conforms to the educational standards of the majority languages.[83]

In a "knowledge society", it is particularly important that the provision of education in RMLs meets the same standards of quality as education in majority languages. The lack of suitable materials or specialist teachers has a clear impact on the persistence of prejudice, with the result that they are not seen as valid for an education that can integrate students socially. The perception that teachers, teaching material or the actual educational content may be of a lower level is a clear disincentive to the learning of minority languages and helps sustain any prejudice against them.

> The language which is the vehicle of instruction has a crucial role in that it is the key to classroom communication and consequently to pupils' acquisition of knowledge. A great deal of research has confirmed that types of education based on the mother tongue significantly increase the chances of educational success and can even give better results.[84]

The Committee of Experts draws attention to the need for multilingualism to be seen as an added value and not as an obstacle when it comes to the teaching of RMLs.[85] In fact, the committee has called for an immediate cessation of the practice of segregating Romani-speakers and placing them in classrooms for students with special needs, observing that this "infringes basic human rights" and is totally contrary to the principles of the Charter.[86] Segregation in classrooms for struggling students has clear discriminatory connotations and is an obvious incentive for families to opt for education in the majority language so as to avoid any likely social segregation.

---

83. The Netherlands 2001, 27.
84. Recommendation 1740 (2006) on the place of the mother tongue in school education.
85. Slovakia 2007, 61.
86. Ibid. In similar terms, Hungary 2004, 46.

A further problem to the positive assessment of multilingualism is the treatment of RMLs in the education system as if they were foreign languages, even in areas where they are traditionally spoken. The Committee of Experts noted this issue in relation to German in Denmark and stated that "this could be one of the factors hampering the recognition of the special status of the German language and culture as elements of Denmark's cultural wealth, both by public authorities and by the general public".[87] An assessment should also be made of the type of subjects taught in the RMLs, encouraging their use in the provision of all kinds of knowledge, without limiting them to subjects with lower social status.

6.2. Demographic problems and remoteness of schools

A common problem for speakers from different communities speaking RMLs is that these communities are often in economically depressed areas, which as a result suffer from depopulation caused by emigration.[88] This situation has repercussions for the education system, in that there is no comprehensive network of schools, making it necessary for students to travel long distances to attend classes in the regional or minority language.

When schools are closed because of falling pupil numbers, there should be measures to maintain the teaching of minority languages in the new centres catering for pupils who have been moved. However, the Committee of Experts notes that this sometimes does not happen, which creates "negative repercussions on the use of a regional or minority language in the community. Indeed schools have a crucial role in the maintenance of minority languages".[89]

Some member states that have ratified the Charter and opted for the provision of education in RMLs have stipulated relatively low numbers of students as a threshold. The Committee of Experts considers that "the adoption of the same numerical criteria for minority languages as for official languages does not always lead to the best results and encourages the authorities to continue with the flexible approach in implementing legal requirements".[90] Even with this flexible approach, with lower numbers than required for majority-language schools, it may still prove difficult in sparsely populated areas to gather the

---

87. Denmark 2004, Finding D.
88. In general, these minorities experience more acute demographic decline than is seen in the EU member states as a whole, with an estimated drop in 2020 of 11% in pupils aged 5 to 9 years, but with a much sharper projected decrease (40%) for the 10-14 age bracket, see Eurydice, "Key data on education in Europe 2009", 16 July 2009, (http://eacea.ec.europa.eu/education/eurydice/documents/key_data_series/105EN.pdf), p. 13.
89. Hungary 2004, 56; Slovakia 2007, 186.
90. Germany 2002, 432.

minimum number of students required to ensure access to education in RMLs. A solution must also be found to provide continuity for this offer once studies in the regional or minority language have begun but where, subsequently, the minimum number required may not be reached. In demographically-threatened groups there is a risk that the existence of sufficient demand may change over time and a guarantee needs to be found to ensure the necessary continuity.

The speakers of some minority languages place special emphasis on the need for the provision of education linked to vocational training to avoid high emigration rates.[91]

6.3. Costs of education provision in regional or minority languages

Related in some cases to the aforementioned population problems, one difficulty encountered in the teaching of RMLs is fact that there are additional costs for speakers who opt for education in RMLs. Furthermore, there has been a trend, much more acute in recent years, for the authorities to embark on cost-cutting exercises which have an impact on the offer of courses available in minority languages.

Cost-cutting policies in education may result in the closure of schools teaching in RMLs, particularly in areas with lower populations.[92] In some cases, these financial problems have led to the virtual disappearance of the teaching of minority languages. In Sweden the abolition of conditional aid for education in Finnish in 1991 led to a sharp reduction in bilingual classes (300 classes in 1991, 76 in 1997 and only a handful in 2003).[93]

In various states the teaching of minority languages falls outside the public system and relies on private schools run by the speakers themselves or by other institutions. Private schools often receive public subsidies to operate. Funding problems in the teaching of RMLs outside the state school system by private entities are frequent.[94] The Committee of Experts comments favourably on cases in which "it was decided that the Danish private schools should be treated on an equal footing with the public schools".[95]

---

91. "The Upper Sorbian speakers view technical and vocational education as an area of priority, given the general demographic development and high rates of outward migration by young persons from the Upper Sorbian language area. According to the representatives of the speakers, there are a number of Sorbian-speaking companies who expressed their wish to take on Sorbian-speaking apprentices, which indicates that there is indeed a demand for education in or of Upper Sorbian at this level" (Germany 2006, 103).
92. Armenia 2006, 45; Germany 2002, 135.
93. Sweden 2003, 187.
94. Austria 2005, 84.
95. Germany 2006, 51.

6.4. Other organisational measures with disincentive effects

There may also be measures which indirectly deter people from learning RMLs. For example, the need to sit assessment tests in the majority language may prompt pupils to cease their studies of minority languages.[96] A similar outcome was seen in Finland with the abolition of the compulsory examination of the second national language in secondary education.[97] Similar effects are caused by the failure to set learning attainment targets specifically for the minority language, thereby creating inequalities in the organisational aspects of the education system for the teaching of the state language and minority languages. The Committee of Experts highlighted this problem in the case of the Netherlands, encouraging the authorities "to establish such targets to strengthen the situation of Frisian in secondary education".[98]

A fall in the number of pupils studying minority languages may also be caused by excessively flexible arrangements for exemptions from teaching RMLs.[99]

The lack of appropriate educational material for teaching of/in RMLs has also been identified as an obstacle.[100] Print runs are small and this makes it more complex to ensure high-quality teaching material in RMLs. The Committee of Experts recommends that original textbooks be written rather than translating those written in the majority language. Nor would it appear to be the best approach to use textbooks from another state with the same language, as they may not be geared to the relevant education system.[101] Furthermore, producing original textbooks would make it possible to reflect the history and culture of the minority language (leading to fuller compliance with Article 8.1g) and would lead to longer use at school.[102]

7. Best practice in implementation of the ECRML in education

Because education is so important for the preservation of languages that are part of the European heritage, the monitoring reports provide a detailed review

---

96. The Netherlands 2004, 74. The on-the-spot visits indicated that families and teachers had been urged to abandon the use of Frisian in order to improve results in such tests.
97. Finland 2007, 106. "The Committee of Experts believes that in the long run, this development could have a considerable negative effect on students' motivation to learn the second national language thus leading to a further weakening of the Finnish-speaking population's skills in Swedish and of the Swedish-speaking populations' skills in Finnish".
98. The Netherlands, 2004, 90.
99. See ibid., 91. The educational inspectorate recommended a change in the authority responsible for granting exemptions since 37.5% of secondary schools were exempted from teaching Frisian.
100. Spain 2005, 493
101. Sweden 2003, 191.
102. Croatia 2005, 70.

of failures to comply with the undertakings entered into, and raise speakers' awareness of the shortcomings found in education systems. Education is probably the first area of action when embarking on a protection policy for RMLs – it should be noted that protection measures are adopted even for the official majority languages of states. For this reason, it is worthwhile highlighting the good practices identified by the Committee of Experts in their reports, involving application of the principle of positive action.

There are measures relating to education funding and organisation of the education system.

With regard to support for the teaching of regional languages, Switzerland offers an interesting approach in paying for auxiliary staff to help with the integration of non-Romansh speakers.[103] In this way, linguistic minorities are not identified as being in need of reinforcement or support (when in reality they tend to be more often bilingual) but rather it is the pupils who are non-speakers of the minority language in the same classes who are given assistance. This approach also makes it possible to incorporate new speakers of the regional or minority language in areas where it is traditionally spoken, in accordance with Article 7.1g of the Charter.

A further practice of note seen in several countries is the provision of additional public funding to schools, enabling them to honour the undertakings entered into, even where the schools in question are private. In Denmark, private schools which offer teaching in German are given additional funding to meet the expenses inherent in bilingual education.[104] Norway also provides special financial support through the Sami Parliament with funding to councils to arrange for education in Sami.[105]

There are also cases of additional funding for schools that teach in the RMLs to cover both regular expenses and cultural activities and exchanges. In this way, the language encounters new, non-formal opportunities for ensuring diversity in modes of expression. However, one problem which must be highlighted concerns the instability of funding where it is not ensured in the long term.[106]

One way of avoiding falling numbers of pupils studying RMLs is to adopt organisational measures which, in the territories where they are traditionally spoken, make such teaching the general rule unless there is a specific request for other models where they exist. In Austria, for example, children enrolled in bilingual primary schools are automatically registered for bilingual

---

103. Switzerland 2001, 58.
104. Denmark 2004, 51.
105. Norway 2003, 89.
106. Hungary 2007, 69.

instruction. Guardians must make an explicit request if they wish the children to be given monolingual instruction. The Committee of Experts understood that the extension of this practice to secondary education was under discussion and encouraged the authorities in this direction.[107]

8. Conclusions

The importance of education for the protection of European linguistic diversity means that this aspect can be seen as the hard core of the Charter in terms of the extent of the undertakings that can be entered into, the place accorded to education in the number of undertakings that must be accepted, and its presence in parts II and III of the Charter.

Examination of the successive reports of the Committee of Experts suggests a need for a systematic approach and bilingual instruction models in view of the evidence that residual-presence models in the teaching of RMLs (e.g. Sunday schools, one hour per week, use of certain teaching material) do not seem to be effective.[108]

Thought must also be given to the need to ensure that the instruments of ratification allow for continuity in the undertakings entered into, so as to nurture full student proficiency through a gradual acquisition of knowledge of RMLs. In this regard, of special importance is the presence of teaching of/ in the regional or minority language in pre-school education. The fact that many minority languages are no longer passed on from generation to generation makes education the focus for the recovery of the language.

Equally worrying is the lack of continuity and absence of RMLs in secondary, vocational and university education. The need for RMLs to cover technical and specialised uses and be close to the job supply is crucial to their survival.

Mention should be made of the need, once the initial development stage has passed, for the Committee of Experts' reports to assess those aspects which are relevant to implementation of the undertakings that are not listed explicitly in the Charter, such as teaching material, the type of subjects taught in the RMLs and whether or not there are attainment tests to ensure that the way education is organised does not give rise to any bias unfavourable to these languages.

It is also necessary, within the flexibility inherent in the undertakings of Part III of the Charter, that the monitoring activity produces a degree of standardisation of practices or models corresponding to each level of

---

107. Austria 2005, 93.
108. As indicated by the recommendations of the Committee of Ministers to Hungary (Recommendation RecChL(2004)4): "move to forms of bilingual education for Part III languages."

undertaking, so that there are no wide discrepancies between the various solutions adopted for the same undertaking in the different states or for different languages.[109]

References

Arzoz, Xabier (2009), "Language rights as legal norms", *European Public Law*, Vol. 15, No. 4, pp. 541-74.

Arzoz, Xabier (2010), "Accommodating linguistic difference: five normative models of language rights", *European Constitutional Law Review*, No. 6, pp. 102-22.

Bastardas Boadas, Albert (2003), "Ecodinámica sociolingüística: comparaciones y analogías entre la diversidad lingüística y la diversidad biológica", *Llengua i Dret*, No. 39, p. 129.

Committee of Experts (2006), *The Committee of Experts' interpretation and evaluation practice concerning the implementation of articles on education of the European Charter for Regional or Minority Languages*, MIN-LANG (2006) 3. Strasbourg: Council of Europe.

Council of Europe (2000), *European Charter for Regional or Minority Languages and Explanatory Report*. Strasbourg: Council of Europe Publishing.

Dunbar, Robert (2001), "Minority language rights in international law", *International and Comparative Law Quarterly*, No. 50, pp. 90-120.

Pons Parera, Eva (2006), "Los derechos lingüísticos en el marco internacional y comunitario europeo" in José Manuel Pérez Fernández (ed.), *Estudios jurídicos sobre el estatuto jurídico de las lenguas en España*. Barcelona: Atelier.

Thornberry, Patrick (1991), *International law and the rights of minorities*. Oxford: Clarendon Press.

Urrutia Libarona, Iñigo (2005), *Derechos lingüísticos y euskera en el sistema educativo*. Iruña: Lete.

Urrutia, Iñigo and Lasagabaster, Iñaki (2008), "Language rights and community law", *European Integration Online Papers*, Vol. 12, http://eiop.or.at/eiop/index. php/eiop/article/view/2008_004a.

---

109. "Inconsistencies such as these have been criticised as unfortunately making the Committee of Experts appear arbitrary in its approach to the charter, though perhaps a more generous view would point out that what probably needs to be done in the circumstances is a closer monitoring of the Committee of Experts' reports so as to avoid such inconsistencies in the future – and to move away from any accusations of inconsistency or arbitrariness" – F. de Varennes (2008), "Language protection and the European Charter ... *quo vadis?*", p. 31.

Varennes, Fernand (de) (2001), "Language rights as an integral part of human rights", *International Journal on Multicultural Societies*, Vol. 3, No. 1.

Varennes, Fernand (de) (2008), "Language protection and the European Charter for Regional or Minority Languages: *quo vadis?*" in Robert Dunbar and Gwynedd Parry (eds), *The European Charter for Regional or Minority Languages: legal challenges and opportunities*. Strasbourg: Council of Europe Publishing.

Woehrling, Jean-Marie (2008), "The European Charter for Regional or Minority Languages and the principle of non-discrimination" in *The European Charter for Regional or Minority Languages: legal challenges and opportunities*. Strasbourg: Council of Europe Publishing.

Appendix: Ratifications

Article 8		
Paragraph and subparagraph		
1	a.i	**Czech Republic:** Polish (Moravian-Silesian region) **Finland:** Sami and Swedish **Germany:** Romani (*Land* Berlin) **Poland:** Belarusian, Czech, Hebrew, Yiddish, Karaim, Kashub, Lithuanian, Lemko, German, Armenian, Romani, Russian, Slovak, Tatar and Ukrainian **Romania:** Croatian, German, Hungarian, Slovak, Turkish, and Ukrainian **Slovakia:** Hungarian **Slovenia:** Italian **Spain:** Catalan (Catalonia), Basque (in the Navarra "Basque-speaking zone"), Basque (Basque Country), Catalan (Balearic Islands), Valencian (Valencia) and Galician (Galicia) **Switzerland:** Italian **United Kingdom:** Welsh and Scottish-Gaelic
	a.ii	**Austria:** Burgenland Croatian (*Land* Burgenland) and Hungarian (*Land* Burgenland) **Czech Republic:** Polish (Moravian-Silesian region) **Germany:** Romani (*Land* Berlin) **Netherlands:** Frisian (province of Friesland) **Romania:** Bulgarian, Czech and Serbian **Slovakia:** Ruthenian and Ukrainian **Slovenia:** Hungarian
	a.iii	**Bosnia and Herzegovina:** Albanian, Montenegrin, Czech, Italian, Hungarian, Macedonian, German, Polish, Romanian, Rysin, Slovak, Slovenian, Turkish, Ukrainian, Jewish (Yiddish and Ladino) and Romani **Croatia:** Italian, Serbian, Hungarian, Czech, Slovak, Ruthenian and Ukrainian **Denmark:** German (Southern Jutland)

	Germany: Upper Sorbian (Free State of Saxony), North Frisian (*Land* Schleswig-Holstein), Romani (*Land* Hesse) and Romanes (*Land* Hesse) **Hungary:** Romani **Montenegro:** Albanian and Romani **Norway:** Sami **Romania:** Russian **Serbia:** Albanian, Bosnian, Bulgarian, Hungarian, Romani, Romanian, Ruthenian, Slovakian, Ukrainian and Croatian **Slovakia:** Bulgarian, Croatian, Czech, German, Polish and Romani **Sweden:** Sami, Finnish and Meänkieli **Ukraine:** Belarusian, Bulgarian, Gagauz, Greek, Jewish, Crimean Tatar, Moldovan, German, Polish, Russian, Romanian, Slovak and Hungarian **United Kingdom:** Irish
a.iv	**Armenia**: Assyrian, Yezidi, Greek, Russian and Kurdish **Austria:** Slovenian (*Land* Carinthia), Czech (*Land* Vienna), Slovakian (*Land* Vienna), Slovenian (*Land* Styria) and Hungarian (*Land* Vienna) **Czech Republic:** Slovak **Germany:** Danish (*Land* Schleswig-Holstein), Lower Sorbian (*Land* Brandenburg), North Frisian (*Land* Schleswig-Holstein), Sater Frisian (*Land* Lower Saxony), Low German (Free Hanseatic City of Bremen, Free and Hanseatic City of Hamburg and *Länder* of Mecklenburg-Western Pomerania, Lower Saxony and Schleswig-Holstein), Romani (*Land* Baden-Württemberg), Romani (*Land* Hesse), Romani (*Land* Rhineland-Palatinate), Low German (*Land* Brandenburg), Low German (*Land* Saxony-Anhalt) and Romanes (*Land* Hesse) **Hungary:** Croatian, German, Romanian, Serbian, Slovak, Slovenian and Beás **Montenegro:** Albanian and Romani **Serbia:** Albanian, Bosnian, Bulgarian, Hungarian, Romani, Romanian, Ruthenian, Slovakian, Ukrainian and Croatian **Switzerland:** Romansh and Italian
b.i	**Czech Republic:** Polish (Moravian-Silesian Region) **Finland:** Sami and Swedish **Germany:** Romani (*Land* Berlin) **Poland:** Belarusian, Czech, Hebrew, Yiddish, Karaim, Kashub, Lithuanian, Lemko, German, Armenian, Romani, Russian, Slovak, Tatar and Ukrainian **Romania:** Croatian, German, Hungarian, Serbian, Slovak, Turkish and Ukrainian **Slovakia:** Hungarian **Slovenia:** Italian **Spain:** Catalan (Catalonia), Basque (in the Navarra "Basque-speaking zone"), Basque (Basque Country), Catalan (Balearic Islands), Valencian (Valencia) and Galician (Galicia) **Switzerland:** Romansh and Italian **United Kingdom:** Welsh and Scottish-Gaelic
b.ii	**Austria:** Burgenland Croatian (*Land* Burgenland), Slovenian (*Land* Carinthia) and Hungarian (*Land* Burgenland) **Czech Republic:** Polish (Moravian-Silesian region) **Germany:** Romani (*Land* Berlin)

281

		Montenegro: Albanian and Romani (Republic of Montenegro) **Netherlands:** Frisian (province of Friesland) **Romania:** Bulgarian and Czech **Slovakia:** Ruthenian and Ukrainian **Slovenia:** Hungarian
	b.iii	**Germany:** Low German (Free Hanseatic City of Bremen), Low German (Free and Hanseatic City of Hamburg), Low German (*Land* Mecklenburg-Western Pomerania), Low German (*Land* Schleswig-Holstein) and Romani (*Land* Berlin) **Romania:** Russian **Slovakia:** Bulgarian, Croatian, Czech, German, Polish and Romani
	b.iv	**Armenia**: Assyrian, Yezidi, Greek, Russian and Kurdish **Bosnia and Herzegovina:** Albanian, Montenegrin, Czech, Italian, Hungarian, Macedonian, German, Polish, Romanian, Rysin, Slovak, Slovenian, Turkish, Ukrainian, Jewish (Yiddish and Ladino) and Romani **Croatia:** Italian, Serbian, Hungarian, Czech, Slovak, Ruthenian and Ukrainian **Czech Republic:** Slovak **Denmark:** German (Southern Jutland) **Germany:** Danish (*Land* Schleswig-Holstein), Upper Sorbian (Free State of Saxony), Lower Sorbian (*Land* Brandenburg), North Frisian (*Land* Schleswig-Holstein), Romani (*Land* Berlin), Romani (Free and Hanseatic City of Hamburg), Romani (*Land* Hesse), Low German (*Land* Brandenburg), Low German (*Land* Saxony-Anhalt) and Romanes (*Land* Hesse) **Hungary:** Croatian, German, Romanian, Serbian, Slovak, Slovenian, Romani and Beás **Montenegro:** Albanian and Romani **Norway:** Sami **Serbia:** Albanian, Bosnian, Bulgarian, Hungarian, Romani, Romanian, Ruthenian, Slovakian, Ukrainian and Croatian **Sweden:** Sami, Finnish and Meänkieli **Ukraine:** Belarusian, Bulgarian, Gagauz, Greek, Jewish, Crimean Tatar, Moldovan, German, Polish, Russian, Romanian, Slovak and Hungarian **United Kingdom:** Irish
	c.i	**Czech Republic:** Polish (Moravian-Silesian Region) **Finland:** Sami and Swedish **Poland:** Belarusian, Czech, Hebrew, Yiddish, Karaim, Kashub, Lithuanian, Lemko, German, Armenian, Romani, Russian, Slovak, Tatar and Ukrainian **Romania:** German, Hungarian, Serbian, Slovak, Turkish and Ukrainian **Slovakia:** Hungarian **Slovenia:** Italian **Spain:** Catalan (Catalonia), Basque (in the Navarra "Basque-speaking zone"), Basque (Basque Country), Catalan (Balearic Islands), Valencian (Valencia), and Galician (Galicia) **Switzerland:** Italian **United Kingdom:** Welsh and Scottish-Gaelic

c.ii	**Czech Republic:** Polish (Moravian-Silesian Region) **Romania:** Croatian **Slovakia:** Ruthenian and Ukrainian **Slovenia:** Hungarian
c.iii	**Austria:** Burgenland Croatian (*Land* Burgenland), Slovenian (*Land* Carinthia) and Hungarian (*Land* Burgenland) **Denmark:** German (Southern Jutland) **Germany:** Danish (*Land* Schleswig-Holstein), Low German (Free Hanseatic City of Bremen), Low German (Free and Hanseatic City of Hamburg), Low German (*Land* Mecklenburg-Western Pomerania) and Low German (*Land* Schleswig-Holstein) **Montenegro:** Albanian and Romani (Republic of Montenegro) **Netherlands:** Frisian (province of Friesland) **Romania:** Bulgarian, Czech and Russian **Slovakia:** Bulgarian, Croatian, Czech, German, Polish and Romani **Switzerland:** Romansh and Italian
c.iv	**Armenia**: Assyrian, Yezidi, Greek, Russian and Kurdish **Bosnia and Herzegovina:** Albanian, Montenegrin, Czech, Italian, Hungarian, Macedonian, German, Polish, Romanian, Rysin, Slovak, Slovenian, Turkish, Ukrainian, Jewish (Yiddish and Ladino) and Romani **Croatia:** Italian, Serbian, Hungarian, Czech, Slovak, Ruthenian and Ukrainian **Denmark:** German (Southern Jutland) **Germany:** Danish (*Land* Schleswig-Holstein), Upper Sorbian (Free State of Saxony), Lower Sorbian (*Land* Brandenburg), North Frisian (*Land* Schleswig-Holstein), Romani (Free and Hanseatic City of Hamburg), Romani (*Land* Hesse), Low German (*Land* Brandenburg), Low German (*Land* Saxony-Anhalt) and Romanes (*Land* Hesse) **Hungary:** Croatian, German, Romanian, Serbian, Slovak Slovenian, Romani and Beás **Montenegro:** Albanian and Romani (Republic of Montenegro) **Norway:** Sami **Serbia:** Albanian, Bosnian, Bulgarian, Hungarian, Romani, Romanian, Ruthenian, Slovakian, Ukrainian and Croatian **Sweden:** Sami, Finnish and Meänkieli **Ukraine:** Belarusian, Bulgarian, Gagauz, Greek, Jewish, Crimean Tatar, Moldovan, German, Polish, Russian, Romanian, Slovak and Hungarian **United Kingdom:** Irish
d.i	**Finland:** Swedish **Romania:** German and Hungarian **Slovakia:** Hungarian **Slovenia:** Italian **Spain:** Catalan (Catalonia), Basque (in the Navarra "Basque-speaking zone"), Basque (Basque Country), Catalan (Balearic Islands), Valencian (Valencia) and Galician (Galicia) **Switzerland:** Italian

283

d.ii	**Czech Republic:** Polish (Moravian-Silesian region) **Finland:** Sami **Slovakia:** Ruthenian and Ukrainian **Slovenia:** Hungarian
d.iii	**Denmark:** German (Southern Jutland) **Germany:** Danish (*Land* Schleswig-Holstein), Low German (Free and Hanseatic City of Hamburg) and Low German (*Land* Mecklenburg-Western Pomerania) **Poland:** Belarusian, Czech, Hebrew, Yiddish, Karaim, Kashub, Lithuanian, Lemko, German, Armenian, Romani, Russian, Slovak, Tatar and Ukrainian **Slovakia:** Bulgarian, Croatian, Czech, German, Polish and Romani **Switzerland:** Romansh and Italian
d.iv	**Armenia**: Assyrian, Yezidi, Greek, Russian and Kurdish **Austria:** Burgenland Croatian (*Land* Burgenland), Slovenian (*Land* Carinthia) and Hungarian (*Land* Burgenland) **Bosnia and Herzegovina:** Albanian, Montenegrin, Czech, Italian, Hungarian, Macedonian, German, Polish, Romanian, Rysin, Slovak, Slovenian, Turkish, Ukrainian, Jewish (Yiddish and Ladino) and Romani **Croatia:** Italian, Serbian, Hungarian, Czech, Slovak, Ruthenian and Ukrainian **Germany:** Upper Sorbian (Free State of Saxony), Romani (*Land* Hesse) and Romanes (*Land* Hesse) **Hungary:** Croatian, German, Romanian, Serbian, Slovak Slovenian, Romani and Beás **Montenegro:** Albanian and Romani (Republic of Montenegro) **Norway:** Sami **Romania:** Bulgarian, Czech, Russian, Serbian, Slovak, Turkish and Ukrainian **Serbia:** Albanian, Bosnian, Bulgarian, Hungarian, Romani, Romanian, Ruthenian, Slovakian, Ukrainian and Croatian **Sweden:** Sami, Finnish and Meänkieli **Ukraine:** Belarusian, Bulgarian, Gagauz, Greek, Jewish, Crimean Tatar, Moldovan, German, Polish, Russian, Romanian, Slovak and Hungarian **United Kingdom:** Welsh, Scottish-Gaelic and Irish
e.i	**Finland:** Swedish **Germany:** Romani (*Land* Berlin) **Romania:** German and Hungarian **Slovakia:** Hungarian
e.ii	**Croatia:** Italian, Serbian, Hungarian, Czech, Slovak, Ruthenian and Ukrainian **Denmark:** German (Southern Jutland) **Finland:** Sami **Germany:** Danish (*Land* Schleswig-Holstein), Upper Sorbian (Free State of Saxony), North Frisian (*Land* Schleswig-Holstein), Sater Frisian (*Land* Lower Saxony), Low German (Free Hanseatic City of Bremen, Free and Hanseatic City of Hamburg and the *Länder* of Mecklenburg-Western Pomerania, Lower Saxony and Schleswig-Holstein) and Romani (*Land* Berlin)

		Montenegro: Albanian and Romani (Republic of Montenegro) **Netherlands:** Frisian (province of Friesland) **Norway:** Sami **Poland:** Belarusian, Czech, Hebrew, Yiddish, Karaim, Kashub, Lithuanian, Lemko, German, Armenian, Romani, Russian, Slovak, Tatar and Ukrainian **Romania:** Bulgarian, Russian, Serbian, Slovak and Turkish **Serbia:** Albanian, Bosnian, Bulgarian, Hungarian, Romani, Romanian, Ruthenian, Slovakian, Ukrainian and Croatian **Slovakia:** Bulgarian, Croatian, Czech, German, Polish, Romani, Ruthenian and Ukrainian **Switzerland:** Romansh and Italian
	e.iii	**Armenia**: Assyrian, Yezidi, Greek, Russian and Kurdish **Austria:** Burgenland Croatian (*Land* Burgenland), Slovenian (*Land* Carinthia), Hungarian (*Land* Burgenland), Slovenian (*Land* Styria) and Hungarian (*Land* Vienna) **Bosnia and Herzegovina:** Romani **Czech Republic:** Polish (Moravian-Silesian Region) and Slovak (territory of the Czech Republic) **Germany:** Lower Sorbian (*Land* Brandenburg), Romani (*Land* Baden-Württemberg), Romani (*Land* Berlin), Romani (*Land* Hesse), Romani (*Land* North Rhine-Westphalia), Romani (*Land* Rhineland-Palatinate), Low German (*Land* North Rhine-Westphalia) and Romanes (*Land* Hesse) **Hungary:** Croatian, German, Romanian, Serbian, Slovak, Slovenian, Romani and Beás **Romania:** Croatian and Ukrainian **Slovenia:** Italian and Hungarian **Spain:** Catalan (Catalonia), Basque (in the Navarra "Basque-speaking zone"), Basque (Basque Country), Catalan (Balearic Islands), Valencian (Valencia) and Galician (Galicia) **Sweden:** Sami, Finnish and Meänkieli **Ukraine:** Belarusian, Bulgarian, Gagauz, Greek, Jewish, Crimean Tatar, Moldovan, German, Polish, Russian, Romanian, Slovak and Hungarian **United Kingdom:** Welsh, Scottish-Gaelic and Irish
	f.i	**Finland:** Swedish **Germany:** Low German (Free Hanseatic City of Bremen) **Netherlands:** Frisian (province of Friesland) **Romania:** Hungarian **Slovakia:** Hungarian **Spain:** Catalan (Catalonia), Basque (in the Navarra "Basque-speaking zone"), Basque (Basque Country), Catalan (Balearic Islands), Valencian (Valencia) and Galician (Galicia) **Switzerland:** Italian
	f.ii	**Croatia:** Italian, Serbian, Hungarian, Czech, Slovak, Ruthenian and Ukrainian **Denmark:** German (Southern Jutland) **Finland:** Sami **Germany:** Danish (*Land* Schleswig-Holstein) and Low German (Free and Hanseatic City of Hamburg)

285

		Norway: Sami **Slovakia:** Bulgarian, Croatian, Czech, German, Polish, Romani, Ruthenian and Ukrainian **United Kingdom:** Welsh and Irish
	f.iii	**Armenia**: Assyrian, Yezidi, Greek, Russian and Kurdish **Austria:** Burgenland Croatian (*Land* Burgenland), Slovenian (*Land* Carinthia), Hungarian (*Land* Burgenland), Romani (*Land* Burgenland), Slovenian (*Land* Styria) and Hungarian (*Land* Vienna) **Bosnia and Herzegovina:** Romani **Czech Republic:** Polish (Moravian-Silesian region) **Germany:** Danish (*Land* Schleswig-Holstein), Upper Sorbian (Free State of Saxony), Lower Sorbian (*Land* Brandenburg), North Frisian (*Land* Schleswig-Holstein), Sater Frisian (*Land* Lower Saxony), Low German (*Land* Lower Saxony), Low German (*Land* Lower Saxony), Romani (Federal Republic of Germany), Low German (*Land* Brandenburg) and Romanes (federal territory) **Hungary:** Croatian, German, Romanian, Serbian, Slovak and Slovenian, Romani and Beás **Montenegro:** Albanian and Romani (Republic of Montenegro) **Romania:** German, Russian, Turkish and Ukrainian **Serbia:** Albanian, Bosnian, Bulgarian, Hungarian, Romani, Romanian, Ruthenian, Slovakian, Ukrainian and Croatian **Slovenia:** Italian and Hungarian **Sweden:** Sami, Finnish and Meänkieli **Switzerland:** Romansh and Italian **Ukraine:** Belarusian, Bulgarian, Gagauz, Greek, Jewish, Crimean Tatar, Moldovan, German, Polish, Russian, Romanian, Slovak and Hungarian **United Kingdom:** Scottish-Gaelic
	g	**Austria:** Burgenland Croatian (*Land* Burgenland), Slovenian (*Land* Carinthia) and Hungarian (*Land* Burgenland) **Bosnia and Herzegovina:** Albanian, Montenegrin, Czech, Italian, Hungarian, Macedonian, German, Polish, Romanian, Rysin, Slovak, Slovenian, Turkish, Ukrainian, Jewish (Yiddish and Ladino) and Romani **Croatia:** Italian, Serbian, Hungarian, Czech, Slovak, Ruthenian and Ukrainian **Czech Republic:** Polish (Moravian-Silesian region) and Slovak (territory of the Czech Republic) **Denmark:** German (Southern Jutland) **Finland:** Sami and Swedish **Germany:** Danish (*Land* Schleswig-Holstein), Upper Sorbian (Free State of Saxony), Lower Sorbian (*Land* Brandenburg), North Frisian (*Land* Schleswig-Holstein), Sater Frisian (*Land* Lower Saxony), Low German (Free Hanseatic City of Bremen, Free and Hanseatic City of Hamburg and the *Länder* of Mecklenburg-Western Pomerania, Lower Saxony and Schleswig-Holstein), Romani (Federal Republic of Germany), Low German (*Land* Brandenburg), Low German (*Land* North Rhine-Westphalia), Low German (*Land* Saxony-Anhalt)

286

		Hungary: Croatian, German, Romanian, Serbian, Slovak and Slovenian, Romani and Beás **Montenegro:** Albanian and Romani **Netherlands:** Frisian (province of Friesland) **Norway:** Sami **Poland:** Belarusian, Czech, Hebrew, Yiddish, Karaim, Kashub, Lithuanian, Lemko, German, Armenian, Romani, Russian, Slovak, Tatar and Ukrainian **Romania:** Bulgarian, Czech, Croatia, German, Hungarian, Serbian, Slovak, Turkish and Ukrainian **Serbia:** Albanian, Bosnian, Bulgarian, Hungarian, Romani, Romanian, Ruthenian, Slovakian, Ukrainian and Croatian **Slovakia:** Bulgarian, Croatian, Czech, German, Polish, Romani, Ruthenian, Hungarian and Ukrainian **Slovenia:** Italian and Hungarian **Spain:** Catalan (Catalonia), Basque (in the Navarra "Basque-speaking zone"), Basque (Basque Country), Catalan (Balearic Islands), Valencian (Valencia) and Galician (Galicia) **Sweden:** Sami, Finnish and Meänkieli **Switzerland:** Romansh and Italian **Ukraine:** Belarusian, Bulgarian, Gagauz, Greek, Jewish, Crimean Tatar, Moldovan, German, Polish, Russian, Romanian, Slovak and Hungarian **United Kingdom:** Welsh, Scottish-Gaelic and Irish
	h	**Austria:** Burgenland Croatian (*Land* Burgenland), Slovenian (*Land* Carinthia) and Hungarian (*Land* Burgenland) **Croatia:** Italian, Serbian, Hungarian, Czech, Slovak, Ruthenian and Ukrainian **Czech Republic:** Polish (Moravian-Silesian Region) **Denmark:** German (Southern Jutland) **Finland:** Sami and Swedish **Germany:** Danish (*Land* Schleswig-Holstein), Upper Sorbian (Free State of Saxony), Lower Sorbian (*Land* Brandenburg), North Frisian (*Land* Schleswig-Holstein), Low German (Free Hanseatic City of Bremen), Low German (Free and Hanseatic City of Hamburg), Low German (*Land* Mecklenburg-Western Pomerania), Low German (*Land* Schleswig-Holstein), Romani (Federal Republic of Germany), Low German (*Land* North Rhine-Westphalia), Low German (*Land* Saxony-Anhalt), Romanes (federal territory) **Hungary:** Croatian, German, Romanian, Serbian, Slovak and Slovenian, Romani and Beás **Montenegro:** Albanian and Romani **Netherlands:** Frisian (province of Friesland) **Norway:** Sami **Poland:** Belarusian, Czech, Hebrew, Yiddish, Karaim, Kashub, Lithuanian, Lemko, German, Armenian, Romani, Russian, Slovak, Tatar and Ukrainian **Romania:** Bulgarian, Croatian, German, Hungarian, Serbian, Slovak, Turkish and Ukrainian **Slovakia:** Bulgarian, Croatian, Czech, German, Polish, Romani, Ruthenian, Hungarian and Ukrainian **Slovenia:** Italian and Hungarian

287

		Spain: Catalan (Catalonia), Basque (in the Navarra "Basque-speaking zone"), Basque (Basque Country), Catalan (Balearic Islands), Valencian (Valencia) and Galician (Galicia) **Sweden:** Sami, Finnish and Meänkieli **Switzerland:** Romansh and Italian **Ukraine:** Belarusian, Bulgarian, Gagauz, Greek, Jewish, Crimean Tatar, Moldovan, German, Polish, Russian, Romanian, Slovak and Hungarian **United Kingdom:** Welsh, Scottish-Gaelic and Irish
	i	**Austria:** Burgenland Croatian (*Land* Burgenland), Slovenian (*Land* Carinthia) and Hungarian (*Land* Burgenland) **Czech Republic:** Polish (Moravian-Silesian Region) and Slovak **Denmark:** German (Southern Jutland) **Finland:** Sami and Swedish **Germany:** Danish (*Land* Schleswig-Holstein), Upper Sorbian (Free State of Saxony), Lower Sorbian (*Land* Brandenburg), North Frisian (*Land* Schleswig-Holstein), Sater Frisian (*Land* Lower Saxony), Low German (Free and Hanseatic City of Hamburg), Low German (*Land* Schleswig-Holstein), Low German (*Land* Mecklenburg-Western Pomerania), Low German (*Land* Lower Saxony), Romani (*Land* Hesse), Romanes (*Land* Hesse) **Hungary:** Croatian, German, Romanian, Serbian, Slovak, Slovenian, Romani and Beás **Netherlands:** Frisian (province of Friesland) **Norway:** Sami **Poland:** Belarusian, Czech, Hebrew, Yiddish, Karaim, Kashub, Lithuanian, Lemko, German, Armenian, Romani, Russian, Slovak, Tatar and Ukrainian **Romania:** Bulgarian, Czech, Croatian, German, Hungarian, Serbian, Slovak, Turkish and Ukrainian **Slovakia:** Bulgarian, Croatian, Czech, German, Polish, Romani, Ruthenian, Hungarian and Ukrainian **Slovenia:** Italian and Hungarian **Spain:** Catalan (Catalonia), Basque (in the Navarra "Basque-speaking zone"), Basque (Basque Country), Catalan (Balearic Islands), Valencian (Valencia) and Galician (Galicia) **Sweden:** Sami, Finnish and Meänkieli **Switzerland:** Romansh and Italian **Ukraine:** Belarusian, Bulgarian, Gagauz, Greek, Jewish, Crimean Tatar, Moldovan, German, Polish, Russian, Romanian, Slovak and Hungarian **United Kingdom:** Welsh and Scottish-Gaelic

Article 8.2. Education (II)

Adriano Previtali[1]
University of Fribourg/Freiburg

1. Introduction

2. Interpretation and comment

3. Prospects

References

Appendix: Ratifications

Article 8.2 – Education

With regard to education and in respect of territories other than those in which the regional or minority languages are traditionally used, the Parties undertake, if the number of users of a regional or minority language justifies it, to allow, encourage or provide teaching in or of the regional or minority language at all the appropriate stages of education.

1. Introduction

Teaching regional or minority languages (RMLs) outside the regions in which they are traditionally used complements and expands the goals pursued by the first paragraph of Article 8 of the Charter. Teaching these languages is no doubt one of the most effective means of guaranteeing their survival and dissemination, giving practical expression to the ultimate purpose of the Charter, which is to promote Europe's linguistic diversity and cultural heritage (see also Article 7.1a. and c of the Charter). It is true that, like the other clauses of the Charter, Article 8.2 is relatively non-prescriptive. However, despite its clear limitations, this article could help to achieve this goal at least partly.

The relatively high number of states that have agreed to apply the article clearly shows that the principle of the territoriality of languages – which, as we shall see, is mitigated in part by Article 8.2 of the Charter – is not necessarily one of the dogmas of European language policy, especially in the always very delicate sphere of education. The increased mobility of people between different

---

1. I would like to thank my colleagues at the University of Fribourg/Freiburg, Jean-Luc Gassmann and Christine Verdon, for re-reading this paper.

countries and within countries has forced many states to assess whether it is still feasible to pursue traditional language policies based on protecting the linguistic uniformity of various regions or whether it would not be more reasonable to guarantee peace between languages and the integration of the various population groups living on the same territory through the promotion of plurilingualism. These are crucial and urgent issues for RMLs as they are the most severely penalised by the inflexible application of the principle of territoriality. Investigating Article 8.2 of the Charter also makes it possible to review these key aspects of language policy and education.

2. Interpretation and comment

There are two limits on the material scope of the provision in question. Firstly, Article 8.2 applies only to RMLs which are recognised as such by a state.[2] This restriction gives parties the right to limit the effectiveness of this article considerably. Secondly, the article applies only to the sphere of education. The concept must, however, be interpreted in the broadest possible sense because it encompasses all levels of education mentioned in the first paragraph of Article 8. Neither literal nor systematic interpretations make it possible to restrict the idea of education that is intended. Instead they confirm that there is a logical consistency between the definitions of education given in the first and second paragraphs. The fact that the aim of the article is to support and promote RMLs outside the territories where they are traditionally used is not an appropriate argument to justify a more restrictive interpretation of what was intended. There is, after all, no evidence that it would be materially impossible in these regions to achieve this goal in any of the types or levels of education referred to in Article 8 paragraph 1. Thus, for example, a desire to preserve the linguistic homogeneity of territories and contribute to the integration of inhabitants speaking a minority or regional language does not necessarily warrant limiting the list of types of education falling within the scope of the article. The same applies to the costs connected with supporting these languages outside the territories referred to.[3] In this connection, Article 7.1f also highlights the obligation to make suitable forms and methods of education available at all appropriate stages.

Its territorial scope is most certainly one of the main defining features of this rule. Unlike most of the other provisions of the Charter, which are governed by the principle of territoriality, Article 8.2 makes an explicit exception to this principle and provides for the possibility of supporting RMLs outside their traditional areas of use. The only other article to state explicitly that it makes

---

2. See the summary table at the end of the comment on Article 8.2 of the Charter.
3. These arguments might form the basis for public interests allowing states to concentrate activities in some education sectors rather than others (see also below).

a similar exception is Article 12.2, with regard to cultural activities and facilities. Other exceptions to the principle of territoriality arise implicitly from articles 9, on judicial authorities, and 11, on the media, as the right to use an RML in the higher courts or in the national media inevitably amounts to agreeing to the use of these languages outside the territories in which they are traditionally used, because most higher courts and national media companies lie outside these languages' territorial boundaries.[4]

There are two main reasons which warranted the introduction of this extra-territorial aspect in Article 8.2 of the Charter. Firstly, the principle of territoriality is no longer sufficient for the effective protection of RMLs in our increasingly mobile societies.[5] This is especially true in view of the fact that, as well as being spoken by a minority of the population, these languages are often used in peripheral or economically or socially less-favoured regions and that this in turn increases migratory movements towards majority language regions.[6] As a result, it is simply no longer possible to protect and promote these languages if activities are confined within the regions in which they are traditionally used.

Secondly, the exception to the principle of the territoriality of languages confirms the Charter's modern approach to language policy. It reflects its authors' desire to promote plurilingualism at national level, fostering peaceful coexistence between several languages and in particular avoiding conflict at local and regional levels between the majority national language(s) and the RMLs. This choice also enhances the Charter's precursory role in the sphere of second language learning, as sound knowledge of one's mother tongue generally helps people to learn other languages and so contributes indirectly to the integration into a new cultural context of migrants from regions in which RMLs are traditionally used.

The rule applies to territories in which RMLs are not traditionally used. The wording of the article is not as felicitous as it could be. The decision to delimit the territorial scope of Article 8.2 of the Charter in negative terms makes it less clear. It would have been preferable to use a positive expression such as: "the

---

4. See also V. Piergigli (2001), *Lingue minoritarie e identità culturali*. Milan: Giuffrè, p. 44.
5. See Explanatory Report, paragraph 89.
6. The Committee of Experts noted, in its first report on the situation in Germany, that the traditional Sorbian territory had seen a drastic decline in its population (50%) over a decade, leading to the closure of over 300 schools; Germany 2002, 431. The committee also noted of Sweden: "the situation of the Finnish language is very special because more than 95% of the speakers live outside the Finnish administrative area". The situation with regard to the teaching of this language had been deteriorating for a long time and Finnish was clearly now taught as a mother tongue only as a result of the private initiatives of Sweden's Finnish community; Sweden 2003, 210; Sweden 2006, 186.

Parties undertake to allow, encourage or provide teaching in regional or minority languages … which would also take place outside the territory in which these languages are traditionally used".[7]

It is not specified in the Charter exactly what is meant by the word "traditionally". To understand this word, we have to start with its two main meanings, while bearing in mind that these two aspects overlap and complement one another. The first component of the word is a temporal one linked to the length of time for which a language has been present in a given territory. To qualify as a language that is traditionally used in the territory, the language in question needs to have been used there for a very long time. It would be impossible and most probably unreasonable to attempt to put a lower limit on this period of time. The presumption must be, however, that the language needs to have been used in the region for several generations or several centuries.[8] Secondly, the word traditionally implies that the language has influenced the region's culture, ways and customs. This meaning highlights the cultural aspect of languages and, in particular, the relationship of mutual exchange always existing between a language and the territory in which it is used.

To be used traditionally in a given territory within the meaning of the Charter, the RML concerned does not have to be the only language spoken on the territory or the majority language in the region, or be recognised by the state as a national, official or semi-official language. The only deciding factors are the social and linguistic aspects referred to above, namely the length of the language's presence and its historic and cultural ties with the territory. In other words it is enough for a language to have existed for a suitably long time in a given region and established a particularly intense relationship with that region for it to qualify.

A contrario, regions which do not share these characteristics are the "other" territories (in Article 8.2 of the Charter) where states must implement measures to support RMLs.

By ratifying Article 8.2, the parties undertook to take measures for supporting RMLs. This is an instruction directed at the state authorities. Therefore, this article does not grant private individuals or organisations from the linguistic communities concerned any directly enforceable subjective rights or collective rights which may be relied on directly.[9] It is of course regrettable that the article does not have any direct legal effect, but it does not mean that the rule lacks any normative content. In accordance with articles 26 and 27 of the Vienna

---

7. The same comment applies to Article 12.2 of the Charter.
8. See also Article 1, paragraph a of the Charter and paragraph 31 of the Explanatory Report.
9. See also Explanatory Report, paragraph 11.

Convention on the Law of Treaties of 23 May 1969, the parties are required to honour their international commitments and hence to take the appropriate measures to achieve the goal pursued by the rule in question.

To ensure the effectiveness of the right to be taught an RML outside the area in which it is traditionally used, the states commit themselves to take three types of measure, which may be applied simultaneously or in combination. They must:

- authorise teaching of such languages in these territories. The parties undertake to allow the provision of such teaching. In other words, they must refrain from directly or indirectly obstructing public or private actions designed to pursue this goal. There is a particular need to avoid adopting laws or administrative practices in the education or language policy spheres which prevent or hinder the teaching of RMLs, especially through excessively strict application of the principle of the territoriality of languages. It is also important not to discourage those who are interested in learning such languages from doing so. Accordingly, the teaching in question should not have to compete with compulsory classes; it should not be provided at hours that are too inconvenient or at excessive cost in countries where education is not completely free of charge;

- encourage the teaching of such languages. The verb that is used here clearly emphasises the state's duty to adopt a proactive policy in this field. To honour this commitment, it is not enough for the parties to refrain from obstructing teaching; they are required to take active measures. Measures may, of course, vary in type and intensity. The state should begin by supporting the activities of public authorities or private bodies in the sector. Several measures are possible including financial support, particularly for the training and salaries of the teachers involved and the costs of producing and purchasing teaching materials,[10] logistical support, especially the provision of teaching premises, and co-ordination of the various activities. However, the simple fact of supporting these activities economically is not yet enough to fully honour the commitment made at the international level. To put into practice the obligation of encouraging the dissemination of the languages covered by Article 8.2, the states must also adopt measures conducive to the emergence and development of such activities. The parties should for instance enact legislation – or encourage local authorities to do so if responsibility for education lies with them – whose aim would be to create the right conditions for schools to introduce teaching in RMLs in

---

10. The shortage of adequately trained teachers and suitable teaching material has also been denounced several times by the Committee of Experts, e.g: Sweden 2003, 98; Norway 2007, 134; Application of the Charter in Norway, 4th monitoring cycle (2010), paragraph 156.

areas outside the territories where they are traditionally used. This goal may be pursued, in particular, through at least partial recognition of such courses, the establishment of exchange programmes between teachers and the promotion of activities to foster links with regions where RMLs are traditionally used;

- provide teaching in RMLs. In this case, the state adopts direct measures to enable these languages to be taught, such as setting up lessons in them as part of the general school curriculum or the provision of optional courses offered directly by state-run establishments or indirectly by state-certified private establishments.

The efficiency of these three types of measure depends largely on how much the state has publicised them. The authorities therefore have a duty to inform the various stakeholders in the education system of their duties under the Charter and pupils and parents of their rights.[11]

Article 8.2 gives states broad discretion to choose one or more of the measures described above. This flexibility is accounted for in part by the subtlety of linguistic issues, the complexity of education systems and the costs to states of taking such measures. However, the relatively broad nature of the commitments entered into means that it is not always easy to assess whether they are being honoured.[12] As a result, it is difficult to imagine criticising a state party for choosing one support or promotion measure rather than another – even if it may appear to be less effective to an observer from the outside. Despite this discretion being left to the states, it would nonetheless be difficult for any single state not to take any measures at all, to adopt methods that were clearly not adequate for it to honour its international commitments[13] or to leave it almost entirely to RML communities themselves or to private bodies to ensure that

---

11. The Committee of Experts has also denounced the existence of practical obstacles to the effective provision of teaching of regional or minority languages. In Sweden for example it noted that: "many parents are not well-informed about the statutory right for their children to receive mother-tongue education" and denounced the fact that "head teachers and municipal authorities often are not fully aware of their obligation to provide Sami mother-tongue education" (Sweden 2006, 104).

12. See also Woehrling (2005), op. cit., Strasbourg: Council of Europe Publishing, p. 162.

13. For example having taking note of the "limits of the present model for mother-tongue education in terms of language preservation", the Committee of Experts encouraged the Swedish authorities to "devise or reinforce alternative models of language teaching for Sami" (Sweden 2006, 106). The same committee also denounced the situation of the teaching of Sami in Finland; in particular, it asserted that despite the adoption of certain general measures, there was clearly a lack of continuity in the teaching of this language, and invited the authorities to remedy the situation (Finland 2004, 118).

Article 8.2 of the Charter was being implemented.[14] This is particularly true if the state cannot prove, for example, that RMLs do not require educational support outside the territories in which they are traditionally used or that the number of speakers in these territories is too low to warrant the introduction of such measures (see also below). In such scenarios it has to be asserted that the state has failed to honour its commitments to the international community, even though the effectiveness of the penalties provided for in the event of a violation of the Charter is somewhat limited (see Article 16 of the Charter).[15]

States' undertakings are not absolute. In accordance with the principle of proportionality, Article 8.2 provides for two restrictions of the parties' obligations:

- firstly, states undertake to adopt the measures required by the Charter only if the number of RML speakers in the territory concerned justifies it. The purpose of this restriction is to avoid excessive costs and disproportionate efforts by the state if there is no real demand. The authors of the Charter did not stipulate a minimum number of speakers and so, once again, they have given states a considerable degree of latitude. Two comments must be made. Firstly, it is clearly reasonable to require that measures are introduced only if there is a sufficient critical number of people who may be interested in the service. This is not just because of the economic reasons referred to above but also because sometimes a critical mass is needed to guarantee the quality and consistency of the teaching provided. Secondly, states should not take an excessively inflexible view of the number of speakers needed. One should keep in mind that the overall aim of the Charter is to protect languages which are, by definition, more vulnerable than majority languages. Consequently, the most pragmatic interpretation of Article 8.2 would be to avoid fixing excessively high thresholds, which may not be achieved at all, or achieved only under very special circumstances.[16] To avoid this outcome, relatively large territories need to be taken

---

14. A typical example of this is the problem with the teaching of Catalan in Spain, where it would seem that, apart from the Official Language School in Madrid, it is almost exclusively the autonomous communities or private civic, social or cultural institutions which take responsibility for teaching Catalan outside the territories in which it is traditionally used; Spain 2008, paragraph 230.

15. On the other hand, it is possible that the state's domestic law will include more efficient control mechanisms and that these will, for example, allow the national courts to punish the authorities for their negligent conduct and possibly even order them to take the appropriate measures within a reasonable period of time.

16. It should be underlined that several states have rather low thresholds and the Committee of Experts tries to ensure that requirements are not excessive. For instance, Norway has a minimum of three pupils for the teaching of Sami and 10 for classes in Sami to be set up (see Norway 2001, 67). Under Hungary's legislation on the subject, teaching in a minority or regional language

into account when calculating the number of speakers, particularly in sparsely populated areas. Otherwise, there is a risk that the territorial scope of the Charter will be excessively restricted and the rule in question will only apply in the largest cities or the most densely populated regions. To ensure that Article 8.2 of the Charter is also applied in peripheral regions, alternative measures need to be adopted such as distance learning programmes,[17] courses in administrative centres during school holidays when it is more convenient for people to attend, or courses over short periods to make it easier for people to attend even if they are coming from far away;[18]

- secondly, states are not required to arrange teaching at all academic levels. Article 8.2 grants states the right to arrange for this type of teaching at the appropriate stage. Again, the decision on the practical application and hence the real content of the legal rule is left to the national authorities' discretion. Depending on the different education systems, the parties may spread teaching of the language over several years or confine it to certain years. Two issues need to be raised. Firstly, the Charter's general objective of promoting RMLs can be more properly achieved in the education field if several stages in the speakers' academic careers are catered for.[19] This makes it possible to interact with speakers at various levels and hence to provide a more solid, in-depth knowledge of the languages in question. Similarly, it has to be ensured that all speakers are treated equally and, wherever possible, that certain types of education or training – particularly technical and vocational branches – are not being excluded from arrangements to provide such teaching.

---

is provided if the parents of at least eight pupils request it and supplementary lessons may be arranged if this threshold is not reached; Hungary 2004, 81. In Austria, under Burgenland's Kindergarten Act of 1995, Croatian must be used in addition to German in the municipalities of the Burgenland other than those prescribed by the law if at least 25% of parents ask for it to be used when enrolling their children; Austria 2005, 147. In Sweden, Sami must be taught in principle as soon as one pupil asks for it; Sweden 2006, 104.

17. This solution – which does, of course, have its drawbacks such as the detached nature of the teacher–pupil relationship – has been adopted in several countries (see, among others, Norway 2007, 135; Sweden 2006, 106).

18. Boarding school-type arrangements are also a means of encouraging attendance on such courses. The possibility has been exploited in Tromsø in Norway for the purposes of Sami teaching (see Norway 2007, 135).

19. Without going so far as considering the German authorities' choice to be in breach of the Charter, the Committee of Experts asked them for further information to check whether "North Frisian can be taught at levels other than the university one" (Germany 2002, 182). The authorities' reply to the effect that this language was taught at a *Hauptschule* in Nordfriesland prompted the Committee of Experts to state, laconically, that Germany had "partly fulfilled" its undertaking; Germany 2006, 271ff.

Article 8.2 of the Charter offers states two possible ways of organising the relevant teaching in practice. Apart from the difference in the costs of the two options, the parties' choice is entirely free. They are expected to adopt the approach which most closely corresponds to their language and education policy. States may:

- choose to grant the RML in question teaching language status. In such cases, speakers are able to attend courses given entirely or, more probably, partly in their own language. Clearly this option makes it possible to ensure more effective language learning. Apart from special cases where particularly large communities are concentrated in given territories, there are inherent difficulties in adopting this approach in practice and these are not just economic in nature. The decision to recognise such languages as teaching languages must also be weighed against the effects of this choice on the integration of these language communities. In other words, states must ensure that this approach does not lead to the creation of linguistic and cultural ghettoes. More generally speaking, the recognition of an RML as a teaching language must never be allowed to restrict the equal opportunities of speakers of these languages. This would be a paradoxical outcome, at odds with the Charter's ultimate purpose, which is to promote and protect the rights of members of linguistic minorities. Teaching the aforementioned languages must not therefore have the effect of undermining teaching of the region's majority language or foreign languages;[20]

- introduce teaching of the RML. In such cases as well, states must respect the limits which we have just described for teaching of the language and ensure that the speakers attending such classes have equal opportunities. States are also given a great deal of freedom in this area as to how they organise the teaching (see also above).

3. Prospects

Hence, Article 8.2 suffers the same limitations as most of the other provisions of the European Charter for Regional or Minority Languages, particularly the fact that it is not directly applicable and it gives the states too much freedom in choosing what practical measures to implement in order to achieve the Charter's goals. It may not be possible to translate into action the main novelty of Article 8.2, namely the promotion of plurilingualism through rejection of the excessively inflexible application of the principle of territoriality of languages, if the signatory states confine themselves to a minimalist

---

20. Thus it is not acceptable for states to reduce teaching of other languages to offset the economic burden of introducing teaching in an RML or so as to comply with upper limits on total language teaching hours in school curricula.

interpretation and application of the article. Such an attitude would be contrary to these states' international undertakings and should therefore be condemned by the Charter's supervisory bodies. Another means of enhancing the Charter's binding force is to insist on the fact that the European Court of Human Rights will refer to it when interpreting articles of the European Convention on Human Rights which directly or indirectly protect freedom of language and the right to education, particularly articles 8 and 14 of the Convention and Article 2 of the Additional Protocol to the Convention.[21] From the domestic law point of view, national courts are required to request the authorities to comply with this international legal instrument, particularly through an interpretation in keeping with Article 8.2 of the Charter of their national legislation on language and education. Objectively, to hope for anything more from Article 8.2 would be unrealistic. However, it would be a shame not to make use of all the potential of this provision and underestimate its capacity to give structure and purpose to language policies designed to promote plurilingualism.

References

Explanatory Report to the European Charter for Regional or Minority Languages.

Piergigli, Valeria (2001), *Lingue minoritarie e identità culturali*. Milan: Giuffrè.

Reports by the Committee of Experts (referred to directly in the text).

Woehrling, Jean-Marie (2005), *The European Charter for Regional or Minority Languages: a critical commentary*. Strasbourg: Council of Europe Publishing.

---

21. The Charter should not be regarded as an alternative to the other protective instruments drawn up by the Council of Europe (Article 4.1 of the Charter). It complements them from a cultural rights point of view (see also J.-M. Woehrling, *The European Charter ... a critical commentary*, pp. 16-7).

Appendix: Ratifications

Article 8	
Paragraph 2	
	Germany: Danish (the Danish language area in the *Land* of Schleswig-Holstein); Upper Sorbian (the Upper Sorbian language area in the Free State of Saxony); North Frisian (the North Frisian language area in the *Land* of Schleswig-Holstein); Romani (the *Länder* of Berlin, Hesse and North Rhine-Westphalia); Low German (in the *Länder* of Schleswig-Holstein and North Rhine-Westphalia) **Austria:** Burgenland Croatian (the Burgenland Croatian language area in the *Land* of Burgenland); Slovenian (the Slovenian language area in the *Land* of Carinthia); Hungarian (the Hungarian language area in the *Land* of Burgenland) **Denmark:** German (in southern Jutland) **Spain:** languages protected and preserved in the territories where they are traditionally spoken, namely Catalan, Basque, Galician and Aranese **Finland:** Sami and Swedish **Hungary:** Croatian, German, Romanian, Serbian, Slovak, Slovenian, Romani and Beás **Norway:** Sami **Netherlands:** Frisian (in the province of Fryslân) **Poland:** Belarusian, Czech, Hebrew, Yiddish, Karaim, Kashub, Lithuanian, Lemko, German, Armenian, Romani, Russian, Slovak, Tatar and Ukrainian **Czech Republic:** Polish (in the Moravian-Silesian region in the territory of the districts of Frydek-Místek and Karviná); Slovak (throughout the territory of the Czech Republic) **Romania:** Bulgarian, Czech, Croatian, German, Hungarian, Russian, Slovak and Turkish **United Kingdom:** Scottish-Gaelic, Irish **Slovenia:** Italian, Hungarian **Sweden:** Sami, Finnish, Meänkieli **Ukraine:** Belarusian, Bulgarian, Gagauz, Greek, Jewish, Crimean Tatar, Moldovan, German, Polish, Russian, Romanian, Slovak and Hungarian

Article 9. Judicial authorities

Anna M. Pla Boix
University of Girona

1. Introduction

2. The use of regional or minority languages (RMLs) in judicial proceedings
   2.1. General conditions
       2.1.1. Definition of the judicial districts in which the measures of Article 9.1 are applicable
       2.1.2. Situation of each of the RMLs
       2.1.3. General condition that the use of the facilities afforded by Article 9.1 must not be considered by the judge to hamper the "proper administration of justice"
   2.2. General scope of the provisions of Article 9.1
       2.2.1. RMLs in criminal proceedings
           a) Conduct of criminal proceedings in RMLs (Article 9.1a.i)
           b) Right of the accused in criminal proceedings to use his/her RML (Article 9.1a.ii)
           c) Requests and evidence in an RML (Article 9.1a.iii)
           d) Production of documents connected with the proceedings in an RML (Article 9.1a.iv)
       2.2.2. Regional and minority languages in the civil and administrative courts
           a) Conduct of proceedings in RMLs (articles 9.1b.i and 9.1c.i)
           b) Use of RMLs in personal appearances before the court
           c) Production of documents and evidence in RMLs
   2.3. Translation and interpretation costs in judicial proceedings

3. Validity of legal documents drafted in an RML (Article 9.2)
   3.1. General validity of documents drafted in an RML (Article 9.2a)
   3.2. Conditional validity of legal documents drafted in an RML (Article 9.2b)
   3.3. Validity limited to *inter partes* relations (Article 9.2c)

4. Translation of legislative texts (Article 9.3)

5. Shortcomings in implementation of the guarantees of Article 9: recommendations and good practices
   5.1. Duty to inform members of the public and all legal operators of their linguistic rights in the judicial sphere
   5.2. Guarantee of linguistic proficiency of judicial staff

5.3. Duty to guarantee the availability of legal glossaries in the different RMLs

5.4. Duty to guarantee the availability of translators and interpreters of RMLs

5.5. Duty to ensure that computer programs and other technical facilities in courts permit proper use of RMLs

5.6. Duty to ensure that dialectal differences do not dissuade citizens from using RMLs before the judicial authorities

References

Appendix: Ratifications

Article 9 – Judicial authorities

1. The Parties undertake, in respect of those judicial districts in which the number of residents using the regional or minority languages justifies the measures specified below, according to the situation of each of these languages and on condition that the use of the facilities afforded by the present paragraph is not considered by the judge to hamper the proper administration of justice:

   a. in criminal proceedings:

      i. to provide that the courts, at the request of one of the parties, shall conduct the proceedings in the regional or minority languages; and/or

      ii. to guarantee the accused the right to use his/her regional or minority language; and/or

      iii. to provide that requests and evidence, whether written or oral, shall not be considered inadmissible solely because they are formulated in a regional or minority language; and/or

      iv. to produce, on request, documents connected with legal proceedings in the relevant regional or minority language,

if necessary by the use of interpreters and translations involving no extra expense for the persons concerned;

   b. in civil proceedings:

      i. to provide that the courts, at the request of one of the parties, shall conduct the proceedings in the regional or minority languages; and/or

      ii. to allow, whenever a litigant has to appear in person before a court, that he or she may use his or her regional or minority language without thereby incurring additional expense; and/or

      iii. to allow documents and evidence to be produced in the regional or minority languages,

if necessary by the use of interpreters and translations;

   c. in proceedings before courts concerning administrative matters:

      i. to provide that the courts, at the request of one of the parties, shall conduct the proceedings in the regional or minority languages; and/or

ii. *to allow, whenever a litigant has to appear in person before a court, that he or she may use his or her regional or minority language without thereby incurring additional expense; and/or*

iii. *to allow documents and evidence to be produced in the regional or minority languages,*

if necessary by the use of interpreters and translations;

d. *to take steps to ensure that the application of sub-paragraphs i and iii of paragraphs b and c above and any necessary use of interpreters and translations does not involve extra expense for the persons concerned.*

2. *The Parties undertake:*

a. *not to deny the validity of legal documents drawn up within the State solely because they are drafted in a regional or minority language; or*

b. *not to deny the validity, as between the parties, of legal documents drawn up within the country solely because they are drafted in a regional or minority language, and to provide that they can be invoked against interested third parties who are not users of these languages on condition that the contents of the document are made known to them by the person(s) who invoke(s) it; or*

c. *not to deny the validity, as between the parties, of legal documents drawn up within the country solely because they are drafted in a regional or minority language.*

3. *The Parties undertake to make available in the regional or minority languages the most important national statutory texts and those relating particularly to users of these languages, unless they are otherwise provided.*

1. Introduction

The primary aim of the Charter being to protect and promote regional or minority languages (RMLs), the judicial sphere is undoubtedly one of the key settings for guaranteeing that protection. It comes as no surprise, therefore, that Article 9 provides for an extensive catalogue of rights in this sector.

An analysis of the provisions of this article prompts a preliminary observation of a strictly terminological nature. The article is entitled "Judicial authorities" in the authentic English version of the Charter and "Justice" in the authentic French version. These are somewhat ambiguous titles which do not correspond strictly to its content. In fact, the provisions of Article 9 go far beyond the substantive scope of "Judicial authorities" or "Justice". As we will see, while the article does indeed cover certain linguistic rights before the criminal, civil and administrative courts (Article 9.1), it also safeguards other rights relating to the validity of legal documents (Article 9.2) and the translation of legal texts (Article 9.2). It can therefore be said that the title of the article is somewhat inappropriate if we consider the general scope of its provisions.

However that may be, these are rules of great symbolic significance because many states throughout history have forbidden the use of RMLs in these public spheres, restricting court proceedings to the "national" languages traditionally used by the state authorities.[1] Even today, in many states, the use of the national language in public institutions, and especially the justice system, "is considered a matter of principle and of fundamental value which cannot be compromised in any way".[2]

Article 9 of the Charter therefore seeks to rectify this situation. Its aim is to guarantee and promote the use of RMLs in the judicial sphere, which is one of the areas of public life least open to the languages protected by the Charter. In its periodical evaluation reports, the Committee of Experts has criticised some serious shortcomings in implementation of the guarantees of Article 9. It has done so from an essentially pragmatic perspective, in keeping with the realistic and practical vision suggested by the wording of the document. As we will see, the committee's reports are not limited to identifying instances of non-compliance by the contracting parties with Article 9 of the Charter. Taking into account the particular circumstances of each RML, they also propose practical solutions to concrete problems, with the aim of increasing the effective presence of these languages in a public sphere which is crucial for preserving their vitality. It has been noted in the literature that the presence of RMLs in the public and judicial arena constitutes "an essential aspect of the concerns of citizens in modern society" and "an essential factor in stimulating and modernising them, updating their terminology and developing their potential in these fields".[3]

2. The use of RMLs in judicial proceedings

2.1. General conditions

As will be seen below, Article 9.1 of the Charter provides for a wide range of measures which seek to guarantee the use of RMLs in proceedings before the

---

1. In Spain, for example, the Nueva Planta Decree of 16 January 1716 for Catalonia required judicial proceedings to be conducted in Castilian. In France, the Villers-Cotteret Ordinance of 1539 imposed French as the language of the judicial authorities. According to the literature, this ordinance "has acquired special emblematic force and has become one of the factors most frequently invoked against acceding to the charter". Further, "although many countries have not in the past had any specific law on language in the public sphere, in recent times there has been a mushrooming of increasingly rigid constitutional and legislative provisions on the matter". See J.-M. Woehrling (2005), *The European Charter for Regional or Minority Languages: a critical commentary*. Strasbourg: Council of Europe, p. 161.
2. See J.-M. Woehrling (1998), "Problems raised by the use of regional or minority languages before public and judicial authorities", in *International Conference of the European Charter for Regional or Minority Languages*. Regional or Minority Languages No. 1. Strasbourg: Council of Europe Publishing, p. 25.
3. See Woehrling (2005), op. cit., p. 161.

criminal, civil and administrative courts. However, in view of the potential difficulties raised by the provisions of this article, its applicability has been made subject, expressly, to three general conditions being met: first, they may only be applied in some judicial districts; secondly, in implementing them account must be taken of the particular situation of each of the RMLs protected; and lastly, the use of the facilities afforded by the paragraph must not be considered by the judge to hamper the proper administration of justice.

2.1.1. Definition of the judicial districts in which the measures of Article 9.1 are applicable

Under the terms of the Charter itself, the provisions of Article 9.1 may only be applied in respect of those judicial districts in which the number of residents using the RML justifies the measures specified. This is therefore a stipulation in keeping with the general rule on which the majority of the Charter's provisions are based, the aim of which is to protect RMLs in the geographical area in which they are traditionally spoken.

The Committee of Experts has specified that for higher courts located outside the territory in which the RML is used, it is a matter for the state concerned to take account of the special nature of the judicial system and its hierarchy of instances.[4] As may be seen, this is a somewhat ambiguous requirement in that it does not specify expressly the number of persons which would justify implementation of the linguistic guarantees before the various courts. It will be for the contracting states to specify the judicial districts in which they will be implemented, as posited by certain interpretative debates reflected in the periodic reports of the Committee of Experts.

For example, in its 2010 report on the application of the Charter in Hungary, the committee urged the Hungarian authorities to identify the judicial districts in which the number of residents speaking minority languages justified the organisational measures guaranteed in Article 9. Starting from this premise, the committee went on to say that "the presence of a local minority self-government could become the basis for the concrete implementation of Hungary's obligations under Article 9 of the Charter, given that municipalities in which a local minority self-government is active are obliged to have announcements and forms translated into the minority language, upon request".[5]

In 2001, in the first evaluation round on application of the Charter in Hungary, the Committee of Experts had provided certain interpretative criteria, noting the desirability of specifying the geographical areas in which the concentration

---

4. Explanatory Report, paragraph 90.
5. Application of the Charter in Hungary, 4th monitoring cycle (2010), paragraphs 109-10.

of minority language speakers made it viable, in practice and not only in theory, to implement organisational measures for guaranteeing the provisions of Article 9. In the words of the committee, certain provisions of the article would only be operational if the courts took measures to ensure that proceedings in which minority languages were used were "practically possible", adding that "to take such measures in advance, however, is only possible in a geographical area where there is a certain concentration of speakers of a given minority language, with the resulting probability that a certain number of cases will occur where the mechanism is used". Proceeding on the assumption that the adoption of such organisational measures throughout the national territory for the six languages protected by the Charter is "practically impossible", the committee recommended that the authorities "should accordingly examine the question whether it would not be sensible to construct a specific legislative device for the use of minority languages before the courts, a normative mechanism that would be limited in geographical scope to the main areas of settlement of the linguistic minorities". In the words of the committee, "this would formally restrict the scope of minority rights, but would enable the State to create an operational system that ensures the use of minority languages before courts".[6]

In any event, when it comes to specifying what number or proportion of speakers of an RML would justify implementation of the measures provided for in Article 9.1 in a given judicial district, the specific characteristics of each of these measures will have to be taken into consideration. For example, legal commentators have noted that the conduct of the entire proceedings in a court case in the RML may require a larger number of speakers than where provision is simply made for certain documents drafted in that language to be admitted as evidence in the hearing of the case. It will therefore be for the contracting states to conduct an analysis of the undertakings and measures provided for in Article 9.1 of the Charter in order to specify the geographical range best suited to them.[7]

2.1.2. Situation of each of the RMLs

The implementation of the measures provided for in Article 9.1 of the Charter will depend, in the terms of the article itself, on the situation of each RML. As legal commentators have stressed, this requirement "is merely a reminder which is valid for the whole of Part III".

Very briefly, the following stand out among the most important factors to be taken into account in assessing the particular circumstances of each language:

---

6. Hungary 2001, 46.
7. Woehrling (2005), op. cit., p. 166.

- First, the number of litigants, judges, prosecutors, court clerks, lawyers, witnesses and experts who know or speak the RML in question. If the litigants and legal operators know the language, its use before the courts will raise fewer difficulties than in the case of unfamiliarity with the language, which means constant recourse to translators and interpreters in the hearing of cases.

- Secondly, it should be pointed out that some RMLs have developed an appropriate legal terminology, while others have never been used in the judicial sphere and are therefore still lacking in legal vocabulary. This fact may represent a serious obstacle to the use of these languages in judicial proceedings, as noted in evaluation reports of the Committee of Experts, such as Armenia 2009[8] or Norway 2010.[9]

- Thirdly, it also needs to be considered whether the speakers of RMLs are fluent in the other official languages of the courts. If this is not the case, the use of the RML in the courts by litigants who are unfamiliar or insufficiently familiar with the official language becomes essential to guarantee the fundamental right to a defence and equality of arms between the parties to the proceedings.

- Lastly, legal commentators have noted other relevant factors. For example, some RMLs play a decisive role in the country's social and political life and so must have regular access to the courts to maintain that status. Other languages have more of an impact in cultural life and their habitual presence in the judicial sphere is therefore unnecessary.[10]

In any event, it will be for the contracting states to conduct a detailed analysis of the situation of each of their RMLs in order to decide what measures will be necessary to guarantee their use in the judicial system, while bearing in mind that, as the Committee of Experts has stressed, the parties have an obligation to remove the obstacles mentioned in order to ensure that their undertakings are honoured.

2.1.3. *General condition that the use of the facilities afforded by Article 9.1 must not be considered by the judge to hamper the "proper administration of justice"*

Article 9 of the Charter makes the guarantees of paragraph 1 subject to the condition that "the use of the facilities afforded by the present paragraph is not considered by the judge to hamper the proper administration of justice".

---

8. Armenia 2009, 146-7.
9. Norway 2010, 162-3. The lack of legal terminology in Sami was already noted in the previous report; Norway 2007, 139-40.
10. Woehrling (2005), op. cit., p. 167.

This is a provision which raises serious doubts as to its interpretation. It reflects, *prima facie*, the Charter's concern to uphold the fundamental principles of justice. However, as the Explanatory Report itself stresses, this legitimate concern does not justify any general restriction of a party's undertakings under Article 9.1, because the undertakings in question do not, per se, hamper the proper administration of justice. This condition must therefore be given a restrictive interpretation.

In laying down this condition, the authors of the Charter were taking a simple precaution: to avoid situations of abuse of the possibilities afforded by the article which might detract from the proper administration of justice. Only in certain duly justified and exceptional cases is the judge authorised by the Charter to restrict or even rule out the use of RMLs in the conduct of judicial proceedings. The Explanatory Report of the Charter makes this point when it says that "abuse of the possibilities offered will have to be determined by the judge in individual cases".[11]

The assessment of this condition must therefore meet the following requirements in all cases: first, the obstacle to the proper administration of justice must be assessed by means of a reasoned judicial decision applicable to the specific case;[12] secondly, a judicial decision of this kind should only be given if it is found that the use of an RML guaranteed in Article 9.1 of the Charter does indeed jeopardise the proper administration of justice, with due attention both to the type of proceedings and to the specific circumstances of the case; thirdly, such an assessment may only be made where strictly necessary and on an exceptional basis – that is, a mere complication or difficulty arising from the use of the RML in the conduct of the proceedings is not equivalent to misuse or to an obstacle justifying a restriction of the state's undertakings in this field – and, lastly, legal commentators have pointed out that if the contracting state's domestic legal system authorises the use of RMLs in the conduct of judicial proceedings, any decision by the judge to rule out their use in a particular case on the grounds that it would hamper the proper administration of justice must be provided for under the state's domestic law.[13]

---

11. Explanatory Report, paragraph 91 *in fine*.
12. Moreover, since the decision falls to the judge, it should be open to appeal or review.
13. In the words of Jean-Marie Woehrling (2005), *The European Charter … a critical commentary*, p. 168, "there has to be appropriate provision in the law of the contracting state. If there is a rule of internal law that procedural steps can be carried out in a regional or minority language, a judge can only place restrictions on it if internal law allows him to do so. In other words, this charter provision allowing judges to make exceptions to the language rules is not self-executing; it must be transposed into internal law." Furthermore, other sources note that this exception in Article 9.1 of the Charter is only applicable in respect of those aspects on which the Charter goes further than domestic legislation, but not in respect of other aspects of the

In any event, the assessment of this condition will not be legitimate unless the contracting state takes relevant measures to fulfil its undertakings. As has already been emphasised, the Charter requires the parties to take all the necessary measures to ensure that the undertakings they have accepted are consistent with the proper administration of justice. This condition in Article 9.1 of the Charter should therefore be given a clearly restrictive interpretation.

2.2. General scope of the provisions of Article 9.1

Article 9.1 provides for a wide range of measures which – as indicated by the conjunctions "and/or" – are cumulative and alternative.[14] As will be seen below, the provisions guarantee the use of RMLs before the criminal, civil and administrative courts and offer options adapted to the nature of each category.

2.2.1. RMLs in criminal proceedings

In criminal proceedings, Article 9.1a of the Charter offers contracting states the following undertakings: a) to ensure that the courts, at the request of one of the parties, conduct the proceedings in the RML; b) to guarantee the accused the right to use his/her RML; c) to ensure that requests and evidence, whether written or oral, are not considered inadmissible solely because they are formulated in an RML; d) to produce, on request, documents connected with legal proceedings in the RML.

Contracting states taking on these undertakings, which may be adopted cumulatively or on an alternative basis, must, if necessary, have recourse to interpreters and translations involving no extra expense for the persons concerned.

a) Conduct of criminal proceedings in RMLs (Article 9.1a.i)

Under Article 9.1a.i of the Charter, contracting parties undertake to ensure that the criminal courts, at the request of one of the parties, conduct the proceedings in an RML.

The expression "conduct the proceedings in the RMLs" implies that the relevant RML is used in the courtroom and in those stages of the proceedings in which the party speaking that language takes part. However, it will be for each state to determine the precise scope of the expression "conduct the

---

Charter already guaranteed by the state's domestic legislation, because, as stated in Article 4, the Charter seeks to increase the level of protection of regional or minority languages, not to reduce it or make further exceptions to their use.

14. Explanatory Report, paragraph 92: "A distinction is made between criminal, civil and administrative proceedings and the options provided for are adapted to the particular nature of each. As is indicated by the words 'and/or', some of these options may be adopted cumulatively".

proceedings" in the light of the specific characteristics of its judicial system.[15] The state therefore enjoys a certain degree of discretion in interpreting the procedural scope of this provision, which must in all cases comply with the hermeneutic criteria specified.

Furthermore, for the purposes of this provision of the Charter, the word "party" must be interpreted in a broad sense. It includes not only the accused but also the prosecution and any civil parties to the proceedings. In this connection, it should be remembered that Article 9.1a.i provides for the conduct of proceedings in an RML "at the request of one of the parties". However, this undertaking will be deemed to be fulfilled if the RML is used automatically in the hearing of the criminal case without any of the parties having explicitly requested its use. In any event, as legal commentators have stressed, in stipulating the need for a request from one of the parties, the authors of the Charter "may have had in mind proceedings occurring simultaneously in both the official language and the RML (in that if only one party wishes to use the latter, the other parties must be intending to use the official language)".[16] If proceedings are conducted in two languages, viz. in the RML and the official language, this undertaking under Article 9.1a.i of the Charter will therefore require the provision of free translation and interpretation services.

The implementation of this guarantee has, however, given rise to problems which the Committee of Experts, in its periodical evaluation reports, and always adopting a pragmatic approach, has attempted to diagnose and resolve by proposing practical measures. According to the Committee of Experts, in a number of contracting states the undertakings of Article 9.1 are only guaranteed on a formal, purely theoretical level, and it has made it clear to the authorities of these states that the domestic rules which should guarantee them are not being applied in practice.[17]

The problems identified in implementing the guarantee contained in Article 9.1a.i are of several kinds. Among these problems, the Committee of Experts has identified the following: unfamiliarity with the RML on the part of judicial staff; unfamiliarity on the part of citizens with the right to use their RML in court proceedings; the lack of legal terminology in some RMLs; the lack of translators and interpreters; and, by way of example, attention has been drawn to a certain "diglossic inertia" whereby citizens willingly forego the use of their RML in judicial proceedings to avoid being seen as causing problems which might be harmful to their interests.

---

15. Explanatory Report, paragraph 94.
16. Woehrling (2005), op. cit., p. 169.
17. See, for example, Austria 2005, 152-3.

However that may be, this undertaking in Article 9.1a.i of the Charter grants the parties to criminal proceedings a right which they may exercise even if those requesting the use of their RML in proceedings know and can express themselves properly in the official language used by the court.

b) Right of the accused in criminal proceedings to use his/her RML (Article 9.1a.ii)

Various international instruments prohibit the conduct of criminal proceedings in a language which the accused does not understand. Indeed, the requirement that the accused should understand the language of the court is a guarantee inherent in the fundamental rights to a defence and to a fair trial.

Within the Council of Europe, Article 6 of the Convention for the Protection of Human Rights and Fundamental Freedoms already guarantees the right of everyone charged with a criminal offence "to be informed promptly, in a language which he understands and in detail, of the nature and cause of the accusation against him" (Article 6.3a) and the right "to have the free assistance of an interpreter if he cannot understand or speak the language used in court" (Article 6.3e). Both rights are guaranteed, also explicitly, in Article 14.3 of the International Covenant on Civil and Political Rights[18] and are reproduced in numerous other international instruments relating to particular sectors or to minorities.[19]

Under all these provisions, the right to the assistance of an interpreter is recognised only in the case of persons who do not understand or speak the language used by the court. The Charter seeks to strengthen this protection and guarantees the right of persons charged with an offence to use their own RML to defend themselves, even if they know the official language in which the proceedings are conducted. It therefore affords additional protection to the speakers of RMLs, as confirmed in the Explanatory Report.

This report stresses that Article 9.1a.ii, whereby the parties undertake to guarantee the accused the right to use his/her RML, "goes beyond the right of the

---

18. Article 14.3 expressly recognises the right of everyone charged with an offence, during the proceedings, "to be informed promptly and in detail in a language which he understands of the nature and cause of the charge against him" (paragraph a) and the right "to have the free assistance of an interpreter if he cannot understand or speak the language used in court" (paragraph f).

19. For example, Article 40.2 b.vi of the Convention on the Rights of the Child, articles 16 and 18 of the International Convention on the Protection of the Rights of Migrant Workers and Members of their Families, adopted by the United Nations; or Article 10.3 of the Framework Convention for the Protection of National Minorities, adopted by the Council of Europe. This last reads as follows: "The Parties undertake to guarantee the right of every person belonging to a national minority to be informed promptly, in a language which he or she understands, of the reasons for his or her arrest, and of the nature and cause of any accusation against him or her, and to defend himself or herself in this language, if necessary with the free assistance of an interpreter".

accused, as laid down in Article 6, paragraph 3e, of the European Convention on Human Rights, to have the free assistance of an interpreter if he cannot understand or speak the language used in court". According to the Explanatory Report, this provision of the Charter is based on the consideration that, even if speakers of an RML are able to speak the official language, when it comes to justifying themselves before a court of law they may feel the need to express themselves in the language which is emotionally closest to them or in which they have greater fluency. It would therefore run counter to the purpose of the Charter for its application to be limited to situations of practical necessity.[20] It should be noted that the Committee of Experts has confirmed this interpretation in a number of periodical monitoring reports, including the reports on Croatia in 2001,[21] Armenia in 2006,[22] and Slovakia and the Czech Republic in 2009.[23]

The Committee of Experts has also observed that the right of the accused to use his/her RML in judicial proceedings entails certain obligations for the state authorities: it entails a duty to inform the accused of the linguistic right in question even where he/she knows the official language used by the court;[24] and the authorities of the contracting state must adopt appropriate organisational measures and provide the facilities needed to realise this right.

Lastly, given that this provision of Article 9.1a.ii goes beyond the human rights aspect in the strict sense, in granting the accused freedom of choice, and requires the provision of facilities in keeping with his/her decision, it was considered reasonable to leave it to the discretion of states whether to accept it or not and limit its application to certain judicial districts.[25]

In any event, as legal commentators have clearly emphasised, this subparagraph represents an alternative to the undertaking provided for in the preceding subparagraph 9.1a.i, and this guarantee comes into play "in cases where subparagraph i seems unworkable".[26] Furthermore, if a state accepts the undertaking in the preceding subparagraph (guarantee that criminal courts will conduct proceedings in RMLs), it necessarily includes within its ambit the undertaking in subparagraph 9.1a.ii. The latter, in guaranteeing the right of the accused to use his/her RML, has a more restrictive scope. It is confined to the oral and written submissions of the accused, in which he/she will be able to use his/her RML, while the rest of the proceedings may be conducted in another, official language.

---

20. Explanatory Report, paragraph 95.
21. Croatia 2001, 62.
22. Armenia 2006, 80-2.
23. Slovakia 2007, 121 and 126. See also Slovakia 2009, 83 and 85; and Czech Republic, 2009, 170.
24. For example, Armenia 2006, 80 and 82.
25. Explanatory Report, paragraph 95.
26. Woehrling (2005), op. cit., p. 170.

c) Requests and evidence in an RML (Article 9.1a.iii)

Article 9.1a.iii of the Charter provides that requests and evidence may not be considered inadmissible solely because they are formulated in an RML. Its scope is not limited to written documents but also includes oral evidence. In accordance with this undertaking, requests and evidence, whether written or oral, in an RML must be admitted into the proceedings in the same way as if they were submitted in the official language.

Unlike Article 9.1a.i, this undertaking does not imply that the rest of the proceedings must be conducted in the RML. It applies only to requests and evidence. It therefore differs from the guarantee contained in the preceding subparagraph (Article 9.1a.ii) and may be accepted in combination with it.

Lastly, it should be stressed that the evaluation reports of the Committee of Experts show that the implementation of this provision of the Charter does not give rise to undue difficulties of interpretation or to shortcomings in terms of practical implementation. It only requires the provision of translation and interpretation services in RMLs, which, as this subparagraph itself points out *in fine*, will not entail additional costs for the persons concerned.

d) Production of documents connected with the proceedings in an RML (Article 9.1a.iv)

The final subparagraph of Article 9.1a provides for an undertaking by parties to produce, on request, documents connected with legal proceedings in an RML.

This is an undertaking which will be honoured at the request of a party to the proceedings. Its scope extends to all "documents connected with legal proceedings", an expression which must be interpreted as including all the written material placed in the case file. In any event, it is a clause which covers not only evidence submitted by the party requesting the use of an RML, but all the written documents relating to the proceedings. Also, it differs from the undertaking in subparagraph i because it does not require the proceedings to be conducted in the RML, but simply guarantees the translation of documents. This is without prejudice to the fact that, in both cases, the guarantees apply upon prior request by one of the parties. It will be for the court to provide the documents in the RML, adopting the relevant measures to that end.[27] In any event, under Article 9.1a *in fine*, the cost of translation may not be charged to the party concerned.

---

27. Armenia 2006, 87-8. See also Armenia 2009, 130.

2.2.2. Regional and minority languages in the civil and administrative courts

In proceedings before the civil and administrative courts, subparagraphs b and c of Article 9.1 of the Charter offer contracting states the following options: i) to ensure that the courts, at the request of one of the parties, conduct the proceedings in an RML; ii) to allow litigants required to appear in person before a court to use their RML without thereby incurring additional expense; iii) to allow documents and evidence to be produced in RMLs. The text adds that, in the event of a contracting party accepting these undertakings, which may be adopted cumulatively or on an alternative basis, because the words "and/or" are used in the list, recourse must be had, where necessary, to interpreters and translations.

In analysing these undertakings, we must first explain what is to be understood, for the purposes of the Charter, by "proceedings before courts concerning administrative matters" (Article 9.1c) and "civil proceedings" (Article 9.1b). The Explanatory Report advocates a broad interpretation of the word "courts". Depending on the specific provisions in each state relating to the administration of justice, it must be understood as also covering other bodies performing a judicial function – defined as the function of deciding disputes independently and impartially on the basis of the law – even if they are not courts in the strict sense of the term. This is particularly relevant in the case of "proceedings before courts concerning administrative matters".[28]

Furthermore, legal writers have argued that, for the purposes of Article 9.1b of the Charter, "civil proceedings" include all those not coming under criminal or administrative jurisdiction. Their scope may therefore include both commercial proceedings and cases concerning social matters, in so far as they are not heard by administrative courts.[29] In any event, this will depend on each state's specific provisions relating to the administration of justice.

a) Conduct of proceedings in RMLs (articles 9.1b.i and 9.1c.i)

Under Article 9.1 of the Charter the parties undertake to ensure that the civil courts (Article 9.1b.i) and courts competent in administrative matters (Article 9.1c.i) "conduct the proceedings in the RMLs" at the request of one of the parties. As already stated in the section devoted to an analysis of this clause as it relates to criminal courts, the phrase "conduct the proceedings" means that the whole proceedings should be conducted in the RML at the request of one of the parties. This is therefore the undertaking with the widest scope. However, it

---

28. Explanatory Report, paragraph 93.
29. Woehrling (2005), op. cit., p. 171 *in fine*: "Civil proceedings must logically be taken to mean those which are neither criminal nor administrative. The concept therefore includes commercial proceedings and those held before tribunals dealing with social matters, in so far as they are not administrative courts."

will be for each state to determine the precise scope of the expression "conduct the proceedings" in the light of the specific characteristics of its judicial system.

Where this undertaking is concerned, we refer to our comments on Article 9.1a.i of the Charter on criminal proceedings, with one qualification relating to translation and interpretation costs. In criminal proceedings, the use of translators or interpreters is provided for under this undertaking, but it must not involve any extra expense for the parties. In civil and administrative courts, however, if it is necessary to have recourse to interpreters and translations, the costs involved may or may not be charged to the persons concerned depending on whether the contracting state has accepted the undertaking in Article 9.1d of the Charter, and in the alternative, if it has not, depending on the provisions of the state's domestic legislation. Article 9.1d of the Charter guarantees that the state will take the necessary steps to ensure that the application of these undertakings and any necessary use of interpreters and translations do not "involve extra expense for the persons concerned". If a contracting state does not accept Article 9.1d of the Charter, responsibility for bearing the costs of translation and interpretation will be determined in accordance with the state's domestic legislation.

b) Use of RMLs in personal appearances before the court

Under articles 9.1b.ii (civil proceedings) and 9.1c.ii (proceedings before courts concerning administrative matters), contracting parties undertake to "allow, whenever a litigant has to appear in person before a court, that he or she may use his or her regional or minority language without thereby incurring additional expense". This is an undertaking which, in principle, does not give rise to any doubts as to its interpretation. It guarantees use of the RML in personal appearances before the court.

Legal writers have specified that it refers to oral submissions of the parties, who may be questioned in their RML when they appear before the court. It has also been noted that its scope also covers oral statements made by witnesses or experts participating in the proceedings.[30] The provision guarantees explicitly that such personal appearances involving the use of RMLs may not entail additional expense, even if interpreters are needed.

c) Production of documents and evidence in RMLs

Lastly, articles 9.1b.iii and 9.1c.iii provide for an undertaking by contracting states to allow documents and evidence to be produced in RMLs. Their scope is therefore confined to written items such as requests, submissions, statements by the defence or evidence. The initiative, however, lies with the parties to the proceedings.

---

30. Ibid., p. 172.

The additional expense involved in having documents and evidence translated will be charged to the persons concerned or borne by the judicial authorities depending on whether the contracting state has accepted paragraph 9.1d of the Charter, and if not, depending on the provisions of the state's domestic legislation.

In its reports, the Committee of Experts verifies that the contracting states' domestic legal provisions do not exclude the validity of documents and evidence produced in RMLs. In a number of reports, the committee notes that the honouring and effective implementation of this undertaking in administrative proceedings depends on recognition of the right to use the RML with full validity and effectiveness in dealings with the administrative authorities, on its use by the authorities themselves and on the rules relating to translation of documents contained in the case file.[31]

2.3. Translation and interpretation costs in judicial proceedings

The requirements of equivalence and accuracy which apply to translation in general are compounded, in the field of legal translation, by variables such as the format or syntax of legal texts and the terminology or phraseology specific to the legal world. For this reason, some legal writers argue that persons performing translation or interpretation duties in judicial proceedings should have some legal training, especially if one bears in mind the implications of their work for an understanding of documents filed in judicial proceedings and their faithful reproduction in another language.

Article 9 of the Charter says nothing about this. It only refers explicitly to translation and interpretation services when specifying who will be required to bear any extra expense involved in their use in order to comply with its provisions. Hence:

- in criminal proceedings, the use of interpreters and translations will not involve any extra expense for the persons concerned (Article 9.1a);
- where parties appear in person before the court in civil and administrative cases (articles 9.1b.ii and 9.1c.ii), it is specified that the cost may not be charged to the parties to the proceedings;
- in other cases, it will depend on whether the state accepts the undertaking in Article 9.1d, which specifies that the parties undertake to "take steps to ensure that the application of sub-paragraphs i and iii of paragraphs b and c above and any necessary use of interpreters and translations does not involve extra expense for the persons concerned". Consequently, if the state accepts this undertaking, it will bear the additional costs involved in

---

31. For example, Croatia 2001, 69.

translation and interpretation. As legal commentators have stressed, "the implication is that not only is the expenditure incurred not to be charged to the party which has used a regional or minority language, but it is not to be included in the cost of the proceedings and therefore cannot be charged to whichever party loses either".[32] In other words, the term "persons concerned" in Article 9.1d must be given a broad interpretation. It refers to all parties to the proceedings. If, however, the state does not accept the undertaking in Article 9.1d, responsibility for bearing the cost of translation or interpretation will be determined in accordance with the provisions of its domestic legislation.

Lastly, in its evaluation reports the Committee of Experts has criticised the fact that certain states do not ensure effective implementation of the undertakings in Article 9 of the Charter because of problems connected with court translation and interpretation services. For example, in its reports on Finland in 2007[33] and Slovakia in 2009,[34] it criticises the fact that the shortage of translators and interpreters in some RMLs is a serious obstacle to use of those languages in the justice system.

3. Validity of legal documents drafted in an RML (Article 9.2)

Paragraph 2 of Article 9 refers to the validity of legal documents drafted in an RML. Following the pattern of Part III of the Charter, this provision distinguishes three different types of undertaking which contracting states may accept as regards recognition of the validity of legal documents drafted in these languages. The enumeration of these three types of undertaking is connected by means of the disjunctive conjunction "or", expressing an alternative or option. For this reason, the Committee of Experts has stressed in various reports, such as Hungary 2001, Denmark 2004 or Montenegro 2010, that parties may not subscribe to all three for the same language.[35] Contracting states are faced with three distinct alternatives from which they must choose, listed in descending order according to their scope.

---

32. Woehrling (2005), op. cit., pp. 173-4.

33. Finland 2007, 210.

34. Slovakia 2009, 84-8.

35. Denmark 2004, 78. In the words of the committee, "the sub-paragraphs (a), (b) and (c) are alternative options, and it shall therefore consider options (b) and (c) redundant". For this reason, Denmark having accepted all three, "it shall thus only evaluate Denmark's compliance with sub-paragraph (a), which necessarily includes the undertakings under sub-paragraph (b) and (c)". See also Hungary 2001, 53. In the words of the report, "Hungary has chosen all options under Article 9 paragraph 2. These three options of Article 9.2 are however alternatives and Hungary should therefore have opted for only one of them." Likewise, Application of the Charter in Montenegro, 1st monitoring cycle (2010), paragraph 114.

Article 9.2 of the Charter states that the parties undertake: a) not to deny the validity of legal documents drawn up within the state solely because they are drafted in an RML; or b) not to deny the validity, as between the parties, of legal documents drawn up within the country solely because they are drafted in an RML, and to provide that they can be invoked against interested third parties who are not users of these languages on condition that the contents of the document are made known to them by the person(s) who invoke(s) it; or c) not to deny the validity, as between the parties, of legal documents drawn up within the country solely because they are drafted in an RML.

As regards the scope of Article 9.2, four preliminary points need to be made: first, it is limited in as much as it does not indicate all the conditions for the validity of a legal document but stipulates that the fact that a legal document is drafted in an RML cannot by itself be a ground for denying its validity; secondly, its provisions do not by any means preclude a contracting state from providing for additional formalities such as, for example, the inclusion of a formula of certification in the official language; thirdly, Article 9.2 is without prejudice to the application of treaties and conventions on mutual assistance in legal matters, because, as the Explanatory Report to the Charter points out, "the question of the languages to be used is explicitly dealt with" in each of them;[36] lastly, these provisions have to be interpreted in the light of the provisions of articles 10 and 13 of the Charter.

As legal writers have emphasised, the primary aim of Article 9.2 is to guarantee the validity of legal documents drafted in an RML in "private legal transactions between individuals". In this connection, "legal documents exchanged between public corporate bodies are not formally excluded" from its sphere of application.[37] As regards the use of RMLs by the public authorities, the provisions of Article 10 of the Charter, entitled "Administrative authorities and public services", will apply.[38] Legal documents signed between public authorities and private individuals will, as a rule, be subject to the provisions of Article 9.2.

Legal documents relating to economic and social matters fall, in principle, under the provisions of Article 13, entitled "Economic and social life".[39] That does not mean, however, that all documents having an impact on economic activity fall outside the scope of Article 9.2. In fact, the question of which documents come within the scope of the two provisions – articles 9.2 and 13 of the Charter – has given rise to a certain amount of interpretative debate. Legal commentators have noted that "it seems reasonable to regard all private

---

36. Explanatory Report, paragraph 98.
37. Woehrling (2005), op. cit., p. 175.
38. See commentary on Article 10 of the Charter.
39. See commentary on Article 13 of the Charter by Dr Urrutia in this volume.

legal documents as covered by Article 9.2, even if they are also referred to in other articles of the charter". Consequently, if a contracting state does not accept the undertakings of Article 13 on the validity of legal documents drafted in an RML but accepts those of Article 9.2, these documents will have to be deemed valid under the latter provision. Lastly, if a contracting state accepts the undertakings of both provisions, it will have to comply with both "and therefore apply the one that goes further".[40]

The substance and scope of the provisions of Article 9.2 of the Charter are outlined below.

3.1. General validity of documents drafted in an RML (Article 9.2a)

Article 9.2 of the Charter provides for an undertaking on the part of contracting parties not to deny the validity of legal documents drawn up within the state solely because they are drafted in an RML.

It therefore guarantees the general validity of legal documents drafted in an RML,[41] both *inter partes* and with respect to third parties, including public authorities. For this reason, public authorities of contracting states which have accepted this paragraph may not refuse to recognise the legal effects of such documents on the ground that they are not drafted in an official language.

However, this does not preclude the setting of additional conditions for the validity of the documents in question. The wording used in Article 9.2a when it requires states "not to deny the validity" of documents "solely because they are drafted in a regional or minority language" suggests, as noted in the Explanatory Report, that states may provide for additional formalities such as the inclusion of a formula of certification in the official language.[42]

In its evaluation reports the Committee of Experts analyses the legal systems of the contracting states to check whether or not they restrict the validity of legal documents by reference to the language in which they are drafted.[43]

3.2. Conditional validity of legal documents drafted in an RML (Article 9.2b)

Article 9.2b provides for an undertaking by contracting states not to deny the validity, as between the parties, of legal documents drawn up within the country

---

40. Woehrling (2005), op. cit., p. 175.

41. "This refers to documents such as contracts, unilateral transactions (declarations, wills, etc), acts of incorporation or articles of association, records of proceedings, etc." See ibid., p. 176.

42. Explanatory Report, paragraph 97.

43. For example, Austria 2005, 245. In the words of the report, "the Austrian legal system does not restrict the validity of legal documents by reference to the language in which they are drafted. The Committee of Experts considers this undertaking fulfilled."

solely because they are drafted in an RML, and to provide that they can be invoked against interested third parties who are not users of these languages on condition that the contents of the document are made known to them by the person(s) who invoke(s) it.

The Explanatory Report specifies that paragraph b of Article 9.2 "implies that the contents of the document invoked by the party using the regional or minority language are made known, directly or indirectly (advertisement, state information service, etc.), to the other party or to interested third parties who do not speak the regional or minority language, in a form they can understand".[44] It can therefore be said that this provision contains a guarantee of conditional validity: if the document is to be invoked against third parties who do not speak the RML, its contents must be made known to them in a form they can understand – in practice, translated into the official language. If, however, it can be shown that the third party knows the language in question, translation will be unnecessary.

3.3. Validity limited to *inter partes* relations (Article 9.2c)

The last paragraph of Article 9.2 of the Charter provides for an undertaking by contracting parties not to deny the validity, as between parties, of legal documents drawn up within the country solely because they are drafted in an RML.

This last clause is undoubtedly the most restrictive. It restricts the validity of legal documents drafted in an RML to relations between the parties to proceedings.

4. Translation of legislative texts (Article 9.3)

The last paragraph of Article 9 of the Charter provides for an undertaking by contracting parties to make available in the RMLs "the most important national statutory texts and those relating particularly to users of these languages, unless they are otherwise provided".

The aim of this provision is to ensure the translation of a broad catalogue of legislative texts into RMLs. Translations are guaranteed "unless they are otherwise provided". According to the Committee of Experts, these final words of Article 9.3 refer to "cases where the text already exists in an RML because it has already been translated into a similar or identical language which is the official language of another state".[45] It will therefore be taken into consideration whether a translation of the statutory text in question already exists because, for example, the translation has already been carried out by private

---

44. Explanatory Report, paragraph 97.
45. Ibid., paragraph 99.

institutions dedicated to the promotion of these RMLs or by foreign states whose official language is similar or identical.

However that may be, by means of this undertaking contracting states take on a duty to guarantee the translation of two specific types of text: first, "the most important national statutory texts"; and secondly, legislative texts which particularly concern the speakers of RMLs. This requires interpretation.

Prima facie, the phrase "most important national statutory texts" refers to legislative provisions of the state as a whole. Consequently, its scope does not include provisions adopted by sub-state or local authorities, despite the fact that it is precisely at these sub-state levels that the main provisions relating to RMLs are usually adopted.

Furthermore, the expression "statutory texts" in the authentic English version ("*textes législatifs*" in the authentic French version) also gives rise to doubts as to its interpretation: does its scope include only acts of parliament or, adopting a broader interpretation, does it also include other legal instruments? In this connection, legal writers have focused on the literal interpretation of the authentic versions of the Charter. Hence, "*textes législatifs*" in French means, in the strict sense, texts adopted by the national parliament and therefore does not include government regulations. However, as regards the expression "statutory texts" in the authentic English version, it has been noted that it "seems to include delegated legislation (statutory instruments), that is, government regulations".[46] In any event, Article 9.3 of the Charter refers explicitly to the "most important" statutory provisions, the determination of which will be left to the discretion of each state.

This provision of the Charter also provides for an undertaking by contracting parties to ensure the translation of the statutory texts "relating particularly to users of [regional or minority] languages". This phrase raises no problems of interpretation. It covers all the provisions having a direct influence on the legislative status of these languages.

It should be stressed that, in its evaluation reports, the Committee of Experts has specified that it is not enough to translate the statutory provisions: it is also necessary to harmonise these translations and take measures to improve access to statutory texts that have already been translated. It comments to this effect, for example, in its 2010 report on Norway.[47] The Committee of Experts also notes that some RMLs lack appropriate legal terminology, which makes translation of the legal provisions in question even more difficult.[48] Lastly, in

---

46. Woehrling (2005), op. cit., p. 177.
47. Norway 2010, 168. See also Sweden 2009, 107-9.
48. Armenia 2009, 146-7.

accordance with the pragmatic vision which guides interpretation of Article 9 of the Charter, the Committee of Experts has stated that the official translations of statutory provisions guaranteed in Article 9.3 must be carried out without undue delay. To quote from the 2005 and 2008 evaluation reports on Spain:

> The Committee of Experts reminds the Spanish authorities that a systematic translation of the relevant legal text into Catalan is a crucial part of the context for the fulfilment of the undertakings that Spain entered into under Article 9 of the Charter ... in the view of the Committee of Experts, the absence of a Catalan version of the most relevant pre-1998 legislation and the mentioned delay in the publication of the Catalan version of the Official Gazette represent serious obstacles to an effective use of the Catalan language in the field of justice in Catalonia.

To remedy this, the Committee of Experts went on to recommend that the Spanish authorities adopt practical measures to ensure that the most important national statutory texts and those relating particularly to users of RMLs, in this case Catalan, "are regularly and in the due time available".[49] According to the committee, if statutory provisions are not translated within a reasonable time, the requirements of Article 9.3 of the Charter are not met.

5. Shortcomings in implementation of the guarantees of Article 9: recommendations and good practices

The justice system is one of the areas of public life least open to the presence of RMLs. Indeed, in its periodical evaluation reports, the Committee of Experts has criticised some serious shortcomings in implementation of the guarantees of Article 9 of the Charter. It has done so from an essentially pragmatic perspective, in keeping with the realistic and practical vision suggested by the wording of the document: it has not only identified instances of non-compliance with the contracting states' undertakings, but, as we will see below, has proposed practical ways of remedying them.

This pragmatic approach to the shortcomings identified in implementation of Article 9 is based essentially on two premises: first, the particular circumstances of each RML are taken into consideration and the most appropriate mechanisms for guaranteeing compliance with the Charter in each case are identified and assessed; and second, any approach based on theory or principles is avoided in order to guarantee practical solutions to concrete problems.[50]

---

49. In the view of the Committee of Experts, "the publication of an official translation at the same time as the publication of the official Castilian version would be the most appropriate measure". See Spain 2005, 239-41. See also Spain 2008, 248-54.

50. J.-M. Woehrling (1998), "Problems raised...", p. 28.

This pragmatic approach can be seen in many of the committee's evaluation reports, such as Croatia 2008,[51] Denmark 2004,[52] Hungary 2010[53] and Montenegro 2010.[54] In all these reports, the committee criticises the fact that the undertakings of Article 9 of the Charter are only fulfilled on a formal, strictly theoretical level and it expressly draws the attention of the state authorities to the fact that the domestic rules that should guarantee them are not applied. The importance of promoting practical implementation of the undertakings in question also emerges from many recommendations of the Committee of Ministers to various contracting states, such as Austria and Serbia 2009,[55] Germany 2008[56] or Switzerland 2004.[57]

These reports by the Committee of Experts and recommendations by the Committee of Ministers emphasise the need to take the necessary measures to ensure the effective right to use the RML in question before the courts. A number of them reiterate that "in the absence of any practical implementation ... the undertakings remain only formally fulfilled".[58] In fact, the point is made that fulfilment of the undertakings of Article 9 of the Charter "requires that the formal provisions in the law are followed by some degree of practical implementation". If this is not the case, the committee notes that the undertakings are only formally fulfilled and therefore requests the authorities of the contracting state to remedy their non-compliance.[59]

---

51. Croatia 2008, 124-5: "The Committee of Experts concludes that the undertakings are formally fulfilled with regard to all languages, but only fulfilled in practice in relation to Italian. The Committee of Experts encourages the authorities to take measures to ensure that these undertakings are implemented in practice for all other regional or minority languages" (p. 125).
52. Denmark 2004, 75-6, where the Committee of Experts, referring to the German minority, said: "75. Although the right to submit documents and evidence in German is guaranteed under Danish legislation, the Committee of Experts was unable to obtain information on the use made of this right by members of the German-speaking minority in practice. 76. The Committee of Experts considers therefore that this undertaking is only formally fulfilled."
53. Hungary 2010, 113-5, 119-21 and 125-7. For example, with reference to the right of the accused in criminal proceedings to use his/her regional or minority language: "113. In the third evaluation report, the Committee of Experts considered this undertaking formally fulfilled and urged the Hungarian authorities to take practical measures so that the undertaking is implemented in practice ... 115. On the whole, the Committee of Experts considers this undertaking only formally fulfilled."
54. Montenegro 2010, 111.
55. Recommendations of the Committee of Ministers: Austria (2009), 4 and Serbia (2009), 5.
56. Recommendation of the Committee of Ministers: Germany (2008), 5, where the following recommendation is made: "take resolute action to establish a structured policy for making it possible in practice to use regional or minority languages in dealings with the administration and, where relevant, in the courts".
57. Recommendation of the Committee of Ministers: Switzerland (2004), 2.
58. Germany 2008, 147-50, with reference to Upper Sorbian, and paragraphs 223-5, with reference to Lower Sorbian.
59. Montenegro 2010, 111.

The Committee of Experts is aware of the practical difficulties experienced by some states in strictly implementing all the guarantees of Article 9 of the Charter, and especially those set out in paragraph 1. For this reason, it does not require the immediate achievement of absolute and ideal compliance, but it does require them to make real and tangible efforts going beyond mere reform of its domestic rules. Furthermore, the Committee of Experts identifies in its evaluation reports a broad catalogue of practical measures for guaranteeing effective implementation of the provision. Many of these are set out explicitly in the recommendations of the Committee of Ministers on application of the Charter in the different contracting states. Some of the more outstanding of these measures are outlined below.

5.1. Duty to inform members of the public and all legal operators of their linguistic rights in the judicial sphere

According to the Committee of Experts, the guarantees provided for in Article 9.1 of the Charter are not fulfilled in practice if the contracting state fails to provide information about the right to use RMLs in judicial proceedings.

A typical example may be found in the 2010 report on Hungary, where the committee explicitly requests the Hungarian authorities to "actively inform citizens about the possibility to use a minority language in courts". Proceeding on this basis, the committee goes on to state that Article 9 of the Charter "places a duty on the authorities to make sure that minority language speakers are made aware of this right". The committee therefore "considers that judicial staff could provide the relevant information in a general way and, moreover, encourage the use of minority languages through bi- or multilingual notices and signs in/ on court buildings, and information in public announcements of court forms".[60] These practical measures to provide information about the right to use an RML before the courts are also proposed in numerous other evaluation reports, such as Slovak Republic 2009,[61] Croatia 2008[62] or Spain 2005.[63] In all these reports, the committee adopts a pragmatic approach and outlines concrete measures for achieving this objective.[64]

---

60. Hungary 2010, 111-2.
61. Slovakia 2009. For example, with reference to the Romani language, paragraph 84 of the report states: "In conclusion, the Committee of Experts reiterates the need to clarify the legal framework and to encourage a certain degree of implementation in practice, for example through bi- or multilingual notices and signs in/on court buildings, and information in public announcements or summons". See also Hungary 2007, 107.
62. Croatia 2008, 124-5.
63. Spain 2005, with reference, for example, to the use of Catalan, see 233-4.
64. For example, in the case of Spain 2005, see paragraph 234 *in fine*, where the Committee of Experts states that "in order to fully implement the requirement for the courts located in Catalonia

For its part, the Committee of Ministers, in several recommendations, has explicitly set out the duty of contracting states to provide information about the right to use RMLs in judicial proceedings, for example its recommendations to Armenia 2009[65] and Hungary 2010.[66]

5.2. Guarantee of linguistic proficiency of judicial staff

According to the Committee of Experts, to ensure effective compliance with the rights set out in Article 9.1 of the Charter, judicial staff – more especially judges and prosecutors – must be in a position to respect litigants' judicial rights. This means guaranteeing a certain knowledge of the RML among judicial staff. In this connection, the Committee of Experts has repeatedly criticised the fact that their unfamiliarity with RMLs creates a sometimes insuperable obstacle to full compliance with the undertakings of Article 9.1. It has raised this criticism in numerous evaluation reports.[67]

According to the committee, in some countries, such as Spain, the limited percentage of judicial staff capable of speaking RMLs, especially among judges and prosecutors, "still constitutes an additional obstacle to the chosen undertakings being properly implemented".[68] However, the Committee of

---

to conduct the proceedings in Catalan at one party's request and the other undertakings at issue, the following measures seem to be necessary: (i) the introduction, in the legal framework, of formal guarantees corresponding to the undertakings entered into under Article 9 paragraph 1.a.i, 1.a.ii, 1.b.i and 1.c.i; (ii) provision for the parties to be specifically informed, at the relevant stage of the proceedings concerned, of the possibilities inherent to the undertakings entered into by Spain under Article 9 and (iii) adequate practical and organisational measures".

65. Recommendation of the Committee of Ministers: Armenia (2009), 2 ("Ensure the use of regional or minority languages before courts and inform courts and the public on the rights and duties related to Article 9 of the Charter").

66. Recommendation of the Committee of Ministers: Hungary (2010), 5.

67. For example, Finland 2001, 74-6, 83, 86-7; Finland 2004, 76; Spain 2005 and 2008; Sweden 2008, 95; Austria 2009, 132.

68. Spain 2005, 232. On the political and academic debate, see A. M. Pla Boix (2005), *El règim jurídic de les llengües a l'Administració de Justícia*. Collecció Institut d'Estudis Autonòmics No. 41. Barcelona: Generalitat de Catalunya. On the linguistic proficiency of judicial staff in Spain, see A. M. Pla Boix (2007), "El perfil lingüístic del personal al servei de l'Administració de Justícia. Comentari a la STC 270/2006 de 13 de setembre", *Revista Jurídica de Catalunya*, No. 2. Also A. M. Pla Boix (2006), "La valoració del coneixement de la llengua autonòmica cooficial en la provisió de places judicials: estat de la qüestió. Comentari a la STC 253/2005 de 10 d'octubre", *Revista Jurídica de Catalunya*, No. 2, pp. 123-50. In the case of Catalonia, the most recent attempt to guarantee the linguistic proficiency of judges, prosecutors and other judicial staff working in that region, in keeping with the provisions of the Charter as interpreted by the Committee of Experts, is to be found in Article 33 of the Catalan Statute of Autonomy as revised by Law 6/2006 of 19 July 2006 (BOE (Official Gazette) No. 172 of 20 July 2006), which was subsequently challenged before the Constitutional Court. Its constitutionality was confirmed by Constitutional Court judgment 31/2010 of 28 June 2010.

Experts has not confined itself to diagnosing the problem, but has analysed the factors involved and proposed corrective measures to improve the linguistic skills of judicial and administrative staff.[69] It has also recommended that some contracting states adopt further measures to promote knowledge of RMLs among all legal operators, and especially among lawyers.[70]

Among the reasons for the inadequate linguistic proficiency of judicial staff, the committee has identified: contracting states' domestic legal framework, which does not always guarantee that sufficient judges, prosecutors and other staff working in the justice system are familiar with the RMLs used by members of the public seeking justice; the system for filling judicial posts, which, according to the committee, sometimes precludes consolidation of the use of these languages in courts;[71] or certain provisions on the conduct of judicial proceedings, under which the language used sometimes depends on the choice of language at the previous police investigation stage.[72]

The situation is aggravated by the tendency of citizens to willingly forego the use of their RML when appearing before a court. By foregoing their language in favour of the court's official language, they ensure that they are understood without any need for a translator or interpreter. In this context, the Committee of Experts criticises the fact that, in using their RML, citizens often see themselves as "trouble-makers", which may be detrimental to them in the hearing of the case. One example of this is the 2004 report on the

---

69. Finland 2007, 120-4, 209, 211-2. See also the Netherlands 2008, 111.

70. Slovenia 2007, 90.

71. For example, Spain 2005, 232. In the words of the Committee of Experts: "the problem is aggravated by the fact that a system based on a customary rotation of judges leads either to judges not being encouraged to learn a regional or minority language when they know it might no longer be useful after a transfer, or to losing the investment spent on language training when a judge with the necessary linguistic skills is transferred to an autonomous community where those skills are no longer relevant. As a result, a review of the current training and career structure seems to be indispensable".

72. Finland 2001, 76. In the words of the Committee of Experts: "In practice, this right cannot always be exercised for two main reasons. Firstly, the lack of officers, lawyers and judges with sufficient command of Swedish makes the choice of the Swedish language too difficult to manage for the proceedings. As Swedish-speakers are bilingual, they prefer not to ask for their mother tongue to be the language of the proceedings, as they may risk not being correctly understood or even being seen as 'trouble-makers'. The Public Prosecutor and other state agents use the language of the defendant if they are required to know this language. Secondly ... the language chosen by the police in its statements depends on the officer's mother tongue and not on that of the defendant. As the instruction language remains the same during the proceedings that may follow this, in practice [,] excludes the possibility for the defendant to use a different language (as he or she has a sufficient command of the language of the proceedings). Swedish-speakers are very often confronted with this situation."

application of the Charter in Finland, where the committee notes that the right to use an RML in courts of law, in this case Swedish, is not always guaranteed because some litigants "felt constrained to give up using Swedish, or requesting to use Swedish, because it created an atmosphere which is not always very positive in judicial proceedings, the individual having the feeling that he or she may be considered as a 'trouble maker'".[73] A similar observation is found in the 2001 report on Hungary, where the committee notes that "since speakers of minority languages in Hungary all live in a situation of 'diglossia', having a good command of the national language, judicial practice will inevitably have a tendency to restrict the formula to foreigners without any serious command of Hungarian", adding that "since the assistance of interpreters is costly and makes the procedure cumbersome, accused persons that are users of a minority language, but can also speak Hungarian, are afraid to be perceived as trouble-makers if they use their right to speak in the minority language before the court".[74]

For all these reasons, the Committee of Ministers has explicitly urged some states to ensure that a certain proportion of judicial staff have a knowledge of the RML. This is the case, for example, in its recommendations to Spain in 2005 and 2008, where it calls for the adoption of "the necessary legal and practical measures to ensure that an adequate proportion of the judicial staff posted in the autonomous communities concerned by the application of Article 9 of the Charter have a working knowledge of the relevant languages".[75]

5.3. Duty to guarantee the availability of legal glossaries in the different RMLs

In this connection, the Committee of Experts has noted in various evaluation reports, such as Armenia 2009[76] or Norway 2010,[77] that some RMLs lack appropriate legal terminology, which hinders implementation of the undertakings in Article 9 of the Charter.

It has also criticised the fact that some states which have accepted the undertaking in Article 9.3 do not ensure effective translation of their statutory provisions. According to the committee, it is not enough to translate statutory provisions: it is also necessary to harmonise these translations, take measures

---

73. Finland 2004, 76.
74. Hungary 2001, 45-6. See also Austria 2005, 152.
75. Recommendations of the Committee of Ministers: Spain (2005) and (2008), 1.
76. Armenia 2009, 146-7.
77. Norway 2010, 162-3. The previous report had pointed out the lack of legal terminology in Sami: Norway 2007, 139-40.

to improve access to legislative texts that have already been translated and ensure that texts are translated without undue delay. It comments to this effect, for example, in its 2010 report on Norway.[78] According to the Committee of Experts, the fact that some RMLs lack adequate legal terminology makes translation of the legal provisions in question even more problematical.[79]

5.4. Duty to guarantee the availability of translators and interpreters of RMLs

In numerous other evaluation reports, such as Finland 2007[80] or Slovakia 2009,[81] the Committee of Experts also criticises the lack of translators and interpreters for some RMLs, which seriously hampers the use of these languages in judicial proceedings. For this reason, it has in some cases recommended measures such as informing the court of the use of an RML sufficiently in advance to ensure the provision of translation and interpretation services.[82]

5.5. Duty to ensure that computer programs and other technical facilities in courts permit proper use of RMLs

Similarly, the Committee of Experts has specified in numerous evaluation reports that the guarantees in Article 9.1 require contracting states to ensure that computer programs used in courts permit proper use of RMLs. For example, in its report on the application of the Charter in Austria in 2009, the Committee of Experts observed that "the computer software used in the courts cannot reproduce the diacritics of the Slovenian alphabet in documents" and therefore urged "the Austrian authorities to solve the practical problems relating to the use of diacritical signs".[83]

5.6. Duty to ensure that dialectal differences do not dissuade citizens from using RMLs before the judicial authorities

Lastly, the Committee of Ministers has pointed out that, in some contracting states, the dialectal differences exhibited by their RMLs may prove dissuasive to their speakers when it comes to using them before the judicial authorities.

---

78. Norway 2010, 168. Another typical example is Sweden 2008, 107-9.
79. Armenia 2009, 146-7.
80. Finland 2007, 210.
81. Slovakia 2009, 84, 88.
82. United Kingdom 2004, 139, on the use of Welsh. See C. F. Huws (2008), "Chartering new territories in Welsh language judicial proceedings", in *The European Charter for Regional or Minority Languages: legal challenges and opportunities*. Regional or Minority Languages No. 5. Strasbourg: Council of Europe Publishing.
83. Austria 2009, 227-8.

For this reason in some evaluation reports, such as Czech Republic 2009, the committee has reminded the authorities that the provisions of Article 9 of the Charter apply not only to the standard forms of RMLs but also to their variants traditionally spoken in a specific geographical area.[84]

References

Huws, Catrin Fflur (2008), "Chartering new territories in Welsh language judicial proceedings" in *The European Charter for Regional or Minority Languages: legal challenges and opportunities*, Regional or Minority Languages No. 5. Strasbourg: Council of Europe Publishing.

Pla Boix, Anna M. (2005), *El règim jurídic de les llengües a l'Administració de Justícia*, Col·lecció Institut d'Estudis Autonòmics No. 41. Barcelona: Generalitat de Catalunya.

Pla Boix, Anna M. (2006), "La valoració del coneixement de la llengua autonòmica cooficial en la provisió de places judicials: estat de la qüestió. Comentari a la STC 253/2005 de 10 d'octubre", *Revista Jurídica de Catalunya*, No. 2.

Pla Boix, Anna M. (2007), "El perfil lingüístic del personal al servei de l'Administració de Justícia. Comentari a la STC 270/2006 de 13 de setembre", *Revista Jurídica de Catalunya*, No. 2.

Woehrling, Jean-Marie (1998), "Problems raised by the use of regional or minority languages before public and judicial authorities" in *International Conference of the European Charter for Regional or Minority Languages*. Regional or Minority Languages No. 1. Strasbourg: Council of Europe Publishing.

Woehrling, Jean-Marie (2005), *The European Charter for Regional or Minority Languages: a critical commentary*. Strasbourg: Council of Europe Publishing.

---

84. Czech Republic 2009, 169.

Appendix: Ratifications

Article 9		
Paragraph and subparagraph		
1	a.i	**Finland:** Swedish. **Norway:** Sami. **Spain:** Basque (Autonomous Community of the Basque Country; Historical Community of Navarra), Catalan (Autonomous Community of Catalonia, Balearic Islands), Valencian (Autonomous Community of Valencia) and Galician (Autonomous Community of Galicia). **Slovenia:** Italian and Hungarian. **Switzerland:** Italian.
	a.ii	**Armenia:** Assyrian, Yezidi, Greek, Russian and Kurdish. **Austria**: Burgenland Croatian (*Land* Burgenland), Slovenian (*Land* Carinthia) and Hungarian (*Land* Burgenland). **Bosnia and Herzegovina:** Albanian, Montenegrin, Czech, Italian, Hungarian, Macedonian, German, Polish, Romanian, Romani, Rysin, Slovak, Slovenian, Turkish, Ukrainian and Jewish (Yiddish and Ladino). **Croatia:** Italian, Serbian, Hungarian, Czech, Slovak, Ruthenian and Ukrainian. **Czech Republic:** Polish (Moravian-Silesian region and in the territory of the districts of Frydek-Místek and Karviná) and Slovak. **Finland:** Sami and Swedish. **Germany:** Upper Sorbian (Free State of Saxony) and Lower Sorbian (*Land* Brandenburg). **Hungary:** Croatian, German, Romanian, Serbian, Slovak, Slovenian, Romani and Béas. **Montenegro:** Albanian and Romani. **Netherlands:** Frisian (province of Friesland). **Norway:** Sami. **Romania:** Bulgarian, Czech, Croatian, German, Hungarian, Russian, Serbian, Slovak, Turkish and Ukrainian. **Serbia:** Albanian, Bosnian, Bulgarian, Hungarian, Romani, Romanian, Ruthenian, Slovakian, Ukrainian and Croatian. **Slovakia:** Bulgarian, Croatian, Czech, German, Polish, Romani, Ruthenian, Ukrainian and Hungarian. **Slovenia:** Italian and Hungarian. **Spain:** Basque (Autonomous Community of the Basque Country; Historical Community of Navarra), Catalan (Autonomous Community of Catalonia, Balearic Islands), Valencian (Autonomous Community of Valencia) and Galician (Autonomous Community of Galicia). **Sweden:** Sami, Finnish and Meänkieli. **Switzerland:** Romansh and Italian. **United Kingdom:** Welsh.

| a.iii | **Armenia:** Assyrian, Yezidi, Greek, Russian and Kurdish.
Austria: Burgenland Croatian (*Land* Burgenland), Slovenian (*Land* Carinthia and Hungarian (*Land* Burgenland).
Bosnia and Herzegovina: Albanian, Montenegrin, Czech, Italian, Hungarian, Macedonian, German, Polish, Romanian, Romani, Rysin, Slovak, Slovenian, Turkish, Ukrainian and Jewish (Yiddish and Ladino).
Czech Republic: Polish (Moravian-Silesian region and in the territory of the districts of Frydek-Místek and Karviná) and Slovak.
Finland: Sami and Swedish.
Germany: Upper Sorbian (Free State of Saxony) and Lower Sorbian (*Land* Brandenburg).
Hungary: Croatian, German, Romanian, Serbian, Slovak, Slovenian, Romani and Béas.
Montenegro: Albanian and Romani.
Netherlands: Frisian (province of Friesland).
Norway: Sami.
Romania: Bulgarian, Czech, Croatian, German, Hungarian, Russian, Serbian, Slovak, Turkish and Ukrainian.
Serbia: Albanian, Bosnian, Bulgarian, Hungarian, Romani, Romanian, Ruthenian, Slovakian, Ukrainian and Croatian.
Slovakia: Bulgarian, Croatian, Czech, German, Polish, Romani, Ruthenian, Ukrainian and Hungarian.
Slovenia: Italian and Hungarian.
Spain: Basque (Autonomous Community of the Basque Country; Historical Community of Navarra), Catalan (Autonomous Community of Catalonia, Balearic Islands), Valencian (Autonomous Community of Valencia) and Galician (Autonomous Community of Galicia).
Sweden: Sami, Finnish and Meänkieli.
Switzerland: Romansh and Italian.
Ukraine: Belarusian, Bulgarian, Gagauz, Greek, Jewish, Crimean Tatar, Moldovan, German, Polish, Russian, Romanian, Slovak and Hungarian.
United Kingdom: Welsh. |
| a.iv | **Armenia:** Assyrian, Yezidi, Greek, Russian and Kurdish.
Croatia: Italian, Serbian, Hungarian, Czech, Slovak, Ruthenian and Ukrainian.
Czech Republic: Polish (Moravian-Silesian region and in the territory of the districts of Frydek-Místek and Karviná) and Slovak.
Finland: Sami and Swedish.
Hungary: Croatian, German, Romanian, Serbian, Slovak, Slovenian, Romani and Béas.
Montenegro: Albanian and Romani.
Norway: Sami.
Slovenia: Italian and Hungarian.
Spain: Basque (Autonomous Community of the Basque Country; Historical Community of Navarra), Catalan (Autonomous Community of Catalonia, Balearic Islands), Valencian (Autonomous Community of Valencia) and Galician (Autonomous Community of Galicia).
Sweden: Sami, Finnish and Meänkieli. |

331

1	b.i	**Finland:** Swedish. **Norway:** Sami. **Slovenia:** Italian and Hungarian. **Spain:** Basque (Autonomous Community of the Basque Country; Historical Community of Navarra), Catalan (Autonomous Community of Catalonia, Balearic Islands), Valencian (Autonomous Community of Valencia) and Galician (Autonomous Community of Galicia). **Switzerland:** Italian.
	b.ii	**Armenia:** Assyrian, Yezidi, Greek, Russian and Kurdish **Austria**: Burgenland Croatian (*Land* Burgenland), Slovenian (*Land* Carinthia) and Hungarian (*Land* Burgenland). **Bosnia and Herzegovina:** Albanian, Montenegrin, Czech, Italian, Hungarian, Macedonian, German, Polish, Romanian, Romani, Rysin, Slovak, Slovenian, Turkish, Ukrainian and Jewish (Yiddish and Ladino). **Croatia:** Italian, Serbian, Hungarian, Czech, Slovak, Ruthenian and Ukrainian. **Czech Republic:** Polish (Moravian-Silesian region and in the territory of the districts of Frydek-Místek and Karviná) and Slovak. **Finland:** Sami and Swedish **Germany:** Upper Sorbian (Free State of Saxony). **Hungary:** Croatian, German, Romanian, Serbian, Slovak, Slovenian, Romani and Béas. **Montenegro:** Albanian and Romani. **Norway:** Sami. **Romania:** Bulgarian, Czech, Croatian, German, Hungarian, Russian, Serbian, Slovak, Turkish and Ukrainian. **Serbia:** Albanian, Bosnian, Bulgarian, Hungarian, Romani, Romanian, Ruthenian, Slovakian, Ukrainian and Croatian. **Slovakia:** Bulgarian, Croatian, Czech, German, Polish, Romani, Ruthenian, Ukrainian and Hungarian. **Slovenia:** Italian and Hungarian. **Spain:** Basque (Autonomous Community of the Basque Country; Historical Community of Navarra), Catalan (Autonomous Community of Catalonia, Balearic Islands), Valencian (Autonomous Community of Valencia) and Galician (Autonomous Community of Galicia). **Sweden:** Sami, Finnish and Meänkieli. **Switzerland:** Romansh and Italian. **United Kingdom:** Welsh.
	b.iii	**Austria**: Burgenland Croatian (*Land* Burgenland), Slovenian (*Land* Carinthia) and Hungarian (*Land* Burgenland). **Bosnia and Herzegovina:** Albanian, Montenegrin, Czech, Italian, Hungarian, Macedonian, German, Polish, Romanian, Romani, Rysin, Slovak, Slovenian, Turkish, Ukrainian and Jewish (Yiddish and Ladino). **Croatia:** Italian, Serbian, Hungarian, Czech, Slovak, Ruthenian and Ukrainian. **Czech Republic:** Polish (Moravian-Silesian region and in the territory of the districts of Frydek-Místek and Karviná) and Slovak (all over the territory of the Czech Republic).

		Denmark: German (Southern Jutland). **Finland:** Sami and Swedish. **Germany:** Danish (*Land* Schleswig-Holstein), Upper Sorbian (Free State of Saxony), Lower Sorbian (*Land* Brandenburg), North Frisian (*Land* Schleswig-Holstein), Sater Frisian (*Land* Lower Saxony), Low German (Free Hanseatic City of Bremen, Free and Hanseatic City of Hamburg, *Land* Mecklenburg-Western Pomerania, Schleswig-Holstein, North Rhine-Westphalia), Romani and Romanes. **Hungary:** Croatian, German, Romanian, Serbian, Slovak, Slovenian, Romani and Béas. **Montenegro:** Albanian and Romani. **Netherlands:** Frisian (province of Friesland). **Norway:** Sami. **Romania:** Bulgarian, Czech, Croatian, German, Hungarian, Russian, Serbian, Slovak, Turkish and Ukrainian. **Slovakia:** Bulgarian, Croatian, Czech, German, Polish, Romani, Ruthenian, Ukrainian and Hungarian. **Slovenia:** Italian and Hungarian. **Spain:** Basque (Autonomous Community of the Basque Country; Historical Community of Navarra), Catalan (Autonomous Community of Catalonia, Balearic Islands), Valencian (Autonomous Community of Valencia) and Galician (Autonomous Community of Galicia). **Sweden:** Sami, Finnish and Meänkieli. **Switzerland:** Romansh and Italian. **Ukraine:** Belarusian, Bulgarian, Gagauz, Greek, Jewish, Crimean Tatar, Moldovan, German, Polish, Russian, Romanian, Slovak and Hungarian. **United Kingdom:** Welsh and Scottish-Gaelic.
1	c.i	**Finland:** Swedish. **Slovenia:** Italian and Hungarian. **Spain:** Basque (Autonomous Community of the Basque Country; Historical Community of Navarra), Catalan (Autonomous Community of Catalonia, Balearic Islands), Valencian (Autonomous Community of Valencia) and Galician (Autonomous Community of Galicia). **Switzerland:** Italian.
	c.ii	**Armenia:** Assyrian, Yezidi, Greek, Russian and Kurdish. **Austria**: Burgenland Croatian (*Land* Burgenland), Slovenian (*Land* Carinthia) and Hungarian (*Land* Burgenland). **Bosnia and Herzegovina:** Albanian, Montenegrin, Czech, Italian, Hungarian, Macedonian, German, Polish, Romanian, Romani, Rysin, Slovak, Slovenian, Turkish, Ukrainian and Jewish (Yiddish and Ladino). **Croatia:** Italian, Serbian, Hungarian, Czech, Slovak, Ruthenian and Ukrainian. **Czech Republic:** Polish (Moravian-Silesian region and in the territory of the districts of Frydek-Místek and Karviná) and Slovak. **Finland**: Sami and Swedish. **Germany:** Upper Sorbian (Free State of Saxony). **Hungary:** Croatian, German, Romanian, Serbian, Slovak, Slovenian, Romani and Béas.

		Montenegro: Albanian and Romani. **Netherlands:** Frisian (province of Friesland). **Romania:** Bulgarian, Czech, Croatian, German, Hungarian, Russian, Serbian, Slovak, Turkish and Ukrainian. **Serbia:** Albanian, Bosnian, Bulgarian, Hungarian, Romani, Romanian, Ruthenian, Slovakian, Ukrainian and Croatian. **Slovakia:** Bulgarian, Croatian, Czech, German, Polish, Romani, Ruthenian, Ukrainian and Hungarian. **Slovenia:** Italian and Hungarian. **Spain:** Basque (Autonomous Community of the Basque Country; Historical Community of Navarra), Catalan (Autonomous Community of Catalonia, Balearic Islands), Valencian (Autonomous Community of Valencia) and Galician (Autonomous Community of Galicia). **Sweden:** Sami, Finnish and Meänkieli. **Switzerland:** Romansh and Italian. **United Kingdom:** Welsh.
	c.iii	**Armenia:** Assyrian, Yezidi, Greek, Russian and Kurdish. **Austria**: Burgenland Croatian (*Land* Burgenland), Slovenian (*Land* Carinthia) and Hungarian (*Land* Burgenland). **Bosnia and Herzegovina:** Albanian, Montenegrin, Czech, Italian, Hungarian, Macedonian, German, Polish, Romanian, Romani, Rysin, Slovak, Slovenian, Turkish, Ukrainian and Jewish (Yiddish and Ladino). **Croatia:** Italian, Serbian, Hungarian, Czech, Slovak, Ruthenian and Ukrainian. **Czech Republic:** Polish (Moravian-Silesian region and in the territory of the districts of Frydek-Místek and Karviná) and Slovak. **Denmark:** German (Southern Jutland). **Finland:** Sami and Swedish. **Germany:** Danish (*Land* Schleswig-Holstein), Upper Sorbian (Free State of Saxony), Lower Sorbian (*Land* Brandenburg), North Frisian (*Land* Schleswig-Holstein), Sater Frisian (*Land* Lower Saxony), Low German (Free Hanseatic City of Bremen, Free and Hanseatic City of Hamburg, *Land* Mecklenburg-Western Pomerania, Schleswig-Holstein, North Rhine-Westphalia), Romani and Romanes. **Hungary:** Croatian, German, Romanian, Serbian, Slovak, Slovenian, Romani and Béas. **Montenegro:** Albanian and Romani. **Netherlands:** Frisian (province of Friesland). **Romania:** Bulgarian, Czech, Croatian, German, Hungarian, Russian, Serbian, Slovak, Turkish and Ukrainian. **Slovakia:** Bulgarian, Croatian, Czech, German, Polish, Romani, Ruthenian, Ukrainian and Hungarian. **Slovenia:** Italian and Hungarian. **Spain:** Basque (Autonomous Community of the Basque Country; Historical Community of Navarra), Catalan (Autonomous Community of Catalonia, Balearic Islands), Valencian (Autonomous Community of Valencia) and Galician (Autonomous Community of Galicia). **Sweden:** Sami, Finnish and Meänkieli. **Ukraine:** Belarusian, Bulgarian, Gagauz, Greek, Jewish, Crimean Tatar, Moldovan, German, Polish, Russian, Romanian, Slovak and Hungarian. **United Kingdom:** Welsh.

| 1 | d | **Armenia:** Assyrian, Yezidi, Greek, Russian and Kurdish.
Austria: Burgenland Croatian (*Land* Burgenland), Slovenian (*Land* Carinthia) and Hungarian (*Land* Burgenland).
Croatia: Italian, Serbian, Hungarian, Czech, Slovak, Ruthenian and Ukrainian.
Czech Republic: Polish (Moravian-Silesian region and in the territory of the districts of Frydek-Místek and Karviná) and Slovak.
Finland: Sami and Swedish.
Germany: Upper Sorbian (Free State of Saxony).
Montenegro: Albanian and Romani.
Norway: Sami.
Romania: Bulgarian, Czech, Croatian, German, Hungarian, Russian, Serbian, Slovak, Turkish and Ukrainian.
Serbia: Albanian, Bosnian, Bulgarian, Hungarian, Romani, Romanian, Ruthenian, Slovakian, Ukrainian and Croatian.
Slovakia: Bulgarian, Croatian, Czech, German, Polish, Romani, Ruthenian, Ukrainian and Hungarian.
Slovenia: Italian and Hungarian.
Spain: Basque (Autonomous Community of the Basque Country; Historical Community of Navarra), Catalan (Autonomous Community of Catalonia, Balearic Islands), Valencian (Autonomous Community of Valencia) and Galician (Autonomous Community of Galicia).
Sweden: Sami, Finnish and Meänkieli.
Switzerland: Italian.
United Kingdom: Welsh. |
| 2 | a | **Austria:** Burgenland Croatian (*Land* Burgenland), Slovenian (*Land* Carinthia) and Hungarian (*Land* Burgenland).
Czech Republic: Polish (Moravian-Silesian region and in the territory of the districts of Frydek-Místek and Karviná) and Slovak.
Denmark: German (Southern Jutland).
Finland: Sami, Swedish
Germany: Danish (*Land* Schleswig-Holstein), Upper Sorbian (Free State of Saxony), Lower Sorbian (*Land* Brandenburg), North Frisian (*Land* Schleswig-Holstein), Sater Frisian (*Land* Lower Saxony), Low German (Free Hanseatic City of Bremen, Free and Hanseatic City of Hamburg, *Länder* Mecklenburg-Western Pomerania, Schleswig-Holstein, North Rhine-Westphalia, Brandenburg, Saxony-Anhalt), Romani and Romanes.
Hungary: Croatian, German, Romanian, Serbian, Slovak and Slovenian.
Montenegro: Albanian and Romani.
Norway: Sami
Poland: Belarusian, Czech, Hebrew, Yiddish, Karaim, Kashub, Lithuanian, Lemko, German, Armenian, Romani, Russian, Slovak, Tatar and Ukrainian.
Romania: Bulgarian, Czech, Croatian, German, Hungarian, Russian, Serbian, Slovak, Turkish and Ukrainian.
Serbia: Albanian, Bosnian, Bulgarian, Hungarian, Romani, Romanian, Ruthenian, Slovakian, Ukrainian and Croatian.
Slovakia: Hungarian.
Slovenia: Italian and Hungarian. |

335

		Spain: Basque (Autonomous Community of the Basque Country; Historical Community of Navarra), Catalan (Autonomous Community of Catalonia, Balearic Islands), Valencian (Autonomous Community of Valencia) and Galician (Autonomous Community of Galicia). **Sweden:** Sami, Finnish, and Meänkieli. **Switzerland:** Romansh and Italian.
	b	**Denmark:** German (Southern Jutland). **Hungary:** Croatian, German, Romanian, Serbian, Slovak and Slovenian. **Montenegro:** Albanian and Romani. **Netherlands:** Frisian (province of Friesland). **Serbia:** Albanian, Bosnian, Bulgarian, Hungarian, Romani, Romanian, Ruthenian, Slovakian, Ukrainian and Croatian. **Sweden:** Sami, Finnish and Meänkieli. **United Kingdom:** Welsh.
	c	**Bosnia and Herzegovina:** Albanian, Montenegrin, Czech, Italian, Hungarian, Macedonian, German, Polish, Romanian, Romani, Rysin, Slovak, Slovenian, Turkish, Ukrainian and Jewish (Yiddish and Ladino). **Denmark:** German (Southern Jutland). **Hungary:** Croatian, German, Romanian, Serbian, Slovak and Slovenian. **Montenegro:** Albanian and Romani. **Serbia:** Albanian, Bosnian, Bulgarian, Hungarian, Romani, Romanian, Ruthenian, Slovakian, Ukrainian and Croatian. **Sweden:** Sami, Finnish and Meänkieli. **Ukraine:** Belarusian, Bulgarian, Gagauz, Greek, Jewish, Crimean Tatar, Moldovan, German, Polish, Russian, Romanian, Slovak and Hungarian.
3		**Armenia:** Assyrian, Yezidi, Greek, Russian and Kurdish. **Finland:** Sami and Swedish. **Montenegro:** Albanian and Romani. **Norway:** Sami. **Romania:** Bulgarian, Czech, Croatian, German, Hungarian, Russian, Serbian, Slovak, Turkish and Ukrainian. **Serbia:** Albanian, Bosnian, Bulgarian, Hungarian, Romani, Romanian, Ruthenian, Slovakian, Ukrainian and Croatian. **Slovakia:** Ruthenian, Ukrainian and Hungarian. **Spain:** Basque (Autonomous Community of the Basque Country; Historical Community of Navarra), Catalan (Autonomous Community of Catalonia, Balearic Islands), Valencian (Autonomous Community of Valencia) and Galician (Autonomous Community of Galicia). **Sweden:** Sami, Finnish and Meänkieli. **Switzerland:** Romansh and Italian. **Ukraine:** Belarusian, Bulgarian, Gagauz, Greek, Jewish, Crimean Tatar, Moldovan, German, Polish, Russian, Romanian, Slovak and Hungarian. **United Kingdom:** Irish.

Article 10. Administrative authorities and public services

Jutta Engbers
Lawyer, Friesoythe, Germany

1. Introduction

2. Article 10.1: Reasonableness
    2.1. Article 10.1: Structure
    2.2. Article 10.1a: Ensuring the use of the language
        2.2.1. Article 10.1a.i: Extensive use in administrative matters
        2.2.2. Article 10.1a.ii: Staff with a command of the language
        2.2.3. Article 10.1a.iii: Use of the language on request
        2.2.4. Article 10.1a.iv: Applications in the regional or minority language
        2.2.5. Article 10.1a.v: Submission of documents
    2.3. Article 10.1b: (Bilingual) forms, administrative regulations
    2.4. Article 10.1c: Official documents in the regional or minority language (RML)

3. Article 10.2: Local and regional authorities and administrations
    3.1. Allow/encourage
    3.2. Structure
    3.3. Article 10.2a: Comprehensive use
    3.4. Article 10.2b: Use by citizens
    3.5. Article 10.2c and d: Official documents
    3.6. Article 10.2e and f: Assembly meetings
    3.7. Article 10.2g: Place names and signs

4. Article 10.3: Enterprises that provide public services
    4.1. Article 10.3a: Extensive use
    4.2. Article 10.3b: Use of the regional or minority language by service users
    4.3. Article 10.3c: Applications and enquiries

5. Article 10.4: Implementation conditions
    5.1. Article 10.4.a: Translations
    5.2. Article 10.4.b and c: Staff planning
        5.2.1. Article 10.4.b: Recruitment and training
        5.2.2. Article 10.4.c: Deployment in own language area

6. Article 10.5. Choice of name

References

Appendix: Ratifications

Article 10 – Administrative authorities and public services

1. *Within the administrative districts of the State in which the number of residents who are users of regional or minority languages justifies the measures specified below and according to the situation of each language, the Parties undertake, as far as this is reasonably possible:*

   a. i. *to ensure that the administrative authorities use the regional or minority languages; or*

   ii. *to ensure that such of their officers as are in contact with the public use the regional or minority languages in their relations with persons applying to them in these languages; or*

   iii. *to ensure that users of regional or minority languages may submit oral or written applications and receive a reply in these languages; or*

   iv. *to ensure that users of regional or minority languages may submit oral or written applications in these languages; or*

   v. *to ensure that users of regional or minority languages may validly submit a document in these languages;*

   b. *to make available widely used administrative texts and forms for the population in the regional or minority languages or in bilingual versions;*

   c. *to allow the administrative authorities to draft documents in a regional or minority language.*

2. *In respect of the local and regional authorities on whose territory the number of residents who are users of regional or minority languages is such as to justify the measures specified below, the Parties undertake to allow and/or encourage:*

   a. *the use of regional or minority languages within the framework of the regional or local authority;*

   b. *the possibility for users of regional or minority languages to submit oral or written applications in these languages;*

   c. *the publication by regional authorities of their official documents also in the relevant regional or minority languages;*

   d. *the publication by local authorities of their official documents also in the relevant regional or minority languages;*

   e. *the use by regional authorities of regional or minority languages in debates in their assemblies, without excluding, however, the use of the official language(s) of the State;*

   f. *the use by local authorities of regional or minority languages in debates in their assemblies, without excluding, however, the use of the official language(s) of the State;*

   g. *the use or adoption, if necessary in conjunction with the name in the official language(s), of traditional and correct forms of place-names in regional or minority languages.*

3. *With regard to public services provided by the administrative authorities or other persons acting on their behalf, the Parties undertake, within the territory in which regional or minority languages are used, in accordance with the situation of each language and as far as this is reasonably possible:*

a. *to ensure that the regional or minority languages are used in the provision of the service; or*

b. *to allow users of regional or minority languages to submit a request and receive a reply in these languages; or*

c. *to allow users of regional or minority languages to submit a request in these languages.*

4. *With a view to putting into effect those provisions of paragraphs 1, 2 and 3 accepted by them, the Parties undertake to take one or more of the following measures:*

a. *translation or interpretation as may be required;*

b. *recruitment and, where necessary, training of the officials and other public service employees required;*

c. *compliance as far as possible with requests from public service employees having a knowledge of a regional or minority language to be appointed in the territory in which that language is used.*

5. *The Parties undertake to allow the use or adoption of family names in the regional or minority languages, at the request of those concerned.*

1. Introduction[1]

The main provisions of the current Article 10 were a component in the genesis of the Charter from the outset.[2] It was realised, early on, that this article had to cover not only state administrations as such but also bodies responsible for carrying out privatised public functions. There were lengthy discussions on whether and when the individual contracting parties or their internal state subdivisions are allowed/able to take another decision on every concrete measure in relation to the situation of a language and, if so, how such a

---

1. The comments are based on the author's article in S. Boysen et al. (2011), *Europäische Charta der Regional- oder Minderheitensprachen, Handkommentar,* Zurich: Dike.
2. In Resolution 192 (1988) of the Standing Conference of Local and Regional Authorities of Europe, reprinted in Council of Europe, *Preparatory work of the European Charter for Regional or Minority Languages,* No. 5, 2004, still designated as Article 7, without any separation of the rules in the current Article 9; since the 3rd meeting of the ad hoc committee in September 1990 as Article 8 (CAHLR (90) 9); since the 5th meeting in April 1991 as Article 11 (CAHLR (91) 9), and since the 7th meeting in February 1992 as Article 10 (CAHLR (92) 5).

provision must be worded.[3] The double "'reasonableness" provision in Article 10.1 was ultimately included in order to enable individual states to take account, when necessary, of specific regional or linguistic features and needs by implementing active measures.

The basic purpose of Article 10 is to protect or establish the regional or minority language (RML) both orally and in writing, especially as a language of the state administrative authorities and, therefore, in the core area of the state's sphere of responsibility. To achieve this objective, the administrative authorities need to institute effective measures to which the attention of all citizens is drawn and which actively urge the speakers of the RML to use it in their dealings with those authorities.

The Charter presupposes that every speaker of a regional or minority language is able to use the state language.[4] However, Article 10 permits the use of the RML in dealings with the authorities and accordingly recognises the value of linguistic diversity as such. This provision thus extends to communication in the public sphere a person's internationally recognised individual right to use his or her mother tongue at least in the private sphere and between civil society partners.[5] It is in the use of language that an individual human being and an entire society manifest themselves. In Article 10, the state demonstrates respect for the RML by ensuring that its authorities use it in the same way as its speakers in their administrative dealings with state authorities and when exercising their civil rights. The language is thus recognised as an equally valid part of the culture and history of its speakers as citizens of the state[6] and country.[7]

At the same time, Article 10 enables the RML to be used in the context of official acts and thus also guarantees the preservation or extension of its vocabulary, especially at the official (administrative) level and, hence, in the external

---

3. For example, at the 2nd meeting of the ad hoc committee in February 1990, CAHLR (90) 4; the 5th meeting, CAHLR (91) 9, report item 3, No. 14; the 6th meeting, CAHLR (92) 1, report item 3, No. 23, and the statement by the CDCJ (European Committee on Legal Co-operation) of 6.12.1991, CAHLR (1991) 10, Addendum 4.

4. That is, the language that has been generally used up to now by an actual state authority in a concrete situation or must be used as the official language either by law or under the constitution. See for example Article 9.1a and Hungary 2010, 112.

5. M. Nowak, *UN Covenant on Civil and Political Rights, CCPR Commentary*, 2nd edn, 2005, Article 27, marginal note 42.

6. Article 10 thus goes beyond the protection of the language as a mere cultural asset. According to the French delegation's statement at the 5th meeting of the ad hoc committee, CAHLR (91) 9, item 3, No. 15, language is a means of internal state communication and, therefore, a constituent element of democracy.

7. As pointed out in the unequivocal statement made at the 2nd meeting of the ad hoc committee, CAHLR (90) 4, Appendix III, Article 7.

social sphere and to a high written standard. The rule also serves to improve communication between authorities and citizens because in individual cases the RML provides words and expressions that are either more suitable for a specific situation or only occur in the context of that language.

It is not permitted to examine the motivation for using the RML.[8] The Charter protects the languages concerned to enable them to be spoken, written and otherwise used by everyone with the same right to protection.[9] The protection is not limited to specific groups of people or usage contexts.

Although Article 10 protects individual RMLs, the individual obligations that very precisely grant an actual legal entity a right in a specific situation automatically result in the users of those languages having an individual right[10] to use them in dealings with the state. Through the ratification legislation, this internationally recognised effect[11] is incorporated in the national legal order and – perhaps as a result of additional implementing provisions, or a lack of them, or inadequate or (too) imprecise provisions – becomes in conjunction with remedies that already exist in the national legal order an enforceable individual right for clearly definable legal entities in specific situations. These entities may be speakers, non-speakers and juridical persons subject either to private or public law, such as local authorities, with their own rights vis-à-vis the state. These rules are, for example, contained in Article 10.1a and the parallel provisions in paragraphs 3 and 2b and e for the tier of government concerned as well as, in particular, in paragraph 2c, d, e and f[12] with regard to local authorities, where provision is made for use of the language as an individual official or working language[13] on the basis of conditions detailed further down.

The provisions of Article 10 are divided into five paragraphs containing different obligations. Paragraph 1 deals with the administrative authorities of the state,

---

8. Cf. P. Hilpold (2001), *Modernes Minderheitenrecht...*, p. 295, with further references.
9. European Charter for Regional or Minority Languages, Preamble
10. S. Oeter (2010), "10 Jahre Sprachencharta in Deutschland, Erfahrungen aus der Sicht des Expertenkomitees" in J. Peters and G. Diekmann-Dröge (eds), *10 Jahre Europäische Sprachencharta in Niedersachsen*, p. 31ff.
11. An individual right must be assumed to exist when a provision accords an actual legal entity a specified right, even if the international treaty itself does not provide for the filing of an individual complaint to enforce it and irrespective of whether the national legal order guarantees the right to file such a complaint. See the comprehensive discussion by P. Hilpold (2006), "Minderheitenschutz im Völkerbundsystem", in C. Pan and B. S. Pfeil (eds), *Zur Entstehung des modernen Minderheitenschutzes in Europa. Handbuch der europäischen Volksgruppen*, Vol. 3, pp. 156, 173ff.
12. Detailed at the end of each provision.
13. These are provisions pertaining to the use of official languages in individual cases. Cf. P. Hilpold (2003), "Der Ortsnamenstreit in Kärnten und in Südtirol aus rechtsvergleichender und völkerrechtlicher Sicht", *Juristiche Blätter*, p. 97.

paragraph 2 with the local and regional administrative authorities and paragraph 3 with entities that provide public services and services of general interest on behalf of public bodies, while paragraph 4 contains implementing provisions on the actual use of the RML. Paragraph 5 refers to the use of names that only exist in the RML.

2. Article 10.1: Reasonableness

Whether the situation of a language justifies considering it reasonable to expect a measure to be taken is up to the state to decide on the basis of an indeterminate legal concept that can be fully examined by the courts. It requires a review of the current situation of the language in the actual area in which it is used, that is, not only the establishment of the number of speakers compared to the population as a whole[14] but also in relation to the inhabitants affected by the measure concerned and to any other languages, the frequency of their use, the situations in which they are used and, perhaps, their vocabulary. Reasonableness depends, firstly, on the administrative burden on the state, and account must be taken of the fact that the Charter generally calls for proactive protection. Secondly, it depends on an assessment of the actual ability to use the language and its actual use: the specific need. However, it is necessary here to focus not only on the existing situation but also on the need of the language for support in the situation concerned, because the individual measures have been signed up to by the state itself in the context of that situation. It is clearly not possible to make use of services if none are available, so it is not enough to wait for the speakers of a language to make demands.[15] Rather, a prognosis has to be made whether services would be used or are necessary to guarantee the protection chosen for the preservation and protection of that language.

The decision has to be made separately for each individual RML and every measure as well as for each administrative district as the case may be. If the language is not limited to one or more administrative districts or if the state has taken no decision or enacted no rules on implementing the provisions of the Charter, the latter's direct applicability in the states or countries concerned follows automatically from the ratification law.[16]

---

14. Minority languages that are used within a limited geographical area are regionally just as important as more widespread languages. The territoriality principle, which underlies Swiss law, for example, and according to which a specific percentage of the total population is sufficient or required, does not meet the demands of Article 10; see the comprehensive discussion by D. Richter (2011), "The model character of Swiss language law" in A. L. Kjaer and S. Adamo (eds), *Linguistic diversity and European democracy*, p. 192, with further references.

15. Cf. the Committee of Ministers recommendation in respect of Germany (2006), 1.

16. As stated in Secretariat Memorandum CAHLR (91) 13.

A purely economic approach is not possible. By signing the Charter, the state has in principle shown that it regards the language concerned as needing protection and has selected certain individual measures from the obligations laid down in Article 10 as being necessary for that language. The state's observance of the Charter is not measured according to its budgetary situation.

Laying down a minimum percentage of speakers within the total population normally does not meet the requirements of this decision on reasonableness because it usually excludes the protection afforded by Article 10,[17] especially when no precise details are given of the continuity in terms of time that must be demonstrated by the (minimum) proportion of the total population made up by the speakers of this RML[18] in order to reflect the actual situation of the language in a specific area correctly and with sufficient statistical certainty. Generally, a fixed percentage that is not achieved at all or is only achieved in a single municipality is not in keeping with the spirit of the Charter. For example, the Committee of Experts has established that a 20% quota must be regarded as an unacceptable hurdle because the Charter generally justifies protective measures where the percentage is significantly below that figure. This applies in particular to smaller minorities, such as the Croatian or German minority in Slovakia, which only achieve this percentage in one municipality in that country. In these cases, the Committee of Experts emphasises that the provisions of Article 10 also fulfil their function to afford protection in municipalities with a minority of less than 20%.[19] In an individual case, a single-digit percentage may be appropriate. The state concerned has signed up to certain conditions of the Charter and, accordingly, declared its willingness to protect and foster the RML. Minimum percentages are therefore at most permissible to distinguish areas in fringe regions of the geographical distribution of the languages concerned where there is no actual need, and only after consulting the group of speakers involved, in order not to undermine the purpose of the provision.[20] Here too, however, it must not be forgotten

---

17. There is generally no fixed number in international law. Cf. P. Hilpold, "Der Ortsnamenstreit in Kärnten und in Südtirol…", p. 102.

18. The political, economic or personal motives of the people surveyed or the (lack of) motivation on the part of those conducting the survey therefore often alter the results, as do the motives of certain groups with regard to minority rights. See the comprehensive discussion of the issue, taking Austria as an example, by Hilpold, "Der Ortsnamenstreit in Kärnten und in Südtirol", pp. 292ff.

19. Slovakia 2007, 323ff; Committee of Ministers recommendation in respect of Slovakia (2007); Slovakia 2007, 345; Committee of Ministers recommendation in respect of Slovakia (2009); Application of the Charter in Ukraine, 1st monitoring cycle (2010), paragraph 383ff; Committee of Ministers recommendation in respect of Ukraine (2010).

20. Slovakia 2007, 323ff; Jean-Marie Woehrling (2005), *The European Charter for Regional or Minority Languages: a critical commentary*. Strasbourg: Council of Europe, p. 182.

that when the distribution of a language is limited to a local area the necessary administrative costs are also significantly reduced.[21]

2.1. Article 10.1: Structure

The provisions of subparagraphs a, b and c set out alternative undertakings relating to the use of the RML, listed in order of decreasing intensity. It can also be concluded from the system employed here that the measures must generally be applied country-wide for the language concerned unless the state has made other stipulations, since the state has already decided which of the conditions was appropriate for which language in which sphere of activity when it signed up to the provision.

2.2. Article 10.1a: Ensuring the use of the language

Ensuring the use of the language within the meaning of Article 10.1a means that the measure chosen must be secured in structural terms, that is to say there needs to be a legislative act for the implementation of the obligation chosen.[22] In this connection, the Committee of Experts considers that, in addition to acts of parliament and/or delegated legislation, purely administrative instructions, such as ministerial decrees or circulars, may suffice. In federal states it is also necessary to ensure the necessary measures are taken by the tier of government responsible, for example the federation must exert its influence over the *Länder*, cantons, etc.[23] The text of the Charter alone is not sufficient, even if it has been incorporated into domestic law by the implementing legislation and is therefore directly applicable.[24]

2.2.1. Article 10.1a.i: Extensive use in administrative matters

The provision in subparagraph i guarantees comprehensive protection and puts the RML on an equal footing in every respect in the state administration, both with regard to administrative staff and all staff in the administrative district. The use of the language by the administrative authorities means its external use in the form of decisions, rules and regulations, publications and communications and its internal use, in work instructions, notices, administrative objectives and assessments. The provision calls for both its oral and written use, including via the modern electronic media. Its use only in oral or electronic

---

21. As in the case of Sater Frisian, only spoken in a single municipality (Saterland) in Lower Saxony, Germany.

22. Hungary 2010, 140; Slovakia 2007, 325; Committee of Ministers recommendation in respect of Germany (2006), 1.

23. Germany 2008, 19.

24. Cf. J. Engbers (2010), "En Urdell över Platt of bale jie Seeltersk, Niederdeutsch und Saterfriesisch in der Justiz", in J. Peters and G. Diekmann-Dröge, *10 Jahre Europäische Sprachencharta in Niedersachsen*, p. 96ff.

communications is not enough as it must cover all areas of administration;[25] it is not permitted only to use the RML when expressly asked to do so.

2.2.2. Article 10.1a.ii: Staff with a command of the language

Subparagraph ii limits this obligation significantly to staff of state administrative authorities with outside contacts, that is, those who communicate with citizens irrespective of the authority's internal structure. Every member of staff, whatever his or her function, who may be contacted by a citizen must have the necessary command of the language. Here, too, this covers written, electronic and oral contacts.

A limit is imposed in that the administrative authority only has to respond in the RML when it has been contacted in that language. However, the context calls for a proactive approach by the administrative authorities, which must not only permit the use of the RML by all individuals who want to contact them but also actively encourage that use by providing both written and oral information.[26] Thus, in external dealings, the administrative authority has the same obligation as in subparagraph i above.

2.2.3. Article 10.1a.iii: Use of the language on request

This provision calls for at least one member of the administrative authority's staff present[27] to be able to respond to enquiries or applications in an RML and process and answer them both orally and in writing. A structured policy is required.[28] Furthermore, the authority must actively and fully draw attention to this possibility.

The user of the RML may be referred to that member of staff but without (*de facto*) forcing him or her to switch to the state language or creating *de facto* obstacles in any other way.[29] The official referring the member of the public must accordingly have at least a basic command of the RML. A mere indirect reference to allegedly additional administrative work or a situation in which the person concerned has to justify the use of the RML constitutes undue discrimination.

---

25. Bilingual forms, etc. are, however, sufficient.

26. Hungary 2007, 134; Hungary 2010, Finding G; Committee of Ministers recommendation in respect of Hungary (2004); Denmark 2007, 73; Committee of Ministers recommendation in respect of Denmark (2004), 2; Germany 2006, 760; Germany 2008, 28, 102, 105, 151, 160, 324, 370, 382, 404, 629, 643, 688, 693, 720, 744ff., 751, 756, 792.

27. A single staff member with a command of the language may be sufficient. Cf. Woehrling (2005), op. cit., p. 183.

28. Cf. the Committee of Ministers recommendations in respect of Germany (2006), 1 and 5, and Austria (2009), 4.

29. Slovakia 2007, 327; Committee of Ministers recommendation in respect of Slovakia (2007); Slovakia 2009, 348; Committee of Ministers recommendation in respect of Slovakia (2009).

A (written) reply by the authorities in response to a letter in the RML and referring to the attached text in the state language is just as insufficient as simply forwarding forms and other material in the state language.

2.2.4. Article 10.1a.iv: Applications in the regional or minority language (RML)

Article 10.1a.iv limits the administrative authority's obligation to a passive competence, but this implies the condition that, for example, all members of staff recognise the RML, thus ensuring from the organisational point of view that applications and enquiries can at least be forwarded without further ado to a member of staff with at least a passive command of the language, to enable him or her to process and/or translate them into the state language. In oral communication, a passive command is not enough as the conversational situation in the state language results *de facto* in the rejection of applications in the RML. The authorities concerned must also actively and especially draw attention in the RML to the possibility of using it. Officials who have dealings with the public must therefore at least have a basic command of the RML because the administrative authority is obliged to encourage its use. Non-verbal means of expression that prevent or impede its actual use are not permitted either.

The state must make active efforts and perhaps enact legislation to make forms available at the authorities' offices in the RML concerned or explicitly waive formal requirements for applications in RMLs.

2.2.5. Article 10.1a.v: Submission of documents

This provision concerns an entirely different aspect and actually has no direct influence on administrative action but only stipulates that documents to be submitted, typically written evidence or proof, are just as legally valid in the RML as in the state language. It is immaterial whether the person submitting the documents speaks the RML himself or herself because "use" here is to be understood as having a broad meaning in order to guarantee practical protection for the language. For example, the Committee of Experts called on Hungary to amend its Administrative Procedure Act in such a way that people with a command of Hungarian were also able to submit documents in RMLs.[30]

It is enough for the language to be passively recognised by the administration in order to be able to distinguish the documents from foreign documents. However, an actual knowledge of the language is not required because a translation, which, pursuant to Article 10.4, must be free of charge to the person submitting the document(s), may if necessary be made.

---

30. Hungary 2001, 54; Committee of Ministers recommendation in respect of Hungary (2001); Hungary 2007, 135ff.

The administrative authorities' obligation is limited to actively disseminating information, for example by systematically translating printed forms and installing bilingual signs on and in public buildings,[31] which requires a specific basis in domestic law[32] for the RML. However, this is not enough on its own when virtually no use is made of these services and the respect for the RML needed to bring about that use is not present.[33] In order to implement this provision effectively, the authorities must take practical measures. For example, the Committee of Experts recommends establishing what staff in the relevant authorities have a knowledge of the RMLs in order to identify any possible staff shortages, which must be dealt with through the specific appointment or transfer of qualified personnel.[34]

2.3. Article 10.1b: (Bilingual) forms, administrative regulations

This provision guarantees extensive use of the RML in daily communication, both within an authority and with users, through the extremely small amount of administrative work involved in a one-off translation or bilingual versions of texts and forms. This indirectly results in the development of terminology in that language adapted to the current legal/administrative situation and in that terminology being made available to its speakers, which has the effect of giving them strong psychological motivation and is thus very important for implementation of the Charter.[35] The provision refers to the administration's "bulk business".[36]

In principle, a form is in general use when it is employed every time for the same administrative act. As the administration normally only uses forms when it expects a large number of applications or when standardised action proves to be the efficient way forward, this provision generally covers all forms that are already in use or are being (newly) employed in the state language.

---

31. See for example the brochure *Plattdütsk – die Regionalsprache im Wirtschaftsleben und in der Verwaltung*, Ostfriesische Landschaft, 2nd edn, 2005.
32. Germany 2005, 568ff., 624ff., 691ff.; Germany 2008, 625.
33. Cf. also J. Engbers, "Perspektiven und Probleme im Justizbereich Niedersachsen bei der praktischen Umsetzung der europäischen Sprachencharta", paper given at a meeting of regional and national divisional heads (*Länder*-Bund-Referententreffen), Aurich, 9.6.2010, available at (Stand: 05/2011): www.mwk.niedersachsen.de/live/live.php?navigation_id=6257&article_id=19089&_psmand=19.
34. Hungary 2001 and Committee of Ministers Recommendation RecChL(2001)4; Hungary 2004 and Committee of Ministers Recommendation RecChL(2004)4.
35. Woehrling (2005), op. cit., p. 185.
36. For example, applications for identity cards, marriage licences, subsistence and other benefits, or forms for residents' registration, local taxes and charges (waste disposal, dog licences and tax on second residences).

Administrative regulations are subordinate legislation that direct actual administrative action or constitute explanations of printed forms.[37] Internal administrative guidelines and staff guidance information are accordingly also covered despite the equivocal wording, even though they have no (or only an indirect) effect on citizens. They affect the population because this provision refers to all speakers, whether they are staff of the administrative authority itself or residents administered by it. Accordingly, whether a text also falls within the scope of this rule depends exclusively on how often it is used in the administration.

These (bilingual) forms must generally be used, or forms only in the RML must be provided, automatically, even if the person concerned applies to the administrative authority in the state language. This is something which can also be dealt with by staff with no command of the other language. When an active legislative measure is enacted for each RML, the administrative authority must be authorised to issue the relevant texts and forms, if necessary in individual areas of administration, and obliged to draw attention to these provisions or forms.[38]

2.4. Article 10.1c: Official documents in the regional or minority language (RML)

This provision authorises authorities to draw up documents and decisions in the RML concerned, that is, to carry out original administrative action in that language in a legally binding manner. Such documents not only relate to administrative acts, decisions and orders but also other regulatory or non-regulatory written communications, which may be addressed either to a single individual or a large number of people and may be drawn up internally between various members of staff or administrative units.[39]

This provision calls for legislative action by the state in order, if necessary, to provide conflicting or open legal rules of the state with the relevant exemption clause or rules providing for exceptions and to lay down the precise scope of the provision concerned.[40] Furthermore, the state or country must draw the relevant administrative authorities' attention to this possibility, for example by means of ministerial decrees or circulars.[41]

---

37. Including ordinances, decrees, work instructions, notices, implementing provisions, samples, etc.
38. Woehrling (2005), op. cit., p. 185.
39. Ibid.
40. Ibid.
41. Hungary 2007, 143.

3. Article 10.2: Local and regional authorities and administrations

The provisions of this paragraph refer, even if this is actually missing from subparagraph b owing to an editorial oversight,[42] to regional or local authorities in the functional sense. The local authority is always the state entity closest to the citizen.[43] In each case, this is the lower tier of administration.

The regional authority is the lower administrative entity's hierarchical superior, that is, a medium-level administrative body responsible for a geographical region. An authority may take on a dual function and be both the local authority for one field and the regional authority for another. If a tier of administration is abolished or its structure changed, the obligations arising from Article 10.2 refer to the authority that takes over the functions concerned. However, the rules in Article 10.1 apply where an authority is responsible for a constituent entity of a federal state (e.g., a *Land* in Germany, canton in Switzerland) or even an authority directly responsible for the entire state. A regional authority thus need be responsible only for a geographically defined part of the state or, in federal systems, the *Land*, province or canton.

The term "authority" covers both the lower and middle tiers of state administration as well as local government bodies at all levels. The authority or local government body responsible for a particular matter must be specified in an individual case with regard to each language.

3.1. Allow/encourage

The parties undertake to allow and/or encourage the individual elements specified in paragraph 2. These provisions complement one another and do not constitute alternatives.[44] Merely allowing in the sense of passively standing by is not enough.[45] Rather, depending on the individual case, active legislative or administrative action is required.

As local and regional authorities often directly carry out both state and local government functions, the domestic responsibilities of contracting parties to the Charter have been taken into account in this wording. If state functions are carried out directly by local or regional authorities, the implementation of these provisions must be brought about by enacting the relevant legal rules. In the

---

42. Explanatory Report to the European Charter for Regional or Minority Languages, paragraph 102.
43. Cities, municipalities, districts etc.
44. Woehrling (2005), op. cit., p. 191.
45. Application of the Charter in Ukraine, 1st monitoring cycle (2010), paragraphs 385ff; Slovakia 2007, 329ff.

area of local government, on the other hand, states are obliged to adapt the legal framework accordingly or enact further measures.[46]

In federal states, the state as a whole has external obligations and must consequently ensure effective implementation of the provisions at the domestic level.[47] However, it is rarely responsible (on its own) internally. The *Länder*/cantons, etc. are in some cases bound in different ways via the ratification laws. Whether the federal state or the *Länder*/cantons have the relevant responsibility vis-à-vis the regional and local authorities depends on the national distribution of responsibilities concerning the individual subject-area.

At any rate, it is necessary for the constituent state to draw the authorities' attention to the possibility allowed and urge them to inform their citizens in turn. The form in which they are to be encouraged to make use in a specific case of the possibilities available is not stipulated, but an overall structural approach is called for. This approach must, at least from the point of view of the individual states, lead to the increased use of the language concerned. It is not enough merely to wait or for the state to point out that the legal situation does not rule out the measures permitted.[48] Whether a particular measure fits in with such an overall approach and whether it or the approach itself is suitable must be examined at regular intervals in the light of actual developments. In individual cases, the constituent states are entitled to make a non-verifiable prognosis.

Under their powers of self-government, the local and regional authorities, as territorial entities, have an enforceable right vis-à-vis the state in regard to this provision of Article 10.2.

3.2. Structure

The provisions of Article 10.2 are structured hierarchically with decreasing intensity; at any rate, subparagraph a covers all the subsequent provisions. The provisions concerning council meetings/assemblies are identical to those for both local and regional institutions.

3.3. Article 10.2a: Comprehensive use

The use of the RML within the authority refers to communication between the authority's staff and also between the staff of various authorities at the same or a superior level of administration but not the higher administrative tier of the state administration. This applies to every type of internal official communication,

---

46. For example, by making the necessary funds available. Explanatory Report, paragraph 105.
47. Cf., for example, Germany 2008, 19.
48. Woehrling (2005), op. cit., p. 186; Explanatory Report, paragraph 105; Finland 2001, 167 on the use of Sami in council meetings.

such as orders and calls for job applications, and to assessments. This provision also covers every external communication by the authority. This applies both to regulatory communications, such as decisions and local laws[49] and to information for citizens or statements on fiscal matters.[50] It covers not only written and electronic but also oral communication. The RML must therefore be fully used as an official language with equal status.

The implementation of the provision presupposes a structural underpinning, that is to say an administrative rule has at least to be adopted within the regional or local authority.[51]

Only when every citizen who enters into contact with the relevant authority and every staff member of an authority is able to invoke this right will the relevant implementing legislation be sufficient to meet the contracting state's obligation; or the lack/inadequacy of such legislation, combined with ratification of the obligation under the Charter, will lead to an enforceable right under the provisions of domestic law.[52] In the area of local government, each territorial entity also has an enforceable right vis-à-vis the state under the same conditions.

3.4. Article 10.2b: Use by citizens

The wording of this provision limits the use of the RML to citizens. This nonetheless requires at least an active command of the language by officials who deal with those citizens because this would otherwise be an active impediment to use of the RML in an actual conversation.[53] In written communication, a passive command is sufficient for many staff because they can if necessary either forward applications to officials able to speak the language or use/process/ forward existing written forms.

Even if requests for application forms are not made in the RML, the relevant forms must be made available to enable citizens to exercise this right.

The provision only provides for oral or written applications to be received, and there is no express requirement for the authority to reply in the RML. However, the purpose of Article 10 can only be achieved when the language is also used by the regional or local authority because continuous use of the state language constitutes a *de facto* obstacle to the use of the RML, not only in oral communication. Especially in the area of local government, there is accordingly a need

---

49. For example, the notification of obligations to clear snow in front of properties, urban development plans or by-laws relating to fees and charges.
50. Award of building contracts, acquisition of materials, etc.
51. Or enacted by the state. Cf. Woehrling (2005), op. cit., p. 186.
52. Cf. S. Oeter, "10 Jahre Sprachencharta in Deutschland…", pp. 45, 31ff.
53. Woehrling (2005), op. cit., p. 191.

for a decision on when and why, despite this provision, the RML should not be used in the reply. In the area of direct state administration, at least letters to citizens and/or the reasons for decisions must be written in the RML[54] in order to guarantee its practical use and comply with the sense of the provision. Even if there is normally no provision for this language to be used for replies to/ decisions on an enquiry or application, it is not permissible for a reply or decision only or normally to be given in the state language.

The state government level must if necessary ensure by means of legislative measures that the local or regional authorities can avail themselves of the possibility and draw their attention to this by issuing notices and guidelines.[55] Furthermore, the local and regional authorities must inform potential users and urge them to exercise their right. These measures only suffice if they lead to the actual use of the language.[56] For citizens, the provision constitutes an individually enforceable right under the aforementioned conditions.

3.5. Article 10.2c and d: Official documents

The provisions of Article 10.2c and d are identical, but subparagraph c refers to regional and subparagraph d to local authorities. Official documents as defined in the relevant domestic legal rules can be published in an RML.[57] However, this also covers all kinds of publications produced by an authority.[58]

The publications do not have to be published at the same time as those in the state language, that is, they are not necessarily bilingual.[59] However, in the case of official documents they must not only be in the legally prescribed form

---

54. Woehrling (2005), op. cit., p. 191, considers it necessary for the regional or local authority expressly to decide whether or why the regional or minority language should not be used for drawing up replies/decisions. As any necessary forms are to be made available in this language, a reply in the state language is a clear instance of disregarding the regional or minority language and therefore not permissible.

55. The establishment by a contracting party that there are no contrary legal provisions is therefore not sufficient. See also Woehrling (2005), op. cit., p. 191.

56. As in the case of Germany, where the possibility of using Low German in dealings with staff of various towns and localities is publicised by means of stickers. See in this connection Switzerland 2008, 82.

57. If legal rules exist for this, they must also be complied with in order to show the equal status and rank of the publication.

58. Advertising, information booklets, event calendars, tourist material (e.g., the Bealach na Gaeltachta hiking maps, etc. in Donegal, Ireland).

59. For example, "Upptäck Samekulturen i Idre", information on the culture of the Sami in Idre, Dalarna, Sweden, updated annually since 2006 in Sami and Swedish.

but also in the same form to show that they have the same status and to reach the same target group. A symbolic or summary translation is not sufficient.[60]

Legislative measures have to be enacted to insert the relevant provisions or adapt contrary provisions. Furthermore, states must take action to draw their local and regional authorities' attention to the changes made.[61] Under the conditions mentioned, the local authorities have an enforceable right under domestic law in accordance with their powers of local self-government.

3.6. Article 10.2e and f: Assembly meetings

The provisions of subparagraphs e and f employ the same wording to provide for the use of the RML in meetings of the assemblies of the local or regional administrative authorities.[62] This is an important instance of the state's recognition of this language. Active civic commitment either in this language too or only in this language has a direct influence on the administration/state, which in turn, and in a way that plays well with the public, shows its appreciation and respect for speakers as committed citizens, thus effectively and proactively protecting their language. Especially in council meetings, the use of the RML in addition to the state language is a manifestation of living democracy and the integration of all citizens with a pacifying effect[63] because all linguistic cultures are given equal recognition as part of the state and the process of self-government.

As council (assembly) meetings reflect the long-term population, all RMLs should be spoken in addition to the state language in order to show and foster the mutual respect and tolerance of the languages as having equal status and equal rights.[64] Furthermore, in this way it will be possible to achieve at least a certain passive command of the language by all inhabitants and bring about respect for this language as part of the culture of the locality.

Depending on the situation, the provisions of subparagraphs e and f can and must lead to the state language taking a back seat. When a council (assembly) member or, indeed, a person in the public gallery states that he or she does not understand the RML, that does not rule out its use but if necessary leads to a translation being made or to the comment itself being translated into the RML.[65]

---

60. Slovakia 2007, 333; Slovakia 2009, 352.
61. Germany 2005, 638ff; Germany 2008, 636ff.
62. That is, cantonal parliaments, local, rural, district, town, city and county councils (parliaments).
63. The pacifying effect was already a key aspect of the protection of minorities in the League of Nations system, cf. P. Hilpold, "Der Ortsnamenstreit in Kärnten und in Südtirol…", p. 158.
64. S. Oeter, "10 Jahre Sprachencharta in Deutschland…", p. 46.
65. Which is normally unnecessary as the speakers of the regional or minority language are normally bilingual. Cf. Woehrling (2005), op. cit., p. 192.

Exclusion of the RML is not permitted. This applies to *de facto* obstacles, irrespective of their form, and also to instances where members of the council (assembly) or listeners in the public gallery/local residents have no command of the language.[66]

The provisions cover both the council (assembly) meeting itself and all committees, sub-committees and other sub-bodies set up by the council (assembly).

Implementation requires the enactment of the relevant legal or administrative rules[67] and an obligation on the part of the state authorities responsible to draw the attention of the (often unpaid) council/assembly chairs to the most effective way of putting these provisions into practice.[68] If need be, interpreters must be kept available or the translation services of individual council (assembly) members must be drawn on, but this must be done in such a way that it does not result in the RML taking a back seat but, rather, in an incentive to use it.[69] Both the members of the council (assembly) and everyone entitled to speak at its meetings have an enforceable right under domestic law to use the RML.

3.7. Article 10.2g: Place names and signs

Article 10.2g is extremely important in practice because when it is implemented the state's acceptance of the RML is particularly obvious, especially to citizens who do not speak this language. The clear identification of the geographical distribution of an RML also has the effect of strengthening the identity of its speakers.

This provision covers the names of streets and squares as well as field names, names of localities and, accordingly, street and place-name signs in individual districts.[70] It also covers the names of specific buildings, especially public buildings like town halls, schools, hospitals, community centres and libraries.[71] When new streets, places or areas are given names, the RML must first be used in its geographical area of distribution.

---

66. Or indeed a statement that the person taking the minutes has no command of the language.
67. Germany 2006, 408 with respect to Low German; Germany 2008, 639ff.
68. For example, simultaneous interpretation or at least similarly effective measures must be provided in order to ensure the actual use of the language. Cf. Switzerland 2008, 97; Hungary 2007, 150ff; 2 Slovakia 2009, 354; Germany 2006, 760.
69. Woehrling (2005), op. cit., p. 192.
70. Slovakia 2007, 341; Slovakia 2009, 358
71. For example, in the area of Brandenburg (Germany) where Sorbian is spoken, all public buildings clearly display their Sorbian name, and signs in towns are in both Sorbian and German. Cf. section 11.2 of the Brandenburg Act on the Sorbs/Wends (Gesetz zur Ausgestaltung der Rechte der Sorben (Wenden) im *Land* Brandenburg); Hungary 2007, 154; Hungary 2010, 151.

The provision also covers the names of commercial/private establishments. The owners and operators of businesses and establishments are accordingly entitled to use a name in the RML.[72] However, the use exclusively in that language of the commercial name of a private company or organisation cannot be prescribed.

When new names are given and in cases of "back-translation" from the state language, it is necessary to ensure a dignified choice of words that meets the purpose of this rule. The term in the RML need not necessarily be an exact translation of the one in the state language.[73]

Whether a name in the state language is necessary in addition to the one in the RML – that is, bilingual or even trilingual names – has to be decided in each individual case by taking due account of the purpose of this rule. Direction/ street signs or names of buildings must be easily readable and meet the purpose of this provision; their outward appearance must correspond to the equivalent in the state language[74] unless other interests of the state must also be taken into account, like road safety or easy traffic flows, to make it clear that the RML has equal status.

The state is obliged[75] to draw attention to this possibility and issue the relevant administrative instructions to all authorities responsible[76] so that the provision is applied uniformly or exemptions are granted from any contrary rules that may exist. Furthermore, it is necessary to ensure proper implementation of the provision so that the choice of signs does not result in the language concerned being up- or downgraded. For example, in Hungary only a comparatively small proportion of localities with minority local self-government also have official place names in the minority language and these are normally limited to place entry signs and a few signs on public buildings. Suitable means of guaranteeing actual implementation include financial incentives for co-official signs and supervision by an authority, for example the road traffic department.[77]

---

72. For a different viewpoint, see Woehrling (2005), op. cit., p. 193. Woehrling regards only the state as having a direct obligation, but also concludes from the necessary implementing legislation and articles 7.1d, 7.2 and 13c that such a right exists.

73. This may differ significantly both in the case of historical names and new housing developments, which may bear traditional area names in the regional or minority language but the names of poets and writers in the state language. Cf. Woehrling (2005), op. cit., p. 193.

74. Cf. Slovakia 2007, 337ff; Slovakia 2009, 356ff.

75. See the Committee of Ministers recommendation in respect of Germany (2006), 1, and in respect of Austria (2009), 4.

76. This does not necessarily mean that language group representatives are entitled to demand such signs.

77. Hungary 2007, 153; Hungary 2010, 151.

4. Article 10.3: Enterprises that provide public services

Public services within the meaning of Article 10.3 are those provided either by a legal entity that is separate from the state administration and is in most cases subject to private law or by private firms. They are services of general interest, especially those providing for everyday needs.[78] The important factor is not the legal form of the undertaking[79] but only the form of action. If it is subject to private law but the work is carried out on behalf of the state administration, or instead of the administration under the supervision of a state body, the activity falls within the scope of Article 10.3. The aim of this rule is to ensure that the provision protecting the RML in articles 10.1 and 10.2 also, and especially, remains valid or guaranteed when the state has the functions concerned carried out by external service providers.[80] Administrative restructuring or changes in the orientation of the state administration should have no influence on the effectiveness of the protection of the RML.

Some of the services concerned may at the same time fall within the scope of the more specific rules of Article 13, Article 12 or Article 11. These provisions are more comprehensive in that they not only cover public services but also every kind of economic,[81] cultural[82] or media[83] activity subject to the conditions laid down. At the same time, the rules overlap in one core area, though Article 10.3 contains less precise rules and it guarantees only a minimum in the area of direct public services.

The obligations arising from Article 10.3 are subject to three cumulative conditions that are identical to those of Article 10.1. Therefore, in accordance with the wording of that provision, a separate decision has to be taken for each individual language and each service, and the decision also has to grant speakers an individual right to the extent necessary. The exclusion of individual services or establishments for other reasons, such as economic considerations, or with reference to other establishments in which the RML is used, is not permissible.[84]

In terms of content, the provisions of Article 10.3a to c for protecting the language decrease in intensity, so the provision in subparagraph a includes the provision in subparagraphs b and c, while the provision in subparagraph b fully

---

78. For example, public transport (bus/rail), post, water supplies, sewage disposal, waste disposal, road building and maintenance, libraries, schools, etc.
79. Subject to private or public law, a single enterprise or a mixed undertaking in the so-called public–private partnership format, or through appointees, such as notaries.
80. Woehrling (2005), op. cit., p. 194.
81. Details at Article 13.
82. Details at Article 12.
83. Details at Article 11.
84. Woehrling (2005), op. cit., p. 195.

includes that in subparagraph c. These are alternative rules. In all these provisions, the use of the state language must not be excluded.[85]

For implementation of the provisions of subparagraphs a to c, it is necessary, in addition to the adoption by the state of the relevant legislative measures[86] for the companies concerned, to issue the relevant work instructions or guidelines. Local government administrations, territorial entities or administrative authorities must, for example, guarantee through their interests in companies or other bodies that active support will be provided for use of the RML within the enterprise, and this support also comprises information calling on users to exercise their right.

Furthermore, when a specific service is organised it is necessary to take account of the language question and, if need be, establish bilingual access and, through the relevant staff planning, make a multilingual team available. Initial and in-service training measures, including measures for staff with no knowledge of the language, need to be provided, as do forms, notices, work instructions and communications to users or the public that are either bilingual or only in the RML.[87] If necessary, provision should be made for using a particular service in different languages. For example, the lending section of a library could be multilingual, and media in various languages could be made available at the same time. Another possibility is to enable ticket machines to be operated in several languages.

4.1. Article 10.3a: Extensive use

This provision corresponds to that of Article 10.1a.i and gives both the user and every member of staff an individual right in accordance with the afore-mentioned conditions to use or provide the facility or service in the RML, which may be a full working language alongside the state language.

4.2. Article 10.3b: Use of the regional or minority language by service users

This provision corresponds to a very large extent to the one in Article 10.1a.ii and gives the speakers of the RML an individual right in accordance with the conditions mentioned therein to use their language when utilising or requesting the service provided by an establishment or authority. This language must therefore neither be rejected as unauthorised nor lead to the speaker being turned away or not dealt with because he or she is not understood.

---

85. Ibid.
86. Cf. Hungary 2004, 111; Hungary 2007, 156; Hungary 2010, 154; Committee of Ministers recommendation on Slovakia (2007), 1; Slovakia 2009, 360.
87. Woehrling (2005), op. cit., p. 196.

In spite of the wording, the service or product (such as a travel ticket) does not necessarily have to be provided in the same language. The service may only be in the form of action taken or in another language, but any advice must be given in the user's language.

4.3. Article 10.3c: Applications and enquiries

The provision in subparagraph c corresponds to the one in Article 10.1a.iv and merely requires the receipt of enquiries and applications in the RML, with the consequence that they have to be accepted without objection and then processed. If it is necessary to make use of the service in a specific form, printed forms must be made available in the RML.

Although the application can be processed in that language or a reply or consultation may follow, the speaker has no right to this or to the provision of the service in that language.[88]

5. Article 10.4: Implementation conditions

In order to meet the obligations arising from articles 10.1 to 10.3, the contracting parties must choose at least one of the measures mentioned in subparagraphs a, b and c. Although only the direct contracting parties are bound externally, in federal states the tier of government responsible is bound via the implementing legislation in the context of the ratification legislation. Putting into effect means enacting provisions under domestic law which directly bring about the application of a measure by the administrative authorities.[89] It is not enough to rely only on the initiative of individual authorities or indeed private undertakings. The responsibility to provide a guarantee is so manifest here that under domestic law the person concerned must be granted an enforceable individual right.[90]

5.1. Article 10.4a: Translations

The terms "translation" and "interpretation" are used here as mutually intensifying synonyms since they refer to both oral and written translation in both directions – into the RML or into the state language. It is important that a proper and accurate translation be made into the other language.

The demand depends on the actual situation. It is not absolutely necessary to provide for a translation when everyone involved has a sufficient command of the RML, but the need arises as soon as one party wants a translation or clearly requires one, and staff must be made aware for example of any typical linguistic

---

88. Ibid.
89. Ibid., p. 188; S. Oeter, "10 Jahre Sprachencharta in Deutschland…", p. 32.
90. Committee of Ministers recommendation in respect of Hungary (2001), 3; Hungary 2004, 111.

shortcomings.[91] Other obstacles, such as the need for the number of speakers to exceed a specific proportion of the total population, are not permissible.[92]

It is up to the state concerned to stipulate the form of interpretation, for instance, whether an interpreter has to be professionally qualified. The provision only specifies the result, that is to say a proper translation. It may therefore be worthwhile investing in multilingual initial and in-service staff training or in setting up a team of translators.

The provision is framed in such a way as to ensure that no costs may be incurred by the person concerned[93] since an obstacle of this kind and the *de facto* check on his or her motivation associated with it would otherwise undermine the necessary protection of the RML. Otherwise, everyone prefers in practice to use the state language.

5.2. Article 10.4b and c: Staff planning

These provisions call for active staff planning by the state in order to guarantee a sufficient number of staff with a knowledge of the RML in administrations or individual authorities. In the case of subparagraph c, differences in dialect should be taken into account in the regional deployment of staff.

5.2.1. Article 10.4b: Recruitment and training

It is up to the state to decide whether linguistically competent individuals are recruited, that is, whether they must already have a command of the language when appointed or whether existing staff acquire the necessary capabilities through initial and in-service training.[94]

The attention of all staff, including those with no command of an RML, must be drawn to the protected status of these languages and the rights of their speakers associated with that status. Staff must continue to be given further training to ensure they positively support or respond to the use of a language and if necessary refer the speaker to a linguistically competent colleague. Moreover, all staff in the region concerned should be required to have a basic understanding of the RMLs so that they recognise the languages involved and, for example, are able to deal properly with applications and documents.

---

91. The actual situation also has to be taken into account. It may be that sufficient protection is only provided if a translation facility is made available from the outset.
92. Cf. Slovakia 2007, 252; Committee of Ministers recommendation in respect of Slovakia (2007), 1; Slovakia 2009, 364; Committee of Ministers recommendation in respect of Slovakia (2009), 1.
93. Woehrling (2005), op. cit., p. 197.
94. Financial or other incentives (such as training leave) can be created to induce staff to undertake such further training. Ibid., p. 198.

5.2.2. Article 10.4c: Deployment in own language area

This provision gives public service staff – that is, officials already appointed, with the necessary linguistic competence – an individual right to have their knowledge of a language or languages taken into account in a decision on their posting. If they so wish, they should be employed where they can make use of their knowledge of the RML and their linguistic competence is actually necessary for the post concerned. This also applies to the relevant area of distribution in the case of dialectal variations when a knowledge of the specific linguistic variety is important for the post involved. For example, it may only be possible to employ language teachers in a fairly small geographical area whereas for other duties a knowledge of the language may be important but slight dialectal variations have no impact on professional communication with the local speakers.

Linguistic competence must be taken into account as a technical qualification, so that only selection from among individuals with the same language qualifications normally takes place. Only when a partial or very limited/passive knowledge of the language is sufficient for the work concerned are further qualifications on a par with one another, so that a person with otherwise better professional qualifications who learns the RML is to be preferred over a native speaker of that language with lower qualifications.

The state's interest in flexible, mobile staff is maintained because the member of staff only has such a right if it is possible to grant it, that is to say after discretionary powers have been exercised. There is no right to the creation of new posts, but existing posts should be filled in accordance with the aforementioned criteria.[95]

6. Article 10.5: Choice of name

The purpose of paragraph 5 is to provide a lasting guarantee of the use of surnames/house names/family names[96] in the RML. This also means first names, as provided for by Article 8 of the European Convention on Human Rights,[97] because it is only when both names are taken together that they refer to the actual person and his or her membership of a family.[98] The provision would no longer have this purpose if it only referred to family names, since the combination of a first name in the state language and a family name in the RML already leads to discrimination in the designation of individuals, and inter-

---

95. Ibid., p. 199.
96. However, this does not apply to company names, at least not the names of legal entities.
97. Cf. European Court of Human Rights, judgment of 24.10.1996, *Reports of Judgments and Decisions* 1996-V, p. 1602, paragraph 21; *Guillot v. France; Jens Meyer-Ladewig*, EMRK, *Kommentar*, 2nd edn, 2006, Article 8, marginal note 6.
98. For a different viewpoint but with no reasons given, see Woehrling (2005), op. cit., p. 200. Cf., however, Norway 2003, 130; Hungary 2004, 116; the Netherlands 2004, 147.

family traditions are in many cases passed on in first names. Consequently, the relevant names (first names) should not only be permitted when naming newborn babies but also later when changes are made (in a first name or family name) to a form in the RML or when a new name is chosen for the sole purpose of having such a name in that language.[99] Other requirements – for the individuals concerned to give reasons or other obstacles of whatever kind imposed by domestic legislation – are not permissible.[100]

The provision also covers the "restoration" of "mutilated" or distorted forms of names to their original or traditional form in the correct spelling and with any necessary diacritical marks in the RML.[101]

If necessary, the country or state concerned should broaden the scope of provisions governing the use of names or adopt special rules. All particular requirements in the use of names in the RML, as regards their form and their spelling, must be correctly specified. The attention of the group potentially affected should be drawn to this possibility through the proactive dissemination of information,[102] and the relevant administrative staff should be informed of the need for citizen-friendly implementation.[103] In each case, an applicant has an enforceable right under domestic law to use the relevant name because the obligation to grant this right is very clearly worded.[104]

References

Boysen, Sigrid et al. (2011), *Europäische Charta der Regional- oder Minderheitensprachen, Handkommentar*. Zurich: Dike.

Jutta Engbers, "Perspektiven und Probleme im Justizbereich Niedersachsen bei der praktischen Umsetzung der europäischen Sprachencharta", paper given at a meeting of regional and national divisional heads (Länder-Bund-Referententreffen), Aurich, 9.6.2010, available at (Stand: 05/2011): www.mwk.niedersachsen.de/live/live.php?navigation_id=6257&article_id=19089&_psmand=19.

---

99. Considerable use was made of this right in Wales after this was permitted for the first time. Cf. data from the Welsh Language Board and Emyr Lewis, conference speech, conference entitled "The European Charter for Regional or Minority Languages, Legal Challenges and Opportunities", Swansea, 20-21 November 2006.

100. See, with regard to special female forms of names in the case of adoption or German family names, Slovakia 2007, 247ff; Slovakia 2009, 247ff., 368ff; Committee of Ministers recommendation in respect of Slovakia (2007), 1.

101. Cf. Norway 2003, 130; Hungary 2004, 116 re names not originally written in Latin script.

102. For example, by providing a list of proposals for first names when marriages take place in certain areas, as is customary in Hungary for first names in minority languages.

103. Hungary 2004, 115. Provision now complied with in the case of forms of Frisian names. Cf. the Netherlands 2004, 147.

104. S. Oeter, "10 Jahre Sprachencharta in Deutschland...", p. 31.

Engbers, Jutta (2010), "En Urdell över Platt of bale jie Seeltersk. Niederdeutsch und Saterfriesisch in der Justiz" in Jörg Peters and Gabriele Diekmann-Dröge (eds), *10 Jahre Europäische Sprachencharta in Niedersachsen. Symposium an der Carl-von-Ossietzky-Universität Oldenburg am 4. September 2009.* Oldenburg: Isensee, pp. 93-9.

Hilpold, Peter (2001), *Modernes Minderheitenrecht: Eine rechtsvergleichende Untersuchung des Minderheitenrechtes in Österreich und in Italien unter besonderer Berücksichtigung völkerrechtlicher Aspekte.* Vienna: Manz.

Hilpold, Peter (2003), "Der Ortsnamenstreit in Kärnten und in Südtirol aus rechtsvergleichender und völkerrechtlichter Sicht", *Juristische Blätter*, No. 125, 92-105.

Hilpold, Peter (2006), "Minderheitenschutz im Völkerbundsystem" in Christoph Pan and Beate Sibylle Pfeil (eds), *Zur Entstehung des modernen Minderheitenschutzes in Europa. Handbuch der europäischen Volksgruppen*, Vol. 3. Vienna: Springer, pp. 156-89.

Nowak, Manfred, *UN Covenant on Civil and Political Rights*, CCPR Commentary, 2nd edn, 2005.

Oeter, Stefan (2010), "10 Jahre Sprachencharta in Deutschland: Erfahrungen aus der Sicht des Expertenkomitees" in Jörg Peters and Gabriele Diekmann-Dröge (eds), *10 Jahre Europäische Sprachencharta in Niedersachsen. Symposium an der Carl-von-Ossietzky-Universität Oldenburg am 4. September 2009.* Oldenburg: Isensee, pp. 26-49.

Richter, Dagmar (2011), "The model character of Swiss language law" in Anne Lise Kjaer and Silvia Adamo (eds), *Linguistic diversity and European democracy.* Farnham: Ashgate, pp. 189-206.

Woehrling, Jean-Marie (2005), *The European Charter for Regional or Minority Languages: a critical commentary.* Strasbourg: Council of Europe Publishing.

Appendix: Ratifications

Article 10		
Paragraph and subparagraph		
1	a.i	**Finland:** Swedish **Slovenia:** Italian and Hungarian **Spain:** Basque (Autonomous Community of the Basque Country; Historical Community of Navarra), Catalan (Autonomous Community of Catalonia, Balearic Islands), Valencian (Autonomous Community of Valencia) and Galician (Autonomous Community of Galicia) **Switzerland:** Romansh and Italian **United Kingdom:** Welsh
	a.ii	**Romania:** Bulgarian, Czech, Croatian, German, Hungarian, Russian, Serbian, Slovak, Turkish, Ukrainian **Slovakia:** Hungarian
	a.iii	**Austria**: Burgenland Croatian (*Land* Burgenland), Slovenian (*Land* Carinthia) and Hungarian (*Land* Burgenland) **Croatia:** Italian, Serbian, Hungarian, Czech, Slovak, Ruthenian and Ukrainian **Finland:** Sami **Montenegro:** Albanian and Romani **Norway:** Sami **Romania:** Bulgarian, Czech, Croatian, German, Hungarian, Russian, Serbian, Slovak, Turkish, Ukrainian **Slovakia:** Bulgarian, Croatian, Czech, German, Polish, Romani, Ruthenian and Ukrainian **Sweden:** Sami, Finnish and Meänkieli
	a.iv	**Armenia:** Assyrian, Yezidi, Greek, Russian and Kurdish **Bosnia and Herzegovina:** Albanian, Montenegrin, Czech, Italian, Hungarian, Macedonian, German, Polish, Romanian, Romani, Rysin, Slovak, Slovenian, Turkish, Ukrainian and Jewish (Yiddish and Ladino). **Croatia:** Italian, Serbian, Hungarian, Czech, Slovak, Ruthenian and Ukrainian **Czech Republic:** Polish (Moravian-Silesian region and in the territory of the districts of Frydek-Místek and Karviná) and Slovak **Germany:** Upper Sorbian (Free State of Saxony), Lower Sorbian (*Land* Brandenburg) **Hungary:** Romani **Montenegro:** Albanian and Romani **Romania:** Bulgarian, Czech, Croatian, German, Hungarian, Russian, Serbian, Slovak, Turkish, Ukrainian **Serbia:** Albanian, Bosnian, Bulgarian, Hungarian, Romani, Romanian, Ruthenian, Slovakian, Ukrainian and Croatian **Slovakia:** Bulgarian, Croatian, Czech, German, Polish, Romani, Ruthenian and Ukrainian **United Kingdom:** Irish

	a.v	**Armenia:** Assyrian, Yezidi, Greek, Russian and Kurdish **Czech Republic:** Slovak **Denmark:** German (Southern Jutland) **Germany:** Danish (*Land* Schleswig-Holstein), Upper Sorbian (Free State of Saxony), Lower Sorbian (*Land* Brandenburg), North Frisian (*Land* Schleswig-Holstein), Sater Frisian (*Land* Lower Saxony), Low German (Free Hanseatic City of Bremen, Free and Hanseatic City of Hamburg, Mecklenburg-Western Pomerania, Lower Saxony, Schleswig-Holstein) **Hungary:** Croatian, German, Romanian, Serbian, Slovak, Slovenian and Béas **Montenegro:** Albanian and Romani **Netherlands:** Frisian (Province of Friesland) **Romania:** Bulgarian, Czech, Croatian, German, Hungarian, Russian, Serbian, Slovak, Turkish, Ukrainian **Serbia:** Albanian, Bosnian, Bulgarian, Hungarian, Romani, Romanian, Ruthenian, Slovakian, Ukrainian and Croatian **Sweden:** Sami, Finnish and Meänkieli
	b	**Armenia:** Assyrian, Yezidi, Greek, Russian and Kurdish **Croatia:** Italian, Serbian, Hungarian, Czech, Slovak, Ruthenian and Ukrainian **Finland:** Sami and Swedish **Hungary:** Romani **Norway:** Sami **Romania:** German, Hungarian **Slovenia:** Italian and Hungarian **Spain:** Basque (Autonomous Community of the Basque Country; Historical Community of Navarra), Catalan (Autonomous Community of Catalonia, Balearic Islands), Valencian (Autonomous Community of Valencia) and Galician (Autonomous Community of Galicia) **Switzerland:** Romansh and Italian **United Kingdom:** Welsh
	c	**Austria**: Burgenland Croatian (*Land* Burgenland), Slovenian (*Land* Carinthia) and Hungarian (*Land* Burgenland) **Bosnia and Herzegovina:** Albanian, Montenegrin, Czech, Italian, Hungarian, Macedonian, German, Polish, Romanian, Romani, Rysin, Slovak, Slovenian, Turkish, Ukrainian and Jewish (Yiddish and Ladino). **Croatia:** Italian, Serbian, Hungarian, Czech, Slovak, Ruthenian and Ukrainian **Finland:** Sami and Swedish **Germany:** Sater Frisian (*Land* Lower Saxony area), Low German (Free Hanseatic City of Bremen, Free and Hanseatic City of Hamburg, Mecklenburg-Western Pomerania, Lower Saxony, Schleswig-Holstein) **Hungary:** Croatian, German, Romanian, Serbian, Slovak, Slovenian, Romani and Béas **Montenegro:** Albanian and Romani **Netherlands:** Frisian (Province of Friesland) **Norway:** Sami **Romania:** German, Hungarian **Serbia:** Albanian, Bosnian, Bulgarian, Hungarian, Romani, Romanian, Ruthenian, Slovakian, Ukrainian and Croatian **Slovenia:** Italian and Hungarian

		Spain: Basque (Autonomous Community of the Basque Country; Historical Community of Navarra), Catalan (Autonomous Community of Catalonia, Balearic Islands), Valencian (Autonomous Community of Valencia) and Galician (Autonomous Community of Galicia) **Sweden:** Sami, Finnish and Meänkieli **Switzerland:** Romansh and Italian **United Kingdom:** Welsh, Scottish-Gaelic and Irish
2	a	**Bosnia and Herzegovina:** Albanian, Montenegrin, Czech, Italian, Hungarian, Macedonian, German, Polish, Romanian, Romani, Rysin, Slovak, Slovenian, Turkish, Ukrainian and Jewish (Yiddish and Ladino). **Croatia:** Italian, Serbian, Hungarian, Czech, Slovak, Ruthenian and Ukrainian **Finland:** Sami and Swedish **Germany:** Upper Sorbian (Free State of Saxony), Sater Frisian (*Land* Lower Saxony), Low German (Free Hanseatic City of Bremen, Free and Hanseatic City of Hamburg, Mecklenburg-Western Pomerania, Lower Saxony, Schleswig-Holstein) **Netherlands:** Frisian (Province of Friesland) **Norway:** Sami **Slovakia:** Hungarian **Slovenia:** Italian and Hungarian **Spain:** Basque (Autonomous Community of the Basque Country; Historical Community of Navarra), Catalan (Autonomous Community of Catalonia, Balearic Islands), Valencian (Autonomous Community of Valencia) and Galician (Autonomous Community of Galicia) **Switzerland:** Romansh and Italian **Ukraine:** Belarusian, Bulgarian, Gagauz, Greek, Jewish, Crimean Tatar, Moldovan, German, Polish, Russian, Romanian, Slovak and Hungarian **United Kingdom:** Welsh and Scottish-Gaelic
	b	**Armenia:** Assyrian, Yezidi, Greek, Russian and Kurdish **Austria**: Burgenland Croatian (*Land* Burgenland), Slovenian (*Land* Carinthia) and Hungarian (*Land* Burgenland) **Bosnia and Herzegovina:** Albanian, Montenegrin, Czech, Italian, Hungarian, Macedonian, German, Polish, Romanian, Romani, Rysin, Slovak, Slovenian, Turkish, Ukrainian and Jewish (Yiddish and Ladino). **Croatia:** Italian, Serbian, Hungarian, Czech, Slovak, Ruthenian and Ukrainian **Czech Republic:** Polish (Moravian-Silesian region and in the territory of the districts of Frydek-Místek and Karviná) and Slovak **Finland:** Sami and Swedish **Germany:** Upper Sorbian (Free State of Saxony), Lower Sorbian (*Land* Brandenburg), Sater Frisian (*Land* Lower Saxony), Low German (Free Hanseatic City of Bremen, Free and Hanseatic City of Hamburg, Mecklenburg-Western Pomerania, Lower Saxony, Schleswig-Holstein) **Hungary:** Croatian, German, Romanian, Serbian, Slovak, Slovenian, Romani and Béas **Montenegro:** Albanian and Romani **Netherlands:** Frisian (Province of Friesland)

365

		Norway: Sami **Poland:** Belarusian, Czech, Hebrew, Yiddish, Karaim, Kashub, Lithuanian, Lemko, German, Armenian, Romani, Russian, Slovak, Tatar and Ukrainian **Romania:** Bulgarian, Czech, Croatian, German, Hungarian, Russian, Serbian, Slovak, Turkish, Ukrainian **Serbia:** Albanian, Bosnian, Bulgarian, Hungarian, Romani, Romanian, Ruthenian, Slovakian, Ukrainian and Croatian **Slovakia:** Bulgarian, Croatian, Czech, German, Polish, Romani, Ruthenian, Ukrainian and Hungarian **Slovenia:** Italian and Hungarian **Spain:** Basque (Autonomous Community of the Basque Country; Historical Community of Navarra), Catalan (Autonomous Community of Catalonia, Balearic Islands), Valencian (Autonomous Community of Valencia) and Galician (Autonomous Community of Galicia) **Sweden:** Sami, Finnish and Meänkieli **Switzerland:** Romansh and Italian **United Kingdom:** Welsh, Scottish-Gaelic and Irish
	c	**Croatia:** Italian, Serbian, Hungarian, Czech, Slovak, Ruthenian and Ukrainian **Finland:** Sami and Swedish **Germany:** Sater Frisian (*Land* Lower Saxony), Low German (Free Hanseatic City of Bremen, *Land* Lower Saxony) **Netherlands:** Frisian (Province of Friesland) **Norway:** Sami **Romania:** Bulgarian, Czech, German, Hungarian **Serbia:** Albanian, Bosnian, Bulgarian, Hungarian, Romani, Romanian, Ruthenian, Slovakian, Ukrainian and Croatian **Slovakia:** Bulgarian, Croatian, Czech, German, Polish, Romani, Ruthenian, Ukrainian and Hungarian **Slovenia:** Italian and Hungarian **Spain:** Basque (Autonomous Community of the Basque Country; Historical Community of Navarra), Catalan (Autonomous Community of Catalonia, Balearic Islands), Valencian (Autonomous Community of Valencia) and Galician (Autonomous Community of Galicia) **Sweden:** Sami, Finnish and Meänkieli **Switzerland:** Romansh and Italian **Ukraine:** Belarusian, Bulgarian, Gagauz, Greek, Jewish, Crimean Tatar, Moldovan, German, Polish, Russian, Romanian, Slovak and Hungarian **United Kingdom:** Welsh
	d	**Austria:** Burgenland Croatian (*Land* Burgenland), Slovenian (*Land* Carinthia) and Hungarian (*Land* Burgenland) **Croatia:** Italian, Serbian, Hungarian, Czech, Slovak, Ruthenian and Ukrainian **Finland:** Sami and Swedish **Germany:** Sater Frisian (*Land* Lower Saxony), Low German (Free Hanseatic City of Bremen, *Land* Lower Saxony) **Montenegro:** Albanian and Romani **Netherlands:** Frisian (Province of Friesland)

		Norway: Sami **Romania:** Bulgarian, Czech, Croatian, German, Hungarian, Russian, Serbian, Slovak, Turkish, Ukrainian **Serbia:** Albanian, Bosnian, Bulgarian, Hungarian, Romani, Romanian, Ruthenian, Slovakian, Ukrainian and Croatian **Slovakia:** Bulgarian, Croatian, Czech, German, Polish, Romani, Ruthenian, Ukrainian and Hungarian **Slovenia:** Italian and Hungarian **Spain:** Basque (Autonomous Community of the Basque Country; Historical Community of Navarra), Catalan (Autonomous Community of Catalonia, Balearic Islands), Valencian (Autonomous Community of Valencia) and Galician (Autonomous Community of Galicia) **Sweden:** Sami, Finnish and Meänkieli **Switzerland:** Romansh and Italian **Ukraine:** Belarusian, Bulgarian, Gagauz, Greek, Jewish, Crimean Tatar, Moldovan, German, Polish, Russian, Romanian, Slovak and Hungarian **United Kingdom:** Welsh and Scottish-Gaelic
e		**Czech Republic:** Polish (Moravian-Silesian region and in the territory of the districts of Frydek-Místek and Karviná) and Slovak **Finland:** Sami and Swedish **Germany:** Sater Frisian (*Land* Lower Saxony), Low German (Free Hanseatic City of Bremen, Free and Hanseatic City of Hamburg, *Land* Lower Saxony), Romani (*Land* Hesse) **Hungary:** Croatian, German, Romanian, Serbian, Slovak, Slovenian, Romani and Béas **Netherlands:** Frisian (Province of Friesland) **Norway:** Sami **Romania:** Bulgarian, Czech, German, Hungarian, Turkish, Ukrainian **Slovenia:** Italian and Hungarian **Spain:** Basque (Autonomous Community of the Basque Country; Historical Community of Navarra), Catalan (Autonomous Community of Catalonia, Balearic Islands), Valencian (Autonomous Community of Valencia) and Galician (Autonomous Community of Galicia) **Switzerland:** Romansh and Italian **Ukraine:** Belarusian, Bulgarian, Gagauz, Greek, Jewish, Crimean Tatar, Moldovan, German, Polish, Russian, Romanian, Slovak and Hungarian **United Kingdom:** Welsh, Scottish-Gaelic and Irish
f		**Armenia:** Assyrian, Yezidi, Greek, Russian and Kurdish **Czech Republic:** Polish (Moravian-Silesian region and in the territory of the districts of Frydek-Místek and Karviná) and Slovak **Finland:** Sami and Swedish **Germany:** Sater Frisian (*Land* Lower Saxony), Low German (Free Hanseatic City of Bremen, Free and Hanseatic City of Hamburg, Mecklenburg-Western Pomerania, Lower Saxony, Schleswig-Holstein), Romani (*Land* Hesse) **Hungary:** Croatian, German, Romanian, Serbian, Slovak, Slovenian, Romani and Béas **Netherlands:** Frisian (Province of Friesland)

		Norway: Sami **Romania:** Bulgarian, Czech, Croatian, German, Hungarian, Russian, Serbian, Slovak, Turkish, Ukrainian **Slovakia:** Bulgarian, Croatian, Czech, German, Polish, Romani, Ruthenian, Ukrainian and Hungarian **Slovenia:** Italian and Hungarian **Spain:** Basque (Autonomous Community of the Basque Country; Historical Community of Navarra), Catalan (Autonomous Community of Catalonia, Balearic Islands), Valencian (Autonomous Community of Valencia) and Galician (Autonomous Community of Galicia) **Switzerland:** Romansh and Italian **Ukraine:** Belarusian, Bulgarian, Gagauz, Greek, Jewish, Crimean Tatar, Moldovan, German, Polish, Russian, Romanian, Slovak and Hungarian **United Kingdom:** Welsh, Scottish-Gaelic and Irish
	g	**Armenia:** Assyrian, Yezidi, Greek, Russian and Kurdish **Bosnia and Herzegovina:** Albanian, Montenegrin, Czech, Italian, Hungarian, Macedonian, German, Polish, Romanian, Romani, Rysin, Slovak, Slovenian, Turkish, Ukrainian and Jewish (Yiddish and Ladino). **Croatia:** Italian, Serbian, Hungarian, Czech, Slovak, Ruthenian and Ukrainian **Czech Republic:** Polish (Moravian-Silesian region and in the territory of the districts of Frydek-Místek and Karviná) **Finland:** Sami and Swedish **Germany:** Upper Sorbian (Free State of Saxony), Lower Sorbian (*Land* Brandenburg), North Frisian (*Land* Schleswig-Holstein), Sater Frisian (*Land* Lower Saxony) **Hungary:** Croatian, German, Romanian, Serbian, Slovak, Slovenian, Romani and Béas **Montenegro:** Albanian and Romani **Netherlands:** Frisian (Province of Friesland) **Norway:** Sami **Poland:** Belarusian, Czech, Hebrew, Yiddish, Karaim, Kashub, Lithuanian, Lemko, German, Armenian, Romani, Russian, Slovak, Tatar and Ukrainian **Romania:** Bulgarian, Czech, Croatian, German, Hungarian, Russian, Serbian, Slovak, Turkish, Ukrainian **Serbia:** Albanian, Bosnian, Bulgarian, Hungarian, Romani, Romanian, Ruthenian, Slovakian, Ukrainian and Croatian **Slovakia:** Bulgarian, Croatian, Czech, German, Polish, Romani, Ruthenian, Ukrainian and Hungarian **Slovenia:** Italian and Hungarian **Spain:** Basque (Autonomous Community of the Basque Country; Historical Community of Navarra), Catalan (Autonomous Community of Catalonia, Balearic Islands), Valencian (Autonomous Community of Valencia) and Galician (Autonomous Community of Galicia) **Sweden:** Sami, Finnish and Meänkieli **Switzerland:** Romansh and Italian **Ukraine:** Belarusian, Bulgarian, Gagauz, Greek, Jewish, Crimean Tatar, Moldovan, German, Polish, Russian, Romanian, Slovak and Hungarian **United Kingdom:** Welsh, Scottish-Gaelic and Irish

3	a	**Croatia:** Italian, Serbian, Hungarian, Czech, Slovak, Ruthenian and Ukrainian **Finland:** Swedish **Montenegro:** Albanian and Romani **Romania:** Bulgarian, Czech, Croatian, German, Hungarian, Russian, Serbian, Slovak, Turkish, Ukrainian **Slovenia:** Italian and Hungarian **Spain:** Basque (Autonomous Community of the Basque Country; Historical Community of Navarra), Catalan (Autonomous Community of Catalonia, Balearic Islands), Valencian (Autonomous Community of Valencia) and Galician (Autonomous Community of Galicia) **Switzerland:** Italian **United Kingdom:** Welsh
	b	**Croatia:** Italian, Serbian, Hungarian, Czech, Slovak, Ruthenian and Ukrainian **Finland:** Sami **Germany:** Upper Sorbian (Free State of Saxony), Lower Sorbian (*Land* Brandenburg) **Norway:** Sami **Romania:** Bulgarian, Czech, Croatian, German, Hungarian, Russian, Serbian, Slovak, Turkish, Ukrainian **Slovakia:** Hungarian **Spain:** Basque (Autonomous Community of the Basque Country; Historical Community of Navarra), Catalan (Autonomous Community of Catalonia, Balearic Islands), Valencian (Autonomous Community of Valencia) and Galician (Autonomous Community of Galicia) **Switzerland:** Romansh and Italian
	c	**Armenia:** Assyrian, Yezidi, Greek, Russian and Kurdish **Bosnia and Herzegovina:** Albanian, Montenegrin, Czech, Italian, Hungarian, Macedonian, German, Polish, Romanian, Romani, Rysin, Slovak, Slovenian, Turkish, Ukrainian and Jewish (Yiddish and Ladino). **Croatia:** Italian, Serbian, Hungarian, Czech, Slovak, Ruthenian and Ukrainian **Czech Republic:** Slovak **Germany:** Upper Sorbian (Free State of Saxony), Lower Sorbian (*Land* Brandenburg), Romani (*Land* Hesse) **Hungary:** Croatian, German, Romanian, Serbian, Slovak, Slovenian, Romani and Béas **Romania:** Bulgarian, Czech, German, Hungarian, Turkish, Ukrainian **Serbia:** Albanian, Bosnian, Bulgarian, Hungarian, Romani, Romanian, Ruthenian, Slovakian, Ukrainian and Croatian **Slovakia:** Bulgarian, Croatian, Czech, German, Polish, Romani, Ruthenian, Ukrainian and Hungarian **United Kingdom:** Irish

369

4	a	**Austria**: Burgenland Croatian (*Land* Burgenland), Slovenian (*Land* Carinthia) and Hungarian (*Land* Burgenland) **Czech Republic:** Polish (Moravian-Silesian Region and in the territory of the districts of Frydek-Místek and Karviná) and Slovak **Finland:** Sami and Swedish **Germany:** Lower Sorbian (*Land* Brandenburg), Sater Frisian (*Land* Lower Saxony), Low Germany (*Land* Lower Saxony) **Hungary:** Croatian, German, Romanian, Serbian, Slovak, Slovenian, Romani and Béas **Montenegro:** Albanian and Romani **Netherlands:** Frisian (Province of Friesland) **Norway:** Sami **Slovakia:** Bulgarian, Croatian, Czech, German, Polish, Romani, Ruthenian, Ukrainian and Hungarian **Slovenia:** Italian and Hungarian **Spain:** Basque (Autonomous Community of the Basque Country; Historical Community of Navarra), Catalan (Autonomous Community of Catalonia, Balearic Islands), Valencian (Autonomous Community of Valencia) and Galician (Autonomous Community of Galicia) **Sweden:** Sami, Finnish and Meänkieli **Switzerland:** Romansh and Italian **United Kingdom:** Welsh and Irish
	b	**Finland:** Sami and Swedish **Romania:** Bulgarian, Czech, Croatian, German, Hungarian, Russian, Serbian, Slovak, Turkish, Ukrainian **Slovenia:** Italian and Hungarian **Spain:** Basque (Autonomous Community of the Basque Country; Historical Community of Navarra), Catalan (Autonomous Community of Catalonia, Balearic Islands), Valencian (Autonomous Community of Valencia) and Galician (Autonomous Community of Galicia). **Switzerland:** Italian **United Kingdom:** Welsh
	c	**Armenia:** Assyrian, Yezidi, Greek, Russian and Kurdish **Bosnia and Herzegovina:** Albanian, Montenegrin, Czech, Italian, Hungarian, Macedonian, German, Polish, Romanian, Romani, Rysin, Slovak, Slovenian, Turkish, Ukrainian and Jewish (Yiddish and Ladino). **Denmark:** German (Southern Jutland) **Germany:** Danish (*Land* Schleswig-Holstein), Upper Sorbian (Free State of Saxony), Lower Sorbian (*Land* Brandenburg), North Frisian (*Land* Schleswig-Holstein), Sater Frisian (*Land* Lower Saxony), Low German (Free and Hanseatic City of Hamburg, *Land* Mecklenburg-Western Pomerania, *Land* Lower Saxony, *Land* Schleswig-Holstein), Romani (*Land* Hesse) **Hungary:** Croatian, German, Romanian, Serbian, Slovak, Slovenian, Romani and Béas **Montenegro:** Albanian and Romani **Netherlands:** Frisian (Province of Friesland)

		Romania: Bulgarian, Czech, Croatian, German, Hungarian, Russian, Serbian, Slovak, Turkish, Ukrainian **Serbia:** Albanian, Bosnian, Bulgarian, Hungarian, Romani, Romanian, Ruthenian, Slovakian, Ukrainian and Croatian **Slovakia:** Bulgarian, Croatian, Czech, German, Polish, Romani, Ruthenian, Ukrainian and Hungarian **Slovenia:** Italian and Hungarian **Spain:** Basque (Autonomous Community of the Basque Country; Historical Community of Navarra), Catalan (Autonomous Community of Catalonia, Balearic Islands), Valencian (Autonomous Community of Valencia) and Galician (Autonomous Community of Galicia) **Switzerland:** Romansh and Italian **Ukraine:** Belarusian, Bulgarian, Gagauz, Greek, Jewish, Crimean Tatar, Moldovan, German, Polish, Russian, Romanian, Slovak and Hungarian
5		**Armenia:** Assyrian, Yezidi, Greek, Russian and Kurdish **Austria**: Burgenland Croatian (*Land* Burgenland), Slovenian (*Land* Carinthia) and Hungarian (*Land* Burgenland) **Bosnia and Herzegovina:** Albanian, Montenegrin, Czech, Italian, Hungarian, Macedonian, German, Polish, Romanian, Romani, Rysin, Slovak, Slovenian, Turkish, Ukrainian and Jewish (Yiddish and Ladino). **Croatia:** Italian, Serbian, Hungarian, Czech, Slovak, Ruthenian and Ukrainian **Czech Republic:** Polish (Moravian-Silesian region and in the territory of the districts of Frydek-Místek and Karviná) and Slovak **Denmark:** German (Southern Jutland) **Finland:** Sami and Swedish **Germany:** Danish (*Land* Schleswig-Holstein), Upper Sorbian (Free State of Saxony), Lower Sorbian (*Land* Brandenburg), North Frisian (*Land* Schleswig-Holstein), Sater Frisian (*Land* Lower Saxony) **Hungary:** Croatian, German, Romanian, Serbian, Slovak and Slovenian **Montenegro:** Albanian and Romani **Netherlands:** Frisian (Province of Friesland) **Norway:** Sami **Poland:** Belarusian, Czech, Hebrew, Yiddish, Karaim, Kashub, Lithuanian, Lemko, German, Armenian, Romani, Russian, Slovak, Tatar and Ukrainian **Romania:** Bulgarian, Czech, Croatian, German, Hungarian, Russian, Serbian, Slovak, Turkish, Ukrainian **Serbia:** Albanian, Bosnian, Bulgarian, Hungarian, Romani, Romanian, Ruthenian, Slovakian, Ukrainian and Croatian **Slovakia:** Bulgarian, Croatian, Czech, German, Polish, Romani, Ruthenian, Ukrainian and Hungarian **Slovenia:** Italian and Hungarian **Spain:** Basque (Autonomous Community of the Basque Country; Historical Community of Navarra), Catalan (Autonomous Community of Catalonia, Balearic Islands), Valencian (Autonomous Community of Valencia) and Galician (Autonomous Community of Galicia) **Sweden:** Sami, Finnish and Meänkieli **Switzerland:** Romansh and Italian **United Kingdom:** Welsh, Scottish-Gaelic and Irish

Article 11. Media

Robert Dunbar
University of the Highlands and Islands
Tom Moring
University of Helsinki

1. Introduction

2. General application
   2.1. Contextual analysis
   2.2. The Charter's strategy on media issues

3. The scope of the provisions: analysis of the position taken by the Committee of Experts
   3.1. Subparagraph 1a
   3.2. Subparagraph 1b
   3.3. Subparagraph 1c
   3.4. Subparagraph 1d
   3.5. Subparagraph 1e
   3.6. Subparagraph 1f
   3.7. Subparagraph 1g
   3.8. Paragraph 2
   3.9. Paragraph 3

4. Good practice

5. Conclusions

References

Appendix: Ratifications

Article 11 – Media[1]

1. *The Parties undertake, for the users of the regional or minority languages within the territories in which those languages are spoken, according to the situation of each language, to the extent that the public authorities, directly or indirectly, are competent, have power or play a role in this field, and respecting the principle of the independence and autonomy of the media:*

---

1. This chapter builds on an earlier publication by T. Moring and R. Dunbar (2008), *The European Charter for Regional or Minority Languages and the media*. Regional or Minority Languages, No. 6. Strasbourg: Council of Europe Publishing, which for the purpose of this chapter has been revised and updated.

   a. *to the extent that radio and television carry out a public service mission:*

       i. *to ensure the creation of at least one radio station and one television channel in the regional or minority languages; or*

      ii. *to encourage and/or facilitate the creation of at least one radio station and one television channel in the regional or minority languages; or*

     iii. *to make adequate provision so that broadcasters offer programmes in the regional or minority languages;*

   b. iv. *to encourage and/or facilitate the creation of at least one radio station in the regional or minority languages; or*

      v. *to encourage and/or facilitate the broadcasting of radio programmes in the regional or minority languages on a regular basis;*

   c. vi. *to encourage and/or facilitate the creation of at least one television channel in the regional or minority languages; or*

     vii. *to encourage and/or facilitate the broadcasting of television programmes in the regional or minority languages on a regular basis;*

   d. *to encourage and/or facilitate the production and distribution of audio and audiovisual works in the regional or minority languages;*

   e. viii. *to encourage and/or facilitate the creation and/or maintenance of at least one newspaper in the regional or minority languages; or*

     ix. *to encourage and/or facilitate the publication of newspaper articles in the regional or minority languages on a regular basis;*

   f. x. *to cover the additional costs of those media which use regional or minority languages, wherever the law provides for financial assistance in general for the media; or*

     xi. *to apply existing measures for financial assistance also to audiovisual productions in the regional or minority languages;*

   g. *to support the training of journalists and other staff for media using regional or minority languages.*

2. *The Parties undertake to guarantee freedom of direct reception of radio and television broadcasts from neighbouring countries in a language used in identical or similar form to a regional or minority language, and not to oppose the retransmission of radio and television broadcasts from neighbouring countries in such a language. They further undertake to ensure that no restrictions will be placed on the freedom of expression and free circulation of information in the written press in a language used in identical or similar form to a regional or minority language. The exercise of the above-mentioned freedoms, since it carries with it duties and responsibilities, may be subject to such formalities, conditions, restrictions or penalties as are prescribed by law and are necessary in a democratic society, in the interests of national security, territorial integrity or public safety, for the prevention of disorder or crime, for the protection of health or morals, for the protection of the reputation or rights of others, for preventing disclosure of information received in confidence, or for maintaining the authority and impartiality of the judiciary.*

> 3. *The Parties undertake to ensure that the interests of the users of regional or minority languages are represented or taken into account within such bodies as may be established in accordance with the law with responsibility for guaranteeing the freedom and pluralism of the media.*

1. Introduction

Part III of the Charter includes a provision dealing specifically with media. This is expressly discussed in the Explanatory Report,[2] which starts from the fact that global development of the media sector is leading to a weakening of the cultural influence of less widely-spoken languages. This claim, echoed by researchers in language retention and media studies,[3] is further argued in the Explanatory Report. It says "[t]he time and space which regional or minority languages can secure in the media is vital for their safeguard" and that "[t]oday no language can keep its influence unless it has access to new forms of mass communications. The development of these throughout the world and the progress of technology are leading to the weakening of the cultural influence of less widely-spoken languages."

The argument of size of market is one basic argument for public intervention in the field of the media,[4] and the Explanatory Report echoes this argument in noting that "regional and minority languages represent a small cultural market. Despite the new opportunities offered them by the advances in broadcasting technology, it remains true that to have access to the media they need public support."

2. General application

2.1. Contextual analysis

To provide a background to the importance of media to language, we need to take the discussion on functional aspects of media provisions in the context of regional or minority language (RML) usage somewhat further. The Charter approaches media from three separate, yet interrelated, viewpoints: (1) the role of the media as vehicles for pursuing tolerance, (2) the importance of

---

2. See the Explanatory Report, paragraph 74.
3. Cf. J. A. Fishman (2001), "From theory to practice (and vice versa): review, reconsideration and reiteration" in J. A. Fishman, *Can threatened languages be saved?* Clevedon: Multilingual Matters, pp. 473-4; B. Busch (2004), *Sprachen im Disput. Medien und Öffentlichkeit in multilingualen Gesellschaften.* Klagenfurt: Drava Diskurs 13; T. Moring and C. Husband (2007), "The contribution of Swedish-language media in Finland to linguistic vitality", *International Journal of the Sociology of Language*, Vol. 187/188, pp. 75-101.
4. Cf. G. F. Lowe and C. S. Nissen (eds) (2011), *Small among giants: television broadcasting in smaller countries.* Göteborg: Nordicom.

maintaining media as carriers of the language itself, and (3) the importance of cross-border communication in situations where the language can be enhanced by its use in "identical or similar form" in a neighbouring country.

In the light of the importance of media for the daily usage of a language, a goal for any language must be to maximise services in the language, the ultimate goal being that it is served by all types of media in full. This would mean not only all types of media platforms (newspaper, radio, television, Internet and other new platforms such as those provided by mobile communication techniques). It also means that different media genres, spanning youth programmes and popular culture to news and documentary programmes, should be offered to the speakers of the language on a daily basis. In this light, ambiguities in Article 11 should, in principle, be resolved in such a manner that maximises the time, space and scope that the RMLs can secure in the media and which maximises their access to new forms of mass communication.

The types of media that are expressly included in Article 11 are confined to radio, television, newspapers and audiovisual production, but policies in the field of media also spill over to undertakings on cultural activities/facilities in more general terms. Thus the undertakings regarding media under the Charter cannot be restricted to the types of media outlets expressly mentioned in Article 11 paragraph 1. In this regard, it is important to note that different types of media, such as newspapers, radio, television, Internet and mobile services serve different purposes of communication. They are also used during different parts of the day.[5]

New technologies still seek their role in this context. It is evident that the Internet and other electronic platforms have a huge impact, and that the objectives of the Charter in this field cannot today be reached if these media are neglected. However, the provisions of the Charter do not expressly define how these matters should be assessed in the field of the media.

It is important to understand that substituting one medium for another in the service of audiences in an RML will not meet the objectives of the Charter. The requirements, as set out in Article 11 paragraph 1, are independently formulated for each medium. By deduction from the principles set out in Article 12, we consider the undertakings of Article 11 paragraph 1 also to include the new media. Regarding new media, the Committee of Experts could take a similar approach as in Article 11 paragraph 1, meaning that states would be expected

---

5. T. Moring (2007), "Functional completeness in minority language media" in M. Cormack and N. Hourigan (eds), *Minority language media: concepts, critiques and case studies*. Clevedon: Multilingual Matters, pp. 17-33; T. Moring and R. Dunbar (2008), *The European Charter for Regional or Minority Languages and the media.*

to develop new media in the same levelled fashion as they are expected to develop radio, television or newspapers. The actual monitoring of policies in the new media field would, however, have to be done under Article 12 paragraphs 1 and 2. In light of the reasoning presented above, this is well in tune with requirements to meet the main objective of the Charter, to safeguard the languages and support their use. At the same time, as the provisions under Article 12 are less precisely formulated with respect to the new requirements arising due to developments in the field of the media, the states parties here are faced with a challenge to develop an approach that is consistent with the spirit of the Charter, as reflected in regard to other types of media. In more recent monitoring, the Committee of Experts has shown sensitivity to this issue (see section 3 of this chapter).

Among the challenges here are developments in the way that broadcasting is arranged, and the emergence of new services that have the character of media but are not specifically mentioned in the Charter. At the same time, the amount of available programming has increased enormously. Services that take over cultural functions of broadcasting or the printed press are also already provided on the web. The changes do not concern only broadcast media. Publishers of traditional newspapers have, in some cases, turned to Internet publishing in addition to or even instead of print publishing. New news platforms resembling newspapers have also been established on the Web, without a printed version.

A consequence of the arguments presented above is that, in the light of the Charter, the approach to be taken by authorities with respect to such new developments is that they are to be considered as complementary to, not substitutes for, the services that bind the state party. It is, however, important that new media developments are encouraged also in RMLs. There are several provisions in the Charter that can reasonably be considered to cover the new developments in full. The most obvious provisions available are those in Article 11 paragraph 1d and f. The former provision requires the state party to encourage and/ or facilitate the production and distribution of audio and audiovisual works in the RMLs. The latter includes alternative provisions: either to cover the additional costs of those media which use RMLs, wherever the law provides for financial assistance in general for the media, or to apply existing measures for financial assistance also to audiovisual productions in the RMLs.

In addition to new types of media, we understand audio and audiovisual works also to cover new platforms carrying developments of traditional types of media. If new platforms take on functions from television and radio, the application should, *mutatis mutandis*, be monitored on the same grounds as these services, but under the relevant provisions. As noted, subparagraphs 1a to c of Article 12 (Cultural activities and facilities) may be of increasing importance in this

377

context. We find this article, which refers to "the use of new technologies", actually includes provisions that cover all types of requirement for production and distribution of new media products in the RML, as well as the translation of new media into the language and out of the language with whatever means are proper to serve these functions.

We also wish to point to the relevance of Article 14 (Transfrontier exchanges) in the light of new technological development, as a complement to the provision in Article 11 paragraph 2. The latter provision requires the states parties to guarantee freedom of direct reception of radio and television broadcasts from neighbouring countries. Transfrontier exchanges may be both hindered and facilitated by new media technology. Article 14 paragraph a, by referring to the fields of culture, education and information, explicitly addresses this issue. The first part of Article 14 paragraph b, which refers to facilitation and/or promotion of co-operation across borders, includes the same provision, although in more general terms. These provisions may be of importance, for example, in cases where new technologies threaten to hinder or reduce transfrontier reception of radio and television programmes or Internet content. These paragraphs may also be of importance in proactive measures to improve access to media, where this has not earlier been possible, by using the possibilities offered by new technology.

2.2. The Charter's strategy on media issues

With regard to the substantive provisions of Article 11, these are set out in three paragraphs. Paragraph 1 has seven separate subparagraphs, a to g. Subparagraphs a, b and c apply to radio and television broadcasting. Subparagraph a applies "to the extent that radio and television carry out a public service mission"; subparagraphs b and c make no reference to such a mission and can therefore be considered complementary in offering provisions meant to apply to radio and television broadcasting where such a public service mission is not at hand, or where it is appropriate to include provisions pertaining to private broadcasters.

Subparagraph d of paragraph 1 refers to the obligation of the state to encourage and/or facilitate the production and distribution of audio and audiovisual works in the RML. An ambiguity here is whether either term would contemplate material that is made available online through websites accessible with computers; indeed, it is not clear into which category of media mentioned in Article 11 Web-based materials should be considered to fall.

Subparagraph e.i of paragraph 1 of Article 11 refers to the obligation of the state to encourage and/or facilitate the creation and/or maintenance of at least one newspaper in the RML, while subparagraph e.ii refers to the obligation of the state to encourage and/or facilitate the publication of newspaper articles in the RML. With respect to subparagraph e.i, the most difficult question is that of what constitutes a "newspaper" in the RML, and we will return to how this question has been interpreted in more detail in section 3.

Subparagraph f also contains separate, alternative provisions. Subparagraph f.i obliges states to cover the additional costs of those media which use RMLs, wherever the law provides for financial assistance in general for the media. Subparagraph f.ii obliges the state to apply existing measures for financial assistance to audiovisual productions in the RML.

Subparagraph g obliges states to support the training of journalists and other staff for media using RMLs. While the term "journalist" is not entirely free from ambiguity, the reference to "other staff" engaged in media is potentially very wide, and would probably include types of media employee who might not qualify as "journalists".

Paragraph 2 of Article 11 contains three distinct aspects and presumably all three would have to be satisfied. First, the state guarantees the freedom of direct reception of radio and television broadcasts from neighbouring countries in a language used in identical or similar form to an RML. Significantly, the Explanatory Report to the Charter effectively expands the scope of this provision. It provides at paragraph 111 that the guarantee of freedom of reception relates not only to obstacles to reception of programmes which have been deliberately erected, but also "passive obstacles resulting from failure of the competent authorities to take any action to make such reception possible". Second, the state agrees not to oppose the retransmission of radio and television broadcasts from neighbouring countries in an RML. Third, the state undertakes to ensure that no restrictions will be placed on the freedom of expression and free circulation of information in the written press in a language used in identical or similar form to an RML. Paragraph 2 concludes by providing that the exercise of all three of these aspects may be subject to such formalities, conditions, restrictions and penalties as are prescribed by law and are necessary in a democratic society for a range of purposes listed in the paragraph, such as national security, the protection of health and morals, the prevention of crime and disorder, the protection of the rights and reputation of others, and so forth. As is noted in paragraph 112 of the Explanatory Report, the limitation is identical to that which applies in respect of the right to freedom of expression, set out in Article 10 of the European Convention on Human Rights ("the ECHR"). It should be noted that paragraph 112 of the Explanatory Report provides that, for those states which are parties to the European Convention on Transfrontier Television, the circumstances and conditions under which the freedoms guaranteed by Article 11 paragraph 2 of the Charter can be restricted will be determined by that convention. This would seem to imply that the authors of the Charter did indeed intend that, otherwise, the extent of the restriction should be determined by reference to Article 10 of the ECHR.

A particularly complicated matter is raised by securing rights and interests of the rights-holders in relation to paragraph 2 of Article 11. The Explanatory Report explicitly mentions this aspect (paragraph 112): "Moreover, the provisions of this paragraph do not affect the need for copyright to be respected." The solving of problems in this field may require active participation by the state party and the licence holders.[6]

Finally, paragraph 3 of Article 11 of the Charter requires the state to undertake to ensure that the interests of the users of RMLs are represented or taken into account within bodies having responsibility for guaranteeing the freedom and pluralism of the media. Paragraph 113 of the Explanatory Report indicates that the words "or taken into account" were inserted in response to the difficulties involved in determining who are the representatives of users of RMLs. The sort of regulatory body to which this provision applies is, however, not altogether obvious.

As public intervention in the media is sensitive, in line with principles of freedom of the media,[7] the Explanatory Report (paragraph 107) argues that "The public authorities act in this field essentially by encouragement and the provision of aid". As has been expressly argued by the Committee of Experts, promoting RML broadcasting through financial incentives is not to be considered an infringement of sensitivities about state intervention in the media.[8]

3. The scope of the provisions: analysis of the position taken by the Committee of Experts

Given the centrality of the media in any effort to maintain and promote a minoritised language, it is not surprising that the Committee of Experts has examined virtually all of the paragraphs and subparagraphs of Article 11 in considerable detail. The reports based on the monitoring of the Charter bear witness to the fact that the speakers frequently bring up problems in regard to media services and wish to improve availability – in quantity, quality, scheduling and technical transmission – to media offerings in their language. There have indeed been positive developments in the media sector with improvement of services to meet the speakers' demands, sometimes assisted by the opportunities emerging from technological development. But also drawbacks and new problems have emerged due to reorganisation of the media sector, technological obstacles or other changes.

---

6. For examples, see T. Moring and S. Godenhjelm (2011), "Broadcasting for minorities in big and small countries", in G. F. Lowe and C. S. Nissen (eds), *Small among giants*.

7. Article 10 of the European Convention on Human Rights (ECHR).

8. This is expressly argued in the report by the Committee of Experts in Germany 2008, 4.

States have predominantly opted for the lower-level undertakings in regard to broadcasting – to offer programmes in the languages instead of full radio stations or television channels (subparagraphs 11.1a.iii, b.ii, c.ii) – though in some cases the actual services may be at higher levels. Undertakings in regard to audio- and audiovisual services (subparagraph 11.1d) and encouraging or facilitating of newspapers (subparagraph 11.1e.i) are chosen in a majority of cases; however, the actual provision of a newspaper has in many cases not been fulfilled or has been fulfilled at a quite modest level.

States usually undertake to guarantee freedom of direct reception of radio and television broadcasts from neighbouring countries (paragraph 11.2); this, however, does not exclude problems in reception of kin-state programmes in practice.

3.1. Subparagraph 1a

Given the importance of both television and radio broadcasting, subparagraphs 1a, b and c have attracted particular attention. Subparagraph 1a of Article 11 requires states to ensure, where radio and television carry out a public service mission, the creation of at least one radio station and one television channel in the RMLs. This provision contains a number of ambiguities which the Committee of Experts have sought to address. One is the concept of a "public service mission". Based on the Explanatory Report to the Charter, this concept seemed to comprise both "public broadcasting" (that is, state-owned broadcasting) and private sector, commercial broadcasting, where the state imposed on the private sector certain public service obligations. In some of their earlier reports, the Committee of Experts seemed willing to consider private sector provision in the context of subparagraph 1a.i; in its report on the initial UK state report, for example, the broadcasting of "certain amounts of Welsh-language program-ming" on other "regional and commercial stations" other than the public sector BBC Radio Cymru service was noted by the Committee of Experts, though not commented on.[9] In its third report on Germany, in 2008, the Committee of Experts recognised that, because of major changes in the nature of broadcasting since the Charter was concluded in 1992, the traditional distinction between monolithic public service broadcaster and private broadcasters has eroded,[10] prompting a different approach to how it will deal with subparagraphs 1a, b and c, and this change of approach is considered further, below.

One aspect of this changing media environment is the effects of privatisation, a phenomenon which has been particularly significant in the former socialist states of eastern and central Europe. In its first report on Serbia, for example, the

---

9. Paragraph 160.
10. Paragraph 17.

Committee of Experts found that Serbia was in the process of privatising local television and radio broadcasters. Even though it found that private broadcasters played an important role in the provision of programmes in RMLs, the Committee of Experts found that the Serbian authorities had taken no regulatory measures to ensure that such broadcasters would continue to make adequate provision for programmes in RMLs, and in a box recommendation encouraged the Serbian authorities to ensure that the privatisation of local broadcasters would not "negatively affect the offer of programmes in the RMLs".[11]

Another issue which the Committee of Experts has had to deal is whether, in order to be a "radio station" or "television channel" within the meaning of subparagraph 1a, broadcasting had to be solely through the medium of the minority language. The Committee of Experts seems to accept that this is not necessary. In its report on the initial UK state report, for example, in which the Committee of Experts found that the UK's undertaking under subparagraph 1a.i was fulfilled, they noted that S4C, the "Welsh language television channel", broadcasts 5.14 hours a day in Welsh (though these are broadcast in "prime time", a concept not further defined) and that it broadcast 17.94 hours a day in English.[12] Thus, a channel which broadcasts three quarters of its output in the majority language can nonetheless be considered to be a minority language "television channel", rather than a television channel which broadcasts programmes in the minority language. Although the Committee of Experts did not specifically address this, it may be that the condition may nonetheless have been fulfilled because there were a certain minimum number of hours broadcast, and that such broadcasting was at peak times, ensuring widest possible access to the Welsh-language programming. The Committee of Experts may also have been influenced by the fact that S4C was created specifically to ensure the presence of Welsh on television, and has a strongly Welsh-language identity.

In their first report on Slovenia, in contrast, the Committee of Experts concluded that the undertaking under subparagraph 1a.i in respect of Hungarian was not fulfilled; even though a certain amount of time was granted to programmes in Hungarian (2 hours a week, divided into four slots of 30 minutes each), this was below the legal standard of 30 minutes per day and was "in the context of one of the Slovenian-speaking channels".[13] In a box which followed these comments, the Committee of Experts encouraged the state authorities to consider ways towards proper implementation of the undertaking and to take interim measures to increase the level of television programming. They did not, however, suggest that such increased levels of programming should not

---

11. Paragraph 215 and subsequent box recommendation.
12. Paragraph 161.
13. Paragraphs 141-2.

be on Slovenian-speaking channels. Thus, in spite of the reference in the treaty provision to a "television channel", the primary concern seems not whether the channel which carries the programming is primarily a majority-language one, but more the actual number of hours per day that are broadcast in the minority language. It would appear that 30 minutes per day, four days a week, is unsatisfactory, but that about five hours per day, much of it at peak times, as is the case in Wales, would be satisfactory.

With regard to what constitutes a "radio station", though it is unclear from the Committee of Experts' reports whether the various minority-language "stations" which they considered also broadcast programmes in the majority language, it is again clear that the committee is primarily concerned with actual numbers of broadcasting hours. In respect of the UK, for example, the Committee of Experts found that the subparagraph 1a.i undertaking was satisfied in respect of Welsh, where it was noted[14] that the BBC Radio Cymru service broadcasts about 100 hours of Welsh-medium programming per week. In respect of Slovenia, the committee found that the undertaking was satisfied in respect of Hungarian, noting[15] that an autonomous studio set up in Lendava/Lendva broadcasts 13 hours and 15 minutes per day. As the Committee of Experts has not yet determined that the undertaking has not been satisfied, it is difficult, though, to determine what amount of daily programming, in terms of hours, would not be considered satisfactory.

Two other issues that have been raised by the Committee of Experts in the context of subparagraph 1a are the question of digital broadcasting and the use of repeat programming. With regard to the use of digital broadcasting, the Committee of Experts observed that the use of such a medium, which requires special technical requirements for reception, "runs the risk of excluding a minority from the mass media".[16] On the one hand, the exploitation of new technologies such as digital broadcasting should be encouraged, but on the other hand, the presence of minority-language programming on such technologies should not be at the expense of the presence of such programming on more widely available formats; the Committee of Experts has shown that it places primary emphasis on the real access of speakers of RMLs to minority-language radio and television broadcasting.

The switch over to digital broadcasting in certain states such as the UK presents a slightly different issue, but one which also relates to the general availability of minority-language broadcasting. In its third report on the UK, the Committee

---

14. See United Kingdom 2004, 160.
15. Slovenia 2004, 139.
16. See United Kingdom 2004, 161-2.

of Experts noted that a Gaelic-language digital television service, BBC ALBA, had been created in 2008, and it commented favourably on a number of aspects of the new service, including the number of hours broadcast per day and the range of programming. It noted, however, that the service was only available on satellite platform, with the result that only some of the potential viewers could address the channel, and that the relevant regulator had delayed a decision on whether the new service would be available on Freeview, ensuring access on all digital platforms. The committee underlined the importance of "widening the footprint of the service", indicating that it is important that the new service gets a place on Freeview with other public service broadcasters, and they encouraged the authorities to do what they could to make this happen.[17]

With respect to the use of repeat programming as part of the programming mix, the Committee of Experts has merely noted its use, without much further comment; in its first report on the UK, the committee found that the UK's undertaking in respect of Welsh had been fulfilled, even though there was considerable repeat programming, thereby suggesting that the use of some repeat programming is presumably acceptable. The Committee of Experts has not yet provided any further guidance on how much repeat programming is acceptable. Given the costs of television production, there is the real danger that broadcasters may try to satisfy their obligations by the use of increasing amounts of repeat programming, and at some point, this may result in questions about whether obligations under subparagraph 1a.i are being met.

With respect to subparagraph 1a.ii (to encourage and/or facilitate the creation of at least one radio station and one television channel in the RMLs), the Committee of Experts has had only one opportunity to consider its implementation, in the context of the UK state report in relation to Scottish-Gaelic. The obligation under this subparagraph is to "encourage and/or facilitate" the creation of at least one radio station and one television channel in the RML. In respect of Gaelic radio broadcasting, the Committee of Experts considered in its first report on the UK that the undertaking was only partly fulfilled, and in respect of television, they found that it was not fulfilled. The Committee of Experts noted that radio services were mainly provided by the BBC. They found that 50-60 hours were broadcast per week, that the programming was multi-genre and included news and current affairs programmes, and that the service was available online, meaning that Gaelic speakers in other parts of the UK and elsewhere in the world had access to Gaelic programmes. They also noted, though, that there were some parts of Scotland that were not receiving broadcasts because of gaps in the transmission infrastructure. It appears that it was this latter difficulty – the gaps in reception in Scotland – rather than the number

---

17. Paragraph 276.

of hours and content, which led the Committee of Experts to conclude that the subparagraph 1a.ii obligation was only partly fulfilled in respect of radio broadcasting, as they specifically encouraged the UK Government to "take appropriate action to ensure that all of Scotland can receive Radio nan Gaidheal".[18]

The Committee of Experts described in some detail the situation of Gaelic television broadcasting.[19] They noted that the BBC provides regular Gaelic programming, mostly broadcast for two hours on one day a week, and that the BBC offered a total of 24 hours of television output in 2001/2. They also noted that the UK broadcasting regulator requires a private sector television channel to offer not less than 90 minutes of Gaelic programmes per week, and that about 150 hours of Gaelic television programmes are broadcast per year. Given that the Committee of Experts' conclusion was that the UK's undertaking under subparagraph 1a.ii was not fulfilled in respect of television, it is clear that this level of programming does not constitute the "encouragement and/or facilitation" of the creation of a television channel in the RML. A significant factor leading to the Committee of Experts' conclusion appears to be that the UK legislation dealing with broadcasting matters at the time of the first report on the UK, the Communication Act, did "not expressly provide for the promotion or establishment of a Gaelic TV channel".[20] The Committee of Experts were told by UK Government officials that this new legislation "would 'enable' a channel to be established, 'should funding become available'", although the Committee of Experts noted that there was no evidence from the state authorities that such funding would, in fact, be made available. Their conclusion is important: "Compliance with the undertaking chosen by the UK requires more than simply creating a legal framework within which a channel can exist; it requires positive action (including where necessary funding) on the part of the Authorities". Thus, setting a framework which potentially allows the undertaking to be met is not sufficient. It would appear that the Committee of Experts is taking a results-oriented approach to determining whether this undertaking is satisfied; their conclusion appears to suggest that the degree to which the state is meeting its commitments to "encourage and/or facilitate" the desired outcome, the establishment of a TV channel, will be determined by the extent to which such a channel actually exists. There is no doubt that the UK has taken some steps – both the legislative changes in the Communications Act which ultimately have permitted the creation of a channel, and already significant funding of Gaelic-medium broadcasting, something that was noted by the Committee of Experts,[21] could be considered to be "encouragement and/or facili-

---

18. See United Kingdom 2004, 262 and 264.
19. Ibid., 259-61.
20. Ibid., 263.
21. Ibid., 261.

tation" – but the fact that such steps were not sufficient to ensure the outcome of a Gaelic TV channel seems to have proved decisive. Thus, the Committee of Experts seems to interpret subparagraph 1a.ii as imposing a quite significant obligation on the state; indeed, it seems to approach the subparagraph 1a.i obligation as one of "ensuring" the creation of a television channel.

It appears, therefore, that the Committee of Experts contemplates that television programming provided on existing majority-language television channels will not be enough to fulfil the undertaking in subparagraph 1a.ii, and that to do so a special purpose minority-language channel must be the aim of state policy and practice. It would appear, based on the earlier discussion of subparagraph 1a.i, that such a channel would not have to broadcast exclusively in the minority language, but it would seem that, without a channel specifically created to cater for minority-language users, the undertaking will not be satisfied.

Of the three options in subparagraph 1a of Article 11, subparagraph 1a.iii (to make adequate provision so that broadcasters offer programmes in the RMLs) is by far the undertaking which is chosen most frequently by states,[22] and unlike subparagraph 1a.ii, the Committee of Experts has had the opportunity to consider this provision on very many occasions. Subparagraph 1a.iii is undoubtedly the "weakest" undertaking in subparagraph 1a, as it does not refer to the creation of a "station" or a "channel", but only to the making of "adequate" provision so that broadcasters having a public service obligation to offer "programmes" in the RMLs. Perhaps the most significant issue in this subparagraph is the meaning of the phrase "adequate provision". The Committee of Experts' comments on this provision suggest that their primary focus is on the number of hours of programming in the RMLs; reference has also been made to the regularity of such programming, to matters relating to the accessibility of such programming – the times during the day when such programming is broadcast and whether, where programming is broadcast in digital format, it is also accessible in analogue – and to financial support for such programming. The Committee of Experts has reiterated in a number of its reports the great importance of the electronic media, and in particular television, for the promotion of RMLs in modern societies, and in particular that "a regular and predictable (e.g. weekly) presence of a regional or minority language on radio and television can enhance considerably its social prestige".[23]

On the total numbers of hours of radio and television programming, the Committee of Experts has not been prescriptive in setting clear quantitative standards. Given the diversity in the situation of RMLs throughout Europe, in

---

22. See Appendix 1: Ratifications.
23. See, for example, Slovakia 2009, 124; see also Switzerland 2004, 118.

technical and regulatory standards and in financial conditions in different states, it would hardly be possible or even desirable to be prescriptive. It would, however, be desirable for the committee to be as consistent as possible: where, in particular, different RMLs are in broadly comparable situations, and where the states involved are also broadly comparable, it would seem desirable for the committee to seek to ensure that provision is broadly comparable. Based on a consideration of the committee's work on this subparagraph, the existence of such inconsistencies does not appear to be a serious problem.

As just noted, the Committee of Experts has not been prescriptive about the total number of hours of programming broadcast in RMLs. Thus, in their first report on the Netherlands, the committee generally found that one hour per day of regional television programming in Frisian and eight hours per day of regional radio programming in Frisian fulfilled the undertaking.[24] In their first report on Hungary too, the Committee of Experts concluded that the undertaking had been fulfilled. They found there were regular weekly radio programmes in all six RMLs covered by Part III, including over 13 hours per week in Slovak, Croatian, German and Romanian, over 6 hours per week in Serbian and about 1 hour per week in Slovenian.[25] The amount of television programming in these languages was not specified, but clearly seemed to be less, with the Committee of Experts noting "weekly and/or biweekly programmes are broadcast on public television" in all the six Part III languages. With regard to television at least, it seems that the regularity with which programmes are broadcast, rather than total number of hours, is the most important consideration. In some cases, the quantity of programming comes close to what might be considered acceptable under subparagraph 1a.i.[26]

Sometimes, relatively small amounts of programming in RMLs appear to be acceptable to the Committee of Experts. For example, in its first report on Sweden, the committee found that the state broadcaster transmitted 107 hours of television programmes in Finnish in 1999 and 116 hours in 2001. The committee also noted that, during their on-the-spot visit, representatives of the Finnish community "confirmed that the situation in the media was felt to be fair", and it would appear that the Committee of Experts may, in applying concepts such as "adequate provision" that are inherently difficult to apply in fixed quantitative terms and which always have a subjective element, place

---

24. See the Netherlands 2001, 58.
25. See Hungary 2001, 63.
26. For example, in Norway 2001, 80, the Committee of Experts found that over 1 500 hours of Sami radio programmes were broadcast per year (a little over 4 hours per day); in Switzerland 2001, they found the state broadcaster's Romansh service put out 14 hours of radio programmes a day and had about 100 employees.

considerable emphasis on the perceptions of users of the languages themselves.[27] In the first report on Sweden, the Committee of Experts found that even dramatically smaller amounts of television programming in Sami were acceptable; they noted there were 17 hours of Sami television per year in 2000 and 39 hours in 2001, and that the figures for "own production" were rising, which was described as encouraging. In the same report, the committee found that, in spite of dramatically lower levels of television broadcasting in Meänkieli, the obligation was nonetheless "partly fulfilled": in 2001, only 4.35 hours were broadcast, made up of three 30-minute programmes, with repeats, and that this was down from 5.12 hours per annum in 1999.[28]

In its first report on Montenegro, in respect of radio broadcasting in Albanian, a 3-minute and a 30-minute programme each day on Radio Montenegro, a 45-minute programme on a local radio station broadcast five days a week and another local radio station which broadcast 70% of its programming in Albanian allowed the Committee of Experts to conclude that Montenegro's obligations were fulfilled.[29] However, it is clear that there must be a point at which hours are so small and programming is therefore so irregular that the Committee of Experts will conclude that the undertaking has not been fulfilled. In its report on the UK, the committee found that provision for Irish-language radio programming on BBC, the public broadcaster, of 5 hours per week was satisfactory, but that television programming on the BBC, which amounted to only 16 hours per year (of which 13 hours were repeat programmes for adult learners of Irish), was insufficient and the undertaking under subparagraph 1a.iii in relation to television was not fulfilled.[30] In its second report on Austria, the Committee of Experts considered that a 25-minute television programme broadcast six times a year and a 45-minute programme broadcast four times a year on the state broadcaster ORF in Hungarian were insufficient.[31] In its first report on the Czech Republic, the committee found that one 5-minute insert of Polish-language broadcasting per week on television was insufficient, and that the Czech Republic's obligations were therefore not fulfilled.[32] But the numbers of hours of Irish broadcasting were not significantly lower than those which the committee found satisfactory for Sami in Sweden, and this does raise questions. There are some differences which, though not explicitly articulated by the Committee of Experts, may help to explain the difference in approach: one is that the number of hours of Sami television broadcasting was increasing; a second may be the

---

27. See Sweden 2003, 235 and 237.
28. See Sweden 2003, 126 and 349.
29. Paragraphs 150 and 154.
30. See United Kingdom 2004, 350 and 354.
31. Paragraphs 330-2.
32. Paragraph 208.

large numbers of hours of repeat Irish-language broadcasting; and a third may be the relative demographic position of the two communities, because there are much larger numbers of Irish-speakers, based on UK census returns, in Northern Ireland than Sami-speakers in Sweden. Similar examples can be found also elsewhere.

The most detailed consideration of and guidance with respect to subparagraph 1a.iii was given in the first two Committee of Experts' reports on Croatia. Factually, little had changed between the two reports, although the committee had more detailed information on the precise nature of the programming at the time of the second report. In the first report, they noted that, with respect to television, Croatian law imposed an obligation on the state public broadcaster to produce and broadcast programmes that offer informative material for users of RMLs, and that there was a weekly television news magazine, *Prizma*, an information programme for national minorities which is normally produced in an RML with subtitles in Croatian; as the Committee of Experts did not indicate otherwise, it seems that this satisfied the undertaking. They noted that they had little information on existing radio programmes in RMLs, but that they were "aware of the fact that various radio programmes are actually produced" in RMLs, and found on this basis that the undertaking was fulfilled for Italian, Hungarian, Czech and Serbian.[33] In many ways, these were both surprising conclusions, if only because so little about the precise situation seems to have been known, and very little information seems to have been available on precisely how many hours were broadcast, at what times and so forth.

In the second report on Croatia, by contrast, the Committee of Experts had more information and concluded that the undertaking was no longer fulfilled. First, the committee clarified that private broadcasting, even if regulated by the state, did not come within subparagraph 1a, where they noted that the imposition by law of obligations on private broadcasters concerning the presence of minority-language programmes related to a different obligation than that set out in subparagraph 1a.iii.[34] The result appears to be that, in spite of the provisions in the Explanatory Report to the Charter, which seem to contemplate that the "public service mission" referred to in subparagraph 1a could cover private broadcasters who are under a public service obligation, recent monitoring has treated public broadcasters (in the sense of publicly-owned state broadcasters or publicly subsidised broadcasters) under subparagraph 1a, and private broadcasters, even those who are put under significant obligations, under subparagraphs 1b and 1c.

---

33. Croatia 2001, 93-4.
34. Croatia 2005, 161.

With respect to the public sector television broadcasting provided by Croatia, the Committee of Experts noted that the situation had not changed since the first report, but that they had additional information about the *Prizma* programme, the primary means by which Croatia seeks to satisfy its undertaking with respect to television. In total, 51 programmes of 55 minutes each were broadcast, and the amount of time for the various RMLs ranged from 30 minutes in total for Ruthenian, to 239 minutes per year (about 4 hours) for Czech, 290 minutes (almost 5 hours) for Serbian and 312 minutes (slightly over 5 hours) for Italian. The Committee of Experts also noted that information received during the on-the-spot visit indicated that the presence in the media for some languages had worsened, and that *Prizma* represented an "inadequate format" as it conveyed a "folklore image" of regional and minority languages in Croatia.[35]

The Committee of Experts began by making an important policy statement about television broadcasting in general: it underlined "the great importance of television for the protection and promotion or regional and minority languages in modern societies". It also noted that the presence of such languages in the media served another crucial purpose, namely "the raising of the awareness of the majority population". Such a policy orientation was reiterated by the committee in its second report on Switzerland (paragraph 118), where it made the following statement:

> The Committee of Experts underlines the great importance of television for the protection and the promotion of regional or minority languages in modern societies. Among other things, a real presence of a regional or minority language on television can enhance considerably its social prestige, which … is a crucial factor for minority language protection and promotion.

On the basis of such a policy orientation, the Committee of Experts found in its second report on Croatia that the format of *Prizma* "may therefore be seen as granting to regional or minority languages an almost symbolic visibility on the Croatian public television, in that it does not allow each language to develop an autonomous and significant presence". In addition, they noted that users of the languages could not be certain whether their language would appear in any specific *Prizma* programme, and that this reduced the attractiveness and therefore the effectiveness of the broadcasting provided. It concluded by saying that "an autonomous and significant presence" is a feasible objective, and they pointed to the autonomous half-hour weekly programme in Hungarian that is available in Croatia. Based on the foregoing considerations and on "the ever-growing importance of the media in modern societies", the committee revised the conclusion from its first report on Croatia, finding that the subparagraph 1a.iii undertaking was no longer fulfilled for television broadcasting.[36]

---

35. See Croatia 2005, 162-3.
36. Ibid., 165.

A somewhat different though related issue is the imposition of quotas requiring certain percentages of broadcasting through the medium of the official language. In its first report on Ukraine, the Committee of Experts noted that, under Ukrainian broadcasting legislation, at least 75% of broadcasting had to be through the medium of Ukrainian, a percentage that was subsequently increased to 80, then to 85%. This quota applied even in areas of the country where minorities comprised up to 50% of the population. While the Committee of Experts noted that this rule was meant to protect and promote the state language, they stated that "an overall exclusion of the use of the national minority languages in the nation-wide public service and private broadcasting sectors is not compatible with Article 11 of the Charter",[37] and in a box recommendation the Committee of Experts encouraged the authorities to revise the regulations for broadcasting in RMLs covered by the Charter, though they were not prescriptive as to how those regulations should be revised. Later in their report, the Committee of Experts expressed the view that the quota system hampers the accomplishment of the Ukraine's undertaking and that reducing the quota would benefit minority-language broadcasting, and encouraged the authorities to review the system in order to ensure that the presence of programmes in RMLs responding to the needs of the speakers is not subject to excessive limitations.[38]

The Committee of Experts has also been critical of other forms of regulation to protect the position of the majority language which disadvantage minority-language broadcasters.[39] In its second report on Slovakia, it noted a requirement that all private broadcasters which broadcast programmes in an RML must provide subtitles in Slovak, placing such broadcasters at a competitive disadvantage. They concluded that the Slovak undertaking was not fulfilled,[40] and in a box recommendation encouraged the authorities to remove the existing restrictive requirements for private broadcasters.

In respect of radio broadcasting, the Committee of Experts also had additional information. They found that the main public radio broadcaster broadcasts a 60-minute weekly programme for national minorities, though it is presented in Croatian and mainly concerns cultural matters; but they also found that some regional stations broadcast relatively small amounts of material in certain of the RMLs, but such broadcasts took place on a regular basis – for example, daily news bulletins in Italian at specified times, a daily information programme in Italian lasting up to 15 minutes, a half-hour daily Italian programme in

---

37. Paragraph 448.
38. Paragraphs 486-7.
39. Here, the Committee of Experts' position coincides with principles tabled by the OSCE in *Guidelines on the use of minority languages in the broadcast media* (OSCE, 2003).
40. Paragraphs 130-1, 257-9, 379-81, 510-11, 646-7 and 807-8.

another region, a half-hour daily programme in Hungarian in one region, a weekly programme in Czech and a weekly programme in Slovak (see paragraph 167). On the basis of this information, the Committee of Experts concluded that the subparagraph 1a.iii undertaking in respect of public radio was fulfilled in respect of these languages – Italian, Hungarian, Czech and Slovak. The committee recommended that Croatia take the necessary measures to develop television programmes for each Part III language and to introduce an offer of radio programmes in Serbian, Ruthenian and Ukrainian, "following the models used for the other languages". Thus, as noted above, it would appear that very small numbers of overall hours of television and radio broadcasting can satisfy the requirements of subparagraph 1a.iii; what seems to be of greater importance is the regularity and predictability of such broadcasting, and also the content, which, it seems, should be contemporary and should avoid stereotypical or overly folkloric depictions of the languages or their users.

A related issue which has arisen, particularly in relation to television, is the time slots which RML programmes occupy. In addition to regularity of programming, an important consideration is broadcasting at times of the day that make such programming accessible to the users of the languages. In the case of Hungary, for example, the Committee of Experts noted in its first report that the time slots allotted to minority-language programmes "have given rise to complaints from the representatives of the minority languages" and that while the Hungarian undertaking had been "formally fulfilled", "further efforts" were needed "to come to functional arrangements in questions of detail" such as time slots.[41] Similar problems were cited in the second report on Hungary, with the Committee of Experts noting complaints that some half-hour television programming was available only in the early afternoon, "when students and workers can hardly watch TV". They went on to "encourage" the Hungarian authorities to "strengthen the offer and to improve the time-slot and the time-frame available for minority language television programmes".[42] Again, though, the Committee of Experts was not prescriptive; it did not indicate a general policy on time slots. So, while it is possible to say that timing of programmes in minority languages is a matter that is relevant under this provision, it is not possible to say precisely what sort of schedule would be acceptable. The Committee of Experts did base its conclusions on the perceptions of users of the languages, and therefore what is acceptable to such users will be an important consideration. This principle – consideration of the perceptions of the users themselves in assessing compliance – is one which emerges elsewhere in the Committee of Experts' reports

---

41. Paragraph 63.
42. See Hungary 2001, 120 and 123.

and is an important underlying principle when interpreting terms such as "adequate provision"; adequacy is determined at least in part by the perceptions of the users of the languages themselves.

The importance of accessibility of programming is also raised by the use of digital as opposed to analogue broadcasting technology. In the first report on Sweden, the Committee of Experts noted in respect of Meänkieli that there was concern among users of the language that a greater proportion of radio broadcasting was being transmitted digitally, which effectively excluded most listeners from being able to listen to the programmes.[43] In its second report on Hungary, the committee noted that one of the main problems facing minority-language radio broadcasting was the use of a frequency for such broadcasts that modern radio sets were not capable of receiving; they concluded that, because of such problems, the undertaking in respect of radio broadcasting could be considered only "partly fulfilled",[44] and in a box which followed this discussion they "urged the Hungarian authorities to ensure that programmes in minority languages are transmitted on frequencies which can be received by ordinary radio sets". This is a case where the Committee of Experts has demonstrated that it is not acceptable that media services in minority languages are subjected to requirements that unreasonably impose extra cost or effort on them, compared to similar services in the majority language.

A final set of issues which the Committee of Experts will consider in determining whether levels of radio and television broadcasting are "adequate" under subparagraph 1a.iii is related to resource issues. In its first report on the Netherlands, for example, while the committee found that the undertaking was fulfilled in respect of Frisian broadcasting, they noted that the broadcaster received "exactly the same funding" for Frisian programming as it did for Dutch-language programming, and concluded that "as it is more costly to produce programmes in Frisian, there is an evident need for special, earmarked support" for the broadcaster "in order to take account of its special task";[45] the Committee of Experts encouraged the government to take into account the special needs of broadcasting in Frisian and "to consider increasing its financial support". Likewise, while the committee found in its first report on Sweden that the undertaking was fulfilled in respect of Finnish broadcasting, it encouraged the Swedish authorities to collaborate with broadcasters and representatives of Finnish-speakers to ensure that Finnish-language programming does not suffer unfairly as a result of budgetary constraints, "including, if necessary, ring-fenced funds for Finnish language programmes".

---

43. See Sweden 2003, 353.
44. See Hungary 2004, 122-3.
45. See the Netherlands 2001, 59.

3.2. Subparagraph 1b

Subparagraph 1b.i of the Charter requires states to encourage and/or facilitate the creation of at least one radio station in the RML. As suggested above, the Committee of Experts now seems to interpret the provisions in both subparagraph 1b and c as applying to private-sector commercial broadcasters rather than public broadcasters, even if such private-sector broadcasters are subject to fairly close government regulation in the public interest, and even if they receive significant financial support from government. In Austria, for example, radio broadcasters such as Radio dva and AGORA have been funded largely or wholly by the government or, more recently, to a significant extent by the state broadcaster ORF. Even though they are not, strictly speaking, publicly owned (only publicly subsidised), they were nonetheless considered by the Committee of Experts in the context of Austria's obligations under subparagraph 1b.[46]

Two major issues have arisen in respect of subparagraph 1b: first, in relation to subparagraph 1b.i, what constitutes a radio "station" and, second, in relation to subparagraph 1b.ii, what measures are implied by the words "encourage and/ or facilitate". With regard to what constitutes a "station", does this word imply that minority-language programmes constitute the only or the main output? The Committee of Experts has not specifically addressed this; for example, in its second report on Norway, it noted that out of 300 local radio stations, four broadcast in Sami, though it did not specify whether these stations broadcast exclusively in Sami.[47] In its second report on Switzerland, the committee found that, in spite of the fact that certain private stations were obliged by the licensing laws to broadcast a number of programmes in Romansch and Italian, there was insufficient evidence that such quotas were enforced, and they also commented that there was no "private radio station in Romansch".[48] In the box which followed this discussion, the Committee of Experts encouraged the authorities to take measures to encourage and/or facilitate the creation of at least one radio station in Romansch and to ensure that the licensing laws were implemented. Thus, it would appear that the provision of some programming in the RML is not enough to satisfy subparagraph 1b.i; unfortunately, the Committee of Experts did not specify what level of programming would constitute the outlet as a "station" broadcasting in the RML. This question of how much minority-language programming must be broadcast before a radio station can be one which is considered to meet this undertaking is an important one, because subparagraph 1b.ii, an alternative provision that would appear to be "weaker", can be satisfied with some programming in the RMLs. In order for subpara-

---

46. See Austria 2005, 260-1.
47. See Norway 2003, 132.
48. See Switzerland 2004, 122-3.

graph 1b.i to be a meaningful provision, the level of programming in the RML that would distinguish it from subparagraph 1b.ii should be clear.

The Committee of Experts have clarified that it is necessary for the state to take special measures to satisfy subparagraph 1b.i, and that it is not enough to simply create conditions that would permit the creation of a radio station in the RML. In its first report on Denmark, for example, the Committee of Experts noted that the creation of radio stations in German is subject to the same rules as the creation of any radio station in Denmark, and that the authorities would allow the creation of such a station; however, it also found that no measures had been taken specifically to encourage and/or facilitate the creation of such a station, that no German-language radio stations actually existed and that therefore the undertaking was not fulfilled. It was made clear that Denmark had to "take steps" to satisfy this undertaking. Thus, in its first report on Norway, the committee, in concluding that the undertaking had been fulfilled, noted that there existed special schemes for creating private radio and television stations, though it did not specify the nature of these schemes or what it was that made them sufficient.

Subparagraph 1b.ii provides that states will "encourage and/or facilitate" the broadcasting of radio programmes in the RML. First, it appears that the mere existence of such programmes does not, without evidence of state support, satisfy this provision; this was made clear in the Committee of Experts' first report on the UK, where it found that Irish-language broadcasting did in fact take place but, because the UK authorities had not provided evidence of any "public encouragement or assistance" to private radio stations broadcasting in Irish, the undertaking had not been fulfilled.[49] A sense of the sort of measures which this undertaking contemplates was provided in the first report on Hungary, in which the Committee of Experts noted that the state did subsidise radio programmes in minority languages through the Public Foundation for Minorities and that minority self-governments easily obtained licences for radio programmes. However, it also noted that other applications for licences to broadcast programmes in minority languages had to compete on an equal footing with other applicants and minority-language applicants "have difficulties in meeting the same technical standards as commercial networks". On this basis, it found the undertaking was only partly fulfilled. The Committee of Experts commented that a "bonus system" for minority-language applications would be in the spirit of the subparagraph.[50] The committee seems to be suggesting that a licensing process that applies the same standards to all applications is inadequate, and that special measures should be taken to address any particular difficulties that may, in spite of the formal equality of the legal rules, pose

---

49. See United Kingdom 2004, 356-7.
50. See Hungary 2001, 64.

greater practical barriers to minority-language broadcasters. Thus, they seem to suggest that the subparagraph requires that, at a minimum, measures must be taken to ensure *de facto* as well as formal equality. In their second report on Hungary, the Committee of Experts gave some further indication of the sort of measures that could be taken, such as "ear-marked funding" or "minimum requirements for licensing".[51]

A second ambiguity in subparagraph 1b.ii concerns the question of whether a certain minimum amount or quality of programming is required in order to fulfil this undertaking. The Committee of Experts has not had to consider this issue explicitly, but in its report on the UK it noted the views of representatives of speakers of Scottish-Gaelic that private radio programmes were of "weak quality" and that such programmes were "broadcast on less attractive time-slots".[52] The committee went on to indicate that they would welcome more information about the regularity and time of broadcasting of Gaelic programmes for private radio stations, thereby indicating that such matters were indeed relevant in considering whether the obligations had been met. As with other obligations, though, the Committee of Experts was not prescriptive, and it has not provided more detailed guidance on such issues.

One of the interesting aspects of the expansion of the Internet – a medium which barely existed when the Charter was created and whose pervasiveness in the media landscape could not have been adequately foreseen – is that broadcasters are increasingly using their websites as both a platform for distribution of programming and as a means of providing their users with additional information and another means of interaction. In the context of its comments on Sami in radio and television broadcasting in its fourth report on Norway, the Committee of Experts commented on what it described as "interesting information" in relation to new technology, noting that after NRK Sami Radio relaunched its web pages on the website of the state broadcaster NRK, of which it is an arm, the average monthly use increased by about 50%, and that it is now looking to use the website as its main platform for news updates in both Sami and Norwegian.[53]

3.3. Subparagraph 1c

With regard to subparagraph 1c of the Charter, subparagraph 1c.i provides that states must encourage and/or facilitate the creation of at least one television channel in the RML. In addition to the recurrent question of what constitutes "encouragement" and "facilitation", like subparagraph 1a.i and ii, the

---

51. See Hungary 2004, 126.
52. See United Kingdom 2004, 266.
53. Paragraph 195.

undertaking raises the question of what constitutes a television "channel". The Committee of Experts has had the opportunity of considering this undertaking only once, in respect of Denmark. It found in its first report on Denmark that there was no German-language television channel in southern Jutland nor any measures aimed at creating such a channel. They noted that one local public television channel broadcast a 10-minute television programme once a month, and that this would not even fulfil the requirements of subparagraph 1c.ii, a weaker option that will be considered in a moment. Thus, the Committee of Experts has not yet been able to resolve the ambiguities in this subparagraph.

Subparagraph 1c.ii provides that states must encourage and/or facilitate the broadcasting of television programmes in the RML. As discussed above, in relation to subparagraph 1a, it appears that the reference in subparagraph 1a to a "public service mission" is, in spite of the guidance in the Explanatory Report, interpreted as applying to public broadcasters – in the sense of public-sector, state broadcasting agencies – and that private-sector, commercially owned broadcasters – even where they are subject to considerable regulation – will be dealt with under subparagraphs 1b and 1c. In spite of this, the Committee of Experts seems to have considered programming broadcast by public-sector, state broadcasters in determining that the subparagraph 1c.ii undertaking has been satisfied.

In its first report on Finland, for example, the Committee of Experts referred to programmes in Swedish broadcast by the Swedish branch of the National Broadcasting Company[54] and added that some programmes in Sami are broadcast on "national TV". In its first report on Norway, the committee noted, in concluding that Norway had fulfilled its subparagraph 1c.ii undertaking, that NRK Sami Radio is responsible for television programming in Sami;[55] however, it would appear from the same report that NRK Sami Radio is a public broadcaster, and that its contribution to television broadcasting in Sami was also considered in the context of subparagraph 1a.iii.[56] In the second report on Norway, the Committee of Experts no longer referred to the NRK programming, but only to Sami broadcasts by TV2, described as the private national TV channel.[57] Precisely the same difficulty emerged in the first report on Switzerland, where the contribution of SSR Romansch broadcasts was referred to in the consideration of both subparagraphs 1a.iii and 1c.ii; in this case, though, the Committee of Experts noted this fact, and concluded that the Swiss undertaking under subparagraph 1c.ii was therefore not fulfilled. If, however, subparagraph 1c is to be limited to private-sector broadcasters, it would not seem

---

54. Paragraph 105.
55. Paragraph 82.
56. Paragraph 80.
57. Paragraph 133.

appropriate to consider the contribution of public broadcasters to the satisfaction of these commitments; their contribution would presumably be in respect of the satisfactory implementation of subparagraph 1a.

The Committee of Experts has found that the subparagraph 1c.ii undertaking has not been fulfilled where programmes are not broadcast on a regular basis,[58] but once again the committee has not been prescriptive as to what would constitute an acceptable level of regularity to fulfil this undertaking. For example, in the first report on Finland, the Committee of Experts simply noted that programmes in Swedish are broadcast regularly, and made special reference to news programmes being broadcast daily.[59] It would, however, not appear that programmes had to be broadcast on a daily basis to constitute regular programming; again, though, the committee has not been explicit. The importance of the regularity of broadcast is, however, evident in the Committee of Experts' report on the UK, in which they noted that they had not received any information about the regularity of programmes in Scottish-Gaelic broadcast on private TV channels and stated that they would "welcome" such information in the second state report.[60]

Accessibility of broadcasts is also an issue in respect of subparagraph 1c.ii. In its first report on Finland, the Committee of Experts, in finding that the state had not fulfilled its undertakings in respect of Sami, noted that, although there is a Sami-language teletext service which provides daily news and service pages, users complained that the very high fees for decoders were a practical barrier to access.[61] This is yet another case where the committee has demonstrated that it is not acceptable to subject media services in minority languages to extra constraints.[62] In its second report, the Committee of Experts considered that the Finnish undertaking was now "partly fulfilled". They noted that the Finnish Broadcasting Company now broadcast 10-minute daily news programmes five days a week, but also found that there were no children's programmes in Sami; presumably, this gap was one of the reasons that the Committee of Experts concluded that the Finnish obligation was only partly fulfilled, and if this is the case, it also suggests that, in addition to regularity and accessibility of broadcasts, the range of programming, and particularly the availability of children's programmes, is an important consideration. In its report on the UK, the Committee of Experts noted complaints from NGOs that

---

58. See, for example, Finland 2001, 174, which found that Sami programmes were broadcast only on an "occasional basis".
59. See Finland 2001, 105.
60. See United Kingdom 2004, 271.
61. See Finland 2001, 174.
62. See the example quoted above of Hungarian radio, as reflected in Hungary 2004, 122-3.

private TV programmes in Gaelic were being broadcast at a time when they were not easily accessible for most viewers, and stated that they would "welcome" more information about the times of broadcasting for private TV broadcasts in the second state report.[63]

Finally, the Committee of Experts has also not been prescriptive about what sorts of measures constitute "encouragement" or "facilitation" of private TV broadcasts in minority languages. In its first report on the UK, the committee acknowledged that encouragement of Scottish-Gaelic programming was being made through the Broadcasting Act, which established a body to fund Gaelic television programmes, and the provision of funds to this body. However, it also noted that it was not sure of the effects of such encouragement, as no information was provided as to the regularity of programmes.[64] Thus, the Committee of Experts seems to be implying that measures of encouragement had to be accompanied by tangible effects, in terms of programme availability, before the subparagraph 1c.ii undertaking would be considered to have been fulfilled. In its discussion of the difficulties that are actually faced by minority-language television broadcasting in Hungary, the Committee of Experts noted in its first report that, in applying for a broadcasting licence, commercial broadcasters sometimes made promises about the transmission of minority-language programmes, but that these promises were "practically not monitored and enforced"; in spite of concluding that the subparagraph 1c.ii undertaking was fulfilled, it invited the Hungarian authorities to investigate the possibility of including a restricted "must carry" provision in its cable TV licences in order to ensure the retransmission of minority-language programmes. In its second report, the Committee of Experts found that the subparagraph 1c.ii undertaking was not fulfilled. It noted that no "must carry" measures had been introduced and that retransmission of programmes was still perceived as largely unsatisfactory; more significant was its finding that the Hungarian authorities "still seem to lack a coherent and determined policy in this whole area, particularly as far as private stations are concerned", implying that in order to satisfy the undertaking, states should indeed have some articulated policy.[65]

Interestingly, it appears that a state can satisfy its obligations under subparagraph 1c.ii solely through the retransmission of programmes produced and broadcast in another state. In its first report on Sweden, the Committee of Experts found that the Swedish Radio and TV Act provided for terrestrial transmission of a Finnish TV channel in Stockholm, and that the transmission is carried out through an agreement of reciprocity. While noting that this kind of arrangement

---

63. See United Kingdom 2004, 271.
64. Ibid.
65. See Hungary 2004, 129-31.

is "not entirely satisfactory, since, presumably, there is no specific Sweden content on this channel", the Committee of Experts nonetheless concluded that the undertaking was fulfilled.[66] This is a troubling conclusion, because while retransmission of foreign programming is to be encouraged as an important supplementary measure, it should never be the sole manner by which a state satisfies its obligations in respect of any type of minority-language broadcasting.

One further issue of importance is the basis on which the state distributes broadcast licences: the right to distribute licences to broadcast is a powerful tool of the state that can be used also in the domain covered by the Charter, particularly under Article 11 subparagraphs 1b and c. Irrespective of this, there are several cases where this tool seems to operate against fulfilment of undertakings that the states parties have ratified, rather than in support of fulfilment.[67] In the cases cited, the authorities seem to have based their reasoning on a principal commitment to rules of competition for licences. This would mean that the reason that stations broadcasting in RMLs have not got licences is that they were not sufficiently competitive.

It is suggested that an argument of this type blatantly contradicts the spirit of the Charter and also the undertakings that states have accepted by ratifying Article 11 subparagraph 1b.i.[68] The Charter obliges a state party to take positive measures to add to the presence of RMLs in the media. As is clearly stated in the Explanatory Report to the Charter,[69] the media sector as a whole tends to endanger the position of RMLs. By ratifying the Charter, the state party ties itself to policies intended to rectify this influence. In this context, it is against the purpose of the Charter to require applicants for licences to be on an equal competitive footing in situations where no sufficient supply in the RML is available. On the contrary, the Charter requires – in letter and spirit – a proactive role for the state, in line with the requirement to encourage and/or facilitate services in this field. As with many other undertakings under the Charter, this is a question of the right of a state to use positive discrimination as a means of rectifying the situation of an underprivileged group.

A final issue to consider in the context of subparagraphs 1b and c of the Charter is the question of ambiguities in the ratifications of states parties. In particular,

---

66. See Sweden 2003, 242.
67. Cf. United Kingdom 2004, 355-7, in the case of a private radio station broadcasting in Irish; Application of the Charter in Spain 2005, 427-9, in the case of a private radio station broadcasting in the Basque language in Navarra.
68. We recognise that in the Irish case the undertaking was 11.1b.ii, which does not require a state to encourage or facilitate a radio station, only radio programmes, but the line of argument in both cases is very similar.
69. See paragraphs 2, 10 and 107 of the Explanatory Report.

subparagraphs b.ii and c.ii require states parties to encourage and/or facilitate the broadcasting of (respectively) radio and television programmes in RMLs on a regular basis. The Committee of Experts now appears to interpret these obligations as covering exclusively encouragement and/or facilitation of programmes in the private sector, in the light of the fact that public service provision is dealt with under paragraph 1a. It also relies for its interpretation on paragraph 110 of the Charter's Explanatory Report, which provides that "where broadcasting is conceived as a purely private-sector function, the state can do no more than 'encourage and/or facilitate' (sub-paragraphs b and c)".

If a state which is considering ratification of the Charter has broadcasting media carrying out a public service mission, it should bear this interpretative approach in mind when considering whether to undertake obligations under Article 11 subparagraphs 1b and c. It could be argued that the formulation of subpara-graph 1a indicates that, in all cases where a state party has broadcasting media carrying out a public service mission, provisions under subparagraph 1a should be chosen. This also makes sense in practice, as public service broadcasters almost without exception have an obligation to serve different groups in society, including groups speaking different languages. Only in cases where the state party opts for encouraging and/or facilitating broadcasting services (only or also) through private-sector broadcasters who are not under an obligation to carry out a public service mission would the provisions under subparagraphs 1b and c be relevant. It can be argued that the reason for a division between subparagraph 1a and subparagraphs 1b and c lies basically in the position the state party has with respect to its possibilities for setting obligations for the media. In the first case (1a) the state party clearly has power or plays a role in this field and can decide about obligations of the broadcaster. In the latter case (1b and c), the enhancement of the objectives of the Charter can only be carried out with the help of encouragement and/or facilitation.

The situation may, however, remain unclear even if the principle suggested above is followed. Such problems may further increase with new developments in the media sector. Such problems in the application of the Charter arising out of such developments can already be observed. An example is the case of Scottish-Gaelic in the UK.[70] In the UK, public funding has been available to support production of Scottish-Gaelic programming on private-sector radio and television outlets. In addition, the public broadcaster (BBC) provides services in Scottish-Gaelic. It is likely that these types of mixed solutions will increase in the future, either as applied in the UK by earmarked funding, or by inclusion in licensing conditions, as in Switzerland and Spain, and also in Norway. This development may, obviously, blur the scene even more in the future. It is there-

---

70. See United Kingdom 2004, 258-71.

fore most likely that the Committee of Experts will have to accept the emergence of a grey zone between public service broadcasting and private broadcasting.

It should be noted that the qualifying requirement in Article 11 subparagraph 1a is formulated with great foresight to read "to the extent that radio and television carry out a public service mission". It would not be against the formulation of this article to interpret it to cover cases where the public service is placed as an obligation that is arranged by a private broadcaster. Indeed, this would mean that there would be an obvious overlap between undertakings in Article 1 subparagraph 1a on the one hand and in subparagraphs 1b and c on the other. While this may in some cases be cumbersome with regard to consistency in application and monitoring, it would necessarily not form a substantial problem with respect to the objective of the Charter itself, which requires services in the languages in question to be available.

3.4. Subparagraph 1d

Article 11 subparagraph 1d provides that the state is required to encourage and/ or facilitate the production and distribution of audio and audiovisual works in RMLs. In some cases, states have argued that their obligations under this subparagraph have been satisfied on the basis that funding programmes and competitions of general application are also open on equal terms to applications in respect of works in RMLs. The approach taken by the Committee of Experts does not seem to be completely consistent, either in its internal application, or in respect of what it has said in respect of other provisions, such as subparagraph 1c.ii.

For example, in its first report on Croatia, the Committee of Experts noted that no special measures had been taken to encourage or facilitate minority-language productions, but that there were open competitions in which such works could participate on equal terms. It noted that it understood subparagraph 1c.ii as meaning that active measures of support for minority-language productions should be taken. Partly on this basis, then, it concluded that the undertaking was not fulfilled.[71] By contrast, in its first report on Finland, the Committee of Experts noted that the national production aid for audiovisual works in Swedish applied the same criteria as for productions in Finnish, and therefore the undertaking was fulfilled.[72] It is clear from this that there were separate programmes for the two languages and this may have justified the different approach taken; however, it also seems from the committee's comment that the same conditions are applied to both languages. Under subparagraph 1c.ii, however, the Committee of Experts have concluded that provisions in national legislation about content

---

71. See Croatia 2001, 95.
72. See Finland 2001, 106.

of television programming which treat Dutch and Frisian in a formally equal way, by providing that a certain amount of programming must be in either of those languages, do not fulfil the undertaking. The committee stated forcefully that "in this so-called equality between the majority and minority languages, the minority language always loses".[73] This approach seems wholly justified, and therefore the Committee of Experts should take the same strong stance in respect of all provisions in Article 11 (and elsewhere under the Charter), and require special measures of support for minority languages in order to satisfy provisions such as subparagraph 1d.

The Committee of Experts has also made clear that special means of support must be directed at the minority languages themselves, and not merely to benefit those in areas where speakers of such languages tend to be found. In their first report on Sweden, for example, the Committee of Experts noted that the state had created a regional resource centre for film and video production and a regional film production centre in a county in which Sami-speakers tend to be found. The Committee of Experts noted, though, that it was not clear to what extent the regional resource centre had a specific remit in respect of producing and/or distributing Sami-language works, and therefore considered that it was not in a position to say whether the undertaking had been fulfilled.[74]

3.5. Subparagraph 1e

Subparagraph 1e.i provides that states undertake to encourage and/or facilitate the creation and/or maintenance of at least one newspaper in the RML. In addition to the ambiguity which surrounds phrases like "encourage and/or facilitate", what precisely constitutes a "newspaper" within the meaning of this provision is also unclear. Certainly, not all printed publications will constitute "newspapers". In its second report on Finland, for example, the Committee of Experts distinguished between a "newspaper" and a "periodical", though it did not specify what the difference was.[75] Although a daily newspaper in the RML would clearly qualify under this subparagraph, the Committee of Experts has made clear that less frequent, though regular, publications would also qualify. For example, in its first report on Hungary, the Committee of Experts found "weekly or biweekly newspapers" satisfactory.[76] In its first report on Slovenia, the Committee of Experts found that the undertaking was fulfilled for Hungarian on the basis that the government co-financed a weekly newspaper, a literary periodical and an almanac. It is not clear, however, whether the undertaking

---

73. See the Netherlands 2004, 160.
74. See Sweden 2003, 135.
75. See Finland 2004, 146.
76. See Hungary 2001, 66.

would have been considered fulfilled if the authorities had funded only the literary periodical and the almanac. In its report on the UK, the Committee of Experts found, in concluding that the UK had fulfilled its undertaking in respect of Welsh under subparagraph 1e.i, that there were a number of "periodical news publications available in Welsh", making reference to some which appeared weekly, to a monthly "current affairs magazine", and to local newspapers – or, the Committee of Experts added, "news sheets" – which appeared on mostly a monthly basis.[77] Again, though, it is not clear whether the Committee of Experts would have concluded that the undertaking had been fulfilled by, say, the monthly "news sheets" or the monthly "current affairs magazine" alone, without the weekly publications. The Committee of Experts also noted that the non-existence of a daily newspaper in Welsh was "anomalous", considering other RMLs in Europe which "are in a similar position to Welsh in the UK".[78]

In its second report on Austria, the Committee of Experts appeared to clarify matters somewhat. Reiterating the position it had taken in the first report on Austria, it concluded that a monthly magazine in Hungarian published in Burgenland did not qualify as a newspaper for the purposes of subparagraph 1e[79] and, in a box recommendation, the committee encouraged the authorities to encourage and/or facilitate the creation of at least one newspaper in Hungarian. In its first report on Serbia, the Committee of Experts first also appeared to clarify matters: it stated that "normally, a 'newspaper' has to be published at least weekly" and noted that this was the case for all of Serbia's Part III languages except three. However, it arguably clouded matters once again with its comments on those other three languages. It noted that, with respect to one of them, Bosnian, there were four monthly publications and a quarterly publication, for another, Romani, there was a fortnightly and a monthly publication, and for the last of them, Ukrainian, there were three monthly and two quarterly publications, and that most of these publications received public support. It concluded that Serbia's obligations under subparagraph 1e in respect of these languages had also been fulfilled, based on "the concrete circumstances" – presumably, the relatively small size of the linguistic communities in question, although this was not made explicit – and in particular the number of publications supported.[80] Subsequently, the position appears to have changed again somewhat, when in their second report on Armenia, the Committee of Experts recalled that "the definition of a newspaper is a publication issued at least once a week".[81] So, if a publication appears monthly, it may not qualify, but if it appears less frequently, but is one of several periodical

---

77. See United Kingdom 2004, 164.
78. Ibid., 165.
79. Paragraphs 336-8. See also Czech Republic 2009, 301.
80. Paragraph 267.
81. Paragraph 186. See also Slovakia 2009, 136.

publications, taken as a whole they may satisfy the requirements of the subparagraph. As a result, it is clear that the Committee of Experts has identified a range of print media, differing in frequency of publication and in content, but relevant under this subparagraph. A publication qualifies as a "newspaper" for the purposes of this provision if it is published on a weekly basis; if it is published less frequently than that, it may still qualify, depending on the circumstances. However, what distinguishes a "newspaper" from a "news sheet" or a "periodical" has not been made explicit. Further clarification of the question of frequency and of content would be welcome.

A second issue here is the extent to which the newspaper must be published only in the RML in order to satisfy the subparagraph. In most cases, this has not been considered, and it is likely that most of the newspapers which the Committee of Experts considered were overwhelmingly or exclusively in the RML. In its finding in the first Swedish report that Sweden had not satisfied its undertaking under subparagraph 1e.i in respect of Meänkieli, the committee noted that there was a trilingual newspaper, in Swedish, Finnish and Meänkieli, but that the Meänkieli content was "very small". Reference was also made to a cultural magazine, which was about 50% in Meänkieli.[82] The Committee of Experts encouraged the authorities to explore the possibilities of establishing "a newspaper in Meänkieli". Yet, it is still not clear that this undertaking requires a newspaper to be exclusively in the RML; if some content in the majority language is permitted, the question which has not yet been resolved is that of how much content must be in the RML.

With regard to what constitutes "encouragement" and "facilitation", the Committee of Experts have repeatedly recognised that most newspapers written in RMLs are not commercially viable, and therefore the provision of state subsidies to enable the publication of such newspapers is perhaps the most common means by which the undertaking in subparagraph 1e.i is fulfilled.[83] The first report on Denmark illustrated that other means of "encouragement" and "facilitation" were possible: in this report, the Committee of Experts made reference to public announcements of central, regional or local authorities – presumably, advertising by public bodies – and regretted the decrease in such announcements, recommending that the Danish authorities assess their public information policy.[84] We have seen before, however, that the committee expects measures taken in pursuit of undertakings to be effective. Thus, in concluding in the second report on

---

82. See Sweden 2003, 360-1.
83. See, for example, Hungary 2001, 66; Norway 2001, 84; Switzerland 2001, 145, in respect of Romansch; United Kingdom 2004, 164 and 360, in respect of Welsh and Irish; and Denmark 2004, 92.
84. See Denmark 2004, 92.

Finland that the state had not fulfilled its obligation under subparagraph 1e.i in respect of Sami, the committee noted that, though the government granted annual subsidies to newspapers upon application, these did not seem adequate, as no Sami newspaper actually existed.[85] The increasing financial difficulties being faced by the Romansch daily in Switzerland led the Committee of Experts to emphasise that fulfilment of the Swiss undertaking was at risk and to encourage the Swiss authorities "to look into ways of ensuring that one newspaper in Romansch continues to exist".[86] The focus on effectiveness of state measures led the committee to conclude in its first report on Slovenia that the financial support provided by Slovenia to several Italian-language printed media fulfilled the undertaking, even though most of these were actually published in Croatia and received most of their subsidy (80%) from the Croatian authorities.[87] In some of the committee's more recent reports, there is emerging the suggestion that state support should be systematic and perhaps formalised; thus, in the second report on Slovakia, the Committee of Experts urged the authorities to create a legal basis for continued support of newspapers in RMLs.

Increasingly, newspapers publish much or all of what appears in the traditional paper format online on the paper's website. In its third report on the UK, the Committee of Experts reported that a proposal in 2008 for a subsidy to be provided by the Welsh Assembly government for the creation of a daily Welsh-language newspaper had been delayed, owing to political opposition, and that instead a small amount had been given to a Welsh-language publication to create an online news service.[88] The Committee of Experts emphasised that the employment of new technologies in this way is "a valuable contribution to the fulfilment of this undertaking" but they still encouraged the authorities to pursue further the idea of a printed daily Welsh-language newspaper "as this seems to be a wish of the Welsh-speakers".[89]

Subparagraph 1e.ii contains the slightly less demanding undertaking of encouraging and/or facilitating the publication of "newspaper articles" in the RML. In some of its discussion of this undertaking, the committee has provided further information about what constitutes a "newspaper". To fulfil the undertaking, the articles to which the subparagraph refers must appear in "newspapers". In its first report on Sweden, for example, the Committee of Experts, in finding that the state had not fulfilled its undertaking under subparagraph 1e.ii in respect of Sami, noted that there were two Sami "magazines", but that, in addition to being almost

---

85. See Finland 2004, 146.
86. See Switzerland 2004, 130.
87. See Slovenia 2004, 217.
88. Paragraph 195.
89. Ibid.

exclusively in Swedish, they were "periodicals" and "not newspapers".[90] Again, the Committee of Experts did not make explicit the difference between such publications, although it clearly contemplates that such a difference exists. Given the fact that subparagraph 1e.ii does not require the newspaper to be in the RML, but only that articles in that language appear in it, it is difficult to interpret the import of the Committee of Experts' comment that the publications were "almost exclusively in Swedish". This comment would seem to suggest that the minority language content must be more than simply symbolic, but the minimum threshold of content required for a finding that an "article" has been published remains unclear. If, for example, a newspaper was "almost exclusively" in the majority language, but contained an article in the RML, on what basis would this not fulfil the requirements of the subparagraph?

In its report on the UK, the Committee of Experts noted that a Gaelic organisation funded by the government publishes a "Gaelic-only newspaper", but noted that, according to information provided by speakers of Scottish-Gaelic, this was not a "newspaper" but a "periodical published monthly". The Committee of Experts went on to note that, although this paper and other publications were "much esteemed", "they do not provide support for daily readership in Scottish Gaelic". It is suggested that this final comment may confuse matters somewhat; even under the heavier obligation in respect of "newspapers" contained in subparagraph 1e.i, the Committee of Experts has accepted that a weekly or even biweekly newspaper could qualify, so the reference here to "daily readership" is perplexing. It is important to note that the committee did not refer to a daily publication, and it is understood that, in its view, what was important was that the publication be available frequently enough that, even if it was not produced daily, it could provide useful reading material on a daily basis. A weekly publication might, for example, fill this role. This might be an appropriate approach to take, but the use of the word "daily" may cause some confusion, and may lead states and others seeking to implement the treaty to suppose that a daily publication is being referred to. Thus, the committee may wish to clarify this, when the opportunity presents itself.

With regard to what constitutes "encouragement" and/or "facilitation", the Committee of Experts has indicated that state action must take place: in its first report on the UK, for example, it found that, although newspaper articles in Gaelic appear regularly in some local or regional newspapers, it had no information about whether such articles were supported by any measures taken by the authorities, and therefore they were not in a position to conclude whether the undertaking had been fulfilled.[91] This seems to imply that the existence of

90. See Sweden 2003, 137.
91. See United Kingdom 2004, 277.

articles in the RML, without the existence of any state support, is not sufficient to fulfil the requirements of the undertaking. The Committee of Experts has also indicated that more is required in order to fulfil this undertaking than merely demonstrating that the state guarantees the basic requirement of freedom to publish in RMLs; rather, positive measures are required.[92]

Among the means available to provide support in the field of media, activities by the authorities themselves may have immediate consequences in the media market. One such practice would be advertising in RML newspapers and on private radio and television stations or programmes that are broadcast in these languages. Such practices can have multiple effects. First of all, such practices have an information value, by reaching out to the population speaking the language in question. Secondly, they indicate recognition by the authorities of the value of communication in this language. Thirdly, they provide direct financial revenue in the form of an advertising income for the media. While there are no express regulations in this field, the principle which has been applied elsewhere by the Committee of Experts, that the Charter would require RMLs to be treated at least equally with mainstream media, should apply. If discriminatory practices are introduced, they should operate to the advantage of the underprivileged, not to their detriment. In this respect, then, the Committee of Experts, in their monitoring activity, should start to pay particular attention to how practices in this field have developed and, if necessary,[93] take resolute action to enhance practices that are in favour of media produced in RMLs.

It would appear that the Committee of Experts has gradually arrived at an opinion that the requirement under subparagraph 1e to "encourage and/or facilitate" requires a stricter demonstration of active measures by the state party than was evident in earlier reports. As an example, in its first report on Spain, with respect to Catalan in the Balearic Islands, the Committee of Experts stated:

> According to the limited information received by the Committee of Experts, there is one newspaper published in Catalan in the Balearic Islands, i.e. the "Diario de Baleares". It is however unclear what measures the competent authorities are taking to encourage and/or facilitate its maintenance. The Committee of Experts is therefore not in a position to conclude on this undertaking and encourages the Spanish authorities to clarify this point in their next periodical report.[94]

We would also refer to the argumentation in the same report with respect to Galician: "The Committee of Experts considers that this undertaking is fulfilled but would welcome further information, in the next periodical report, on the type

---

92. See Croatia 2001, 97.
93. Cf. Spain 2005, 573.
94. Paragraph 700.

and amount of support concretely granted to 'O Correo Galego' and to 'A nosa Terra'."[95] Comparing this ruling to earlier rulings on the same article, for example in the first report on Finland, there is a clear difference in approach: "Several newspapers are published in Swedish. Most of them appear more than once a week. The Committee considers this undertaking fulfilled."[96] In the Finnish case, there were subsidies for the press and they were relatively generous for Swedish-language newspapers. The interesting observation is, however, that this was not mentioned in the argumentation leading up to the conclusion that the undertaking had been fulfilled; the committee appeared to have accepted that the end result as such was acceptable, irrespective of how it had been accomplished.

The development in this field should be studied with attention to the requirements placed on the state party in all situations where it in one way or another has bound itself by undertakings in a particular field. It appears as if the committee has arrived at the conclusion that a state that has ratified a particular article in each case should demonstrate activity in line with the undertaking. If the situation on the ground does not require encouragement and/or facilitation, the state cannot consider fulfilling an undertaking by simply sitting on the side and watching things go by themselves. This does not qualify as fulfilment, irrespective of the fact that the situation as such may be satisfactory; the state must actually do something.

The position which the Committee of Experts has developed in later reports appears to be reasonable and consistent, and potentially quite important. As unfortunately has been the case for many languages, changes in the media field have also led to deterioration of services in the media sector. The state party must be encouraged to maintain alertness in this field and to keep the necessary instruments required intact, in order to be able to take active measures to encourage and/or facilitate, if required. In most cases, this would involve instruments of licensing for broadcast media in the private sector, and/or economic supports for broadcast media and the press. A state party that has signed an undertaking can, indeed, be expected to demonstrate its ability to fulfil it in order to secure the desired results.

The arguments raised by different states (such as Germany in its second report) that the state would have very limited scope for intervention in this area are fully dealt with in the Explanatory Report to the Charter,[97] and in the second report on Germany by the Committee of Experts itself (Finding S), and can be disregarded. Likewise, the argument presented by the Swedish authorities in the first periodical report, or the Finnish authorities in the second periodical report, that there are

---

95. Paragraph 958.
96. Paragraph 112.
97. See the Explanatory Report, paragraph 107.

(general) subsidies available for the press and that the Sami could avail themselves of these is comprehensively dealt with in the first report on Sweden[98] and the second report on Finland,[99] and can be disregarded.

3.6. Subparagraph 1f

With regard to Article 11.1f, subparagraph 1f.i obliges states to cover the additional costs of those media which use RMLs. Perhaps the most difficult issue here is the determination of what constitutes the "additional costs" referred to, and the Committee of Experts has been able to provide only limited guidance. In its first report on Hungary, the committee acknowledged that whether the amount of money allocated to minority language media is really sufficient to cover the additional costs of such media "is not clear", recognising that it is "difficult to quantify such additional costs". The fact that Hungary had made "serious efforts" to secure the financial basis of the minority-language media was considered by the committee to be sufficient.[100] Another big issue is whether measures which had been considered by the Committee of Experts in assessing whether another Article 11 provision had been fulfilled should also be considered in determining whether this particular provision had been fulfilled. It appears that the Committee of Experts is willing to accept such "double counting", as it found the subparagraph 1f.i undertaking to have been fulfilled even where the measures had been referred to elsewhere by the state in question.[101]

Subparagraph 1f.ii obliges states to apply existing measures for financial assistance to audiovisual productions in the RML. The question of double counting – just referred to in the context of subparagraph 1f.i – also exists under this provision and, as was the case under that subparagraph, the Committee of Experts seems to tolerate this.[102] Reference has also been made to the principle of "effectiveness" of measures, which underpins the approach taken by the committee in assessing compliance with several Article 11 undertakings: in particular, does the measure in question have any actual impact? In the context of subparagraph 1f.ii, the Committee of Experts seems to take an approach that departs somewhat from this principle of effectiveness. For example, in its first report on Sweden, the Committee of Experts concluded in respect of Sami that where financial assistance of a general nature was, in principle, available to audiovisual works in Sami, the undertaking was "formally" fulfilled, even though there were no examples of

---

98. See Sweden 2003, 136-40.
99. See Finland 2004, 146.
100. See Hungary 2001, 67.
101. See, for example, Hungary 2001, 67; Switzerland 2001, 147 (re Romansch); Sweden 2003, 248 (re Finnish).
102. See, for example, United Kingdom 2004, 279; and Sweden 2003, 141, in respect of Sami.

Sami works that had in fact benefited.[103] They came to the same conclusion with Meänkieli. Similarly, in its first report on the Netherlands, the Committee of Experts noted that there was a national fund for the promotion of cultural broadcasting and, even though "practice shows it to be very difficult for Frisian productions to obtain funding" from this fund, it considered the undertaking "formally" fulfilled. A similar approach was taken in the second report on the Netherlands.[104] Likewise in its report on the UK, the committee noted that, though there were no specific measures for Irish-language productions, these were eligible for assistance from funding sources of general application. Despite hearing evidence that only one Irish script had been financed by this scheme in the last five years, they considered the undertaking to be fulfilled.[105]

3.7. Subparagraph 1g

Subparagraph 1g obliges states to support the training of journalists and other staff for media using RMLs. The Committee of Experts has made clear that specific schemes are required in order to fulfil this undertaking. For example, in its first report on Hungary, the committee noted that the state grants scholarships to minority-language students for studies at Hungarian universities and training institutions and for stays abroad, but that the lack of specific schemes for training minority-language journalists had resulted in a lack of qualified journalists.[106] Thus it concluded that the undertaking was only partly fulfilled and encouraged the Hungarian authorities to establish a scheme for training minority-language journalists. In the report on the UK, the Committee of Experts explored other aspects of what specificity implied. It noted in respect of Scottish-Gaelic the existence at the Gaelic College of a "broad course in television and media", but noted that the course was "not specifically directed towards the training of journalists"; thus they concluded that the undertaking was only partly fulfilled.[107] In respect of Irish, the committee noted in-house training of journalists at the BBC and a pilot training course in Irish-language television and film production, but because of a "lack of continuity" in the courses supported and a shortage of courses focusing "specifically on journalism" the Committee of Experts concluded that the undertaking was only partly fulfilled.[108]

---

103. See Sweden 2003, 141-3.
104. See the Netherlands 2004, 161-3.
105. See United Kingdom 2004, 362-4.
106. See Hungary 2001, 68.
107. See United Kingdom 2004, 280-1.
108. Ibid., 366.

3.8. Paragraph 2

Paragraph 2 of Article 11 contains a number of separate provisions, focusing primarily on cross-border media provision; there is also a provision which echoes the ECHR protection for freedom of expression, subject to the same conditions as are imposed under the ECHR. In spite of the wide ratification of this provision by states which are parties to the Charter, the Committee of Experts has generally found few difficulties in its implementation, and therefore any ambiguities inherent in the provision. Difficulties have been identified on only a few occasions. In its first report on Finland, for example, the Committee of Experts noted with respect to Sami that, although Norwegian and Swedish radio stations collaborated with the Sami Radio, television programmes from Norway or Sweden could not be received and were very rarely transmitted. In spite of this, the committee found that Finland had fulfilled the undertaking, but it considered that, in view of the significant costs of production of programmes in Sami languages, every effort should be made to enable programmes in Sami from Norway and Sweden to be received in Finland, and they suggested that the Finnish authorities provide the necessary means to support the Nordic Sami TV Channel.

This comment raises an interesting issue. As noted in section 3.1, above, the Explanatory Report makes clear that such positive measures of support are implied by the paragraph 2 undertaking. It is a matter of interpretation in each case separately whether, if cross-border transmission is successfully taking place, this qualifies as sufficient or whether further steps should be taken.

In its first report on the Ukraine, the Committee of Experts indicated that it had been informed that foreign programmes distributed in the Ukraine via cable networks must have their programmes dubbed or translated into Ukrainian. The committee concluded that such dubbing or translation of programmes "is not in conformity with the present undertaking".[109]

3.9. Paragraph 3

Finally, paragraph 3 of Article 11 obliges states to ensure that the interests of users of RMLs are represented or taken into account within those bodies responsible for guaranteeing the freedom and pluralism of the media. As noted in section 3.1, above, one of the main difficulties in this provision is the reference to bodies "responsible for guaranteeing freedom and pluralism of the media"; it is not clear, for example, whether a state broadcaster would necessarily qualify. This problem is evident in the first report of the Committee of Experts on Finland. In concluding that this paragraph was satisfied for Swedish-speakers and not for the Sami, the

---

109. Paragraph 562.

Committee of Experts made reference to the Board of Directors of the Finnish Broadcasting Company, the state broadcaster. The Committee of Experts made clear that this board is "a parliamentary body supervising the programme objectives and projects and their support" (they may, in fact, have been referring to the administrative council of the company, rather than the board of directors). In any case, the body referred to seems to be something like the content board of a state broadcaster, which seems rather narrower than a body that "guarantees the freedom and pluralism of the media".[110]

In other reports the Committee of Experts has sought to clarify this distinction. In its first report on Hungary, for example, in finding that the undertaking was fulfilled, the committee noted that the minorities were entitled to delegate one representative to the Hungarian Public Television and the Hungarian Public Radio boards of trustees; the Committee of Experts then clarified that both these boards "may be qualified as bodies with a responsibility for guaranteeing the freedom and pluralism of the media". In the first report on Switzerland, the committee found that representation of Romansch-speakers in the decision-making bodies of SSR, the national radio and television undertaking, was not sufficient, and contrasted this with "bodies responsible for guaranteeing the freedom and pluralism of the media", of which the committee found that they had no evidence. Thus there seems to be some difference of approach being taken here by the Committee of Experts. The difficulty of determining the nature of the regulatory body in question was highlighted in the committee's report on the UK in respect of Welsh. The Committee of Experts referred to a number of bodies which undertake activities in the field, and noted that most would, as a result of 2003 legislation, be merged into one organisation, OFCOM, which was preparing a Welsh-language scheme. The committee noted that, while such a scheme could result in the provision by OFCOM of Welsh-language services, it did not ensure representation of the language in the organisation. Given that it had no information on how the interests of users of Welsh would be taken into account in OFCOM, it was unable to conclude whether the undertaking was fulfilled.[111]

It is suggested that a functional approach should be taken here, in line with the proper principles of treaty interpretation. What this provision seems to be aiming at is to ensure representation on bodies which themselves have some role in ensuring that minority views and minority languages can gain access to the media. Where there is a powerful state broadcaster or a powerful regulatory body which has the power to regulate not all, but at least some of the state's most important media, representation in the decision-making process of that body is what the Committee of Experts should aim at. Once again,

---

110. See Finland 2001, 179.
111. See United Kingdom 2004, 169-70.

the assumptions on which the rather different approaches to fulfilment of paragraph 3 have been taken should be made more explicit. In its second report on Croatia, though, the Committee of Experts did provide very useful guidance as to what sort of representation was required to fulfil the undertaking. There they noted that implementation of paragraph 3 does not require that each individual Part III language should have its own representative on the bodies in question, but it does require that "adequate systems or processes exist to ensure that the interests of speakers of each Part III language are in fact represented or taken into account".[112] Thus, we see here once again the prime importance of the principle of effectiveness in the work of the Committee of Experts.

4. Good practice

On the basis of our analysis, in conclusion we present some definitions and interpretations with a particular focus on the media that interested states parties, NGOs or others interested in this aspect of the Charter may find helpful in their work.

The application of the various paragraphs and subparagraphs in Article 11 is complicated by a number of factors. First, as discussed in section 2.2, above, the treaty provisions contain a number of ambiguities which require clarification and interpretation. Second, the situation of RMLs to which these provisions are applied can differ greatly, and the provisions must be applied in a way that responds to these differences without losing their coherence. Third, as discussed in section 2.1, the nature of the media is itself changing rapidly, in terms of ownership – in particular, the role of the state – in terms of structure, in terms of the regulatory environment, and in terms of technology; in all cases, treaty provisions that were drafted mainly in the late 1980s must respond to a very different media environment. On the basis of our analysis, we present some conclusions that those parties involved in the process of implementation and monitoring of the Charter might find helpful.

Regarding the terms "radio station" and "television channel", the core question is access on an equal basis for each speaker covered by the provision of the Charter. Another aspect of the terms "station" or "channel" has to do with the quantity and quality of programming offered. With regard to content requirements, at least news, information and content carrying cultural expression would have to be given a prominent role in the programming. It would also have to be of a quality that secures its attractiveness in comparison with competing programme supply in other languages. With regard to quantity, we point to the ongoing development of new and targeted radio and television services in the majority languages aimed specifically at serving special audience segments. In this context,

---

112. See Croatia 2005, 180.

it is particularly important that the services in minority languages are developed in a way that caters for availability of programming that can serve such functions in these languages, particularly for children and young people.

Regarding the term "programmes", the core question is servicing the basic needs of a language. Benchmarking here could specify that "programmes" include elements of all the following: news, information and cultural expression. Another aspect of "programmes" has to do with frequency and the length of the broadcasts. Benchmarking here could make reference to regularity and predictability of the broadcasts, with at least a weekly presence but preferably a daily one. Benchmarking the programme length could specify a minimum daily news broadcast of the same nature as that which serves the majority population. A third requirement has to do with scheduling of programmes, where different strategies may be employed to best serve the audience speaking the RML. In any case, broadcasting during or in proximity to peak hours and during normal viewing or listening hours would be required.

Regarding the term "audiovisual production", in the light of recent media developments, this concept should be interpreted widely. It would therefore include not only radio and television, film, video and DVD productions, and so forth, but also multimedia productions of various kinds, as well as Internet-based services and any transformations of traditional audiovisual or print media to be offered in equal or similar forms on new platforms, including mobile communication technology when used for functions that are similar to media.

A "newspaper" within the meaning of Article 11 subparagraph e.i would denote a printed product that appears frequently and regularly, with a capacity to cover news occurring in the society that this newspaper serves. Benchmarking in this respect could be based on the obligations of the Minority Daily Newspaper organisation MIDAS,[113] which requires of its members a publication frequency of at least three times a week. Any reduction below these levels would have to be qualified. A further requirement would be a capacity to deal with, and a focus on, current events. It is unlikely that a publication appearing less than once a week would be sufficient to qualify in this respect. An entertainment- or tourism-promotion focus is inconsistent with the notion of a "newspaper", which would be required to provide the population in the area with content that enhances its capacity to participate in society and the public sphere. Article 11 subparagraph 1f.ii requires the states parties to apply existing measures for financial assistance also to "audiovisual productions" in RMLs. We would interpret this term in such a way that this obligation would also apply to electronic versions of the newspapers on the Web.

---

113. European Association of Daily Newspapers in Minority and Regional Languages (www. midas-press.org).

With reference to the term "additional costs" of media, as used in Article 11 subparagraph 1f.i, we find this section to mean that RML media should be treated fairly by funding schemes available which provide media subsidies. Particular attention should be given to the requirements of minority media in order for them to be competitive, in terms of quality, with mainstream media.

With respect to the term "journalists and other staff", within the meaning of Article 11 paragraph 1g, the questions of who constitutes "journalists" and what sorts of job are covered by "other staff" has so far been answered in very few cases in the assessments of the Committee of Experts. In most states, regular education of journalists in RMLs is either non-existent or very scarce. In accordance with the spirit of the Charter, we interpret this undertaking to mean that training of journalists in the languages is provided for in the same way and to the same extent as for the majority. In addition, further professional training can be provided in order to keep up professional and language skills. Other staff would include persons that form the relevant professional production milieu.

With regard to the phrase "[to] guarantee freedom of direct reception of radio and television broadcasts" from neighbouring countries, which appears in Article 11 paragraph, 2, obstacles in media transmission and reception may be of several kinds. There are technical issues as well as juridical issues that may hamper media transmission and reception. In view of the strong support given in the Explanatory Report to the enhancement in all instances of cross-border viewing (Article 7 subparagraph 1i; Article 14), the question of raising obstacles in media transmission and reception or accepting that such obstacles occur for one reason or another (for example, digitalisation of broadcasting, limitation of Internet content) must be taken seriously. The states parties would be required to actively work in order to remove any such barriers.

Articles 12 and 14 have so far been applied rather haphazardly to media issues, and we feel that this is obviously due to sparse reporting of the situation on the ground in the periodical reports. We suggest that the states parties implementing the Charter better observe that measures in the field of media are expected also to be included under these paragraphs. Developments in the field of media spill over into questions relating to cultural activities and facilities, and transfrontier exchanges. A particular concern in this respect is that media technology is becoming increasingly digitised, which will affect requirements under the provisions of both these articles.

5. Conclusions

Our analysis shows that there is a predominance of attention paid to broadcast media in the Committee of Experts' reports and Committee of Ministers' recommendations.[114] This predominance is consistent, whether we study the absolute number of observations or the numbers relative to the amount of ratifications in each category. The imbalance remains, whether we look at share of boxes and findings of the Committee of Experts or recommendations of the Committee of Ministers. The newspaper sector, in absolute numbers, gets second-most attention in the Committee of Experts' reports.

In spite of numerous ratifications, audiovisual works are almost not referred to at all. Also, the representation of RMLs in bodies with responsibility for freedom of the media and the existence of training for journalists were matters which were rarely given salience in the Committee of Experts' reports. Regarding the relative importance of this sector (particularly new media and youth-oriented media) the parties could, indeed, pay more attention to this field in the future.

There are relatively few ratifications for representation of RMLs in bodies responsible for freedom of the media, or for training of journalists. Looking at the reports, we find little information about how these features are arranged in states parties, which leads us to expect that much could still be done in this field. However, with some exceptions, this fact is not reflected in the boxes and findings of the Committee of Experts or recommendations of the Council of Ministers. The parties should pay attention to obvious shortcomings in this field.

There are two aspects to the provision on representation of RMLs in bodies responsible for freedom of the media which make things somewhat unclear. The first is that the sort of regulatory body described in the Charter itself may not correspond with the regulatory regime for the media which actually exists; and this ambiguity in the treaty itself could be clarified by some statement of policy clarifying the sorts of regulatory bodies which might be covered.

To sum up our analysis of the treatment of undertakings under Article 11 (boxes and findings of the Committee of Experts and recommendations of the Committee of Ministers), we find that the level of attention to this field in the Charter appears to be quite high and consistent. We do, however, find it to be skewed towards the presence of the media in general, and particularly broad-casting media. We find that the parties should give more attention to new media and the discussion of audiovisual production. We also raise the question of whether observations regarding representation of RMLs in bodies responsible for freedom of the media, and regarding training of journalists and other staff are adequately reflected in all the cases covered by these provisions.

---

114. See also T. Moring and R. Dunbar (2008), *The European Charter ... and the media*, Table 1.

We have noted that the Committee of Experts has generally sought to avoid being prescriptive in the application of Article 11 provisions. While, for example, it has, through its practice, provided concrete examples of actions which might be considered to amount to "encouragement" or "facilitation", it has not sought to specify in a prescriptive way what measures must be taken to constitute "encouragement" or "facilitation". In our view, this approach is commendable. It would be inappropriate and, perhaps, not possible to specifically enumerate measures which would have to be taken in the context of the considerable differences that exist between the various RMLs to which the European Charter will be applied.

References

Busch, Brigitta (2004), *Sprachen im Disput. Medien und Öffentlichkeit in multilingualen Gesellschaften*, Drava Diskurs No. 13. Klagenfurt: Drava.

European Convention on Human Rights.

Fishman, Joshua A. (2001), "From theory to practice (and vice versa): review, reconsideration and reiteration" in Joshua A. Fishman (ed.), *Can threatened languages be saved? Reversing language shift, revisited: a 21st century perspective*. Clevedon: Multilingual Matters, pp. 451-83, at 473-4.

Lowe, Gregory Ferrell and Nissen, Christian S. (eds) (2011), *Small among giants: television broadcasting in smaller countries*. Göteborg: Nordicom.

Moring, Tom (2007) "Functional completeness in minority language media" in Mike Cormack and Niamh Hourigan (eds), *Minority language media: concepts, critiques and case studies*. Clevedon: Multilingual Matters.

Moring, Tom and Dunbar, Robert (2008), *The European Charter for Regional or Minority Languages and the media*, Regional or Minority Languages, No. 6. Strasbourg: Council of Europe Publishing.

Moring, Tom and Godenhjelm, Sebastian (2011), "Broadcasting for minorities in big and small countries" in Gregory Ferrell Lowe and Christian S. Nissen (eds), *Small among giants: television broadcasting in smaller countries*. Göteborg: Nordicom.

Moring, Tom and Husband, Charles (2007), "The contribution of Swedish-language media in Finland to linguistic vitality", *International Journal of the Sociology of Language*, No. 187/188, pp. 75-101.

OSCE (2003), *Guidelines on the use of minority languages in the broadcast media.*

"Report by the Committee of Experts of the European Charter for Regional or Minority Languages on the third monitoring cycle on the Application of the Charter in Germany", ECRML (2008) 4.

Vienna Convention on the Law of Treaties.

Appendix: Ratifications

Article 11		
Paragraph and subparagraph		
1	a.i	**Slovenia:** Italian, Hungarian **Spain:** Basque, Catalan, Valencian, Galician **Switzerland:** Italian **United Kingdom:** Welsh (Wales)
	a.ii	**Hungary:** Romani **Poland:** Belarusian, Czech, Hebrew, Yiddish, Karaim, Kashub, Lithuanian, Lemko, German, Armenian, Romani, Russian, Slovak, Tatar, Ukrainian **Romania:** Hungarian **United Kingdom:** Scottish-Gaelic (Scotland)
	a.iii	**Armenia:** Assyrian, Yezidi, Greek, Russian, Kurdish **Bosnia and Herzegovina:** Albanian, Montenegrin, Czech, Italian, Hungarian, Macedonian, German, Polish, Romani, Romanian, Rysin, Slovak, Slovenian, Turkish, Ukrainian and Jewish (Yiddish and Ladino) **Croatia:** Italian, Serbian, Hungarian, Czech, Slovak, Ruthenian, Ukrainian **Czech Republic:** Polish (Moravian-Silesian region), Slovak **Finland:** Saami, Swedish **Hungary:** Croatian, German, Romanian, Serbian, Slovak, Slovenian, Beás **Montenegro:** Albanian, Romani **Netherlands:** Frisian (Friesland) **Norway:** Sami **Poland:** Belarusian, Czech, Hebrew, Yiddish, Karaim, Kashub, Lithuanian, Lemko, German, Armenian, Romani, Russian, Slovak, Tatar, Ukrainian **Romania:** Bulgarian. Czech, Croatian, German, Russian, Serbian, Slovak, Turkish, Ukrainian **Serbia:** Albanian, Bosnian, Bulgarian, Hungarian, Romani, Romanian, Ruthenian, Slovakian, Ukrainian, Croatian **Slovak Republic:** Bulgarian, Croatian, Czech, German, Polish, Romani, Ruthenian, Ukrainian, Hungarian **Sweden:** Sami, Finnish, Meänkieli **Switzerland:** Romansh **Ukraine:** Belarusian, Bulgarian, Gagauz, Greek, Jewish, Crimean Tatar, Moldovan, German, Polish, Russian, Romanian, Slovak, Hungarian **United Kingdom:** Irish (Northern Ireland)
	b.i	**Bosnia and Herzegovina:** Albanian, Montenegrin, Czech, Italian, Hungarian, Macedonian, German, Polish, Romani, Romanian, Rysin, Slovak, Slovenian, Turkish, Ukrainian and Jewish (Yiddish and Ladino) **Denmark:** German (Southern Jutland) **Finland:** Sami, Swedish **Germany:** Romani (*Land* Berlin) **Norway:** Sami **Romania:** Hungarian **Spain:** Basque, Catalan, Valencian, Galician **Switzerland:** Romansh

419

b.ii		**Armenia:** Assyrian, Yezidi, Greek, Russian, Kurdish **Austria:** Burgenland Croatian (*Land* Burgenland), Slovenian (*Land* Carinthia), Hungarian (*Land* Burgenland). Individual requirements: Romani (*Land* Burgenland) **Czech Republic:** Polish (Moravian-Silesian region), Slovak **Denmark:** German (Southern Jutland) **Germany:** Danish (*Land* Schleswig-Holstein), Upper Sorbian (Free State of Saxony), Lower Sorbian (*Land* Brandenburg), North Frisian (*Land* Schleswig-Holstein), Sater Frisian (*Land* Lower Saxony), Low German (*Länder* Bremen, Hamburg, Mecklenburg-Western Pomerania, Lower Saxony, Schleswig-Holstein, Brandenburg, Saxony-Anhalt), Romani (*Land* Berlin, Free Hanseatic City of Hamburg, *Land* Hesse, *Land* Schleswig-Holstein) **Hungary:** Croatian, German, Romanian, Serbian, Slovak, Slovenian, Romani, Beás **Montenegro:** Albanian, Romani **Netherlands:** Frisian (Friesland) **Poland:** Belarusian, Czech, Hebrew, Yiddish, Karaim, Kashub, Lithuanian, Lemko, German, Armenian, Romani, Russian, Slovak, Tatar, Ukrainian **Romania:** Bulgarian. Czech, German, Russian, Serbian, Slovak, Turkish, Ukrainian **Serbia:** Albanian, Bosnian, Bulgarian, Hungarian, Romani, Romanian, Ruthenian, Slovakian, Ukrainian, Croatian **Slovak Republic:** Bulgarian, Croatian, Czech, German, Polish, Romani, Ruthenian, Ukrainian, Hungarian **Ukraine:** Belarusian, Bulgarian, Gagauz, Greek, Jewish, Crimean Tatar, Moldovan, German, Polish, Russian, Romanian, Slovak, Hungarian **United Kingdom:** Scottish-Gaelic (Scotland), Irish (Northern Ireland)
c.i		**Denmark:** German (Southern Jutland) **Romania:** Hungarian **Spain:** Basque, Catalan, Valencian, Galician **Sweden:** Finnish
c.ii		**Armenia:** Assyrian, Yezidi, Greek, Russian, Kurdish **Austria:** Burgenland Croatian (*Land* Burgenland), Slovenian (*Land* Carinthia), Hungarian (*Land* Burgenland) **Bosnia and Herzegovina:** Albanian, Montenegrin, Czech, Italian, Hungarian, Macedonian, German, Polish, Romani, Romanian, Rysin, Slovak, Slovenian, Turkish, Ukrainian and Jewish (Yiddish and Ladino) **Czech Republic:** Polish (Moravian-Silesian region) **Denmark:** German (Southern Jutland) **Finland:** Sami, Swedish **Germany:** Low German (*Länder* Brandenburg, Saxony-Anhalt), Romani (*Land* Berlin, Free Hanseatic City of Hamburg, *Land* Hesse, *Land* Rhinland-Palatinate, *Land* Schleswig-Holstein) **Hungary:** Croatian, German, Romanian, Serbian, Slovak, Slovenian, Romani, Beás **Montenegro:** Albanian, Romani **Netherlands:** Frisian (Friesland)

		Norway: Sami **Poland:** Belarusian, Czech, Hebrew, Yiddish, Karaim, Kashub, Lithuanian, Lemko, German, Armenian, Romani, Russian, Slovak, Tatar, Ukrainian **Romania:** Bulgarian, Czech, Croatian, Russian, Serbian, Slovak, Turkish, Ukrainian **Serbia:** Albanian, Bosnian, Bulgarian, Hungarian, Romani, Romanian, Ruthenian, Slovakian, Ukrainian, Croatian **Slovak Republic:** Bulgarian, Croatian, Czech, German, Polish, Romani, Ruthenian, Ukrainian, Hungarian **Switzerland:** Romansh **Ukraine:** Belarusian, Bulgarian, Gagauz, Greek, Jewish, Crimean Tatar, Moldovan, German, Polish, Russian, Romanian, Slovak, Hungarian **United Kingdom:** Scottish-Gaelic (Scotland)
	d	**Austria:** Burgenland Croatian (*Land* Burgenland), Slovenian (*Land* Carinthia), Hungarian (*Land* Burgenland). Individual requirements: Czech (*Land* Vienna), Slovakian (*Land* Vienna), Romani (*Land* Burgenland), Slovenian (*Land* Styria), Hungarian (*Land* Vienna) **Bosnia and Herzegovina:** Romani **Croatia:** Italian, Serbian, Hungarian, Czech, Slovak, Ruthenian, Ukrainian **Czech Republic:** Polish (Moravian-Silesian region), Slovak **Denmark:** German (Southern Jutland) **Finland:** Saami, Swedish **Germany:** Low German (*Länder* Brandenburg, North Rhine-Westphalia), Romani (the territory of the Federal Republic of Germany) **Montenegro:** Albanian, Romani **Poland:** Belarusian, Czech, Hebrew, Yiddish, Karaim, Kashub, Lithuanian, Lemko, German, Armenian, Romani, Russian, Slovak, Tatar, Ukrainian **Romania:** Bulgarian. Czech, Croatian, German, Hungarian, Russian, Serbian, Slovak, Turkish, Ukrainian **Serbia:** Albanian, Bosnian, Bulgarian, Hungarian, Romani, Romanian, Ruthenian, Slovakian, Ukrainian, Croatian **Slovak Republic:** Bulgarian, Croatian, Czech, German, Polish, Romani, Ruthenian, Ukrainian, Hungarian **Spain:** Basque, Catalan, Valencian, Galician **Sweden:** Sami, Finnish, Meänkieli **Ukraine:** Belarusian, Bulgarian, Gagauz, Greek, Jewish, Crimean Tatar, Moldovan, German, Polish, Russian, Romanian, Slovak, Hungarian **United Kingdom:** Welsh (Wales), Scottish-Gaelic (Scotland), Irish (Northern Ireland)
	e.i	**Armenia:** Assyrian, Yezidi, Greek, Russian, Kurdish **Austria:** Burgenland Croatian (*Land* Burgenland), Slovenian (*Land* Carinthia), Hungarian (*Land* Burgenland). Individual requirements: Slovenian (*Land* Styria), Hungarian (*Land* Vienna) **Czech Republic:** Polish (Moravian-Silesian region), Slovak **Denmark:** German (Southern Jutland) **Finland:** Saami, Swedish **Germany:** Upper Sorbian (Free State of Saxony), Lower Sorbian (*Land* Brandenburg), Romani (*Land* Hesse)

		Hungary: Croatian, German, Romanian, Serbian, Slovak, Slovenian **Montenegro:** Albanian, Romani **Norway:** Sami **Poland:** Belarusian, Czech, Hebrew, Yiddish, Karaim, Kashub, Lithuanian, Lemko, German, Armenian, Romani, Russian, Slovak, Tatar, Ukrainian **Romania:** Bulgarian. Czech, Croatian, German, Hungarian, Russian, Serbian, Slovak, Turkish, Ukrainian **Serbia:** Albanian, Bosnian, Bulgarian, Hungarian, Romani, Romanian, Ruthenian, Slovakian, Ukrainian, Croatian **Slovak Republic:** Bulgarian, Croatian, Czech, German, Polish, Romani, Ruthenian, Ukrainian, Hungarian **Slovenia:** Italian, Hungarian **Spain:** Basque, Catalan, Valencian, Galician **Sweden:** Sami, Finnish, Meänkieli **Switzerland:** Romansh, Italian **Ukraine:** Belarusian, Bulgarian, Gagauz, Greek, Jewish, Crimean Tatar, Moldovan, German, Polish, Russian, Romanian, Slovak, Hungarian **United Kingdom:** Welsh (Wales), Irish (Northern Ireland)
	e.ii	**Armenia**[115] **Bosnia and Herzegovina:** Albanian, Montenegrin, Czech, Italian, Hungarian, Macedonian, German, Polish, Romani, Romanian, Rysin, Slovak, Slovenian, Turkish, Ukrainian and Jewish (Yiddish and Ladino) **Croatia:** Italian, Serbian, Hungarian, Czech, Slovak, Ruthenian, Ukrainian **Germany:** Danish (*Land* Schleswig-Holstein), North Frisian (*Land* Schleswig-Holstein), Sater Frisian (*Land* Lower Saxony), Low German (*Länder* Bremen, Hamburg, Mecklenburg-Western Pomerania, Lower Saxony, Schleswig-Holstein, Brandenburg, Saxony-Anhalt), Romani (the territory of the Federal Republic of Germany) **Hungary:** Romani, Beás **United Kingdom:** Scottish-Gaelic (Scotland)
	f.i	**Hungary:** Croatian, German, Romanian, Serbian, Slovak, Slovenian, Beás **Romania:** German, Hungarian **Slovak Republic:** Hungarian **Switzerland:** Romansh
	f.ii	**Austria:** Burgenland Croatian (*Land* Burgenland), Slovenian (*Land* Carinthia), Hungarian (*Land* Burgenland). Individual requirements: Czech (*Land* Vienna), Slovakian (*Land* Vienna), Romani (*Land* Burgenland), Slovenian (*Land* Styria), Hungarian (*Land* Vienna) **Denmark:** German (Southern Jutland) **Finland:** Sami, Swedish **Germany:** Danish (*Land* Schleswig-Holstein), Upper Sorbian (Free State of Saxony), North Frisian (*Land* Schleswig-Holstein), Sater Frisian (*Land* Lower Saxony), Low German (*Länder* Bremen, Hamburg, Mecklenburg-Western Pomerania, Lower Saxony, Schleswig-Holstein, Brandenburg), Romani (the Territory of the Federal Republic of Germany) **Hungary:** Romani **Montenegro:** Albanian, Romani

		Netherlands: Frisian (Friesland) **Norway:** Sami **Poland:** Belarusian, Czech, Hebrew, Yiddish, Karaim, Kashub, Lithuanian, Lemko, German, Armenian, Romani, Russian, Slovak, Tatar, Ukrainian **Serbia:** Albanian, Bosnian, Bulgarian, Hungarian, Romani, Romanian, Ruthenian, Slovakian, Ukrainian, Croatian **Slovak Republic:** Bulgarian, Croatian, Czech, German, Polish, Romani, Ruthenian, Ukrainian **Spain:** Basque, Catalan, Valencian, Galician **Sweden:** Sami, Finnish, Meänkieli **United Kingdom:** Welsh (Wales), Scottish-Gaelic (Scotland), Irish (Northern Ireland)
	g	**Austria:** Burgenland Croatian (*Land* Burgenland), Slovenian (*Land* Carinthia), Hungarian (*Land* Burgenland) **Bosnia and Herzegovina:** Romani **Denmark:** German (Southern Jutland) **Germany:** Low German (Free Hanseatic City of Bremen, Free Hanseatic City of Hamburg), Romani (the territory of the Federal Republic of Germany) **Hungary:** Croatian, German, Romanian, Serbian, Slovak, Slovenian, Romani, Beás **Norway:** Sami **Poland:** Belarusian, Czech, Hebrew, Yiddish, Karaim, Kashub, Lithuanian, Lemko, German, Armenian, Romani, Russian, Slovak, Tatar, Ukrainian **Romania:** Bulgarian. Czech, Croatian, German, Hungarian, Russian, Serbian, Slovak, Turkish, Ukrainian **Spain:** Basque, Catalan, Valencian, Galician **Switzerland:** Italian **Ukraine:** Belarusian, Bulgarian, Gagauz, Greek, Jewish, Crimean Tatar, Moldovan, German, Polish, Russian, Romanian, Slovak, Hungarian **United Kingdom:** Scottish-Gaelic (Scotland), Irish (Northern Ireland)
2		**Armenia:** Assyrian, Yezidi, Greek, Russian, Kurdish **Austria:** Burgenland Croatian (*Land* Burgenland), Slovenian (*Land* Carinthia), Hungarian (*Land* Burgenland). Individual requirements: Czech (*Land* Vienna), Slovakian (*Land* Vienna), Slovenian (*Land* Styria) **Bosnia and Herzegovina:** Albanian, Montenegrin, Czech, Italian, Hungarian, Macedonian, German, Polish, Romani, Romanian, Rysin, Slovak, Slovenian, Turkish, Ukrainian and Jewish (Yiddish and Ladino) **Croatia:** Italian, Serbian, Hungarian, Czech, Slovak, Ruthenian, Ukrainian **Czech Republic:** Polish (Moravian-Silesian region), Slovak **Denmark:** German (Southern Jutland) **Finland:** Sami, Swedish **Germany:** Danish (*Land* Schleswig-Holstein), Upper Sorbian (Free State of Saxony), Lower Sorbian (*Land* Brandenburg), North Frisian (*Land* Schleswig-Holstein), Sater Frisian (*Land* Lower Saxony), Low German (*Länder* Bremen, Hamburg, Mecklenburg-Western Pomerania, Lower Saxony, Schleswig-Holstein, Brandenburg, North Rhine-Westphalia, Saxony-Anhalt), Romani (the territory of the Federal Republic of Germany) **Montenegro:** Albanian, Romani

		Netherlands: Frisian (Friesland) **Norway:** Sami **Poland:** Belarusian, Czech, Hebrew, Yiddish, Karaim, Kashub, Lithuanian, Lemko, German, Armenian, Romani, Russian, Slovak, Tatar, Ukrainian **Romania:** Bulgarian. Czech, Croatian, German, Hungarian, Russian, Serbian, Slovak, Turkish, Ukrainian **Serbia:** Albanian, Bosnian, Bulgarian, Hungarian, Romani, Romanian, Ruthenian, Slovakian, Ukrainian, Croatian **Slovak Republic:** Bulgarian, Croatian, Czech, German, Polish, Romani, Ruthenian, Ukrainian, Hungarian **Slovenia:** Italian, Hungarian **Spain:** Basque, Catalan, Valencian, Galician **Sweden:** Sami, Finnish, Meänkieli **Switzerland:** Italian **Ukraine:** Belarusian, Bulgarian, Gagauz, Greek, Jewish, Crimean Tatar, Moldovan, German, Polish, Russian, Romanian, Slovak, Hungarian **United Kingdom:** Welsh (Wales), Scottish-Gaelic (Scotland), Irish (Northern Ireland)
3		**Armenia:** Assyrian, Yezidi, Greek, Russian, Kurdish **Bosnia and Herzegovina:** Albanian, Montenegrin, Czech, Italian, Hungarian, Macedonian, German, Polish, Romani, Romanian, Rysin, Slovak, Slovenian, Turkish, Ukrainian and Jewish (Yiddish and Ladino) **Croatia:** Italian, Serbian, Hungarian, Czech, Slovak, Ruthenian, Ukrainian **Finland:** Sami, Swedish **Hungary:** Croatian, German, Romanian, Serbian, Slovak, Slovenian, Romani, Beás **Montenegro:** Albanian, Romani **Poland:** Belarusian, Czech, Hebrew, Yiddish, Karaim, Kashub, Lithuanian, Lemko, German, Armenian, Romani, Russian, Slovak, Tatar, Ukrainian **Romania:** Bulgarian. Czech, German, Hungarian, Russian, Serbian, Slovak, Turkish, Ukrainian **Serbia:** Albanian, Bosnian, Bulgarian, Hungarian, Romani, Romanian, Ruthenian, Slovakian, Ukrainian, Croatian **Slovak Republic:** Bulgarian, Croatian, Czech, German, Polish, Romani, Ruthenian, Ukrainian, Hungarian **Slovenia:** Italian, Hungarian **Spain:** Basque, Catalan, Valencian, Galician **Switzerland:** Romansh, Italian **Ukraine:** Belarusian, Bulgarian, Gagauz, Greek, Jewish, Crimean Tatar, Moldovan, German, Polish, Russian, Romanian, Slovak, Hungarian **United Kingdom:** Welsh (Wales)

---

115. In the first periodical report, the Committee of Experts notes that Armenia in the instrument of ratification does not indicate which subparagraph, e.i or e.ii, has been chosen. These two are alternatives, and the ratification of one excludes the other. The initial report of Armenia deals with undertaking e.i. The Committee therefore assessed the fulfilment of this undertaking. This procedure was also followed in the second monitoring round.

Article 12. Cultural activities and facilities

Elizabeth Craig
University of Sussex

1. Introduction

2. Contextual analysis

3. The scope of the provisions: analysis of the position taken by the Committee of Experts

4. Good practice

5. Conclusions

References

Appendix: Ratifications

Article 12 – Cultural activities and facilities

1. *With regard to cultural activities and facilities – especially libraries, video libraries, cultural centres, museums, archives, academies, theatres and cinemas, as well as literary work and film production, vernacular forms of cultural expression, festivals and the culture industries, including* inter alia *the use of new technologies – the Parties undertake, within the territory in which such languages are used and to the extent that the public authorities are competent, have power or play a role in this field:*

   a. *to encourage types of expression and initiative specific to regional or minority languages and foster the different means of access to works produced in these languages;*

   b. *to foster the different means of access in other languages to works produced in regional or minority languages by aiding and developing translation, dubbing, post-synchronisation and subtitling activities;*

   c. *to foster access in regional or minority languages to works produced in other languages by aiding and developing translation, dubbing, post-synchronisation and subtitling activities;*

   d. *to ensure that the bodies responsible for organising or supporting cultural activities of various kinds make appropriate allowance for incorporating the knowledge and use of regional or minority languages and cultures in the undertakings which they initiate or for which they provide backing;*

e. to promote measures to ensure that the bodies responsible for organising or supporting cultural activities have at their disposal staff who have a full command of the regional or minority language concerned, as well as of the language(s) of the rest of the population;

f. to encourage direct participation by representatives of the users of a given regional or minority language in providing facilities and planning cultural activities;

g. to encourage and/or facilitate the creation of a body or bodies responsible for collecting, keeping a copy of and presenting or publishing works produced in the regional or minority languages;

h. if necessary, to create and/or promote and finance translation and terminological research services, particularly with a view to maintaining and developing appropriate administrative, commercial, economic, social, technical or legal terminology in each regional or minority language.

2. In respect of territories other than those in which the regional or minority languages are traditionally used, the Parties undertake, if the number of users of a regional or minority language justifies it, to allow, encourage and/or provide appropriate cultural activities and facilities in accordance with the preceding paragraph.

3. The Parties undertake to make appropriate provision, in pursuing their cultural policy abroad, for regional or minority languages and the cultures they reflect.

1. Introduction

The inclusion of a provision dealing specifically with cultural activities and facilities can be linked to the overall aims of the European Charter for Regional or Minority Languages ("the Charter"): promoting the use of regional or minority languages and their associated cultural heritage, and allowing speakers access to a "vast cultural heritage" through the avoidance or breaking down of cultural barriers (Explanatory Report, paragraph 116). This is clearly envisaged as a two-way process with Article 12.1a-c encouraging cultural exchange in the aiding and development of translation, dubbing, post-synchronisation and subtitling as means of fostering access to works produced in different languages. Cultural facilities identified in Article 12.1 are libraries, video libraries, cultural centres, museums, archives, academies, theatres and cinemas. Literary work, film productions, vernacular forms of cultural expression, festivals and the cultural industries (including use of new technologies) are listed as relevant cultural activities. Article 12 recognises that public authorities have an important role to play in influencing the conditions in which such facilities are used (Explanatory Report, paragraph 114) with particular emphasis placed on the promotion of appropriate institutional support (Article 12.1d-h). Like many other provisions in the Charter, Article 12.1 applies only "within the territory in which such languages are used and to the extent that the public authorities are competent, have power or play a role in this field". Separate undertakings apply "[i]n respect of territories other than those in which the regional or minority languages are traditionally used" (Article 12.2) and in relation to the pursuit by states parties of "their cultural policy abroad" (Article 12.3).

According to Woehrling, Article 12 of the Charter is important because it recognises that regional or minority languages "can only develop if they are vehicles of quality cultural life".[1] In 2001 a Universal Declaration of Cultural Diversity was adopted by UNESCO, the organisation that has primary responsibility within the UN system for ensuring "the preservation and promotion of the fruitful diversity of cultures". This declaration encapsulates many of the values enshrined in the Charter, recognising the importance of cultural pluralism (Article 2) and cultural rights (Article 5) as well as the importance of access for all cultures "to the means of expression and dissemination" (Article 6). It emphasises the need to preserve cultural heritage (Article 7) and promotes the idea of cultural goods and services "as vectors of identity, values and meaning" (Article 8) as well as the importance of global dissemination (articles 9 and 10). This declaration was followed by the adoption in 2005 of the UNESCO Convention on the Protection and Promotion of the Diversity of Cultural Expressions, which in Article 6 identifies measures that states "may" take in measures aimed at promoting and protecting such diversity within its territories. Meanwhile, there has been a resurgence of interest in the right to take part in cultural life, recognised in both Article 27 of the Universal Declaration of Human Rights, 1948, and Article 15.1 of the International Covenant on Economic, Social and Cultural Rights, 1966.[2] However, the Charter is unique as an instrument imposing precise legal obligations on states specifically in relation to cultural activities and facilities. This chapter considers the significance of the inclusion of Article 12 in the Charter, and key themes and trends that have emerged through the monitoring process.

2. Contextual analysis

The first undertaking in Article 12.1a is "to encourage types of expression and initiative specific to regional or minority languages and foster the different means of access to works produced in these languages". This is a general requirement, which refers to the encouragement of "cultural production"[3] and

---

1. J.-M. Woehrling (2005), *The European Charter for Regional or Minority Languages: a critical commentary*, Strasbourg: Council of Europe, p. 214.
2. See, for example Y. Donders (2007), "The legal framework of the right to take part in cultural life".
3. Woehrling (2005), op. cit., p. 216.

the fostering of means of access to works produced through "publication, production, presentation, diffusion, transmission, and so on".[4] It is therefore unsurprising that all states who have accepted Part III undertakings have chosen to apply Article 12.1a to languages within their territory (see appendix). More specific undertakings are then included in subparagraphs b-h. Article 12.1b refers in particular to the fostering of access to works produced in regional or minority languages in other languages and Article 12.1c is based on the idea of cultural exchange, referring to the fostering of access in regional or minority languages to works produced in other languages. According to Woehrling, such access might be fostered through technical assistance, grant-aid for dubbing, translation, post-synchronisation and subtitling, or through the stimulation of demand for access to such works.[5] More than half of all states parties have accepted these undertakings in relation to Part III languages spoken within their territory (see appendix).

Subparagraphs d and e refer to "bodies responsible for organising or supporting cultural activities", which may be public or private organisations engaged in "standard" cultural activities such as singing, films and theatre.[6] States are required to "ensure" that such bodies "make appropriate allowance for incorporating the knowledge and use of regional or minority languages and cultures in the undertakings which they initiate or for which they provide backing" (Article 12.1d). The role of states is therefore one of "guidance and supervision".[7] They are also required to promote measures to "ensure" such bodies "have at their disposal staff who have a full command of the regional or minority language concerned, as well as of the language(s) of the rest of the population" (Article 12.1e). These undertakings have also been accepted by at least half of states parties (see appendix).

Article 12.1f is the only clause in the Charter to refer to user representatives, requiring states "to encourage direct participation by representatives of the users of a given regional or minority language in providing facilities and planning cultural activities". All states that have accepted Part III undertakings have chosen to apply subparagraph 1f to most Part III languages (see appendix). Article 12.1g provides for the encouragement and/or facilitation of "the creation of a body or bodies responsible for collecting, keeping a copy of and presenting or publishing works produced in the regional or minority languages". This is important because of the weak situation of many regional or minority languages and may require the adaptation of "legislation on legal deposit and archives so

---

4. Explanatory Report, paragraph 115.
5. Woehrling (2005), op. cit., p. 218.
6. Ibid.
7. Explanatory Report, paragraph 117.

that the body envisaged can take part in the conservation of works in regional or minority languages".[8] The majority of ratifying states have chosen to apply this undertaking to most Part III languages (see appendix). The promotion of translation and terminology services is addressed in Article 12.1h, which requires states, "if necessary, to create and/or promote and finance translation and terminological research services, particularly with a view to maintaining and developing appropriate administrative, commercial, economic, social, technical or legal terminology in each regional or minority language". This undertaking appears to be considered by states to be a particularly onerous obligation and Article 12.1h has been accepted by only nine states parties in relation to Part III languages (Finland, Germany, the Netherlands, Norway, Romania, Spain, Sweden, Switzerland and the United Kingdom – see appendix).

Article 12.2, like other provisions of the Charter (e.g. Article 8.2 on education), recognises internal migration as a reality and requires states "to allow, encourage and/or provide appropriate cultural activities and facilities in accordance with the preceding paragraph" in other territories "if the number of users of a regional or minority language justifies it". Whilst the verb "allow" envisages the removal of any restrictive provisions and the verb "encourages" implies state support for the cultural work of private institutions, the verb "provide" implies a more onerous undertaking on the part of public bodies.[9] Article 7.1a, in Part II of the Charter, refers to "the recognition of the regional or minority languages as an expression of cultural wealth". The undertaking in Article 12.3 "to make appropriate provision, in pursuing their cultural policy abroad, for regional or minority languages and the cultures they reflect" is recognised as one way of applying this principle.[10] This undertaking, which has clear links with Article 14 on transfrontier exchanges, recognises that regional and minority languages form part of a state's national cultural heritage and requires some prominence to be given to regional and minority languages in pursuit of cultural policy abroad.[11] Both these undertakings have been accepted by the vast majority of states in relation to most Part III languages (see appendix).

3. The scope of the provisions: analysis of the position taken by the Committee of Experts

Article 12 is not a provision that has attracted much attention, either in the literature or in the Committee of Experts' evaluation reports and subsequent recommendations by the Council of Ministers. Of the 47 reports made public

---

8. Ibid., paragraph 118.
9. Woehrling (2005), op. cit., pp. 222-3.
10. Explanatory Report, paragraph 120.
11. Woehrling (2005), op. cit., p. 223.

by the end of 2009, only 26 make specific reference (in boxes, findings and recommendations of the Committee of Ministers) to cultural life. Specific references to cultural life in boxes in the main body of the evaluation report are unusual in relation to both Article 7[12] and Article 12.[13] Instead, references to cultural life often take the form of a fairly positive assessment included in the committee's main findings[14] with occasional reference to areas of concern such as representation of minority languages in pursuit of cultural policy abroad[15] or to languages in relation to which improvements in the cultural field could be made.[16] Certainly the findings in this area tend to be more positive than the findings in other areas, including in relation to Article 11 on the media.[17] It is therefore fairly unsurprising that the Committee of Ministers rarely makes specific recommendations in this area.[18]. A particular problem that the Committee of Experts appears to have faced under Article 12 is that states sometimes provide little or no information on each of the relevant undertakings,[19] which may explain why committee reports provide little interpretative guidance. However, states that have commented extensively under Article 12 have been commended for doing so.[20] The rest of this section therefore focuses primarily on issues of concern that have been raised by the committee in relation to the application of Article 12 in its evaluation reports.

The committee has shown a particular interest under Article 12.1a in the allocation of funding to encourage types of expression and initiative and to foster

---

12. But see Cyprus 2006, 72 (where the Committee of Experts encouraged the authorities to help Maronites establish a cultural and youth centre under Article 7.1d) and Slovakia 2007, 55 (where the Committee of Experts encouraged the authorities to support the establishment of a cultural organisation for Ruthenian-speakers under Article 7.1e).

13. However, see Finland 2001, 180 (where the Committee of Experts noted that the special fund for the Sami as part of the budget of the Sami Parliament should not exclude the possibility of Sami-speakers applying for other funding as well under Article 12.1a) and Hungary 2007, 193 (where the Committee of Experts urged the authorities to develop a comprehensive medium-term programme for cultural activities and facilities under Article 12.1b).

14. E.g. Austria 2005, Finding Q, and Serbia 2009, Findings I, M, P and S.

15. E.g. Denmark 2004, Finding L, and Germany 2002, Finding P.

16. E.g. Finland 2001, Finding I (Sami), and Germany 2002, Finding Q (Frisian and Low German).

17. Slovakia, 1st and 2nd monitoring cycles (2007, 2009), Finding H; United Kingdom 2004, Finding H, and United Kingdom 2007, Finding I.

18. However, see Recommendation of the Committee of Ministers: Croatia (2001), 3 (on participation of users in planning, funding and organising cultural activities) and recommendations of the Committee of Ministers: Hungary (2001), 4, (2004), 5 and (2007), 6 (on minority self-governments).

19. E.g. Spain 2005 and 2008, in particular the committee's finding in the first cycle that a great number of details in this area were still unknown to it (Finding N) and in the second cycle that it had received very little information in relation to Article 12 for Valencian (Finding G).

20. E.g. Spain 2008, 313-4.

different means of access to works produced in the relevant languages. This is often linked to the concerns expressed by minority-language representatives about the amount of money allocated by the state and about means of (and delays in) distribution.[21] However, such concerns will rarely result in an overall conclusion that the undertaking in Article 12.1a has not been fulfilled or has been fulfilled only partly.[22] Article 12.1a has a particularly wide remit and states that encourage a wide range of cultural activities have been commended for doing so.[23] Meanwhile, the committee has stressed the importance of "modern cultural initiatives" in improving a language's image as a "living language, in particular among younger generations" as well as more traditional cultural expressions.[24] On occasion the committee has gone further and stressed the need for consultation "with a view to identifying the real needs and allocating appropriate funds"[25] and for "concrete" policy planning in this area[26] but these are not phrases that emerge consistently in its comments under Article 12.1a.

The main problem under Articles 12.1b and c has been the failure of states to provide sufficient information on measures taken. Whilst some state reports have lacked specific information on these undertakings,[27] others have focused primarily on translation with insufficient attention paid to "dubbing, post-synchronisation and subtitling activities".[28] This has occasionally led to findings that the relevant undertakings have only been partly fulfilled[29] or, where information had been consistently sought by the committee, to an even stronger conclusion.[30] However, it appears that the committee has adopted a more rigorous approach with some states than with others. For example, it found that the undertaking in Article 12.1b was fulfilled by Hungary in relation to all languages in the first monitoring cycle on the grounds that funds were available for the translation of works produced in minority languages into Hungarian and that this "seemed" to be true also for the other activities listed;[31] and it

---

21. E.g. Armenia 2006, 139-40; Armenia 2009 193-5; Austria 2005, 187 and 334; Austria 2009, 169 and 345; Croatia 2008, 202; Germany 2008, 175; Slovakia 2007, 361; Slovakia 2009, 394.

22. However, see Hungary 2007, 191-3, where concerns about scarce funding along with the lack of long-term planning contributed to a finding that the undertaking was only partly fulfilled.

23. E.g. United Kingdom 2007, 502.

24. Austria 2005, 187. See also Austria 2009, 169.

25. E.g. Finland 2007, 264.

26. E.g. United Kingdom 2004, 369; United Kingdom 2007, 502.

27. E.g. Finland 2001, 117; Application of the Charter in Montenegro, 1st monitoring cycle (2010), paragraphs 179 and 276; Serbia 2009, 287; Slovakia 2007, 168, 276, 363, 447, 527, 578 and 671; Slovakia 2009, 144, 397, 530, 664, 827.

28. E.g. Spain 2005, 444, 583, 838 and 965.

29. E.g. Germany 2002, 278, 345 and 379; Spain 2008, 495; Sweden 2009, 261.

30. E.g. Germany 2008, 453-4 and 711-13.

31. Hungary 2001, 71.

found that the undertaking in Article 12.1c was fulfilled by Serbia on the basis that the Serbian authorities had supported the translation of books into certain minority languages.[32]

Article 12.1d requires states to ensure that relevant bodies "make appropriate allowance for incorporating the knowledge and use of regional or minority languages and cultures in the undertakings which they initiate or for which they provide backing". The key issues here appear to be the involvement (or lack thereof) of representatives of minority language speakers and organisations[33] and, once again, the failure of states to provide adequate information on steps taken.[34] Dialogue with representatives of the speakers of such languages is considered to be particularly important.[35] The committee has stressed that the requirement is to "ensure" that such bodies makes appropriate allowance for such incorporation and that evidence of measures taken and practical examples are required.[36] However, provided there are no concerns raised by the speakers themselves, it appears that the provision of a list of activities in the cultural field funded by the authorities and carried out by relevant organisations may be sufficient.[37]

The personnel requirement in Article 12.1e requires states to provide evidence of minority personnel with capacity in the minority language at the disposal of all bodies responsible for organising or supporting cultural activities in the minority language area.[38] A policy of mere "encouragement" will not be sufficient if this requirement has not been met[39] and the Committee of Experts has expressed concern where such capacity in relevant organisations appears "accidental rather than deliberate".[40] Article 12.1f requires the "encouragement" of direct participation by representatives of language users in providing facilities and planning cultural activities.[41] The committee has indicated that this undertaking requires the state to "secure" direct participation by representatives of users when the bodies providing facilities and planning cultural activities "are an integral part of the state administration"[42] and to provide incentives for

---

32. Serbia 2009, 288-9.
33. E.g. Armenia 2005, 142; Denmark 2007, 100; Slovakia 2007, 169, 277, 364, 579 and 672; United Kingdom 2004, 288.
34. E.g. Denmark 2004, 98; Finland 2001, 117; Spain 2005, 294, 709, 840 and 967.
35. E.g. Armenia 2009, 197-8; Sweden 2003, 157.
36. Germany 2006, 451 and 526-7.
37. E.g. Austria 2009, 172, 277 and 347.
38. E.g. Germany 2002, 203-4; Germany 2006, 309; Germany 2008, 314.
39. E.g. the Netherlands 2001, 96; the Netherlands 2004, 165-6.
40. United Kingdom 2007, 509-10.
41. E.g. United Kingdom 2004, 374, where it was concluded that the undertaking had only been partly fulfilled as the employment of Irish-speakers on various bodies did not appear to be the result of regulations, policy or encouragement on the part of the authorities.
42. E.g. Croatia 2001, 102, and Recommendation of the Committee of Ministers: Croatia (2001), 3.

such participation.[43] For obvious reasons, these are requirements that countries that recognise some form of cultural or territorial autonomy find easier to fulfil.[44] Indeed the committee observed in response to Hungary's initial report that "The whole system of minority self-governments is a perfect embodiment of the content and spirit of Article 12.1f of the Charter" with the Hungarian system "characterised by a high degree of participation of the users of minority languages in the decision-making on issues relating to minority languages".[45]

Article 12.1g deals with archiving, and the main problem here has been the failure of states to provide information for audio and/or audiovisual works, with a lot of states focusing primarily on written publications.[46] One of the Committee of Experts' strengths is of course its ability to respond to developments on the ground and to the concerns of minority-language speakers and, though a Finnish Archive has existed in Sweden since 1975, it is notable that the committee recently concluded that this undertaking had only been partly fulfilled because the funding provided "neither enables the archives to offer their services according to the needs of the speakers, nor to adapt the archives materials to necessary new technologies".[47] As might be expected given the reluctance of some states to select Article 12.1h, which applies to translation and terminological research services, the committee's findings in relation to this undertaking have generally been quite favourable, with Spain being the notable exception due to its failure to provide sufficient information in its reports in the first monitoring cycle.[48]

Article 12.2 is fairly flexibly worded, requiring states "to allow, encourage and/ or provide appropriate cultural activities" in respect of territories other than those where the languages in question are traditionally used. The Committee of Experts has found that the undertaking was fulfilled even if no specific measures were taken to encourage such activities,[49] although it does require that specific examples are provided.[50] The committee has been rather more rigorous in its approach to the requirements of Article 12.3, which relates to

---

43. Germany 2006, 454.
44. E.g. Germany 2002, 162-3; Norway 2001, 89-91; Slovenia 2004, 147-8 and 222-3; Sweden 2003, 158-60. Cf. Spain 2005, 295-6, 448-51, 586-9, 710-11, 841-4 and 968-70.
45. Hungary 2001, 73.
46. E.g. Croatia 2001, 103; Croatia 2005, 185; Finland 2001, 119 and 186; Finland 2007, 153-4; Hungary 2001, 74; Hungary 2007, 197-9; Spain 2008, 506-9, 833-4, 1158-61 and 1002-5.
47. Sweden 2009, 194-5.
48. Spain 2005, 454, 592, 713, 847 and 973.
49. E.g. Denmark 2004, 102; Germany 2002, 165. Cf. United Kingdom 2004, 296, where the conclusion was reached that the undertaking was only "partly fulfilled".
50. E.g. Slovakia 2009, 156, 286, 679, 724 and 836; Slovenia 2004, 149 and 224; Slovenia 2007, 175.

the pursuit of cultural policy abroad. It has stated that this provision "concerns the way in which the country presents its own linguistic and cultural heritage abroad (e.g. cultural exchanges, how regional or minority languages spoken in [the state] and cultures are referred to in European or international exhibitions and events, documentation on the country aimed at the international public, use of bilingual place-names on the official maps in official brochures and guides designed to promote the image of the country abroad, *inter alia*, for tourist purposes".[51] This is a requirement that is often neglected by states even when the assessment of their performance in relation to Article 12 is generally favourable.[52] The Committee of Experts has made it clear that the inclusion of regional or minority languages in the pursuit of cultural policy abroad has an important role to play in raising the prestige of the language and encouraging speakers to use it[53] and has stressed in particular the role that federal authorities have to play in this regard.[54]

4. Good practice

States whose current practice appears to a large extent to meet the requirements of Article 12 include Slovenia (in relation to Hungarian and Italian), Sweden (in relation to Sami, Finnish and Meänkieli) and Switzerland (in relation to Romansch and Italian).[55] Examples of good practice in relation to the general undertaking in Article 12.1a include initiatives such as lectures, language summer camps and literary competitions as well as the co-financing by the Ministry of Culture of cultural centres for the Hungarian and Italian minorities in Slovenia[56] and the adoption of a new law providing for the safeguarding and protection of trilingualism in the Canton of Grisons, Switzerland.[57]

A lot of states have failed to provide sufficient information under subparagraphs 1b and c,[58] and the finding in the first monitoring cycles in relation to Catalan in Catalonia that these undertakings had been fulfilled "in a rather exemplary manner" is therefore significant.[59] Concrete measures identified included

---

51. Slovenia 2004, 151. See also Czech Republic 2009, 232.
52. E.g. Denmark 2004, Finding L; Germany 2002, Finding P; Germany 2006, Finding T; Germany 2008, Finding R.
53. The Netherlands 2004, Finding I.
54. E.g. Germany 2002, 166, 209, 247, 283, 350, 385, 422, 464, 511; Germany 2006, 150-3, 227-30, 313, 388-9, 459, 533-5, 599, 668, 733. See also Germany 2008, e.g. 103-6.
55. See Slovenia 2004; Slovenia 2007; Sweden 2003; Sweden 2006; Sweden 2009; Switzerland 2001, 2004, 2008.
56. Slovenia 2004, 145 and 220.
57. Switzerland 2001, 151.
58. E.g. Slovakia 2007, 168.
59. Spain 2005, 293.

measures to promote the supply of films dubbed and subtitled in Catalan; regulations for subsidies to increase the commercial screening of films dubbed and subtitled in Catalan; the approval of principles on the granting of subsidies for initiatives to promote the commercial release of such films and their presence in video-clubs, bookshops and other commercial outlets.[60] A similar conclusion was reached in relation to the Catalan and Basque languages under Article 12.1h on research and terminological services, with a number of bodies identified as being in charge of developing terminology and a number of specialist terminological projects supported by the relevant authorities.[61] The Committee of Experts also commended the progress made in Wales in the second monitoring cycle with the development of new online databases and specialist glossaries of standard terms.[62]

Examples of good practice under Article 12.1d include the provision of subsidies for a network of Finnish arts centres for children and young people, with one member responsible specifically for developing arts and cultural services for Swedish-speaking children and quotas for performances in Swedish in art forms selected by the speakers themselves.[63] The provision of annual subsidies for the Documentation Centre of the Congress of Poles in the Czech Republic[64] and for the German minority's libraries in Denmark[65] as well as the extensive archives of the national libraries of Scotland and Wales, which are complemented by the archiving work of other organisations, national museums and galleries,[66] have been welcomed under Article 12.1g. Examples of good practice in relation to Article 12.3 include the granting of money to the Hungarian and Italian communities in Slovenia for participation in cultural events in Hungary, Italy and Croatia, and promotion of a booklet in English, "Ethnic minorities in Slovenia",[67] as well as the development of good institutional support structures in Switzerland. These include the existence of a Swiss Arts Council responsible for promoting the state's multicultural image abroad, including the work of Swiss writers and artists; a co-ordinating committee for Switzerland's presence abroad and an Italo-Swiss cultural advisory committee focused on the promotion of cultural co-operation.[68]

---

60. Ibid., 292.
61. Spain 2008, 677-9 and 837-8.
62. United Kingdom 2007, 252-3.
63. Finland 2007, 149.
64. Czech Republic 2009, 227-9.
65. Denmark 2004, 101.
66. United Kingdom 2004, 182 and 291-3.
67. Slovenia 2007, 177-9.
68. Switzerland 2001, 242-4.

5. Conclusions

The greatest problem facing the committee in relation to Article 12 appears to be the continued failure of states to provide sufficient information on the measures that have been taken to fulfil the relevant undertakings, and the committee needs to take a stronger line against consistent offenders if Article 12 is to be taken as seriously as other provisions of the Charter. The committee also needs to be consistent in this regard: findings that an undertaking has been fulfilled even where there is a lack of concrete information on each language protected are not helpful.[69] A second problem is the failure of the committee to provide reassessments where a positive finding has been made in the previous monitoring cycle and no specific complaints have been made by speakers of minority languages or their representatives, whereas more confidence is inspired in the rigour of the monitoring process when a positive initial assessment is followed by a more cautious assessment in the second and third cycles[70] or where there is a request for further information or clarification that is then followed up in the next cycle.[71] There are, however, indications that the committee is beginning to take a more rigorous approach to early ratifying states that are generally considered to have high levels of compliance with the requirements of Article 12. For example, the committee has challenged the Swedish approach to archiving under Article 12.1g, finding in both the first and second cycles that the undertaking had only been partly fulfilled in relation to Finnish.[72] Although further information about a government bill on archiving and the allocation of money to Sweden's Finnish Archives was provided in the third cycle, the committee found that the undertaking was still only partly fulfilled as the funding provided did not enable "the archives to offer their services according to the needs of the speakers" or "to adapt archives materials to necessary new technologies".[73]

Some inconsistency in the committee's approach under Article 12 has already been noted and it appears hard to predict with any certainty what the committee's findings in relation to specific undertakings will be, given the range of formulations used by the committee, including "seems to be fulfilled", "fulfilled at present", "formally fulfilled", "only partly fulfilled" and "not fulfilled". The usefulness of such findings is questionable; a highlighting of good practice and areas of concern, followed by specific undertakings in line with the practice

---

69. E.g. Croatia 2001, 101.
70. Cf. Hungary 2001, Finding G, when it was observed that the Hungarian system was in full conformity with its undertakings under Article 12 with the references to obstacles to transferring cultural bodies and institutions to self-government in Hungary 2007, Finding J.
71. Slovakia 2007, 275 and 362.
72. Sweden 2003, 277; Sweden 2006, 220.
73. Sweden 2009, 194.

under relevant human rights treaties, would appear more appropriate in this context. This is particularly so in light of the challenges facing the committee in responding to instruments of ratification that appear to promise the same levels of protection for a range of different languages.[74] The committee's current approach suggests a much more rigorous approach to the interpretation of Article 12, and a fleshing out of its requirements, than is suggested by the findings highlighted by this contribution and the committee's response to the reports of states that have recently acceded to the Charter.[75]

References

Donders, Yvonne (2007), "The legal framework of the right to take part in cultural life" in Yvonne Donders and Valdimir Volodin (eds), *Human rights in education, science and culture*. Paris: UNESCO/Aldershot: Ashgate, pp. 231-72.

Woehrling, Jean-Marie (2005), *The European Charter for Regional or Minority Languages: a critical commentary*. Strasbourg: Council of Europe Publishing.

Appendix: Ratifications

Article 12		
Paragraph and subparagraph		
1	a	**Armenia:** Assyrian, Yezidi, Greek, Russian, Kurdish **Austria:** Burgenland Croatian (*Land* Burgenland), Slovenian (*Land* Carinthia), Hungarian (*Land* Burgenland) **Bosnia and Herzegovina:** Albanian, Montenegrin, Czech, Italian, Hungarian, Macedonian, German, Polish, Romanian, Rysin, Slovak, Slovenian, Turkish, Ukrainian, Jewish (Yiddish and Ladino), Romani **Croatia:** Italian, Serbian, Hungarian, Czech, Slovak, Ruthenian, Ukrainian **Czech Republic:** Polish (Moravian-Silesian region), Slovak **Denmark:** German (Southern Jutland) **Finland:** Sami, Swedish **Germany:** Upper Sorbian (Free State of Saxony), Lower Sorbian (*Land* Brandenburg), North Frisian (*Land* Schleswig-Holstein), Sater Frisian (Lower Saxony), Low German (Bremen, Hamburg, Mecklenburg-Western Pomerania, Lower Saxony, Schleswig-Holstein) **Hungary:** Croatian, German, Romanian, Serbian, Slovak, Slovenian, Romani, Beás **Montenegro:** Albanian, Romani **Netherlands:** Frisian (Friesland) **Norway:** Sami

---

74. E.g. ratification instruments of Poland and Serbia.
75. E.g. Serbia 2009, 275-91.

		Poland: Belarusian, Czech, Hebrew, Yiddish, Karaim, Kashub, Lithuanian, Lemko, German, Armenian, Romani, Russian, Slovak, Tatar, Ukrainian **Romania:** Bulgarian, Czech, Croatian, German, Hungarian, Russian, Serbian, Slovak, Turkish, Ukrainian **Serbia:** Albanian, Bosnian, Bulgarian, Hungarian, Romani, Romanian, Ruthenian, Slovakian, Ukrainian, Croatian **Slovak Republic:** Bulgarian, Croatian, Czech, German, Polish, Romani, Ruthenian, Ukrainian, Hungarian **Slovenia:** Italian, Hungarian **Spain:** Basque, Catalan, Valencian, Galician **Sweden:** Sami, Finnish, Meänkieli **Switzerland:** Romansh, Italian **Ukraine:** Belarusian, Bulgarian, Gagauz, Greek, Jewish, Crimean Tatar, Moldovan, German, Polish, Russian, Romanian, Slovak, Hungarian **United Kingdom:** Welsh (Wales), Scottish-Gaelic (Scotland), Irish (Northern Ireland)
	b	**Denmark:** German (Southern Jutland) **Finland:** Sami, Swedish **Germany:** Upper Sorbian (Free State of Saxony), Lower Sorbian (*Land* Brandenburg), North Frisian (*Land* Schleswig-Holstein), Sater Frisian (Lower Saxony), Low German (Bremen, Mecklenburg-Western Pomerania, Lower Saxony, Schleswig Holstein) **Hungary:** Croatian, German, Romanian, Serbian, Slovak, Slovenian, Romani, Beás **Montenegro:** Albanian, Romani **Netherlands:** Frisian (Friesland) **Poland:** Belarusian, Czech, Hebrew, Yiddish, Karaim, Kashub, Lithuanian, Lemko, German, Armenian, Romani, Russian, Slovak, Tatar, Ukrainian **Romania:** Bulgarian. Czech, Croatian, German, Hungarian, Russian, Serbian, Slovak, Turkish, Ukrainian **Serbia:** Albanian, Bosnian, Bulgarian, Hungarian, Romani, Romanian, Ruthenian, Slovakian, Ukrainian, Croatian **Slovak Republic:** Bulgarian, Croatian, Czech, German, Polish, Romani, Ruthenian, Ukrainian, Hungarian **Spain:** Basque, Catalan, Valencian, Galician **Sweden:** Sami, Finnish, Meänkieli **Switzerland:** Romansh, Italian **Ukraine:** Belarusian, Bulgarian, Gagauz, Greek, Jewish, Crimean Tatar, Moldovan, German, Polish, Russian, Romanian, Slovak, Hungarian **United Kingdom:** Welsh (Wales)
	c	**Finland:** Sami, Swedish **Germany:** Danish (Schleswig Holstein), Upper Sorbian (Free State of Saxony), Lower Sorbian (*Land* Brandenburg), North Frisian (*Land* Schleswig-Holstein), Sater Frisian (Lower Saxony), Low German (Bremen, Mecklenburg-Western Pomerania, Lower Saxony, Schleswig Holstein) **Hungary:** Croatian, German, Romanian, Serbian, Slovak, Slovenian, Romani, Beás

		Montenegro: Albanian, Romani **Poland:** Belarusian, Czech, Hebrew, Yiddish, Karaim, Kashub, Lithuanian, Lemko, German, Armenian, Romani, Russian, Slovak, Tatar, Ukrainian **Romania:** Bulgarian, Czech, Croatian, German, Hungarian, Russian, Serbian, Slovak, Turkish, Ukrainian **Serbia:** Albanian, Bosnian, Bulgarian, Hungarian, Romani, Romanian, Ruthenian, Slovakian, Ukrainian, Croatian **Slovak Republic:** Bulgarian, Croatian, Czech, German, Polish, Romani, Ruthenian, Ukrainian, Hungarian **Spain:** Basque, Catalan, Valencian, Galician **Sweden:** Finnish, Sami **Switzerland:** Romansh, Italian **Ukraine:** Belarusian, Bulgarian, Gagauz, Greek, Jewish, Crimean Tatar, Moldovan, German, Polish, Russian, Romanian, Slovak, Hungarian **United Kingdom:** Welsh (Wales)
	d	**Armenia:** Assyrian, Yezidi, Greek, Russian, Kurdish **Austria:** Burgenland Croatian (*Land* Burgenland), Slovenian (*Land* Carinthia), Hungarian (*Land* Burgenland) **Denmark:** German (Southern Jutland) **Finland:** Sami, Swedish **Germany:** Danish (Schleswig Holstein), Upper Sorbian (Free State of Saxony), Lower Sorbian (*Land* Brandenburg), North Frisian (*Land* Schleswig-Holstein), Sater Frisian (Lower Saxony), Low German (Bremen, Hamburg, Mecklenburg-Western Pomerania, Lower Saxony, Schleswig-Holstein) **Hungary:** Romani, Beás **Netherlands:** Frisian (Friesland) **Norway:** Sami **Poland:** Belarusian, Czech, Hebrew, Yiddish, Karaim, Kashub, Lithuanian, Lemko, German, Armenian, Romani, Russian, Slovak, Tatar, Ukrainian **Romania:** Bulgarian, Czech, Croatian, German, Hungarian, Russian, Serbian, Slovak, Turkish, Ukrainian **Slovak Republic:** Bulgarian, Croatian, Czech, German, Polish, Romani, Ruthenian, Ukrainian, Hungarian **Slovenia:** Italian, Hungarian **Spain:** Basque, Catalan, Valencian, Galician **Sweden:** Sami, Finnish, Meänkieli **Switzerland:** Italian **Ukraine:** Belarusian, Bulgarian, Gagauz, Greek, Jewish, Crimean Tatar, Moldovan, German, Polish, Russian, Romanian, Slovak, Hungarian **United Kingdom:** Welsh (Wales), Scottish-Gaelic (Scotland), Irish (Northern Ireland)
	e	**Bosnia and Herzegovina:** Albanian, Montenegrin, Czech, Italian, Hungarian, Macedonian, German, Polish, Romanian, Rysin, Slovak, Slovenian, Turkish, Ukrainian, Jewish (Yiddish and Ladino), Romani **Denmark:** German (Southern Jutland) **Finland:** Sami, Swedish

439

		Germany: Danish (Schleswig Holstein), Upper Sorbian (Free State of Saxony), Lower Sorbian (*Land* Brandenburg), North Frisian (*Land* Schleswig-Holstein), Sater Frisian (Lower Saxony), Low German (Bremen, Mecklenburg-Western Pomerania) **Netherlands:** Frisian (Friesland) **Norway:** Sami **Poland:** Belarusian, Czech, Hebrew, Yiddish, Karaim, Kashub, Lithuanian, Lemko, German, Armenian, Romani, Russian, Slovak, Tatar, Ukrainian **Romania:** Bulgarian, Czech, Croatian, German, Hungarian, Russian, Serbian, Slovak, Turkish, Ukrainian **Slovak Republic:** Bulgarian, Croatian, Czech, German, Polish, Romani, Ruthenian, Ukrainian, Hungarian[2] **Slovenia:** Italian, Hungarian **Spain:** Basque, Catalan, Valencian, Galician **Sweden:** Sami **Switzerland:** Romansh, Italian **United Kingdom:** Welsh (Wales), Scottish-Gaelic (Scotland), Irish (Northern Ireland)
	f	**Armenia:** Assyrian, Yezidi, Greek, Russian, Kurdish **Austria:** Slovenian (*Land* Carinthia) **Bosnia and Herzegovina:** Albanian, Montenegrin, Czech, Italian, Hungarian, Macedonian, German, Polish, Romanian, Rysin, Slovak, Slovenian, Turkish, Ukrainian, Jewish (Yiddish and Ladino), Romani **Croatia:** Italian, Serbian, Hungarian, Czech, Slovak, Ruthenian, Ukrainian **Czech Republic:** Polish (Moravian-Silesian region), Slovak **Denmark:** German (Southern Jutland) **Finland:** Sami, Swedish **Germany:** Danish (Schleswig Holstein), Upper Sorbian (Free State of Saxony), Lower Sorbian (*Land* Brandenburg), North Frisian (*Land* Schleswig-Holstein), Sater Frisian (Lower Saxony), Low German (Bremen, Hamburg, Mecklenburg-Western Pomerania, Lower Saxony, Schleswig-Holstein) **Hungary:** Croatian, German, Romanian, Serbian, Slovak, Slovenian, Romani, Beás **Montenegro:** Albanian, Romani **Netherlands:** Frisian (Friesland) **Norway:** Sami **Poland:** Belarusian, Czech, Hebrew, Yiddish, Karaim, Kashub, Lithuanian, Lemko, German, Armenian, Romani, Russian, Slovak, Tatar, Ukrainian **Romania:** Bulgarian. Czech, Croatian, German, Hungarian, Russian, Serbian, Slovak, Turkish, Ukrainian **Serbia:** Albanian, Bosnian, Bulgarian, Hungarian, Romani, Romanian, Ruthenian, Slovakian, Ukrainian, Croatian **Slovak Republic:** Bulgarian, Croatian, Czech, German, Polish, Romani, Ruthenian, Ukrainian, Hungarian **Slovenia:** Italian, Hungarian **Spain:** Basque, Catalan, Valencian, Galician **Sweden:** Sami, Finnish, Meänkieli **Switzerland:** Romansh, Italian

		Ukraine: Belarusian, Bulgarian, Gagauz, Greek, Jewish, Crimean Tatar, Moldovan, German, Polish, Russian, Romanian, Slovak, Hungarian **United Kingdom:** Welsh (Wales), Scottish-Gaelic (Scotland), Irish (Northern Ireland)
	g	**Bosnia and Herzegovina:** Albanian, Montenegrin, Czech, Italian, Hungarian, Macedonian, German, Polish, Romanian, Rysin, Slovak, Slovenian, Turkish, Ukrainian, Jewish (Yiddish and Ladino), Romani **Croatia:** Italian, Serbian, Hungarian, Czech, Slovak, Ruthenian, Ukrainian **Czech Republic:** Polish (Moravian-Silesian region), Slovak **Denmark:** German (Southern Jutland) **Finland:** Sami, Swedish **Germany:** Danish (Schleswig Holstein), Upper Sorbian (Free State of Saxony), Lower Sorbian (*Land* Brandenburg), North Frisian (*Land* Schleswig-Holstein), Sater Frisian (Lower Saxony), Low German (Bremen, Hamburg, Lower Saxony, Schleswig Holstein) **Hungary:** Croatian, German, Romanian, Serbian, Slovak, Slovenian, Romani, Beás **Netherlands:** Frisian (Friesland) **Norway:** Sami **Poland:** Belarusian, Czech, Hebrew, Yiddish, Karaim, Kashub, Lithuanian, Lemko, German, Armenian, Romani, Russian, Slovak, Tatar, Ukrainian **Romania:** Bulgarian, Czech, Croatian, German, Hungarian, Russian, Serbian, Slovak, Turkish, Ukrainian **Slovak Republic:** Bulgarian, Croatian, Czech, German, Polish, Romani, Ruthenian, Ukrainian, Hungarian **Spain:** Basque, Catalan, Valencian, Galician **Sweden:** Sami, Finnish, Meänkieli **Switzerland:** Romansh, Italian **Ukraine:** Belarusian, Bulgarian, Gagauz, Greek, Jewish, Crimean Tatar, Moldovan, German, Polish, Russian, Romanian, Slovak, Hungarian **United Kingdom:** Welsh (Wales), Scottish-Gaelic (Scotland)
	h	**Finland:** Sami, Swedish **Germany:** Upper Sorbian (Free State of Saxony), Lower Sorbian (*Land* Brandenburg), North Frisian (*Land* Schleswig-Holstein), Low German (Mecklenburg-Western Pomerania) **Netherlands:** Frisian (Friesland) **Norway:** Sami **Romania:** Bulgarian, Czech, Croatian, German, Hungarian, Russian, Serbian, Slovak, Turkish, Ukrainian **Spain:** Basque, Catalan, Valencian, Galician **Sweden:** Finnish, Sami **Switzerland:** Romansh, Italian **United Kingdom:** Welsh (Wales), Scottish-Gaelic (Scotland), Irish (Northern Ireland)
2		**Armenia:** Assyrian, Yezidi, Greek, Russian, Kurdish **Austria:** Burgenland Croatian (*Land* Burgenland), Slovenian (*Land* Carinthia), Hungarian (*Land* Burgenland)

		Bosnia and Herzegovina: Albanian, Montenegrin, Czech, Italian, Hungarian, Macedonian, German, Polish, Romanian, Rysin, Slovak, Slovenian, Turkish, Ukrainian, Jewish (Yiddish and Ladino), Romani **Czech Republic:** Polish (Moravian-Silesian region), Slovak **Denmark:** German (Southern Jutland) **Finland:** Sami, Swedish **Germany:** Danish (Schleswig Holstein), Upper Sorbian (Free State of Saxony), Lower Sorbian (*Land* Brandenburg), North Frisian (*Land* Schleswig-Holstein), Sater Frisian (Lower Saxony), Low German (Lower Saxony) **Hungary:** Croatian, German, Romanian, Serbian, Slovak, Slovenian, Romani, Beás **Montenegro:** Albanian, Romani **Netherlands:** Frisian (Friesland) **Norway:** Sami **Poland:** Belarusian, Czech, Hebrew, Yiddish, Karaim, Kashub, Lithuanian, Lemko, German, Armenian, Romani, Russian, Slovak, Tatar, Ukrainian **Romania:** Bulgarian, Czech, Croatian, German, Hungarian, Russian, Serbian, Slovak, Turkish, Ukrainian **Serbia:** Albanian, Bosnian, Bulgarian, Hungarian, Romani, Romanian, Ruthenian, Slovakian, Ukrainian, Croatian **Slovak Republic:** Bulgarian, Croatian, Czech, German, Polish, Romani, Ruthenian, Ukrainian, Hungarian **Slovenia:** Italian, Hungarian **Spain:** Basque, Catalan, Valencian, Galician **Sweden:** Sami, Finnish, Meänkieli **Switzerland:** Romansh, Italian **Ukraine:** Belarusian, Bulgarian, Gagauz, Greek, Jewish, Crimean Tatar, Moldovan, German, Polish, Russian, Romanian, Slovak, Hungarian **United Kingdom:** Welsh (Wales), Scottish-Gaelic (Scotland), Irish (Northern Ireland)
3		**Armenia:** Assyrian, Yezidi, Greek, Russian, Kurdish **Austria:** Burgenland Croatian (*Land* Burgenland), Slovenian (*Land* Carinthia), Hungarian (*Land* Burgenland) **Czech Republic:** Polish (Moravian-Silesian region), Slovak **Denmark:** German (Southern Jutland) **Finland:** Sami, Swedish **Germany:** Danish (Schleswig Holstein), Upper Sorbian (Free State of Saxony), Lower Sorbian (*Land* Brandenburg), North Frisian (*Land* Schleswig-Holstein), Sater Frisian (Lower Saxony), Low German (Bremen, Hamburg, Mecklenburg-Western Pomerania, Lower Saxony, Schleswig-Holstein) **Hungary:** Croatian, German, Romanian, Serbian, Slovak, Slovenian, Romani, Beás **Netherlands:** Frisian (Friesland) **Norway:** Sami **Poland:** Belarusian, Czech, Hebrew, Yiddish, Karaim, Kashub, Lithuanian, Lemko, German, Armenian, Romani, Russian, Slovak, Tatar, Ukrainian

Romania: Bulgarian, Czech, Croatian, German, Hungarian, Russian, Serbian, Slovak, Turkish, Ukrainian
Slovak Republic: Bulgarian, Croatian, Czech, German, Polish, Romani, Ruthenian, Ukrainian, Hungarian
Slovenia: Italian, Hungarian
Spain: Basque, Catalan, Valencian, Galician
Switzerland: Romansh, Italian
Ukraine: Belarusian, Bulgarian, Gagauz, Greek, Jewish, Crimean Tatar, Moldovan, German, Polish, Russian, Romanian, Slovak, Hungarian
United Kingdom: Welsh (Wales), Scottish-Gaelic (Scotland), Irish (Northern Ireland)

Article 13. Economic and social life

Iñigo Urrutia Libarona
University of the Basque Country

1. Introduction

2. General application
    2.1. Economic and social sectors as objectives and principles of the Charter
    2.2. Delimiting the concept of economic and social activities
    2.3. The Charter's strategy on economic and social activities

3. Commentary on the provisions: analysis of the Committee of Experts' position
    3.1. Economic and social activities across the country
        3.1.1. Eliminating provisions prohibiting or limiting the use of regional or minority languages (RMLs) in documents relating to economic or social life
        3.1.2. Prohibition of restrictive clauses in internal regulations of companies and private documents
        3.1.3. Opposition to practices designed to discourage the use of RMLs
        3.1.4. Facilitating and/or encouraging the use of RMLs by other means
    3.2. Economic and social activities in the territory in which regional languages are spoken
        3.2.1. Procedures for using the languages in financial documents
        3.2.2. Use of RMLs in the public sector
        3.2.3. Use of RMLs in the social services
        3.2.4. Safety instructions in RMLs
        3.2.5. Information on the rights of consumers

4. Recommendations and good practice: by way of conclusion

References

Appendix: Ratifications

Article 13 – Economic and social life

1. With regard to economic and social activities, the Parties undertake, within the whole country:

   a. to eliminate from their legislation any provision prohibiting or limiting without justifiable reasons the use of regional or minority languages in documents relating to economic or social life, particularly contracts of employment, and in technical documents such as instructions for the use of products or installations;

b. to prohibit the insertion in internal regulations of companies and private documents of any clauses excluding or restricting the use of regional or minority languages, at least between users of the same language;

c. to oppose practices designed to discourage the use of regional or minority languages in connection with economic or social activities;

d. to facilitate and/or encourage the use of regional or minority languages by means other than those specified in the above sub-paragraphs.

2. With regard to economic and social activities, the Parties undertake, in so far as the public authorities are competent, within the territory in which the regional or minority languages are used, and as far as this is reasonably possible:

a. to include in their financial and banking regulations provisions which allow, by means of procedures compatible with commercial practice, the use of regional or minority languages in drawing up payment orders (cheques, drafts, etc.) or other financial documents, or, where appropriate, to ensure the implementation of such provisions;

b. in the economic and social sectors directly under their control (public sector), to organise activities to promote the use of regional or minority languages;

c. to ensure that social care facilities such as hospitals, retirement homes and hostels offer the possibility of receiving and treating in their own language persons using a regional or minority language who are in need of care on grounds of ill-health, old age or for other reasons;

d. to ensure by appropriate means that safety instructions are also drawn up in regional or minority languages;

e. to arrange for information provided by the competent public authorities concerning the rights of consumers to be made available in regional or minority languages.

1. Introduction

The use of a language in social and economic circles is perhaps the primary means of measuring its vitality. The vitality of a language does not depend only on its legal status or recognition, but also, and above all, on its penetration and use in the economic, industrial, commercial and social spheres. In fact, the bulk of communication between regional- or minority-language speakers occurs in environments other than contacts with the public authorities.[1] The aim of

---

1. According to R. Dunbar (2008), "Definitively interpreting the European Charter for Regional or Minority Languages: the legal challenges" in R. Dunbar and G. Parry, *The European Charter for Regional or Minority Languages: legal challenges and opportunities*. Strasbourg: Council of Europe Publishing, p. 41, about 90% of all communications are with actors other than the public sectors.

protecting and promoting regional and minority languages must not be confined to official or public fields, which would in any case be incomplete and unsatisfactory. The socio-economic field is extremely important for the development and future of regional or minority languages (RMLs).[2]

In an increasingly globalised and interrelated world, regional and/or minority languages are facing intense challenges. The opening up of markets, freedoms of movement and settlement, and side effects of economic globalisation like deregulation and privatisation have obvious repercussions on all languages. Economic freedoms are not linguistically neutral. They favour some languages and put others under pressure, regardless of their status, producing mutual imbalances.[3] Even though this is a global phenomenon, the mechanisms for coping with this effect are not the same for official languages and RMLs.

Nevertheless, instead of the traditional approach of analysing the influence of the economy on languages (and linguistic diversity), we might take the opposite tack. Languages and linguistic diversity also influence the economy. Linguistic knowledge and language learning can be important for economic success.[4] From the economic angle, RMLs should be valued to the extent that they can contribute to economic and social development, injecting life into the language. From a purely economic point of view, plurilingualism is also an opportunity to be seized, a positive factor. In the final analysis, economic factors can be used to protect and promote RMLs and their social development. Bearing in mind that the European Charter for Regional or Minority Languages ("the Charter") does not directly grant rights to the users of RMLs, this economic and social perspective is important for interpreting the scope of the Charter. This approach did not pass unnoticed by the Committee of Experts, who advanced in this direction in connection with transfrontier co-operation.[5] This approach involving promotion and enhancement of plurilingualism has also been adopted by the European Union.[6]

---

2. See the reflections of L. A. Grenoble and L. J. Whaley (2006), *Saving languages*. Cambridge: Cambridge University Press, pp. 18 and 125. In the same sense see L. Hinton and K. L. Hale (2001), *The green book of language revitalization in practice*. San Diego: Academic Press, p. 3. For an historical point of view see X. Irujo and I. Urrutia (2010), *A legal history of the Basque language*. Donostia: Society for Basque Studies, *in toto*.

3. This is why, in the light of the pressure exerted by economic freedoms on language, many states have reacted by enacting language legislation in defence of their official languages. France provides an outstanding example in this connection; see R. Debbasch (1992), "La reconnaissance constitutionnelle de la langue française", *Revue Française de Droit Constitutionnelle*, No. 11, p. 461.

4. Until now this perspective has been very little analysed; see D. Crystal (2000), *Language death*. Cambridge: Cambridge University Press, p. 31. See also F. Grin, C. Sfreddo and F. Vaillancourt (2010), *The economics of the multilingual workplace*. New York: Routledge, p. 250.

5. See Slovenia 2004, 158.

6. See Council Conclusions of 22 May 2008 on multilingualism: 2008/C 140/10 (OJ C 140/14 6.6.2008).

The socio-economic sector is vital for the development of languages, but it is extremely complex in legal terms. There are various reasons for this complexity. Firstly, we must consider that the main stakeholders in the social and economic sectors are private individuals, who work within a framework characterised by the freedom principle. In the economic and social systems which operate in the member states of the Council of Europe, intervention by the public authorities in economic and social life is confined to establishing a general framework by means of legislation and regulations. In the private sphere, unlike in the public or institutional fields, the public authorities have limited scope for influencing linguistic behaviour and rules on the part of economic stakeholders, as this area involves such fundamental rights as freedom of expression and basic individual liberties such as freedom of the press, trade and industry, freedom of settlement, movement, etc.

The principle of freedom of language is inseparable from the socio-economic sector, although this does not mean that all state intervention is prohibited here. From the legal angle, it would be wrong to assert that the public authorities are powerless to intervene in the socio-economic field to safeguard languages. To comprehend the framework for the legitimate development of language policy measures, we must start from the fact that freedom of expression is not incompatible with a policy of promoting RMLs, as the Committee of Experts has rightly stressed: "freedom of expression … is not compromised by facilitating or promoting the use of regional or minority languages".[7] On the other hand, freedom of expression would be incompatible with compulsory exclusive use of the official language in the socio-economic sector. The Human Rights Committee has ruled that imposing the use of a single official language (in commercial signposting) to the exclusion of any others was a disproportionate measure and therefore an infringement of freedom of expression.[8] The aforementioned committee has specified that the aim of safeguarding a vulnerable language in the economic sphere can be considered a legitimate goal in respect of which some degree of attachment to freedom of expression might be deemed justified.[9]

The capacity of member states for intervening in the socio-economic sphere depends on a wide range of factors: first of all, the type of social or economic activity in question, since not all such activities are homogeneous in terms of

---

7. Germany 2002, 59.
8. Human Rights Committee, *John Ballantyne et al v. Canada*. Communication Nos. 359/1989, 385/1989, UN Doc. CCPR/C/47/D/385/1989 (1993), paragraph 11.4.
9. R. Leckey and E. Didier (2004), "The private law of language" in M. Bastarache, *Language rights in Canada*, 2nd edn. Cowansville: Yvon Blais, p. 472; J. Woehrling (1987), "La réglementation linguistique de l'affichage public et de la liberté d'expression. *PG Québec c. Chaussure Brown's Inc*", *McGill Law Journal*, Vol. 32.

the informational aspect of the message or the involvement of public interests or third party rights, as in the case of consumers' and users' rights.[10] Secondly, the transfer of legislative powers in the commercial and economic field from the government departments closest to the RMLs to remoter levels (state or European Union) means involving a great many bodies in designing and planning policies to promote RMLs. Thirdly, we must consider the major discrepancies between European states in terms of the framework within which their socio-economic services have to develop: this, combined with the enormous dynamism of the sector, which is constantly changing thanks to the processes of liberalisation, and under the influence of budget cuts deriving from the world economic downturn affecting the welfare state,[11] is raising enormous obstacles to the emergence of a general European framework for promoting regional and minority languages.

In view of the complexity of all the aforementioned factors, let us now go on to analyse the approach and strategy adopted in the Charter vis-à-vis the socio-economic sector, which is mainly governed by Article 13.

2. General application

2.1. Economic and social sectors as objectives and principles of the Charter

The Charter pinpoints the major importance for RMLs of their use in fields unconnected with the public authorities, including therefore the social and economic areas. As the Explanatory Report points out, the aim of the Charter is to facilitate the use of such languages, *inter alia*, in "economic and social life and cultural activities".[12] The Explanatory Report adds that this objective is also geared to compensating any unfavourable conditions in the past and preserving and developing the languages as a living facet of Europe's cultural identity. This perspective is very important in a field like the socio-economic sphere where regional and minority languages are particularly affected by standardising forces

---

10. See I. Urrutia (2008), "Los requisitos lingüísticos en la actividad socioeconómica y en el mundo del audiovisual" in A. Milian (ed.), *Mundialització, lliure circulació i immigració, i l'exigència d'una llengua com a requisit*. Barcelona: Institut d'Estudis Autònomics, pp. 173-310.

11. K. Banting, R. Johnston, W. Kymlicka and S. Soroka (2006), "Do multiculturalism policies erode the welfare state? An empirical analysis" in K. Banting and W. Kymlicka, *Multiculturalism and the welfare state*. Oxford/NY: Oxford University Press, p. 72, highlight that there is no evidence of a consistent pattern of the adoption of multicultural policies leading to erosion of the welfare state.

12. European Charter for Regional or Minority Languages, ETS No. 148: Explanatory Report, paragraph 10.

and the free market.[13] The Charter's objective of protecting and promoting RMLs covers action in the socio-economic and employment fields.

The overall aim of protecting and promoting languages in the private spheres is clearly expressed in some of the provisions of Part II, especially Article 7.1c and d. These two provisions, applicable in areas where RMLs are spoken, require parties to base their policies, legislation and practice on the following objectives and principles: "the need for resolute action to promote regional or minority languages in order to safeguard them", which also affects the socio-economic sphere, and "the facilitation and/or encouragement of the use of regional or minority languages, in speech and writing, in public and private life".

Both these provisions are vital for the Charter system. The former reflects the idea that it is not enough for states to refrain from restricting the development of RMLs, instead requiring a positive, solid support strategy geared to promoting the languages.[14] The Committee of Experts breaks this strategy down into three strands: a legal framework, an organisational structure and an adequate financial framework.[15] Article 7.1d of the Charter lays down that the drive to promote languages must include measures to promote the possibility of freely using RMLs in speech and writing, in both public and private life.

This undertaking refers both to "public life" and "private life", areas which are defined differently in the different legal systems of the states party to the Charter. For the purposes of the Charter, according to the Explanatory Report, the concept of "public life" should be understood as "community life", "that is to say within the framework of institutions, social activities and economic life".[16] The title of Part III of the Charter includes the concept of "public life". Thus, all sectors referred to in Part III are included in the concept of "public life", covering not only relations with the public authorities but also social and

---

13. See the reflections on the threats to regional or minority languages by J.-M. Woehrling (2005), *The European Charter for Regional or Minority Languages: a critical commentary*. Strasbourg: Council of Europe Publishing, p. 46. See also F. Grin (2003), *Language policy evaluation and the European Charter for Regional or Minority Languages*. Basingstoke/New York: Palgrave Macmillan, pp. 99-113.

14. This could be considered as a general expression of the positive aspect of the equality principle, especially as the Explanatory Report points out that "by reason of the weakness of numerous regional or minority languages, the mere prohibition of discrimination is not sufficient to ensure their survival. They need positive support" (paragraph 61). However, according to Woehrling (2005), op. cit., p. 112, the intensity of such a policy may vary in accordance with the situation of each language.

15. Among others, see Denmark 2007, 33; Germany 2006, 24; Finland 2007, 38; Sweden 2006, 28; Norway 2007, 34; Slovenia 2007, 36; Spain 2008, 103; Hungary 2007, 13.

16. ECRML: Explanatory Report, paragraph 62.

economic life. This broad approach[17] has been highlighted by the Committee of Experts, stressing the need for a wide-ranging interpretation of "public life" in its reports on Croatia 2001[18] and Denmark 2004.[19]

However, the main question arising from this undertaking is its extension to socio-economic activities. What does the undertaking to facilitate or encourage the use of RMLs in public life presuppose? Does it involve unlimited access via RMLs to all socio-economic sectors without any kind of restriction? The answer to this question is a clear "no". In accordance with the spirit of the Charter, the place to be granted each language in the socio-economic sector depends on its specific social and legal situation and features. The provision requires the state to promote the languages, but does not set any specific standard of general protection. This is how the specialists have interpreted it,[20] considering it compatible with this undertaking to set limits and restrictions on RMLs provided that the former do not contradict the promotion policy.

The Committee of Experts has noted that this undertaking requires not an exclusively passive attitude permitting the use of the languages, but a really proactive approach (United Kingdom 2004;[21] cf. Denmark 2004).[22] The committee highlights the insufficiency of a merely passive attitude confined to prohibiting discrimination. In its 2008 report on Croatia, it mentioned the low profile of minority languages in public life, criticising the authorities for adopting a reactive rather than proactive approach. The attainment of this objective could not be measured because of the lack of complaints from users of the minority languages, "whereas the implementation of the Charter requires the authorities to take positive measures to encourage and promote

---

17. See P. Thornberry (2002) "The Charter and the role and responsibility of the state" in *From theory to practice: the European Charter for Regional or Minority Languages*. Strasbourg: Council of Europe Publishing, p. 30.
18. Croatia 2001, 34: "public life" fairly wide and can include the use of the language in education, justice, administration, economic and social life, cultural life, the media and cross-border exchanges".
19. Denmark 2004, 36: the word "public" must be interpreted in a broad sense "to include the use of languages in education, the courts, administration, and economic, social and cultural life".
20. See Woehrling (2005), op. cit., p. 114: "what the Charter asks is that, overall, regional languages should have access to public life, even if there are rules and limits imposed, as long those rules and limits do not substantively affect access". See also R. Dunbar in this volume.
21. United Kingdom 2004, 57: "this obligation does not only imply passive permission to use languages in public and private life, but requires the State Party to facilitate and/or encourage the use of the languages in the various public spheres. This would evidently require a pro-active approach".
22. Denmark 2004, 36: "it should be underlined that this obligation does not only imply passive permission to use regional or minority languages in public and private life, but require the state party to facilitate and/or encourage the use of the languages in these specific public spheres. This would evidently require a pro-active approach".

the use of regional or minority languages in public life".[23] The undertaking requires the adoption of measures geared to increasing the presence and visibility of the languages in public life.[24] It would be inappropriate, for the purposes of meeting this requirement, to treat minority languages as foreign languages or to confine promotion activities to the educational and cultural fields,[25] never mind a policy having the effect of reducing its use and visibility.[26] The provision requires states to adopt a clear policy to promote the use of the languages in question, which policy may vary in form depending on the specific characteristics of each language (legislation, funding programmes, constancy of political support, etc.).[27]

Nonetheless, it must be said that the Committee of Experts' reports have not devoted excessive attention to the protection afforded by Article 7.1d vis-à-vis the socio-economic sector. In analysing the extent to which states facilitate or encourage the use of the relevant languages in the socio-economic sector, the committee usually refers to its comments on Part III of the Charter, particularly Article 13.[28] The exception is in the 2006 report on Sweden: "the Committee of Experts' attention has been drawn to the lack of a structured approach to the provisions of healthcare in regional or minority languages. There is a growing need for healthcare and elderly care services in regional or minority languages. The problem seems to be particularly urgent for Finnish-speakers due to the fact that the number of Swedish-Finnish retired persons is rapidly increasing, whereas the number of Finnish-speaking social care personnel seems to be decreasing. The Committee of Experts is concerned about the situation as described. It encourages the authorities to take measures to improve the situation and come back to the Committee of Experts in the next periodical report."[29]

How are we to analyse this approach? The committee concentrates its questions on the lack of resources to guarantee health care and treatment for elderly persons in RMLs on the basis of Article 7.1d of the Charter. In order to understand the situation, we must realise that Sweden has adopted only one undertaking from Part III relating to the socio-economic sector, namely that set out in Article 13.1a, not 13.2c, which explicitly refers to the social services

---

23. Croatia 2008, 18.
24. Spain 2005, 129: "measures aimed at increasing the presence and visibility in public life": this could depend heavily on the extent of their recognition at the national level.
25. Germany 2002, 59.
26. Spain 2005, 119: "a clear policy of encouragement of the use of Basque in the official sphere and in public life and some elements actually suggest a decline in the use of Basque in this sphere in the 'mixed zone' [of Navarra]".
27. See United Kingdom 2004, 57; Hungary 2001, 24.
28. Article 13 is discussed below in sections 2.2 and 4 (the third point).
29. Sweden 2006, 40.

(hospitals, retirement homes and hostels, etc.). Given the obviously serious problem in the health and social welfare sector and the fact that Sweden has accepted few practical undertakings from Part III of the Charter, the committee apparently focuses its doubts on the country's compliance with Article 7.1d. In the following report on Sweden (3rd monitoring cycle) in 2009, the committee highlighted the major and growing importance of this subject for speakers of regional languages and for the authorities, concluding with the following: "the Committee of Experts ask the authorities to investigate, in co-operation with speakers, whether the undertakings concerning these areas could be part of an extended ratification instrument".[30] In conclusion, given the obviously serious problem in this sector, Article 7.1d of the Charter would appear to require the implementation of a structured and proactive policy in the health sector and services for the elderly, which might be perfectly realisable by adopting specific undertakings from Part III and putting them into practice.

2.2. Delimiting the concept of economic and social activities

The main Charter article dealing with social and economic activities is Article 13, entitled "Economic and social life". The first question to be tackled is how to delimit the concept in order to differentiate it from other related Charter concepts.

In delimiting the concepts of "economic life" and "social life", neither the Charter nor the Explanatory Report gives any clue to their meanings for the purposes of the Charter. In many cases, the references are specific (contracts of employment, technical documents, instructions for the use of products or installations, internal regulations of companies, payment orders, cheques), which means there are no problems. In other cases, however, the Charter contains a hybrid, non-specific reference – "documents relating to economic and social life" (Article 13.1a), "economic and social activities" (Article 13.1c) and "economic and social sectors" (Article 13.2b). Broadly speaking, for legal purposes, there is a strict borderline between economic and social activities. Both share the fact of operating in a general environment characterised by limited or non-existent public intervention.[31] These fields are primarily subject to private law.

---

30. Sweden 2009, 33-4.
31. For legal purposes, the really important factor might be how difficult it is to identify link-up points for establishing linguistic measures. For instance, the implementation of consumers' rights in a specific social or economic activity would facilitate the introduction of promotional measures; similarly, the (varying) capacity for intervention by the public authorities in the banking sector facilitates (to varying degrees) the application of a language policy to financial documents.

At all events, national delimitation of the concepts of "economic life" and "social life" is of little importance for the purposes of the Charter. There are three reasons for this. Firstly, the main focus of Article 13 in establishing language undertakings is the principle of non-discrimination. Secondly, the search for the appropriate means and tools available within each internal legal order to implement the undertakings is a domestic matter for the state parties. Fulfilling the undertakings of the Charter is a matter for the member states under international law, though they cannot be allowed to adopt a passive attitude through lack of supervision of the relevant field of activity. Thirdly, even though the undertakings are confined to the jurisdiction of the public authorities, the use of languages in the private economic and social spheres can reasonably be promoted by means of incentives which do not give rise to theoretically insuperable difficulties.

Much greater importance attaches to the issue of identifying the scope of Article 13 and differentiating it from other provisions of the Charter, particularly Article 10.3 on public services. A wide range of socio-economic activities can take the form of public services if they are geared to meeting citizens' fundamental needs. The reality of public services and other services of general interest is complex and heterogeneous, involving many activities ranging from major network industries (energy, postal services, transport and telecommunications) to health, education and the social services. Article 10.3 of the Charter lays down few demarcation guidelines here, covering public services in general as provided by the administrative authorities or other agencies acting on their behalf. The purpose stated for the activity does not help differentiate the scopes of articles 10.3 and 13, given that private companies operating under the supervision of public bodies which provide socio-economic public services also fall within the ambit of Article 10.3. Nor do the legal regulations governing service provision help define the areas covered by articles 10.3 and 13 respectively, since, as the Explanatory Report points out, Article 10.3 deals with "bodies providing public services, whether under public or private law, where they remain under public control: postal services, hospitals, electricity, transport, and so on".[32] Similarly, the criterion of operational or functional dependence is of little help, since it is applicable not only to Article 10.3 but also to Article 13.2b on "the economic and social sectors directly under their control (public sector)".

In the final analysis, while socio-economic activities unconnected with the public services fall exclusively within the ambit of Article 13 of the Charter, other activities described as public services are also subject to Article 10.3, provided that these activities are conducted under the supervision or direction of the public authorities. One of the aims of the authors of the Charter was to extend Article 13.3 to public service activities, regardless of the public or private

---

32. ECRML: Explanatory Report, paragraph 102 (*in fine*).

status of those providing them and of the economic sector in question.[33] This aim must be regarded as positive, since an approach based exclusively on the public status of the body providing the public service would be unsatisfactory and incomplete in a context of liberalisation and privatisation in Europe, factors which are liable to affect language guarantees.[34] The important thing is not the public or private status of the agency providing the service but the "publicness" of the service itself. The existence of public services is the linkage point for implementing the measures for promoting RMLs (Article 13.2), as is the fact of providing economic and social services subject to public supervision (Article 13.2c) or social care services, regardless of who is providing them (Article 13.2c).

Articles 10.3 and 13 of the Charter must be interpreted in a complementary manner, or else one will exclude the other.[35] Considering that Article 10.3 sets out alternative higher- or lower- level undertakings, the higher level "ensur[ing] that the regional or minority languages are used in the provision of the service", it is possible that in some cases these undertakings are stricter than those set out in Article 13.2b, which, in connection with the public sector (in general), requires "organis[ing] activities to promote the use of regional or minority languages" in the economic and social sectors (including the public services, though not exclusively there). Sometimes it is the other way round, because the undertaking on hospitals and social care facilities (public and private) in Article 13.2c is stricter than that in Article 10.3c. Ultimately, the fulfilment of undertakings vis-à-vis socio-economic services must be analysed on the basis of maximum complementarity and the undertakings adopted by the states parties. The Committee of Experts has usually adopted this approach, which we consider correct, in analysing this matter.[36]

2.3. The Charter's strategy on economic and social activities

One of the Charter's objectives is to provide regional and minority languages with room for development in social and economic activities. In view of the authorities' limited capacity for influencing social and economic sectors, the

---

33. See Woehrling (2005), op. cit., p. 195: "the authors of the Charter decided to devote a special subparagraph to such activities because in some countries it may be easier to promote languages in the context of service provision than in the more formal context of administrative measures reflecting exercise of official powers. Sometimes it is the other way round, being more difficult to cater for regional or minority languages in a public service context".
34. On this concern see Germany 2008, 38.
35. I agree with the opinion of Woehrling (2005), op. cit., pp. 195-6.
36. See Spain 2008, 279, analysing the undertakings from the angle of Article 10.3, and paragraph 1183 of the same report analysing the undertakings from the angle of Article 13.2b, whereby the same postal and transport agencies are responsible in both cases.

Charter adopts a twofold strategy. On the one hand, it advocates eliminating measures to prohibit or discourage the use of these languages in economic and social life, and, on the other, it encourages the adoption of a series of positive measures.

This approach involves implementing the principle of non-discrimination.[37] Other conventions also advocate the approach based on the principle of equality and non-discrimination,[38] but Article 13 of the Charter displays certain distinctive features. Firstly, it covers the negative aspect of the equality principle relating to the elimination of restrictions on the grounds of language, as well as the positive dimension relating to promoting action to encourage the use of the language in the social and economic fields. This has prompted the Committee of Experts to declare that "by reason of their relative economic and political weakness, minority languages are at an inherent disadvantage … It is necessary and appropriate for this imbalance to be redressed by positive measures."[39] Such positive measures should not apply exceptionally or solely to special cases: "the Committee of Experts observes that states parties to the Charter are obliged to actively promote regional or minority languages in all domains of public life, not limited to 'extremely unfavourable living conditions'."[40]

The second distinctive aspect concerns protection of the principle of non-discrimination, which in this case refers to the "use of regional or minority languages" in the socio-economic field. The subject of the protection efforts and beneficiary of the anti-discrimination measures is the use (and the users)

---

37. See paragraph 122 of the Explanatory Report.
38. Non-discrimination is central to many international treaties, including Article 14 of the Convention for the Protection of Human Rights and Fundamental Freedoms and Article 2 of the Universal Declaration of Human Rights of 10 December 1948. Similarly, we might mention Article 2.2 of the International Covenant on Economic, Social and Cultural Rights of 16 December 1966, and Article 27 of the International Covenant on Civil and Political Rights, of the same date, which requires more positive action (see General Observation No. 23, General comments adopted by the Human Rights Committee, Article 27 – Rights of minorities, 50th Session period, UN Doc. HRI/GEN/1/Rev.7 at 183 (1994), paragraph 6.2), and articles 4.2 and 15 of the Framework Convention for the Protection of National Minorities of 1 February 1995. There are, however, substantial differences between the Framework Convention and the ECRML in this field. The Framework Convention requires parties to create the conditions necessary for the "effective participation" of persons belonging to minorities in cultural, social and economic life (paragraph 80 of the Explanatory Report to the Framework Convention), and the ECRML only refers to specific language services in areas relevant to social and economic life. The two texts differ in scope. It might be said that both instruments operate in parallel, only converging on the fact that both cover the negative and positive dimensions of the equality principle.
39. See Germany 2002, 59.
40. See Serbia 2009, 70.

of the RMLs.[41] The Charter does not operate from the angle of preventing the users of the regional languages from being discriminated against in exercising rights in the socio-economic sector, but is geared to ensuring development of these languages in this sector. This approach is particularly interesting in the socio-economic sector, which involves the free play of market rules, allowing stakeholders to influence events. In the final analysis, this clause requires states parties to eliminate any measures liable to harm the use of RMLs in the socio-economic sphere, as specified in Article 13.

Thirdly, the equality-based approach does not involve any kind of restriction on the use of official languages or strict uniformity in the treatment of all languages. Like Article 7.2, Article 13.1a refers to provisions "prohibiting or limiting without justifiable reasons the use of regional or minority languages". What is prohibited is unjustified differentiated treatment, although the level of protection is established by the undertakings of Article 13 which are adopted in each case, having regard to the situation of each language. Accordingly, national legislation requiring use of the Slovak language in the functioning of the health services prompts the following comment from the committee: "the Committee of Experts encourages the Slovak authorities to take the necessary steps to remove the clauses of Act No. 270/1995 which lead to unjustified distinction, exclusion, restriction or preference relating to the use of regional or minority languages in Slovakia".[42] Unjustifiable distinctions are incompatible with the Charter.

Fourthly, the twofold approach combining non-discrimination and positive action is designed as a means of preventing assimilation and encouraging integration. The Committee of Experts has highlighted the fact that merely applying anti-discriminatory measures can have assimilatory effects on the languages in question and the cultural identity of those speaking them: "The Committee of Experts underlines that integration in line with the principles set out in the Charter, is one which allows for a full participation in economic, social and political life, combined with the preservation of one's linguistic and cultural identity".[43] "Integration under the Charter must enable both full participation in economic, social and political life and the opportunity to preserve one's linguistic and cultural identity".[44] The social and economic development of RMLs via positive measures is the means of securing integration.

---

41. See Woehrling (2005), op. cit., p. 123: "the use of a language is here regarded not as a mode of exercising a freedom, but as a freedom in itself". See also J.-M. Woehrling (2008), "The European Charter for Regional or Minority Languages and the principle of non-discrimination" in R. Dunbar and G. Parry, *The European Charter ... legal challenges and opportunities*, p. 69.
42. Slovakia 2007, 76.
43. Hungary 2004, 43.
44. Slovenia 2004, 88.

The Charter also adopts a twofold geographical strategy responding to the characteristics of the economic sector. The capacity of the public authorities for intervention here depends on the structure of legal and other responsibilities in the economic field. The market clause is usually linked to state (or, where appropriate, federal) competence in the economic field. Areas where RMLs are spoken, which often have regional political or administrative powers, usually have limited competences in the economic sector. This is why the two paragraphs of Article 13 of the Charter draw a distinction between undertakings in the socio-economic field applicable to the whole country (paragraph 1), to be implemented mainly under general national legislation, and those applicable in the territory where the RMLs are spoken (paragraph 2).

This twofold approach requires the active participation of all local and regional administrative levels in promoting the languages in the socio-economic sector, although this can sometimes prove difficult. The Committee of Experts has highlighted the inappropriateness of state passivity based on the argument that the fulfilment of the undertakings regarding economic and social life is a matter for the autonomous communities and private social initiative.[45] Conversely, the failure to fulfil undertakings in the socio-economic field by local and regional authorities cannot be considered as justifying state inaction either.[46] Under international law, responsibility for compliance with the Charter lies with the state (the central authorities), even if the Charter's requirements must be enforced in accordance with the national apportionment of powers and responsibilities.[47]

3. Commentary on the provisions: analysis of the Committee of Experts' position

Article 13 comprises two paragraphs. The first deals with economic and social activities throughout the whole country, while the second concerns economic and social activities in the territory in which RMLs are spoken. We shall analyse these two paragraphs separately below.

---

45. Spain 2008, 69: "The Committee of Experts reiterates that, as for other provisions, the promotion of regional or minority languages is not the exclusive responsibility of the respective Autonomous Communities and that the central authorities are responsible for implementing this undertaking" (See also, in this very same sense, United Kingdom 2004, 34).

46. Sweden 2006, 22: "the central authorities remain responsible at the international level for obligations that Sweden has assumed under the Charter. They should therefore deploy all efforts to ensure that these undertakings are complied with, *inter alia*, by informing municipalities of their obligations under the Charter, providing them with the necessary technical and financial support, giving detailed instructions, supervising implementation, as well as by using appropriate incentives, and when necessary, sanctions."

47. Spain 2008, 65; United Kingdom 2004, 34.

3.1. Economic and social activities across the country

The first three undertakings in this paragraph have a negative wording, as they express the principle of non-discrimination, unlike the fourth and final undertaking.

3.1.1. Eliminating provisions prohibiting or limiting the use of regional or minority languages (RMLs) in documents relating to economic or social life

The undertaking set out in Article 13.1a has the specificity of explicitly mentioning the actual manner in which states must comply with it, namely by means of legislative reforms. Although, broadly speaking, ratifying the Charter requires states to bring their domestic legislation into line with the text, fulfilling this undertaking explicitly requires the state to amend its legislation where the latter contains provisions prohibiting or limiting the use of the languages in question. This approach is the same as that of Article 7.2 of the Charter, of which Article 13.1a is a sectoral extension.

In accordance with this undertaking, states must eliminate from their legislation any provisions prohibiting or limiting without justifiable reasons the use of RMLs in documents relating to economic or social life. The object of this requirement is the legislation setting out the prohibition or limitations, rather than the fact of prohibiting or limiting the use of the languages in documents relating to social and economic life, which are covered not by this subparagraph but by 13.1c. Nor does the provision cover any limitations or prohibitions which might arise *de facto* where RMLs are to be used in documents relating to social and economic life, where protection is not explicitly provided for in legislation. The word "legislation" should be interpreted in the broad sense to include other forms of prescriptions such as regulations. Consequently, the undertaking is fulfilled where the laws or statutes *de facto* comprise no formal prohibitions on the use of languages.

The Committee of Experts has invariably interpreted the provision in this manner. The undertaking is considered fulfilled unless there are formal legal prohibitions excluding or limiting the use of RMLs in the documents in question.[48] Confirmation

---

48. Croatia 2001, 104; Germany 2002, 131, 167; Hungary 2001, 76; Spain 2005, 980; Sweden 2003, 170, 284, 393; Finland 2001, 190: "There are no provisions in Finnish legislation prohibiting the use of Sami in economic and social activities. The Committee considers this undertaking fulfilled". United Kingdom 2004, 186: "there are no areas of public life in which there are provisions prohibiting the use of the language. The Committee considers this undertaking fulfilled"; Denmark 2004, 104: "the undertaking is considered fulfilled since the Danish Act on the Employer's Duty to inform the Employee of the Terms of Employment does not specify the language in which the contract of employment should be drawn up".

of the lack of a formal prohibition is sufficient for the committee to conclude that the undertaking has been fulfilled, although in some cases it has also set out a positive appraisal of certain standards and practices. In paragraph 123 of the 2001 report on Finland, the committee considered this undertaking fulfilled because contracts of employment could be drawn up in the minority language, adding that there was also a policy of translating laws, regulations and provisions in labour law into the minority language.[49] In other cases, the committee has deemed positive the adoption of an anti-discrimination provision at domestic level as a measure against practices relevant to this undertaking;[50] it has also approved the existence of domestic (municipal) legislation requiring the use of bilingual signs in companies and economic organisations.[51] The same applies to prescriptions on language policy and consumers' rights which, though they do not comprise a specific prohibition on including restrictive clauses, are geared to promoting Catalan in the socio-economic sphere.[52]

This undertaking refers to provisions prohibiting the use of regional languages in documents relating to economic and social life, explicitly mentioning "contracts of employment and technical documents such as instructions for the use of products or installations". We may first note that the provision does not refer to oral use of the languages, which aspect was deliberately omitted.[53] The Committee of Experts addressed this point in its report on Finland when it stated that the fact that sometimes in practice, especially in some larger enterprises, there is no real incentive to use Swedish does not prevent the undertaking from being fulfilled.[54] Nevertheless, we can conclude that a legal prohibition of the oral use of languages in activities is incompatible with Article 7.2 of the Charter, which refers gener-ally to the "use" of languages. A lack of measures to promote such use is also inconsistent with this undertaking.

In connection with the documents mentioned in this provision, the expression "technical documents such as instructions for the use of products or installa-tions" deserves particular attention. In many cases, under EU legislation on labelling and presentation of products, it is possible for legislation to require

---

49. Finland 2001, 123.
50. Germany 2006, 83.
51. Slovenia 2004, 153, 228.
52. Spain 2008, 321.
53. J.-M. Woehrling (2005), *The European Charter ... a critical commentary*, p. 225: "whereas the initial version of the Charter submitted to the CLRAE referred to 'acts' of social and economic life as well as 'documents' relating to social and economic activity, Article 13.1.a mentions only 'documents relating to economic and social life'."
54. Finland 2001, 123.

technical documents to be drafted in the official languages of the EU.[55] This undertaking does not oppose such requirements. Where legislation requires use of the official language, this undertaking will require the use of RMLs not to be (legally) restricted.[56]

The list of documents contained in Article 13.1a is open-ended, rather than exhaustive. In addition to the documents mentioned, it also covers other documents relating to social and economic life. Under Article 13.1a, the Committee of Experts has considered documents relating to contracts of employment,[57] economic activities[58] the registration of associations and foundations, notarial registrations and registered goods,[59] financial and technical documentation, statutes of associations, unions and companies,[60] and bilingual signposting in companies and economic organisations.[61]

The 2001 report on the Netherlands highlights the non-fulfilment of this undertaking on the grounds that the names of associations and foundations cannot be registered in RMLs at the Chamber of Commerce.[62] The following report had inquired about legislative reforms to allow registration of association and foundations in the minority language (without any need for translation if the activity is conducted in the Province of Friesland), although this would not apply to specified companies. Another legislative reform permits notarial registrations in the minority language, but not the listing of registered goods. Despite these exceptions, which would suggest non-fulfilment of the undertaking, the committee notes positive developments and therefore concludes that the undertaking is fulfilled.[63] This illustrates its dynamic reading of the Charter.

The undertaking does not lay down a radical prohibition. What is required is to eliminate legal prohibitions or limitations which lack "justifiable reasons". Neither Article 13.1a nor Article 7.2 specifies which reasons are deemed justified, but such reasons, which must be formulated by the state party, must be compatible with the objectives of the Charter and be proportionate to the aims

---

55. See for example Article 16.2 and 3 of Directive 2000/13/EC of the European Parliament and of the Council of 20 March 2000 on the approximation of the laws of the member states relating to the labelling, presentation and advertising of foodstuffs.
56. Denmark 2004, 104. In connection with technical documents (instructions for use, etc.), legislation sometimes requires them to be available in Danish, although this does not prevent the provision of the same information in German as well, so that the undertaking is fulfilled.
57. Denmark 2004, 104; Finland 2001, 123.
58. Finland 2001, 190.
59. The Netherlands 2004, 175-6.
60. Slovakia 2007, 175, 285, 370, 454, 534.
61. Slovenia 2004, 153, 228.
62. The Netherlands 2001, 101.
63. The Netherlands 2004, 175-6.

pursued.[64] Obviously, any attempt to discourage the use of RMLs and exclusively promote the use of the official language is incompatible with the Charter. The Committee of Experts referred to this in its 2007 report on Slovakia, analysing the compatibility with the Charter of national legislation requiring use of the majority language in specified activities:

> legal documents related to labour relations, financial and technical documentation, statutes of associations, unions and companies. *Prima facie* this appears to be a limitation to the use of a regional or minority language, such as Romani (Hungarian, German, Ruthenian, Ukrainian, …). No justification for this limitation has been given to the Committee of Experts by the Slovak authorities. The Committee of Experts considers therefore that this undertaking is not fulfilled. … The Committee of Experts encourages the authorities to eliminate from their legislation any provision prohibiting or limiting without justifiable reasons the use of regional or minority languages in documents relating to economic and social life.[65]

This undertaking does not involve any limitation on legislation requiring the use of the state's official language, although if this requirement is exclusive it is indeed incompatible with the Charter provision.

3.1.2. Prohibition of restrictive clauses in internal regulations of companies and private documents

The undertaking set out in Article 13.1b concerns banning the inclusion of prohibitive or restrictive clauses in the internal regulations of companies and private documents. In connection with internal regulations and private documents,[66] the question is what this undertaking requires of the states parties and whether it can be fulfilled, as in the previous case, by a mere formal finding of non-existence of such restrictive clauses, or a request to eliminate such clauses if any are found to exist.

The Committee of Experts has accompanied this undertaking with a certain requirement vis-à-vis legal action, reflected in the expression "to prohibit". It is not enough to note the non-existence of restrictive or prohibitive clauses in private documents: legislation must cover prohibition of such clauses. In its 2001 report on Croatia, the committee noted that Croatian legislation contained no provisions

---

64. Woehrling (2005), op. cit., p. 124.
65. Slovakia 2007, 175, 285, 370, 454, 534.
66. In connection with private documents, the undertaking requires prohibiting clauses that exclude or limit the use of regional or minority languages "at least between users of the same language". The reference to users of the same language is confusing. It is illogical to contemplate clauses limiting the use of the regional or minority language in the case of persons who do not speak the language; such situations simply preclude communication. What the provision appears to be saying, albeit in a confused and confusing manner, is that clauses limiting the use of regional or minority languages must be prohibited among users of these languages.

preventing the use of RMLs in the internal regulations of companies or private documents. However, the committee did state that no information had been provided on the existence of any explicit general prohibition of clauses excluding or restricting the use of RMLs "as required by 13.1b", which would suggest that this undertaking is not fulfilled.[67] On another occasion, the Committee of Experts pointed out that "this provision requires legal action prohibiting the insertion of clauses excluding or restricting the use of Basque in internal regulations of companies".[68] According to the committee's case law, this undertaking requires legal measures prohibiting the inclusion in the internal regulations of companies and private documents of clauses excluding or restricting the use of RMLs.

However, according to the Committee of Experts' interpretation, the Charter does not require one single definite formulation or a specific means of implementing this prohibition. The committee considered it sufficient for the Penal Code to lay down criminal-law consequences for cases of unjustified limitations or restrictions on the exercise of the freedoms and rights recognised by the constitution or legislation on linguistic grounds.[69] In the case of the Basque language, the undertaking is fulfilled if "this undertaking has been included *expresis verbis* in Law No. 6/2003 of 22 December 2003 on the Statute of Consumers and Users, that comprises a Chapter dealing with the language rights of consumers and users, in particular Article 42 paragraph 2.b".[70] However, in the case of Catalan, the undertaking is deemed fulfilled if there is legislation establishing regulations for the use of Catalan in this field: "No reference was made to a specific provision that would prohibit the insertion of clauses restricting the use of the regional or minority language, but the purpose of these laws is the promotion of the use of Catalan in this sphere".[71] This is a case of implicit fulfilment of the undertaking, in that the legislation goes further than merely prohibiting limitative clauses by promoting and encouraging the use of the language.

At all events, it must be remembered that this undertaking is applicable to the whole of the country, not just the territory where RMLs are spoken, as the Committee of Experts has pointed out.[72] The territorial nature of the undertaking requires the legislation adopted by the central authorities (applicable nationwide) to contain the prohibitive clause referred to by the committee, bearing in mind that it may be insufficient for such clauses to be included exclusively in the legislation of the regions or municipalities in which RMLs are spoken.

---

67. Croatia, 2001, 105, finding a non-fulfilment of the undertaking. See also Slovakia 2007, 176 and 286. Cf. Spain 2005, 310.
68. Spain 2008, 521.
69. Croatia 2005, 189.
70. Spain 2008, 684.
71. Ibid., 321.
72. Spain 2005, 310.

3.1.3. Opposition to practices designed to discourage the use of RMLs

This refers not to documents but to practices designed to discourage the use of the languages in question, and the undertaking is to oppose such practices. Considering that the practices in question are those implemented in the private sector, the text of this paragraph is limited and ambiguous. What role do the public authorities play in this field? What kind of practices are supposed to be discouraging the use of RMLs? Since the undertaking mentions that the state must oppose them, what kind of public action must it take? Must it demand compliance in a legal context, and in the event of non-compliance, can judicial channels be used?

Some, but not all, of the ambiguous aspects of this provision have been clarified by the Committee of Experts. Firstly, it seems clear that the expression "to oppose" requires more than a mere passive attitude, and a certain "burden of positive action" must be assumed to exist, whereby "oppose" would mean "counteract". The objective would be to "counteract practices aimed at preventing minority language use in economic and social activities".[73] The committee holds that it is not enough merely to contend that such practices are "opposed": states must adopt specific measures to ensure such opposition.[74] In the final analysis, the undertaking to "oppose" such practices requires the adoption of specific measures.

It may happen that users of an RML are discouraged from speaking it out of fear of a hostile reaction from others (this can take on particular importance in the socio-economic field). Since a mere reaction is liable to be insufficient here, the committee went one step further:

> The Committee of Experts takes the view that in order to fulfil this undertaking, some positive action is required by the authorities, such as awareness-raising and promotion of tolerance of regional or minority languages.[75]

---

73. Armenia 2006, 148.

74. The Committee of Experts reacted to an assertion that practices geared to preventing the use of languages were being "opposed" by stressing the need to indicate the practical or specific measures taken to guarantee this (Croatia 2001, 106), although it did not deem that the undertaking was not fulfilled. Similarly, the absence of information on practical action to "oppose" prevents verification of whether the undertaking is fulfilled (Slovenia 2004, 230). Along the same lines, the lack of information on practical measures does not enable the committee to conclude that the undertaking is fulfilled (Slovakia 2007, 287). Conversely, a lack of information on the existence of practices geared to discouraging the use of regional or minority languages is not sufficient to deem the undertaking fulfilled, and the committee requested specific information on the adoption of practical measures to oppose such practices (Denmark 2004, 105); it concluded that in the absence of such information it was not in a position to conclude whether or not this undertaking was fulfilled.

75. Croatia 2008, 208.

This line of doctrine highlighting the need for states to adopt practical measures going further than a mere reaction or response to individual cases is reiterated in other reports by the Committee of Experts.[76]

The committee has noted a variety of instruments for implementing such positive measures: enactment of new legislation to recognise language rights in the health field and laying down linguistic obligations for private health agencies (to provide linguistic services),[77] a constitutional and legislative guarantee on the use of the RML in the socio-economic sphere,[78] anti-discrimination legislation providing a legal basis for opposing the practices mentioned in the undertaking,[79] and language policy legislation laying down indirect rules on penalties for non-compliance with specific provisions. All these approaches are considered sufficient for the undertaking to be declared fulfilled.[80]

Nevertheless, it must be said that in many cases fulfilment of this undertaking can cause problems linked to a lack of state jurisdiction in domestic law over private bodies.[81] In such cases, states must not hesitate to adopt promotional measures. The Committee of Experts has expressed very positive opinions on various campaigns to promote multilingualism in companies and the presentation of awards to companies promoting the use of RMLs.[82]

At all events, the undertaking is very difficult, indeed impossible, to implement where domestic legislation lays down compulsory use of the official language in economic and social activities. By the same token, the refusal to use names in the minority languages in postal services (postcode) and the railways has been considered as a non-fulfilment of this undertaking.[83] It should be remembered that the scope of the undertaking is not confined to the territory in which the RML is spoken, but covers the whole country.[84]

3.1.4. Facilitating and/or encouraging the use of RMLs by other means

The undertaking set out in Article 13.1d is very broad and non-specific. This is why the Committee of Experts has pointed out that it "leaves open a broad

---

76. Finland 2001, 191: noting a decline in the use of the Sami language because economic players mainly use Finnish, the committee concluded that "positive action is necessary to reverse this tendency". See also Croatia 2005, 191-3.

77. On this basis the committee found that the Finnish authorities actively opposed practices geared to discouraging the use of Sami (Finland 2004, 155). The legislative amendment is sufficient in this case.

78. Finland 2001, 124.

79. Germany 2008, 777; Serbia 2009, 292.

80. Spain 2008, 324.

81. The Netherlands 2004, 178-9.

82. Serbia 2009, 292.

83. The Netherlands 2001, 102.

84. United Kingdom 2004, 187 and 299.

range of options of ways in which the use of regional or minority languages can be facilitated or encouraged".[85] The distinctive feature of this undertaking is its positive wording, requiring the means of implementing it not to be confined to eliminating or excluding standards or practices with negative effects on RMLs. In this connection, the committee has observed that "it can indeed be confirmed that the measures envisaged should be positive, and not only to eliminate or discourage negative practice",[86] including efforts "to facilitate and/or encourage the use of the regional or minority language on buildings, the oral use of the language in public areas, such as in railway stations or airports, use of bilingual brochures in tourism, giving rewards to companies that are actually using the regional or minority language, initiating a campaign of bilingualism, etc".[87]

It is difficult to draw conclusions from an analysis of the Committee of Experts' reports in connection with this undertaking, owing to the wide range of realities covered by regional and minority languages and the extensive case law on activities implemented by the public authorities in individual cases, but two basic aspects might be highlighted.[88] First of all, in pronouncing on the fulfilment, or non-fulfilment, of this undertaking, the committee takes account of the situation of the RML in question, so that specific actions which may be considered sufficient for fulfilment in some situations may prove insufficient in others. There is no one standard parameter or minimum action for formal fulfilment of the undertaking.[89] Fulfilment depends on the action and its effectiveness in the situation of a specific language. Secondly, the Committee of Experts does not examine simply the promotional activity implemented or the form it takes, but rather concentrates on its effectiveness. It is not enough to adopt provisions or multiply activities. What is required is for the activities to be effective. Even where the promotional measures are based on legislation, the existence of a legal provision does not prove that it is observed, which means that an analysis is needed of whether it is applied and effective.[90]

---

85. Armenia 2006, 150; Austria 2005, 279; Germany 2006, 158 among others.
86. Finland 2004, 157.
87. Armenia, 2006, 150; Finland 2004, 157; Germany 2006, 235.
88. The broad discretion granted to states by this provision should be interpreted in accordance with the objectives and principles of the Charter. In all cases the recognition of a wide margin of manoeuvre for the state raises the question of the limits and framework within which the Committee of Experts must assess the measures adopted; see the comments of T. Moring and R. Dunbar (2008), *The European Charter for Regional or Minority Languages and the media*. Strasbourg: Council of Europe Publishing, p. 23.
89. The same applies to other provisions of the Charter. See T. Moring and R. Dunbar (2008), *The European Charter ... and the media*, p. 94.
90. Slovenia 2004, 231-4; Spain 2005, 984.

The following are examples of areas in which promotional activities have been conducted:

- action to promote the use of RMLs by public bodies involved in the socio-economic sector: ministries' publication of information and press notes also in the RML; use of these languages on the websites of bilingual municipalities; job adverts in government departments published in both languages;[91]

- promotional activities targeting the public services;[92]

- promotional activities to raise awareness of linguistic rights and the Charter;[93] public awareness campaigns on the use of these languages by consumers and promoting the latter with posters and pin badges;[94]

- action to promote the use of the languages in the private sector: incentives to produce glossaries and terminology;[95] incentives to use the languages in literature and the religious sphere;[96] encouraging activities in economic sectors working in the minority language;[97] grants for creating cultural infrastructures;[98] use of the language in the tourist and museum fields;[99] co-operation projects with private agencies;[100] campaigns to promote the use of the language in the private sector, setting up an advisory group on the use of the language in the private sector, incentives for creating clusters to develop projects in Irish;[101] subsidies for bodies operating in the socio-economic sector for language training, service provision in the RML, promoting its use in industrial, professional, commercial, advertising, cultural, voluntary, sporting, leisure and other activities;[102] adapting texts, promoting use of the language in computer

---

91. Finland 2007, 156: fulfilment.
92. Spain 2008, 1018-9.
93. Denmark 2004, 106; Germany 2002, 169; the latter report states, re the Frisian language, that the existence of brochures with information about the language situation of Frisian-speakers and about the implications of the Charter is likely to encourage the use of the minority language among the general public. "The committee believes that this work also has an effect in the economic and social sphere and therefore considers the obligation fulfilled" (paragraph 212); Germany 2006, 395.
94. Germany 2006, paragraph 673 (badges and stickers, etc.).
95. Austria 2009, 284.
96. Austria 2009, 253.
97. Denmark 2004, 107.
98. Germany 2006, 395.
99. Ibid., 604.
100. United Kingdom 2004, 378.
101. United Kingdom 2007, 520.
102. Spain 2005, 312-6.

programs;[103] policy of translating banking, tourist and health insurance texts, use of Romansh in advertising and signposting, descriptions of products, invoices, correspondence with consumers, etc.[104]

This undertaking may be implemented in a variety of ways: economic subsidies (Austria 2009, 179); granting of linguistic rights for consumers, with corresponding obligations on companies (Spain 2004, 314); co-operation between the public and private sectors (ibid.); tax relief (Spain 2008, 1017); mandatory linguistic requirements (Slovenia 2004, 155-9); transfrontier co-operation (Slovenia 2004, 158); legislation (Spain 2004, 723, 858 and 954; Spain 2008, 1018-9); and promotional strategies (Spain 2004, 601). It must be stressed that the committee takes account not only of the means of implementation but also of their effectiveness. Furthermore, the action must be sufficient for a finding that the state is implementing a genuine promotional policy, co-ordinating activities with a view to increasing and supporting the use of the relevant languages in the socio-economic field, with regard to their particular situation. These activities must be incorporated in a structured, comprehensive promotional policy which is also tailored to the specific language.

For all the variety of case histories, a more modest promotional policy is liable to prove insufficient to fulfil the undertaking.[105] The absence of legal obstacles to the use of languages is not enough to fulfil this undertaking.[106] Nor is it sufficient for RMLs to be promoted at the direct initiative of private bodies, since private action cannot replace the state's undertaking to take concrete action.[107] Obviously, a totally passive attitude on the part of the authorities responsible for the socio-economic sector, reflected by a failure to adopt measures to promote or facilitate the use of (for example) Basque in Navarra and the complete omission of linguistic rights in the consumer field (in comparison with other autonomous communities), points to non-fulfilment of this undertaking.[108] The utter non-existence of a promotional policy in the socio-economic sphere equals non-fulfilment.

---

103. Ibid., 601.
104. Switzerland 2001, 168.
105. Granting types of specific economic aid to promote the use of Upper Sorbian in religious services is considered as only partially fulfilling the undertaking (Germany 2008, 254 and 255).
106. Austria 2005, 278.
107. Austria 2009, 285.
108. Spain 2008, 528.

3.2. Economic and social activities in the territory in which regional languages are spoken

Article 13.2 of the Charter is applicable in areas where RMLs are spoken.[109] Beyond the geographical delimitation, this paragraph must be interpreted on the basis of two concepts defining its scope: firstly, the undertakings which it sets out are applicable only "in so far as the public authorities are competent" and "as far as this is reasonably possible". The competence criterion presupposes that this paragraph will apply in so far as the public authorities (state and region) are empowered to act (intervene) in the socio-economic fields mentioned in the various indents. This means that the undertakings have to be fulfilled in so far as the public authorities are competent to regulate and manage these fields.[110] Bearing in mind that the power to intervene may vary from one state party to the next, jurisdiction for the fulfilment of the undertakings must be the main criterion for states in adopting these undertakings under Article 13.2. Once the latter are adopted, the states cannot adduce a lack of jurisdiction to fulfil them, which can in any case be done by adopting incentive or promotional measures.

This interpretation must also be borne in mind in analysing the scope of the clause "as far as this is reasonably possible". The adoption of undertakings under Article 13.2 depends on the state's capacity for fulfilling them. The option of adopting undertakings which can reasonably be fulfilled in the light of the situation of each RML is a criterion which is mainly operative only at the time of ratifying the Charter.[111] In fact, this clause cannot be used to relativise the scope of the undertakings accepted: this was the interpretation adopted by the Committee of Experts, as noted below.

3.2.1. Procedures for using the languages in financial documents

The undertaking set out in Article 13.2a refers to the possibility of using RMLs in drawing up payment orders (cheques, drafts, etc.) and in financial documents. However, the undertaking does not require unconditional guarantees of the use of such languages in this kind of document. It requires procedures for using these languages to be set out (in accordance with commercial practice) in financial and banking regulations. According to the Committee of Experts, a legally established obligation on making this type of document available to customers "at least in Catalan" points to the fulfilment of the undertaking.[112] Domestic banking and financial regulations facilitating the use of the RML in

---

109. See *supra* the commentary on Article 1b of the Charter by Eduardo Ruiz Vieytez in this volume.
110. See Woehrling (2005), op. cit., p. 228.
111. I agree with Jean-Marie Woehrling, ibid., p. 96.
112. Spain 2005, 317.

drawing up financial documents whenever the customer so wishes also point to fulfilment of the undertaking.[113] Conversely, where domestic regulations do not cover facilities or procedures for using the languages, a finding of non-fulfilment ensues.[114]

The general tenor of the Committee of Experts' opinion is that merely implementing the principle of non-discrimination is insufficient to fulfil this undertaking. The latter requires certain formal guarantees (by means of regulations). In its latest conclusions, the Committee of Experts appears to favour a reading which combines the formal and substantive criteria; for instance, the obvious fact that financial documents are only available to citizens in the majority languages has elicited a finding of non-fulfilment.[115] Similarly, the finding that even though a number of banks have adopted apposite measures, in the great majority of cases no financial and banking documents are available in Galician has led to a declaration of partial fulfilment of the undertaking.[116] In conclusion, the undertaking involves fulfilling the formal (prescriptive) guarantee and the substantive guarantee (via effective implementation).

3.2.2. Use of RMLs in the public sector

The undertaking set out in Article 13.2b is characterised by its subject, viz. the public sector conducting economic or social activities. This concerns companies or other types of bodies operating directly under public control and conducting activities in these sectors. The combination of both criteria (public supervision/control and type of activity) delimits the scope of this undertaking.

There are major differences between states parties in their modes of management of socio-economic services or activities, so the scope of this undertaking can vary considerably from one state to the next. Broadly speaking, without prejudice to the configuration of the management system (public, private or hybrid) or the scope of the control exercised by public authorities under each state's domestic legislation, this undertaking might be considered to cover: public transport (by rail, road, air and sea), including the corresponding infrastructures; postal services; banking under the direct control of the public authorities; waste collection and disposal; general-interest infrastructures and services (energy, gas, telecommunications, telephone); publicly-owned accommodation (homes, residential centres), and so on.

---

113. Finland 2001, 126.
114. Slovenia 2004, 160.
115. Slovenia 2007, 187.
116. Spain 2008, 1180.

The main point of this paragraph is that the services must be provided under the direct control of the public authorities. The Committee of Experts has stressed that the undertaking does not refer solely to activities conducted under the direct control of central government but it also covers activities controlled by local and regional authorities[117] or any agency exercising authority.[118] In specifying the scope of this undertaking, the Committee of Experts has apparently adopted a broad interpretation that includes companies "owned or controlled by public bodies".[119] This means not only bodies which depend directly on the public authorities (companies operating on 100% public capital) but also those over which the public authorities exercise direct or effective control. Although the committee has not adopted an unequivocal position on this subject, we should not disregard activities conducted by private bodies under the direct control of the public authorities, for instance during the conclusion of contracts (for the management of public services),[120] agreements and other types of deals, including subsidies for providing specific services, conducting certain activities or drawing up specified agreements.[121] Therefore, the scope of this undertaking is similar to that of Article 10.3 of the Charter, although it transcends the field of public services.

The undertaking refers to "organis[ing] activities to promote the use of regional or minority languages". The wording is certainly broad and ambiguous, and is in any case much less specific than that of Article 10.3 (or 1.4), which refers to (linguistic) conditions in public services. Article 13.2b merely demands the implementation of "action" to promote use of languages. According to the Committee of Experts' case law, the fact of guaranteeing the use of RMLs in providing the service and informing customers ensures fulfilment of the undertaking.[122] The same applies to organising staff supervision and training programmes (Spain 2008, 327-30), guaranteeing use of the language in signposting and documentation in public banks and railway stations, including public notices (Switzerland 2001, 170-1) and public announcements (Switzerland 2001, 297).

In so far as the undertaking demands concrete action, merely recognising in legislation the right to use the languages in receiving the service from the public sector would only suggest formal fulfilment.[123] Non-implementation of activities by the authorities to promote the use of the Frisian language in the social

---

117. Spain 2005, 467; United Kingdom 2007, 263.
118. Finland 2004, 159.
119. United Kingdom 2007, 263.
120. Ibid.
121. In this sense see Spain 2008, 327-30.
122. Finland 2001, 127; Finland 2004, 159.
123. Spain 2008, 697.

and economic sectors under the direct control of the Dutch authorities points to non-fulfilment.[124] By the same token, lack of action to promote Galician in the railway, postal and airport services, linked to the lack of Galician-speaking staff capable of providing such services in companies under central government control, led to a finding of non-fulfilment.[125] This undertaking is incompatible with a passive attitude on the part of the public authorities.[126]

Although Article 13.2b leaves states a broad margin of discretion in implementing promotional activities, analysis of the Committee of Experts' reports highlights the need for such activities to be subject to some kind of planning in this sector. Mere selective activities are not enough: the action must be taken in the context of an action programme reflecting the idea of promoting the use of the language in the socio-economic sector. The intensity of the measures depends on the extent of the control exercised by the public authorities over the public sector.

3.2.3. Use of RMLs in the social services

The Article 13.2c undertaking has proved the most problematical of all those set out in Article 13, having given rise to the largest number of recommendations of the Committee of Ministers on the socio-economic sector. This provision refers to social services (setting out a non-exhaustive list including hospitals, retirement homes and hostels). The undertaking is to ensure that users of RMLs can be treated and accommodated in these languages.

The first question to be addressed is the scope of this undertaking. The aim of ensuring the use of RMLs between patients or users and social service staff may correspond to a variety of objectives: first of all, guaranteeing communication where the patients or users do not know the majority language, and secondly, guaranteeing the principle of equal opportunities, that is, catering for freedom of use of the RML. Both the German and Danish authorities claim that since members of the linguistic minorities are bilingual, in practice there are no language barriers or problems of communication between them and social service staff speaking the official language. However, the state cannot use the fluency of RML speakers in the official state language as a reason for remaining passive in this regard.[127] In this connection, the Committee of Experts holds

---

124. The Netherlands 2008, 143, which refers to inactivity on the part of the Ministry of Economic Affairs.
125. Spain 2008, 1183.
126. Slovenia 2007, 131-2.
127. "[I]n this context the Committee of Experts would like to emphasise that the Charter aims to promote the use of regional or minority languages in public and private life. Therefore, in the opinion of the Committee of Experts the fluency of regional or minority language speakers in the official majority language does not justify a lack of active promotion of these languages" (Denmark 2004, 21; Germany 2002, 59).

that this is no reason for exempting the authorities from fulfilling this undertaking, which requires systematic treatment, embracing a bilingual human resources policy for its fulfilment.[128] The undertaking concerns guaranteeing the use of the language in the practical provision of social services, not just as a means of solving communication difficulties.[129] In order to fulfil this undertaking, guarantees must be provided that citizens can use the services in their own language.[130] Nevertheless, the undertaking does not embrace the right to the introduction of services in the region, the availability of the service in the nearest hospital being deemed sufficient,[131] and transfrontier co-operation can also be used to guarantee the service.[132]

The objective of the undertaking has been strictly defined: "The Committee of Experts considers that Article 13 paragraph 2c requires the authorities to ensure certain results".[133] It is not enough to conduct selective activities: fulfilment of the undertaking requires the result of ensuring the effective use of RMLs.[134] Fulfilling the undertaking necessitates a proactive and systematic approach based on prior planning, making a merely reactive (case-by-case) approach insufficient. Nor is it sufficient for fulfilment of the undertaking for domestic legislation to recognise the right to use the RML in this type of situation. The undertaking requires this right to be ensured in practice and in an effective manner via measures geared to concrete implementation.[135]

The objective having been established in these terms, the committee requires states parties to implement a structured policy to systematise the guaranteed use of RMLs: "A systematic approach is necessary to fulfil the undertaking".[136]

---

128. Germany 2002, 170, followed, on the very next line, by "the committee encourages the authorities to take the necessary measures to increase and make more systematic the possibility for the persons concerned to be received and treated in Danish in social care facilities. This should include a bilingual human resources policy" (see also Germany 2002, 286, 320, 354, 426, 468; Denmark 2004, 108).
129. United Kingdom 2004, 189; Slovakia 2007, 179, 289.
130. Finland 2001, 128.
131. Slovenia 2004, 62.
132. Denmark 2007, 109.
133. Slovakia 2007, 181, 459, 539, 682; Germany 2008, 184: "the Committee of Experts underlines that the current undertaking requires the authorities to ensure that Upper Sorbian is used in these establishments which can only be achieved by a bilingual human resources policy".
134. United Kingdom 2007, 273-4: "The Committee of Experts acknowledge the positive steps being taken. However, since the undertaking requires the authorities to ensure that Welsh is used in social care services, the Committee of Experts must conclude that the undertaking is not fulfilled at present" and in box "The Committee of Experts urges the authorities to strengthen their efforts to ensure that health and social care facilities offer services in Welsh".
135. The Netherlands 2004, 186; Finland 2004, 92; Spain 2005, 607; Spain 2008, 1118.
136. Germany 2008, 595.

Furthermore, "a bilingual human resources policy should be an integral component of this approach".[137] Clearly, the main problem in fulfilling this undertaking would be a lack of staff qualified in use of the regional languages. The committee stresses that the authorities must guarantee adequate staffing in order to achieve the result set out in this provision.[138] This must be done in a planned manner, and may involve language requirements for access to posts, as the committee has explicitly recommended in one case,[139] and also further language training and other organisational measures.[140] At all events, it must be understood that the mere adoption of measures is not enough and that what is needed is to ensure the right to use the RML, which is only possible if qualified staff are available.

Another problem which may arise is where social and health services do not come under the public sector but are provided by private or voluntary institutions, which can make it difficult for the public authorities to intervene. In connection with this problem, as mentioned by the German authorities, the Committee of Experts once again observed that the aim of the undertaking was to ensure the right to use the language, and demanded a structured approach for its fulfilment. The requisite strategy should be tailored to the state's capacity for intervention, as fulfilment of the undertaking embraced a guarantee on achieving results.[141]

The Committee of Experts has also asserted that the provision cannot be complied with by providing for translation, because this does not facilitate direct communication between users of RMLs and the health care staff.[142] Similarly, domestic legislation which provides for the normal use of the official language in health care services, allowing the use of other languages only where the patients do not know the former, is incompatible with the undertaking.[143] Again, where the measures adopted are ineffective or insufficient, Article 13.2c of the Charter is infringed.[144]

---

137. Denmark 2007, 112; Germany 2002, 163, 170, 286, 320, 354, 426, 468; Germany 2006, 163; Germany 2008, 184, 598, 721.
138. Armenia 2006, 150; Finland 2001, 195; Finland 2004, 162-3.
139. Finland 2007, Finding F.
140. Norway 2001, 94, Germany 2008, 466.
141. Germany 2006, 465.
142. Norway 2007, 177.
143. Slovakia 2007, 181, 459, 539, 682.
144. Spain 2008, 535, noting the non-availability of Basque-language health care facilities for citizens in Navarra, the lack of medical information in Basque, the exclusive use of Spanish in documents providing instructions on treatment and the implementation of a linguistic policy for staff recruitment whereby knowledge of Basque is required for only 0.7% of jobs in the sector.

3.2.4. Safety instructions in RMLs

The aim of Article 13.2d is to ensure by appropriate means that safety instructions are also drawn up in RMLs.

The Committee of Experts has had occasion to pronounce on the scope of this undertaking in response to the claim by the Spanish authorities that "safety" is fully guaranteed in Spain because all users of RMLs also know the official state language, in which safety instructions are always set out. The Committee of Experts rejected this argument on the grounds that the undertaking refers, precisely, to promoting the use of the languages in the area of safety instructions.[145] This provision is not primarily or exclusively aimed at guaranteeing safety, but rather ensuring the use of the languages in safety instructions,[146] which is a very different matter. This aim, moreover, is clarified by the wording of the undertaking, which stipulates that the instruction should also be drawn up in RMLs.

In connection with the scope of the undertaking, the Committee of Experts points out that safety instructions cover a broader field, for instance safety notices on construction sites and in lifts, fire instructions, etc.[147] The committee has also included product labelling in the RML in this provision, primarily where safety instructions are concerned,[148] and has further referred to legislation on consumers' rights.

The Committee of Experts has rarely pronounced on this undertaking to date because it is difficult to draw any general conclusions on the means of complying with it.[149] Clearly, if safety information is published in the minority languages the undertaking is fulfilled.[150] In any case, the committee would seem to focus

---

145. The committee underlines that it is by making regional or minority languages a means of communication in modern daily life, to which the present undertaking, among others, is conducive, that they can be preserved as living and mature languages. The argument that RML-speakers know the majority language anyway could after all be invoked in any of the fields covered by the Charter, which would make it pointless (Spain 2005, 321).
146. On this aspect, see Woehrling (2005), op. cit., p. 230.
147. Spain 2005, 472.
148. Ibid., 473; Spain 2008, 336. Furthermore, although this is a subject more relevant to Article 13.2e, reference is also made to translating legislation on consumers' rights (Norway 2001, 95).
149. Following Woehrling (2005), op. cit., in paragraph 231 the phrase "appropriate means" seeks to give a contracting state sufficient latitude. It must set in train a reasoned strategy based on the specific situation of each language. See also S. Oeter (2004), "The impact of implementing the Charter" in *The European Charter for Regional or Minority Languages and the French dilemma*, Regional or Minority Languages, No. 4. Strasbourg: Council of Europe Publishing, p. 70.
150. Finland 2001, 129.

on the need for systematic, rather than merely selective, action from the public authorities if the undertaking is to be fulfilled.[151] On the other hand, legislative action is insufficient to fulfil it, as a guarantee must also be provided that this legislation is actually effective.[152]

3.2.5. *Information on the rights of consumers*

Article 13.2e requires states parties to arrange for information provided by the competent public authorities concerning the rights of consumers to be made available in RMLs. The Committee of Experts has mentioned the scope of this provision, pointing out that this undertaking refers not to guaranteeing (language) rights of consumers but to providing information on rights in the RML.[153] It is a question not of recognising linguistic rights but of providing information on the general rights of consumers in these languages. Nor is it a case of arranging for the provision in the RML of information which producers must give consumers under general legislation. The scope of this Charter provision is more limited, referring exclusively to information supplied by the public authorities.[154] In fact, the undertaking is fulfilled where, as the Committee of Experts has pointed out, the legislation on consumer affairs is made available to consumers in the RML: "being acts adopted by the Catalan institutions, they are also available in the Catalan language. The Committee of Experts considers that this undertaking is fulfilled".[155] A problem might arise where consumers' rights are also set out in national (i.e. not only regional) legislation, which would then also have to be translated (in line with Article 9.3 of the Charter). Where no legalisation on this subject is available in the RML and there are no translations of the general consumer information provided by the public authorities, the undertaking is not fulfilled.[156] Nevertheless, it is evident that translating the legislation on consumption can be a valid means of fulfilling the undertaking, as what it requires is the availability of consumer information for RML-speaking consumers in their languages.

---

151. Slovenia 2007, 195.

152. Spain 2008, 705.

153. Spain 2005, 735; Finland 2001, 130.

154. See the opinion of Woehrling (2005), op. cit., p. 231.

155. Spain 2005, 325.

156. Ibid., 476: "The Committee of Experts observes that the present undertaking is concerned with making available information on consumers' rights in Basque, at least for the 'Basque-speaking zone'. According to the information at the disposal of the Committee of Experts, no such information exists. The Committee of Experts therefore considers that the present undertaking is therefore not fulfilled". See also Spain 2008, 541.

4. Recommendations and good practice: by way of conclusion

From the quantitative angle, of the 45 reports analysed, 17 contain Committee of Experts' recommendations on the socio-economic sector, giving rise to 10 recommendations of the Committee of Ministers (concerning seven states parties). Having regard to the importance of this field for the survival and development of languages, it might seem that the committee has not been overly attentive to it (as compared to other fields covered by the Charter). This highlights the legal complexity of public intervention and action in this sector. At all events, the quantitative aspect must be seen in perspective.

In connection with the quantitative aspect, we might single out a number of considerations from the reports and recommendations by way of conclusion. First of all, both the Committee of Experts and the Committee of Ministers have highlighted the major importance of the socio-economic sector for the survival of minority-language communities, and therefore the need for positive public action to guarantee opportunities for development of RMLs in the economy, employment and society in general.[157] Socio-economic development of languages is also deemed essential from the angle of the integration principle.[158]

Secondly, promoting RMLs in the economic and social sectors is seen not as a mere means but as an actual end in itself. The aim is not to overcome the obstacles which might arise from using RMLs in having recourse to social services or conducting economic activities, but to guarantee their availability in these RMLs. The fact of users of an RML having sufficient knowledge of the majority language should not prevent its active use and promotion in all sectors of socio-economic life.[159] The approach involves not only overcoming language barriers[160] or refraining from limiting the use of the said languages in this field, but also, and above all, ensuring opportunities for using them to provide socio-economic services.[161]

This requires designing and implementing a structured linguistic policy. Such a general linguistic policy on the socio-economic sector must involve all territorial levels of the public administration and cater for the specific situation and reality of each language. The state must not behave as if it were a linguistically homogeneous entity;[162] measures are needed at the state level

---

157. United Kingdom 2004, Finding K.
158. Recommendation of the Committee of Ministers to Hungary (2004), point 1.
159. Denmark 2004, Finding F, 24.
160. Germany 2008, 542.
161. Denmark 2007, Finding K.
162. See F. de Varennes (2002), "Linguistic diversity in the Europe of tomorrow" in *From theory to practice: The European Charter for Regional or Minority Languages*. Strasbourg: Council of Europe Publishing, pp. 18-20.

to enhance national plurilingualism. Nor must the state's action be merely reactive, devoid of planning and confined to a specific timescale.[163] The dynamism of the Charter necessitates implementing it via structured and ad hoc policies facilitating gradual progress and analysis of the latter. Such policies must set clear targets geared to guaranteeing the use of these languages in the socio-economic sphere.

Thirdly, we must mention issues arising from implementation of the Charter's undertakings. Three questions are raised by implementation of Article 13 under specific legislation. There is a noticeable practice in some states of ratifying the Charter undertakings that are already provided for in their domestic language legislation (state or region). Yet it has to be said that the existence of a satisfactory domestic legislative framework does not mean per se fulfilment of the undertakings of the Charter. The results are the important thing for the purposes of the Charter, and there may be a wide gap between the legislative framework and the actual practice of economic actors.[164] It is extremely important to analyse the results. A case-by-case analysis is required of the effectiveness of the measures adopted and the compatibility of the practical results with the undertakings of the Charter.[165] However, it would also be wrong to conclude that the implementation of states' domestic legislation has nothing to do with the Charter. The means of implementing domestic legislation may represent a vital instrument for ensuring fulfilment of the Charter's objectives.[166] Lastly, if domestic legislation limits or restricts the use of RMLs in the socio-economic sector, it must definitely be reviewed.[167]

---

163. Hungary 2007, Finding C.

164. Slovenia 2007, Finding O: "regarding social and economic activities, there is wide gap between the legislative framework and the actual practice of economic actors. There is a clear need for a more proactive approach by the authorities with a view to ensuring a more systematic enforcement of the applicable legislation and promoting the bilingual character of the relevant areas". See also Recommendation of the Committee of Ministers to Slovenia (2007), point 4: "take proactive measures to reduce the gap between the legislative framework and practical implementation regarding the use of Hungarian and Italian in the provisions of public services, in economic and social activities". See also Croatia 2001, Finding D.

165. Finland 2001, Finding F; Finland 2004, 93 (in box); Finland 2007, 166 and 282; Norway 2007, Finding H, highlighting that "the existing legal framework is in some cases still not implemented". See also Recommendation of the Committee of Ministers to Croatia (2001), point 1.

166. Germany 2006, Finding F; Recommendation of the Committee of Ministers to Germany (2006), point 1.

167. Slovakia 2007, Finding D; and Recommendation of the Committee of Ministers to Slovakia (2007), point 1: "improve and complete the legislative framework in the light of the obligations entered into by Slovakia upon its ratification of the Charter and in particular: ... review the restrictions on the use of regional or minority languages arising as a consequence of the State Language Act".

Fourthly, we should consider the socio-economic sector that has attracted the largest number of recommendations, viz. social welfare and hospitals. As pointed out above, the undertaking set out in Article 13.2c of the Charter requires the result of using RMLs under a structured linguistic policy which comprises a specific language policy for health care and social welfare staff, recruiting staff with knowledge of the languages and promoting in-house training.[168]

As a final overall observation, I would say that, despite the legal difficulties of intervening in the socio-economic sector, the Charter has set out on an under-explored and complicated road, one which is tremendously important for the future of languages. It has adopted an approach transcending the traditional view of the principle of non-discrimination, venturing into the territory of positive action. The Committee of Experts has delimited the scope of the Charter's provisions in a clear and enlightening manner, with helpful references to good practice. Particular mention should go to those practices which complement the language dimension with the active aspect of a subjective right, granting linguistic rights to consumers and users,[169] encouraging co-operation among regional governments in exchanging and comparing experience and experiments comprising and developing the Committee of Experts' recommendations,[170] and many more besides.

References

Banting, Keith, Johnston, Richard, Kymlicka, Will and Soroka, Stuart (2006), "Do multiculturalism policies erode the welfare state? An empirical analysis" in Keith Banting and Will Kymlicka, *Multiculturalism and the welfare state.* Oxford/New York: Oxford University Press.

Blair, Philip (2004), "The European Charter for Regional or Minority Languages" in *The European Charter for Regional or Minority Languages and the French dilemma*, Regional or Minority Languages, No. 4. Strasbourg: Council of Europe Publishing.

Crystal, David (2000), *Language death*. Cambridge: Cambridge University Press.

---

168. Germany 2006, Finding U: "Structured policies and corresponding measures, such as a bilingual human resources policy, are needed for the fulfilment of Germany's undertakings with respect to the use of regional or minority languages"; Germany 2008, Finding S; United Kingdom 2007, Finding J. See also Recommendations of the Committee of Ministers to Finland (2001), point 4; (2005), point 3; and (2007), point 4; Recommendation of the Committee of Ministers to Norway (2007), point 3; recommendations of the Committee of Ministers to the United Kingdom (2004), point 6; and (2007), point 5.
169. Spain 2005, 734-5.
170. Sweden 2003, Finding J; Spain 2008, Finding F.

Debbasch, Roland (1992), "La reconnaissance constitutionnelle de la langue française", *Revue Française de Droit Constitutionnelle*, No. 11, pp. 457-68.

Dunbar, Robert (2008), "Definitively interpreting the European Charter for Regional or Minority Languages: the legal challenges" in Robert Dunbar and Gwynedd Parry (eds), *The European Charter for Regional or Minority Languages: legal challenges and opportunities*. Strasbourg: Council of Europe Publishing.

Grenoble, Lenore A. and Whaley, Lindsay J. (2006), *Saving languages: an introduction to language revitalization*. Cambridge: Cambridge University Press.

Grin, François (2003), *Language policy evaluation and the European Charter for Regional or Minority Languages*. Basingstoke/New York: Palgrave Macmillan.

Grin, François, Sfreddo, Claudio and Vaillancourt, François (2010), *The economics of the multilingual workplace*. New York: Routledge.

Hinton, Leanne and Hale, Kenneth L. (2001), *The green book of language revitalization in practice*. San Diego: Academic Press.

Irujo, Xabier and Urrutia, Iñigo (2010), *A legal history of the Basque language (1789-2009)*. Donostia: Society for Basque Studies/Eusko Ikaskuntza.

Leckey, Robert and Didier, Emmanuel (2004), "The private law of language" in Michel Bastarache (ed.), *Language rights in Canada*, 2nd edn. Cowansville: Yvon Blais.

Moring, Tom and Dunbar, Robert (2008), *The European Charter for Regional or Minority Languages and the media*. Strasbourg: Council of Europe Publishing.

Oeter, Stefan (2004), "The impact of implementing the Charter" in *The European Charter for Regional or Minority Languages and the French dilemma,* Regional or Minority Languages, No. 4. Strasbourg: Council of Europe Publishing.

Poggeschi, Giovani (2010), *I dititti linguistici*. Rome: Carocci Editore.

Thornberry, Patrick (2002), "The charter and the role and responsibility of the state" in *From theory to practice: the European Charter for Regional or Minority Languages*, Regional or Minority Languages, No. 3. Strasbourg: Council of Europe Publishing.

Urrutia, Iñigo (2008), "Los requisitos lingüísticos en la actividad socioeconómica y en el mundo del audiovisual" in Antoni Milian (ed.), *Mundialització, lliure circulació i immigració, i l'exigència d'una llengua com a requisit*. Barcelona: Institut d'Estudis Autònimics, pp. 173-310.

Urrutia, Iñigo (2010), "Libre competencia, prohibición de ayudas de Estado y fiscalidad lingüística" in Iñigo Urrutia et al., *Estudios jurídicos sobre fiscalidad lingüística: incentivos fiscales como instrumento de política lingüística*. Cizur Menor: Aranzadi Thomson Reuters.

Varennes, Fernand (de) (2002), "Linguistic diversity in the Europe of tomorrow" in *From theory to practice: the European Charter for Regional or Minority Languages*, Regional or Minority Languages, No. 3. Strasbourg: Council of Europe.

Woehrling, Jean-Marie (2005), *The European Charter for Regional or Minority Languages: a critical commentary*. Strasbourg: Council of Europe Publishing.

Woehrling, Jean-Marie (2008), "The European Charter for Regional or Minority Languages and the principle of non-discrimination" in Robert Dunbar and Gwynedd Parry (eds), *The European Charter for Regional or Minority Languages: legal challenges and opportunities*. Strasbourg: Council of Europe Publishing.

Woehrling, José (1987), "La réglementation linguistique de l'affichage public et de la liberté d'expression", *PG Québec c. Chaussure Brown's Inc.*", *McGill Law Journal*, Vol. 32, p. 885.

Appendix: Ratifications

Article 13		
Paragraph and subparagraph		
1	a	**Croatia:** Italian (county of Istarska), Czech (county of Bjelovarsko-bilogorska), Hungarian, Slovak, Ruthenian, Ukrainian (Osjecko-baranjska and Vukovarsko-srijemska counties), Serbian. **Denmark:** German (Southern Jutland). **Finland:** Sami, Swedish. **Germany:** Danish (*Land* Schleswig-Holstein), Upper Sorbian (Free State of Saxony), Lower Sorbian (*Land* Brandenburg), North Frisian (*Land* Schleswig-Holstein), Sater Frisian (*Land* Lower Saxony), Low German (Free Hanseatic City of Bremen; Free and Hanseatic City of Hamburg and the *Länder* of Mecklenburg-Western Pomerania, Lower Saxony, Schleswig-Holstein). Romani. Low German (North Rhine-Westphalia). **Hungary:** Croatian, German, Romanian, Serbian, Slovak, Slovenian. **Montenegro:** Albanian, Romani. **Netherlands:** Frisian (Friesland). **Romania:** Bulgarian, Czech, Croatian, German, Hungarian, Russian, Serbian, Slovak. **Slovakia:** Bulgarian, Croatian, Czech, German, Polish, Romani, Ruthenian, Ukrainian, Hungarian. **Slovenia:** Italian, Hungarian. **Spain:** Basque (Autonomous Community of the Basque Country; Historical Community of Navarra), Catalan (Autonomous Community of Catalonia, Balearic Islands), Valencian (Autonomous Community of Valencia), Galician (Autonomous Community of Galicia). **Sweden:** Sami, Finnish, Meänkieli. **United Kingdom:** Welsh, Scottish-Gaelic.

	b	**Armenia:** Assyrian, Yezidi, Greek, Russian, Kurdish **Croatia:** Italian (county of Istarska), Czech (county of Bjelovarsko-bilogorska), Hungarian, Slovak, Ruthenian, Ukrainian (Osjecko-baranjska and Vukovarsko-srijemska counties), Serbian. **Montenegro:** Albanian, Romani. **Poland:** Belarusian, Czech, Hebrew, Yiddish, Karaim, Kashub, Lithuanian, Lemko, German, Armenian, Romani, Russian, Slovak, Tatar, Ukrainian. **Romania:** Bulgarian, Czech, Croatian, German, Hungarian, Russian, Serbian, Slovak, Turkish, Ukrainian. **Slovakia:** Bulgarian, Croatian, Czech, German, Polish, Romani, Ruthenian, Ukrainian, Hungarian. **Slovenia:** Italian, Hungarian. **Spain:** Basque (Autonomous Community of the Basque Country; Historical Community of Navarra), Catalan (Autonomous Community of Catalonia, Balearic Islands), Valencian (Autonomous Community of Valencia), Galician (Autonomous Community of Galicia). **Ukraine:** Bulgarian, Belarusian, Gagauz, Greek, Jewish, Crimean Tatar, Moldovan, German, Polish, Russian, Romanian, Slovak, Hungarian.
	c	**Armenia:** Assyrian, Yezidi, Greek, Russian, Kurdish **Bosnia and Herzegovina:** Albanian, Montenegrin, Czech, Italian, Hungarian, Macedonian, German, Polish, Romanian, Rysin, Slovak, Slovenian, Turkish, Ukrainian, Jewish (Yiddish and Ladino), Romani. **Croatia:** Italian (county of Istarska), Czech (county of Bjelovarsko-bilogorska), Hungarian, Slovak, Ruthenian, Ukrainian (Osjecko-baranjska and Vukovarsko-srijemska counties), Serbian. **Czech Republic:** Polish, Slovak. **Denmark:** German (Southern Jutland). **Finland:** Sami, Swedish. **Germany:** Danish (*Land* Schleswig-Holstein), Upper Sorbian (Free State of Saxony), Lower Sorbian (*Land* Brandenburg), North Frisian (*Land* Schleswig-Holstein), Sater Frisian (*Land* Lower Saxony), Low German (Free Hanseatic City of Bremen, Free and Hanseatic City of Hamburg and the *Länder* of Mecklenburg-Western Pomerania, Lower Saxony, Schleswig-Holstein). Romani. Low German (North Rhine-Westphalia). **Montenegro:** Albanian, Romani **Netherlands:** Frisian (Friesland). **Poland:** Belarusian, Czech, Hebrew, Yiddish, Karaim, Kashub, Lithuanian, Lemko, German, Armenian, Romani, Russian, Slovak, Tatar, Ukrainian. **Romania:** German, Hungarian **Serbia:** Albanian, Bosnian, Bulgarian, Hungarian, Romani, Romanian, Ruthenian, Slovakian, Ukrainian, Croatian. **Slovakia:** Bulgarian, Croatian, Czech, German, Polish, Romani, Ruthenian, Ukrainian, Hungarian. **Slovenia:** Italian, Hungarian. **Spain:** Basque (Autonomous Community of the Basque Country; Historical Community of Navarra), Catalan (Autonomous Community of Catalonia, Balearic Islands), Valencian (Autonomous Community of Valencia), Galician (Autonomous Community of Galicia). **Ukraine:** Bulgarian, Belarusian, Gagauz, Greek, Jewish, Crimean Tatar, Moldovan, German, Polish, Russian, Romanian, Slovak, Hungarian. **United Kingdom:** Welsh, Scottish-Gaelic.

	d	**Armenia:** Assyrian, Yezidi, Greek, Russian, Kurdish **Austria:** Burgenland Croatian (*Land* Burgenland); Slovenian (*Land* Carinthia); Hungarian (*Land* Burgenland); individual requirements: Slovenian (*Land* Styria), Hungarian (*Land* Vienna). **Bosnia and Herzegovina:** Albanian, Montenegrin, Czech, Italian, Hungarian, Macedonian, German, Polish, Romanian, Rysin, Slovak, Slovenian, Turkish, Ukrainian, Jewish (Yiddish and Ladino), Romani. **Denmark:** German (Southern Jutland). **Finland:** Sami, Swedish. **Germany:** Danish (*Land* Schleswig-Holstein), Upper Sorbian (Free State of Saxony), Lower Sorbian (*Land* Brandenburg), North Frisian (*Land* Schleswig-Holstein), Sater Frisian (*Land* Lower Saxony), Low German (Free and Hanseatic City of Hamburg and the *Länder* of Mecklenburg-Western Pomerania, Lower Saxony, Schleswig-Holstein). Romani. Low German (North Rhine-Westphalia). **Montenegro:** Albanian, Romani. **Netherlands:** Frisian (Friesland). **Poland:** Belarusian, Czech, Hebrew, Yiddish, Karaim, Kashub, Lithuanian, Lemko, German, Armenian, Romani, Russian, Slovak, Tatar, Ukrainian. **Romania:** Hungarian **Slovenia:** Italian, Hungarian. **Spain:** Basque (Autonomous Community of the Basque Country; Historical Community of Navarra), Catalan (Autonomous Community of Catalonia, Balearic Islands), Valencian (Autonomous Community of Valencia), Galician (Autonomous Community of Galicia). **Switzerland:** Romansh, Italian. **United Kingdom:** Irish (Northern Ireland).
2	a	**Finland:** Swedish. **Montenegro:** Albanian, Romani. **Slovenia:** Italian, Hungarian. **Spain:** Basque (Autonomous Community of the Basque Country; Historical Community of Navarra), Catalan (Autonomous Community of Catalonia, Balearic Islands), Valencian (Autonomous Community of Valencia), Galician (Autonomous Community of Galicia).
	b	**Armenia:** Assyrian, Yezidi, Greek, Russian, Kurdish **Finland:** Sami, Swedish. **Montenegro:** Albanian, Romani. **Netherlands:** Frisian (Friesland). **Poland:** Belarusian, Czech, Hebrew, Yiddish, Karaim, Kashub, Lithuanian, Lemko, German, Armenian, Romani, Russian, Slovak, Tatar, Ukrainian. **Slovenia:** Italian, Hungarian. **Spain:** Basque (Autonomous Community of the Basque Country; Historical Community of Navarra), Catalan (Autonomous Community of Catalonia, Balearic Islands), Valencian (Autonomous Community of Valencia), Galician (Autonomous Community of Galicia). **Switzerland:** Romansh, Italian. **United Kingdom:** Welsh.

483

c	**Armenia:** Assyrian, Yezidi, Greek, Russian, Kurdish **Denmark:** German (Southern Jutland) **Finland:** Sami, Swedish. **Germany:** Danish (*Land* Schleswig-Holstein), Upper Sorbian (Free State of Saxony), Low German (Free Hanseatic City of Bremen, Free and Hanseatic City of Hamburg, *Länder* Mecklenburg-Western Pomerania, Schleswig-Holstein). **Montenegro:** Albanian, Romani. **Netherlands:** Frisian (Friesland). **Norway:** Sami. **Romania:** German, Hungarian. **Slovakia (declaration):** Bulgarian, Croatian, Czech, German, Polish, Romani, Ruthenian, Ukrainian, Hungarian. **Slovenia:** Italian, Hungarian. **Spain:** Basque (Autonomous Community of the Basque Country; Historical Community of Navarra), Catalan (Autonomous Community of Catalonia, Balearic Islands), Valencian (Autonomous Community of Valencia), Galician (Autonomous Community of Galicia). **United Kingdom:** Welsh.
d	**Finland:** Swedish. **Montenegro:** Albanian, Romani. **Norway:** Sami. **Romania:** German, Hungarian. **Slovenia:** Italian, Hungarian. **Spain:** Basque (Autonomous Community of the Basque Country; Historical Community of Navarra), Catalan (Autonomous Community of Catalonia, Balearic Islands), Valencian (Autonomous Community of Valencia), Galician (Autonomous Community of Galicia).
e	**Czech Republic:** Polish, Slovak. **Finland:** Swedish. **Montenegro:** Albanian, Romani. **Romania:** German, Hungarian. **Slovenia:** Italian, Hungarian. **Spain:** Basque (Autonomous Community of the Basque Country; Historical Community of Navarra), Catalan (Autonomous Community of Catalonia, Balearic Islands), Valencian (Autonomous Community of Valencia), Galician (Autonomous Community of Galicia). **United Kingdom:** Welsh.

Article 14. Transfrontier exchanges

Eva Pons Parera
University of Barcelona

1. Introduction: the external context
2. General scope: the internal context
   2.1. Transfrontier co-operation as an objective and principle of Part II of the Charter
   2.2. The cross-cutting nature of transfrontier co-operation: how it is connected with other provisions of Part III
      2.2.1. The establishment and dissemination of communication media (Article 11.2)
      2.2.2. Cultural activities (Article 12.3)
      2.2.3. Educational and vocational training activities (Article 8)
3. Definition of transfrontier exchanges in Article 14 of the Charter
   3.1. Paragraph a of Article 14
   3.2. Paragraph b of Article 14
4. The provisions of Article 14: analysis of the position of the Committee of Experts
   4.1. The inclusion of a variety of transfrontier linguistic situations
   4.2. The different players involved in transfrontier exchanges
   4.3. Openness regarding the forms and instruments of transfrontier co-operation
   4.4. Some outstanding questions
5. Recommendations and good practice: by way of a conclusion
References

Article 14 – Transfrontier exchanges

The Parties undertake:

a. *to apply existing bilateral and multilateral agreements which bind them with the States in which the same language is used in identical or similar form, or if necessary to seek to conclude such agreements, in such a way as to foster contacts between the users of the same language in the States concerned in the fields of culture, education, information, vocational training and permanent education;*

b. *for the benefit of regional or minority languages, to facilitate and/or promote co-operation across borders, in particular between regional or local authorities in whose territory the same language is used in identical or similar form.*

1. Introduction: the external context

Frontiers were traditionally linked with the idea of separation and were thus viewed solely in terms of geographical or political boundaries between states. Nowadays, however, the idea of a frontier is also associated with the relations established between citizens and institutions on both sides, so that the frontier is seen less as a dividing line and more as a bridge permitting contact between border areas. In the new context, transfrontier exchange relations are clearly a growing phenomenon. Citizens, associations, businesses and local and regional authorities establish relations across borders mainly with a view to co-operation, weaving a complex web of contacts and exchanges which frequently take on an institutionalised form. All this points to the importance of a phenomenon in which globalisation (in the sense of transcending borders) and proximity (as a new form of neighbourly relations) combine in a particular way.

The importance of transfrontier relations is reflected in a growing interest in their regulation. Public international law has usually been the branch of law applied to this area, since it is concerned with managing the relations between states, and the existence of a frontier naturally presupposes the existence of two subjects of international law. In the European context, we should mention the initial work of two international organisations: the Council of Europe and the Organization for Security and Co-operation in Europe (OSCE). The development of the process of European integration will entail the increasing involvement of the European Union (EU), which needs transfrontier areas to test its reliability, authenticity and legitimacy. Co-operation between the different European organisations and their co-ordinated action have led to the emergence of certain international standards on this issue. And this is also providing the impetus for the development of domestic law geared to facilitating and guaranteeing the effectiveness of these transfrontier relations.

The foregoing constitutes what we might call the external context of the regulation of transfrontier exchanges by the European Charter for Regional or Minority Languages (hereinafter "ECRML" or "the Charter"), to which its Article 5 refers in expressly requiring compliance with states' other obligations under international law, including the principle of the sovereignty and territorial integrity of states. This context significantly influences both the wording of Article 14 ECRML and its practical application (as we will see, the monitoring reports on the application of the Charter by states contain frequent references to other international instruments as the framework for these transfrontier relations).

It should be remembered that, among its general aims, the Council of Europe, the organisation responsible for drawing up the Charter, seeks to foster co-operation between member states and safeguard human rights, including the rights of members of minorities. These aims find concrete expression in an interest in establishing a general framework for transfrontier relations in Europe. Initially, the European Outline Convention on Transfrontier Co-operation between Territorial Communities or Authorities, signed in Madrid in 1980, recognised the special role played in relations of this kind by territorial authorities or communities located on either side of the frontier. Article 2 of this instrument, which has been ratified by the great majority of states parties,[1] defines transfrontier co-operation as "any concerted action designed to reinforce and foster neighbourly relations between territorial communities or authorities within the jurisdiction of two or more contracting parties and the conclusion of any agreement and arrangement necessary for this purpose". One of the most important effects of this instrument was recognition of the importance and legitimacy of the involvement of territorial authorities in relations of this kind, with the corresponding obligation for states not to hinder them. The convention contains suggested models for formalising transfrontier relations (for example, co-operation instruments or setting up co-operation bodies with or without legal personality).

In 1995, in a field more closely related to language issues, the Council of Europe adopted the Framework Convention for the Protection of National Minorities (hereinafter FCNM), which establishes a European system for the protection of minorities. Article 10.1 of the Framework Convention safeguards the general right of minorities to use their own language in public:

> The Parties undertake to recognise that every person belonging to a national minority has the right to use freely and without interference his or her minority language, in private and in public, orally and in writing.

Article 17.1 FCNM expressly recognises the importance of transfrontier relations between groups sharing the same linguistic identity:

> The Parties undertake not to interfere with the right of persons belonging to national minorities to establish and maintain free and peaceful contacts across frontiers with persons lawfully staying in other States, in particular those with whom they share an ethnic, cultural, linguistic or religious identity, or a common cultural heritage.

Article 17.2 FCNM, on the right to participate in activities of non-governmental organisations at national and international level, is on similar lines. Thus, as with the European Outline Convention on Transfrontier Co-operation between Territorial Communities or Authorities, the FCNM places essentially negative obligations on parties not to hinder cross-border contacts. The FCNM Explanatory Report offers no further detail on the types of undertaking entered into by states, merely emphasising their importance for maintaining and

---

1. Of the 25 Council of Europe member states which have ratified the ECRML, only four have not ratified the 1980 convention, namely Cyprus, Montenegro, Serbia and the United Kingdom.

developing the culture of persons belonging to minorities, and the link between these undertakings and the work of the OSCE.[2] In line with the general approach of the treaty, Article 17 always refers to "persons" belonging to minorities, without identifying any form of institutional grouping of such persons as an embodiment of collective rights.[3] The intention behind this approach was to facilitate the accession of most Council of Europe member states.[4]

The missions of the OSCE include paying special attention to neighbourly relations between states and migrants' relations with their countries of origin, as a useful way of preventing and/or facilitating the resolution of conflicts between member states. This organisation's work has contributed significantly to a change of attitude from distrust of relations of this kind, viewed by states as a possible threat to their territorial integrity, to recognition of their beneficial role in fostering peaceful coexistence and respect for human and minority rights.[5] The policy documents issued by the OSCE lay down standards for the treatment of minorities which meet with wide acceptance among its member states. The work of the High Commission for National Minorities, a body set up in 1992, also lays emphasis on facilitating cross-border contacts between minorities, as a requirement founded on minority rights,[6] and reinforces links with the Council of Europe and the EU.

The EU, too, has gradually developed a specific policy on transfrontier relations. The different aspects of this policy point to an increasing communitarisation of this phenomenon, reflected in a common European law in this field. These aspects

---

2. Explanatory Report FCNM, paragraphs 83-4. The latter states: "The provisions of this article are largely based on paragraphs 32.4 and 32.6 of the Copenhagen Document of the CSCE", and adds, in regard to the scope of the provision, that "It was considered unnecessary to include an explicit provision on the right to establish and maintain contacts within the territory of a state, since this was felt to be adequately covered by other provisions of the Framework Convention, notably Article 7 as regards freedom of assembly and of association".
3. See Explanatory Report FCNM, paragraphs 31 and 37.
4. All the ratifying states of the Charter except Luxembourg have also ratified the FCNM.
5. See in particular the document of the Copenhagen Meeting of the Conference on the Human Dimension of the CSCE, II.19: "The participating States affirm that freer movement and contacts among their citizens are important in the context of the protection and promotion of human rights and fundamental freedoms. They will ensure that their policies concerning entry into their territories are fully consistent with the aims set out in the relevant provisions of the Final Act, the Madrid Concluding Document and the Vienna Concluding Document. While reaffirming their determination not to recede from commitments contained in CSCE documents, they undertake to implement fully and improve present commitments in the field of human contacts, including on a bilateral and multilateral bases."
6. This body has dealt specifically with this question: e.g., the Bolzano/Bozen Recommendations on National Minorities in Inter-State Relations (2 October 2008) explain how states can provide support and assistance to persons belonging to national minorities resident in other countries without inflaming inter-ethnic or bilateral relations.

include, firstly, the promotion of joint projects between border regions and areas, especially via Interreg (European programmes for cross-border co-operation projects). Secondly, we should note the role played by the euroregions as focal points of transfrontier relations between member states. Another example is the progress in institutionalisation of transfrontier co-operation relations through the creation of the European Grouping of Territorial Co-operation (Regulation (EC) No. 1082/2006 of the European Parliament and the Council), an instrument which each state must adapt to its domestic legal system.

2. General scope: the internal context

The above overview of the external context of the Charter shows how far Europe has come in attempting to standardise and regulate relations across state borders. In the framework described, the Charter's main contribution lies in applying the general aim of facilitating or promoting transfrontier co-operation to languages. Despite its apparent obviousness, the importance of this detail should not be under-estimated: while it seems today that no one disputes the benefits of cross-border co-operation in, for example, economic and security matters, the question becomes more complex in the case of issues directly related to personal and/or collective identities, such as language; this in turn calls for a more complex approach.

The Charter's references to transfrontier relations must be set in the context of the general aim of this instrument for the protection of the European linguistic heritage represented by regional or minority languages (RMLs), which are defined in articles 1 and 2 of the Charter. As pointed out by J.-M. Woehrling in one of the first commentaries on the text, "many regional or minority languages are spoken in identical or similar form in more than one country. Cross-border exchanges are therefore of considerable value to them, increasing the number of speakers and the amount of cultural output of all kinds."[7] The importance of these exchanges for the Charter's general objectives is expressed via the different references to trans-frontier relations (Article 7.1 in Part II, and articles 11.2, 12.3 and 14 in Part III), reflecting the priority accorded to them as a key means or resource for achieving the objectives of protecting and promoting European linguistic diversity.

The significance of the Charter's contribution in this field must be assessed in relation to the international instruments mentioned above. They ensure the elimination of obstacles to cross-border relations, but the Charter goes a step further in placing a positive obligation on states to "foster" or "promote" this type of exchange for the benefit of RMLs. This perspective, a new development

---

7. J.-M. Woehrling (2005), *The European Charter for Regional or Minority Languages: a critical commentary*. Strasbourg: Council of Europe Publishing, p. 232.

in terms of international standards, is of fundamental importance in an analysis of Article 14, the direct object of our study, in the internal context of the Charter.

2.1. Transfrontier co-operation as a general objective and principle of Part II of the Charter

Article 7, in Part II of the Charter, sets out the objectives and principles which constitute the necessary framework for the preservation of regional or minority languages.[8] These objectives and principles are applicable in the territory in which those languages are spoken, taking into account the "situation of each language", a detail which introduces the possibility of an element of graduated compliance with the general obligation placed on parties to base their "policies, legislation and practice" on those objectives and principles.

Of the various subparagraphs of Article 7.1, the one most directly related to Article 14 is subparagraph i, which refers to:

> the promotion of appropriate types of transnational exchanges, in the fields covered by this Charter, for regional or minority languages used in identical or similar form in two or more States.

The general sense of this provision is explained in the Explanatory Report to the Charter thus: "It is necessary that groups speaking the same regional or minority language have the possibility of engaging in cultural exchanges and in general of developing their relations, in order to contribute together to the preservation and enrichment of their language." The definition of the object of protection is therefore nuanced: whereas Article 7.1i refers to languages as the direct beneficiaries of these exchanges, in line with the general approach adopted in the Charter, it is accepted in practice that groups of speakers are the ultimate target of the objective set, which is subsequently confirmed in the implementation process. The assumption underlying application of the provision is the sharing of languages, identified in fairly vague terms as languages "used in identical or similar form in two or more states", which, in line with the definitions in articles 1 and 2, is intended to cover the variety of linguistic situations present in Europe.[9]

As regards the other components of this undertaking, attention should first be drawn to the introduction of a positive obligation to promote, which goes further than mere non-existence of impediments or the elimination of obstacles by states. Secondly, we should note the openness of the provision on the possible

---

8. Explanatory Report, paragraph 57.

9. In this respect the Charter adopts a cautious approach as it does not stipulate any requirements that have to be satisfied before we can say that a language is "used in identical or similar form in two or more States", which thus makes it possible to cover a wide range of situations involving transitional forms, variants or dialects of the same language with varying degrees of inter-comprehension.

forms of transnational exchanges, which only have to be "appropriate" to the aim pursued, with the result that, under Part II, states are free to introduce the arrangements or mechanisms which they consider most appropriate to bring about these transnational exchanges, taking due account of any internal or external, international constraints.[10] Thirdly, we should note the general nature of the fields to which the obligation applies, which correspond to all those covered by the Charter, without being strictly limited to cultural aspects. As we will see, these last two elements help to differentiate Article 7.1i from the content of the obligations in Article 14, which contains more specific commitments. However, implementation practices often tend to blur these distinctions, which means that activities relating to transnational exchanges can be cited by states or evaluated by the Committee of Experts under either Part II or Part III.

Regarding the scenarios for implementation of the undertaking to promote transnational exchanges, the Explanatory Report lays special emphasis on those cases – without excluding others – in which the same RML in one state is recognised as the state/majority language in another state (which sociolinguistics usually refers to by the term "kin state", meaning the state under whose jurisdiction another state's "exogenous minorities" fall). In line with the precautions suggested by Article 5 of the Charter regarding respect for the territorial integrity of states, the accent is placed here on the cultural benefits to minority groups (Explanatory Report, paragraph 69):

> By definition, regional or minority languages are spoken in the state concerned by a relatively small number of speakers: for the purpose of mutual enrichment in the cultural sphere, the latter may need to be able to rely on the cultural resources available, across frontiers, to other groups speaking the same or a similar language. This is particularly important where a regional language in one state corresponds to a major cultural language, or even the national language, of another state and where transfrontier co-operation can enable the regional community to benefit from cultural activity in that more widespread language.

Furthermore, in order to help define the content of subparagraph i within Article 7.1, it is necessary to distinguish it from subparagraph e, which reads as follows:

> the maintenance and development of links, in the fields covered by this Charter, between groups using a regional or minority language and other groups in the State employing a language used in identical or similar form, as well as the establishment of cultural relations with other groups in the State using different languages.

---

10. See Explanatory Report, paragraph 70: "However, the states are left free to work out the most suitable arrangement for bringing such transnational exchanges about, especially bearing in mind the domestic and international constraints which some of them may face."

According to the Explanatory Report, subparagraph e refers to groups located in different administrative divisions of the same state, while subparagraph i adds a further dimension, concerning the need to promote these exchanges also between groups located in different states. The reference to "groups" in this report[11] once again introduces a nuance regarding the omission of speakers (identified collectively as a group, linguistic minority, national minority, people, etc.) from the text of Article 7.1 of the Charter. As in the case of transfrontier relations, a positive view of these relations as contributing to better mutual understanding and more harmonious coexistence of languages within states is promoted here.[12]

One question posed by the relationship between subparagraphs e and i of Article 7 is this: should the Charter's effectiveness in fostering relations between groups sharing the same language in different states be placed on the same level as its effectiveness in fostering relations between groups in the same state? The question is relevant if we consider the fact that only subparagraph i is subsequently expanded on and given more concrete expression in Part III (in articles 11.2, 12.3 and 14; see below, section 2.2), which might suggest the apparent paradox of more intensive involvement of the Charter in transfrontier linguistic situations than in those resulting from states' internal political and administrative divisions, both types of situation being covered by the aim of protecting RMLs by promoting contacts between speakers. Furthermore, the restrictions and precautions affecting subparagraph i in terms of the need to respect the principle of the sovereignty and integrity of states (Article 5)[13] cannot be applied in the same way to paragraph e, and it therefore seems inconsistent with the aims of the Charter to argue for lower standards in relations between groups with languages spoken in identical or similar form within the same state. We therefore consider that an interpretative criterion can be derived from the

---

11. The exacts words used in paragraph 69 of the Explanatory Report are: "the idea that such relations must also be able to develop across national frontiers if groups speaking the same or similar regional or minority languages are spread over several states".

12. Paragraph 68 of the Explanatory Report expresses this concern not to encourage separatism or marginalisation within states: "Admittedly, such awareness of a shared identity between speakers of a regional or minority language must not be reflected negatively in exclusiveness or marginalisation in relation to other social groups. The objective of promoting cultural relations with speakers of different regional or minority languages therefore serves the goal both of cultural enrichment and of enhanced understanding between all groups in the state."

13. In connection with Article 7.1i, the Explanatory Report has this to say: "It is important that states should recognise the legitimacy of such relations and not consider them suspect in terms of the loyalty which every state expects of its nationals or regard them as a threat to their territorial integrity. A language group will feel all the more integrated in the state of which it is a part if it is recognised as such and if cultural contacts with its neighbouring communities are not hindered" (paragraph 69, continued).

text, according to which the provisions of Part III referring to contacts between speakers of the same language living in different states can, on the basis of their systematic link with Article 7.1e, be applied by analogy to the promotion of relations between groups speaking the same language within a state, except where an argument based on the Charter itself militates against this.[14]

2.2. The cross-cutting nature of transfrontier co-operation: how it is connected with other provisions of Part III

Within the framework of the Charter, the promotion of transfrontier co-operation not only constitutes a general principle and objective, but is a cross-cutting element which is mentioned explicitly in some sectoral undertakings of Part III (specifically in articles 11.2 and 12.3) and implicitly in others (Article 8, for example). These are mainly provisions related to the cultural sectors whose aim is that speakers located on both sides of the border should be able to benefit from activities or resources in their own language. This systematic view of the Charter leads us to regard cross-border co-operation as a resource or instrument used for the implementation of the sectoral commitments set out in other provisions. While not actually emptying the provisions of Article 14 of their substance, this instrumental dimension determines how they are interpreted and applied.

2.2.1. The establishment and dissemination of communication media (Article 11.2)

The sectoral undertaking most obviously related to the theme of transfrontier exchanges is to be found in Article 11.2, which provides as follows:

> The Parties undertake to guarantee freedom of direct reception of radio and television broadcasts from neighbouring countries in a language used in identical or similar form to a regional or minority language, and not to oppose the retransmission of radio and television broadcasts from neighbouring countries in such a language. They further undertake to ensure that no restrictions will be placed on the freedom of expression and free circulation of information in the written press in a language used in identical or similar form to a regional or minority language.

The main aim of the provision is to increase the availability of radio and television programmes in regional or minority languages by making it possible for

---

14. This interpretative criterion may be noted, for example, in connection with the application in Spain of Article 11 within the territory of the Community of Valencia: "Furthermore, during the on-the-spot visit the Committee of Experts was informed that the Valencian authorities allegedly do not allow transmission of Catalan television programmes in Valencia and refuse to grant licences for it. The Committee of Experts invites the authorities to look into the complaints and find the solution in the spirit of the Charter"; Spain 2008, 971.

programmes in such languages to be received from other territories.[15] Transfrontier exchanges therefore stand out as a key resource for guaranteeing the presence of RMLs in those media, independently of the strictness of the commitments entered into by the state concerned under Article 11.1, subparagraph a for television and b for radio. In this connection, the Explanatory Report states:

> However minimal the role of the state may be in relation to the media, it normally at least retains the power to guarantee freedom of communication or take measures involving the elimination of obstacles to such freedom. For this reason, paragraph 2 does not contain the same proviso as paragraph 1 concerning the extent of the competence of public authorities. The undertaking to guarantee freedom of reception relates not only to obstacles deliberately placed in the way of reception of programmes broadcast from neighbouring countries but also to passive obstacles resulting from the failure of the competent authorities to take any action to make such reception possible.[16]

The Explanatory Report has relatively little to say on a topic which deserves maximum attention if the Charter's general aim in this field is to be achieved, as may be inferred from another general statement: "The time and space which regional or minority languages can secure in the media is vital for their safeguard" (Explanatory Report, paragraph 107). When one looks at the reality of most of these languages, the reception of broadcasts from neighbouring countries is essential as a means of increasing the availability of radio and television programmes in which the same or a similar language is used. In particular, the high cost of television production points to the crucial importance of creating economies of scale in order to put the industry on a stronger footing and increase opportunities for disseminating the language.[17]

Article 14a also refers explicitly to "information" as one of the fields in which transfrontier contacts must be fostered between speakers of the same language, through the conclusion and implementation of agreements. Another similarity with Article 11.2 is that both provisions not only require states to eliminate obstacles deliberately placed in the way of the freedom to receive communication media, but also highlight the need for positive action by the authorities to make this possible, with due respect for any limits deriving from other relevant

---

15. See R. Dunbar and T. Moring (2008), *The European Charter for Regional or Minority Languages and the media*, Regional or Minority Languages, No. 6. Strasbourg: Council of Europe Publishing, pp. 69-70.
16. Explanatory Report, paragraph 111.
17. There is no question here of disregarding the cultural aspect. A group of speakers may identify with a specific world of symbols which is not necessarily reflected in the output of other territories where the same language is used. The ideal solution would therefore be complementarity between own output – often necessarily limited by a lack of resources – and the reception of television and radio programmes from other territories.

international instruments.[18] This similarity means that the activities cited by states under Article 14a frequently coincide with those required by Article 11.2 of the Charter. It seems difficult in practice to distinguish the fields covered by the two provisions.[19]

One final clarification is needed regarding the expression "neighbouring countries" in Article 11.2, as distinct from references to "States" in Article 14a and "regional or local authorities" in Article 14b. In our opinion, the ambiguity of the first term, in the context of a systematic interpretation of the Charter, would make it possible to include both states and regional authorities with powers relating to the media as subjects bound by these provisions.[20] If this broad interpretation of Article 11.2, based on the previously analysed interconnection between subparagraphs e and i of Article 7.1, were to be rejected, there would be a risk of a kind of internal contradiction within the text, since the rationale is the same in both cases.

2.2.2. Cultural activities (Article 12.3)

Another provision which should be linked with Article 14 is the third paragraph of Article 12,[21] which provides as follows:

> The Parties undertake to make appropriate provision, in pursuing their cultural policy abroad, for regional or minority languages and the cultures they reflect.

---

18. In connection with possible limits, reference is made to those provided for in Article 10.2 of the European Convention on Human Rights concerning freedom of expression. In the case of television, these provisions are expressed in more concrete terms in the European Convention on Transfrontier Television, which requires states parties to comply with the principle of non-restriction of the retransmission on their territories of programme services which comply with the terms of the convention. The Explanatory Report adds: "Moreover, the provisions of this paragraph do not affect the need for copyright to be respected" (paragraph 112).

19. One possible distinguishing criterion is to include under Article 14 joint or co-operation activities relating to the media which are not confined to eliminating barriers or obstacles to free reception. For example, the Committee of Experts has analysed the following activities under Article 14: a joint programme between Television Ostrava in the Czech Republic and the regional television studio in Katowice, Poland, funded by the EU's Interreg programme (Czech Republic 2009, 241); exchange of programmes whereby the Italian-speaking television channel Koper/Capodistria and the Trieste/Trst regional branch of Italian public television broadcast each other's news once a day, and once a month broadcast a joint documentary devoted to the Italian-speaking minority in Slovenia and the Slovenian-speaking minority in Italy (Slovenia 2004, 238): co-operation between Nordic countries on radio programmes and the production of television programmes in Sami (Sweden 2003, 174).

20. As an additional argument in support of the position defended here, it should be mentioned that the Explanatory Report refers, in connection with Article 11.2, to measures to be adopted by the "competent authorities", a reference which, in accordance with Article 10.2 of the Charter – which recognises the regional authorities as players – should include not only state but also regional authorities.

21. See also the link between the two provisions in Woehrling (2005), op. cit., pp. 223ff.

The aim pursued here is not co-operation for the benefit of the language, but external dissemination of the state's own culture, an aspect which initially distinguishes it from Article 14. In this respect Article 12.3 is more directly related to the objective of Article 7.1a in recognising and disseminating RMLs as cultural assets.[22] Furthermore, the unambiguous reference to policy "abroad" means in this case that the scope of the provision is limited to external relations, with other states or the regions forming part of them.

However, this external policy is often directed towards states with which a linguistic heritage is shared. In such cases, when the state at which this external policy is aimed has groups speaking a shared RML, compliance with this undertaking also involves that of Article 14a if this is done via treaties or agreements; and that of subparagraph b if the RML regions are allowed to participate in the development of this type of external relations (especially in states with a federal structure).

In the process of implementing the Charter, this link between articles 14 and 12.3 becomes obvious,[23] and this seems logical given that the main areas for transfrontier exchanges mentioned in Article 14a partly coincide with the cultural activities referred to in Article 12. As a result, the activities evaluated by the Committee of Experts under both provisions may occasionally coincide in terms of their nature or content without it being possible to identify any strict criterion for delimiting their respective scopes.[24]

2.2.3. Educational and vocational training activities (Article 8)

Despite the fact that Article 8 does not mention transfrontier exchanges in any of its subparagraphs, it is linked to Article 14 by virtue of the enumeration in the latter of "education", "vocational training" and "permanent education" as sectors favoured by the Charter for transfrontier exchanges. This may also be seen from the explicit reference to Article 8 included in the Explanatory Report's commentary on Article 14, where it is noted that the aims pursued by the former

---

22. According to the Explanatory Report to the Charter: "All countries seek to promote their national culture abroad. In order to give a complete and faithful picture of that culture, such promotion should not neglect regional or minority languages and cultures. This undertaking, which is provided for in Article 12, paragraph 3, constitutes one way of applying the principle of the recognition of regional or minority languages embodied in Article 7, paragraph 1.a, of Part II of the charter" (paragraph 120).

23. See, for example, the first periodical report on application of the Charter submitted to the Council of Europe by the Netherlands, where Article 14 is interpreted as referring generally to the state's external policy conducted via specific international policy instruments, for example with other minority-language regions such as Catalonia or Wales (section X).

24. By way of example, see Switzerland 2001, 300, which repeats the comment made under Article 12.3 on the Canton of Ticino's traditional co-operation with the Italian authorities.

provision can sometimes be achieved through recourse to transfrontier exchanges as a means of implementing substantive undertakings in the educational field less expensively (specifically in connection with higher education).[25]

As with the previously mentioned provisions linked to Article 14, references to transfrontier co-operation appear in the process of implementing Article 8 and monitoring compliance with it. In some cases, however, the Committee of Experts has tried to distinguish more clearly between the guarantee of substantive compliance with treaties or agreements, which can be monitored under Article 8, and the undertakings which can be subsumed under Article 14, which would seem to be confined to fostering contacts between speakers of the same RML.[26]

3. Definition of transfrontier exchanges in Article 14 of the Charter

In the above analysis of the internal context of Article 14 in the Charter, attention was drawn to this provision's unusual position: on the one hand, because of its direct link with the principle of fostering transnational exchanges in Article 7.1i, which it sets out in more specific terms;[27] and, on the other hand, because of the role played by transfrontier co-operation as a cross-cutting element which can be used to implement the undertakings set out in certain other substantive fields of Part III of the Charter (especially education, the media and culture). This does not dispense us, however, from examining the concrete meaning of the undertakings contained in the two subparagraphs of Article 14, whose simple structure – in contrast with the complex structure of the other articles in Part III – is in itself a reflection of its unusual nature.

---

25. The exact wording is: "In some circumstances, it [the co-operation envisaged by Article 14] may also be a satisfactory (and less expensive) means of implementing undertakings entered into under other articles of the charter: for example, with respect to the provision of higher education facilities as laid down in Article 8, paragraph 1.e, a bilateral agreement could make arrangements for the students concerned to attend appropriate institutions in a neighbouring state" (paragraph 126 of the Explanatory Report).

26. In some reports by the Committee of Experts one discerns an intention to distinguish between substantive protection of the rights of national minorities in the field of education and the promotion of contacts between speakers. In Czech Republic 2009, 320, after mentioning the treaty on good neighbourly relations with the Slovak Republic and the agreements between the two ministries of culture, the Committee of Experts states: "The guarantee that both countries grant legal protection and support for the newly constituted national minorities, and development among others in the fields of education and culture is enshrined in Article 8 of the Treaty. However, it is not clear to the Committee of Experts how these agreements foster contacts between the Slovak-speakers in both countries."

27. The Explanatory Report clearly endorses this idea when it refers to Article 7.1i to clarify the meaning of Article 14 (in paragraph 124): "This article expands and develops the idea set out in Article 7, paragraph 1.i and reference is therefore made to the explanations given above (see paragraphs 69-70)."

3.1. Subparagraph a of Article 14

Under subparagraph a of Article 14, the parties undertake to:

> apply existing bilateral and multilateral agreements which bind them with the States in which the same language is used in identical or similar form, or if necessary to seek to conclude such agreements, in such a way as to foster contacts between the users of the same language in the States concerned in the fields of culture, education, information, vocational training and permanent education.

This undertaking focuses on the application and conclusion of bilateral or multilateral agreements binding the parties to other states. The specification of these instruments, if only under the fairly broad heading of "agreements", is a plus compared with Article 7.1i, where the question of how transfrontier co-operation is to be implemented is left wide open.

This undertaking is of a goal-oriented nature, the goal being to foster contacts between speakers[28] of the same language situated in two or more states. The Committee of Experts has taken it upon itself to point out that it is not sufficient to prove the existence of agreements or treaties: it is also necessary that both the content and application of existing agreements and the signing of new ones should comply with the purpose of the provision. As we will see later, the position of the Committee of Experts combines a formal criterion (existence of agreements) and a substantive criterion (effective fostering of linguistic contacts) when evaluating states' compliance with their undertakings under Article 14a.[29]

Another defining aspect of subparagraph a of Article 14 is the specification of certain substantive fields or sectors which must be given priority in such contacts and which reflect the Charter's eminently cultural outlook. Without prejudice to that, the setting of stronger obligations in these fields must not be understood in an exclusive sense, given that Article 7.1i promotes transnational exchanges in all fields, so that other forms of co-operation (economic, inter-administrative, etc.) with linguistic implications can also be assessed within the Charter framework.

Lastly, in distinguishing between subparagraphs a and b of Article 14, the undertaking to foster transfrontier exchanges in the former is of a general nature, without any geographical area being specified, that is, the territorial element is not decisive, as it is in subparagraph b, which applies to border areas.[30] This

---

28. On the question of identification of the collective subjects at whom the Charter's cross-border co-operation undertakings are aimed, we refer to the observations made in connection with Article 7.1i (see section 2.1).

29. See below, section 4.3.

30. In this connection, see Woehrling (2005), op. cit., pp. 223ff.

structural division of the provision is specifically noted in the Explanatory Report,[31] though it may prove complicated in practice to draw a dividing line between the activities coming under one subparagraph and those coming under the other. These difficulties of demarcation can be seen in the process of implementation by states[32] and its supervision by the Committee of Experts, despite the distinguishing criteria established by this body, which are analysed later.[33]

3.2. Subparagraph b of Article 14

Under subparagraph b of Article 14, the parties undertake:

> for the benefit of regional or minority languages, to facilitate and/or promote co-operation across borders, in particular between regional or local authorities in whose territory the same language is used in identical or similar form.

The structure of this subparagraph is distinct from that of subparagraph a and closer to the wording of Article 7.1i, though in reverse order. Article 14b first mentions the aim – the benefit of RMLs – and then the undertaking to facilitate and/or promote transfrontier co-operation. The avoidance in subparagraph b of the term "speakers" of these languages is in keeping with the wish of the Charter's drafters not to directly identify ethnic minorities or groups separated by frontiers in order to rule out interpretations designed to undermine the legitimacy of established state frontiers.[34] However, this does not preclude the identification, in the process of implementing the provision, of various collective subjects such as "groups", "communities", "linguistic minorities", "national minorities" or "peoples" as beneficiaries of transfrontier exchanges.[35]

The undertaking to "facilitate and/or promote co-operation across borders" has, in one respect, a broader and more indeterminate content than that relating to the application or signing of agreements in Article 14a; in another respect, its scope seems more limited by virtue of the specific geographical reference to

---

31. "While it is desirable that such co-operation should develop in a general manner, paragraph b underlines that this is particularly the case where one and the same regional language is spoken on either side of the border" (paragraph 125).
32. The case history is very varied: if states have ratified one subparagraph, the reports may cite different types of activity which, on the face of it, also fit under subparagraph b; if states have ratified both subparagraphs, it is not uncommon for activities to be cited under Article 14 without being differentiated by subparagraph; in such cases the Committee of Experts can separate them in its report (in this connection, see below sections 4.3 and 5).
33. See below, section 3.4.
34. See above, in section 2.1 the comments on a similar omission in Article 7.1i and how it is linked to Article 5.
35. See, for example, the references to "communities" in Armenia 2006; to "linguistic minorities" in Germany 2002; to "national minorities" in Czech Republic 2009, and Croatia 2001; and to "peoples" in Finland 2001.

border areas, which is not to be found in subparagraph a or in Article 7.1i (which merely refers to "transnational exchanges" with respect to languages used in two or more states). This seems to be confirmed by the Explanatory Report, although legal opinion is not entirely clear on this point[36] and there is even less consistency in the practical application of the provision.

Another key aspect of this subparagraph is the role given to regional or local authorities on either side of the border as players in co-operative relations. (Article 10.2, referring to "administrative authorities" and "public services", recognises in general terms the role of local and regional authorities in adopting measures to promote the use of RMLs.) Although the 1980 Outline Convention had already established the legitimacy of co-operation between entities of this kind, Article 14b gives it a positive impetus in connection with the objectives of protecting and promoting RMLs. However, as has been rightly noted, this does not exempt states from obligations within the framework of this undertaking because not only is it also binding on decentralised state bodies having legal personality, but states are required to facilitate and promote transfrontier co-operation by establishing an appropriate legal framework and eliminating legal or other obstacles which might hinder the action of local and regional authorities.[37]

Lastly, we should note the failure of subparagraph b of Article 14 to specify the substantive fields to which the undertaking applies, which makes it possible to interpret it in an open-ended way (according to the terms of Article 7.1i), although the cultural and educational sectors, which are mentioned explicitly in subparagraph a, feature prominently in its practical application,[38] thus also contributing to the lack of a clear distinction between the two subparagraphs.[39]

---

36. Woehrling (2005), op. cit., pp. 233ff., says that subparagraph b refers to agreements which affect more particularly border regions when the same language is used in identical or similar form, but in our opinion nothing in this provision justifies confining the undertaking to co-operate to the signing of agreements. As cited in note 31, the Explanatory Report to the Charter endorses this definition of the subparagraph as focusing on regions on both sides of the border where the same language is spoken.
37. See Woehrling (2005), op. cit., pp. 234ff.
38. The Explanatory Report, paragraph 126, without distinguishing explicitly between the two subparagraphs, mentions the following by way of example: "The co-operation envisaged may extend to such matters as school twinnings, teacher exchanges, the mutual recognition of diplomas and circulation of cultural assets (books, films, exhibitions, etc.) and the transfrontier activities of cultural agencies (theatre companies, lecturers, etc.)."
39. The Committee of Experts has contributed to this at least partial overlapping of the substantive fields of application by the special interest it has shown, sometimes through the questions it puts to states.

4. The provisions of Article 14: analysis of the position of the Committee of Experts

Now that the meaning of transfrontier exchanges in Article 14 has been defined, this section focuses on a series of general issues which arise in the process of implementation of the article by states, and supervision of that process by the Committee of Experts. This methodological approach should help to give a clearer idea of the Charter's impact and effectiveness in the area of the promotion of transfrontier exchanges and its influence on European linguistic diversity.

4.1. The inclusion of a variety of transfrontier linguistic situations

An analysis of the application of Article 14 provides an insight into the richness and complexity of the linguistic map of Europe. Of course, it does not cover all European languages, bearing in mind the general scope of the Charter, but those which answer the description of an RML (as defined in articles 1a, 1c and 3.1) and are spoken on the territory of the states which have ratified the Charter, including non-territorial languages and excluding the languages of immigrants. On the basis of this general definition, the Charter embraces a wide variety of linguistic situations where the meaning of transfrontier co-operation and the forms it assumes may vary. So, based on the possible statuses of the various languages concerned, we may identify the following situations:

a. An RML in one country which is the same as the official and majority language of another state party to the Charter (e.g. Danish in Germany, Czech and Slovak in Austria or Polish in the Czech Republic): this situation, described sociolinguistically in terms of linguistic minorities having a "kin state" or "kin languages",[40] is very widespread because of the historic shape of the borders of European countries, which results in some linguistic groups being separated from their state of reference. Transfrontier exchanges take on great importance here,[41] because the speakers of the RML in one country can take advantage of existing provision in the same language in the kin state in the cultural, educational, information and other

---

40. For a comparative analysis of the legal solutions applied to these linguistic groups which "spill over" onto the territory of other states distinct from their state of reference, which tends to adopt a position of vigilance or protection with regard to them, see G. Poggeschi (2010) *Diritti linguistici. Un analisi comparata*. Rome: Carocci, pp. 151-7.

41. This has been stated explicitly in connection with Article 14a of the Charter: "The Committee of Experts observes that the large majority of bilateral or multilateral agreements have been reached with States in which the regional or minority language in question is the official language of the State", a statement which serves to justify the lack of demand for such agreements in the case of speakers of the Romani language, who do not have this possibility. See Germany 2008, 784.

fields, thus helping to offset the shortage of linguistic resources which is usually a consequence of a linguistic group's lack of political structures at state level or the fact that it is too small to produce such resources.

b. RMLs which are the same as the official language of a state which is not a party to the Charter (e.g. Russian in Armenia, Italian in Slovenia, Irish in the United Kingdom or Catalan in Andorra): this is a variant of the previous situation, in which the state where the RML is spoken has ratified the Charter but not the state where the same language is the national or state language. By distinguishing this situation we are able to highlight the fact that the lack of correspondence between the undertakings entered into by states sharing the same language does not directly affect the effectiveness of the Charter. Indeed, in a situation of this kind, the state where the language is a regional or minority language and which has accepted the undertakings of Article 14 of the Charter is required to take the measures provided for by the Charter in the field of transfrontier exchanges. The effects of the Charter therefore extend beyond the territory of ratifying states, giving an impetus to co-operation and exchanges involving other states.

c. The same language is an official language in two signatory states of the Charter (this is the case with Swedish in Finland and Sweden): this is an exceptional situation within the framework of the Charter because the official languages of states are generally excluded from its sphere of protection by Article 1a.ii. Notwithstanding the exceptional nature of this situation, the fact that the language has official status in two or more states is especially favourable to the development of co-operative relations, since one can assume that both will take fairly substantial public action in support of their national languages, thus increasing the opportunities for exchanges.

d. RMLs which are not the official or national language of any state (e.g. Kurdish, Assyrian, Romani, Frisian, Sami or Basque): comparatively speaking, these linguistic realities carry somewhat less weight than situation *a* in the Charter's current field of application. Transfrontier co-operation between groups of speakers of these languages is of special importance for ensuring the continued existence and development of these languages in the cultural, educational, information and other field. In the face of the distrustful attitude of states towards communication between members of minorities which, over the course of time, have been scattered across different states, sometimes out of a fear of possible nationalist or secessionist demands, the Charter asserts the positive value of this communication for languages. The possibilities of co-operation for these languages vary: a distinction may be drawn between languages whose speakers enjoy the benefit of certain political or administrative structures (e.g. Basque,

Sami and Frisian) and those with uncertain institutional support which depend on the initiative of private organisations which may or may not enjoy some form of state framework or state support.[42] Within this situation, there would seem to be a similar distinction to that between subparagraphs a and b, since an RML that is not the state language may enjoy the protection of the Charter on both sides of the border (e.g. Frisian in Germany and Denmark) or not (e.g. Basque or Catalan in Spain and France, or Kurdish in Armenia and Turkey). The lack of reciprocity does not hinder the effectiveness of the Charter here either, but in the latter situation greater difficulties should be expected in stimulating and channelling linguistic co-operation.[43]

Lastly, to complete this systematic analysis of the linguistic situations in which the undertaking to promote transfrontier exchanges is applied, it should be pointed out that, though it is the most common situation, territories where the same language is spoken (with RML status in at least one of them) do not have to be geographically adjacent.[44] In other words, co-operation across borders need not presuppose the existence of a physical border separating two adjacent territories. Such a restriction would not be in keeping with the desire for protection of RMLs expressed in articles 7.1i and 14, transcending borders through the concerted action of players situated in different countries.

4.2. The different players involved in transfrontier exchanges

The identity of the subjects bound by Article 14 is, as already mentioned, one way it differs from Article 7.1i, which merely sets out undertakings of the "Parties" to the treaty. Article 14 refers in subparagraph a to "States" and in subparagraph b to the "regional or local authorities". An analysis of the practical application of the article reveals a range of players involved in transfrontier exchanges within a case history marked by the differing circumstances of the signatory states. Hence, notwithstanding the final responsibility of states as

---

42. In the case of Armenia, for example, with regard to Article 14a, the Committee of Experts accepts the assertion by the state authorities that "bilateral agreements also provide an opportunity for Yezidi, Kurds and Assyrians, who do not have their own ethnic states, to communicate with the corresponding ethnic communities in other countries", together with a number of examples of the exchanges mentioned. Armenia 2009, 226.

43. Of the reality and scale of such difficulties, views differ; for example, a contrast may be seen between the Spanish Government's view of the obstacles stemming from the lack of official recognition of Basque in France (2nd periodical report on the application of the Charter, submitted to the Council of Europe by Spain in December 2006, pp. 492ff.) and the more positive and proactive view of the Autonomous Government of the Basque Country in fostering contacts with regard to the Basque language (pp. 494-6).

44. One negative example is to be found in the United Kingdom's co-operative relations with the province of Nova Scotia in Canada. United Kingdom 2007.

subjects of international law required to guarantee compliance with the under-takings accepted upon ratification, the achievement of the aims prescribed by the article normally requires the more or less concerted action of different players. The following players involved in transfrontier exchanges each have a specific role:

- States: these are the players called on in the first instance to act to secure the conclusion or application of bilateral and multilateral agreements with "other states" (Article 14a). In many countries the state authorities play a clear role in stimulating transfrontier co-operation, not only via agreements, but also via other types of co-operative action; although in some cases the state authorities cite a decentralised internal structure as a reason for leaving the initiative for transfrontier co-operation in the hands of sub-state territorial authorities – without prejudice to formal compliance with the article.[45]

- Regional or federated entities: the fact that a significant number of the ratifying states have a politically decentralised structure results in a signifi-cant role for sub-state political authorities in the development of transfron-tier exchanges. Generally speaking, the existence of these decentralised territorial authorities increases the possibilities for transfrontier co-oper-ation (Article 14b). However, their capacity for action is not the same in all cases: only some federated entities enjoy extensive powers to enter into agreements with states and sub-state authorities as part of their external policy;[46] whereas the majority of regions have more restrictions placed by the domestic legal system on their action in this field, which does not preclude the fact that these authorities are sometimes required to replace the state in performing these functions.[47]

- Local authorities: the local level, which is present in all states, can also play an important role in the field of transfrontier exchanges (Article 14b). Particularly in unitary states (or those with a weak intermediate political and institutional level), municipalities and other, supra-municipal local

---

45. See 2nd report submitted by Spain on application of the Charter in 2006; this report, after recognising that the content of Article 14 "does not correspond to the obligations which the constitutional system attributes to each specific administrative level", mentions as an obstacle the fact that the neighbouring countries, France and Portugal, have a centralised structure for decision making on language policy "whereas in Spain responsibility for a promotional and protective language policy goes virtually exclusively and specifically to the Autonomous Communities" (p. 359).

46. Especially in the case of the *Länder* in Germany (where the ratification instrument states "The separate specification of these provisions for the territories of each individual *Land* is in keeping with the federal structure of the Federal Republic of Germany and takes into account the situation of each of these languages in the *Land* in question") and Austria.

47. See above note 44 on the action of the autonomous communities in Spain.

entities have a key role in stimulating and maintaining co-operative relations with groups in a neighbouring country where the same language is spoken in identical or similar form.[48] The federal structure of some countries is also compatible with the existence of a dynamic co-operation process at the local level as a major level for promoting RMLs.[49]

- Social and cultural bodies: although they are not specifically mentioned in Article 14,[50] various types of body (voluntary associations, NGOs, foundations, etc.) sometimes take the initiative or participate actively in transfrontier exchanges concerning RMLs. The role played by these bodies may vary depending on the institutional support enjoyed by RMLs in each context. The Committee of Experts regards financial support for these bodies from the public authorities as a means of complying with Article 14b. As a result, it has sometimes asked for an explanation when cuts have been made in direct subsidies to organisations working to promote languages through exchanges,[51] without, however, establishing any general policy in this regard.

4.3. Openness regarding the forms and instruments of transfrontier co-operation

A third important aspect of the application of Article 14 is the identification by the Committee of Experts, on the basis of information supplied by states, of important measures for complying with the obligations set out in the Charter. Generally speaking, implementation has left open the types of measure and instrument through which transfrontier exchanges are conducted under this provision. Nevertheless, the Committee of Experts has established a series of formal and substantive criteria as a framework for the activities of the subjects bound by Article 14.

The monitoring performed by the Committee of Experts therefore combines two perspectives: a quantitative, or formal, one (adoption of agreements,

---

48. See, for example, United Kingdom 2004, 380, on district councils; the Netherlands 2001, 107, on the province of Friesland; Armenia 2006, 159, on *marzes* and local authorities; Croatia 2001, 109, on local authorities; and Slovakia, 1st cycle (2007), paragraph 274.
49. See, for example, Germany 2006, 172 and 317-18, on Danish and Frisian respectively.
50. Social and cultural bodies are mentioned, without any special emphasis, in the Explanatory Report to the Charter, which refers to "the transfrontier activities of cultural agencies (theatre companies, lecturers, etc.)" (paragraph 126). This contrasts with the explicit importance attached to these players in Article 17.2 FCNM.
51. For example, in the Netherlands, the Committee of Experts notes the discontinuation of state subsidies for exchange programmes with Denmark on the Frisian language, coinciding with signing of the Charter in 1996, and the fact that the Frisian Council lacks government support for the promotion of similar initiatives.

approval of rules or existence of related bodies)[52] and a qualitative, or substantive, one which complements and nuances the former in view of the requirement that the measures adopted should effectively foster contacts between speakers of the same language and facilitate and/or promote co-operation across borders for the benefit of RMLs.[53] The importance and meaning given by the Committee of Experts to this substantive compliance aspect may vary: in some cases, Article 14a may be deemed to be complied with even in the absence of treaties or agreements, this assessment being based on proven co-operation;[54] although what happens most commonly is that proof of the beneficial effects on languages is required when there are doubts about the relevance and practical application of the formal measures cited by states.

The relative openness of Article 14 with regard to the forms, instruments and actions through which transfrontier co-operation is conducted is reflected in the process of implementing the article, in which the following methods are employed, to varying extents depending on the state concerned:[55]

- Bilateral or multilateral international treaties: as a form of legal document directly subsumable under subparagraph a, international treaties or conventions between sovereign states constitute one of the measures most commonly cited under Article 14. This may involve both the application of treaties with more general co-operation aims[56] and the conclusion and application of specific bilateral or multilateral treaties in the fields identified in Article 14a. In the case of RMLs for which there are no specific treaties, the Committee of Experts usually encourages states to conclude such treaties, in a sense

---

52. For a case in which the absence of bilateral or multilateral co-operation agreements precludes considering that the undertakings of Article 14a are complied with, see Switzerland 2001, 173, in connection with Romansh.

53. In this connection, the Committee of Experts can express an opinion on whether the measures adopted contribute effectively towards eliminating the obstacles to freedom of movement and actively promote cross-border exchanges, so the existence of formal agreements does not dispense states from providing information on how they are applied in fostering contacts between speakers of the same language and what role language plays in the fields provided for under the Charter. See, for example, Czech Republic 2009, 238 and 240, on the application of paragraphs a and b of Article 14 to Polish; Slovakia 2007, 182; and Germany 2006, 786, in both cases for Romanian.

54. This possibility seems more remote in the case of subparagraph a of Article 14, but it does occur in the case of subparagraph b, as may be seen in United Kingdom 2004, 380 and United Kingdom 2006, 522.

55. For the widest and most complete range of instruments and other co-operation arrangements, see Finland 2001 and Finland 2004.

56. Reference was made to these treaties in section 1, above, as forming the external context of the Charter, and they are mentioned very frequently in the reports submitted by states, this information being then reproduced by the Committee of Experts.

giving priority to this type of agreement.[57] However, as already mentioned, the existence of such treaties is not usually considered sufficient: what is required is evidence of how they have been applied or implemented in practice.[58]

- Other types of agreement: the conclusion of other types of agreement (referred to by the terms memorandum, protocol, declaration, etc.) between state authorities, and especially between regional or local authorities (a typical example of the latter being twinnings between towns)[59] is generally assessed by the Committee of Experts as constituting a measure falling within the framework of Article 14. Since there is no requirement that these agreements should take on a specific form, all those forms of agreement provided for under international law and accepted under each state party's domestic legal system will be regarded as complying with the undertaking.

- Setting up new bodies: the existence of stable co-operation bodies is assessed positively by the Committee of Experts as a measure adopted in compliance with Article 14. These may be bodies specialising in linguistic issues[60] or, more usually, bodies with wider responsibilities in the area of co-operation, provided this co-operation also applies to the linguistic field.[61] As regards the latter case, many reports highlight the positive impact of setting up a euroregion as a key factor stimulating transfrontier exchanges in the linguistic field.[62] In accordance with the general criteria already noted, the existence of the body is not considered sufficient: its institutional activity is assessed in the light of such factors as how speakers are

---

57. For example, in Norway 2003, 154, the drawing up of a treaty on the rights of Sami communities is pointed out as being a very positive initiative.

58. The Committee of Experts sometimes regards the non-existence of complaints about the application of these treaties as constituting sufficient evidence, see Slovakia 2007, 291.

59. Examples of twinned towns are to be found in Armenia 2006, 159 (twinnings with towns in Georgia and Iran); and in the 2nd periodic report submitted to the Council of Europe by Croatia in 2003, pp. 63-6, where there is a reference to the existence of a register of co-operation agreements between towns and cities in Croatia and in other countries (among others, Hungary, Slovakia and Slovenia).

60. For example, the North-South Language Implementation Body between the United Kingdom (Northern Ireland) and Ireland, whose aim is to foster transnational contacts and exchanges (United Kingdom 2004, 379).

61. One typical example is the Nordic Council, which comprises four states party to the Charter (Finland, Sweden, Norway and Denmark) together with other territories: Sweden 2003, 171-2; and, in central Europe, Arge Alpen-Adria, a body supporting cultural co-operation whose members include Austria and Germany.

62. Czech Republic 2009, 242; Denmark 2007, 114; Germany 2006, 389; Slovakia 2007, 293, where the setting up of several euroregions is cited as evidence of the smooth functioning of cross-border co-operation with Hungary, although proof is required of the benefits to the RMLs concerned.

represented on it[63] and the effectiveness of this activity in promoting contacts between speakers and fostering linguistic exchanges.[64]

- Carrying out activities: the Committee of Experts also assesses compliance with the undertakings contained in Article 14, and especially in subparagraph b, on the basis of the carrying out of joint or exchange activities in which the state, regional or local authorities participate directly or by means of financial support. It may be seen from the reports that these activities usually relate to the fields of education (pupil or teacher exchanges, teacher training in institutions in the other country, mutual recognition of qualifications), culture (joint organisation of festivals, theatrical or musical performances, poetry recitals), the media (joint broadcasts or reception of broadcasts from other territories, financial support for print media), promotion of the language (information campaigns, activities aimed at young people, funding of research projects), among others. In this way, the Charter helps to stimulate and maintain a positive process of cross-border co-operation, without it always being absolutely necessary to structure it by means of agreements or other instruments.[65]

- Other measures helping to eliminate obstacles to freedom of movement: action to facilitate co-operation required by the article, and especially subparagraph b, also includes a wide range of measures related to that goal: the establishment of certain rights through constitutional rules or legislation; waiving of a visa requirement for nationals of the country with which the language is shared; facilitating free circulation of the press and other cultural or academic materials; or the granting of tax exemptions for exchanges with certain countries and in respect of certain products.

4.4. Some outstanding questions

As pointed out in the preceding pages, Article 14, as a specification of Article 7.1i, operates in a field which was previously the domain of various European organisations working to facilitate and/or promote co-operation across

---

63. See Norway 2001, 96, where the existence of a Sami Parliament is included as an important element in these exchanges, as it represents the Sami population in Norway; and the related case of Finland 2001, 196, where there is a reference to the involvement of various bodies (Sami Council, Parliamentary Sami Council, Arctic Council, Nordic Sami Institute) in the fields of education, employment, culture and the economy of the Sami people.

64. For example, with regard to Arge Alpen-Adria, a body which fosters interregional co-operation, the committee requests information on specific projects or activities for the benefit of Burgenland Croatian: Austria 2004, 197.

65. United Kingdom 2004, 380, regarding the exchanges between district councils in the UK and Ireland, which comply with Article 14b without any special agreement being required to make them more structured. The committee draws attention to the opportunities to increase and further this type of co-operation.

borders. The Charter performs a specific function by gearing transfrontier communication and co-operation towards certain specific objectives, namely protecting RMLs and increasing opportunities for contact between speakers. With regard to the implementation of these general goals, attention should be drawn to three questions still outstanding or awaiting further clarification which affect the scope of Article 14 and its effectiveness in affording protection.

Firstly, the question of the identity of the language for the purposes of implementation of the undertakings set out in the Charter. As we have seen, an expression used repeatedly in several of its provisions is that of territories/ countries/states where "the same language is used in identical or similar form" (articles 7.1i, 11.2 and 14). The identity of the language is therefore a precondition for the implementation of these undertakings. In principle, it is for states to specify which RMLs are protected in their respective territories and, in connection with those languages, to identify the territories with which contacts and exchanges will be established under Article 14. However, there may be cases in which, for various reasons – political disagreements or conflicts, disputes over the standard of the language, etc. – a state bound by the Charter does not recognise the identity of a particular language, and this may detract from the effectiveness of the international instrument.[66]

This question prompts another, concerning the role of the Committee of Experts, as the Charter's monitoring body, in determining what constitutes "the same language". Hitherto this body has adopted a cautious attitude, avoiding explicit pronouncements on the identity of a language when faced with cases which are disputed owing to the existence of different names for a language or different variants on either side of a border. Neither is consideration usually given under the article in question to initiatives aimed at standardising scattered variants,[67] a factor which, from a sociolinguistic perspective, is usually considered important for fostering communication between speakers separated by political or administrative borders. In our opinion, the responsibility of the Committee of Experts for monitoring the proper implementation of the Charter, together with

---

66. The cases in question are very varied: the fragmentation of Romansh and the doubts voiced by the Committee of Ministers in the monitoring process concerning whether it is used in an identical or similar form in other states (Switzerland 2004, 134); the use of the language as a political tool for asserting the individuality of Valencian within the Catalan language, of which it constitutes a variant (Spain 2005, 867-9, where Valencian is linked to Catalan in France, Italy and Andorra, but no examples of interregional co-operation are given); or the difficulty of linking together the variants of the Romani language owing to its low level of standardisation, among others.

67. The question of linguistic standardisation, which is vitally important for revitalising some RMLs, is usually dealt with under Article 12 of the Charter. In one report, however, the committee stresses the importance of developing common standards for the Sami languages and harmonising the different variants spoken in different countries and the terminology (Sweden 2003, 173).

the responsibility that falls to the Committee of Ministers on a political level, should lead to greater involvement in ensuring that undertakings to co-operate across borders (which include states' internal political and administrative divisions) are not flouted through the omission of languages or unjustified denial of their identity, thus having a negative impact on the effectiveness of articles 14, 7.1e and 7.1i. Through greater involvement of the supervisory bodies, a dynamic process of co-operation could be set in motion where there is reasonable evidence that the same RML is spoken, albeit in different variants, outside the territory of the state, especially when this is an important factor in revitalising that language; and, in sociolinguistic terms, that would help to strengthen the view of linguistic unity as consisting of realities characterised by political and administrative fragmentation.

A second question still outstanding, based on analysis of the application of Article 14, concerns the identification of certain objective parameters for determining or measuring the scope of the undertakings set out in the Charter. It may be inferred from the committee's monitoring activity that the article basically comprises "obligations as to activity", consisting in the adoption of instruments or measures to foster contacts between speakers and promote co-operation across borders, with the additional requirement that they should benefit the protection and dissemination of RMLs. But the separate question which is posed here is that of the quantum of activity which states must prove for the undertakings of Article 14 to be considered as complied with: for example, the committee sometimes notes the "high level of compliance" of a particular country, thus indicating the possibility of different levels of compliance; while on other occasions it requires more co-operation activities to be included for the article to be deemed complied with, without it being possible to infer any minimum standard in this regard.

It should be noted that, unlike many other provisions of Part III of the Charter, the article under consideration does not include a clause allowing the undertakings to be varied according to the reality to which they are applied.[68] Without prejudice to this, the monitoring performed by the Committee of Experts with regard to the undertakings derived from Article 14 is not based on any predetermined minima but tends implicitly to graduate or adapt the level of compliance required according to more pragmatic criteria, which lead it to perform low-intensity monitoring in those situations where there is evidence of

---

68. Such as those included in other provisions of the Charter or those of the type "as far as reasonably possible", "if justified by the number of speakers" or "depending on the situation of each language".

free-flowing communication between territories sharing the same language,[69] while the monitoring becomes more intense when problems or shortcomings are detected.[70] The monitoring body's approach can be explained, at least partly, by Article 14's function as an instrument for complying with other substantive undertakings, and it is on these that the emphasis has hitherto been placed in the process of monitoring compliance with the Charter. This does not rule out the possibility that the monitoring criteria might be refined in future, thus avoiding any blurring of the specific profile of Article 14 in relation to other provisions of the Charter.

The final question to be dealt with here, which in various respects underlies the preceding analysis, concerns the difficulty of delimiting precisely and unambiguously the undertakings specific to each of the subparagraphs of Article 14. The origins of this problem are undoubtedly to be found in the process of ratification of the Charter by states, which generally has not reflected a clear awareness on the part of the subject agreeing to be bound by it of the specific content of each subparagraph.[71] This lack of clear distinctions was subsequently reflected in the implementation reports submitted to the Council of Europe by the states parties, and has sometimes been further reflected in the monitoring reports of the Committee of Experts, where activities of the same type are sometimes included under subparagraph a and sometimes under subparagraph b, without there being any fixed guidelines.

While bearing in mind the impossibility of deriving from the implementation process any conclusive criteria for the practical distinction between the two subparagraphs, some observations may nevertheless be made. One criterion used is that of the players involved, so that co-operative relations and exchanges between states are included under subparagraph a, while subparagraph b refers to relations between sub-state territorial authorities,[72] though

---

69. In these cases, after the first monitoring cycle, there is virtually a presumption of compliance which, unless new developments or complaints have been reported, makes it unnecessary for the Committee of Experts to examine Article 14: for example, Finland 2004; Finland 2007; Hungary 2004; Hungary 2007, the omission being explicitly justified in this case (paragraphs 203-4); Norway 2007, where it is explicitly excluded on the ground that it is not a problematical issue; and Sweden 2009.

70. In one case, though, the Committee of Experts held that the state's argument on the sociolinguistic situation, by which the type of cross-border link would depend on how populations were concentrated or dispersed, was insufficient to justify the low level of co-operation activity (re Slovakian, Czech Republic 2009, 322).

71. In fact, the majority of countries ratified both subparagraphs at the same time for the majority of RMLs, while in other cases the choice of one or other of the subparagraphs seems to be based on varying criteria.

72. For example, Denmark 2004, 111-2.

this criterion is contradicted in some reports where regional exchanges are dealt with under subparagraph a.[73] On the other hand, a second general criterion used is based on the type of activity assignable to each subparagraph, with treaties and agreements coming under subparagraph a and other co-operation activities under subparagraph b. However, there is no shortage of exceptions in the committee's monitoring reports where substantive co-operation activities are discussed under subparagraph a and agreements under subparagraph b.

To sum up, where the last question is concerned, it is not easy to tell whether confusion and overlapping between the two subparagraphs of Article 14 in the implementation process has significant effects or not on compliance with the Charter's objectives in this field. Although it is difficult in practice to discern the theoretical connection between the two subparagraphs, once again that is in line with the substantive and, as it were, case-history-based approach which has prevailed in application of the provision, in which the dynamics and results of transfrontier co-operation activities for the benefit of languages and their speakers appear more important to the Committee of Experts than the actual forms taken by those exchanges.

5. Recommendations and good practice: by way of a conclusion

In all the reports of the Committee of Experts examined, there are very few occasions when Article 14 appears in the findings; there are even fewer recommendations of the Committee of Ministers referring directly to the article in question. The explanation for this is connected both with the earlier comments on the flexible criteria applied by the Committee of Experts when verifying compliance with the undertakings set out in the article and with the fact that its monitoring activity has hitherto focused more on application of the Charter in the substantive fields regulated by articles 8 to 13 – and has varied in intensity among these articles, as may be seen from the comments made in this chapter.

However that may be, a number of recommendations and good practices which may help to strengthen transfrontier exchanges for the benefit of RMLs and their speakers can be drawn from the committee's reports. First, the Committee of Experts has pointed out on several occasions that the impetus for transfrontier contacts and co-operation is a responsibility which lies with the different levels of government in each state, in order to comply with the undertakings set out in the relevant provision. The activities of sub-state

---

73. For an example of the unclear distinction between the two subparagraphs, see United Kingdom 2004, 379-80 and United Kingdom 2007, 522-3.

territorial authorities and private bodies in the field of languages are considered particularly legitimate for this purpose, without this exempting states from their responsibilities in eliminating obstacles and positively promoting transfrontier exchanges. The committee accordingly emphasises the shared responsibilities of the different levels of government in the framework of Article 14 and the importance of properly co-ordinating the different players' activities in order to achieve the provision's aims.

Second, the committee's work gives an impetus to formalising transfrontier co-operation. In this connection, it may be observed that, in the successive monitoring cycles, several states which had previously shown a poor level of treaty-related activity subsequently set up the necessary mechanisms to strengthen and formalise co-operative relations with other states and regions. The importance of a substantive approach, giving priority to the reality of a dynamic co-operation process and its positive repercussions for languages, does not preclude the committee from stressing the importance of formalising that co-operation and even prioritising treaties and other types of binding agreements.

Third, the Committee of Experts gives a positive assessment to, and encourages, the institutionalisation of transfrontier co-operation (especially through the setting up of permanent bodies) as a practice with positive effects on the promotion of languages. The existence of bodies of various kinds working in this field not only demonstrates the firmness of the different players' undertaking, but may also encourage greater efficiency and optimisation of the resources devoted to the promotion of languages.

Fourth, the question of the adequacy of resources is another aspect monitored by the Committee of Experts, which may request information from public authorities on their financial involvement in fostering co-operation, although doubts in this regard have not been considered a sufficient ground for a finding of non-compliance.

Lastly, through the monitoring activity of the Committee of Experts the effects of the co-operation requirements of Article 14 are projected on to countries which have not ratified the Charter but which are located within the sphere of influence of the signatory countries. This occurs when the effectiveness and binding nature of the undertakings accepted by the parties are recognised regardless of whether the territories in which the same language is spoken belong to other states parties or not. In this way, the "virtuous circle" set in motion by the application of the Charter helps to spread throughout the European continent, with its relatively fragmented linguistic mosaic, an awareness of the value, and a positive vision, of transfrontier exchanges relating to languages.

References

Dunbar, Robert and Moring, Tom (2008), *The European Charter for Regional or Minority Languages and the media*, Regional and Minority Languages, No. 6. Strasbourg: Council of Europe Publishing.

Poggeschi, Giovanni (2010), *Diritti linguistici. Un analisi comparata*. Rome: Carocci.

Woehrling, Jean-Marie (2005), *The European Charter for Regional or Minority Languages: a critical commentary*. Strasbourg: Council of Europe Publishing.

**Part IV
Application of the Charter**

Articles 15 to 17. Application of the Charter

Iñaki Lasagabaster
University of the Basque Country

1. Introduction

Many international treaties and conventions provide for mandatory submission of reports as a means of making their provisions effective. The procedures and forms laid down in the international legal system for implementing these standards vary widely. We shall confine ourselves to briefly considering the relevant provisions in the human rights field here. The systems for guaranteeing compliance with treaties in this field include mechanisms enabling individuals and other states to demand such compliance, alongside less stringent arrangements such as reporting. Individual human rights protection mechanisms laid down in international treaties are of great legal importance in terms of the individual safeguards on infringed rights. However, they are also important in that they grant an international authority or body the power and competence to judge the actions of state authorities, including the judiciary itself.[1] Yet this does not detract from the fact that the guarantee on the applicability of fundamental rights lies not only, and sometimes not even primarily, in the individual guarantees or quasi-judicial procedures. Their efficacy depends on how well suited the treaties' guarantee mechanisms are to the legislative features of individual signatory states.

Or again, the supervision system may exclusively provide for periodical reports. In this case, consideration should be given to the scope and the real efficacy of the reports. The fact of only providing for reports as an enforcement mechanism might suggest that the provisions in question are not particularly binding or stringent. This limited enforceability may be occasioned by the states parties to the treaty, which sign the instrument precisely because it has little binding force. Furthermore, the difficulty of "judicialising" mandatory compliance with its content would seem to commend this type of procedure. If this is not the case, it might be that the reporting system, as the sole mechanism for guaranteeing the rights laid down in the treaties, simply reflects the weakness of the undertakings accepted. This must be qualified with the consideration that the types of report and procedures for implementing reports vary widely. There are major differences between reporting systems, ranging from highly functional and effective ones to purely theoretical mechanisms. This is why it is so important to analyse the reports provided for under each instrument.

Treaties can provide for mandatory reports detailing specific aspects of their application in the states. Such reports may refer to selective matters or to all relevant regulations; they may be directly commissioned by the signatory state or be based on a decision taken by a body that the treaty itself provides for. The content of the report may therefore vary, as may its periodicity; it may be produced ad hoc or regularly. Reports can pass through special channels depending on whether they are referred to a political or technical body, whether they will be made public or not, and so on. Experience can diverge widely in this field. As we know, it is an institution's mode of functioning that ensures its legitimacy. Experience of the functioning of a reporting system shows whether it can effectively help implement the provisions of the treaty. And experience can prove positive despite possibly defective regulations.

---

1. See I. Lasagabaster (2004), "Introduction" in I. Lasagabaster (ed.), *Convenio europeo de derechos humanos. Comentario sistemático*, 1st edn. Madrid: Thomson/Civitas, p. 25.

2. Periodical reports

Article 15 – Periodical reports

1. *The Parties shall present periodically to the Secretary General of the Council of Europe, in a form to be prescribed by the Committee of Ministers, a report on their policy pursued in accordance with Part II of this Charter and on the measures taken in application of those provisions of Part III which they have accepted. The first report shall be presented within the year following the entry into force of the Charter with respect to the Party concerned, the other reports at three-yearly intervals after the first report.*

2. *The Parties shall make their reports public.*

2.1. General considerations

Periodical reports have a series of common features, there being two different types of periodical reports. The first report is submitted one year after the entry into force of the Charter. Subsequent reports must be presented at three-yearly intervals after the submission of the first report.[2] The reports create a direct obligation, and the obligation arises *ex lege*, without any need for mediation by the bodies provided for in the Charter. The report must be submitted to the Secretary General of the Council of Europe, who deals with it in the manner stipulated by Article 16 of the Charter, as described in section 3 below.

The content of the reports is predetermined. They must provide information on the policy implemented as laid down in Part II of the Charter, and measures taken in pursuance of the provisions of Part III. The difference between these two parts is logical. Part II of the Charter sets out the objectives and principles in this field, developing the provisions of Article 2.1. Part III lays down the requisite measures to promote the use of languages, which is why the report must cover any practical measures adopted. As Part II is confined to setting out objectives and principles, the report must explain the policies adopted, which involves a more general approach.

Despite these specifications, the reports can very widely in form, which creates problems in terms of monitoring and comparative analysis. This is why, in order to ensure that all reports have a similar objective content, a drafting scheme has been devised which must be followed by all reports. The scheme was adopted by the Committee of Ministers at the initiative of the Committee of Experts, and is referred to below.

---

2. Subsequent reports must cover new elements, mainly measures adopted so as to comply with the observations and recommendations of the Committee of Experts of the Committee of Ministers. See E. J. Ruiz Vieytez (2004), *Working together: NGOs and regional or minority languages*. Strasbourg: Council of Europe Publishing, p. 41.

2.2. The first report

The scheme for drafting the first report emerged from the first meeting of the Committee of Experts of the Charter on 28 June 1998. Subsequently, at the 648th meeting of the Ministers' Deputies on 10 November 1998, the Committee of Ministers approved the scheme, as set out below:

Part I

1. Please state main legal act(s) whereby the European Charter for Regional or Minority Languages has been implemented in your State. If you so desire, please mention the general considerations which have guided your country in the ratification process.

2. Please indicate all regional or minority languages, as defined in paragraph a, of Article 1 of the Charter, which exist on your State's territory. Indicate also the parts of the territory of your country where the speakers of such language(s) reside.

3. Please indicate the number of speakers for each regional or minority language. Specify the criteria for the definition of "speaker of regional or minority language" that your country has retained for this purpose.

4. Please indicate the non-territorial languages, as defined in paragraph c, Article 1 of the Charter, used on your State's territory and provide statistical data concerning speakers.

5. Please indicate if any body or organisation, legally established, exists in your State, which furthers the protection and development of regional or minority languages. If so, please list the names and addresses of such organisations.

6. Please indicate if any body or organisation has been consulted on the preparation of this periodical report. In the case of an affirmative answer, specify which one(s).

7. Please indicate the measures taken (in accordance with Article 6 of the Charter) to make better known the rights and the duties deriving from the application of the Charter.

Part II

1. Please indicate what measures your State has taken to apply Article 7 of the Charter to the regional or minority languages referred to in paragraphs 2 and 4 of Part I above, specifying the different levels of government responsible.

2. If appropriate, state any future measures which are envisaged in your country.

Part III

For each regional or minority language chosen at the moment of ratification, as follow from paragraph 2, Article 2 of the Charter, please indicate in which way the paragraphs and/or subparagraphs have been implemented, see Appendix.

When indicating the measures taken in order to implement each paragraph or sub-paragraph chosen, please specify the relevant legal provision and the territory where they are applicable.

2.3. The three-yearly report

The three-yearly report is geared to monitoring public policies implemented in pursuance of the Charter. The aim is not to repeat what has already been said in the first report. The three-yearly report must cover new measures adopted in the relevant field. Where no new measures have been adopted, the report should not repeat information already supplied but rather refer back to such information provided in previous reports.[3] This is the scheme for three-yearly reports as adopted by the Committee of Ministers at the 1056th meeting of the Ministers' Deputies on 6 May 2009:

Part I

Please provide updated information, if any new data exists, about the number and geographic distribution of speakers of regional or minority languages, and the general demographic situation.

Please provide information about changes in the general policies, legislation or practice of your state in respect of regional or minority languages. Please also indicate any developments which are expected to occur during the next monitoring cycle, such as envisaged political or budgetary changes, policy plans or any other elements that may have a direct or indirect effect on the situation of the regional or minority languages in your State.

Please give a detailed account of the legal and/or practical measures that your State has taken to implement each one of the recommendations of the Committee of Ministers.

Part II

Please indicate what measures your State has taken to apply Article 7 of the Charter to the regional or minority languages as defined in paragraph *a* of Article 1 of the Charter, focusing in particular on the following aspects:
- Please provide information, for each regional or minority language, on new developments that have occurred since the last monitoring round concerning the provisions of Article 7;
- Please give a detailed account of the legal and/or practical measures that your State has taken to implement the encouragements and box recommendations of the Committee of Experts given in the previous evaluation report(s).

Part III

For each regional or minority language chosen at the moment of ratification, as follows from paragraph 2 of Article 2 of the Charter, please indicate how the undertakings have been implemented (see Appendix), focusing in particular on the following aspects:
- Please provide information on new developments that have occurred since the last monitoring round.

---

3. See MIN-LANG (2009) 8.

With reference to the most recent evaluation report of the Committee of Experts concerning the implementation of the Charter in your State:
- For undertakings for which the Committee of Experts did not have sufficient information to property evaluate the implementation, please provide detailed information;
- For undertakings which the Committee of Experts considered were not fulfilled, please indicate what steps your State has taken, for each regional or minority language, to implement these undertakings;
- For the encouragements and box recommendations of the Committee of Experts, please give a detailed account of the legal and/or practical measures that your State has taken.

3. Publication of the report

State reports must be made public. Like other documents, and as increasingly required by legislation, the reports should be published on the Internet and be freely accessible. Any associations and bodies which so wish can forward their comments on the state reports to the Committee of Experts.

Article 16 – Examination of the reports

1. *The reports presented to the Secretary General of the Council of Europe under Article 15 shall be examined by a committee of experts constituted in accordance with Article 17.*

2. *Bodies or associations legally established in a Party may draw the attention of the committee of experts to matters relating to the undertakings entered into by that Party under Part III of this Charter. After consulting the Party concerned, the committee of experts may take account of this information in the preparation of the report specified in paragraph 3 below. These bodies or associations can furthermore submit statements concerning the policy pursued by a Party in accordance with Part II.*

3. *On the basis of the reports specified in paragraph 1 and the information mentioned in paragraph 2, the committee of experts shall prepare a report for the Committee of Ministers. This report shall be accompanied by the comments which the Parties have been requested to make and may be made public by the Committee of Ministers.*

4. *The report specified in paragraph 3 shall contain in particular the proposals of the committee of experts to the Committee of Ministers for the preparation of such recommendations of the latter body to one or more of the Parties as may be required.*

5. *The Secretary General of the Council of Europe shall make a two-yearly detailed report to the Parliamentary Assembly on the application of the Charter.*

3.1. Presentation and analysis of the report

Reports submitted by states to the Secretary General are examined by a Committee of Experts. Under the rules of procedure of the Committee of Experts, one or more of its members can be appointed to discharge specific duties in connection with the groundwork on which the committee will subsequently base its decision (Article 17.1). In addition to a rapporteur, the member of the committee appointed by the state in question and a third member also help in drafting the report.[4] The committee's task is to study the report submitted by the state. The presence in the study group of the representative of the state under consideration raises questions, because the committee member appointed by this state cannot vote on the report to be presented to the Committee of Ministers (Article 14.3), and also because the committee members are not state representatives and are not bound by any mandate. This is logical, since the exercise of his/her functions precisely requires such independence and freedom from all accountability. The state's position within a procedure which concerns itself is guaranteed by its direct participation, as shown in the next paragraph. The fact that the state representative is involved alongside the rapporteur and others in the initial examination of the state report might be justified by the fact that (s)he can improve the committee's knowledge of the situation in the state in question.

3.2. Observations submitted to the committee

The committee can receive information directly, as described below. It is not necessary for such information to be submitted to the Secretary General of the Council of Europe. Three questions arise with regard to the observations, viz: 1) who can present the observations, 2) what kind of observations can be submitted, and 3) what is the procedure to be used.

3.2.1. Who can submit observations?

Observations can be submitted by bodies or associations. Individual observations are not permitted, and individuals are not entitled to become involved in this procedure on a personal basis.

The bodies or associations must be legally established. This means that they must have legal personality. The mere fact of being a group of persons dealing with a specific situation does not legitimate them to take part in the procedure. In the same way, associations do not have to have a specific interest in order to participate, or to devote themselves to issues related to the Charter. Any

---

4. See J.-M. Woehrling (2005), *The European Charter for Regional or Minority Languages: a critical commentary*. Strasbourg: Council of Europe Publishing, p. 250.

legally established association can become involved, regardless of the purpose set out in its founding statute. Nor is any specific legal form required. The word "association" should be taken as meaning any method of conferring legal personality on a group of persons in conformity with the domestic legal system. The date on which the association is set up is irrelevant in terms of its involvement in the procedure.

The word "bodies" refers to different modes of conferring legal personality, including both public and private. Therefore, information can be provided by associations or bodies subject to private law or by bodies subject to public law. The latter include the various public administrations, with their different modes of conferring legal personality, as well as bodies within individual administrations. This concerns information submitted by the minister responsible for this subject in the central, autonomous, federal or regional government, whereby the government does not have to submit the information on behalf of the said administration, as its representative. The same sometimes applies to the local level. This provision must be interpreted in an open manner, since the modes of conferring legal personality differ greatly from state to state. In the same way, new modes of conferring legal personality are emerging, in transfrontier co-operation and the European legal systems, such as territorial co-operation groupings.

Although the provision does not explicitly say so, bodies and associations submitting observations must be from the state under examination. Associations from other states cannot be involved. This is geared to preventing inter-party disputes. Organisations which have obtained legal personality under supra-state provisions, as in the case of the European Union, must also be allowed to participate.

3.2.2. What kind of observations?

The participation of associations or other bodies varies according to the part of the Charter concerned. In the case of Part III, the associations or bodies can draw the committee's attention to matters relating to the undertakings adopted by the states on ratifying the Charter. Just as the states' reports differentiate between parts II and III of the Charter, the same distinction is made in the mode of participation of associations and other bodies. The reason is simply the inherent difference between these two parts. Just as the mode of participation differs, so the procedure to be followed for the observations also varies.

Observations submitted by bodies or associations in connection with Part III are transmitted to the state in question for its reply. Such state involvement is deemed justified under the transparency principle.[5] After this consultation procedure, the committee decides whether or not to take account of the said

---

5. Woehrling (2005), op. cit., p. 253.

observations. Clearly, this is a matter for the committee, which finalises the procedure at this point. There is no question of the debate continuing after the committee's decision, as in judicial proceedings. Nor can the Committee of Experts accept the observations if they have not first of all been notified to the state. The observations play a major role in the conclusions presented by the Committee of Experts.

Declarations can be submitted on Part II of the Charter. The difference between parts II and III of the Charter in terms of involving bodies or associations derives from the contrasting content of the two parts. Part II is more general and abstract, laying down objectives and principles, which means that it is appropriate to present declarations in this case. The latter are intended to assess the policy implemented in the state in question. Such an assessment is very important to the committee because, in addition to an intrinsic value of facilitating participation, it provides an insight into other sources and views of the processes and forms of application of the Charter.[6]

3.2.3. Procedure for submission

The procedure to be followed in submitting the observations and declarations provided for differs in the two cases. However, it would not appear that the difference set out in the provision has to be taken literally. In the case of the observations made under Part III by bodies or associations, the committee must transmit them to the state in question. As stated above, such transmission is a consequence of the principle of transparency. But when the provision mentions the declarations on Part II, it does not state that they too must be transmitted. Despite this obvious literal difference, it would be logical for the declarations made by bodies and associations on Part II of the Charter, where they are taken into account by the committee, to have to be transmitted to the states. There is nothing to prevent this, and the aforementioned principle of transparency would commend this approach.[7] The committee sends any observations it receives to the secretariat, which sends acknowledgements of receipt to the bodies and associations submitting them.[8]

---

6. See V. Crnic-Grotic (2010), "The impact of the Charter" in *Minority language protection in Europe: into a new decade*. Strasbourg: Council of Europe Publishing, pp. 36-7.
7. Woehrling (2005), op. cit., p. 254.
8 See rules of procedure of the Committee of Experts for the European Charter for Regional or Minority Languages (as amended by the Committee of Experts on 24 March 2004), Article 17.3 (www.coe.int/t/dg4/education/minlang/aboutcommittee/Rulesprocedure_en.pdf).

3.3. Preparation of the committee's report

3.3.1. Resources used for drafting

The drafting of the committee's report is based initially on the report submitted by the state, as laid down in Article 16.1, and the observations and statements submitted by associations and/or bodies in accordance with Article 16.2. These provide the basic material for preparing the report. The Committee of Experts can also opt for visiting the country in question, on its own initiative, as laid down in Article 17.4 of its rules of procedure. The Committee of Experts can decide, by a simple majority, to send one or more of its members to a country in order to carry out an on-the-spot evaluation of any situation which might be relevant to the implementation of the Charter. In addition to previous material, the Committee of Experts can also use any information from public sources of information as well as public documents from the state in question. The information in question must be either public or generally known.

The committee's rules of procedure also require the committee to liaise with the Advisory Committee of the Framework Convention for the Protection of National Minorities and other specialised bodies of the Council of Europe.

3.3.2. Mode of adoption of the report

Once the rapporteur has presented his/her work to the Committee of Experts, the committee discusses it and holds a vote. Each member of the committee has one vote in this procedure. Decisions must be adopted by a two-thirds majority of votes cast. Failing such a majority, the report is submitted to the Committee of Ministers, presenting the majority and the minority views (Article 18.2 in the rules of procedure). The member of the Committee of Experts appointed by the state under examination does not take part in voting (Article 16 of the rules of procedure). Once the report has been approved, the state is invited to submit its observations, which are appended to the committee's report and jointly submitted to the Committee of Ministers. It should be pointed out that the Committee of Experts' report cannot be amended on the basis of the state's observations.

3.4. Report and recommendations

The Committee of Experts' report must set out proposed recommendations to be presented to the state.[9] The whole document is submitted to the

---

9. R. Dunbar (2008), "Definitively interpreting the European Charter for Regional or Minority Languages: the legal challenges" in R. Dunbar and G. Parry, *The European Charter for Regional or Minority Languages: legal challenges and opportunities*. Strasbourg: Council of Europe Publishing, p. 55, states that neither the Committee of Experts nor the Committee of Ministers holds jurisdiction for interpreting the Charter. Nevertheless, insofar as recommendations are adopted on a consensual basis, it is understood that they involve some degree of consensus on the interpretation of the applicability of the Charter within the meaning of Article 31.1 of the Vienna Convention on the Law of Treaties.

Committee of Ministers for decision. The Committee of Ministers may or may not make observations. Although the Charter says nothing on the subject, the Committee of Ministers publishes the Committee of Experts' report and the recommendations which it (the Committee of Ministers) makes to the state in question. All these documents are freely accessible on the Council of Europe's web page. On the other hand, the proposed recommendations put forward by the Committee of Experts to the Committee of Ministers are not usually published.

The decision of the Committee of Ministers of the Council of Europe is adopted by all its member states, even though some of them have not ratified the Charter. This does not prevent them from taking part in the discussions and the ultimate decision. It has been argued that this participation is geared to ensuring that the non-signatory states to the Charter also help implement the instrument.[10] The Committee of Ministers normally adopts recommendations in the light of the report and the proposals put forward by the Committee of Experts. The Committee of Ministers' recommendations are complex in nature, given that they have no binding force.[11] They are recommendations, non-compliance with which has no legal or political consequences.

3.5. Biannual reports by the Secretary General

The Secretary General of the Council of Europe must present a report on the implementation of the Charter every two years. This report is presented before the Parliamentary Assembly of the Council of Europe. The Secretary General has so far presented five reports: the first on 18 October 2000 (Doc. 8879), the second on 11 November 2002 (Doc. 9540), the third on 3 September 2005 (Doc. 10659), the fourth on 24 October 2007 (Doc. 11442) and the fifth on 21 June 2010 (Doc. 12300).

4. The Committee of Experts

Article 17 – Committee of experts

1 *The committee of experts shall be composed of one member per Party, appointed by the Committee of Ministers from a list of individuals of the highest integrity and recognised competence in the matters dealt with in the Charter, who shall be nominated by the Party concerned.*

2 *Members of the committee shall be appointed for a period of six years and shall be eligible for reappointment. A member who is unable to complete a term of*

---

10. Woehrling (2005), op. cit., p. 255.
11. See F. Benoît-Rohmer and H. Klebes (2005), *Council of Europe law: towards a pan-European legal area*. Strasbourg: Council of Europe Publishing, p. 54. For the opposite view, see note 11.

> *office shall be replaced in accordance with the procedure laid down in para-graph 1, and the replacing member shall complete his predecessor's term of office.*
>
> 3 *The committee of experts shall adopt rules of procedure. Its secretarial services shall be provided by the Secretary General of the Council of Europe.*

4.1. Composition of the Committee of Experts

The Committee of Experts is made up of one member per state party to the Charter. There are fewer experts than there are member states of the Council of Europe. The experts are nominated exclusively by signatory states of the Charter. Each state must submit a list, according to the relevant provisions. The number of persons on the list is not specified, although a shortlist is tradition-ally submitted for the elections.

As for the appointment of other persons to such bodies as the Committee of Experts or judicial bodies, the candidates must fulfil a number of eligibility criteria. The first refers to their integrity and the second to their acknowledged competence in the subjects covered by the Charter. The reference to integrity concerns independence from the appointing authorities. Such independence has been described as having an objective component in its functioning and mode of action, as well as a subjective dimension, which refers to their never having held a position of responsibility in the process of implementing the Charter.[12] The recognised competence refers to specialised knowledge of the specific subjects dealt with in the Charter and their implementation. Such competence can be highlighted by means of publications, professional positions or activities in the relevant policy areas. The Committee of Ministers can reject the list of candidates and request fresh nominations.

4.2. Terms of office of committee members

Committee members have a six-year term of office. If a member resigns before the end of his/her term, (s)he is replaced. The replacement is for the period remaining to run in the replaced member's term. The mode of election is as outlined in the previous paragraph. Committee members can be renewed in office.

4.3. Rules of procedure of the Committee of Experts

The committee approves its rules of procedure. These rules govern the election of the president and vice-presidents, who are appointed for a two-year term. If they resign before the end of the term they are replaced for the remaining period, and their replacement may be re-elected. They are elected by secret ballot,

---

12. Woehrling (2005), op. cit., p. 257.

whereby the members obtaining the majority of votes cast in the first round or the greatest number of votes in subsequent rounds are elected. The president's main duty is to chair meetings and to discharge the other functions assigned him/her by the rules of procedure. The president cannot chair a meeting dealing with a report submitted by the state which nominated him/her to the committee.

The rules go on to deal with matters relating to the functioning of the committee. It is based and meets in Strasbourg, except where a two-thirds majority decides to hold the meeting elsewhere. Meetings are held in English and French. Invitations to the meetings are sent out four weeks in advance, together with the draft agenda. The agenda is approved during the committee meeting. The requisite information documents must be transmitted to committee members, as far as possible one month in advance.

The committee can consult and interview individuals, organisations and states if it considers this necessary to improve the implementation of the Charter. It may also consult other specialist bodies, particularly the Advisory Committee of the Framework Convention for the Protection of National Minorities. The Charter is monitored by means of ongoing dialogue between all those involved.[13]

The rules of procedure govern voting methods and procedures. The list of adopted decisions is subject to a committee vote, as is the summary of proceedings at each committee meeting. The rules of procedure are directly accessible on the Council of Europe web page.

5. Conclusions

Having analysed the instruments which the Charter sets out for its own implementation, we now briefly discuss the legal value of these instruments, particularly that of the reports and recommendations drawn up by the Committee of Experts and the Committee of Ministers. First of all, we should remember that the Charter is an international treaty and that, as such, it can be applied at the domestic level by judges and courts in accordance with the legal value attributed to international provisions under each legal system. This may also vary in accordance with the different types of provisions.[14] Some of the provisions of the Charter are binding and others set out rules or principles geared to maximising or optimising the implementation of other provisions.

---

13. See S. Gramstad (2010), "The Charter's monitoring mechanism: a practical perspective" in *Minority language protection in Europe: into a new decade*, p. 31.
14. J. M. Castells Arteche (2004), "Efectos jurídicos de la ratificación por España de la Carta Europea de las Lenguas regionales o minoritarias", *Revista Vasca de Administración Pública*, No. 69 (II), pp. 223-38; J. Nieva Fenoll (2009), "La invocació directa de la Carta Europea de les llengües regionals o minoritàries als tribunals", *Revista de Llengua i Dret*, No. 52, pp. 183ff.

As in other treaties, this legal value of the Charter as an international treaty comes up against the problem of interpretation. Treaties can set up bodies specifically responsible for interpreting them, that is, with full authority to interpret their content and scope. The Charter assigns this function to neither the Committee of Experts nor the Committee of Ministers, neither of which is therefore the ultimate interpreter of the provisions of the Charter.

The Charter does not provide any judicial solution for its interpretation. In fact, such a solution might have been considered inappropriate, from the angle of legislative policy. This being the case, the scope of the reports and recommendations addressed to states by both the Committee of Experts and the Committee of Ministers requires clarification.

A distinction must be drawn here between the Committee of Ministers and the Committee of Experts. The former operates within the structures of the Council of Europe, which means that it must adhere to the rules of this Organisation and verify, in the Council of Europe context, the value and importance to be attached to the recommendations which it addresses to member states, the member states in question being those that have signed the Charter. The Statute of the Council of Europe establishes the competence of the Committee of Ministers to address recommendations to states. The states must provide information on the measures they have adopted in response to the recommendations. Although this provision seems to lack binding force, it is quite effective when taken in conjunction with the provisions of the Vienna Convention on the Law of Treaties, which lays down that in interpreting a treaty, regard must be had to: (a) any agreement relating to the treaty which was made between all the parties in connection with the conclusion of the treaty, and (b) any instrument which was made by one or more parties in connection with the conclusion of the treaty and accepted by the other parties as an instrument related to the treaty (Article 31 of the Vienna Convention).[15]

Applying these provisions to the mechanisms of the Charter, we can see that the recommendations adopted by the Committee of Ministers fully correspond to the instruments referred to by the Vienna Convention, and that they therefore have the requisite legal value. They can be used, *inter alia*, by judges and courts of law, to interpret the provisions of the Charter. Their legal value is not the result of a judicial construct but the expression of a legal system based on traditional modes of interpretation of international law, namely the major international system created by the Vienna Convention on the Law of Treaties.

The reports of the Committee of Experts cannot have the same value as the Committee of Ministers' recommendations. This does not mean that the reports

---

15. R. Dunbar (2008), "Definitively interpreting the European Charter…", p. 56.

have no value. In international law, and increasingly in administrative law, the decisions, resolutions and reports of international bodies are being assigned the force of soft law. In the context of the Council of Europe, without going any further afield, various types of bodies in the Organisation adopt resolutions which are subsequently regularly used by the national courts. This applies, for instance, to the resolutions adopted by the Congress of Local and Regional Authorities in connection with the European Charter of Local Self-Government. A similar arrangement might be considered for the public use of the reports and other documents of the Committee of Experts and the Committee of Ministers. Soft law as a domestic back-up for resolutions by administrative or judicial bodies is increasingly important in a variety of fields, among them the industrial, economic and environmental sectors. Soft law is also particularly important vis-à-vis decisions, resolutions and reports adopted at the Council of Europe. The importance of these documents is constantly increasing, *inter alia* in the legal field, as can be seen from an overview of case law in the national courts. Such soft law documents are also not void of any legal significance. Seen together with the practice of the Committee of Ministers in taking cognisance of the Committee of Expert's report and adopting recommendations, the positions taken by both organs are transformed into subsequent practice of member states which is of high relevance for the interpretation of the Charter as an international legal treaty.

In conclusion, I would like to stress the importance of the monitoring system implemented under the Charter. A flexible relationship based on mutual trust among the members of the Committee of Experts, the state authorities and the NGOs and inter-state bodies could be highly productive and have a highly positive effect on the implementation of the principles and rights set out in the Charter. The effectiveness of a regulation is measured not only by its strictly legal value, as seen from the judicial angle of recognising subjective rights for citizens. The possibilities provided by the Charter's monitoring process are enormous, although they depend on the will of the states to implement them and a firm and appropriate policy from the Council of Europe, particularly the Committee of Experts. Ensuring timely processing of the reports submitted by the states and proper follow-up to the Committee of Ministers' recommendations would help guarantee effective compliance with the provisions of the Charter.

References

Benoît-Rohmer, Florence and Klebes, Heinrich (2005), *Council of Europe law: towards a pan-European legal area*. Strasbourg: Council of Europe Publishing.

Castells Arteche, José Manuel (2004), "Efectos jurídicos de la ratificación por España de la Carta Europea de las Lenguas Regionales o Minoritarias", *Revista Vasca de Administración Pública*, No. 69 (II).

Crnic-Grotic, Vesna (2010), "The impact of the Charter" in *Minority language protection in Europe: into a new decade*, Regional or Minority Languages, No. 8. Strasbourg: Council of Europe Publishing.

Dunbar, Robert (2008), "Definitively interpreting the European Charter for Regional or Minority Languages: the legal challenges" in Robert Dunbar and Gwynedd Parry (eds), *The European Charter for Regional or Minority languages: legal challenges and opportunities*. Strasbourg: Council of Europe Publishing.

Gramstad, Sigve (2010), "The Charter's monitoring mechanism: a practical perspective" in *Minority language protection in Europe: into a new decade*, Regional or Minority Languages, No. 8. Strasbourg: Council of Europe Publishing.

Lasagabaster, Iñaki (2004), "Introduction" in Iñaki Lasagabaster (ed.), *Convenio europeo de derechos humanos. Comentario sistemático*, 1st edn. Madrid: Thomson/Civitas.

Nieva Fenoll, Jordi (2009), "La invocació directa de la Carta Europea de les llengües regionals o minoritàries als tribunals", *Revista de Llengua i Dret*, No. 52.

Ruiz Vieytez, Eduardo J. (2004), *Working together: NGOs and regional or minority languages*. Strasbourg: Council of Europe Publishing.

Woehrling, Jean-Marie (2005), *The European Charter for Regional or Minority Languages: a critical commentary*. Strasbourg: Council of Europe Publishing.

**Part V
Final provisions**

Articles 18 to 23. Final provisions

Santiago J. Castellà Surribas
University Rovira i Virgili, Tarragona

1. Introduction

2. General scope of the provisions in the light of the purpose of the Charter

3. Analysis of states' practice in the application of the Charter

4. Some conclusions

References

1. Introduction

Examination of Part V of the European Charter prompts us to reflect on the final stage in the process of concluding treaties, focusing on the expression of states' consent to be parties to the Charter. Articles 18 to 23, which constitute Part V under the title "Final provisions", are based on the standard or model clauses used in the legal tradition developed in the different conventions and agreements concluded within the Council of Europe.[1]

This section thus focuses on questions relating to the ways the member states of the Council of Europe express their consent (Article 18), entry into force (Article 19), the possibility for non-member states to accede to the Charter (Article 20), formulation and withdrawal of reservations (Article 21), denunciation or withdrawal of a state (Article 23), final declaration of the languages in which authentic versions of the Charter exist, and procedure for deposit.

All these questions, over and above their strictly literal meaning, allow us to reflect on the formal implications of the various unilateral declarations made by states at the time of ratification, acceptance or approval of, or accession to, the Charter concerning the obligations assumed in respect of the regional or minority languages they wish to protect.

Part V – Final provisions

Article 18
This Charter shall be open for signature by the member States of the Council of Europe. It is subject to ratification, acceptance or approval. Instruments of

---

1. The Explanatory Report on the European Charter for Regional or Minority Languages, paragraph 133, says: "The final clauses contained in Articles 18 to 23 are based on the model final clauses for conventions and agreements concluded within the Council of Europe".

ratification, acceptance or approval shall be deposited with the Secretary General of the Council of Europe.

Article 19

1. *This Charter shall enter into force on the first day of the month following the expiration of a period of three months after the date on which five member States of the Council of Europe have expressed their consent to be bound by the Charter in accordance with the provisions of Article 18.*

2. *In respect of any member State which subsequently expresses its consent to be bound by it, the Charter shall enter into force on the first day of the month following the expiration of a period of three months after the date of the deposit of the instrument of ratification, acceptance or approval.*

Article 20

1. *After the entry into force of this Charter, the Committee of Ministers of the Council of Europe may invite any State not a member of the Council of Europe to accede to this Charter.*

2. *In respect of any acceding State, the Charter shall enter into force on the first day of the month following the expiration of a period of three months after the date of deposit of the instrument of accession with the Secretary General of the Council of Europe.*

Article 21

1. *Any State may, at the time of signature or when depositing its instrument of ratification, acceptance, approval or accession, make one or more reservations to paragraphs 2 to 5 of Article 7 of this Charter. No other reservation may be made.*

2. *Any Contracting State which has made a reservation under the preceding paragraph may wholly or partly withdraw it by means of a notification addressed to the Secretary General of the Council of Europe. The withdrawal shall take effect on the date of receipt of such notification by the Secretary General.*

Article 22

1. *Any Party may at any time denounce this Charter by means of a notification addressed to the Secretary General of the Council of Europe.*

2. *Such denunciation shall become effective on the first day of the month following the expiration of a period of six months after the date of receipt of the notification by the Secretary General.*

Article 23

The Secretary General of the Council of Europe shall notify the member States of the Council and any State which has acceded to this Charter of:

    a. *any signature;*

    b. *the deposit of any instrument of ratification, acceptance, approval or accession;*

  *c. any date of entry into force of this Charter in accordance with Articles 19
  and 20;*

  *d. any notification received in application of the provisions of Article 3,
  paragraph 2;*

  e. any other act, notification or communication relating to this Charter.

*In witness whereof the undersigned, being duly authorised thereto, have signed
this Charter.*

*Done at Strasbourg, this 5th day of November 1992, in English and French, both
texts being equally authentic, in a single copy which shall be deposited in the
archives of the Council of Europe. The Secretary General of the Council of Europe
shall transmit certified copies to each member State of the Council of Europe and
to any State invited to accede to this Charter.*

2. General scope of the provisions in the light of the purpose of the Charter

The Charter, created at the instigation of the Conference of Local and Regional
Authorities of Europe,[2] was adopted as a convention by the Committee of
Ministers of the Council of Europe – a body comprising all the ministers of foreign
affairs of the member states – and opened for signature to the member states on
5 November 1992. Only member states of the Council of Europe may, as nego-
tiating parties, sign the text, that signature having the force of an act of authentication in accordance with the provisions of Article 10 of the 1969 Vienna
Convention on the Law of Treaties.[3] Signature, as a legal act provided for in the
first sentence of Article 18 of the Charter, may be effected only by states which
were members of the Council of Europe at the time when the Charter was adopted
as a convention, or by states which joined the Organisation subsequently. Its
significance lies in the simple expression of interest in the substance of the Charter
as indicating a probable expression of consent in the future; it produces no binding

---

2. See J.-M. Woehrling (1992), "Institutions européennes et droit linguistiques des minorités"
in H. Giordan (ed.), *Les minorités en Europe: droits linguistiques, droits de l'homme*. Paris:
Kime, pp. 517-21; S. Petschen (1989), "Entre la política y el derecho: la Carta europea de las
llenguas regionales o minoritarias", *Revista de Estudios Políticos*, No. 66, pp. 127-44. On the
process of drafting the European Charter, a member of the group of experts in charge of it has
written two interesting articles: L. M. de Puig (1986), "Informe provisional sobre la preparació
d'un projecte de Carta europea de les llengües regionals i minoritàries", *Revista Llengua i Dret*,
No. 8, pp. 79-92; and L. M. de Puig (1991), "Debat i elaboració de la Carta europea de les
Llengües", *Revista Llengua i Dret*, No. 16, pp. 153-72.
3. Article 10 – Authentication of the text. – The text of a treaty is established as authentic
and definitive: (a) by such procedure as may be provided for in the text or agreed upon by the
states participating in its drawing up; or (b) failing such procedure, by the signature, signature
ad referendum or initialling by the representatives of those states of the text of the treaty or of
the Final Act of a conference incorporating the text.

effect linked to the enforceability of the content of the Charter in the signatory state which, having signed the instrument, will then be obliged merely to "refrain from acts which would defeat the object and purpose of a treaty" in accordance with Article 18 of the Vienna Convention of 1969.

Article 18 of the Charter also provides that, when opened for signature, the Charter is subject to ratification, acceptance or approval by the signatory states, all being members of the Council of Europe, as has been said. The three terms correspond to different ways of manifesting a state's consent to take on obligations under the Charter; all three produce identical legal effects, in accordance with the explanation of definitions given by Article 2 of the Vienna Convention of 1969[4] and the rules applying to ratification under that convention's Article 14.2, which provides that "The consent of a State to be bound by a treaty is expressed by acceptance or approval under conditions similar to those which apply to ratification." The Secretary General of the Council of Europe acts as depositary of the instruments of ratification, as is customary for all treaties drawn up in the institutional framework of the Council of Europe.

The formal act of expressing a state's consent to be bound by the Charter takes on material significance, and must be accompanied by a declaration, in accordance with Article 3.1 of the Charter, in which the state specifies each regional or minority language, or official language which is less widely used on the whole or part of its territory, to which the obligations assumed under Part III of the Charter will apply. Article 2 of the Charter regulates the conditions and scope of this declaration, laying down a minimum number of 35 paragraphs or subparagraphs chosen from among the provisions of Part III of the Charter, including at least three chosen from each of articles 8 and 12 and one from each of articles 9, 10, 11 and 13.

It is for the Committee of Experts governed by Article 17 of the Charter, on the basis of its examination of the periodic reports that states are required to submit, to give its opinion on the content of these declarations made at the time of ratification (or accession) and the manner of their compliance with the requirements arising from the Charter. However, apart from this declaration which will mainly affect Part III of the Charter, the rest of the substantive content of the Charter places the same obligation on the states parties, particularly the provisions of Part II, Article 7, which must be applied to all the regional or minority languages spoken in the territory of a state, whether or not they are mentioned in the mandatory declaration made.

---

4. Vienna Convention of 1969, Article 2: "(b) 'ratification', 'acceptance', 'approval' and 'accession' mean in each case the international act so named whereby a State establishes on the international plane its consent to be bound by a treaty".

The state's discretionary options, at the time of ratifying or acceding to the Charter, will thus be limited by the obligation to apply the general aims and principles of Article 7 of Part II to all regional or minority languages – in accordance with the definitions given by Article 1 of the Charter – spoken in its territory; but the Explanatory Report points out that:

> Although the states parties are not free to grant or to refuse a regional or minority language the status which it is guaranteed under Part II of the charter, they are responsible, as authorities for the application of the charter, for deciding whether the form of expression used in a particular area of their territory or by a particular group of their nationals constitutes a regional or minority language within the meaning of the charter.[5]

Those discretionary options will increase in relation to Part III of the Charter, permitting the state to apply none of its provisions to a regional or minority language spoken in its territory, but such complete exclusion must always be based on "reasons compatible with the spirit, objectives and principles of the charter",[6] failing which a minimum of obligations must be entered into. These declarations made by states at the time of entering into obligations under the Charter are of a particular legal kind, since they will determine the substantive content binding on states, giving its full meaning to the definition of the Charter, and this has worked to its advantage as a Charter à la carte.[7]

Such a declaration has similar effects to those of a reservation, although it is not a reservation technically speaking, in the strict sense of the word, and its purpose is not the same as that of a reservation. In fact these declarations do not seek merely to exclude or interpret a provision of the Charter, but to assume – among alternative obligations – those regarded as most appropriate to the actual situation of each regional or minority language. We might therefore say that, by choosing a given provision, technically speaking we are excluding other alternative provisions to the one chosen, and so this coincides with the

---

5. Explanatory Report, paragraph 40.
6. Ibid., paragraph 42.
7. D. Christopoulos (1999), "La question de la protection des minorités dans un ordre public européen: analise critique des travaux élaborés au sein du Conseil de l'Europe, de la CSCE, et de la CEE". Strasbourg: Université R. Schuman (thesis), p. 101, See also the analysis of the different degrees of commitment which a state may enter into, by P. Kovács (1993), "La protection des langues des minorites ou la nouvelle approche de la protection des minorités? Quelques considérations sur la Charte européenne des langues régionales ou minoritaires", *RGDIP*, Vol. 97, No. 2, pp. 414-5. See also H. Harting (1994), "Les travaux du Conseil de l'Europe dans le domaine des minorités", in P. Grigoriou, *Questions de minorités en Europe*. Brussels: Centre Hellénique d'Etudes Europénnes/Presses Interuniversitaires Européennes, p. 289; and J. Verhoeven (1997), "Les principales étapes de la protection internationale des minorités", *RTDH*, No. 30, pp. 200-1.

definition of reservation given by the Vienna Convention of 1969.[8] However, the idea we are seeking to convey, through this digression on the legal nature of this unilateral declaration by the state on the obligations it undertakes, is that we are dealing with a declaration with substantive effects of the first order, and that the real efficacy of the Charter will depend on its correct implementation and subsequent interpretation by the Committee of Experts.

The unilateral declaration may be modified at any time by the state party, as Article 3.2 of the Charter explains. The extension of obligations in respect of one or more regional or minority languages has been, as we shall see, a practice adopted by various states, and has been welcomed by the Committee of Experts as a "dynamic enlargement" of the instrument of ratification. The case of a state party making a fresh declaration reducing the level of protection as compared with that initially accepted would be a different thing, and has not occurred in practice. This paradoxical situation, contrary to the progressive spirit of human rights protection standards, would necessarily lead to a restrictive interpretation of this possibility open to states, if one considers that the said declaration is tantamount to an exclusion reservation, not allowed by the Charter and therefore devoid of effect.

Continuing with our analysis of the final provisions, let us consider some aspects of Article 20 of the Charter, concerning the possibilities of accession, as a way of manifesting their agreement, in the case of states which do not have the status of Council of Europe member states and might be invited by the Committee of Ministers to undertake obligations under the Charter.[9] This provision affords an interpretation in conjunction with the Framework Convention for the Protection of National Minorities,[10] which also came into being in the Council of Europe at the instigation of the Venice Commission. According to Article 27, that instrument is open to accession by non-member states of the Council of Europe, and the Explanatory Report observes that this is a reference in particular to states which are members of the Conference on Security and Co-operation in Europe (CSCE, now OSCE).[11] This is an aspect much emphasised by some states and by the Committee of Experts.

---

8. Vienna Convention (1969), Article 2.1: "(d) 'reservation' means a unilateral statement, however phrased or named, made by a State, when signing, ratifying, accepting, approving or acceding to a treaty, whereby it purports to exclude or to modify the legal effect of certain provisions of the treaty in their application to that State."

9. Germany 2006, 15.

10. See Woehrling (2005), *The European Charter for Regional or Minority Languages: a critical commentary*. Strasbourg: Council of Europe Publishing, p. 265.

11. Framework Convention for the Protection of National Minorities, ETS No. 157, Explanatory Report, paragraph 99, available at http://conventions.coe.int/Treaty/en/Reports/Html/157.htm.

The possibility of reservations envisaged by Article 21 of the Charter[12] is limited to Article 7, specifically paragraphs 2 to 5, paragraph 1 being excluded by the express wish of the authors within the Conference of Local and Regional Authorities of Europe, in response to the idea that a reservation which excluded or modified Article 7.1 would necessarily and logically run counter to the object and purpose of the treaty, and must be regarded as prohibited in the light of Article 19c of the Vienna Convention of 1969, which adopted the precedent found in the advisory opinion of the International Court of Justice on reservations to the Genocide Convention.[13]

It would obviously not make sense to extend the possibility of making reservations to Part III of the Charter, the provisions of which, as we have seen, have to be chosen as alternatives by the states parties, it being possible to establish that if the minimum number of 35 accepted provisions distributed as required by Article 2.2 of the Charter is not attained, this would produce unbalanced protection below the minimum standard required in order to respect the object and purpose of the Charter. The prohibition on making reservations to Part I "General provisions", Part IV "Application of the Charter" and Part V "Final provisions" should be interpreted in the same way, so that its basic, formal content precludes the opportunity of reservations, these consequently being confined to paragraphs 2 to 5 of Article 7.

Now, not all reservations to these paragraphs are to be understood as being possible, but – again in the light of the Vienna Convention of 1969 – only those which are compatible with the object and purpose of the Charter. But who is to decide on that compatibility? Only the Convention on the Elimination of All Forms of Racial Discrimination (CERD) and the last part of Article 20.2 thereof establishes as a criterion of incompatibility an objection to the reservation by two thirds of the states parties;[14] this criterion, by reason of its complexity and the requirement of an active commitment on the part of the states, has been largely resisted by doctrine, leaving to committees set up under human rights conventions – like the Committee of Experts in the case of the Charter – the power to assess the compatibility of the reservation in question in the framework of their general power of interpretation.[15]

---

12. Woehrling (2005), op. cit., p. 265.
13. ICJ, Advisory Opinion, reservations to the Convention on the Prevention and Punishment of the Crime of Genocide, 28 May 1951, Collected Decisions 1951.
14. International Convention on the Elimination of All Forms of Racial Discrimination, adopted and opened for signature and ratification by General Assembly Resolution 2106 A (XX) of 21 December 1965, entry into force 4 January 1969 in accordance with Article 19.
15. See C. Villán Durán (2002), *Curso de derecho internacional de los derechos humanos.* Madrid: Trotta, pp. 244-5.

Another question that may arise is whether the prohibition on reservations also presupposes an absolute bar to so-called interpretative declarations – a question we must answer in the affirmative, since we believe that, this possibility not being clearly set out in the text of the Charter, it is to be understood that the general prohibition on reservations refers both to those which seek to exclude part of the text and to those which seek to modify it by interpreting its meaning; this solution, as well as being in conformity with the rules in force on the law of treaties, draws all its strength from the fact that it makes no sense to permit earlier provisions of the Charter to be interpreted when the Committee of Experts is called upon to find the most uniform interpretation possible of the linguistic diversity and disparity covered by the rules.

The absence of a territorial clause stipulating that the Charter will apply to the entire territory of a state party, and which might be the subject of specific reservations excluding particular territories by reason of their colonial, island or other nature, must be interpreted in the same manner; as the Explanatory Report points out: "it is already an intrinsic characteristic of the present charter that it is concerned especially with particular territories, namely those on which regional or minority languages are used", the states being entitled, under Article 3.1, to gear their obligations to territorial realities.[16]

Reservations must be made either before or at the same time as the state expresses its consent, in accordance with the general law of treaties,[17] set out in Article 21 of the Charter, together with the permanent possibility of unilaterally withdrawing a reservation and the immediate production of effects once officially notified to the Secretary General. However, nothing is said about objections to reservations, whether about their possibility, their effects or their subsequent withdrawal, on which aspects we shall have to rely on the general rules of the law of treaties.[18] The only point of interest is the possibility of dealing with a large number of objections to a reservation as an indication that the reservation in question is incompatible with the object and purpose of the Charter, an option which is not regulated but can be assessed, as it were, by the Committee of Experts.

---

16. Explanatory Report, paragraph 134.
17. See, on this question, J. Bonet (1996), *Las reservas a los tratados internacionales*. Barcelona: J. M. Bosch; A. G. Chueca Sancho (1992), *Las reservas a los tratados de derechos humanos*. Madrid: Ministerio de Justicia, Documentación Jurídica, XIX; R. W. Edwards Jr (1989), "Reservations to treaties", *Michigan Journal of International Law*, Vol. 10, No. 2; and P.-H. Imbert (1982), "La question des réserves et les conventions en matière de droits de l'homme", in Council of Europe, *Proceedings of the fifth international colloquy on the European Human Rights Convention*. Paris: Pedone.
18. See Articles 19 to 23 of the Vienna Convention on the Law of Treaties of 23 May 1969.

The text also regulates the possibility of denunciation or withdrawal by a state party, through notification of the Secretary General of the Council of Europe, which becomes effective after a period of six months following such notification, in keeping with a flexible, permissive trend in the rules of the general law of treaties.[19]

The office of depositary, as the holder of an international function, falls to the institution of the Secretary General of the Council of Europe, as is the custom with conventions adopted in the Council of Europe, in accordance with Article 23 of the Charter. The principal function of the depositary is to centralise notifications received in respect of the various events concerning the Charter, record them in the archives and communicate them to all the member states of the Council of Europe and the signatory states to the Charter. The events expressly referred to in the text of the said article of the Charter are: signature by each state, deposit of an instrument of ratification or accession, entry into force in each state, or – an open-ended clause – "any other act, notification or communication relating to this Charter", which covers notification of reservations, objections, denunciations or withdrawals, and declarations on obligations entered into with regard to regional or minority languages.

Among the particular functions of the international office of depositary, we should also mention certifying authentic copies of the Charter and of any other documents it may be necessary to certify, keeping records of the Charter and its documentation in the Council of Europe archives, and registering them with the Secretary General of the United Nations.[20]

Similarly, (s)he will centralise the periodic reports received from the member states in accordance with Article 15 of the Charter, and will inform the Parliamentary Assembly of the Council of Europe in a biennial report about the application of the Charter (these last two functions cannot be considered as inherent in the office of depositary, except in the framework of the procedures of monitoring, follow-up and control of application of the Charter), as well as providing secretarial services for the Committee of Experts in accordance with the terms of reference contained in Article 17.3 of the Charter.

The authentication of the Charter in the French and English versions presupposes, as the final provision indicates, that both language texts are equally authoritative and that no other language version of the Charter may be regarded as an authentic text, it being assumed *juris tantum* that the terms used in the Charter carry the same meaning in each authentic text; any difference of

---

19. See Article 56 of the Vienna Convention on the Law of Treaties of 23 May 1969.
20. This registration is not mentioned in the Charter, but it derives from Article 80 of the Vienna Convention on the Law of Treaties and Article 102 of the United Nations Charter.

meaning which cannot be resolved must be settled by applying the general criteria for interpretation of treaties,[21] adopting the meaning which best reconciles the texts in French and English, bearing the object and purpose of the Charter in mind.[22]

3. Analysis of states' practice in the application of the Charter

At the end of 2011, 25 member states of the Council of Europe had ratified the Charter, and another eight member states had signed but not yet expressed their consent to be bound by it,[23] leaving 14 member states that had not taken any legal action in relation to the Charter,[24] while no Council of Europe non-member state has agreed to accede to it. Six countries (Albania, "the former Yugoslav Republic of Macedonia", Moldova, the Russian Federation, Georgia and Azerbaijan) committed themselves to ratifying the Charter when acceding to the Council of Europe but have not yet done so.[25] As provided for in Article 19, the Charter entered into force on 1 March 1998, the first day of the month following the three-month period since the first five states deposited their instruments of ratification – Norway, which ratified on 10 November 1993, Finland on 9 November 1994, Hungary on 26 April 1995, the Netherlands on 2 May 1996 and Liechtenstein on 18 November 1997.[26]

The entry into force for the remainder of the states parties has posed no problem, it having been explained and clearly stipulated that this would take place on the first day of the month following the three-month period after the date of the official deposit of their instruments of ratification with the Secretary General of the Council of Europe. The only event worthy of note was the fact that, just a few months after the instrument of ratification was deposited by Serbia and Montenegro on 15 February 2006, Montenegro declared independence (on 3 June 2006) leaving Serbia as the successor state with legal personality, while the new state of Montenegro expressed its desire to continue as party to the conventions to which it had subscribed as the predecessor state with the Council

---

21. Covered by Articles 31 and 32 of the Vienna Convention on the Law of Treaties of 1969.
22. As prescribed by Article 33 of the Vienna Convention on the Law of Treaties of 1969.
23. Azerbaijan, France, Iceland, Italy, Malta, Moldova, Russia and "the former Yugoslav Republic of Macedonia".
24. Albania, Andorra, Belgium, Bulgaria, Estonia, Georgia, Greece, Ireland, Latvia, Lithuania, Monaco, Portugal, San Marino and Turkey.
25. The deadlines for ratification were: 9/11/1996 ("the former Yugoslav Republic of Macedonia"), 13/07/1996 (Moldova), 28/2/1998 (Russia), 27/4/2000 (Georgia), 25/1/2002 (Azerbaijan).
26. A ratification we might describe as one of convenience, since it stated in its declaration that no regional or minority languages within the meaning of the Charter existed in its territory at the time of its ratification, a situation repeated in the four monitoring cycles in which it submitted a brief report to the Committee of Experts.

of Europe, and the Secretary General accepted the updating of its declaration maintaining the existing reservation (declaration).

The possibility of making reservations to paragraphs 2 to 5 of Article 7 has been used only by Croatia, which excluded application of Article 7 paragraph 5. This provides for application, *mutatis mutandis*, of the general principles of the Charter, as recognised in paragraphs 1 to 4, to languages without a specified territory. The limited possibility of reservations permitted by the Charter has led to the practice of reservations being confined to that referred to, no objection having been raised by the other states parties. The gradual adoption of protection measures for the Romani language in Croatia made it possible for the Committee of Experts, in its second evaluation report, to speak of a positive development which will help to create the conditions for Croatia to withdraw its reservation,[27] but that has not yet happened.

Nonetheless, various kinds of declarations different from those envisaged in Article 3.1 of the Charter have proliferated, and the states that have made some of these veritable interpretative declarations, sometimes in exceptional cases, do not hesitate to call them reservations. This is true of Montenegro which, while recognising an earlier declaration by its predecessor state, Serbia and Montenegro, has made a reservation which both the Secretary General and the Committee of Experts are treating as an interpretative declaration. It includes the statement that "As to Article 1.b of the Charter, Serbia and Montenegro declares that the term 'territory in which the regional or minority languages is used' will refer to areas in which regional and minority languages are in official use in line with the national legislation".[28] This declaration is reproduced by Serbia (which, curiously, does not call it a reservation).[29] Furthermore, Croatia, referring to it as a declaration and in very similar terms, asserts that "The Republic of Croatia declares, with regard to Article 1, paragraph b., of the Charter, that pursuant to Croatian legislature, the term 'territory in which the regional or minority languages is used' shall refer to those areas in which the official use of minority language is introduced by the by-laws passed by the local self-government units, pursuant to Article 12 of the Constitution of the Republic of Croatia and Articles 7 and 8 of the Constitutional Law on Human Rights and Freedoms and the Rights of National and Ethnic Communities or Minorities on the Republic of Croatia".[30] The Committee of Experts has no hesitation in pointing out that a declaration with this content may have conse-

---

27. Croatia 2005, 14.
28. Montenegro: reservation contained in the instrument of ratification deposited by the state union of Serbia and Montenegro, on 15 February 2006.
29. Serbia: declaration contained in the instrument of ratification deposited on 15 February 2006.
30. Croatia: declaration contained in the instrument of ratification, deposited on 5 November 1997.

quences at variance with the spirit of the Charter, leaving the decision on its territorial application in the hands of the local authorities.[31]

Declarations on the application of Part II of the Charter to specific languages are also common.[32] Examples are the declarations made by Austria, stating that "Part II of the Charter shall be applied to the Burgenland Croatian, the Slovenian, the Hungarian, the Czech, the Slovakian languages and the Romani language of the Austrian Roma minority upon its entry into force in the Republic of Austria. The objectives and principles laid down in Article 7 of the Charter shall form the bases with regard to these languages", subsequently adding: "At the same time, Austrian law and established administrative practice thus meet individual requirements laid down in Part III of the Charter".[33] Germany has followed suit.[34] In both cases the Committee of Experts considers that this declaration does not permit the protection under Part III of the Charter to be extended, because the minimum number of 35 paragraphs have not been accepted as obligatory, and that an extension which may be positive in the case of territorial languages is not so in the case of languages with a specific territorial scope.[35] The Liechtenstein declaration stating that no regional or minority languages within the meaning of the Charter exist in its territory[36] may be seen as similar in kind; this is in contrast to the absence of a declaration by Luxembourg.

The declarations by Azerbaijan, a signatory but still not a party to the Charter, which made a declaration on the impossibility of applying the Charter in the territories occupied by Armenia until such time as that occupation ceases, may be regarded as territorial reservations.[37] Likewise, the United Kingdom declaration stating that the Charter applies in the Isle of Man,[38] and the one by Denmark

---

31. Croatia 2005, 11.

32. On the concepts employed in the European Charter, see P. Thornberry and M. A. Martín Estebanez (1994), *The Council of Europe and minorities*. COEMIN, pp. 32-3. On the content of these provisions, see F. Albanese (1991), "Ethnic and linguistic minorities en Europe", *Yearbook of European Law*, Vol. 11, pp. 332-6.

33. Austria: declaration contained in the instrument of ratification deposited on 28 June 2001.

34. Germany: declarations contained in a letter dated 16 September 1998, from the Permanent Representation of Germany, handed to the Secretary General at the time of depositing the instrument of ratification on 16 September 1998.

35. Germany 2002, Chapter 3, Findings of the Committee, A, B and C; Austria 2005, 50-2.

36. Liechtenstein: declaration contained in the instrument of ratification deposited on 18 November 1997.

37. Azerbaijan: declaration contained in a *note verbale* handed by the Permanent Representative of Azerbaijan to the Deputy Secretary General at the time of signature of the instrument, on 21 December 2001.

38. United Kingdom: declaration contained in a letter from the Permanent Representative of the United Kingdom, dated 22 April 2003 and registered at the Secretariat General on 23 April 2003.

excluding the application of the Charter in the Faroe Islands and Greenland,[39] are also territorial in character. Curiously, the Netherlands is the only state party to give a concrete answer to the possibility of applying the Charter outside Europe,[40] stating that "The Kingdom of the Netherlands accepts the said Charter for the Kingdom in Europe".[41]

Finally, other declarations of various kinds can be found. At the time of signature and pending confirmation at the time of ratification, France submitted a broad interpretative declaration on compatibility between the existence of linguistic groups and the text of its constitution.[42] Denmark stated its interpretation according to which the requirement of translation accompanying documents presented in a foreign language, as provided for in domestic procedural law, is not at variance with Article 9 paragraphs 1b.iii and 1c.iii of the Charter.[43]

However, if we focus on the declarations derived from the requirement of Article 3.1, we must emphasise their variety, in respect of both form and content, ranging from the most classic formulations including the minimum of 35 provisions accepted for each language protected, to those which give a long list of languages, with different situations and the same obligations accepted for all of them,[44] or those which use indirect techniques, not mentioning the languages but leaving the list, as in Spain's case, to those that are declared official in the respective autonomy statutes.[45] The Committee of Experts is usually perplexed when declarations by the states parties, far from taking advantage of the opportunity to choose the provisions of Part III of the Charter in accordance with the needs and realities of each language, opt for all the languages via a common, identical protection regime.[46] It also demonstrates its uncertainty in the face of broad protection regimes for languages not yet standardised, as with Romani in Germany,[47] or for those with few speakers.

---

39. Denmark: communication contained in a *note verbale* from the Permanent Representation of Denmark, dated 25 August 2000, handed over at the time of deposit of the instrument of ratification on 8 September 2000.

40. Woehrling (2005), op. cit., p. 267.

41. Netherlands: declaration contained in the instrument of acceptance, deposited on 2 May 1996.

42. France: declaration contained in the full powers handed to the Secretary General at the time of signature of the instrument, on 7 May 1999.

43. Denmark: declaration contained in a *note verbale* from the Permanent Representation of Denmark, handed over at the time of deposit of the instrument of ratification on 8 September 2000.

44. As in the case of Croatia, which has declared that the Italian, Serbian, Hungarian, Czech, Slovakian, Ruthenian and Ukrainian languages are equally protected; of Hungary, which gives equal protection to Croatian, German, Romanian, Serbian, Slovakian and Slovenian, and of Ukraine.

45. Spain: declarations contained in the instrument of ratification deposited on 9 April 2001.

46. See, for example, Croatia 2001, 17.

47. Germany 2006, 13.

The extension of declarations provided for, as we have observed, in Article 3.2 of the Charter, has followed a normal course in Germany, which made a fresh declaration on 21 March 2003 extending the languages protected under Part III of the Charter.[48] Cyprus also made a fresh declaration in 2005 declaring Cypriot Maronite Arabic to be a language protected by Part II of the Charter.[49] In 1999, Hungary extended protection to the Romani and Beás languages.[50] And Ukraine has also announced that it will draw up a new instrument of ratification.

It is customary for the Committee of Experts to draw attention in its first reports to languages which merit protection under Part II of the Charter and to request the authorities of states to supply relevant information on them, sometimes mentioning official languages which might deserve to be treated or regarded as minority languages, or the existence of different designations for one and the same language, or extending the scope of application to dialect variants of official languages in another state or minority languages in the same state, making the most of the possibilities afforded by Article 1 of the Charter and advocating extensive interpretations where the scope of application is unclear, as with the Basque language, which is official in only part of the Autonomous Community of Navarra in the case of Spain.

The state's international responsibility and its obligation to fulfil the commitments entered into under the convention is not affected by the federal character of those states, such as Austria, Germany or Spain, in which regulatory authorities below state level hold much of the power in the sphere of juridico-linguistic rules. Likewise, the automatic acceptance of convention rules, which is a feature of monistic systems, in which the international rule needs no transposition in order to be fully effective in the domestic order, taking precedence over national legislation, is not sufficient reason, in the committee's opinion, to refrain from developing the Charter's provisions in the domestic legislative system.

Finally, it is to be noted that, as is customary with treaties on matters relating to human rights protection, there is no precedent for denunciation or withdrawal

---

48. Germany: declaration contained in a letter from the Permanent Representative of Germany, dated 17 March 2003 and registered at the Secretariat General on 21 March 2003.

49. Cyprus: declaration contained in a *note verbale* from the Permanent Representation of Cyprus, dated 5 November 2008, registered at the Secretariat General on 12 November 2008.

50. Hungary: declaration contained in a *note verbale* from the Permanent Representation of Hungary, dated 24 June 2008 – "The Government of the Republic of Hungary, based on the authorisation of the Parliament and according to Article 2, paragraph 2, of the Charter, undertakes to apply the following provisions in respect of the Romani language" – supplemented by a *note verbale* from the Permanent Representation of Hungary, dated 17 July 2008, registered at the Secretariat General on 22 July 2008. – "The Government of the Republic of Hungary, based on the authorisation of the Parliament and according to Article 2, paragraph 2, of the Charter, undertakes to apply the following provisions in respect of the Beás language".

by a state party to the Charter; such an occurrence is highly improbable by reason of the open-ended, optional nature of the Charter, which leaves states a wide margin of discretion.

4. Some conclusions

As the process of signatures to the Charter is at a standstill, new ratifications have slowed down and there have been no accessions, we may assess the final provisions as a whole by pointing to the huge disparity in the declarations made by states when expressing their consent in accordance with Article 3.1 of the Charter. The declarations in question frequently fail to take advantage of the opportunities for choosing and adapting the regional or minority language under Part III of the Charter, and demonstrate various technical shortcomings. Actively assisting the governments of states wishing to ratify or accede to the Charter could help to obviate these problems.

These questions also reflect the tendency to declare that languages not protected by Part III of the Charter will be protected by the aims and principles of Part II, often excluding some languages and giving the Committee of Experts the responsibility of monitoring the existing linguistic situation. In our view, the practice established by the requirement of the Committee of Experts for languages not initially considered to be included in the periodic national reports cannot be transposed into a necessary extension of states' initial declarations. The possibility of extension envisaged in Article 3.2 of the Charter should thus be reserved mainly for the acceptance of new obligations under Article 3.1 of the Charter.

Declarations which do not entail the acceptance of 35 or more provisions of Part III are not regarded by the committee other than as languages protected by Part II of the Charter, thus needlessly lowering the level of protection. The state having demonstrated its wish to undertake commitments, the solution could lie in a protection standard of 35 provisions in the lowest category of obligations that may be accepted.

The proliferation of atypical declarations, which may be disguised forms of interpretative declarations and whose content the Committee of Experts has usually found incompatible with the provisions of the Charter, also strikes us as dangerous.

Finally, the complexity of powers characteristic of federally constituted states must not be an obstacle to meeting the requirement of international responsibility and the development of means of application for the proper implementation of the Charter by the state party.

549

References

Albanese, Ferdinando (1991), "Ethnic and linguistic minorities in Europe", *Yearbook of European Law*, Vol. 11, pp. 332-6.

Bonet, JORDI (1996), *Las reservas a los tratados internacionales*. Barcelona: J. M. Bosch.

Christopoulos, Dimitris (1999), "La question de la protection des minorités dans un ordre públic européen: analise critique des travaux élaborés au sein du Conseil de l'Europe, de la CSCE, et de la CEE". Strasbourg: Université R. Schuman thesis.

Chueca Sancho, Angel G. (1992), *Las reservas a los tratados de derechos humanos*. Madrid: Ministerio de Justicia, Documentación Jurídica, XIX.

Edwards, Richard W. Jr (1989), "Reservations to treaties", *Michigan Journal of International Law*, Vol. 10, No. 2, pp. 362-405.

Harting, Harno (1994), "Les travaux du Conseil de l'Europe dans le domaine des minorités" in Parayotis Grigoriou (ed.), *Questions de minorités en Europe*. Brussels: Centre Hellénique d'Etudes Europénnes/Presses Interuniversitaires Européennes.

Imbert, Pierre Henri (1982), "La question des réserves et les conventions en matière de droits de l'homme" in Council of Europe, *Proceedings of the fifth inter-national colloquy on the European Human Rights Convention*. Paris: Pedone, pp. 87-146.

Kovács, Péter (1993), "La protection des langues minoritaires ou la nouvelle approche de la protection des minorités? Quelques considérations sur la Charte européenne des langues régionales ou minoritaires", *Revue Générale de Droit International Public*, Vol. 97, No. 2.

Petschen, Santiago (1989), "Entre la política y el derecho: la Carta europea de las llenguas regionales o minoritarias", *Revista de Estudios Políticos*, No. 66.

Puig, Lluís Maria (de) (1986), "Informe provisional sobre la preparació d'un projecte de Carta europea de les llengües regionals i minoritàries", *Revista Llengua i Dret*, No. 8.

Puig, Lluís Maria (de) (1991), "Debat i elaboració de la Carta europea de les llengües", *Revista Llengua i Dret*, No. 16.

Thornberry, Patrick and Martín Estebanez, María Amor (1994), *The Council of Europe and minorities*. Strasbourg: Council of Europe Publishing (COEMIN).

Verhoeven, JOE (1997), "Les principales étapes de la protection internationale des minorités", *Revue Trimestrielle des Droits de l'Homme*, No. 30.

Villán Durán, Carlos (2002), *Curso de derecho internacional de los derechos humanos*. Madrid: Trotta.

Woehrling, Jean-Marie (1992), "Institutions européennes et droit linguistiques des minorités" in Henri Giordan (ed.), *Les minorités en Europe: droits linguistiques, droits de l'homme*. Paris: Kime.

Woehrling, Jean-Marie (2005), *The European Charter for Regional or Minority Languages: a critical commentary*. Strasbourg: Council of Europe.

Sales agents for publications of the Council of Europe
Agents de vente des publications du Conseil de l'Europe

BELGIUM/BELGIQUE
La Librairie Européenne -
The European Bookshop
Rue de l'Orme, 1
BE-1040 BRUXELLES
Tel.: +32 (0)2 231 04 35
Fax: +32 (0)2 735 08 60
E-mail: info@libeurop.eu
http://www.libeurop.be

Jean De Lannoy/DL Services
Avenue du Roi 202 Koningslaan
BE-1190 BRUXELLES
Tel.: +32 (0)2 538 43 08
Fax: +32 (0)2 538 08 41
E-mail: jean.de.lannoy@dl-servi.com
http://www.jean-de-lannoy.be

**BOSNIA AND HERZEGOVINA/
BOSNIE-HERZÉGOVINE**
Robert's Plus d.o.o.
Marka Maruliça 2/V
BA-71000, SARAJEVO
Tel.: + 387 33 640 818
Fax: + 387 33 640 818
E-mail: robertsplus@bih.net.ba

CANADA
Renouf Publishing Co. Ltd.
22-1010 Polytek Street
CDN-OTTAWA, ONT K1J 9J1
Tel.: +1 613 745 2665
Fax: +1 613 745 7660
Toll-Free Tel.: (866) 767-6766
E-mail: order.dept@renoufbooks.com
http://www.renoufbooks.com

CROATIA/CROATIE
Robert's Plus d.o.o.
Marasoviçeva 67
HR-21000, SPLIT
Tel.: + 385 21 315 800, 801, 802, 803
Fax: + 385 21 315 804
E-mail: robertsplus@robertsplus.hr

**CZECH REPUBLIC/
RÉPUBLIQUE TCHÈQUE**
Suweco CZ, s.r.o.
Klecakova 347
CZ-180 21 PRAHA 9
Tel.: +420 2 424 59 204
Fax: +420 2 848 21 646
E-mail: import@suweco.cz
http://www.suweco.cz

DENMARK/DANEMARK
GAD
Vimmelskaftet 32
DK-1161 KØBENHAVN K
Tel.: +45 77 66 60 00
Fax: +45 77 66 60 01
E-mail: gad@gad.dk
http://www.gad.dk

FINLAND/FINLANDE
Akateeminen Kirjakauppa
PO Box 128
Keskuskatu 1
FI-00100 HELSINKI
Tel.: +358 (0)9 121 4430
Fax: +358 (0)9 121 4242
E-mail: akatilaus@akateeminen.com
http://www.akateeminen.com

FRANCE
La Documentation française
(diffusion/distribution France entière)
124, rue Henri Barbusse
FR-93308 AUBERVILLIERS CEDEX
Tél.: +33 (0)1 40 15 70 00
Fax: +33 (0)1 40 15 68 00
E-mail: commande@ladocumentationfrancaise.fr
http://www.ladocumentationfrancaise.fr

Librairie Kléber
1 rue des Francs Bourgeois
FR-67000 STRASBOURG
Tel.: +33 (0)3 88 15 78 88
Fax: +33 (0)3 88 15 78 80
E-mail: librairie-kleber@coe.int
http://www.librairie-kleber.com

**GERMANY/ALLEMAGNE
AUSTRIA/AUTRICHE**
UNO Verlag GmbH
August-Bebel-Allee 6
DE-53175 BONN
Tel.: +49 (0)228 94 90 20
Fax: +49 (0)228 94 90 222
E-mail: bestellung@uno-verlag.de
http://www.uno-verlag.de

GREECE/GRÈCE
Librairie Kauffmann s.a.
Stadiou 28
GR-105 64 ATHINAI
Tel.: +30 210 32 55 321
Fax.: +30 210 32 30 320
E-mail: ord@otenet.gr
http://www.kauffmann.gr

HUNGARY/HONGRIE
Euro Info Service
Pannónia u. 58.
PF. 1039
HU-1136 BUDAPEST
Tel.: +36 1 329 2170
Fax: +36 1 349 2053
E-mail: euroinfo@euroinfo.hu
http://www.euroinfo.hu

ITALY/ITALIE
Licosa SpA
Via Duca di Calabria, 1/1
IT-50125 FIRENZE
Tel.: +39 0556 483215
Fax: +39 0556 41257
E-mail: licosa@licosa.com
http://www.licosa.com

NORWAY/NORVÈGE
Akademika
Postboks 84 Blindern
NO-0314 OSLO
Tel.: +47 2 218 8100
Fax: +47 2 218 8103
E-mail: support@akademika.no
http://www.akademika.no

POLAND/POLOGNE
Ars Polona JSC
25 Obroncow Street
PL-03-933 WARSZAWA
Tel.: +48 (0)22 509 86 00
Fax: +48 (0)22 509 86 10
E-mail: arspolona@arspolona.com.pl
http://www.arspolona.com.pl

PORTUGAL
Livraria Portugal
(Dias & Andrade, Lda.)
Rua do Carmo, 70
PT-1200-094 LISBOA
Tel.: +351 21 347 42 82 / 85
Fax: +351 21 347 02 64
E-mail: info@livrariaportugal.pt
http://www.livrariaportugal.pt

**RUSSIAN FEDERATION/
FÉDÉRATION DE RUSSIE**
Ves Mir
17b, Butlerova ul.
RU-101000 MOSCOW
Tel.: +7 495 739 0971
Fax: +7 495 739 0971
E-mail: orders@vesmirbooks.ru
http://www.vesmirbooks.ru

SPAIN/ESPAGNE
Díaz de Santos Barcelona
C/ Balmes, 417-419
ES-08022 BARCELONA
Tel.: +34 93 212 86 47
Fax: +34 93 211 49 91
E-mail: david@diazdesantos.es
http://www.diazdesantos.es

Díaz de Santos Madrid
C/Albasanz, 2
ES-28037 MADRID
Tel.: +34 91 743 48 90
Fax: +34 91 743 40 23
E-mail: jpinilla@diazdesantos.es
http://www.diazdesantos.es

SWITZERLAND/SUISSE
Planetis Sàrl
16 chemin des Pins
CH-1273 ARZIER
Tel.: +41 22 366 51 77
Fax: +41 22 366 51 78
E-mail: info@planetis.ch

UNITED KINGDOM/ROYAUME-UNI
The Stationery Office Ltd
PO Box 29
GB-NORWICH NR3 1GN
Tel.: +44 (0)870 600 5522
Fax: +44 (0)870 600 5533
E-mail: book.enquiries@tso.co.uk
http://www.tsoshop.co.uk

**UNITED STATES and CANADA/
ÉTATS-UNIS et CANADA**
Manhattan Publishing Co
670 White Plains Road
USA-10583 SCARSDALE, NY
Tel.: +1 914 271 5194
Fax: +1 914 472 4316
E-mail: coe@manhattanpublishing.com
http://www.manhattanpublishing.com

Council of Europe Publishing/Editions du Conseil de l'Europe
FR-67075 STRASBOURG Cedex
Tel.: +33 (0)3 88 41 25 81 – Fax: +33 (0)3 88 41 39 10 – E-mail: publishing@coe.int – Website: http://book.coe.int